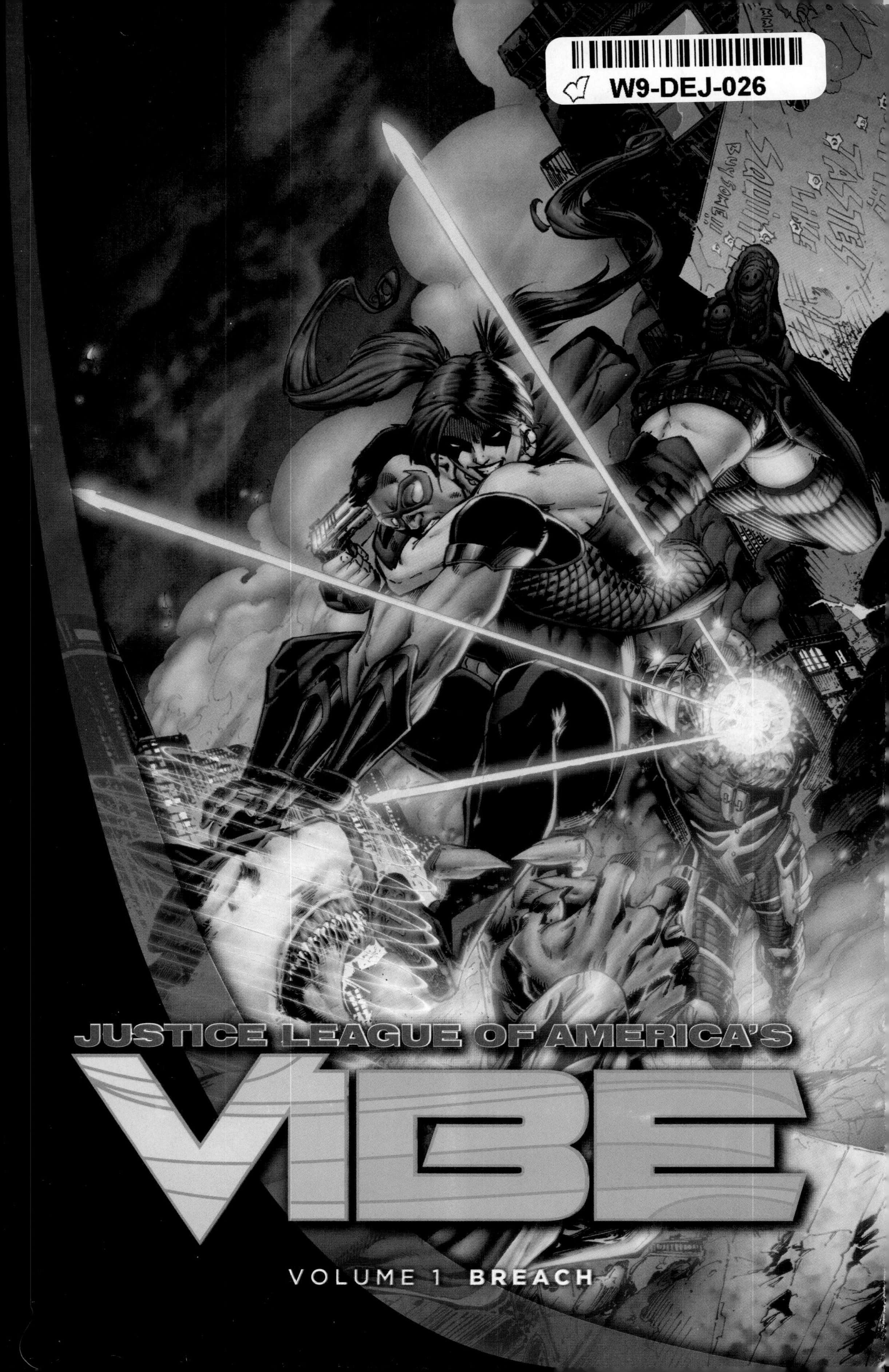

JUSTICE LEAGUE OF AMERICA'S VIBE

VOLUME 1 **BREACH**

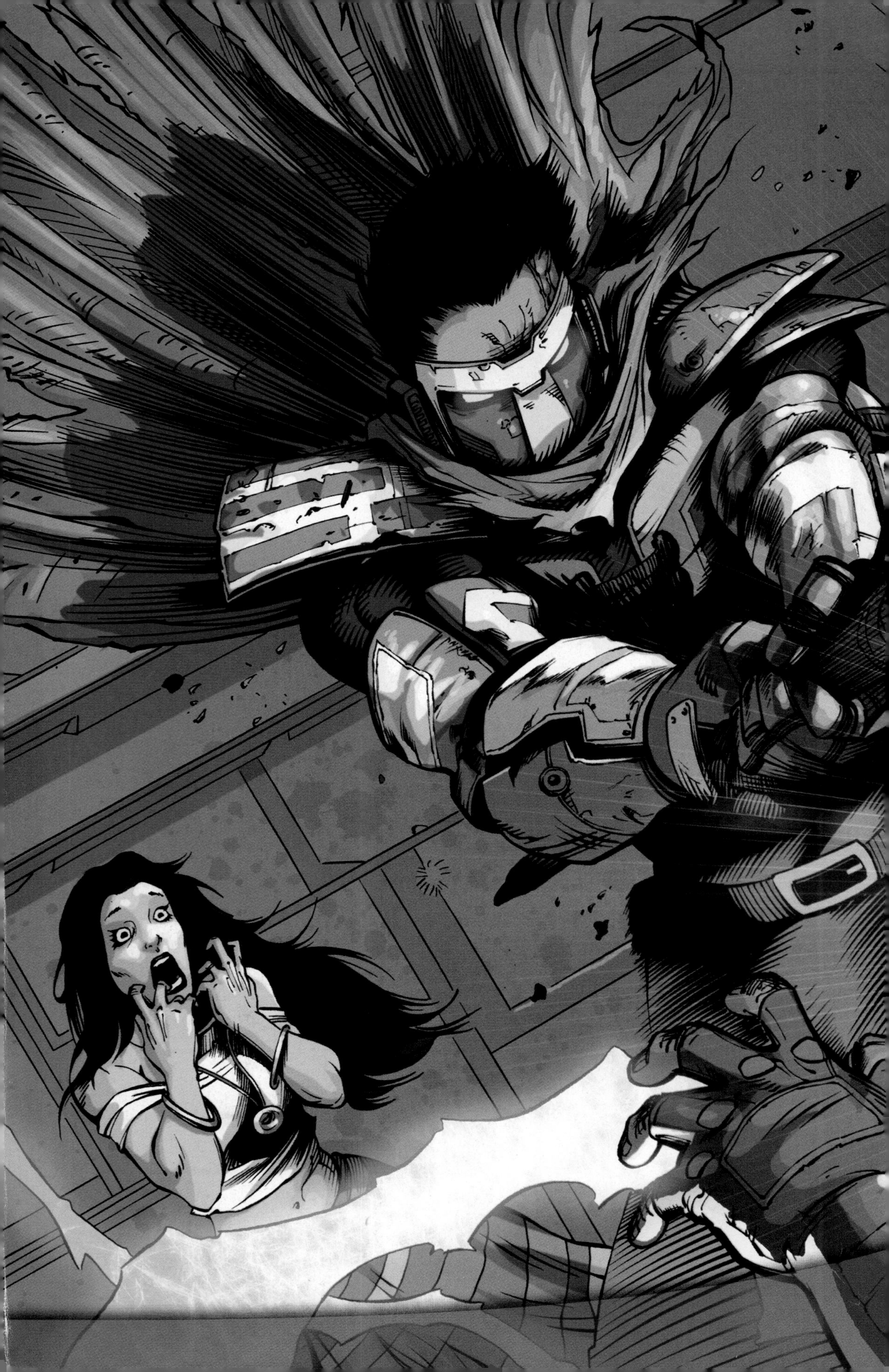

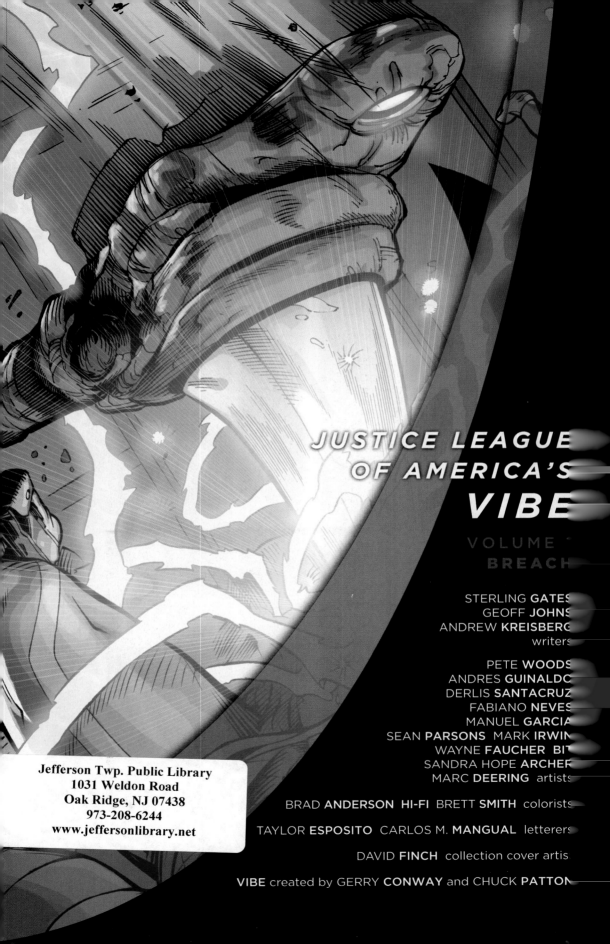

JUSTICE LEAGUE OF AMERICA'S VIBE

VOLUME 1
BREACH

STERLING **GATES**
GEOFF **JOHNS**
ANDREW **KREISBERG**
writers

PETE **WOODS**
ANDRES **GUINALDO**
DERLIS **SANTACRUZ**
FABIANO **NEVES**
MANUEL **GARCIA**
SEAN **PARSONS** MARK **IRWIN**
WAYNE **FAUCHER** BIT
SANDRA HOPE **ARCHER**
MARC **DEERING** artists

BRAD **ANDERSON** HI-FI BRETT **SMITH** colorists

TAYLOR **ESPOSITO** CARLOS M. **MANGUAL** letterers

DAVID **FINCH** collection cover artist

VIBE created by GERRY **CONWAY** and CHUCK **PATTON**

BRIAN CUNNINGHAM Editor – Original Series KATIE KUBERT Associate Editor – Original Series
KATE DURRÉ Assistant Editor – Original Series ROBIN WILDMAN Editor
ROBBIN BROSTERMAN Design Director – Books ROBBIE BIEDERMAN Publication Design

BOB HARRAS Senior VP – Editor-in-Chief, DC Comics

DIANE NELSON President DAN DIDIO and JIM LEE Co-Publishers GEOFF JOHNS Chief Creative Officer
AMIT DESAI Senior VP – Marketing and Franchise Management
AMY GENKINS Senior VP – Business and Legal Affairs NAIRI GARDINER Senior VP – Finance
JEFF BOISON VP – Publishing Planning MARK CHIARELLO VP – Art Direction and Design
JOHN CUNNINGHAM VP – Marketing TERRI CUNNINGHAM VP – Editorial Administration
LARRY GANEM VP – Talent Relations and Services ALISON GILL Senior VP – Manufacturing and Operations
HANK KANALZ Senior VP – Vertigo and Integrated Publishing JAY KOGAN VP – Business and Legal Affairs, Publishing
JACK MAHAN VP – Business Affairs, Talent NICK NAPOLITANO VP – Manufacturing Administration SUE POHJA VP – Book Sales
FRED RUIZ VP – Manufacturing Operations COURTNEY SIMMONS Senior VP – Publicity BOB WAYNE Senior VP – Sales

JUSTICE LEAGUE OF AMERICA'S VIBE VOLUME 1: BREACH

DC Comics, 1700 Broadway, New York, NY 10019
A Warner Bros. Entertainment Company.
Printed by RR Donnelley, Owensville, MO, USA. 6/20/14. First Printing.

ISBN: 978-1-4012-4331-9

Library of Congress Cataloging-in-Publication Data

Johns, Geoff, 1973- author.
Justice League of America's Vibe. Vol. 1, Breach / Geoff Johns, Andrew Kreisberg ; [illustrated by] Pete Woods.
pages cm
ISBN 978-1-4012-4331-9 (pbk.)
1. Graphic novels. I. Kreisberg, Andrew, 1971- author. II. Woods, Pete, illustrator. III. Title. IV. Title: Breach.
PN6728.J87J6555 2014
741.5'973—dc23
2013039604

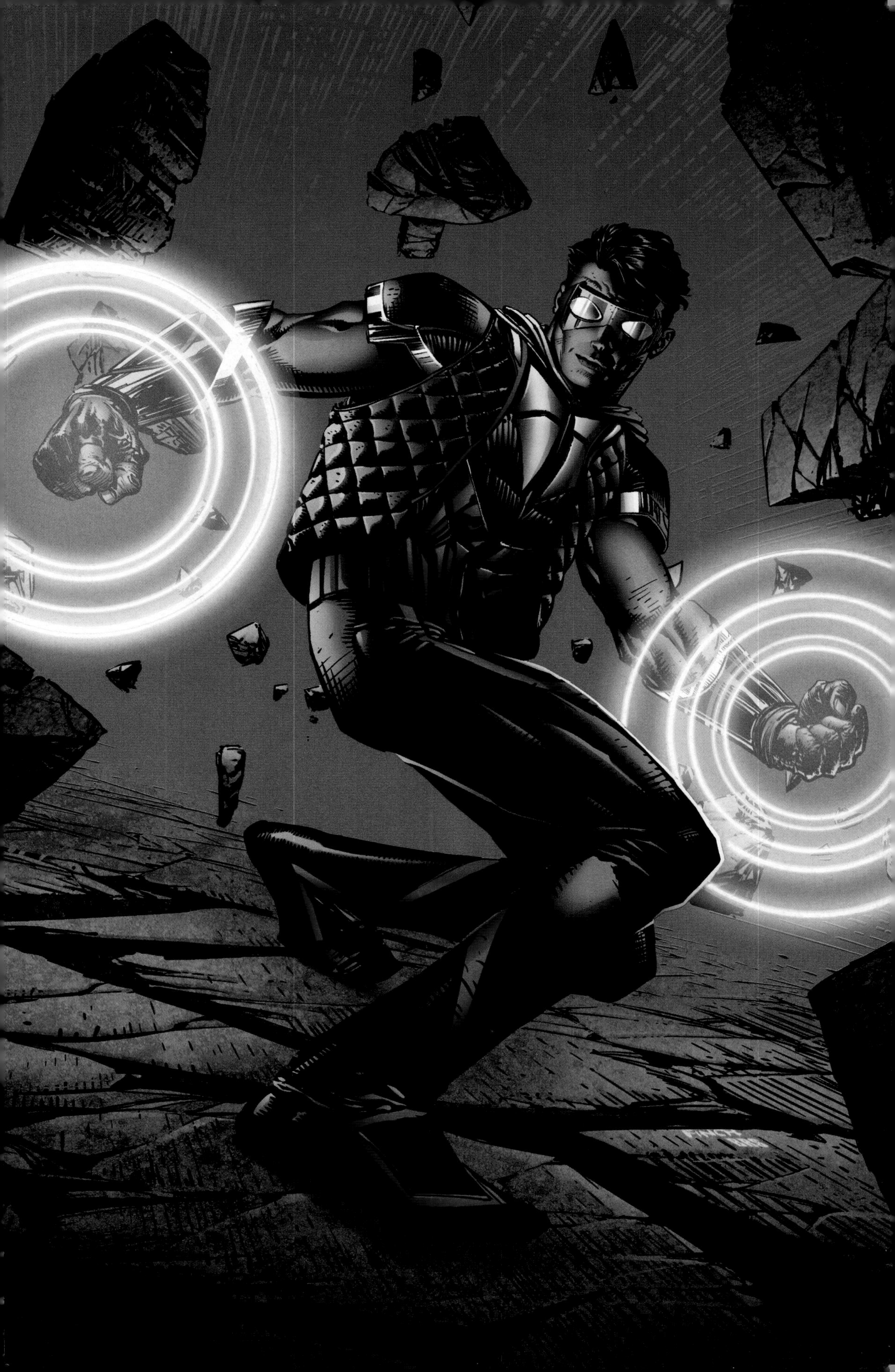

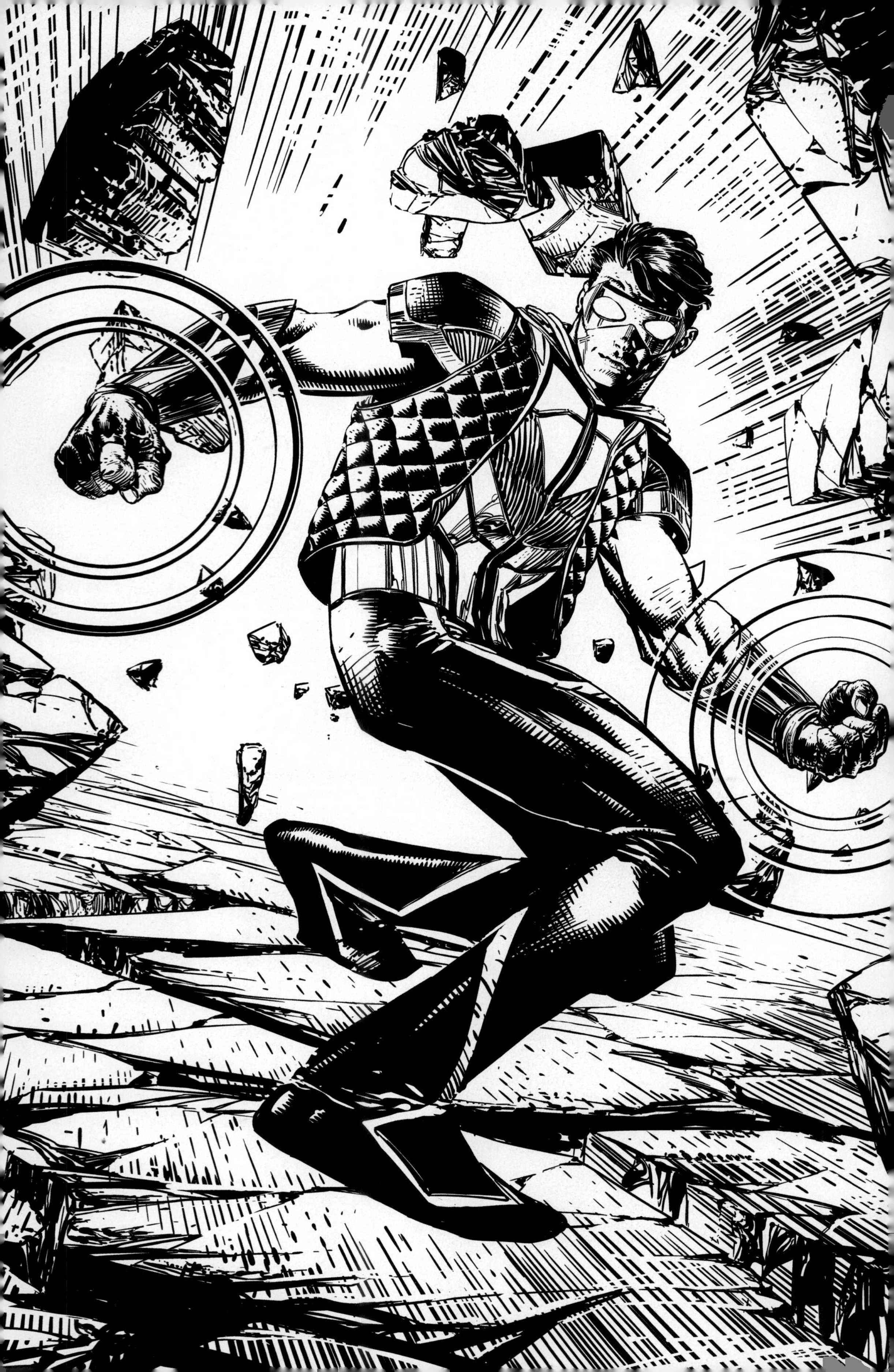

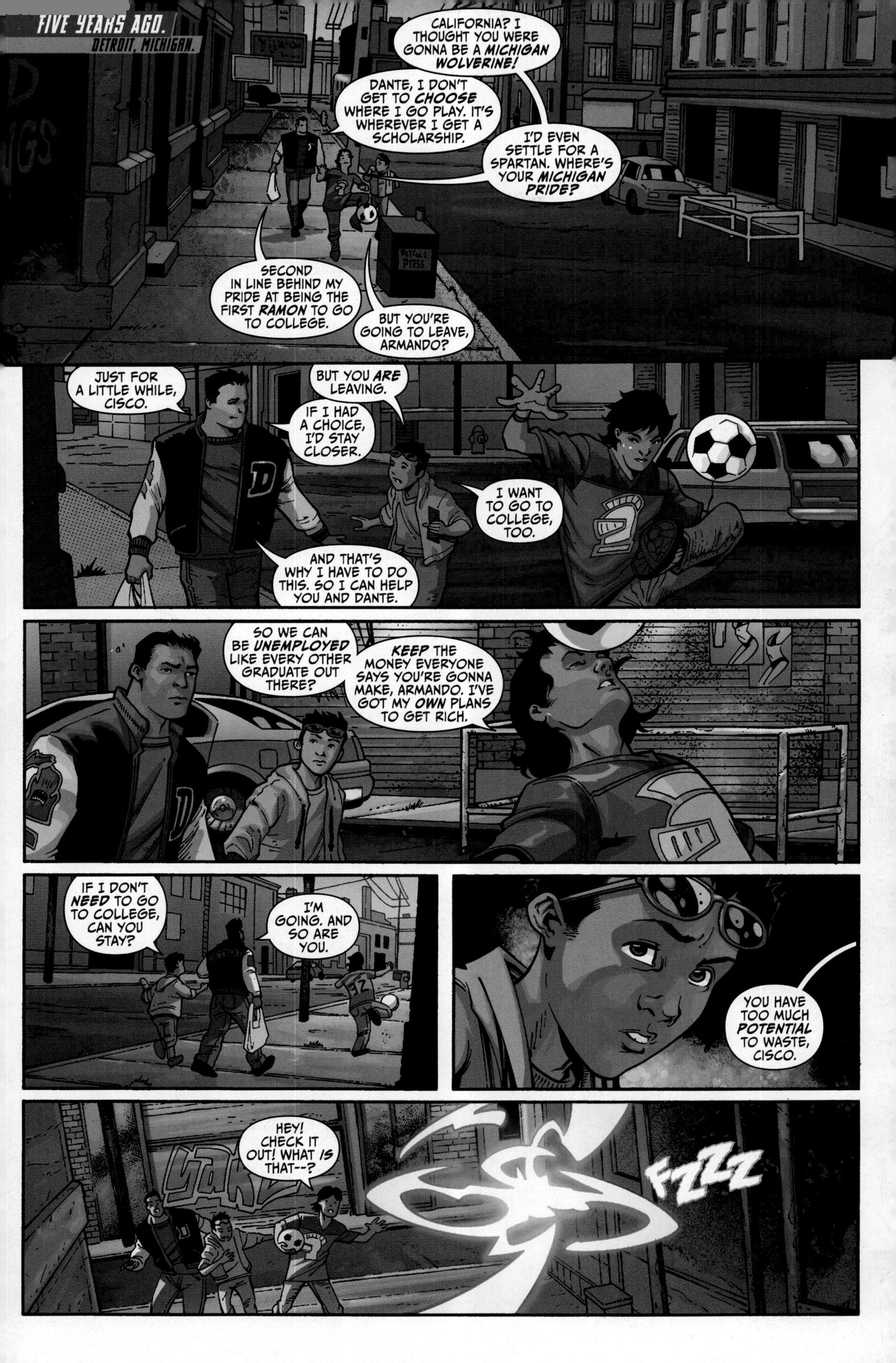
FIVE YEARS AGO.
DETROIT, MICHIGAN.
CALIFORNIA? I THOUGHT YOU WERE GONNA BE A MICHIGAN WOLVERINE!
DANTE, I DON'T GET TO CHOOSE WHERE I GO PLAY. IT'S WHEREVER I GET A SCHOLARSHIP.
I'D EVEN SETTLE FOR A SPARTAN. WHERE'S YOUR MICHIGAN PRIDE?
SECOND IN LINE BEHIND MY PRIDE AT BEING THE FIRST RAMON TO GO TO COLLEGE.
BUT YOU'RE GOING TO LEAVE, ARMANDO?
JUST FOR A LITTLE WHILE, CISCO.
BUT YOU ARE LEAVING.
IF I HAD A CHOICE, I'D STAY CLOSER.
I WANT TO GO TO COLLEGE, TOO.
AND THAT'S WHY I HAVE TO DO THIS. SO I CAN HELP YOU AND DANTE.
SO WE CAN BE UNEMPLOYED LIKE EVERY OTHER GRADUATE OUT THERE?
KEEP THE MONEY EVERYONE SAYS YOU'RE GONNA MAKE, ARMANDO. I'VE GOT MY OWN PLANS TO GET RICH.
IF I DON'T NEED TO GO TO COLLEGE, CAN YOU STAY?
I'M GOING. AND SO ARE YOU.
YOU HAVE TOO MUCH POTENTIAL TO WASTE, CISCO.
HEY! CHECK IT OUT! WHAT IS THAT--?
FZZZ

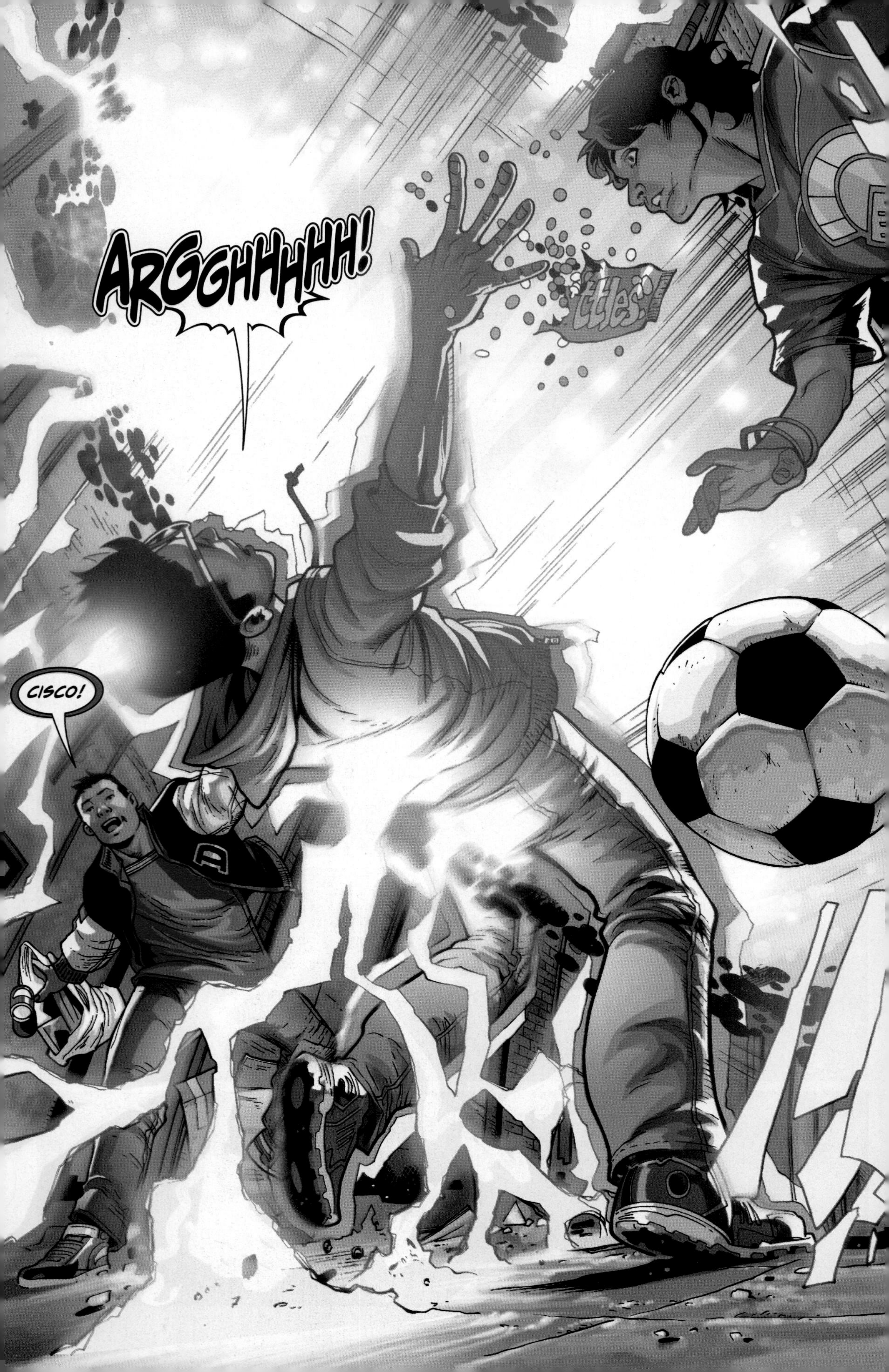
ARGGHHHHH!
CISCO!

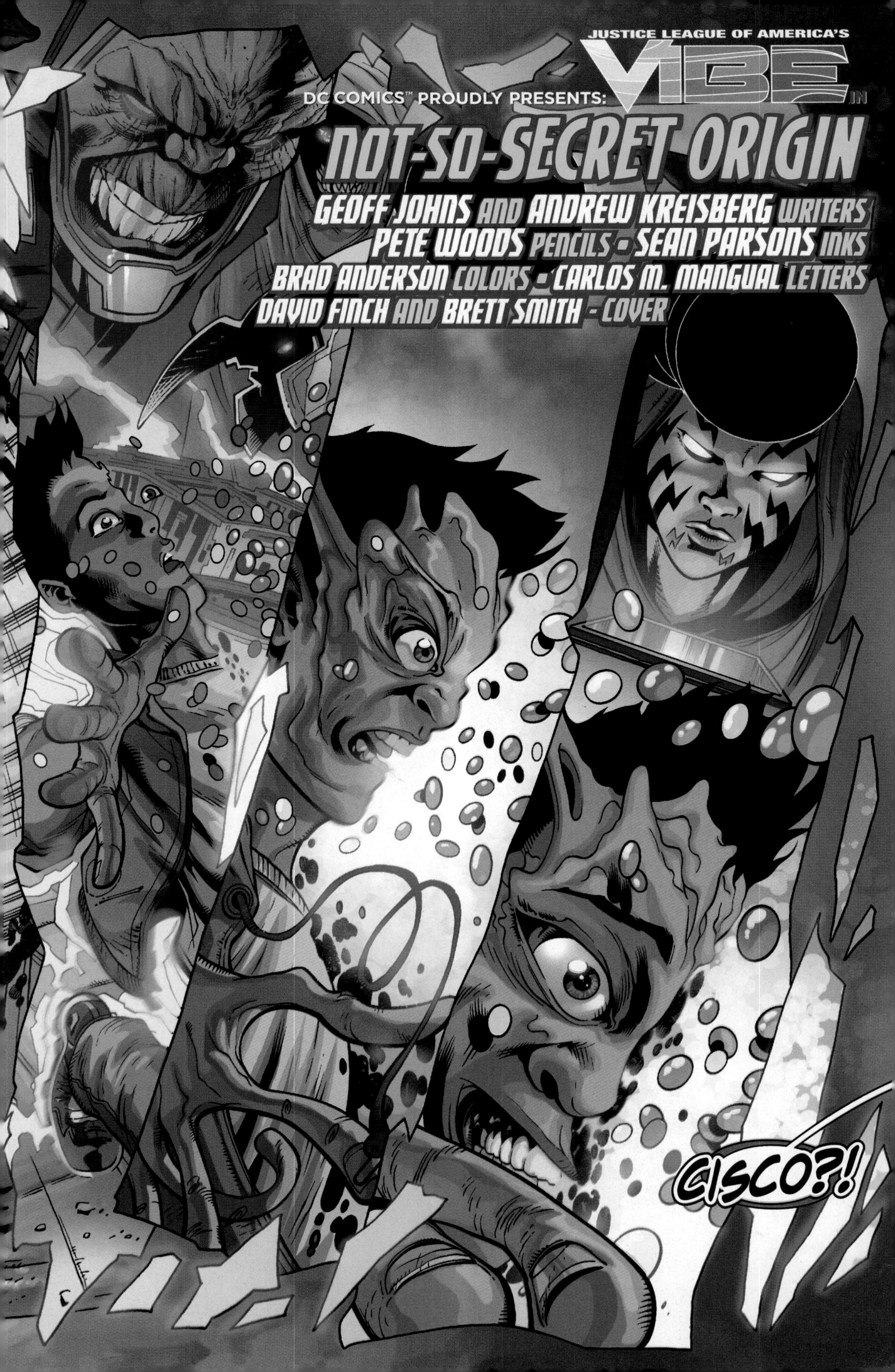
JUSTICE LEAGUE OF AMERICA'S
DC COMICS™ PROUDLY PRESENTS: VIBE IN
NOT-SO-SECRET ORIGIN
GEOFF JOHNS AND ANDREW KREISBERG WRITERS
PETE WOODS PENCILS • SEAN PARSONS INKS
BRAD ANDERSON COLORS • CARLOS M. MANGUAL LETTERS
DAVID FINCH AND BRETT SMITH - COVER
CISCO?!

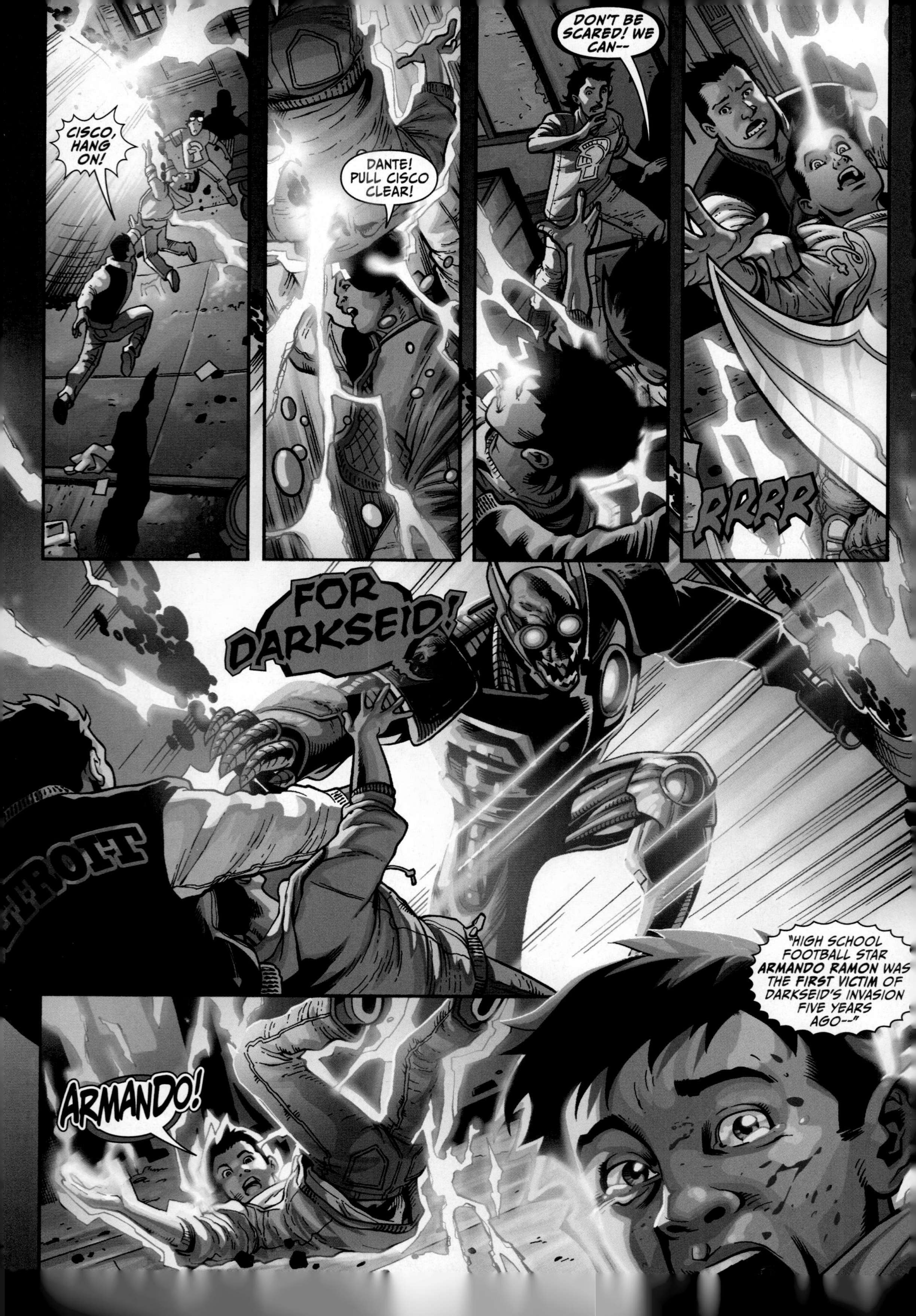
CISCO, HANG ON!
DANTE! PULL CISCO CLEAR!
DON'T BE SCARED! WE CAN--
RRRR
FOR DARKSEID!
"HIGH SCHOOL FOOTBALL STAR ARMANDO RAMON WAS THE FIRST VICTIM OF DARKSEID'S INVASION FIVE YEARS AGO--"
ARMANDO!

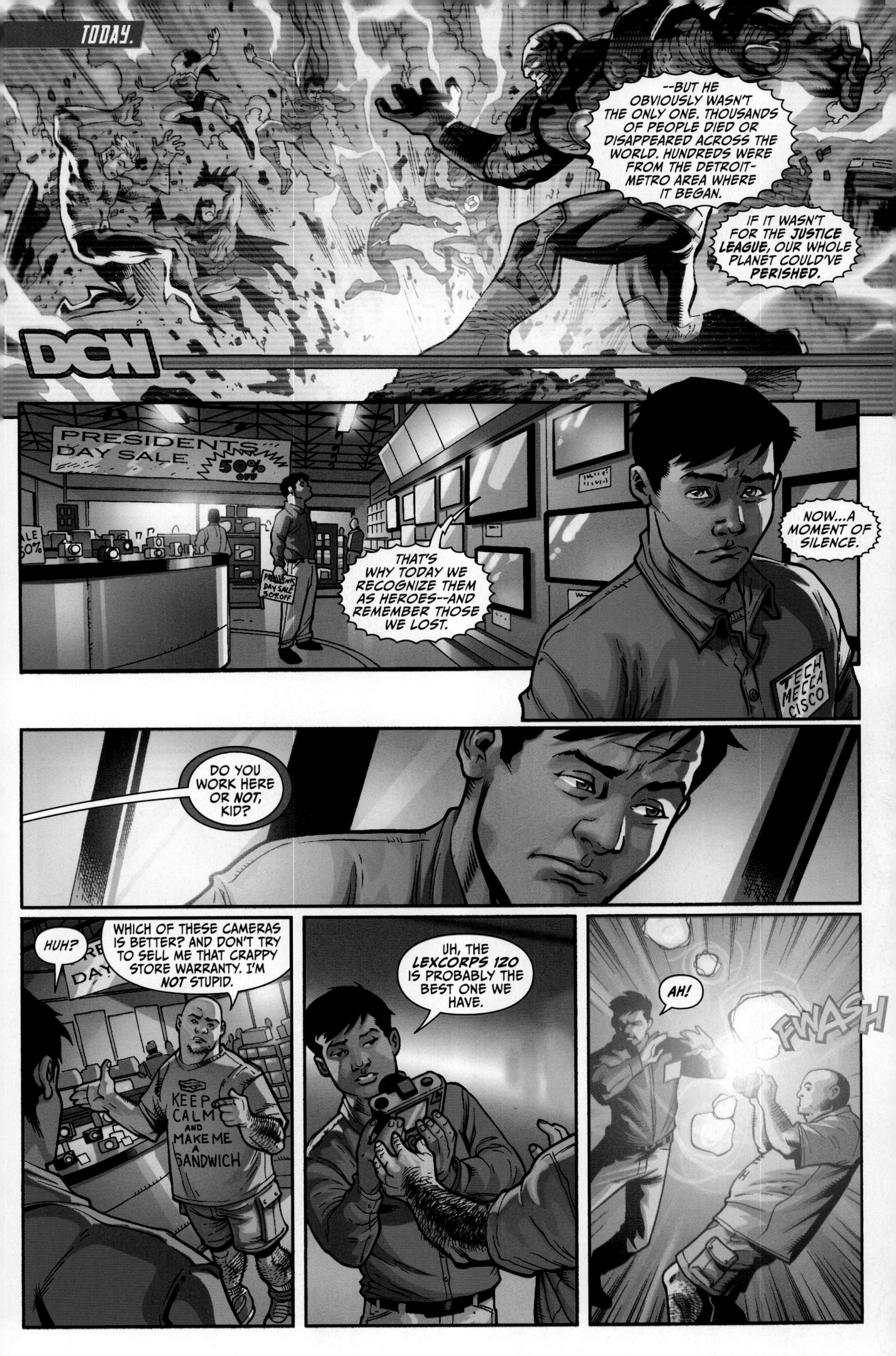

TODAY.
--BUT HE OBVIOUSLY WASN'T THE ONLY ONE. THOUSANDS OF PEOPLE DIED OR DISAPPEARED ACROSS THE WORLD. HUNDREDS WERE FROM THE DETROIT-METRO AREA WHERE IT BEGAN.
IF IT WASN'T FOR THE JUSTICE LEAGUE, OUR WHOLE PLANET COULD'VE PERISHED.
DCN
PRESIDENTS DAY SALE 50% OFF
THAT'S WHY TODAY WE RECOGNIZE THEM AS HEROES--AND REMEMBER THOSE WE LOST.
NOW...A MOMENT OF SILENCE.
TECH MECCA CISCO
DO YOU WORK HERE OR NOT, KID?
HUH?
WHICH OF THESE CAMERAS IS BETTER? AND DON'T TRY TO SELL ME THAT CRAPPY STORE WARRANTY. I'M NOT STUPID.
KEEP CALM AND MAKE ME A SANDWICH
UH, THE LEXCORPS 120 IS PROBABLY THE BEST ONE WE HAVE.
AH!
FWASH

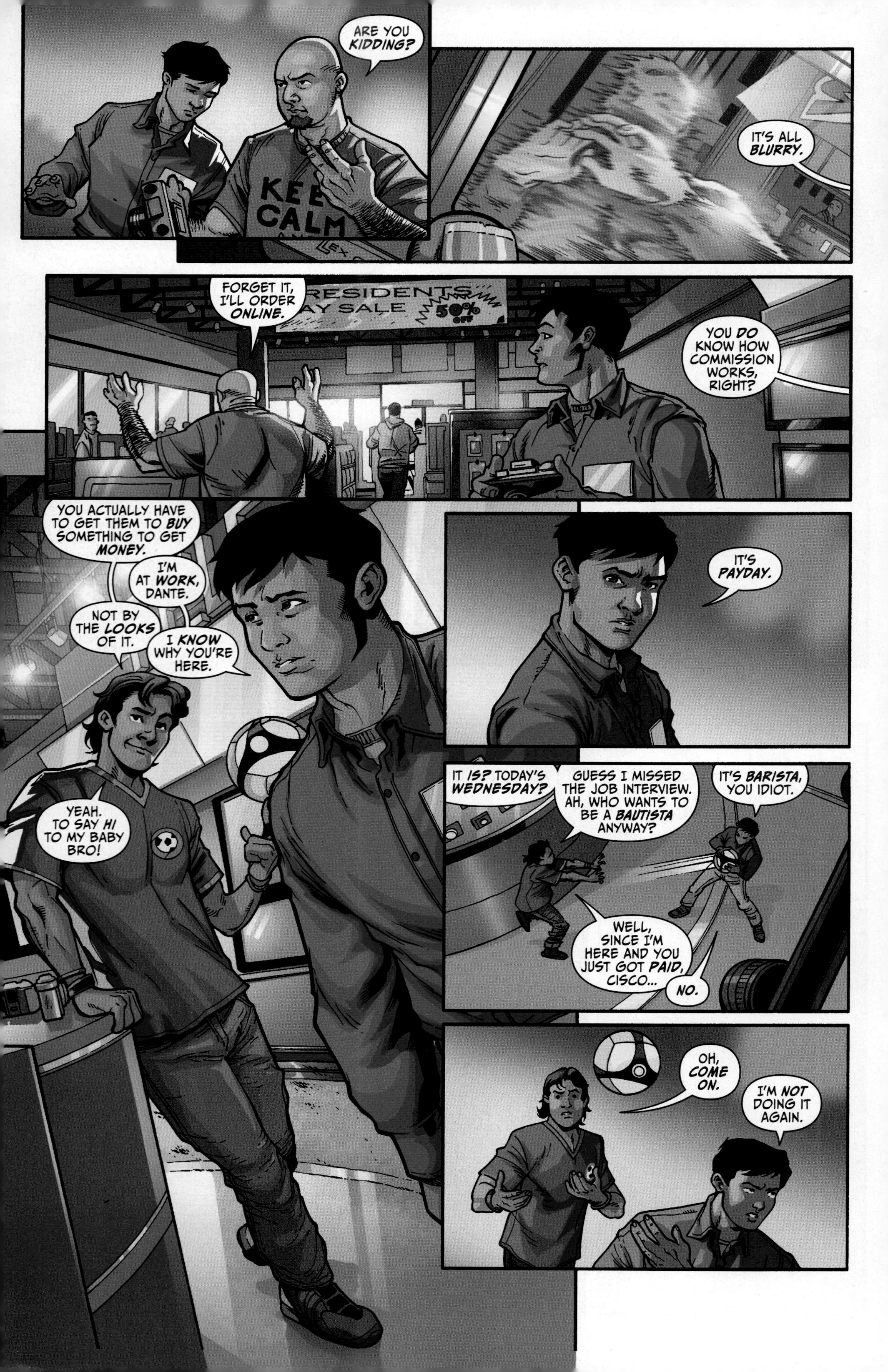
ARE YOU KIDDING?
KEEP CALM
IT'S ALL BLURRY.
PRESIDENTS DAY SALE 50% OFF
FORGET IT, I'LL ORDER ONLINE.
YOU DO KNOW HOW COMMISSION WORKS, RIGHT?
YOU ACTUALLY HAVE TO GET THEM TO BUY SOMETHING TO GET MONEY.
I'M AT WORK, DANTE.
NOT BY THE LOOKS OF IT.
I KNOW WHY YOU'RE HERE.
YEAH. TO SAY HI TO MY BABY BRO!
IT'S PAYDAY.
IT IS? TODAY'S WEDNESDAY?
GUESS I MISSED THE JOB INTERVIEW. AH, WHO WANTS TO BE A BAUTISTA ANYWAY?
IT'S BARISTA, YOU IDIOT.
WELL, SINCE I'M HERE AND YOU JUST GOT PAID, CISCO...
NO.
OH, COME ON.
I'M NOT DOING IT AGAIN.

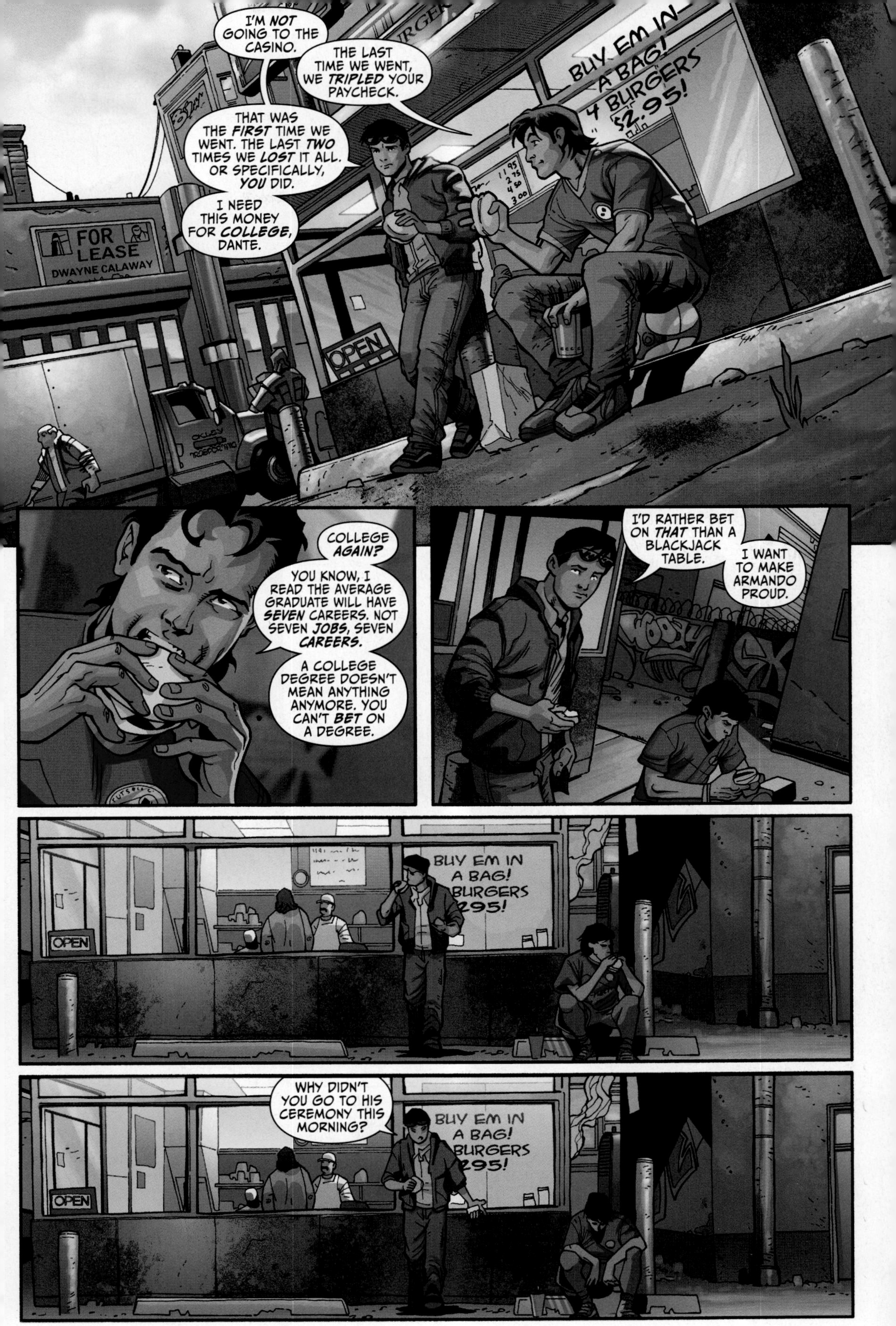
I'M NOT GOING TO THE CASINO.
THE LAST TIME WE WENT, WE TRIPLED YOUR PAYCHECK.
THAT WAS THE FIRST TIME WE WENT. THE LAST TWO TIMES WE LOST IT ALL. OR SPECIFICALLY, YOU DID.
I NEED THIS MONEY FOR COLLEGE, DANTE.
BUY EM IN A BAG! 4 BURGERS $2.95!
FOR LEASE
DWAYNE CALAWAY
OPEN
COLLEGE AGAIN?
YOU KNOW, I READ THE AVERAGE GRADUATE WILL HAVE SEVEN CAREERS. NOT SEVEN JOBS, SEVEN CAREERS.
A COLLEGE DEGREE DOESN'T MEAN ANYTHING ANYMORE. YOU CAN'T BET ON A DEGREE.
I'D RATHER BET ON THAT THAN A BLACKJACK TABLE.
I WANT TO MAKE ARMANDO PROUD.
BUY EM IN A BAG! BURGERS 295!
OPEN
WHY DIDN'T YOU GO TO HIS CEREMONY THIS MORNING?
BUY EM IN A BAG! BURGERS 295!
OPEN

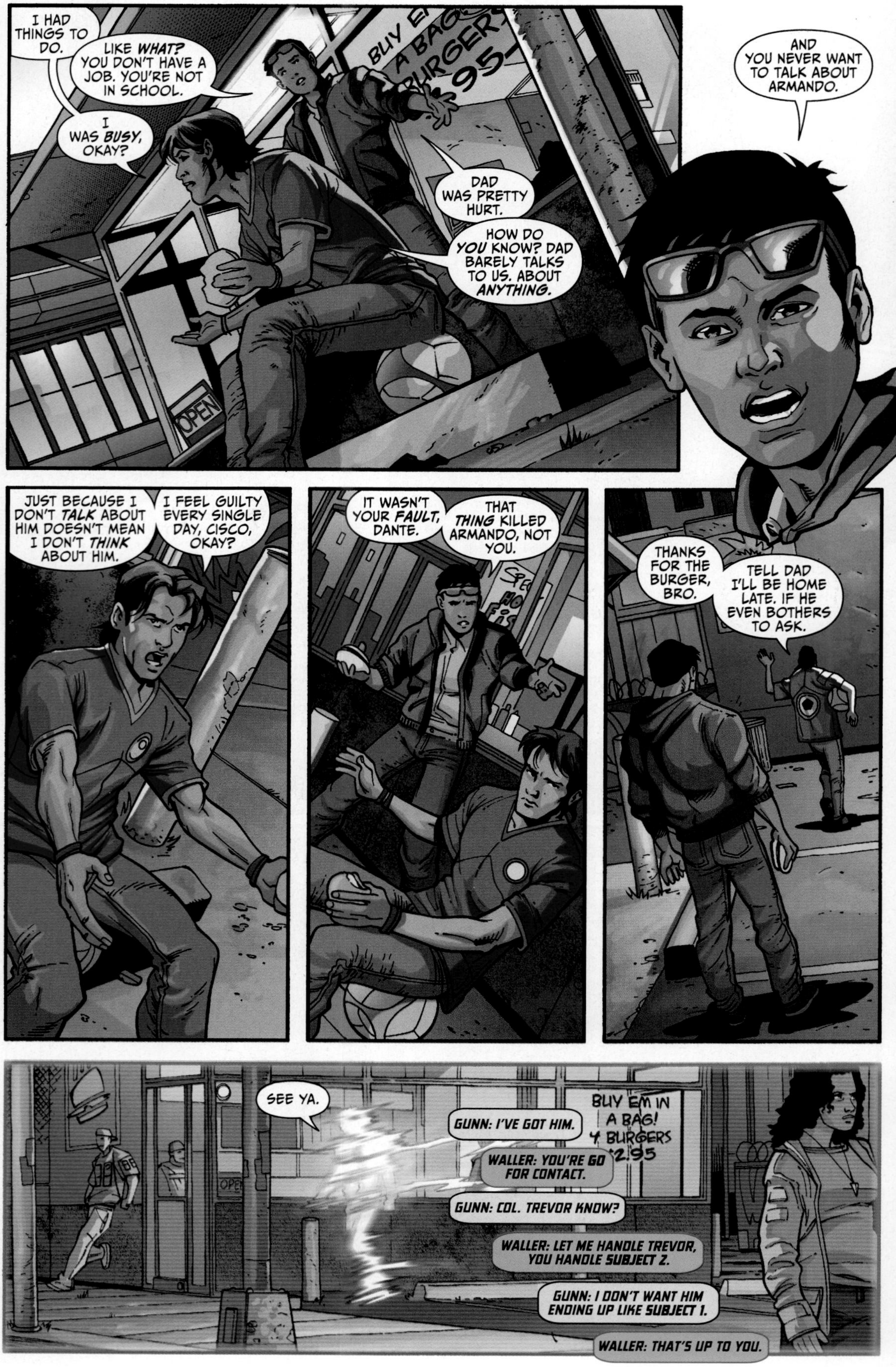
BUY EM IN A BAG 4 BURGERS $2.95
I HAD THINGS TO DO.
LIKE WHAT? YOU DON'T HAVE A JOB. YOU'RE NOT IN SCHOOL.
I WAS BUSY, OKAY?
DAD WAS PRETTY HURT.
HOW DO YOU KNOW? DAD BARELY TALKS TO US. ABOUT ANYTHING.
AND YOU NEVER WANT TO TALK ABOUT ARMANDO.
OPEN
JUST BECAUSE I DON'T TALK ABOUT HIM DOESN'T MEAN I DON'T THINK ABOUT HIM.
I FEEL GUILTY EVERY SINGLE DAY, CISCO, OKAY?
IT WASN'T YOUR FAULT, DANTE.
THAT THING KILLED ARMANDO, NOT YOU.
THANKS FOR THE BURGER, BRO.
TELL DAD I'LL BE HOME LATE. IF HE EVEN BOTHERS TO ASK.
SEE YA.
GUNN: I'VE GOT HIM.
WALLER: YOU'RE GO FOR CONTACT.
GUNN: COL. TREVOR KNOW?
WALLER: LET ME HANDLE TREVOR, YOU HANDLE SUBJECT 2.
GUNN: I DON'T WANT HIM ENDING UP LIKE SUBJECT 1.
WALLER: THAT'S UP TO YOU.

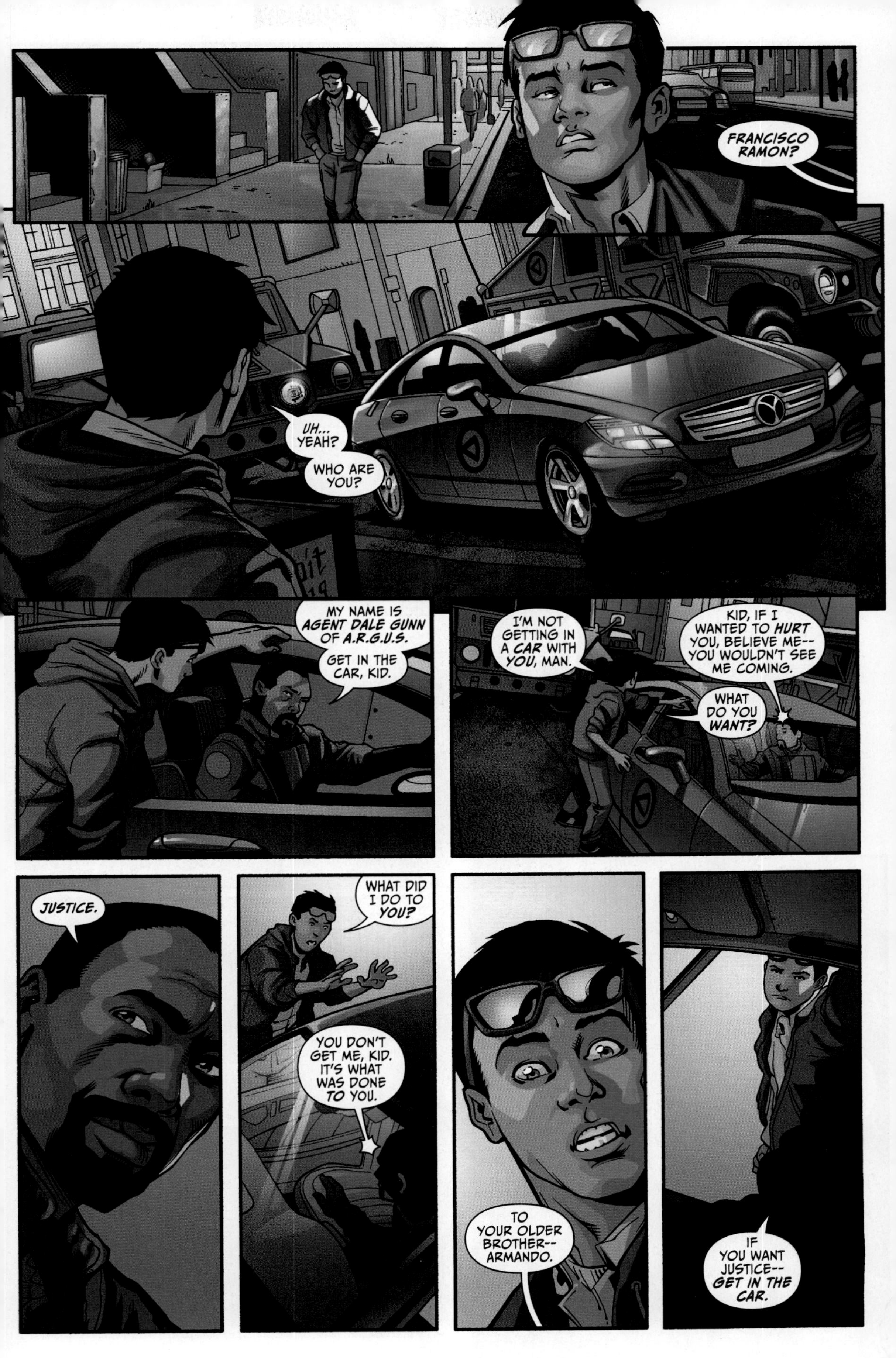
FRANCISCO RAMON?
UH... YEAH?
WHO ARE YOU?
MY NAME IS AGENT DALE GUNN OF A.R.G.U.S.
GET IN THE CAR, KID.
I'M NOT GETTING IN A CAR WITH YOU, MAN.
KID, IF I WANTED TO HURT YOU, BELIEVE ME-- YOU WOULDN'T SEE ME COMING.
WHAT DO YOU WANT?
JUSTICE.
WHAT DID I DO TO YOU?
YOU DON'T GET ME, KID. IT'S WHAT WAS DONE TO YOU.
TO YOUR OLDER BROTHER-- ARMANDO.
IF YOU WANT JUSTICE-- GET IN THE CAR.

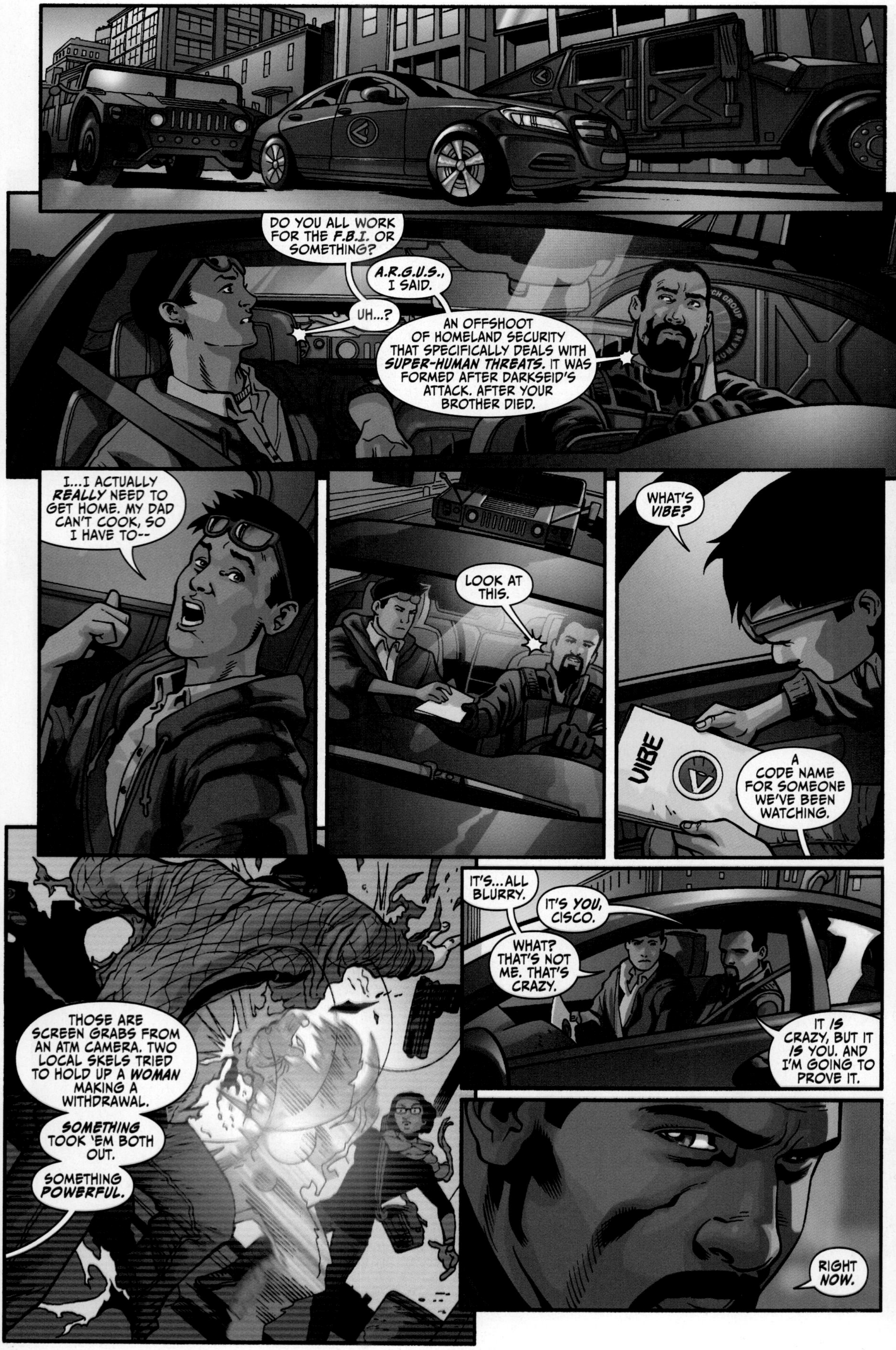
DO YOU ALL WORK FOR THE F.B.I. OR SOMETHING?
A.R.G.U.S., I SAID.
UH...?
AN OFFSHOOT OF HOMELAND SECURITY THAT SPECIFICALLY DEALS WITH SUPER-HUMAN THREATS. IT WAS FORMED AFTER DARKSEID'S ATTACK. AFTER YOUR BROTHER DIED.
I...I ACTUALLY REALLY NEED TO GET HOME. MY DAD CAN'T COOK, SO I HAVE TO--
LOOK AT THIS.
WHAT'S VIBE?
VIBE
A CODE NAME FOR SOMEONE WE'VE BEEN WATCHING.
THOSE ARE SCREEN GRABS FROM AN ATM CAMERA. TWO LOCAL SKELS TRIED TO HOLD UP A WOMAN MAKING A WITHDRAWAL.
SOMETHING TOOK 'EM BOTH OUT.
SOMETHING POWERFUL.
IT'S...ALL BLURRY.
IT'S YOU, CISCO.
WHAT? THAT'S NOT ME. THAT'S CRAZY.
IT IS CRAZY, BUT IT IS YOU. AND I'M GOING TO PROVE IT.
RIGHT NOW.

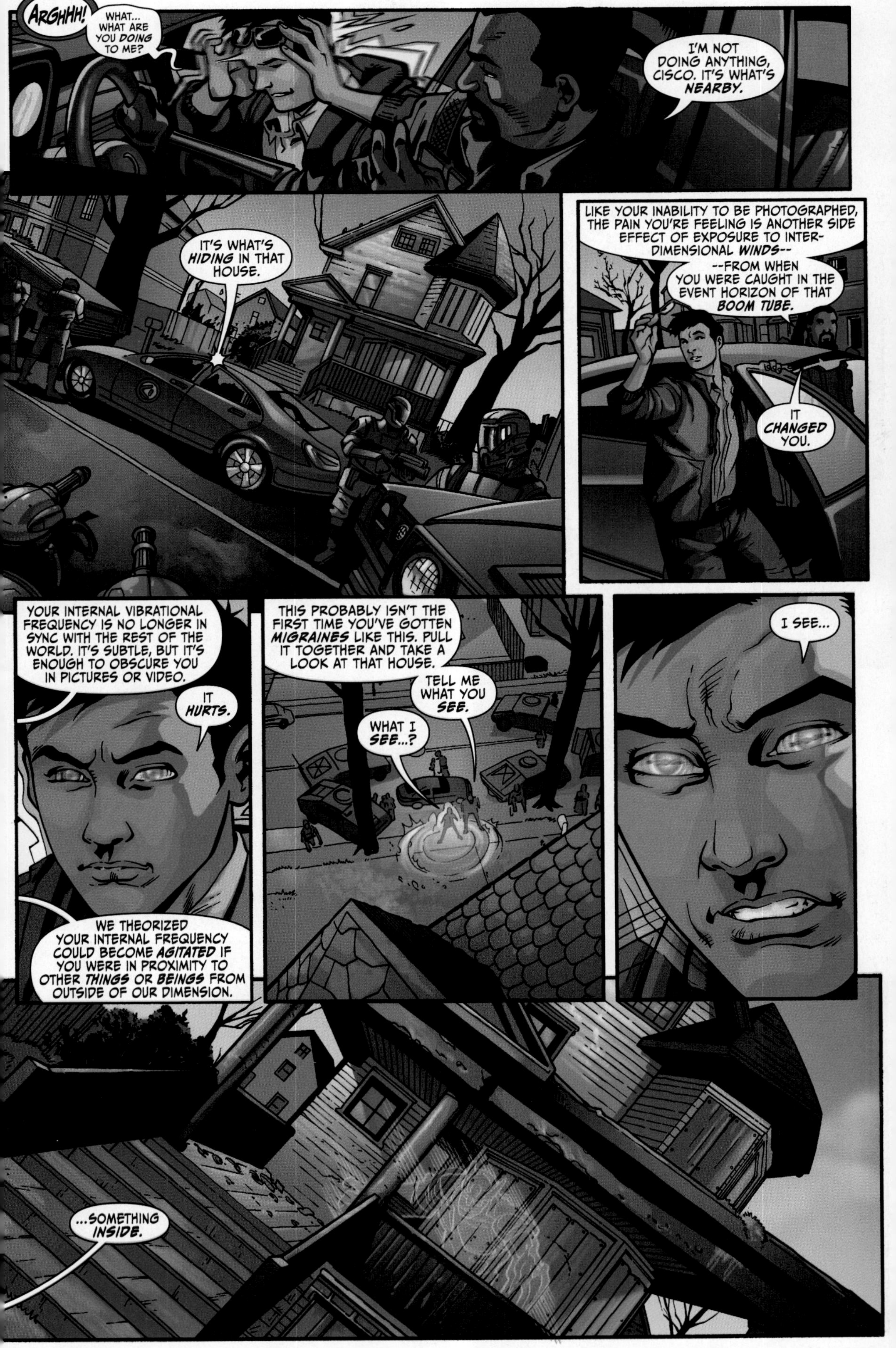
ARGHHH!
WHAT... WHAT ARE YOU DOING TO ME?
I'M NOT DOING ANYTHING, CISCO. IT'S WHAT'S NEARBY.
IT'S WHAT'S HIDING IN THAT HOUSE.
LIKE YOUR INABILITY TO BE PHOTOGRAPHED, THE PAIN YOU'RE FEELING IS ANOTHER SIDE EFFECT OF EXPOSURE TO INTER-DIMENSIONAL WINDS--
--FROM WHEN YOU WERE CAUGHT IN THE EVENT HORIZON OF THAT BOOM TUBE.
IT CHANGED YOU.
YOUR INTERNAL VIBRATIONAL FREQUENCY IS NO LONGER IN SYNC WITH THE REST OF THE WORLD. IT'S SUBTLE, BUT IT'S ENOUGH TO OBSCURE YOU IN PICTURES OR VIDEO.
IT HURTS.
WE THEORIZED YOUR INTERNAL FREQUENCY COULD BECOME AGITATED IF YOU WERE IN PROXIMITY TO OTHER THINGS OR BEINGS FROM OUTSIDE OF OUR DIMENSION.
THIS PROBABLY ISN'T THE FIRST TIME YOU'VE GOTTEN MIGRAINES LIKE THIS. PULL IT TOGETHER AND TAKE A LOOK AT THAT HOUSE.
TELL ME WHAT YOU SEE.
WHAT I SEE...?
I SEE...
...SOMETHING INSIDE.

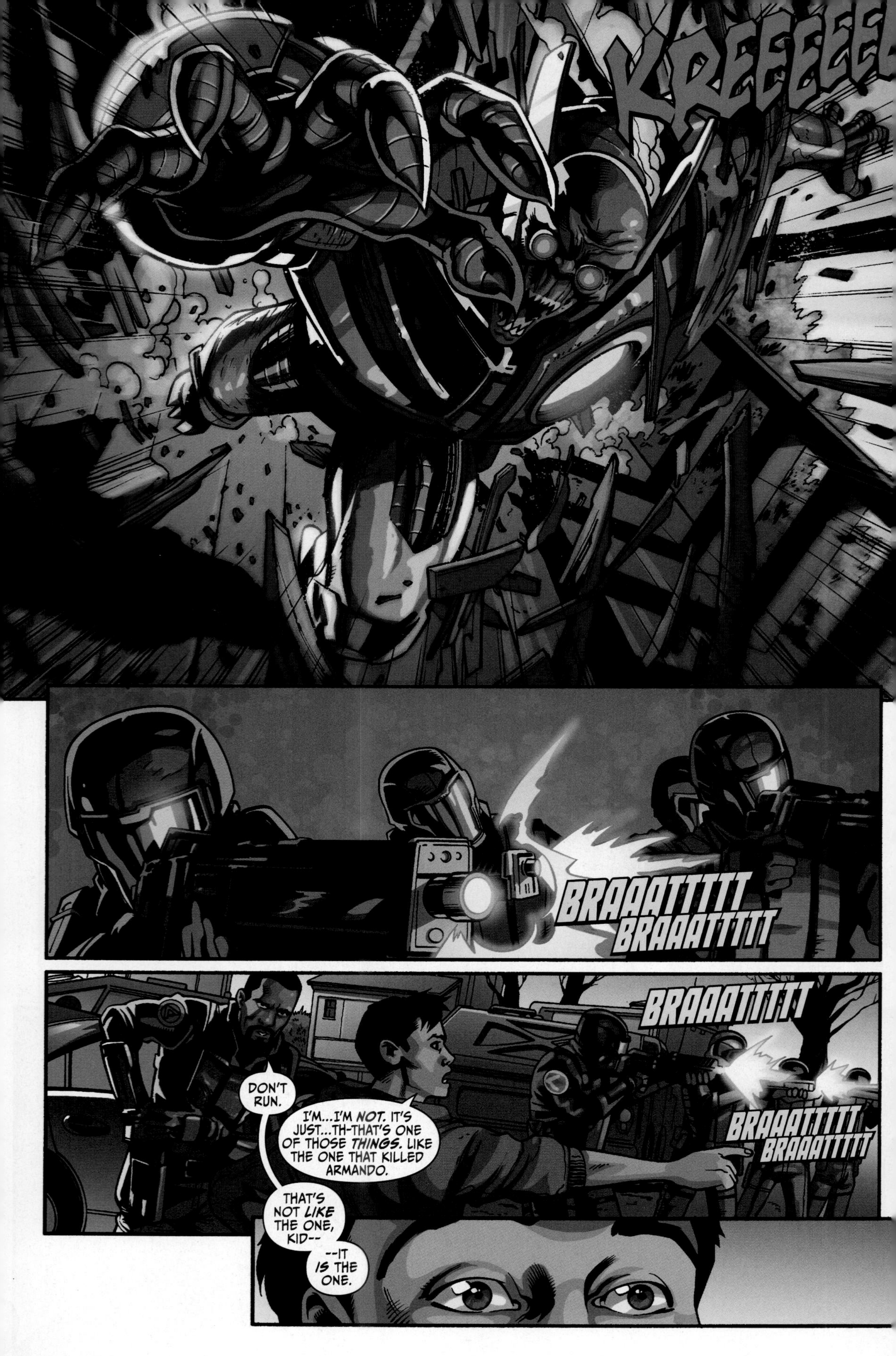
KREEEEEE
BRAAATTTTT
BRAAATTTTT
BRAAATTTTT
BRAAATTTTT
BRAAATTTTT
DON'T RUN.
I'M...I'M NOT. IT'S JUST...TH-THAT'S ONE OF THOSE THINGS. LIKE THE ONE THAT KILLED ARMANDO.
THAT'S NOT LIKE THE ONE, KID--
--IT IS THE ONE.

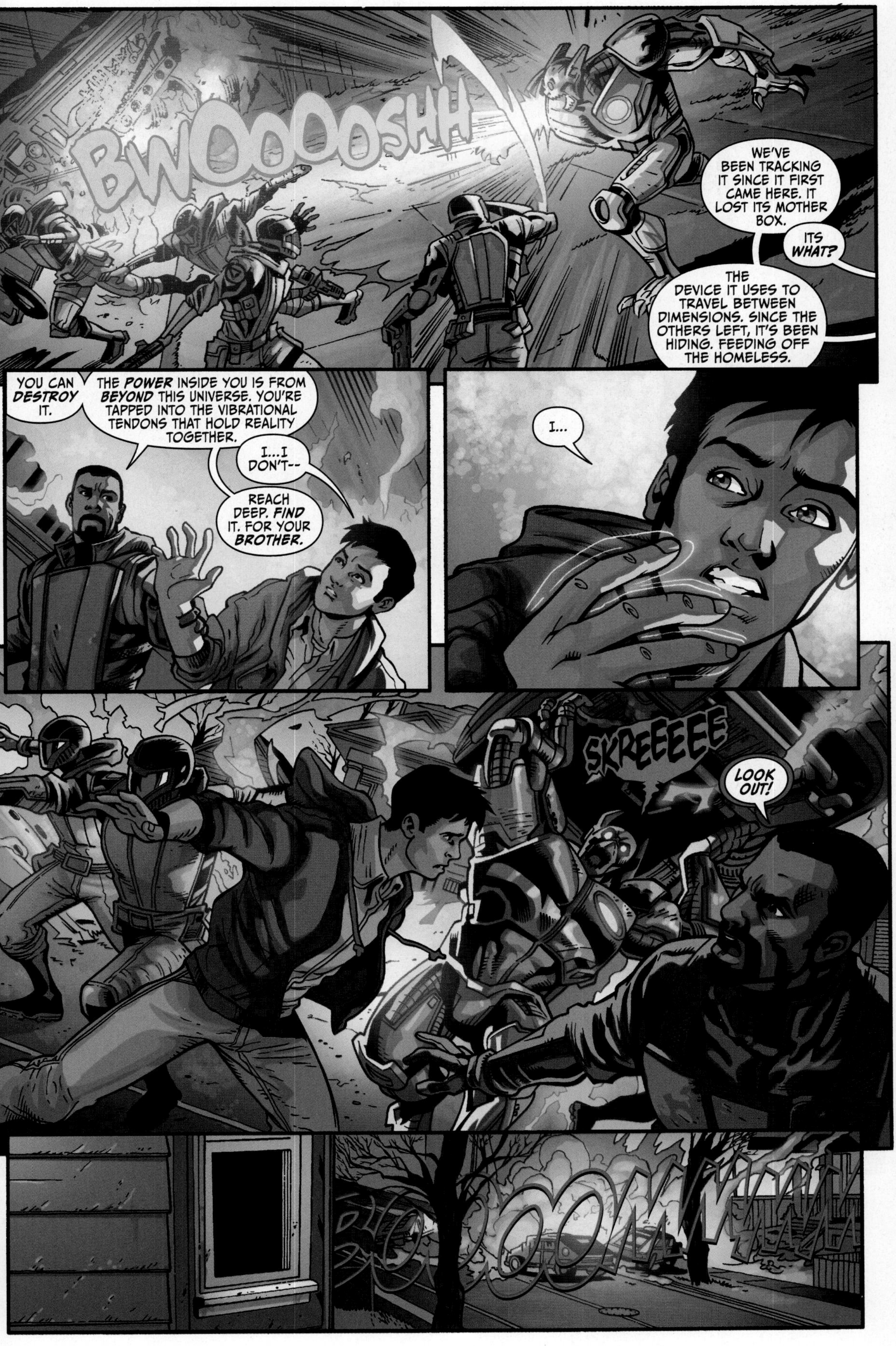
BWOOOOSHH
WE'VE BEEN TRACKING IT SINCE IT FIRST CAME HERE. IT LOST ITS MOTHER BOX.
ITS WHAT?
THE DEVICE IT USES TO TRAVEL BETWEEN DIMENSIONS. SINCE THE OTHERS LEFT, IT'S BEEN HIDING. FEEDING OFF THE HOMELESS.
YOU CAN DESTROY IT.
THE POWER INSIDE YOU IS FROM BEYOND THIS UNIVERSE. YOU'RE TAPPED INTO THE VIBRATIONAL TENDONS THAT HOLD REALITY TOGETHER.
I...I DON'T--
REACH DEEP. FIND IT. FOR YOUR BROTHER.
I...
SKREEEEE
LOOK OUT!

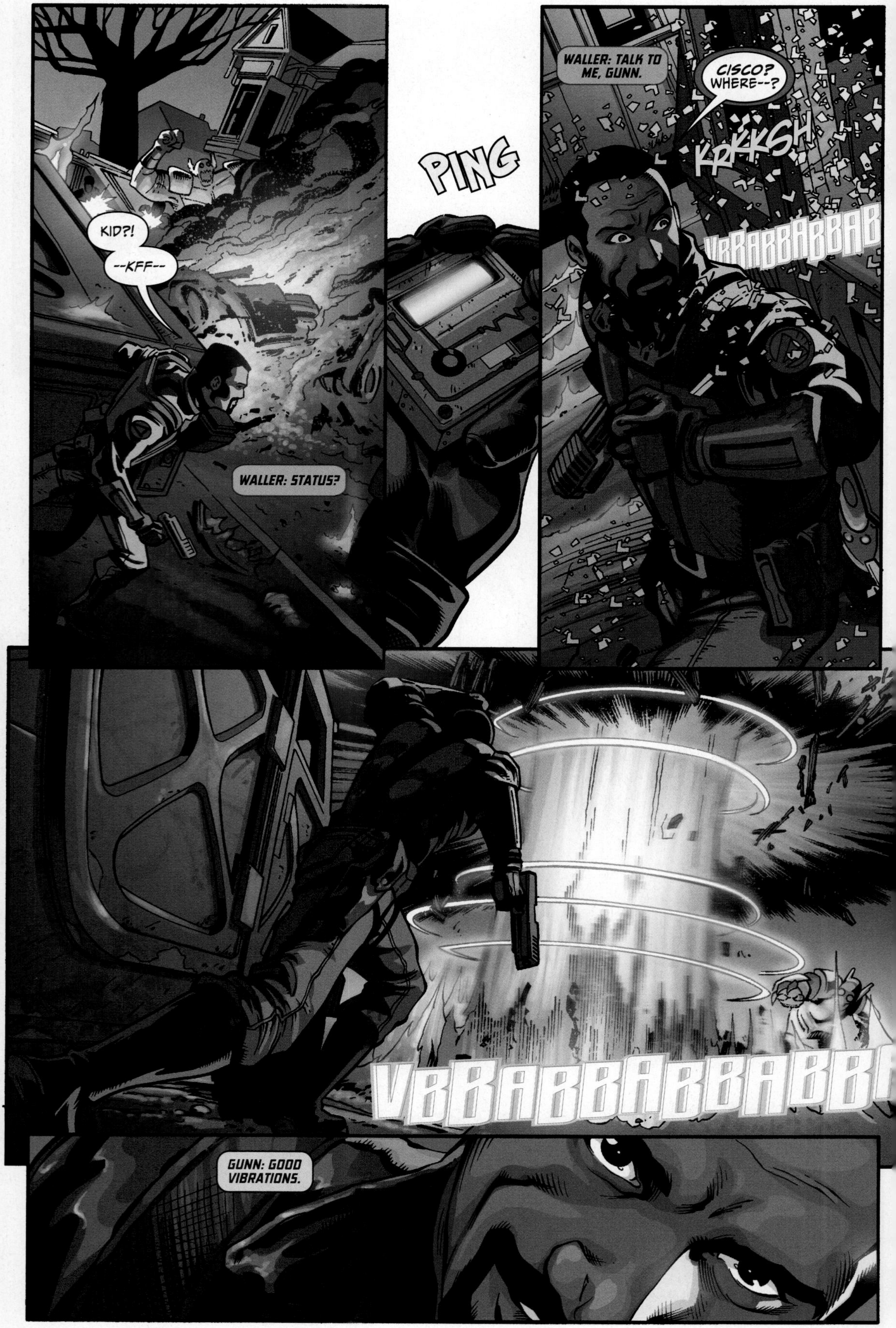
KID?!
--KFF--
WALLER: STATUS?
PING
WALLER: TALK TO ME, GUNN.
CISCO? WHERE--?
KRKKSH
VBRABBABBAB
VBBABBABBABB
GUNN: GOOD VIBRATIONS.

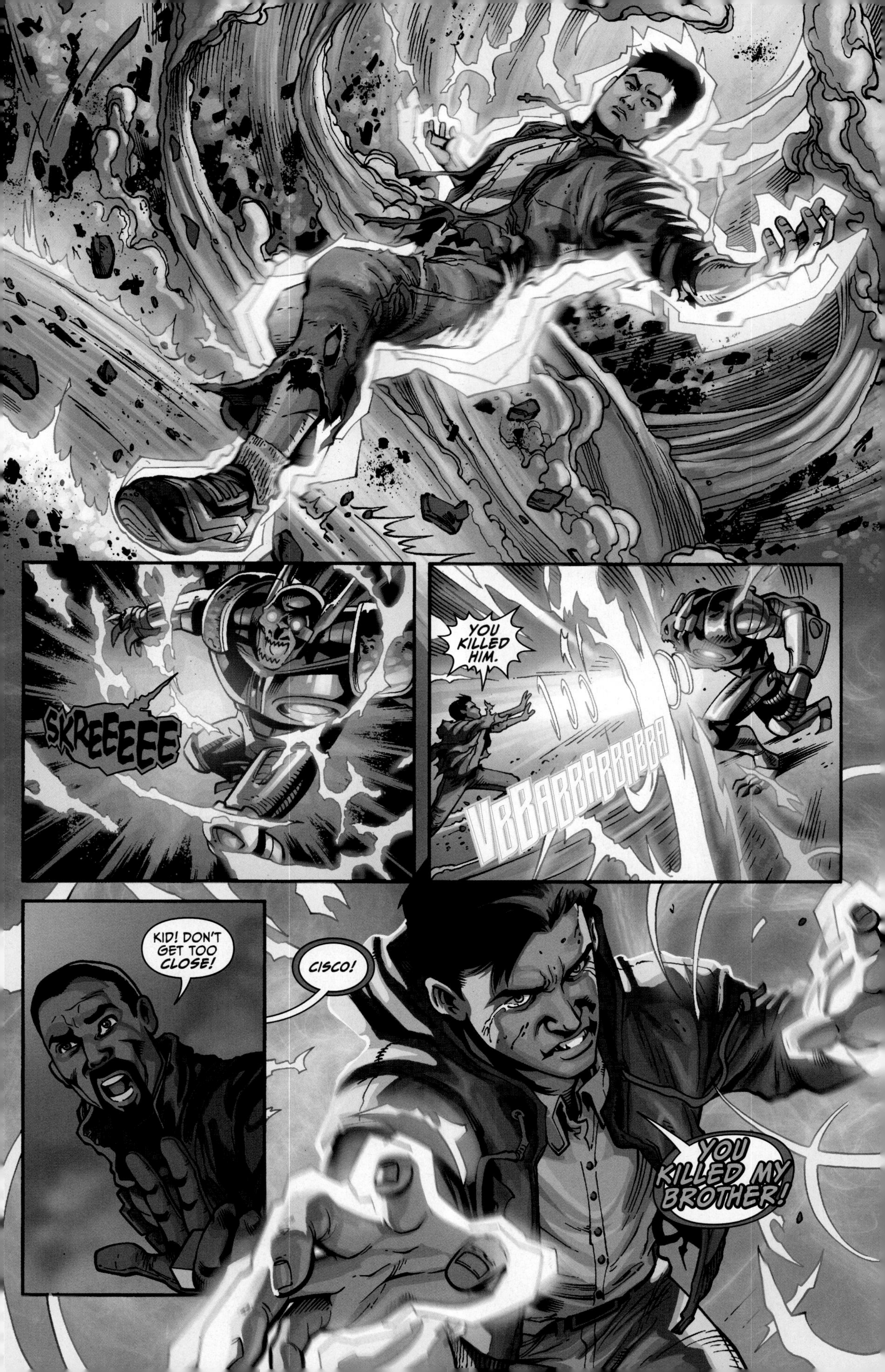
SKREEEEEE
YOU KILLED HIM.
VBBABBABBABBA
KID! DON'T GET TOO CLOSE!
CISCO!
YOU KILLED MY BROTHER!

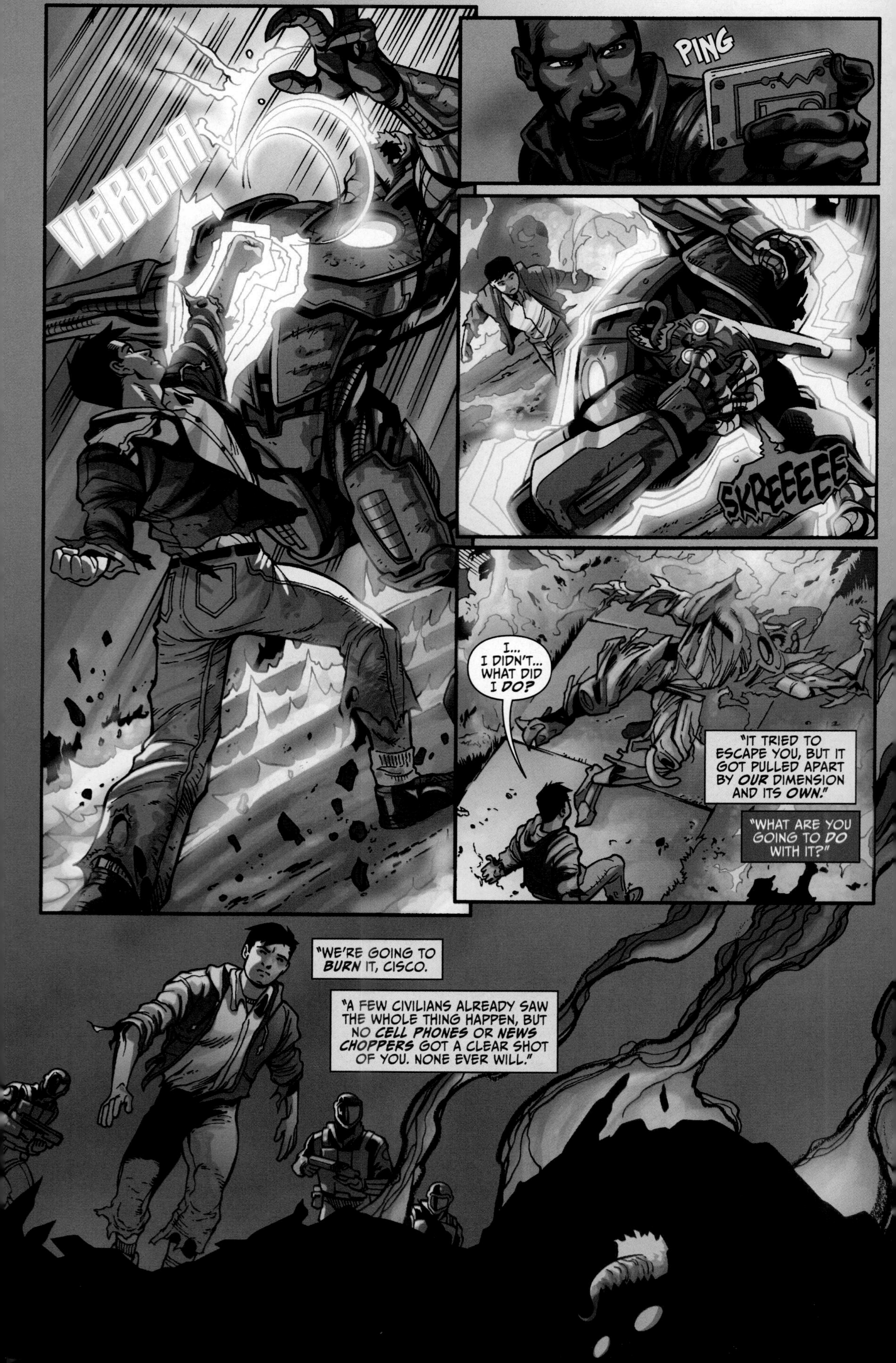
VBBBAA
PING
SKREEEEE
I... I DIDN'T... WHAT DID I DO?
"IT TRIED TO ESCAPE YOU, BUT IT GOT PULLED APART BY OUR DIMENSION AND ITS OWN."
"WHAT ARE YOU GOING TO DO WITH IT?"
"WE'RE GOING TO BURN IT, CISCO.
"A FEW CIVILIANS ALREADY SAW THE WHOLE THING HAPPEN, BUT NO CELL PHONES OR NEWS CHOPPERS GOT A CLEAR SHOT OF YOU. NONE EVER WILL."

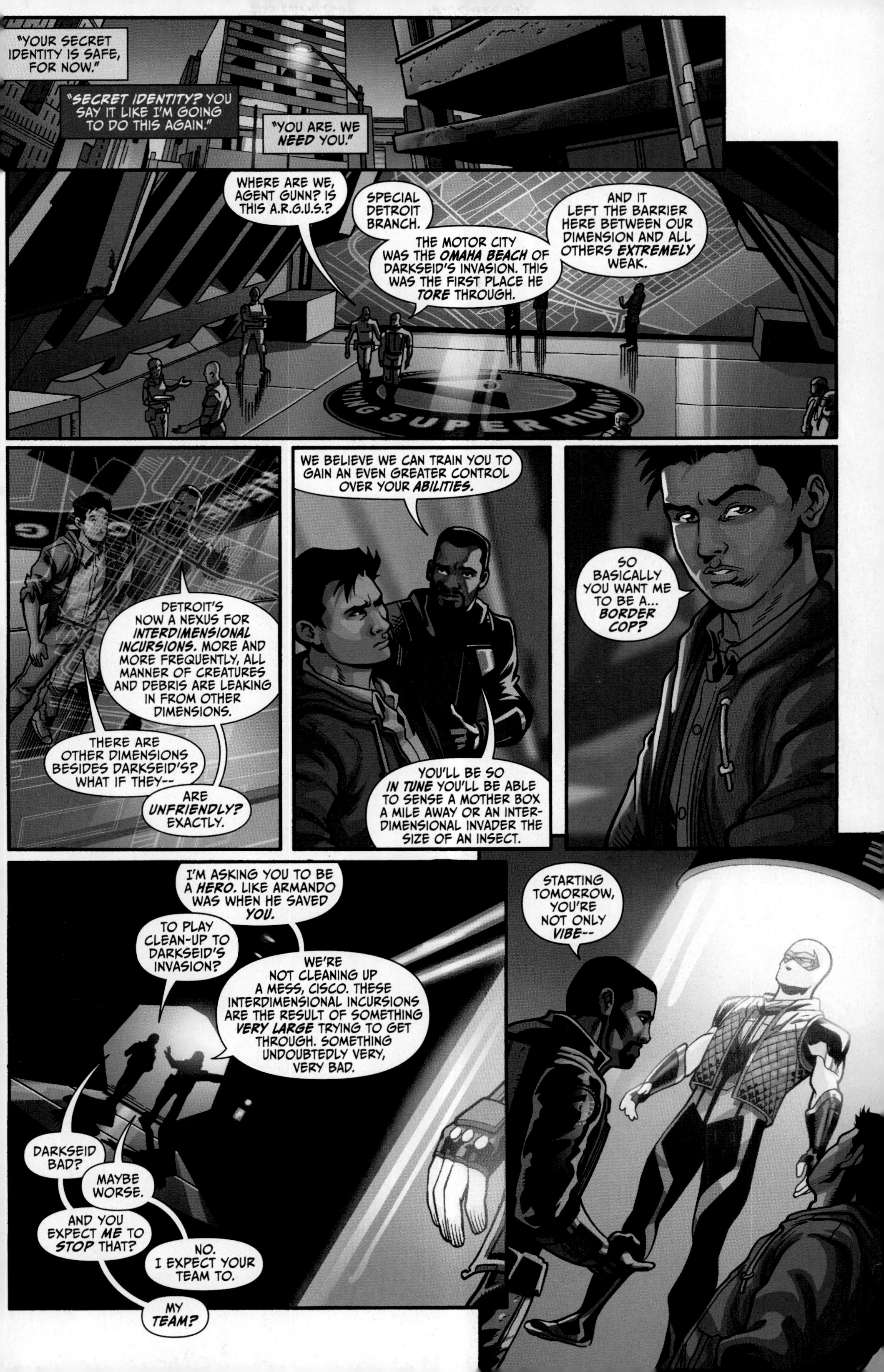
"YOUR SECRET IDENTITY IS SAFE, FOR NOW."
"SECRET IDENTITY? YOU SAY IT LIKE I'M GOING TO DO THIS AGAIN."
"YOU ARE. WE NEED YOU."
WHERE ARE WE, AGENT GUNN? IS THIS A.R.G.U.S.?
SPECIAL DETROIT BRANCH.
THE MOTOR CITY WAS THE OMAHA BEACH OF DARKSEID'S INVASION. THIS WAS THE FIRST PLACE HE TORE THROUGH.
AND IT LEFT THE BARRIER HERE BETWEEN OUR DIMENSION AND ALL OTHERS EXTREMELY WEAK.
SUPER HUMANS
DETROIT'S NOW A NEXUS FOR INTERDIMENSIONAL INCURSIONS. MORE AND MORE FREQUENTLY, ALL MANNER OF CREATURES AND DEBRIS ARE LEAKING IN FROM OTHER DIMENSIONS.
THERE ARE OTHER DIMENSIONS BESIDES DARKSEID'S? WHAT IF THEY--
ARE UNFRIENDLY? EXACTLY.
WE BELIEVE WE CAN TRAIN YOU TO GAIN AN EVEN GREATER CONTROL OVER YOUR ABILITIES.
YOU'LL BE SO IN TUNE YOU'LL BE ABLE TO SENSE A MOTHER BOX A MILE AWAY OR AN INTER-DIMENSIONAL INVADER THE SIZE OF AN INSECT.
SO BASICALLY YOU WANT ME TO BE A... BORDER COP?
I'M ASKING YOU TO BE A HERO. LIKE ARMANDO WAS WHEN HE SAVED YOU.
TO PLAY CLEAN-UP TO DARKSEID'S INVASION?
WE'RE NOT CLEANING UP A MESS, CISCO. THESE INTERDIMENSIONAL INCURSIONS ARE THE RESULT OF SOMETHING VERY LARGE TRYING TO GET THROUGH. SOMETHING UNDOUBTEDLY VERY, VERY BAD.
DARKSEID BAD?
MAYBE WORSE.
AND YOU EXPECT ME TO STOP THAT?
NO. I EXPECT YOUR TEAM TO.
MY TEAM?
STARTING TOMORROW, YOU'RE NOT ONLY VIBE--

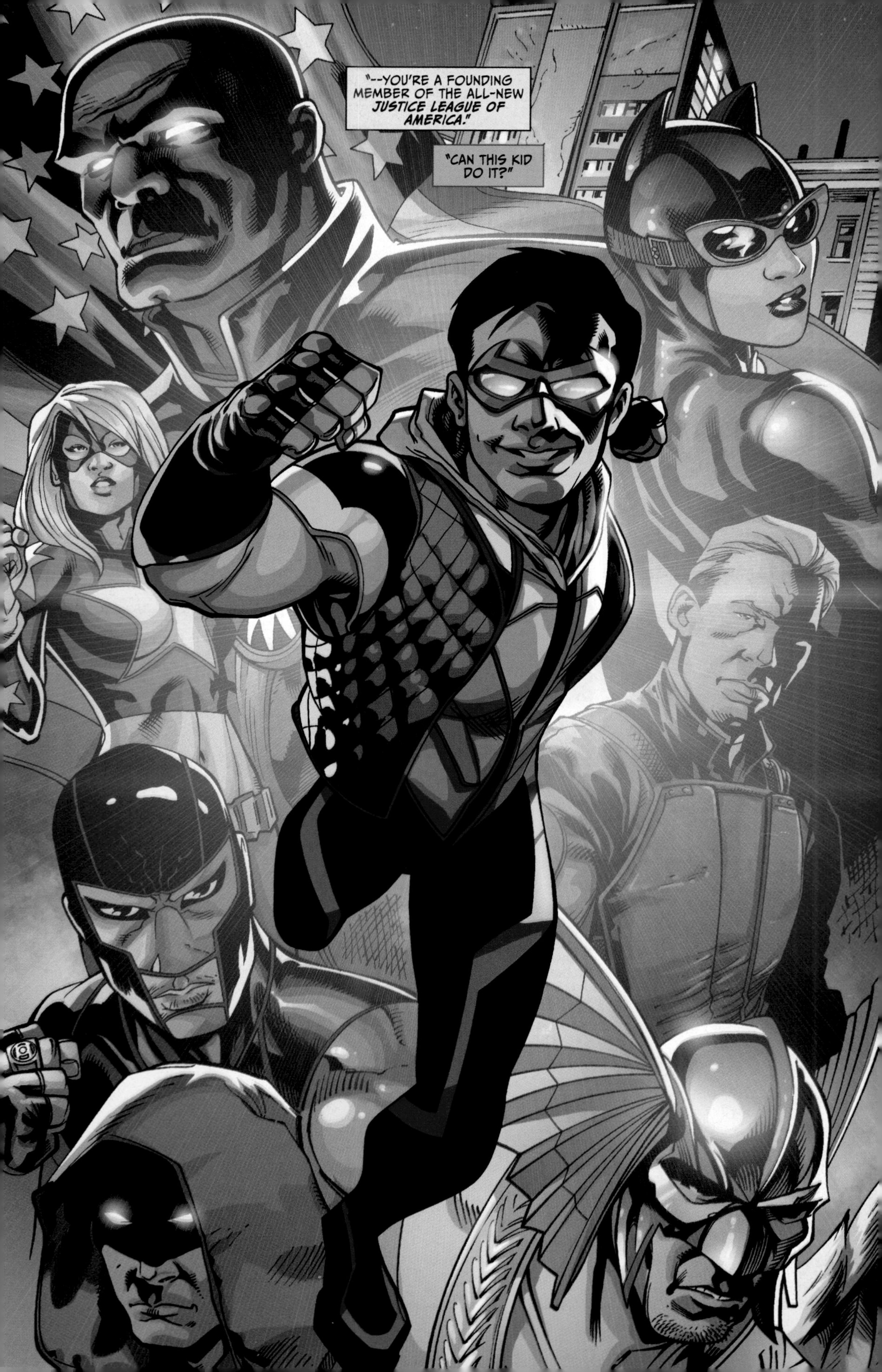
"--YOU'RE A FOUNDING MEMBER OF THE ALL-NEW *JUSTICE LEAGUE OF AMERICA.*"
"CAN THIS KID DO IT?"

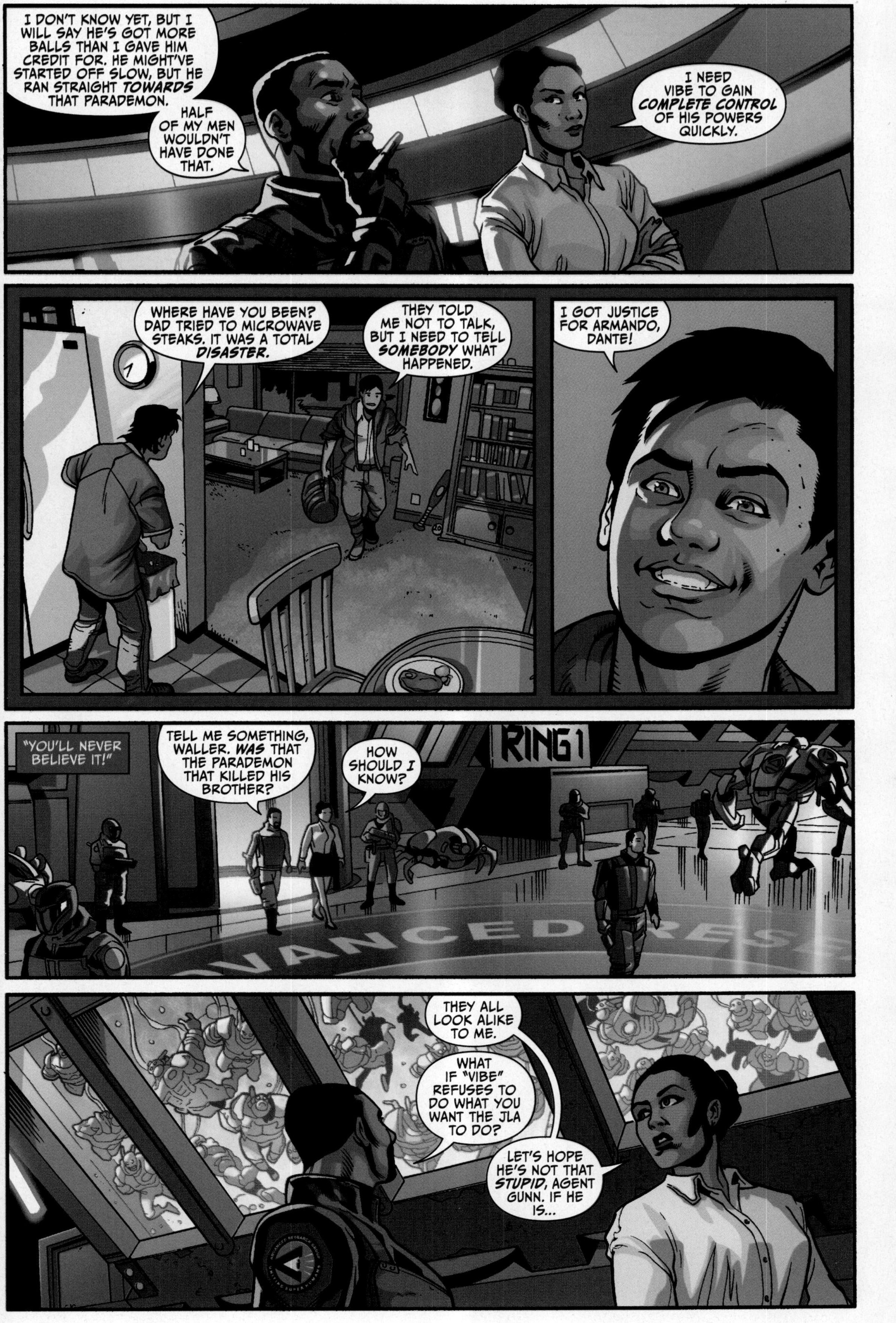
I DON'T KNOW YET, BUT I WILL SAY HE'S GOT MORE BALLS THAN I GAVE HIM CREDIT FOR. HE MIGHT'VE STARTED OFF SLOW, BUT HE RAN STRAIGHT *TOWARDS* THAT PARADEMON.
HALF OF MY MEN WOULDN'T HAVE DONE THAT.
I NEED VIBE TO GAIN *COMPLETE CONTROL* OF HIS POWERS QUICKLY.
WHERE HAVE YOU BEEN? DAD TRIED TO MICROWAVE STEAKS. IT WAS A TOTAL *DISASTER.*
THEY TOLD ME NOT TO TALK, BUT I NEED TO TELL *SOMEBODY* WHAT HAPPENED.
I GOT JUSTICE FOR ARMANDO, DANTE!
"YOU'LL NEVER BELIEVE IT!"
TELL ME SOMETHING, WALLER. *WAS* THAT THE PARADEMON THAT KILLED HIS BROTHER?
HOW SHOULD *I* KNOW?
RING 1
ADVANCED RES
THEY ALL LOOK ALIKE TO ME.
WHAT IF "VIBE" REFUSES TO DO WHAT YOU WANT THE JLA TO DO?
LET'S HOPE HE'S NOT THAT *STUPID*, AGENT GUNN. IF HE IS...

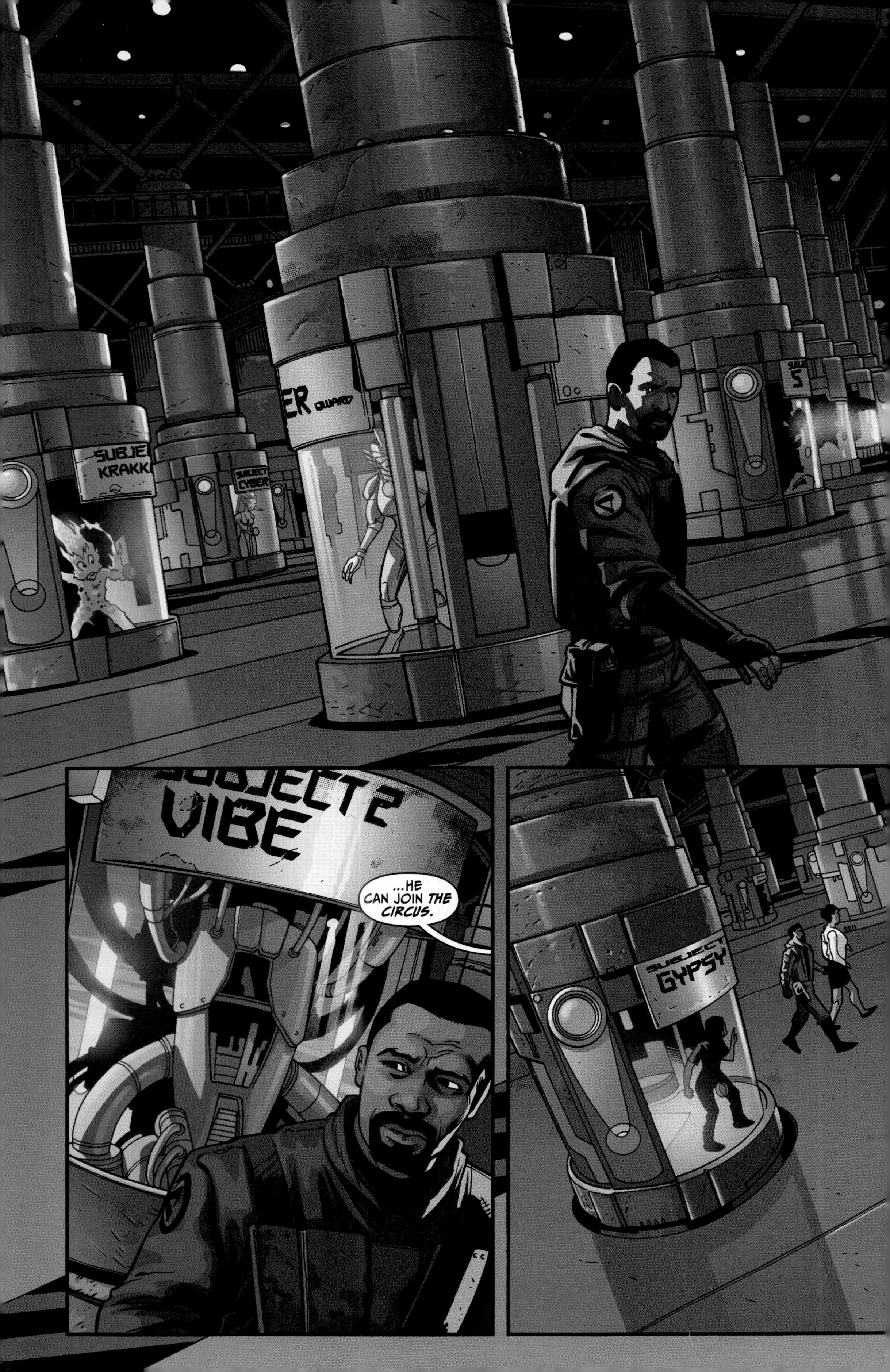
KRAKK
SUBJECT CYBER
VIBE
...HE CAN JOIN THE CIRCUS.
SUBJECT GYPSY

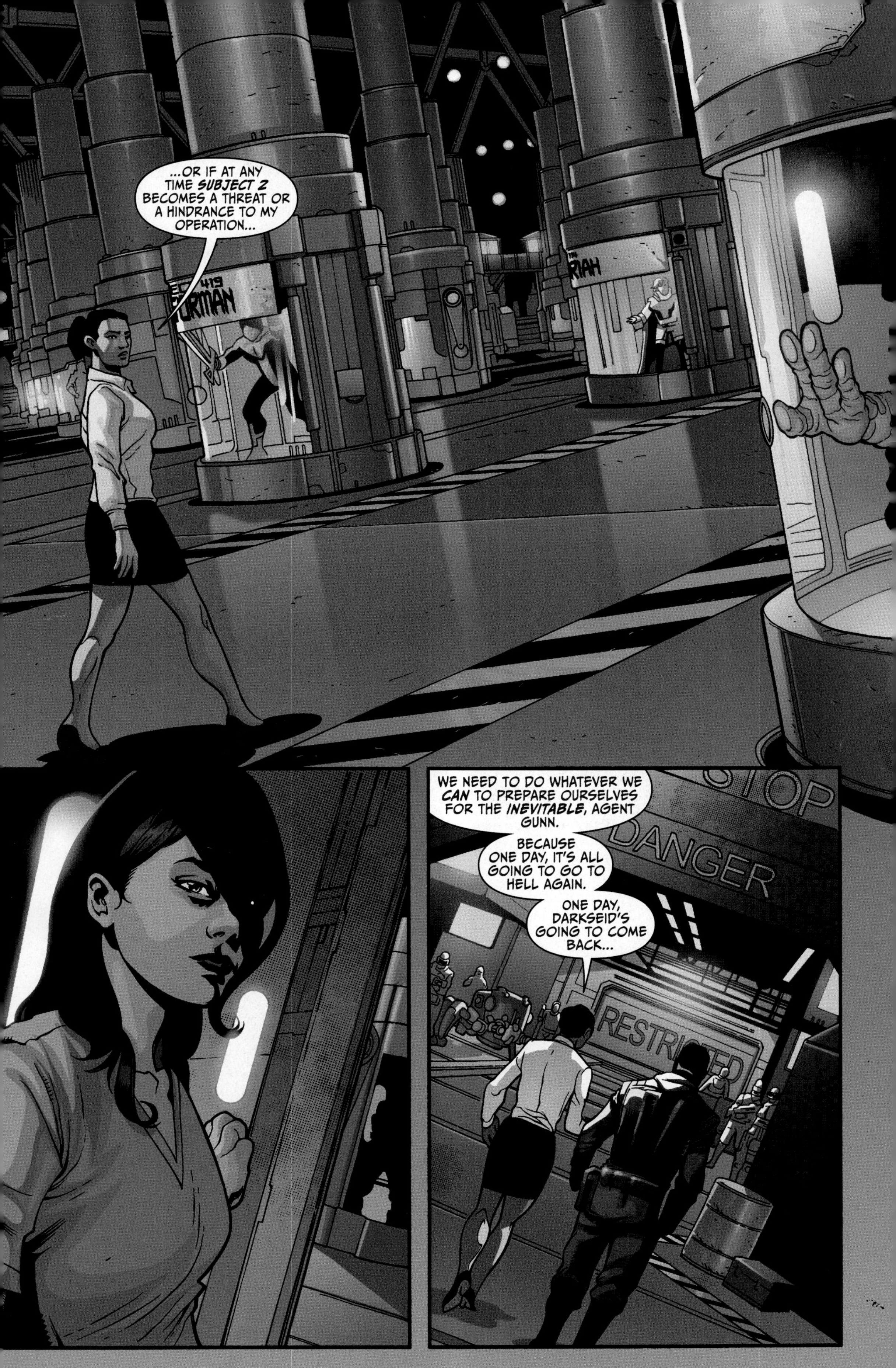
...OR IF AT ANY TIME SUBJECT 2 BECOMES A THREAT OR A HINDRANCE TO MY OPERATION...
WE NEED TO DO WHATEVER WE CAN TO PREPARE OURSELVES FOR THE INEVITABLE, AGENT GUNN.
BECAUSE ONE DAY, IT'S ALL GOING TO GO TO HELL AGAIN.
ONE DAY, DARKSEID'S GOING TO COME BACK...
STOP
DANGER

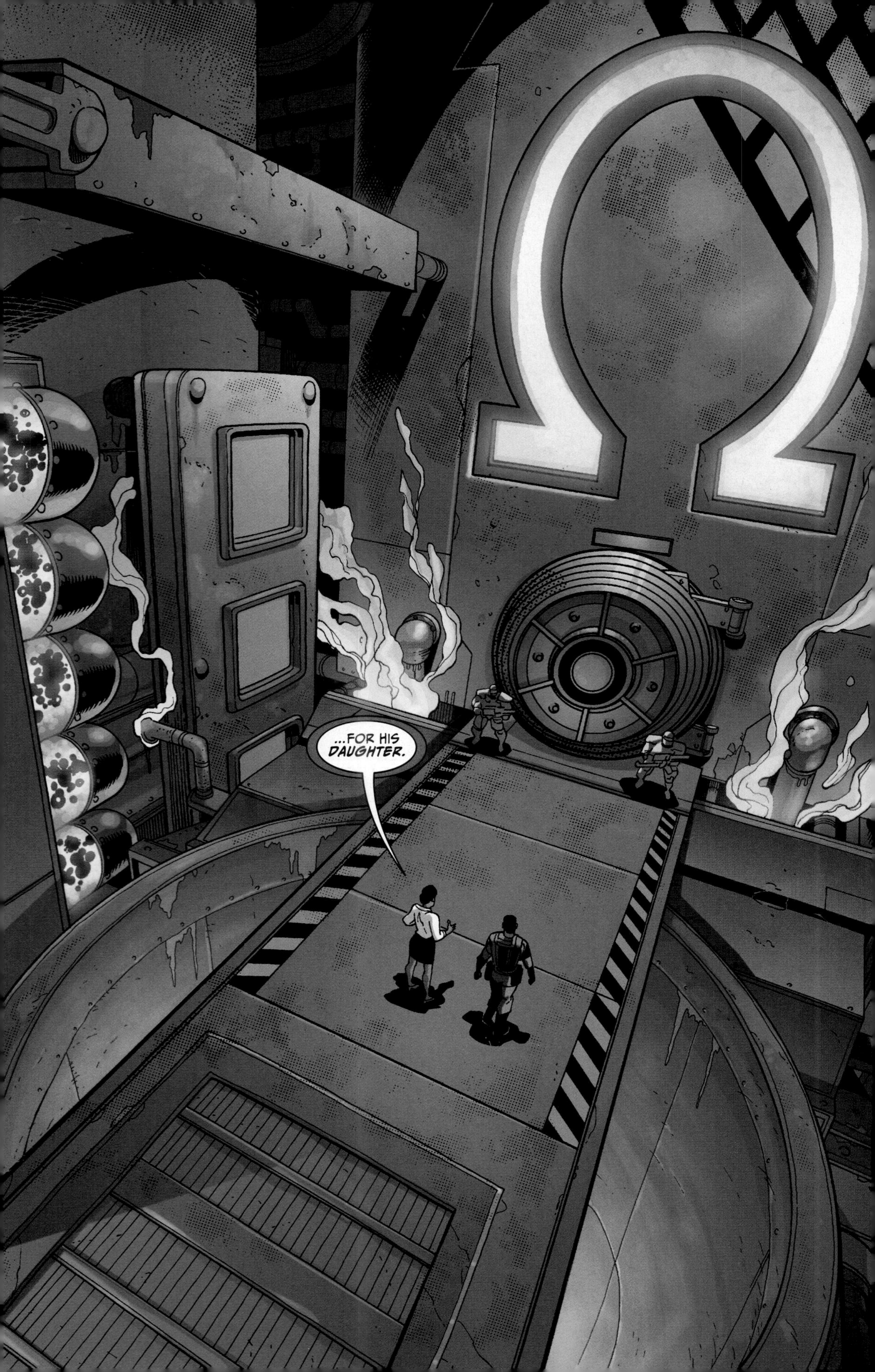
...FOR HIS DAUGHTER.

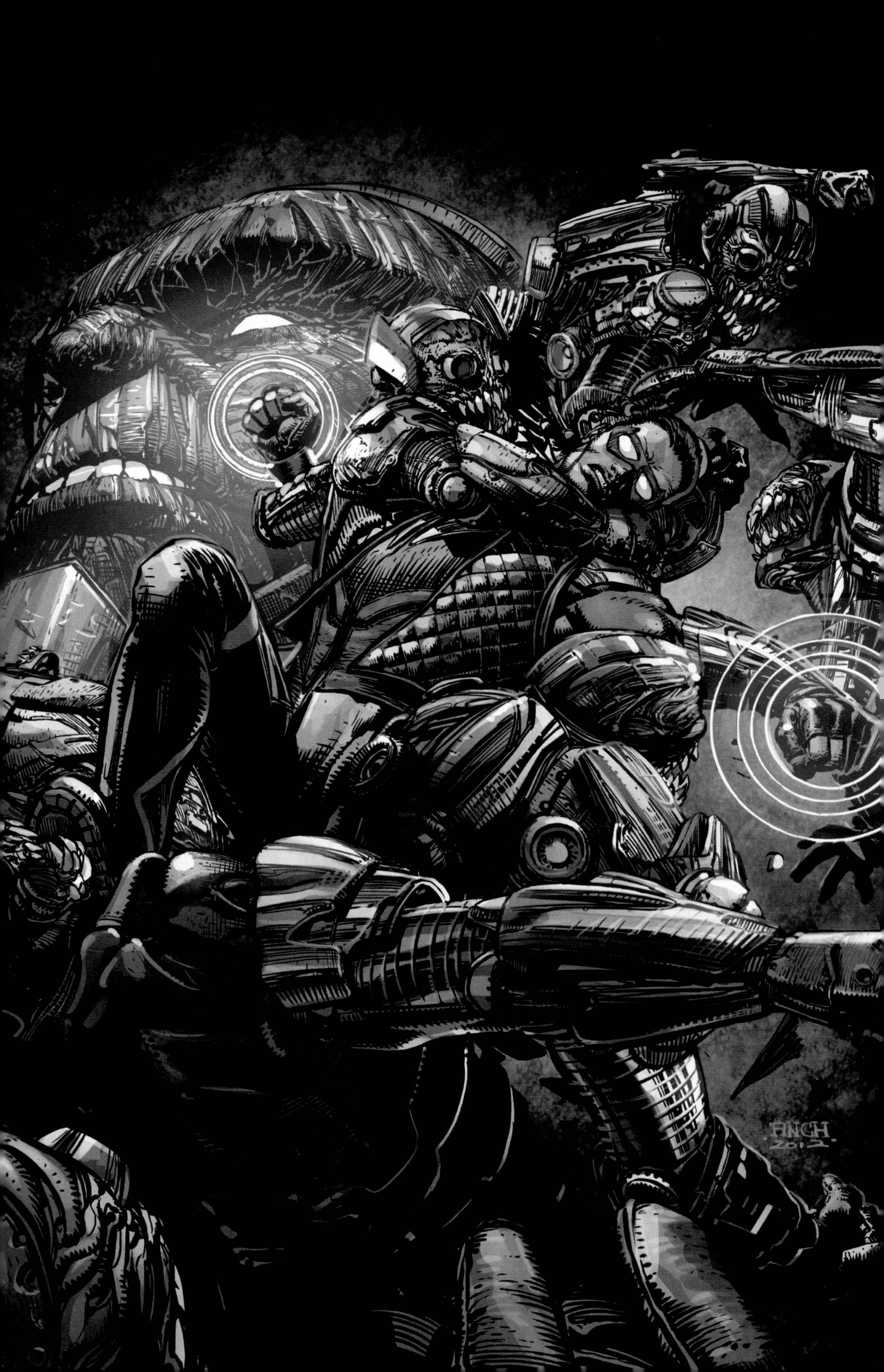
FINCH
2012

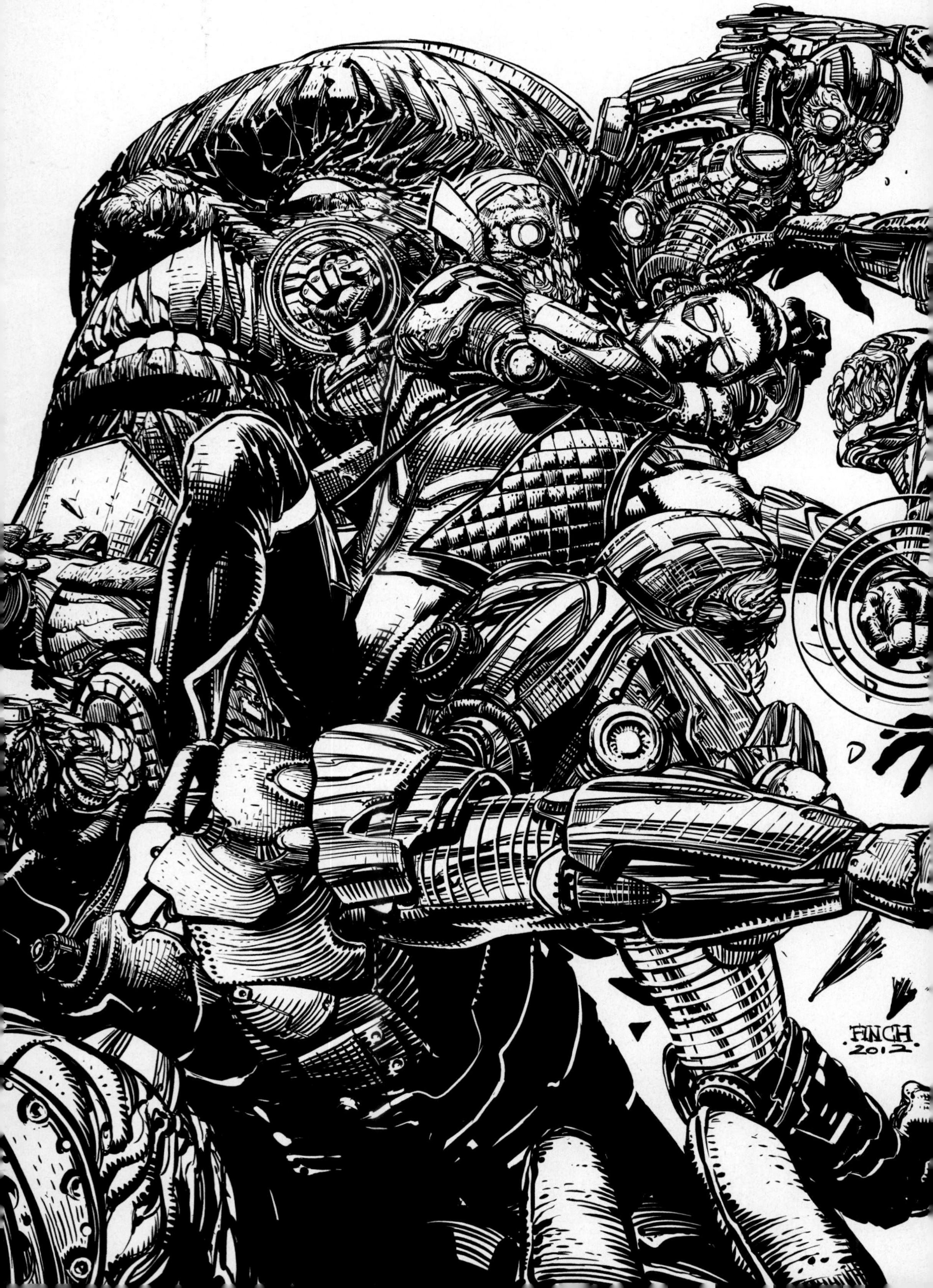
FINCH
2012

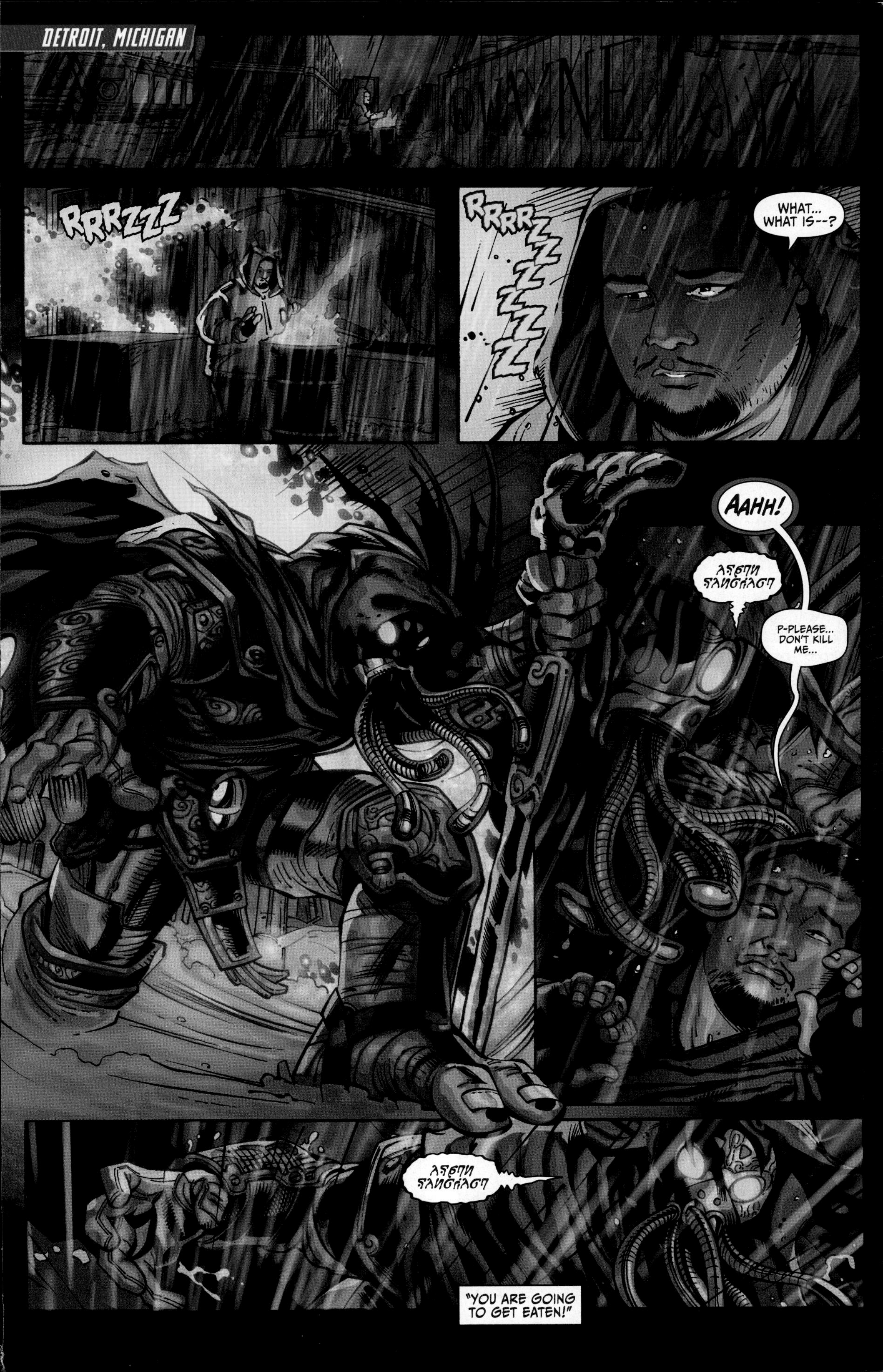
DETROIT, MICHIGAN
RRRZZZ
RRRRZZZZZZZ
WHAT... WHAT IS--?
AAHH!
P-PLEASE... DON'T KILL ME...
"YOU ARE GOING TO GET EATEN!"

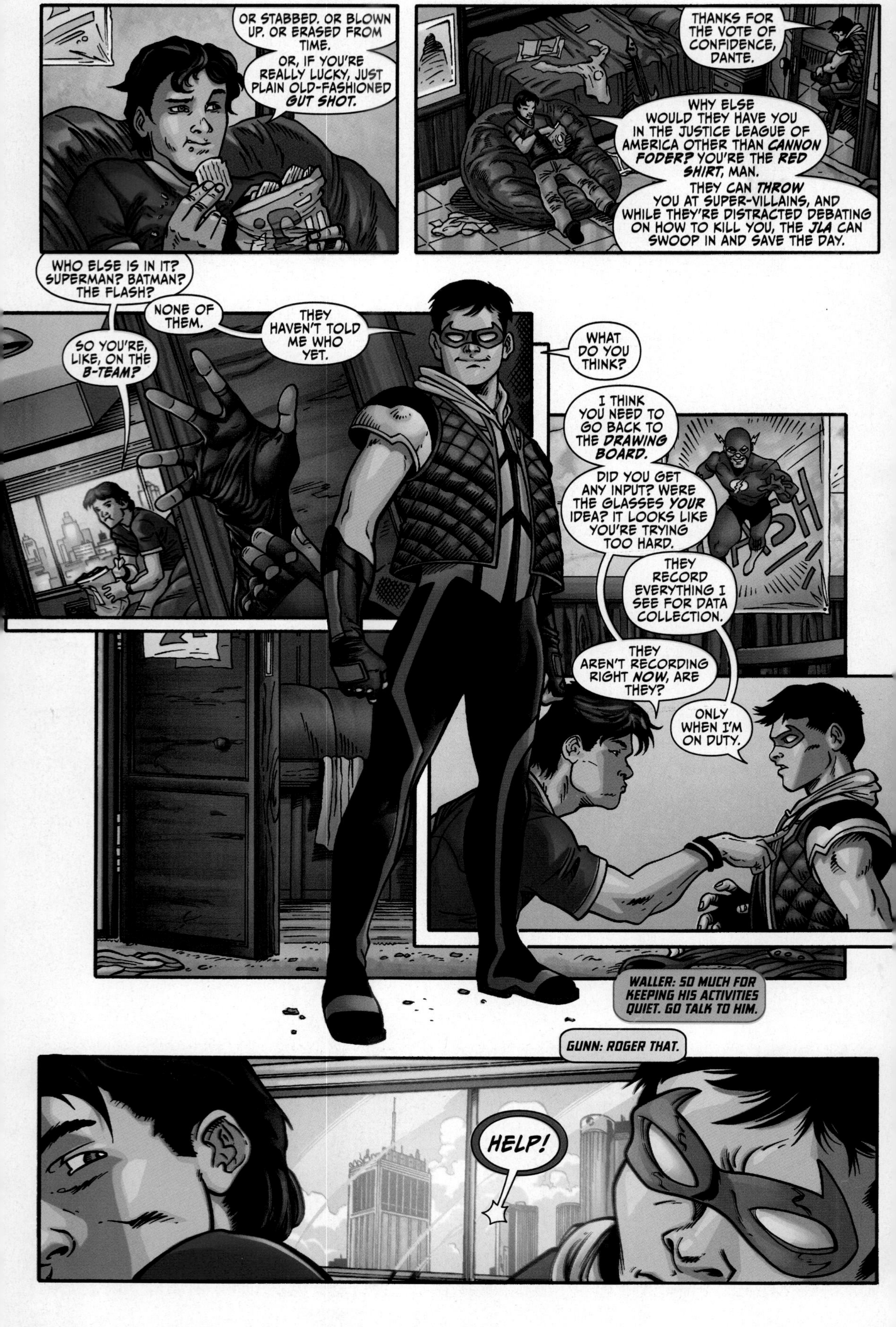
OR STABBED. OR BLOWN UP. OR ERASED FROM TIME.
OR, IF YOU'RE REALLY LUCKY, JUST PLAIN OLD-FASHIONED GUT SHOT.
THANKS FOR THE VOTE OF CONFIDENCE, DANTE.
WHY ELSE WOULD THEY HAVE YOU IN THE JUSTICE LEAGUE OF AMERICA OTHER THAN CANNON FODER? YOU'RE THE RED SHIRT, MAN.
THEY CAN THROW YOU AT SUPER-VILLAINS, AND WHILE THEY'RE DISTRACTED DEBATING ON HOW TO KILL YOU, THE JLA CAN SWOOP IN AND SAVE THE DAY.
WHO ELSE IS IN IT? SUPERMAN? BATMAN? THE FLASH?
NONE OF THEM.
THEY HAVEN'T TOLD ME WHO YET.
SO YOU'RE, LIKE, ON THE B-TEAM?
WHAT DO YOU THINK?
I THINK YOU NEED TO GO BACK TO THE DRAWING BOARD.
DID YOU GET ANY INPUT? WERE THE GLASSES YOUR IDEA? IT LOOKS LIKE YOU'RE TRYING TOO HARD.
THEY RECORD EVERYTHING I SEE FOR DATA COLLECTION.
THEY AREN'T RECORDING RIGHT NOW, ARE THEY?
ONLY WHEN I'M ON DUTY.
WALLER: SO MUCH FOR KEEPING HIS ACTIVITIES QUIET. GO TALK TO HIM.
GUNN: ROGER THAT.
HELP!

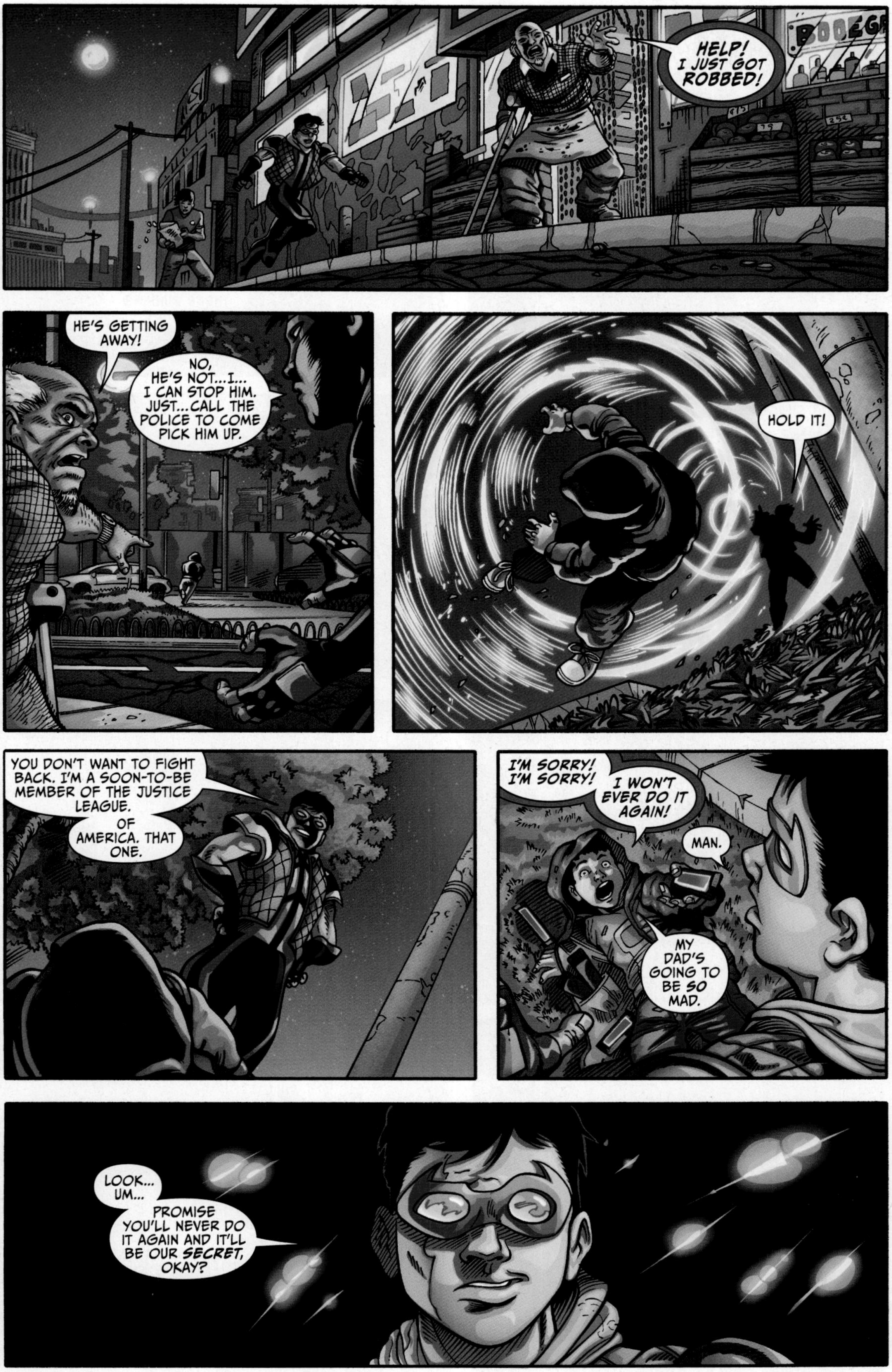
HELP! I JUST GOT ROBBED!
HE'S GETTING AWAY!
NO, HE'S NOT...I... I CAN STOP HIM. JUST...CALL THE POLICE TO COME PICK HIM UP.
HOLD IT!
YOU DON'T WANT TO FIGHT BACK. I'M A SOON-TO-BE MEMBER OF THE JUSTICE LEAGUE.
OF AMERICA. THAT ONE.
I'M SORRY! I'M SORRY!
I WON'T EVER DO IT AGAIN!
MAN.
MY DAD'S GOING TO BE SO MAD.
LOOK... UM...
PROMISE YOU'LL NEVER DO IT AGAIN AND IT'LL BE OUR SECRET, OKAY?

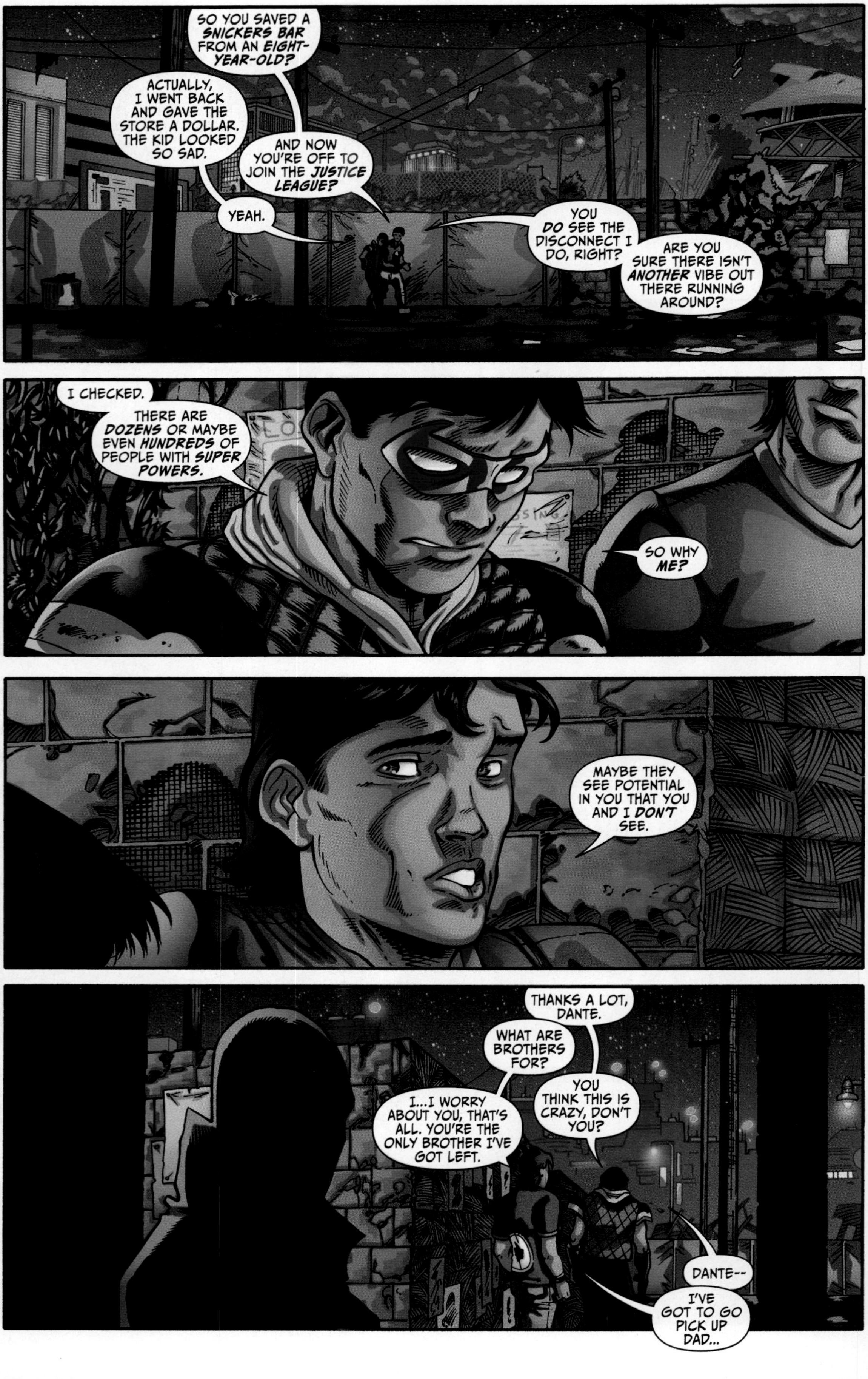
SO YOU SAVED A SNICKERS BAR FROM AN EIGHT-YEAR-OLD?
ACTUALLY, I WENT BACK AND GAVE THE STORE A DOLLAR. THE KID LOOKED SO SAD.
AND NOW YOU'RE OFF TO JOIN THE JUSTICE LEAGUE?
YEAH.
YOU DO SEE THE DISCONNECT I DO, RIGHT?
ARE YOU SURE THERE ISN'T ANOTHER VIBE OUT THERE RUNNING AROUND?
I CHECKED.
THERE ARE DOZENS OR MAYBE EVEN HUNDREDS OF PEOPLE WITH SUPER POWERS.
SO WHY ME?
MAYBE THEY SEE POTENTIAL IN YOU THAT YOU AND I DON'T SEE.
THANKS A LOT, DANTE.
WHAT ARE BROTHERS FOR?
YOU THINK THIS IS CRAZY, DON'T YOU?
I...I WORRY ABOUT YOU, THAT'S ALL. YOU'RE THE ONLY BROTHER I'VE GOT LEFT.
DANTE--
I'VE GOT TO GO PICK UP DAD...

"...I'LL CATCH YOU LATER."

AGENT GUNN?

YOU JUST WIELDED **VIBRATIONAL POWERS** YOU ACQUIRED FROM EXPOSURE TO THE **INTERDIMENSIONAL FORCES** THAT HOLD THE MYRIAD ALTERNATE REALITIES TOGETHER...

...TO STOP A **THIRD GRADER** WITH A SWEET TOOTH.

BIT OF **OVERKILL**, WOULDN'T YOU SAY?

ISN'T THAT WHAT YOU WANT ME TO DO? **HELP** PEOPLE?

I'M NOT SURE YOU'VE REALLY **GRASPED** HOW IMPORTANT YOUR **ROLE** IN THE WORLD IS NOW, CISCO.

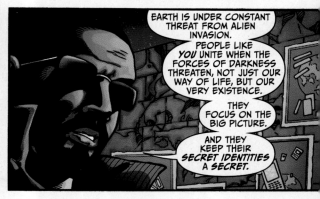

EARTH IS UNDER CONSTANT THREAT FROM ALIEN INVASION.

PEOPLE LIKE **YOU** UNITE WHEN THE FORCES OF DARKNESS THREATEN, NOT JUST OUR WAY OF LIFE, BUT OUR VERY EXISTENCE.

THEY FOCUS ON THE **BIG PICTURE.**

AND THEY KEEP THEIR **SECRET IDENTITIES** A SECRET.

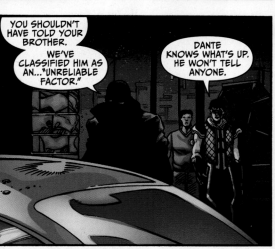

YOU SHOULDN'T HAVE TOLD YOUR BROTHER.

WE'VE CLASSIFIED HIM AS AN..."UNRELIABLE FACTOR."

DANTE KNOWS WHAT'S UP. HE WON'T TELL ANYONE.

I'M NOT THE ONE YOU HAVE TO CONVINCE OF THAT.

AGENT GUNN...YOU TALK ABOUT HOW IMPORTANT WHAT I DO IS, BUT...I KNOW THERE ARE OTHER PEOPLE OUT THERE. WHY **ME?**

WHY DOES THE JLA WANT **ME?**

BECAUSE YOU HAVE A **POWER** NO ONE ELSE DOES. YOU JUST NEED TO LEARN HOW TO USE IT. NOW GO **HOME,** KID.

YOU'RE MEETING THE TEAM **TOMORROW.**

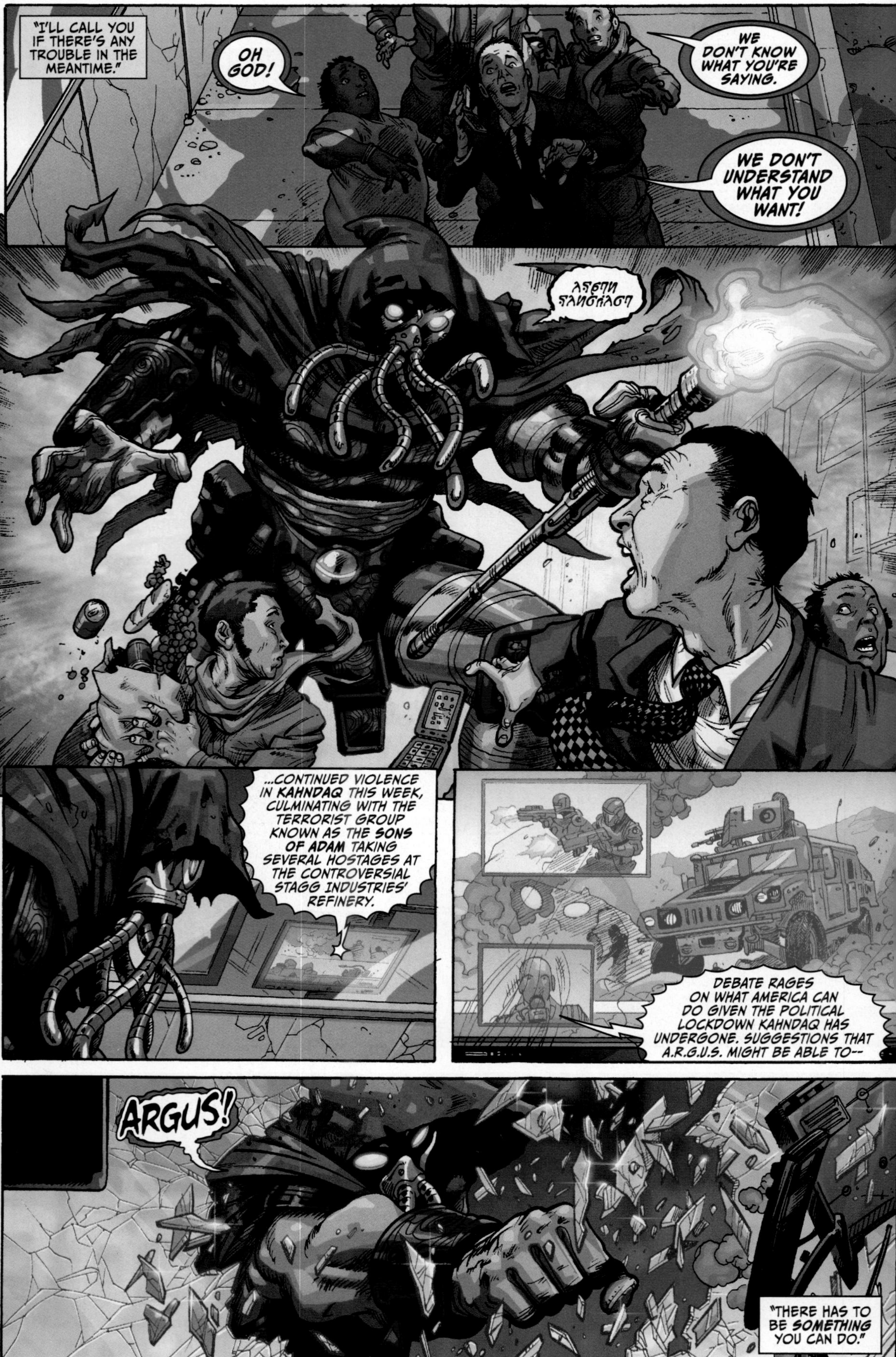
"I'LL CALL YOU IF THERE'S ANY TROUBLE IN THE MEANTIME."
OH GOD!
WE DON'T KNOW WHAT YOU'RE SAYING.
WE DON'T UNDERSTAND WHAT YOU WANT!
...CONTINUED VIOLENCE IN KAHNDAQ THIS WEEK, CULMINATING WITH THE TERRORIST GROUP KNOWN AS THE SONS OF ADAM TAKING SEVERAL HOSTAGES AT THE CONTROVERSIAL STAGG INDUSTRIES' REFINERY.
DEBATE RAGES ON WHAT AMERICA CAN DO GIVEN THE POLITICAL LOCKDOWN KAHNDAQ HAS UNDERGONE. SUGGESTIONS THAT A.R.G.U.S. MIGHT BE ABLE TO--
ARGUS!
"THERE HAS TO BE SOMETHING YOU CAN DO."

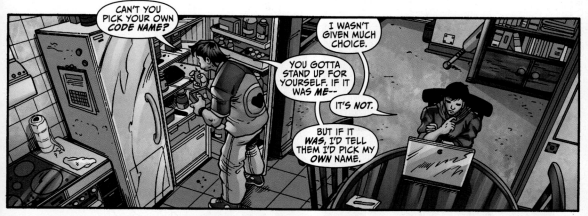

CAN'T YOU PICK YOUR OWN *CODE NAME*?

I WASN'T GIVEN MUCH CHOICE.

YOU GOTTA STAND UP FOR YOURSELF. IF IT WAS *ME*--

IT'S *NOT*.

BUT IF IT *WAS*, I'D TELL THEM I'D PICK MY *OWN* NAME.

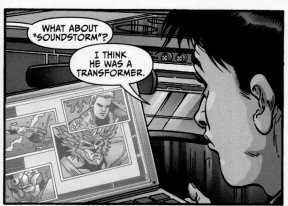

WHAT ABOUT "SOUNDSTORM"?

I THINK HE WAS A TRANSFORMER.

YOU DON'T THINK *HAWKMAN* WILL BE THERE, DO YOU?

IT SAYS HE'S A COP FROM THANAGAR WHO'S NOW WORKING WITH A.R.G.U.S. TO UNCOVER EXTRA-TERRESTRIAL FUGITIVES.

HAWKMAN'S A COOL NAME.

WILL YOU *FORGET* ABOUT IT ALREADY?

ALL I'M SAYING IS YOU CAN'T RUN UP TO *METALLO* OR *BANE* AND SAY...

"THIS IS A JOB FOR *VIBE!*"

THEY WILL LAUGH IN YOUR *FACE*...

...RIGHT BEFORE THEY KILL YOU, I MEAN.

NOW WHAT ARE YOU WORRIED ABOUT?

OTHER THAN HOW DAD IS GOING TO PAY FOR YOUR *FUNERAL*.

I'M WONDERING *WHO* MY TEAMMATES WILL BE IN THE JLA.

IF I CAN FIGURE OUT WHO ELSE IS JOINING, MAYBE I CAN FIGURE OUT WHY THEY WANT *ME*. IF HAWKMAN IS THERE AND THEY'RE HUNTING ALIEN CRIMINALS, MAYBE... MAYBE I CAN HELP THEM LOCATE THEM.

MAYBE I'LL BE LIKE THEIR GPS TO THE *BAD GUYS*.

CISCO? DANTE?

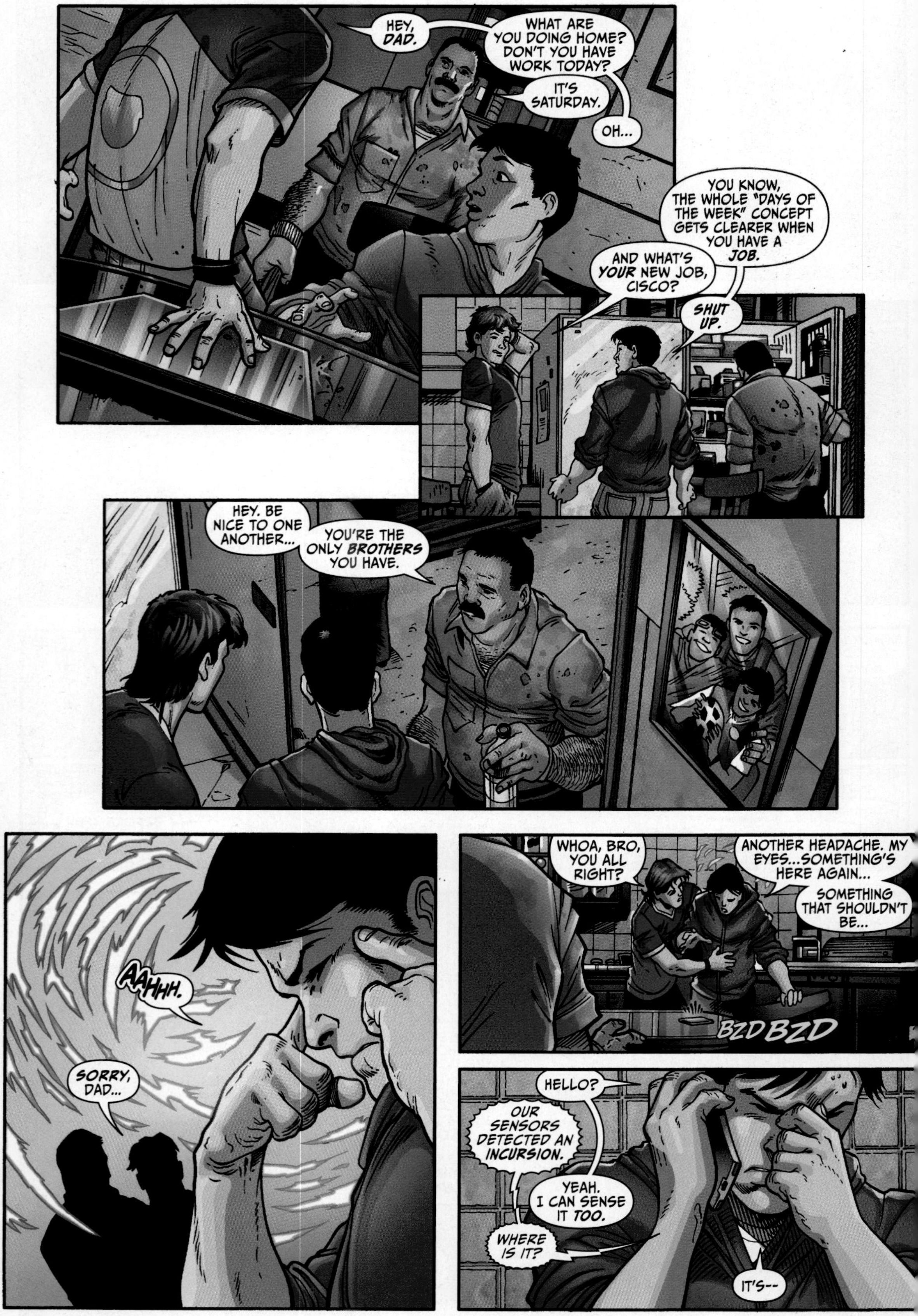
HEY, DAD.
WHAT ARE YOU DOING HOME? DON'T YOU HAVE WORK TODAY?
IT'S SATURDAY.
OH...
YOU KNOW, THE WHOLE "DAYS OF THE WEEK" CONCEPT GETS CLEARER WHEN YOU HAVE A JOB.
AND WHAT'S YOUR NEW JOB, CISCO?
SHUT UP.
HEY. BE NICE TO ONE ANOTHER...
YOU'RE THE ONLY BROTHERS YOU HAVE.
AAHHH.
SORRY, DAD...
WHOA, BRO, YOU ALL RIGHT?
ANOTHER HEADACHE. MY EYES...SOMETHING'S HERE AGAIN...
SOMETHING THAT SHOULDN'T BE...
BZD BZD
HELLO?
OUR SENSORS DETECTED AN INCURSION.
YEAH. I CAN SENSE IT TOO.
WHERE IS IT?
IT'S--

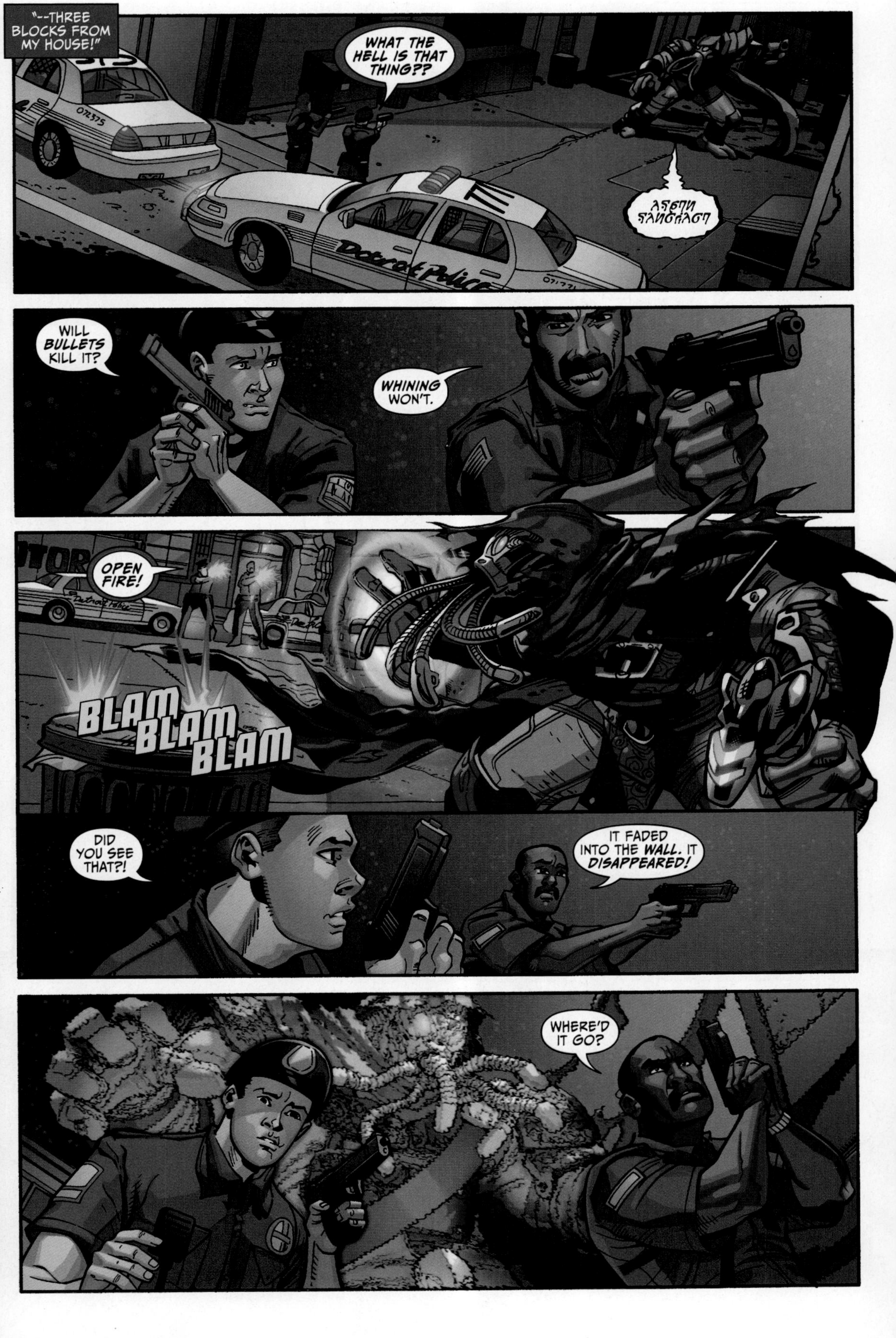
"--THREE BLOCKS FROM MY HOUSE!"
WHAT THE HELL IS THAT THING??
WILL BULLETS KILL IT?
WHINING WON'T.
OPEN FIRE!
BLAM BLAM BLAM
DID YOU SEE THAT?!
IT FADED INTO THE WALL. IT DISAPPEARED!
WHERE'D IT GO?

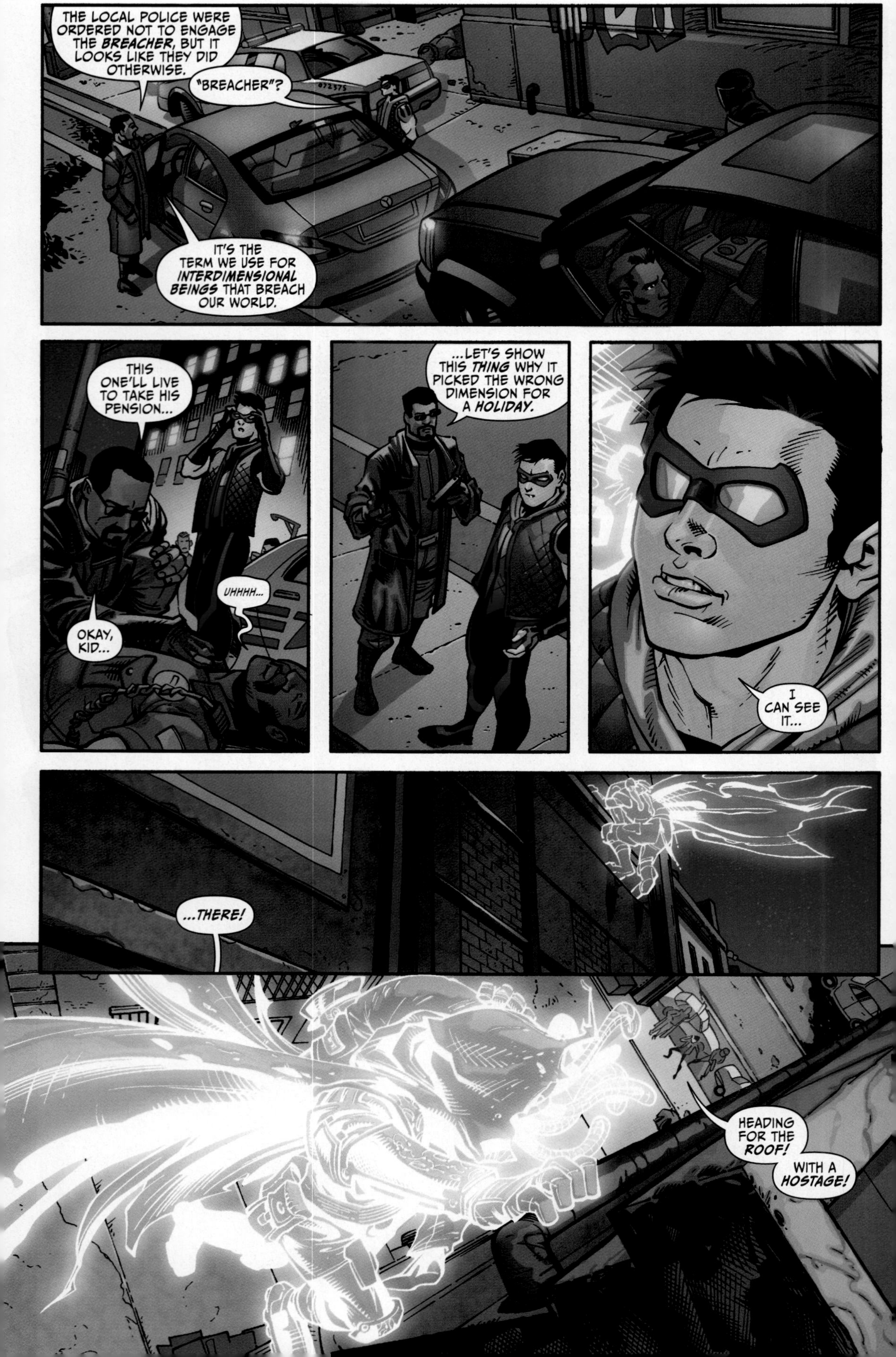
THE LOCAL POLICE WERE ORDERED NOT TO ENGAGE THE *BREACHER*, BUT IT LOOKS LIKE THEY DID OTHERWISE.
"BREACHER"?
IT'S THE TERM WE USE FOR *INTERDIMENSIONAL BEINGS* THAT BREACH OUR WORLD.
THIS ONE'LL LIVE TO TAKE HIS PENSION...
UHHHH...
OKAY, KID...
...LET'S SHOW THIS *THING* WHY IT PICKED THE WRONG DIMENSION FOR A *HOLIDAY*.
I CAN SEE IT...
...*THERE!*
HEADING FOR THE *ROOF!*
WITH A *HOSTAGE!*

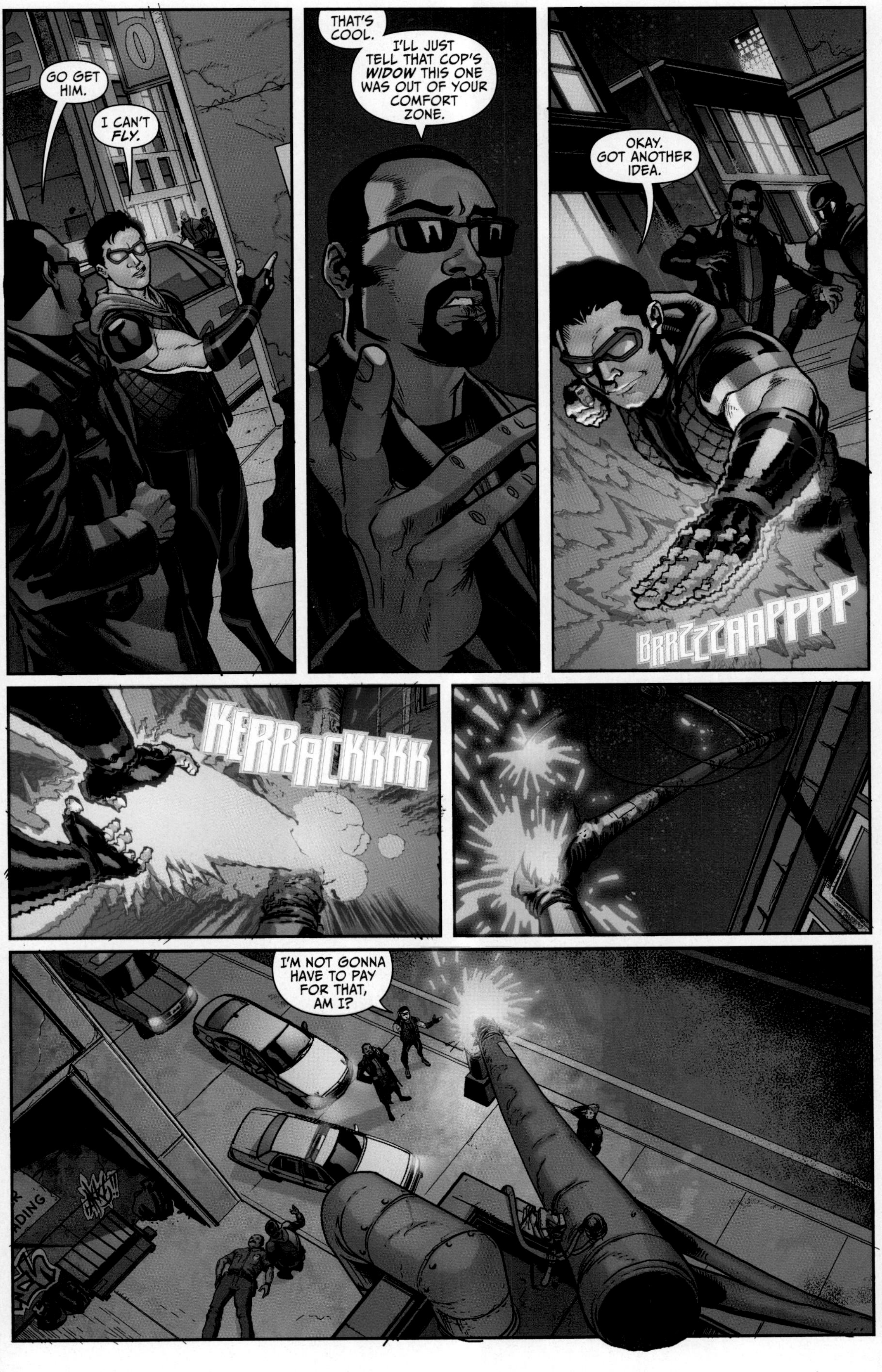
GO GET HIM.
I CAN'T FLY.
THAT'S COOL.
I'LL JUST TELL THAT COP'S WIDOW THIS ONE WAS OUT OF YOUR COMFORT ZONE.
OKAY. GOT ANOTHER IDEA.
BRRZZZAAPPPP
KERRACKKKK
I'M NOT GONNA HAVE TO PAY FOR THAT, AM I?

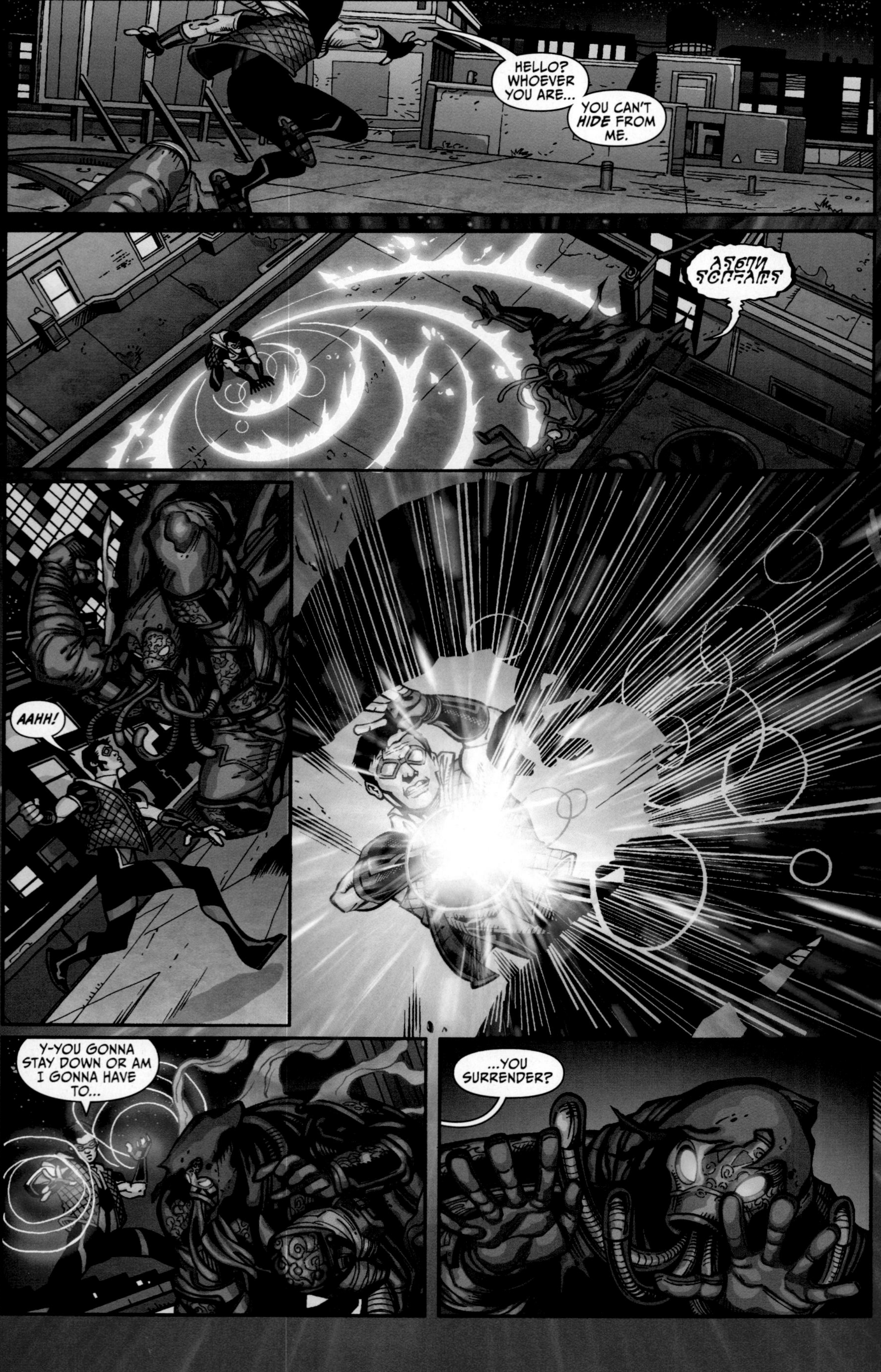
HELLO? WHOEVER YOU ARE...
YOU CAN'T *HIDE* FROM ME.
AAHH!
Y-YOU GONNA STAY DOWN OR AM I GONNA HAVE TO...
...YOU SURRENDER?

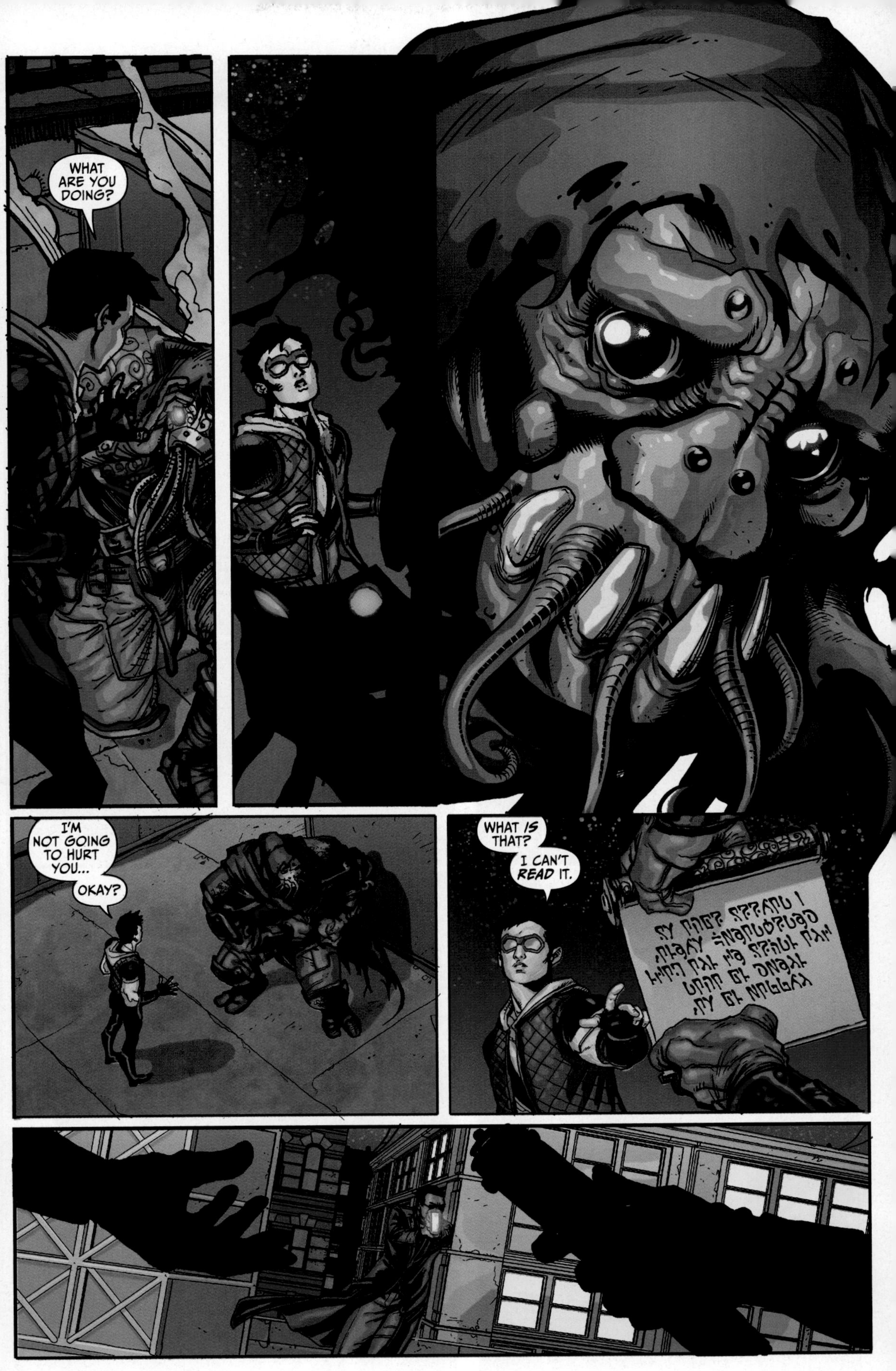
WHAT ARE YOU DOING?
I'M NOT GOING TO HURT YOU...
OKAY?
WHAT *IS* THAT?
I CAN'T *READ* IT.

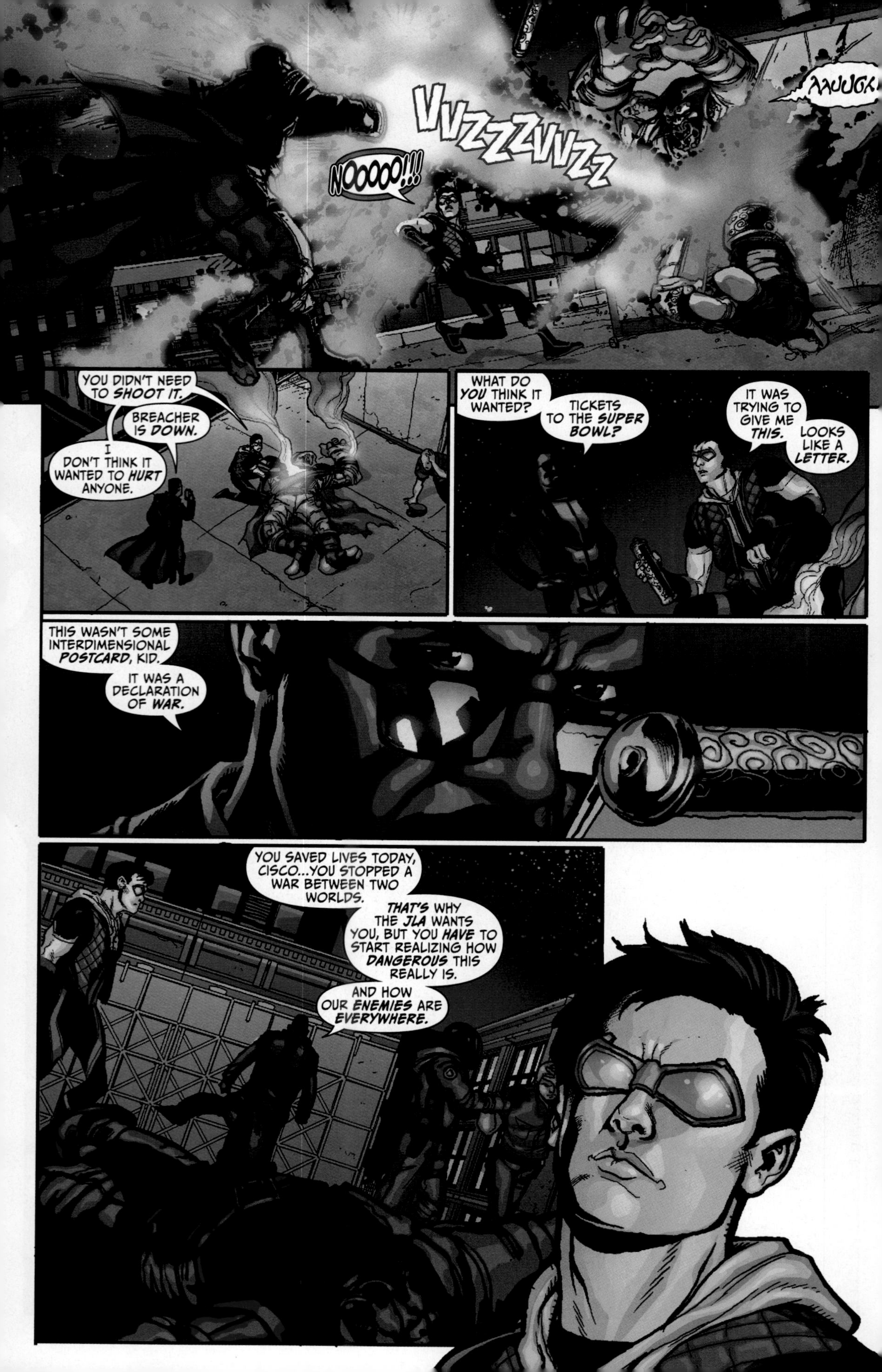

AAUUGK
VVZZZZVVZZ
NOOOOO!!!
YOU DIDN'T NEED TO SHOOT IT.
BREACHER IS DOWN.
I DON'T THINK IT WANTED TO HURT ANYONE.
WHAT DO YOU THINK IT WANTED?
TICKETS TO THE SUPER BOWL?
IT WAS TRYING TO GIVE ME THIS.
LOOKS LIKE A LETTER.
THIS WASN'T SOME INTERDIMENSIONAL POSTCARD, KID.
IT WAS A DECLARATION OF WAR.
YOU SAVED LIVES TODAY, CISCO...YOU STOPPED A WAR BETWEEN TWO WORLDS.
THAT'S WHY THE JLA WANTS YOU, BUT YOU HAVE TO START REALIZING HOW DANGEROUS THIS REALLY IS.
AND HOW OUR ENEMIES ARE EVERYWHERE.

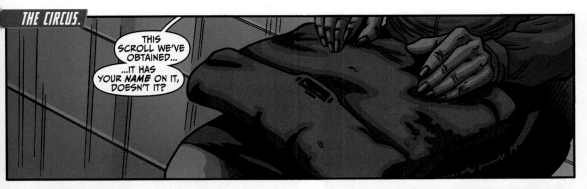

THIS SCROLL WE'VE OBTAINED...

...IT HAS YOUR *NAME* ON IT, DOESN'T IT?

WRITTEN IN YOUR LANGUAGE.

IT'S A *LETTER.* SOMEONE WENT TO A GREAT DEAL OF TROUBLE GETTING THIS TO YOU.

WHAT BECAME OF THE *COURIER?*

HE WAS SENT HOME.

AND I SHOULD BELIEVE THAT... *WHY?*

I DON'T *LIE*...IF I DON'T HAVE TO.

I WANT TO KNOW WHAT THE LETTER SAYS. IF YOU WOULD PLEASE *TRANSLATE*...

ALOUD.

IT'S FROM MY *FATHER.* HE IS ASKING ME TO COME *HOME.*

YOU SEEM TO PREFER A MORE *NOMADIC* EXISTENCE. THAT MAKES YOU SOMETHING OF A TRANS-DIMENSIONAL...

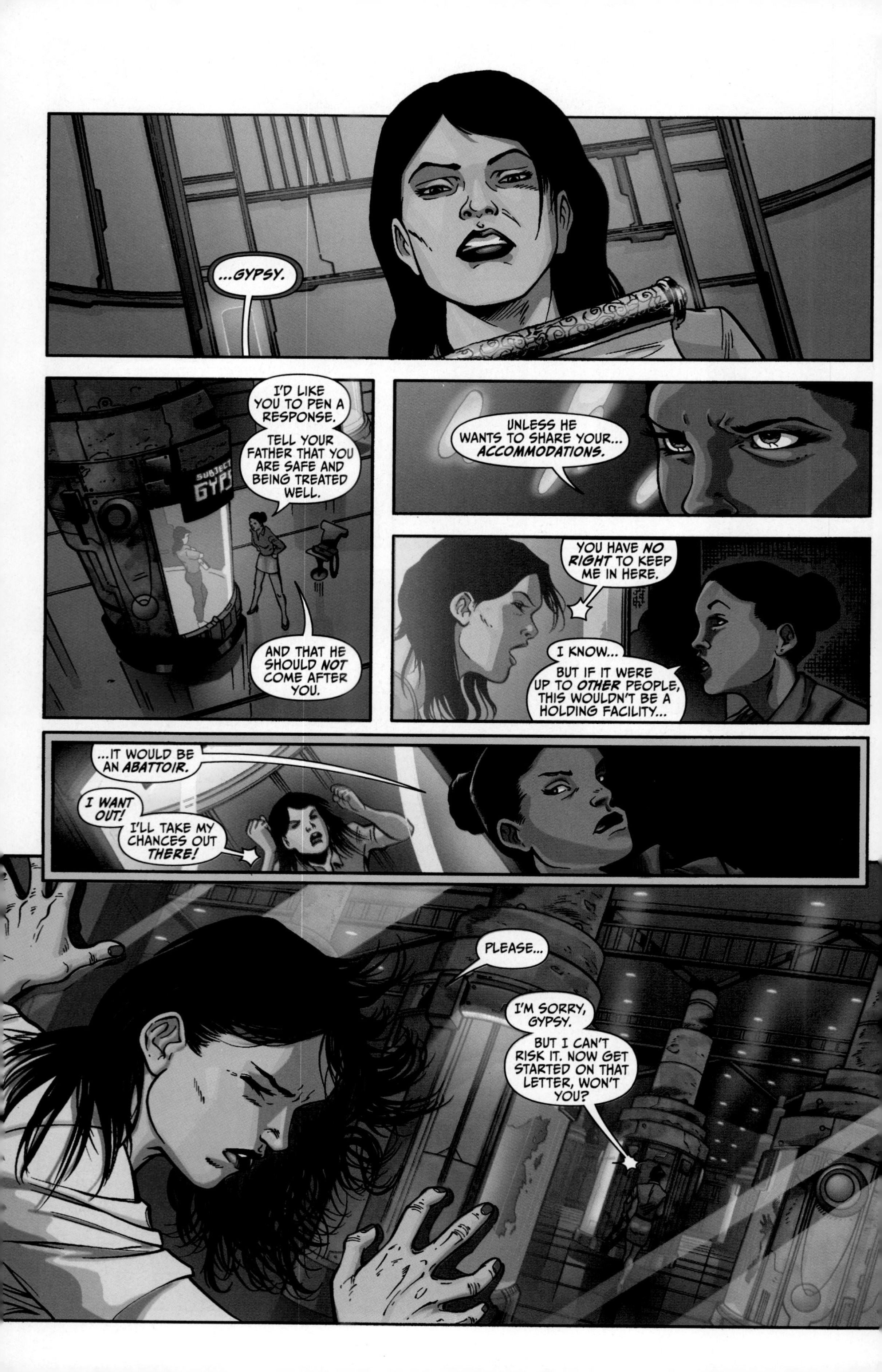
...GYPSY.
I'D LIKE YOU TO PEN A RESPONSE.
TELL YOUR FATHER THAT YOU ARE SAFE AND BEING TREATED WELL.
SUBJECT GYPS
AND THAT HE SHOULD NOT COME AFTER YOU.
UNLESS HE WANTS TO SHARE YOUR... ACCOMMODATIONS.
YOU HAVE NO RIGHT TO KEEP ME IN HERE.
I KNOW...
BUT IF IT WERE UP TO OTHER PEOPLE, THIS WOULDN'T BE A HOLDING FACILITY...
...IT WOULD BE AN ABATTOIR.
I WANT OUT!
I'LL TAKE MY CHANCES OUT THERE!
PLEASE...
I'M SORRY, GYPSY.
BUT I CAN'T RISK IT. NOW GET STARTED ON THAT LETTER, WON'T YOU?

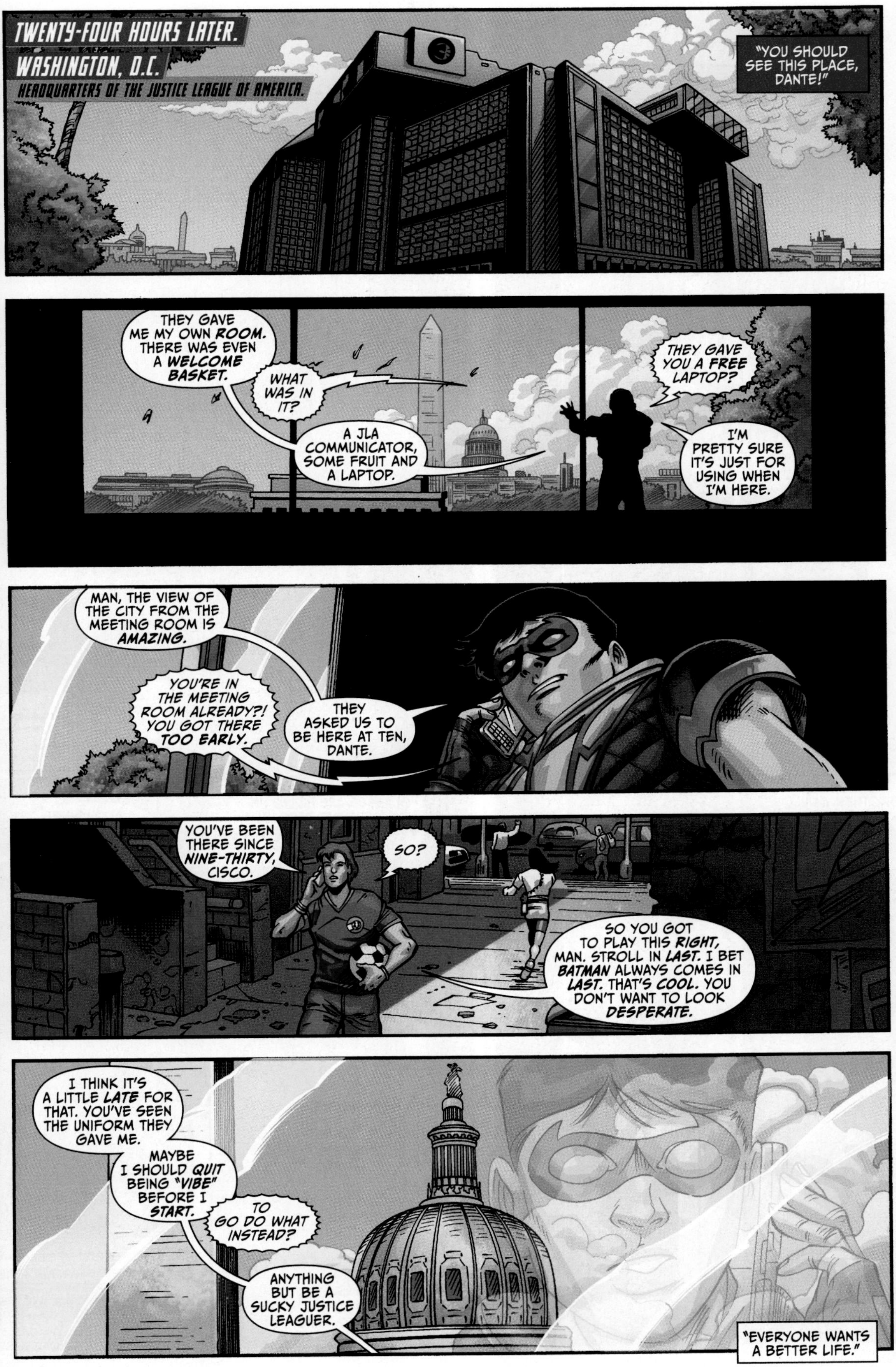
TWENTY-FOUR HOURS LATER.
WASHINGTON, D.C.
HEADQUARTERS OF THE JUSTICE LEAGUE OF AMERICA.
"YOU SHOULD SEE THIS PLACE, DANTE!"
THEY GAVE ME MY OWN ROOM. THERE WAS EVEN A WELCOME BASKET.
WHAT WAS IN IT?
A JLA COMMUNICATOR, SOME FRUIT AND A LAPTOP.
THEY GAVE YOU A FREE LAPTOP?
I'M PRETTY SURE IT'S JUST FOR USING WHEN I'M HERE.
MAN, THE VIEW OF THE CITY FROM THE MEETING ROOM IS AMAZING.
YOU'RE IN THE MEETING ROOM ALREADY?! YOU GOT THERE TOO EARLY.
THEY ASKED US TO BE HERE AT TEN, DANTE.
YOU'VE BEEN THERE SINCE NINE-THIRTY, CISCO.
SO?
SO YOU GOT TO PLAY THIS RIGHT, MAN. STROLL IN LAST. I BET BATMAN ALWAYS COMES IN LAST. THAT'S COOL. YOU DON'T WANT TO LOOK DESPERATE.
I THINK IT'S A LITTLE LATE FOR THAT. YOU'VE SEEN THE UNIFORM THEY GAVE ME.
MAYBE I SHOULD QUIT BEING "VIBE" BEFORE I START.
TO GO DO WHAT INSTEAD?
ANYTHING BUT BE A SUCKY JUSTICE LEAGUER.
"EVERYONE WANTS A BETTER LIFE."

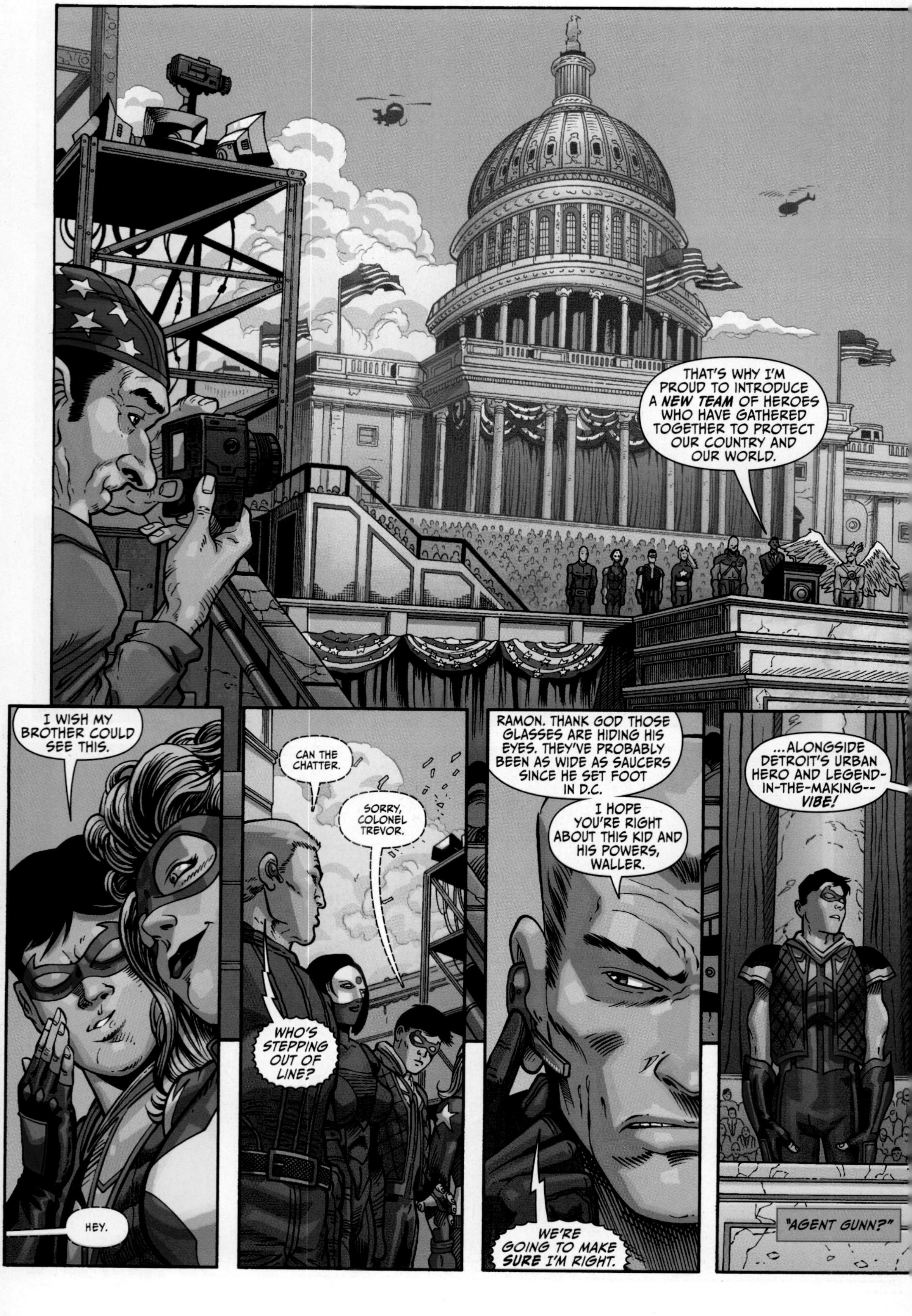
THAT'S WHY I'M PROUD TO INTRODUCE A NEW TEAM OF HEROES WHO HAVE GATHERED TOGETHER TO PROTECT OUR COUNTRY AND OUR WORLD.
I WISH MY BROTHER COULD SEE THIS.
HEY.
CAN THE CHATTER.
SORRY, COLONEL TREVOR.
WHO'S STEPPING OUT OF LINE?
RAMON. THANK GOD THOSE GLASSES ARE HIDING HIS EYES. THEY'VE PROBABLY BEEN AS WIDE AS SAUCERS SINCE HE SET FOOT IN D.C.
I HOPE YOU'RE RIGHT ABOUT THIS KID AND HIS POWERS, WALLER.
WE'RE GOING TO MAKE SURE I'M RIGHT.
...ALONGSIDE DETROIT'S URBAN HERO AND LEGEND-IN-THE-MAKING--VIBE!
"AGENT GUNN?"

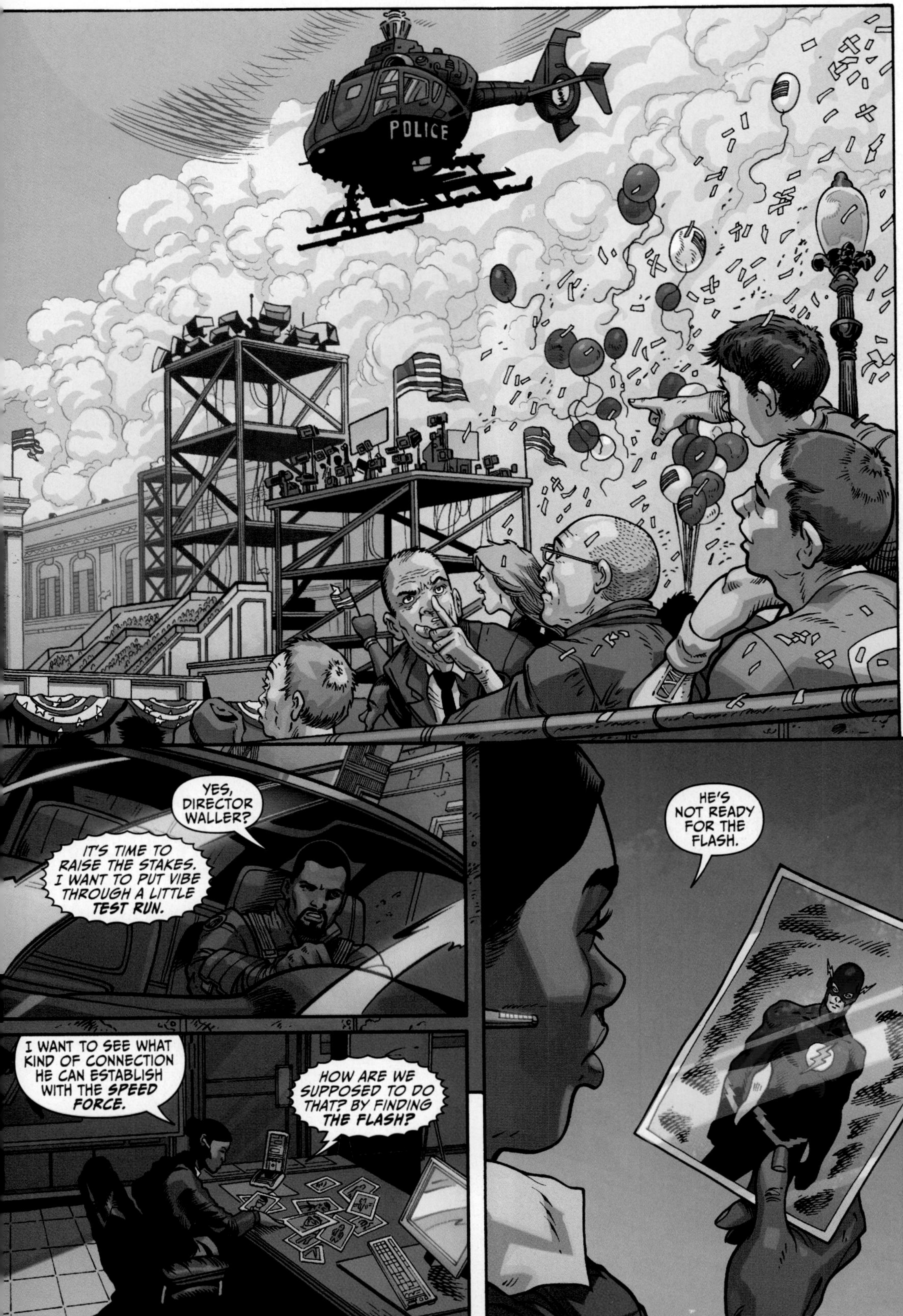
POLICE
YES, DIRECTOR WALLER?
IT'S TIME TO RAISE THE STAKES. I WANT TO PUT VIBE THROUGH A LITTLE TEST RUN.
I WANT TO SEE WHAT KIND OF CONNECTION HE CAN ESTABLISH WITH THE SPEED FORCE.
HOW ARE WE SUPPOSED TO DO THAT? BY FINDING THE FLASH?
HE'S NOT READY FOR THE FLASH.

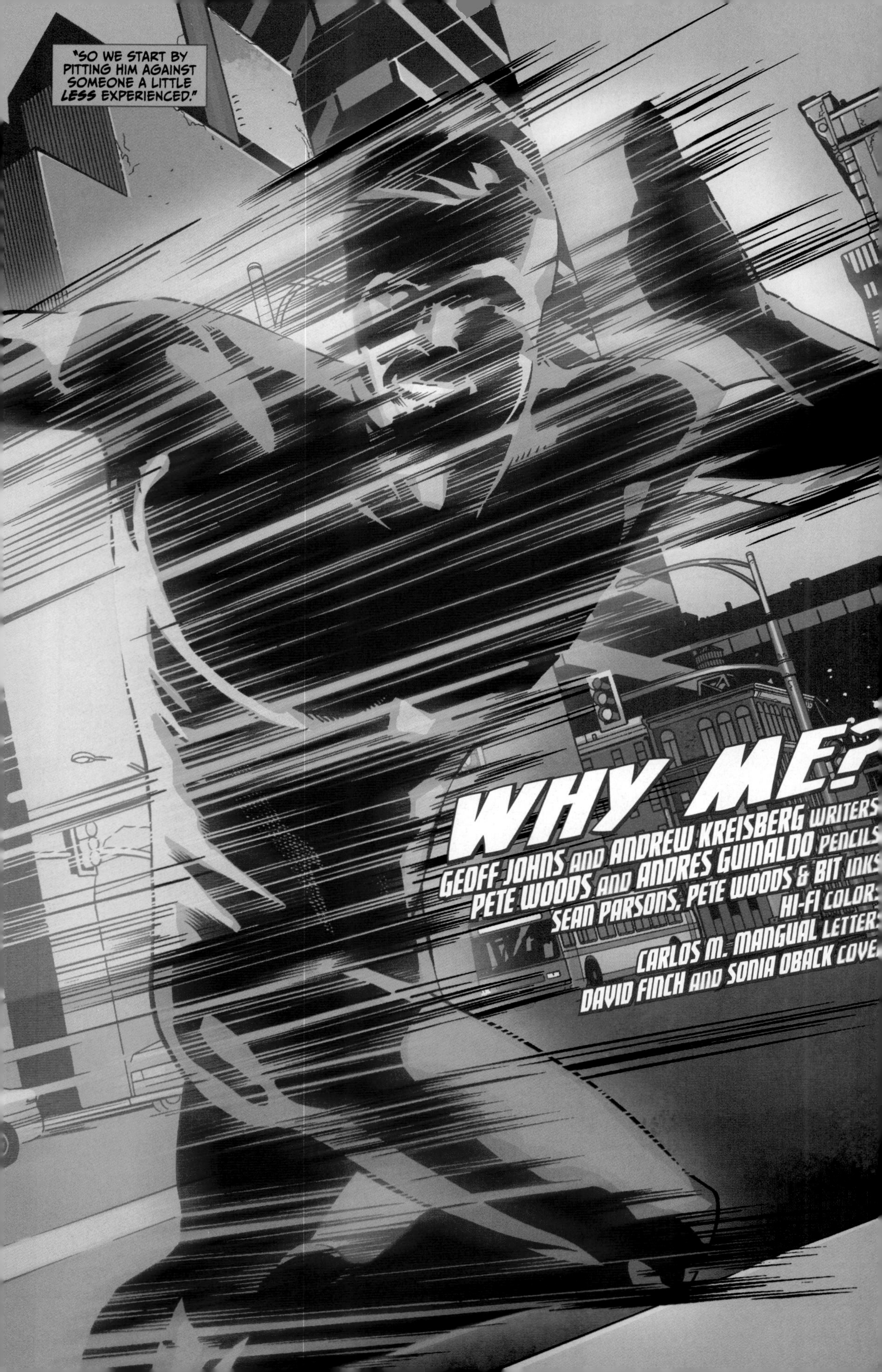
"SO WE START BY PITTING HIM AGAINST SOMEONE A LITTLE LESS EXPERIENCED."
WHY ME?
GEOFF JOHNS AND ANDREW KREISBERG WRITERS
PETE WOODS AND ANDRES GUINALDO PENCILS
SEAN PARSONS, PETE WOODS & BIT INKS
HI-FI COLOR
CARLOS M. MANGUAL LETTER
DAVID FINCH AND SONIA OBACK COVE

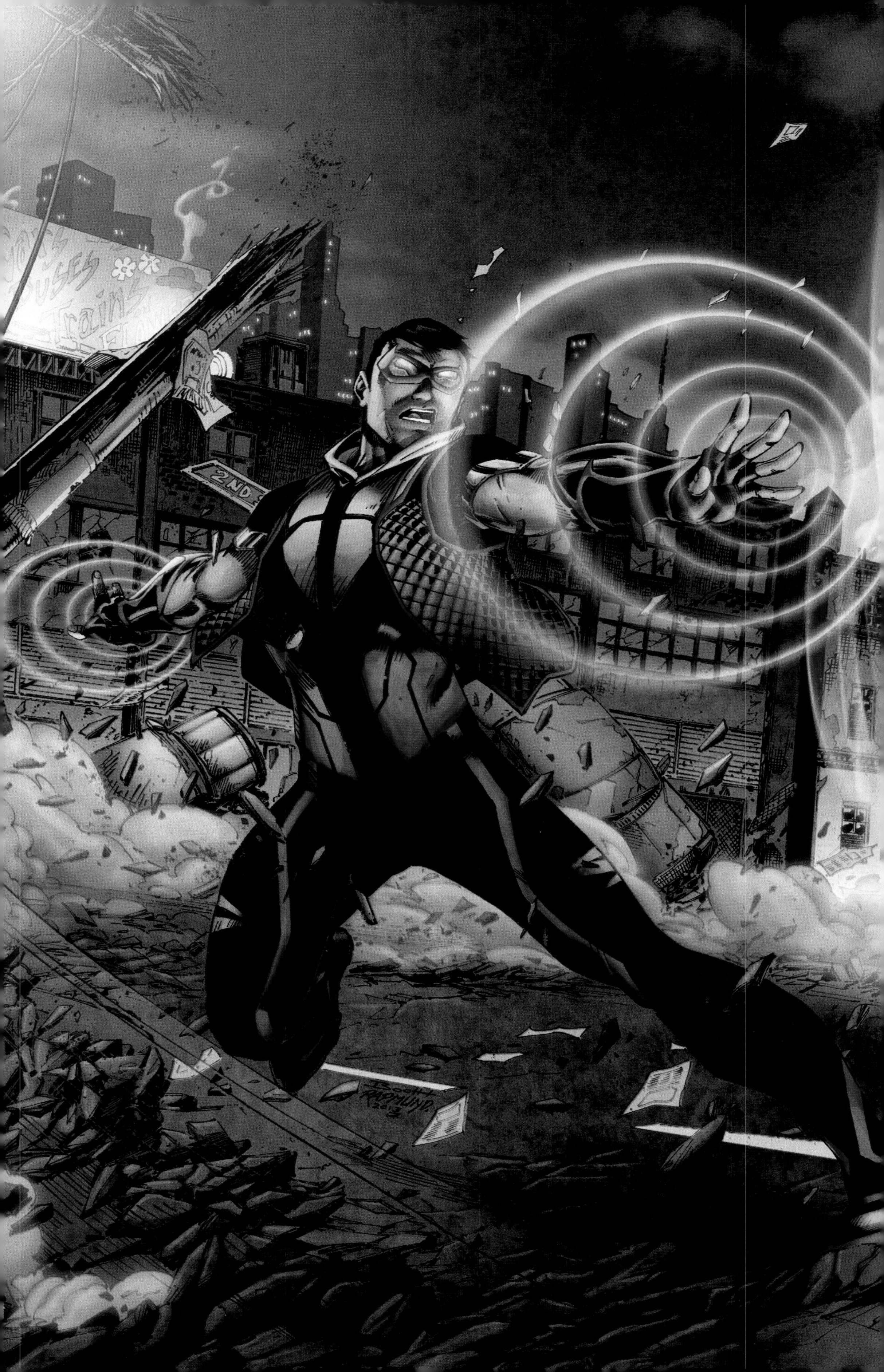

Trains
2ND

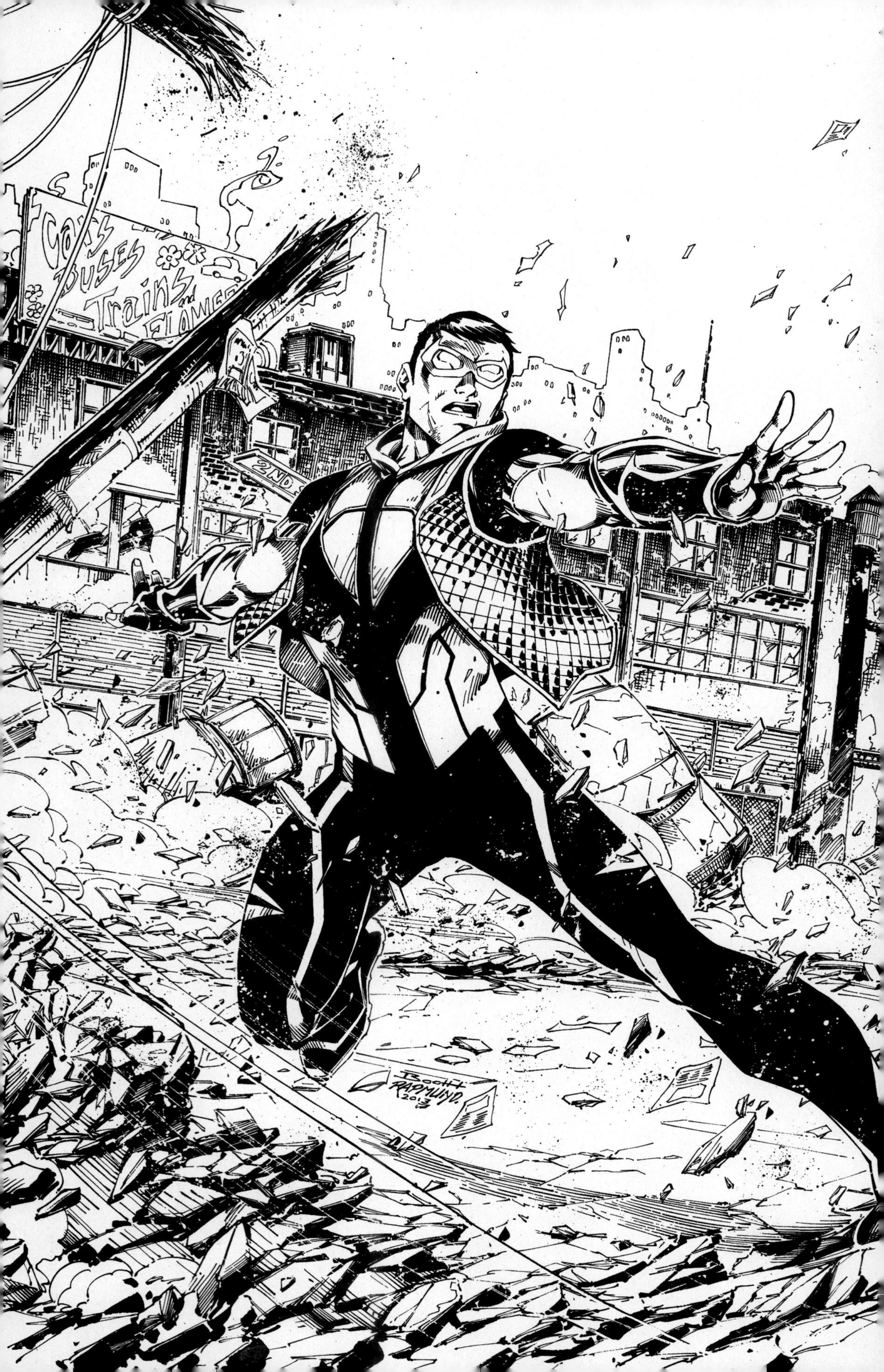

Cars
Buses
Trains and
2ND
Booth
RAPMUND.
2013

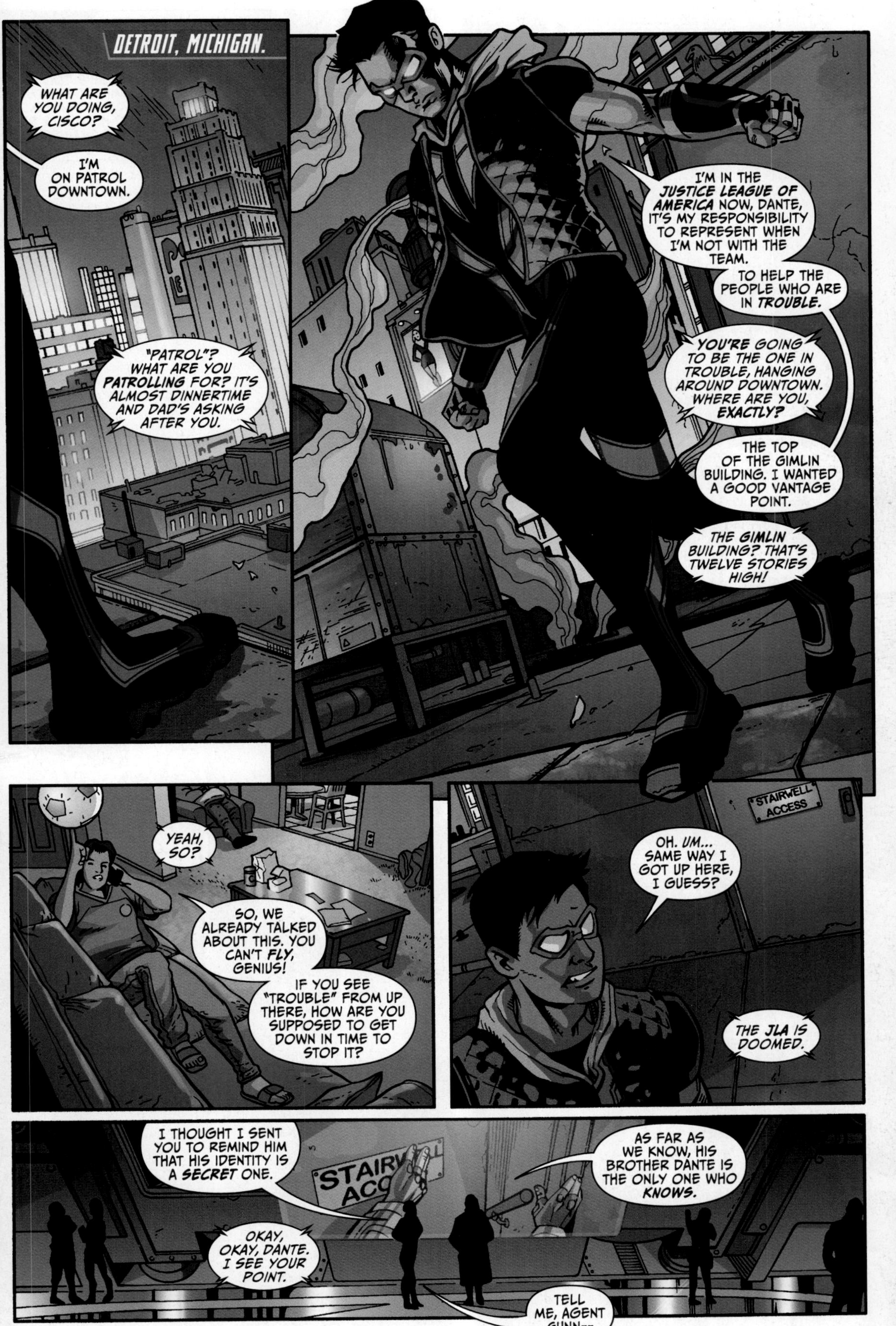
DETROIT, MICHIGAN.
WHAT ARE YOU DOING, CISCO?
I'M ON PATROL DOWNTOWN.
"PATROL"? WHAT ARE YOU PATROLLING FOR? IT'S ALMOST DINNERTIME AND DAD'S ASKING AFTER YOU.
I'M IN THE JUSTICE LEAGUE OF AMERICA NOW, DANTE, IT'S MY RESPONSIBILITY TO REPRESENT WHEN I'M NOT WITH THE TEAM.
TO HELP THE PEOPLE WHO ARE IN TROUBLE.
YOU'RE GOING TO BE THE ONE IN TROUBLE, HANGING AROUND DOWNTOWN. WHERE ARE YOU, EXACTLY?
THE TOP OF THE GIMLIN BUILDING. I WANTED A GOOD VANTAGE POINT.
THE GIMLIN BUILDING? THAT'S TWELVE STORIES HIGH!
YEAH, SO?
SO, WE ALREADY TALKED ABOUT THIS. YOU CAN'T FLY, GENIUS!
IF YOU SEE "TROUBLE" FROM UP THERE, HOW ARE YOU SUPPOSED TO GET DOWN IN TIME TO STOP IT?
STAIRWELL ACCESS
OH. UM... SAME WAY I GOT UP HERE, I GUESS?
THE JLA IS DOOMED.
I THOUGHT I SENT YOU TO REMIND HIM THAT HIS IDENTITY IS A SECRET ONE.
AS FAR AS WE KNOW, HIS BROTHER DANTE IS THE ONLY ONE WHO KNOWS.
OKAY, OKAY, DANTE. I SEE YOUR POINT.
TELL ME, AGENT GUNN--

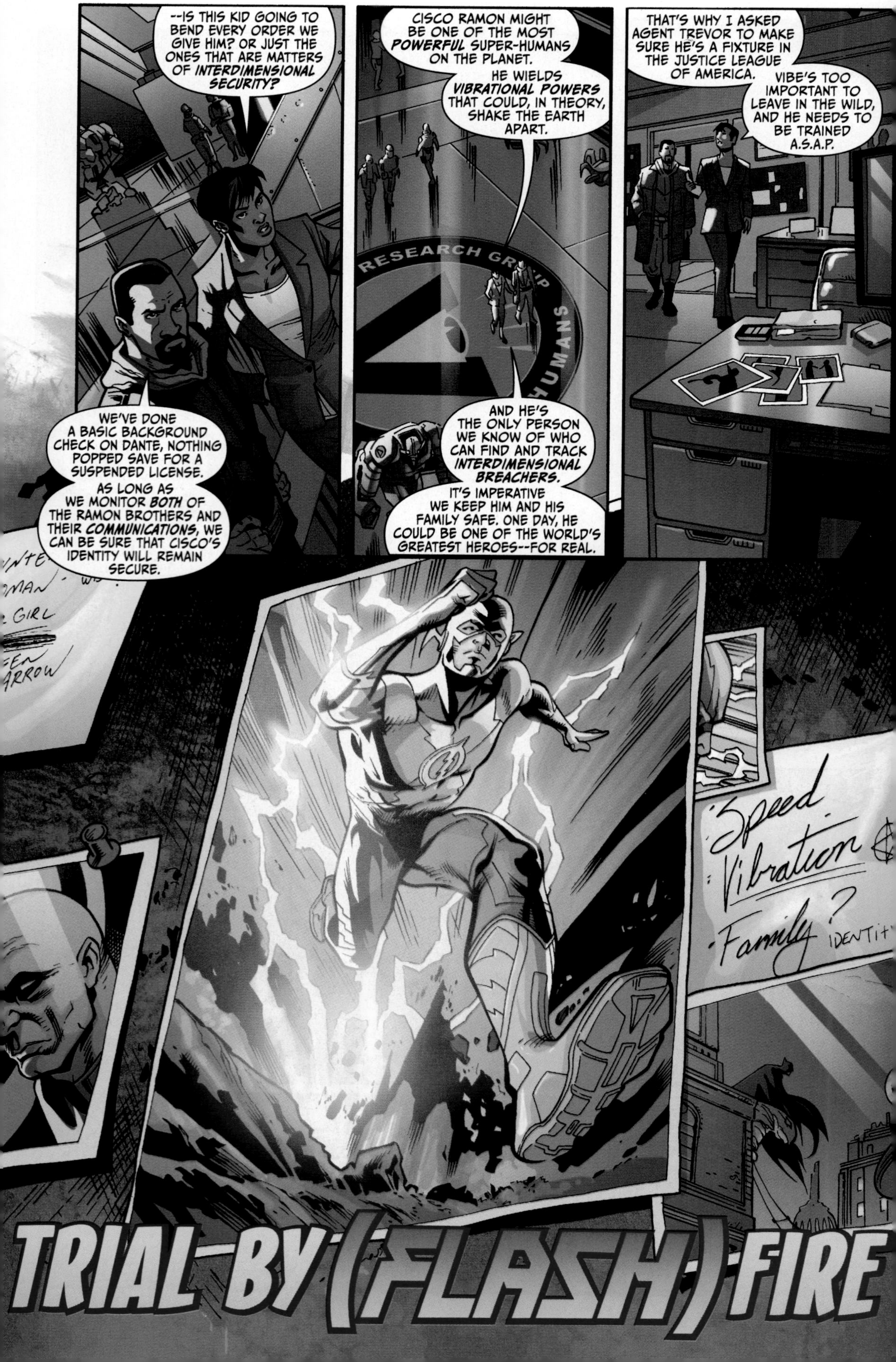
--IS THIS KID GOING TO BEND EVERY ORDER WE GIVE HIM? OR JUST THE ONES THAT ARE MATTERS OF INTERDIMENSIONAL SECURITY?
WE'VE DONE A BASIC BACKGROUND CHECK ON DANTE, NOTHING POPPED SAVE FOR A SUSPENDED LICENSE.
AS LONG AS WE MONITOR BOTH OF THE RAMON BROTHERS AND THEIR COMMUNICATIONS, WE CAN BE SURE THAT CISCO'S IDENTITY WILL REMAIN SECURE.
CISCO RAMON MIGHT BE ONE OF THE MOST POWERFUL SUPER-HUMANS ON THE PLANET.
HE WIELDS VIBRATIONAL POWERS THAT COULD, IN THEORY, SHAKE THE EARTH APART.
RESEARCH GR
HUMANS
AND HE'S THE ONLY PERSON WE KNOW OF WHO CAN FIND AND TRACK INTERDIMENSIONAL BREACHERS.
IT'S IMPERATIVE WE KEEP HIM AND HIS FAMILY SAFE. ONE DAY, HE COULD BE ONE OF THE WORLD'S GREATEST HEROES--FOR REAL.
THAT'S WHY I ASKED AGENT TREVOR TO MAKE SURE HE'S A FIXTURE IN THE JUSTICE LEAGUE OF AMERICA.
VIBE'S TOO IMPORTANT TO LEAVE IN THE WILD, AND HE NEEDS TO BE TRAINED A.S.A.P.
Speed
Vibration
Family?
IDENTIT
TRIAL BY (FLASH) FIRE

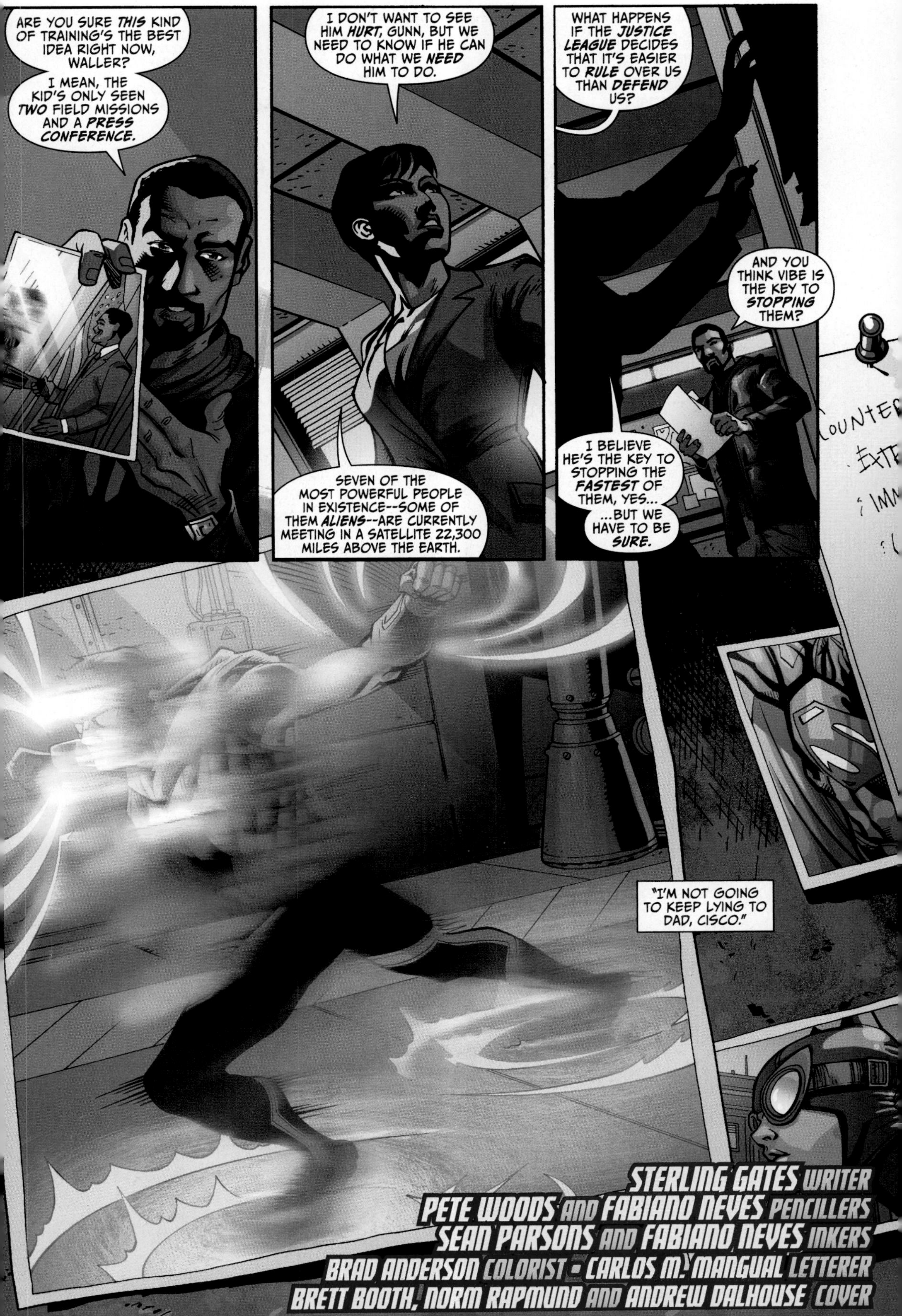

ARE YOU SURE THIS KIND OF TRAINING'S THE BEST IDEA RIGHT NOW, WALLER?
I MEAN, THE KID'S ONLY SEEN TWO FIELD MISSIONS AND A PRESS CONFERENCE.
I DON'T WANT TO SEE HIM HURT, GUNN, BUT WE NEED TO KNOW IF HE CAN DO WHAT WE NEED HIM TO DO.
SEVEN OF THE MOST POWERFUL PEOPLE IN EXISTENCE--SOME OF THEM ALIENS--ARE CURRENTLY MEETING IN A SATELLITE 22,300 MILES ABOVE THE EARTH.
WHAT HAPPENS IF THE JUSTICE LEAGUE DECIDES THAT IT'S EASIER TO RULE OVER US THAN DEFEND US?
AND YOU THINK VIBE IS THE KEY TO STOPPING THEM?
I BELIEVE HE'S THE KEY TO STOPPING THE FASTEST OF THEM, YES...
...BUT WE HAVE TO BE SURE.
"I'M NOT GOING TO KEEP LYING TO DAD, CISCO."
STERLING GATES WRITER
PETE WOODS AND FABIANO NEVES PENCILLERS
SEAN PARSONS AND FABIANO NEVES INKERS
BRAD ANDERSON COLORIST - CARLOS M. MANGUAL LETTERER
BRETT BOOTH, NORM RAPMUND AND ANDREW DALHOUSE COVER

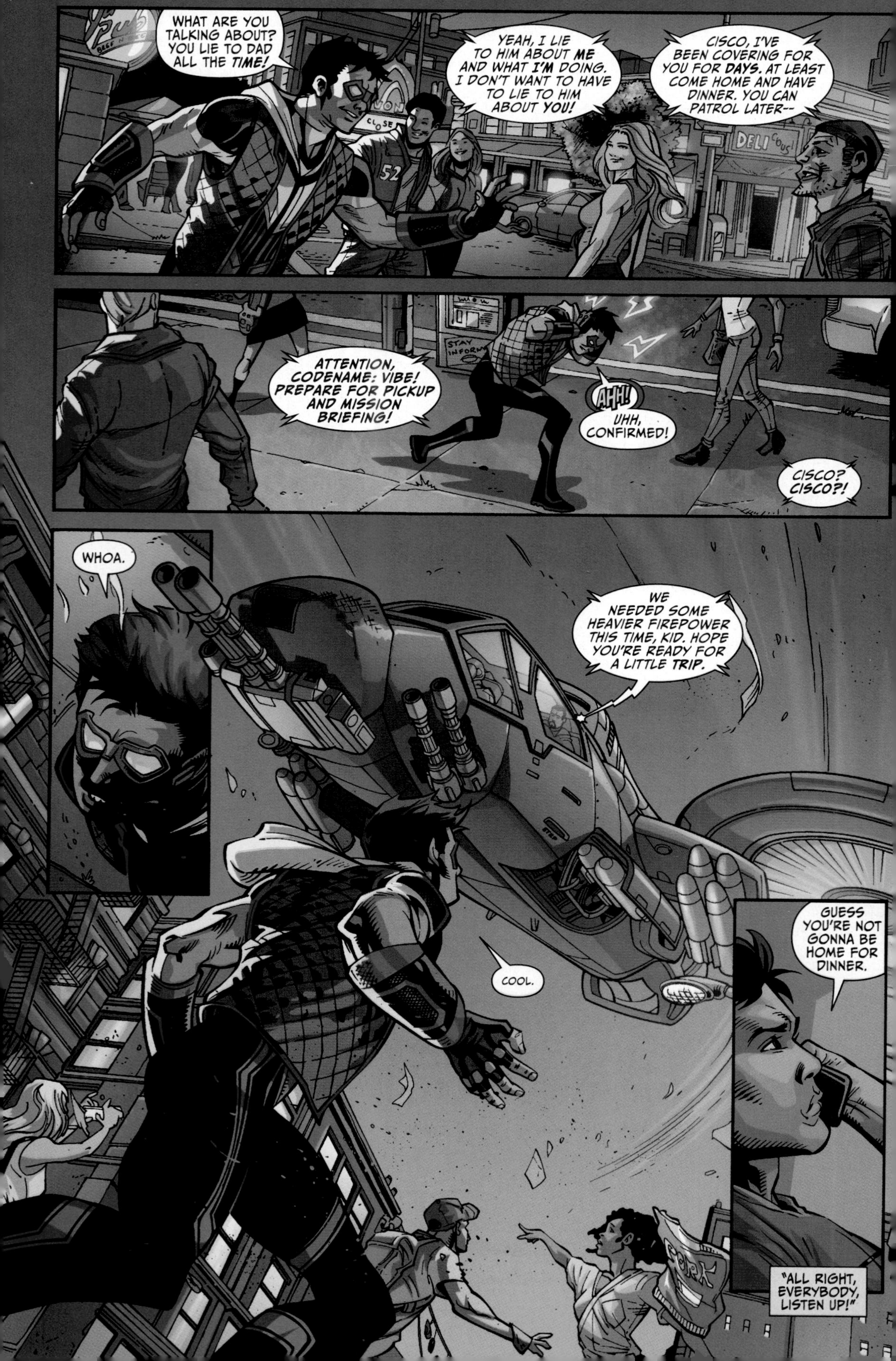
WHAT ARE YOU TALKING ABOUT? YOU LIE TO DAD ALL THE TIME!
YEAH, I LIE TO HIM ABOUT ME AND WHAT I'M DOING. I DON'T WANT TO HAVE TO LIE TO HIM ABOUT YOU!
CISCO, I'VE BEEN COVERING FOR YOU FOR DAYS. AT LEAST COME HOME AND HAVE DINNER. YOU CAN PATROL LATER--
DELI
ATTENTION, CODENAME: VIBE! PREPARE FOR PICKUP AND MISSION BRIEFING!
AHH!
UHH, CONFIRMED!
CISCO? CISCO?!
WHOA.
WE NEEDED SOME HEAVIER FIREPOWER THIS TIME, KID. HOPE YOU'RE READY FOR A LITTLE TRIP.
COOL.
GUESS YOU'RE NOT GONNA BE HOME FOR DINNER.
"ALL RIGHT, EVERYBODY, LISTEN UP!"

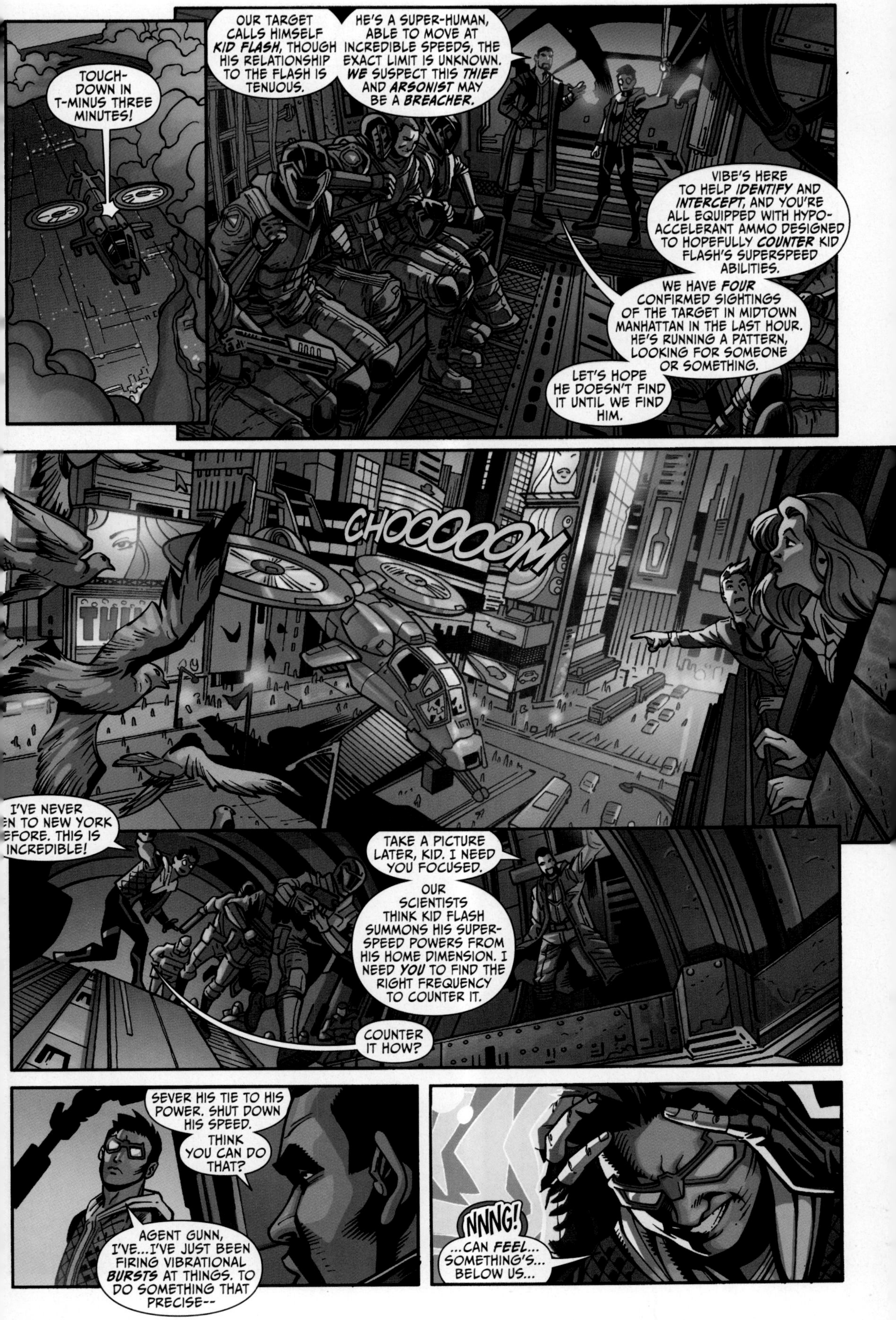
TOUCH-DOWN IN T-MINUS THREE MINUTES!
OUR TARGET CALLS HIMSELF KID FLASH, THOUGH HIS RELATIONSHIP TO THE FLASH IS TENUOUS.
HE'S A SUPER-HUMAN, ABLE TO MOVE AT INCREDIBLE SPEEDS, THE EXACT LIMIT IS UNKNOWN. WE SUSPECT THIS THIEF AND ARSONIST MAY BE A BREACHER.
VIBE'S HERE TO HELP IDENTIFY AND INTERCEPT, AND YOU'RE ALL EQUIPPED WITH HYPO-ACCELERANT AMMO DESIGNED TO HOPEFULLY COUNTER KID FLASH'S SUPERSPEED ABILITIES.
WE HAVE FOUR CONFIRMED SIGHTINGS OF THE TARGET IN MIDTOWN MANHATTAN IN THE LAST HOUR. HE'S RUNNING A PATTERN, LOOKING FOR SOMEONE OR SOMETHING.
LET'S HOPE HE DOESN'T FIND IT UNTIL WE FIND HIM.
CHOOOOOOM
I'VE NEVER EN TO NEW YORK EFORE. THIS IS INCREDIBLE!
TAKE A PICTURE LATER, KID. I NEED YOU FOCUSED.
OUR SCIENTISTS THINK KID FLASH SUMMONS HIS SUPER-SPEED POWERS FROM HIS HOME DIMENSION. I NEED YOU TO FIND THE RIGHT FREQUENCY TO COUNTER IT.
COUNTER IT HOW?
SEVER HIS TIE TO HIS POWER. SHUT DOWN HIS SPEED.
THINK YOU CAN DO THAT?
AGENT GUNN, I'VE...I'VE JUST BEEN FIRING VIBRATIONAL BURSTS AT THINGS. TO DO SOMETHING THAT PRECISE--
NNNG!
...CAN FEEL... SOMETHING'S... BELOW US...

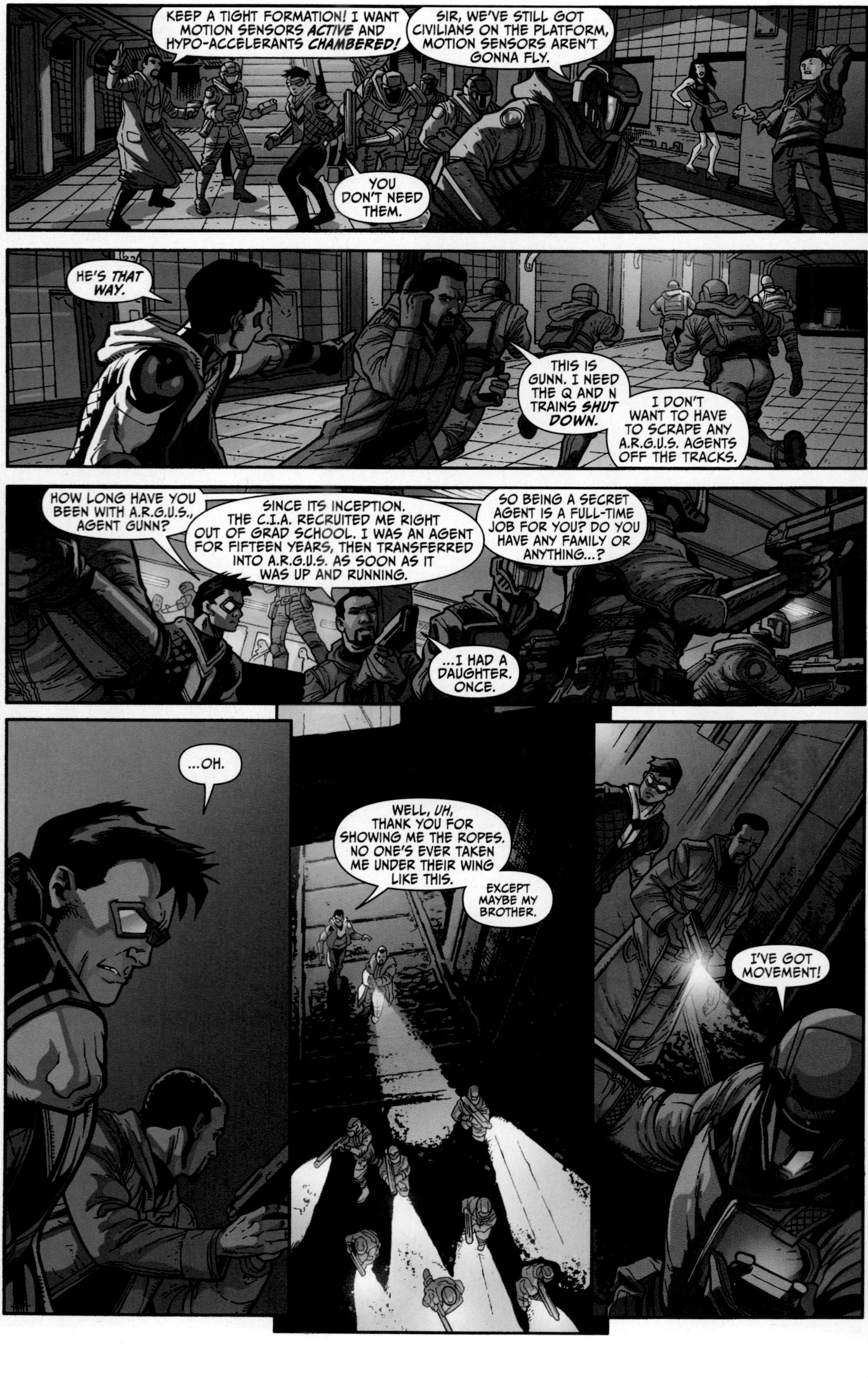
KEEP A TIGHT FORMATION! I WANT MOTION SENSORS ACTIVE AND HYPO-ACCELERANTS CHAMBERED!
SIR, WE'VE STILL GOT CIVILIANS ON THE PLATFORM, MOTION SENSORS AREN'T GONNA FLY.
YOU DON'T NEED THEM.
HE'S THAT WAY.
THIS IS GUNN. I NEED THE Q AND N TRAINS SHUT DOWN.
I DON'T WANT TO HAVE TO SCRAPE ANY A.R.G.U.S. AGENTS OFF THE TRACKS.
HOW LONG HAVE YOU BEEN WITH A.R.G.U.S., AGENT GUNN?
SINCE ITS INCEPTION. THE C.I.A. RECRUITED ME RIGHT OUT OF GRAD SCHOOL. I WAS AN AGENT FOR FIFTEEN YEARS, THEN TRANSFERRED INTO A.R.G.U.S. AS SOON AS IT WAS UP AND RUNNING.
SO BEING A SECRET AGENT IS A FULL-TIME JOB FOR YOU? DO YOU HAVE ANY FAMILY OR ANYTHING...?
...I HAD A DAUGHTER. ONCE.
...OH.
WELL, UH, THANK YOU FOR SHOWING ME THE ROPES. NO ONE'S EVER TAKEN ME UNDER THEIR WING LIKE THIS.
EXCEPT MAYBE MY BROTHER.
I'VE GOT MOVEMENT!

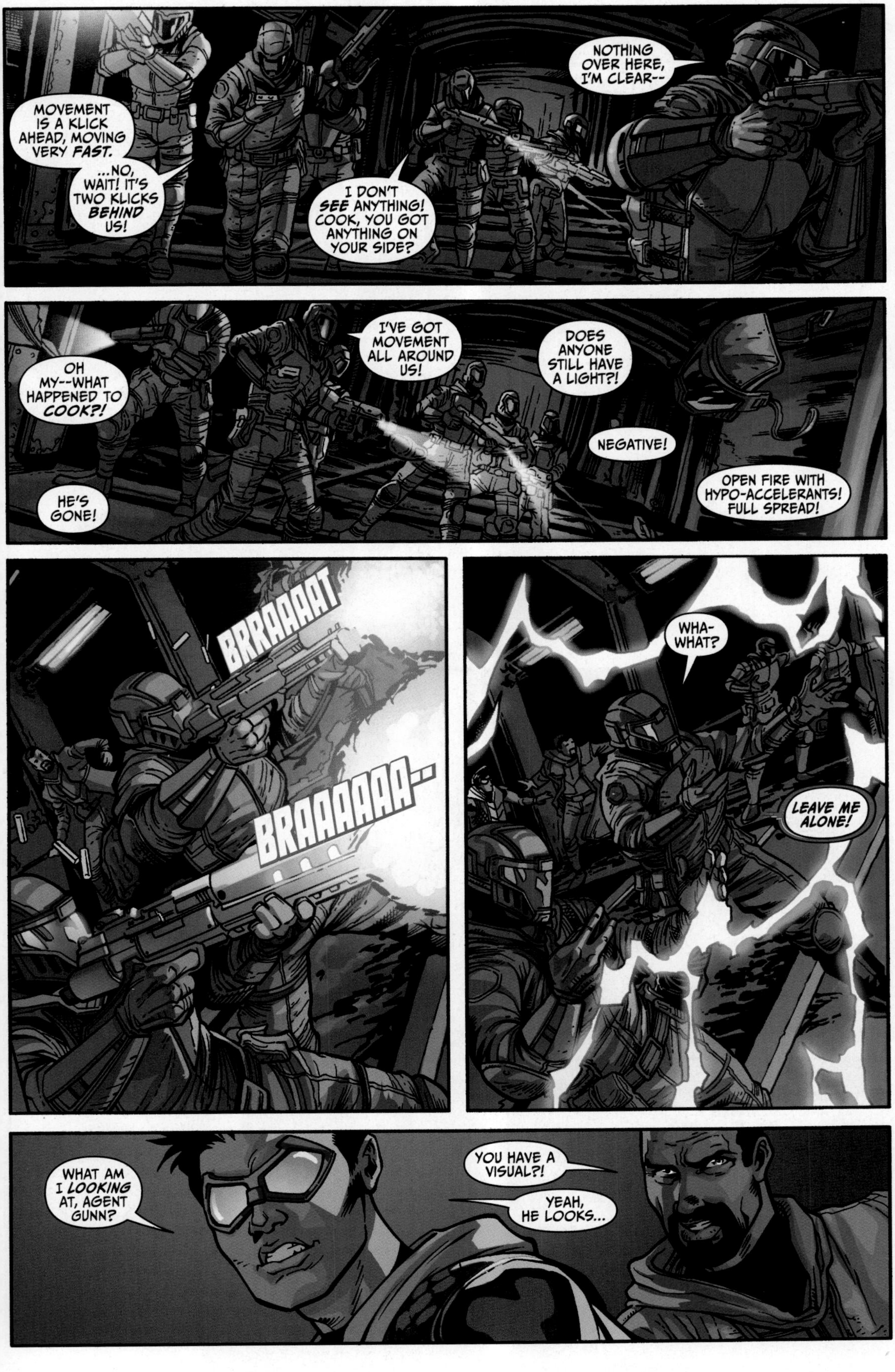
MOVEMENT IS A KLICK AHEAD, MOVING VERY *FAST.*
...NO, WAIT! IT'S TWO KLICKS *BEHIND* US!
I DON'T *SEE* ANYTHING! COOK, YOU GOT ANYTHING ON YOUR SIDE?
NOTHING OVER HERE, I'M CLEAR--
OH MY--WHAT HAPPENED TO *COOK?!*
HE'S GONE!
I'VE GOT MOVEMENT ALL AROUND US!
DOES ANYONE STILL HAVE A LIGHT?!
NEGATIVE!
OPEN FIRE WITH HYPO-ACCELERANTS! FULL SPREAD!
BRRAAAAT
BRAAAAAA--
WHA-WHAT?
LEAVE ME ALONE!
WHAT AM I *LOOKING* AT, AGENT GUNN?
YOU HAVE A VISUAL?!
YEAH, HE LOOKS...

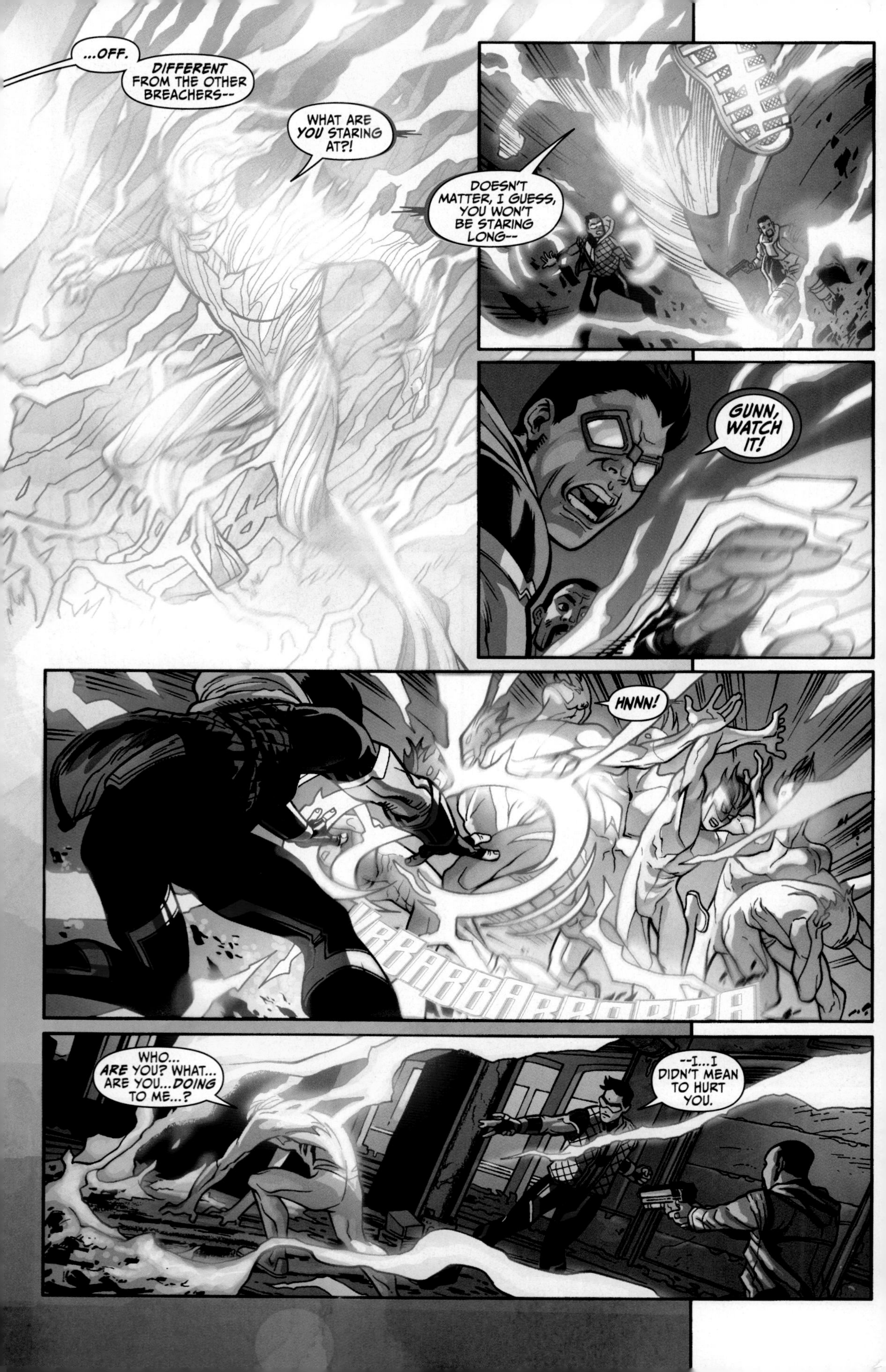
...OFF.
DIFFERENT FROM THE OTHER BREACHERS--
WHAT ARE YOU STARING AT?!
DOESN'T MATTER, I GUESS, YOU WON'T BE STARING LONG--
GUNN, WATCH IT!
HNNN!
WHO... ARE YOU? WHAT... ARE YOU...DOING TO ME...?
--I...I DIDN'T MEAN TO HURT YOU.

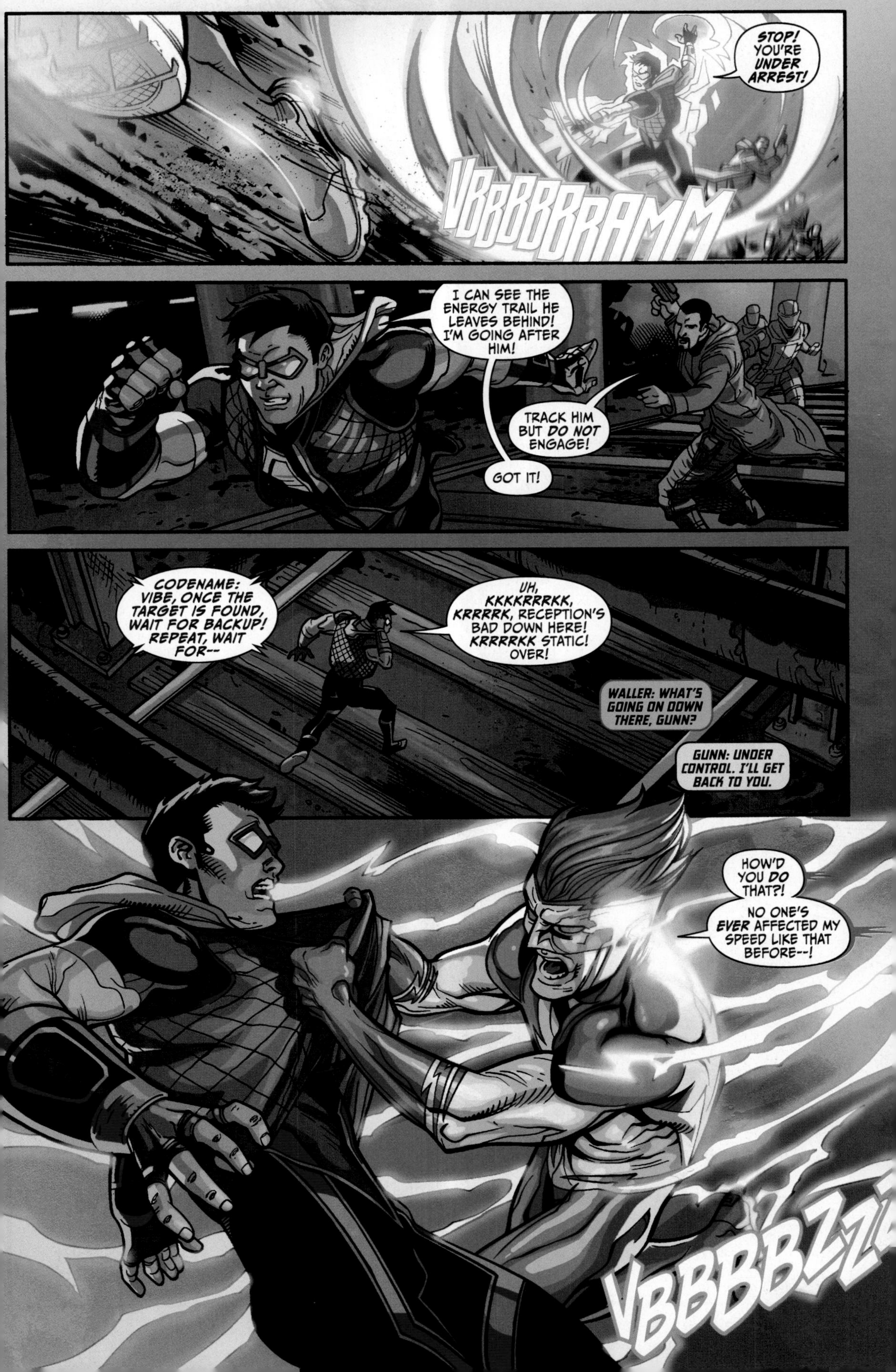
STOP! YOU'RE UNDER ARREST!
VBBBBBRAMM
I CAN SEE THE ENERGY TRAIL HE LEAVES BEHIND! I'M GOING AFTER HIM!
TRACK HIM BUT DO NOT ENGAGE!
GOT IT!
CODENAME: VIBE, ONCE THE TARGET IS FOUND, WAIT FOR BACKUP! REPEAT, WAIT FOR--
UH, KKKKRRRKK, KRRRK, RECEPTION'S BAD DOWN HERE! KRRRRKK STATIC! OVER!
WALLER: WHAT'S GOING ON DOWN THERE, GUNN?
GUNN: UNDER CONTROL. I'LL GET BACK TO YOU.
HOW'D YOU DO THAT?!
NO ONE'S EVER AFFECTED MY SPEED LIKE THAT BEFORE--!
VBBBBZZ

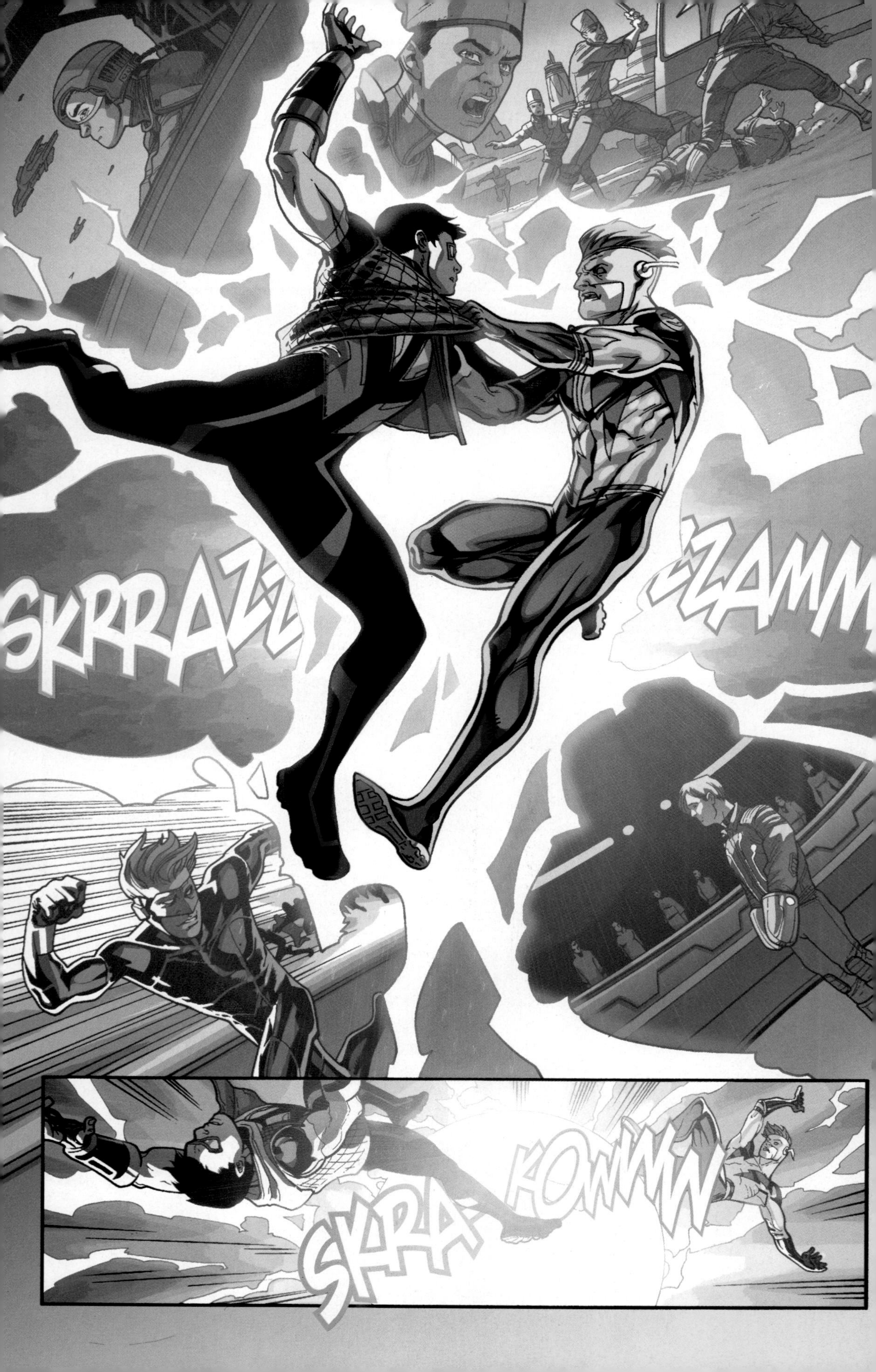
SKRRAZZ
ZAMM
SKRA-KOWWW

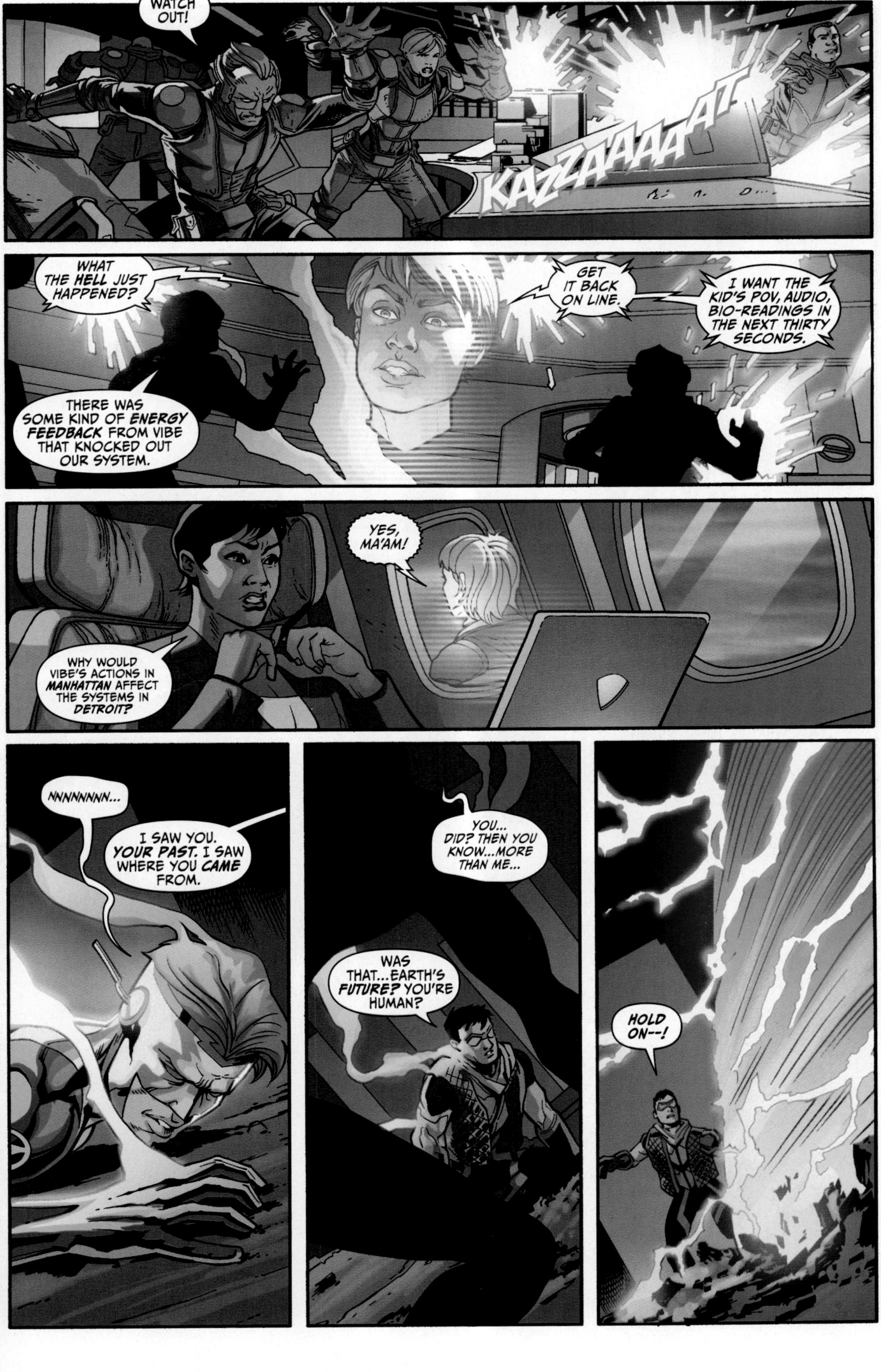
WATCH OUT!
KAZZAAAAAAT
WHAT THE HELL JUST HAPPENED?
THERE WAS SOME KIND OF ENERGY FEEDBACK FROM VIBE THAT KNOCKED OUT OUR SYSTEM.
GET IT BACK ON LINE.
I WANT THE KID'S POV, AUDIO, BIO-READINGS IN THE NEXT THIRTY SECONDS.
YES, MA'AM!
WHY WOULD VIBE'S ACTIONS IN MANHATTAN AFFECT THE SYSTEMS IN DETROIT?
NNNNNNNN...
I SAW YOU. YOUR PAST. I SAW WHERE YOU CAME FROM.
YOU... DID? THEN YOU KNOW...MORE THAN ME...
WAS THAT...EARTH'S FUTURE? YOU'RE HUMAN?
HOLD ON--!

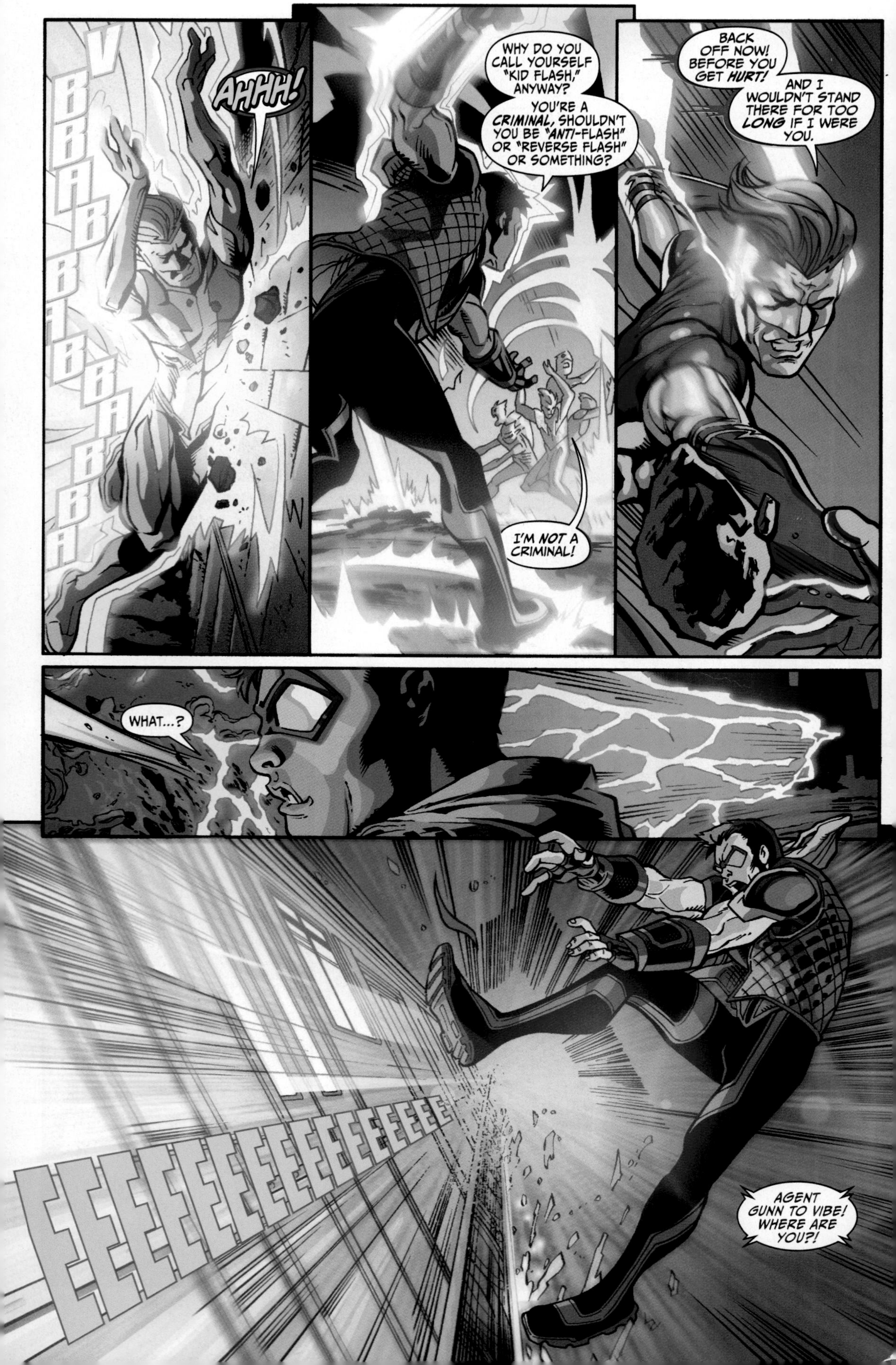
VBBBABBABBABBA
AHHH!
WHY DO YOU CALL YOURSELF "KID FLASH," ANYWAY?
YOU'RE A CRIMINAL, SHOULDN'T YOU BE "ANTI-FLASH" OR "REVERSE FLASH" OR SOMETHING?
I'M NOT A CRIMINAL!
BACK OFF NOW! BEFORE YOU GET HURT!
AND I WOULDN'T STAND THERE FOR TOO LONG IF I WERE YOU.
WHAT...?
EEEEEEEEEEEEEEEEEEE
AGENT GUNN TO VIBE! WHERE ARE YOU?!

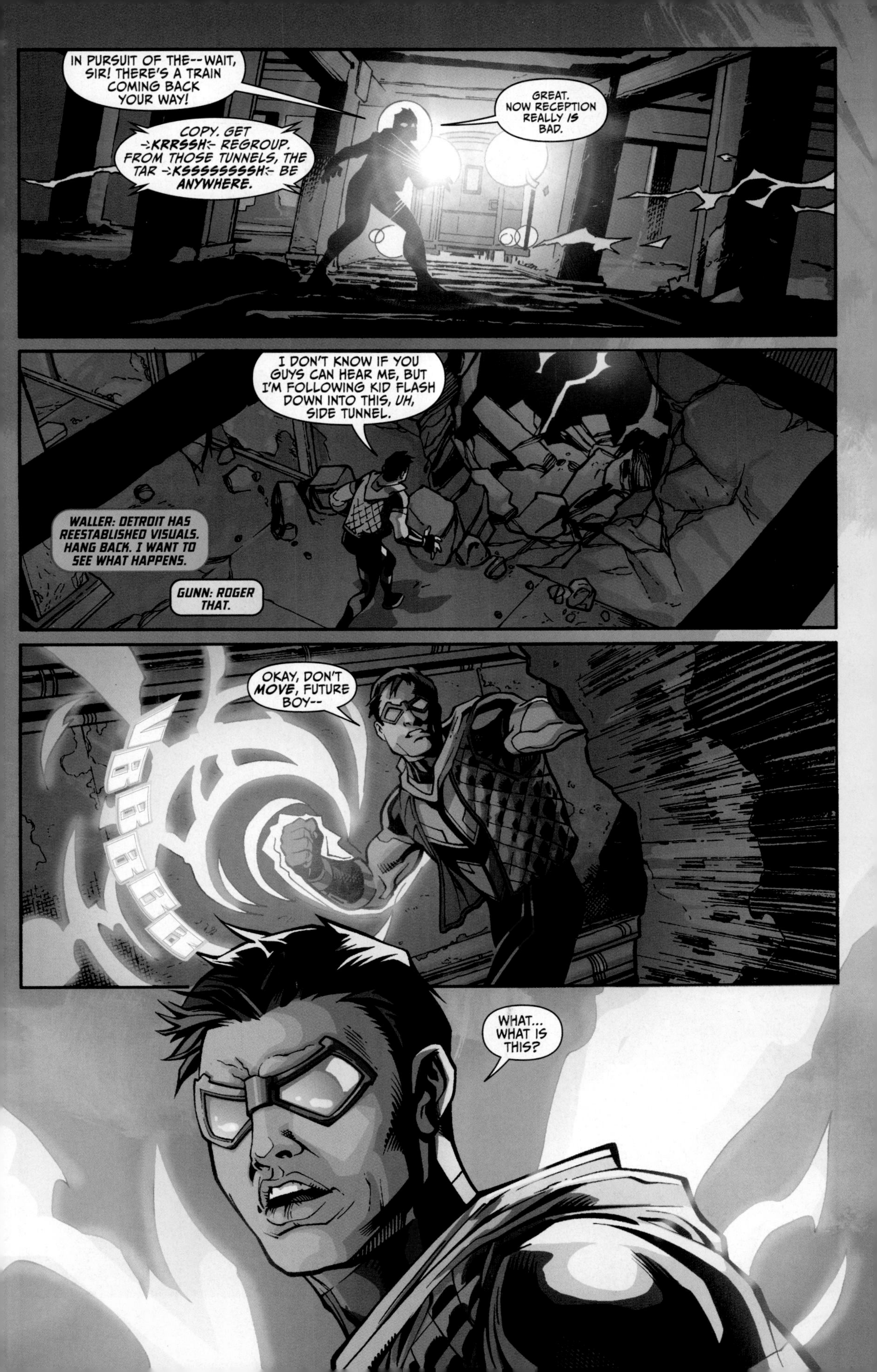
IN PURSUIT OF THE--WAIT, SIR! THERE'S A TRAIN COMING BACK YOUR WAY!
COPY. GET -KRRSSH- REGROUP. FROM THOSE TUNNELS, THE TAR -KSSSSSSSSH- BE ANYWHERE.
GREAT. NOW RECEPTION REALLY IS BAD.
I DON'T KNOW IF YOU GUYS CAN HEAR ME, BUT I'M FOLLOWING KID FLASH DOWN INTO THIS, UH, SIDE TUNNEL.
WALLER: DETROIT HAS REESTABLISHED VISUALS. HANG BACK. I WANT TO SEE WHAT HAPPENS.
GUNN: ROGER THAT.
OKAY, DON'T MOVE, FUTURE BOY--
WHAT... WHAT IS THIS?

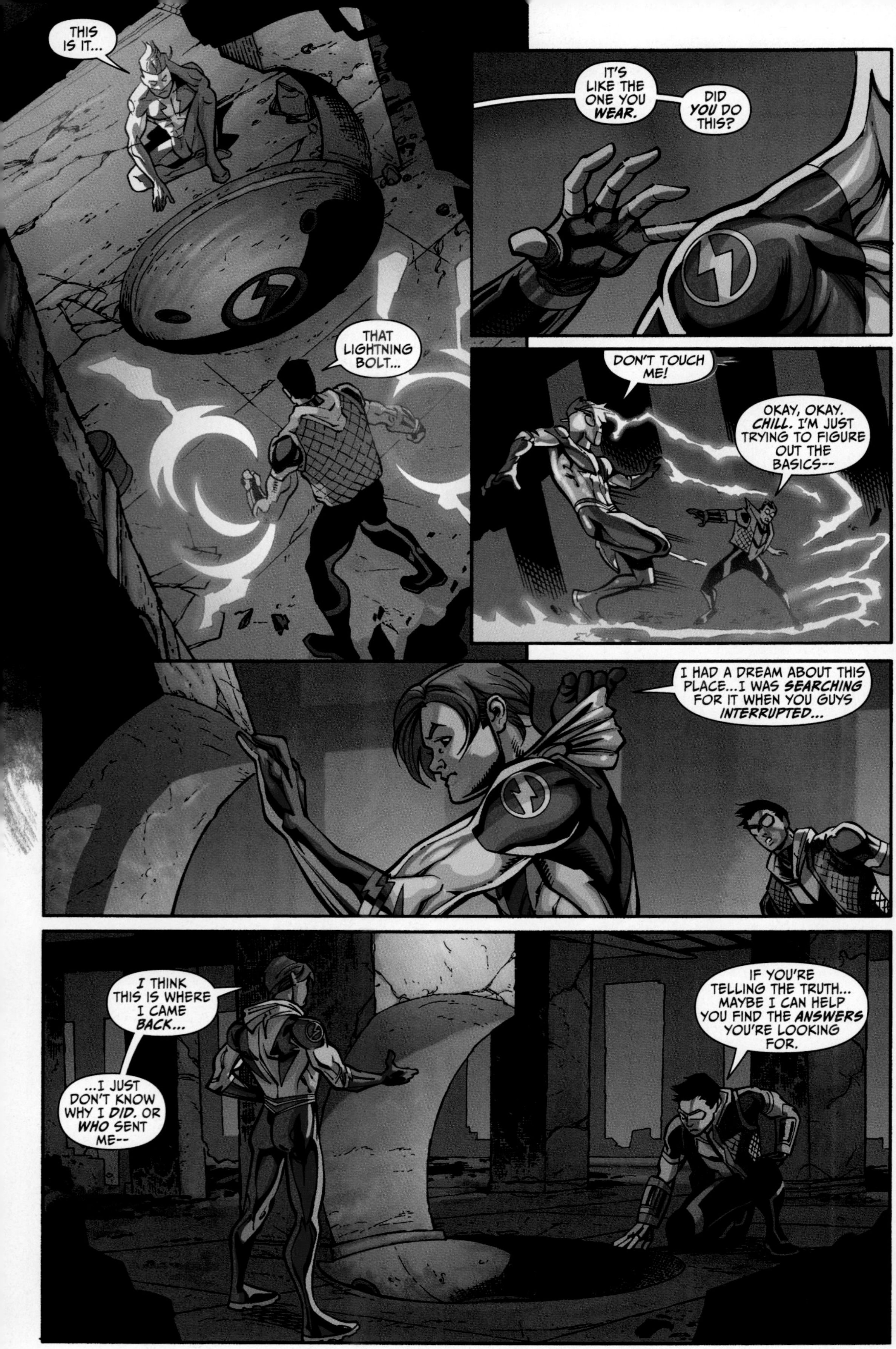
THIS IS IT...
IT'S LIKE THE ONE YOU WEAR.
DID YOU DO THIS?
THAT LIGHTNING BOLT...
DON'T TOUCH ME!
OKAY, OKAY. CHILL. I'M JUST TRYING TO FIGURE OUT THE BASICS--
I HAD A DREAM ABOUT THIS PLACE...I WAS SEARCHING FOR IT WHEN YOU GUYS INTERRUPTED...
I THINK THIS IS WHERE I CAME BACK...
...I JUST DON'T KNOW WHY I DID. OR WHO SENT ME--
IF YOU'RE TELLING THE TRUTH... MAYBE I CAN HELP YOU FIND THE ANSWERS YOU'RE LOOKING FOR.

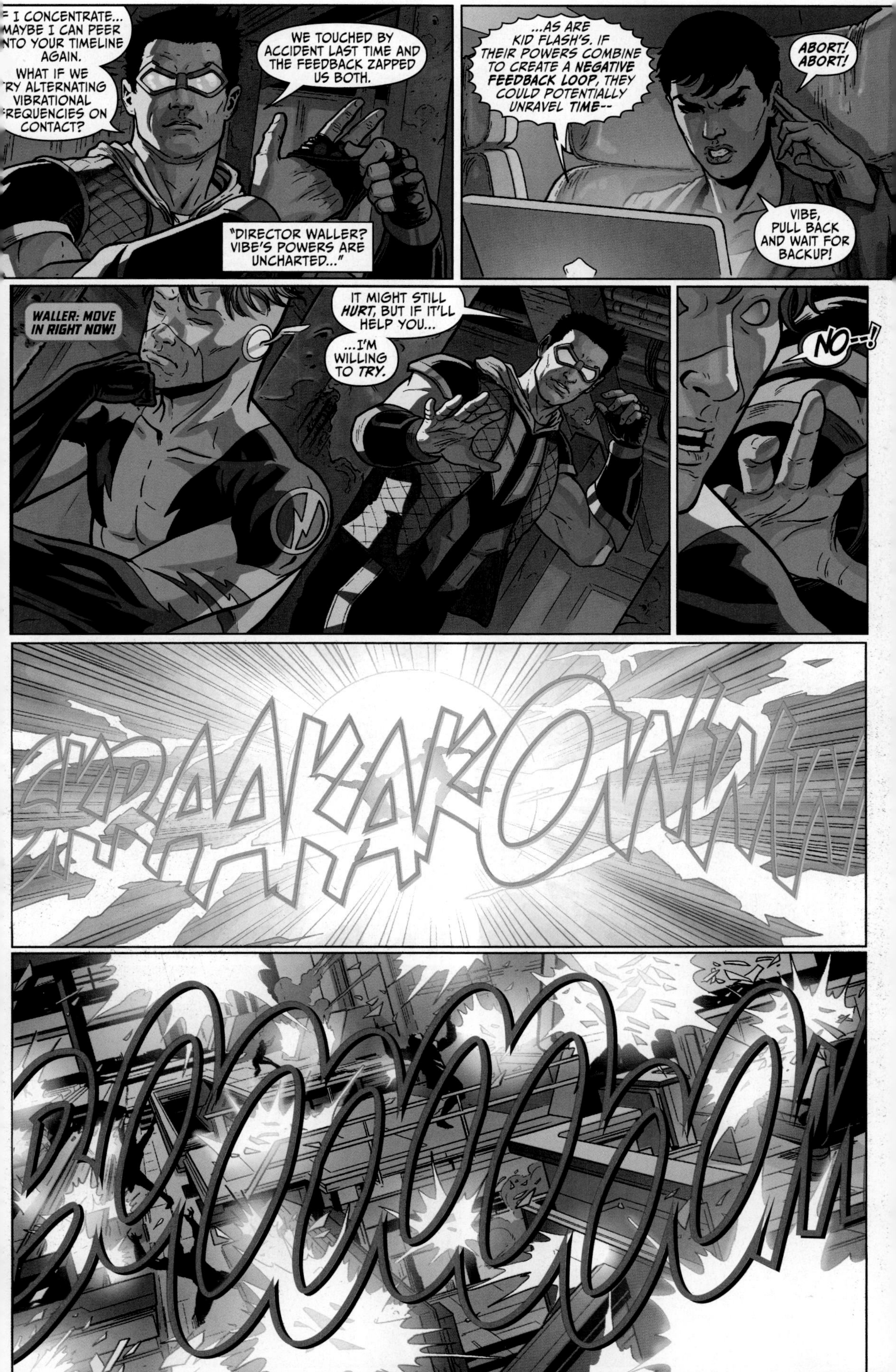

F I CONCENTRATE... MAYBE I CAN PEER NTO YOUR TIMELINE AGAIN.
WHAT IF WE TRY ALTERNATING VIBRATIONAL FREQUENCIES ON CONTACT?
WE TOUCHED BY ACCIDENT LAST TIME AND THE FEEDBACK ZAPPED US BOTH.
"DIRECTOR WALLER? VIBE'S POWERS ARE UNCHARTED..."
...AS ARE KID FLASH'S. IF THEIR POWERS COMBINE TO CREATE A NEGATIVE FEEDBACK LOOP, THEY COULD POTENTIALLY UNRAVEL TIME--
ABORT! ABORT!
VIBE, PULL BACK AND WAIT FOR BACKUP!
WALLER: MOVE IN RIGHT NOW!
IT MIGHT STILL HURT, BUT IF IT'LL HELP YOU...
...I'M WILLING TO TRY.
NO--!

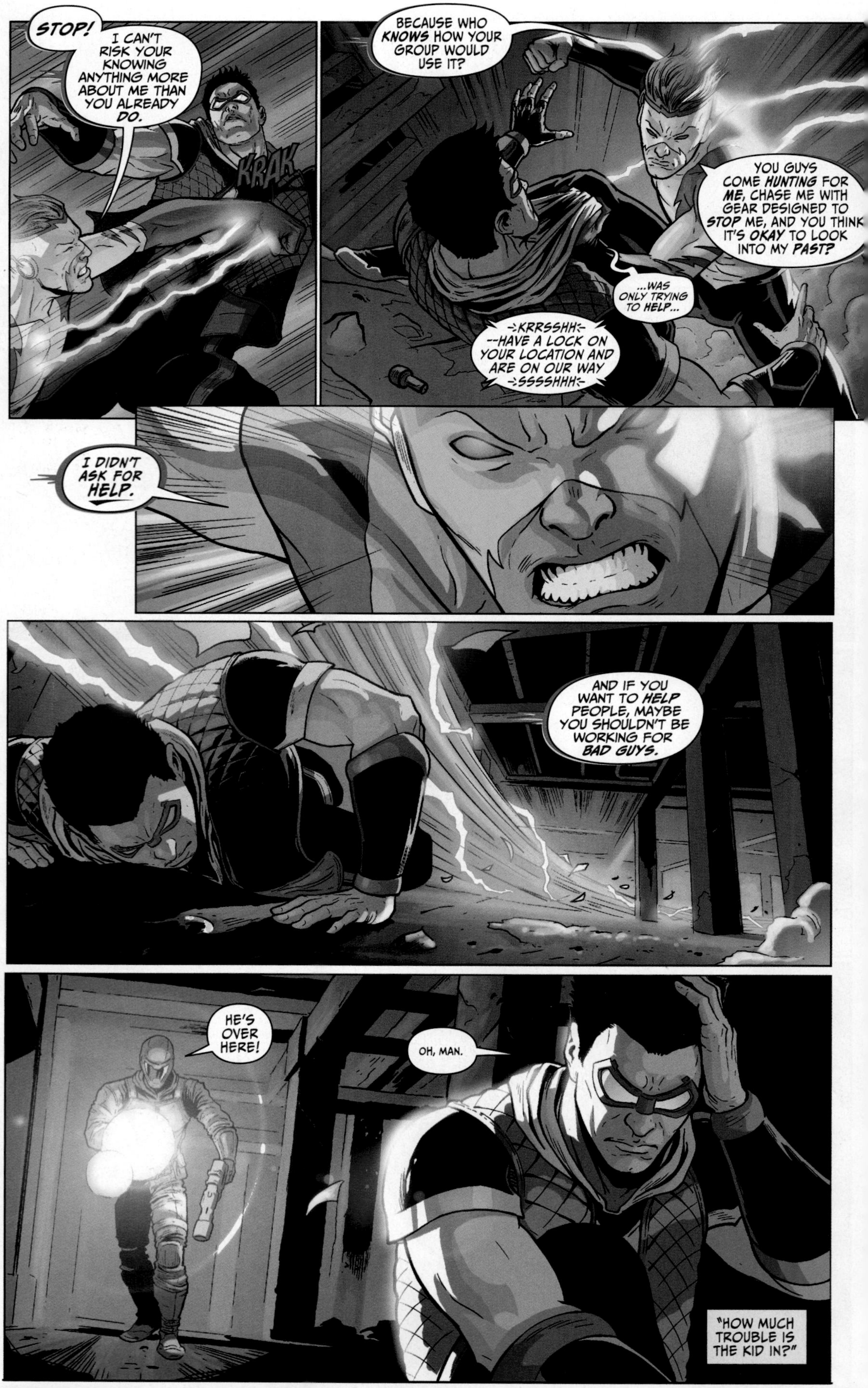
STOP!
I CAN'T RISK YOUR KNOWING ANYTHING MORE ABOUT ME THAN YOU ALREADY DO.
KRAK
BECAUSE WHO KNOWS HOW YOUR GROUP WOULD USE IT?
YOU GUYS COME HUNTING FOR ME, CHASE ME WITH GEAR DESIGNED TO STOP ME, AND YOU THINK IT'S OKAY TO LOOK INTO MY PAST?
...WAS ONLY TRYING TO HELP...
-KRRSSHH- --HAVE A LOCK ON YOUR LOCATION AND ARE ON OUR WAY -SSSSHHH-
I DIDN'T ASK FOR HELP.
AND IF YOU WANT TO HELP PEOPLE, YOU SHOULDN'T BE WORKING FOR BAD GUYS.
HE'S OVER HERE!
OH, MAN.
"HOW MUCH TROUBLE IS THE KID IN?"

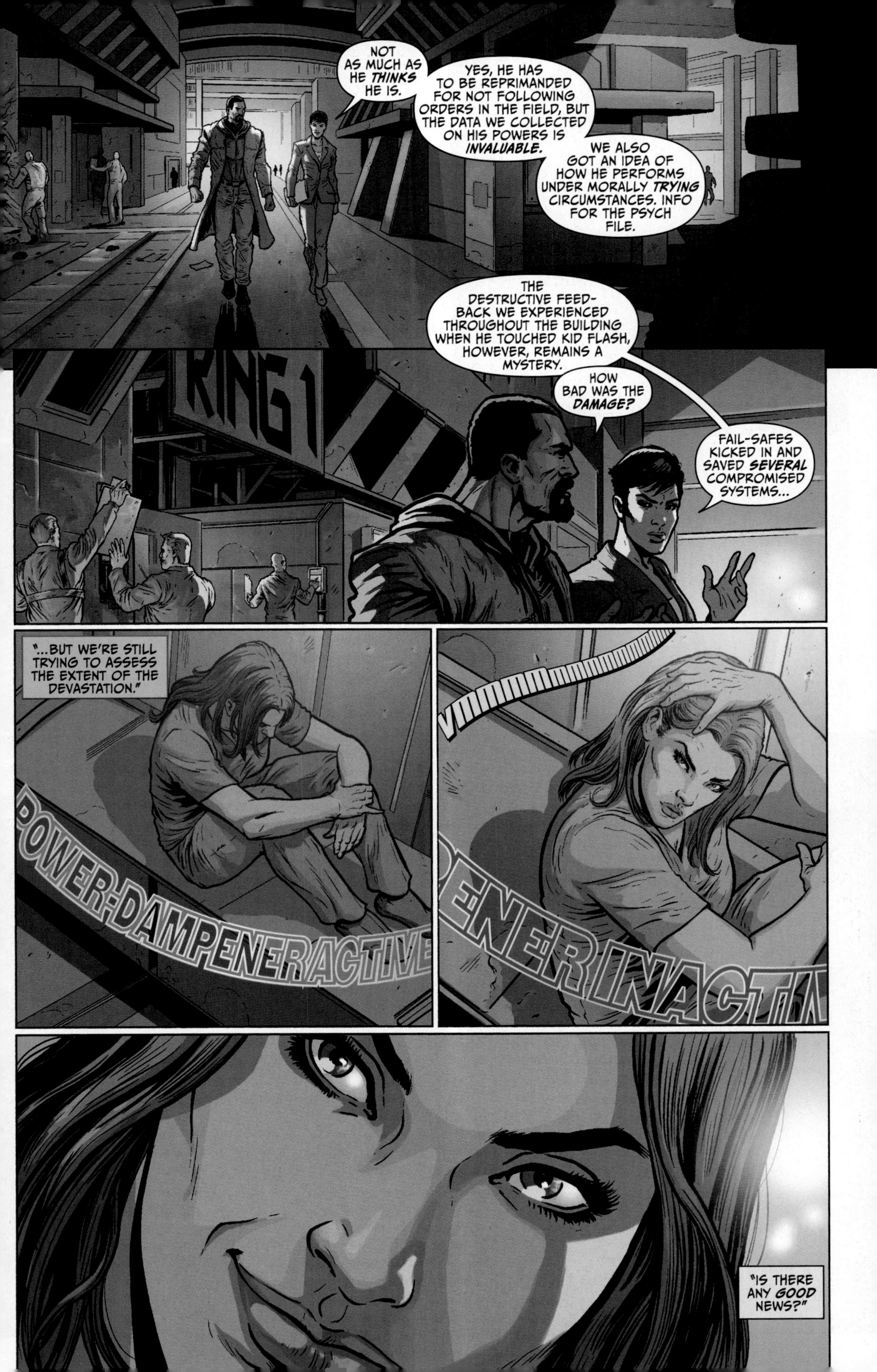
NOT AS MUCH AS HE THINKS HE IS.
YES, HE HAS TO BE REPRIMANDED FOR NOT FOLLOWING ORDERS IN THE FIELD, BUT THE DATA WE COLLECTED ON HIS POWERS IS INVALUABLE.
WE ALSO GOT AN IDEA OF HOW HE PERFORMS UNDER MORALLY TRYING CIRCUMSTANCES. INFO FOR THE PSYCH FILE.
THE DESTRUCTIVE FEED-BACK WE EXPERIENCED THROUGHOUT THE BUILDING WHEN HE TOUCHED KID FLASH, HOWEVER, REMAINS A MYSTERY.
RING 1
HOW BAD WAS THE DAMAGE?
FAIL-SAFES KICKED IN AND SAVED SEVERAL COMPROMISED SYSTEMS...
"...BUT WE'RE STILL TRYING TO ASSESS THE EXTENT OF THE DEVASTATION."
POWER-DAMPENER ACTIVE
VMMMMMMMM
ENER INACTIV
"IS THERE ANY GOOD NEWS?"

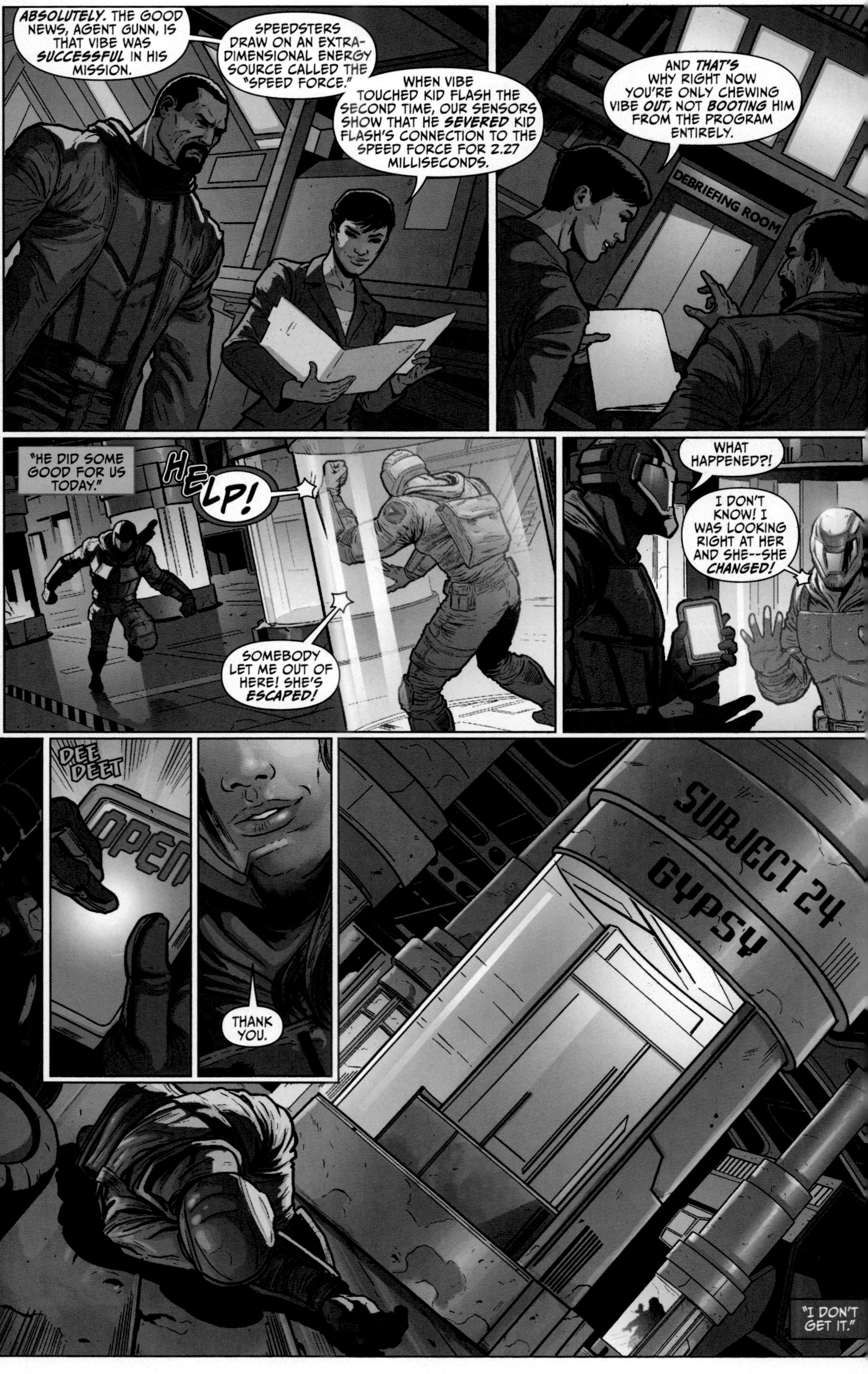

ABSOLUTELY. THE GOOD NEWS, AGENT GUNN, IS THAT VIBE WAS SUCCESSFUL IN HIS MISSION.
SPEEDSTERS DRAW ON AN EXTRA-DIMENSIONAL ENERGY SOURCE CALLED THE "SPEED FORCE."
WHEN VIBE TOUCHED KID FLASH THE SECOND TIME, OUR SENSORS SHOW THAT HE SEVERED KID FLASH'S CONNECTION TO THE SPEED FORCE FOR 2.27 MILLISECONDS.
AND THAT'S WHY RIGHT NOW YOU'RE ONLY CHEWING VIBE OUT, NOT BOOTING HIM FROM THE PROGRAM ENTIRELY.
DEBRIEFING ROOM
"HE DID SOME GOOD FOR US TODAY."
HELP!
SOMEBODY LET ME OUT OF HERE! SHE'S ESCAPED!
WHAT HAPPENED?!
I DON'T KNOW! I WAS LOOKING RIGHT AT HER AND SHE--SHE CHANGED!
DEE DEET
OPEN
THANK YOU.
SUBJECT 24
GYPSY
"I DON'T GET IT."

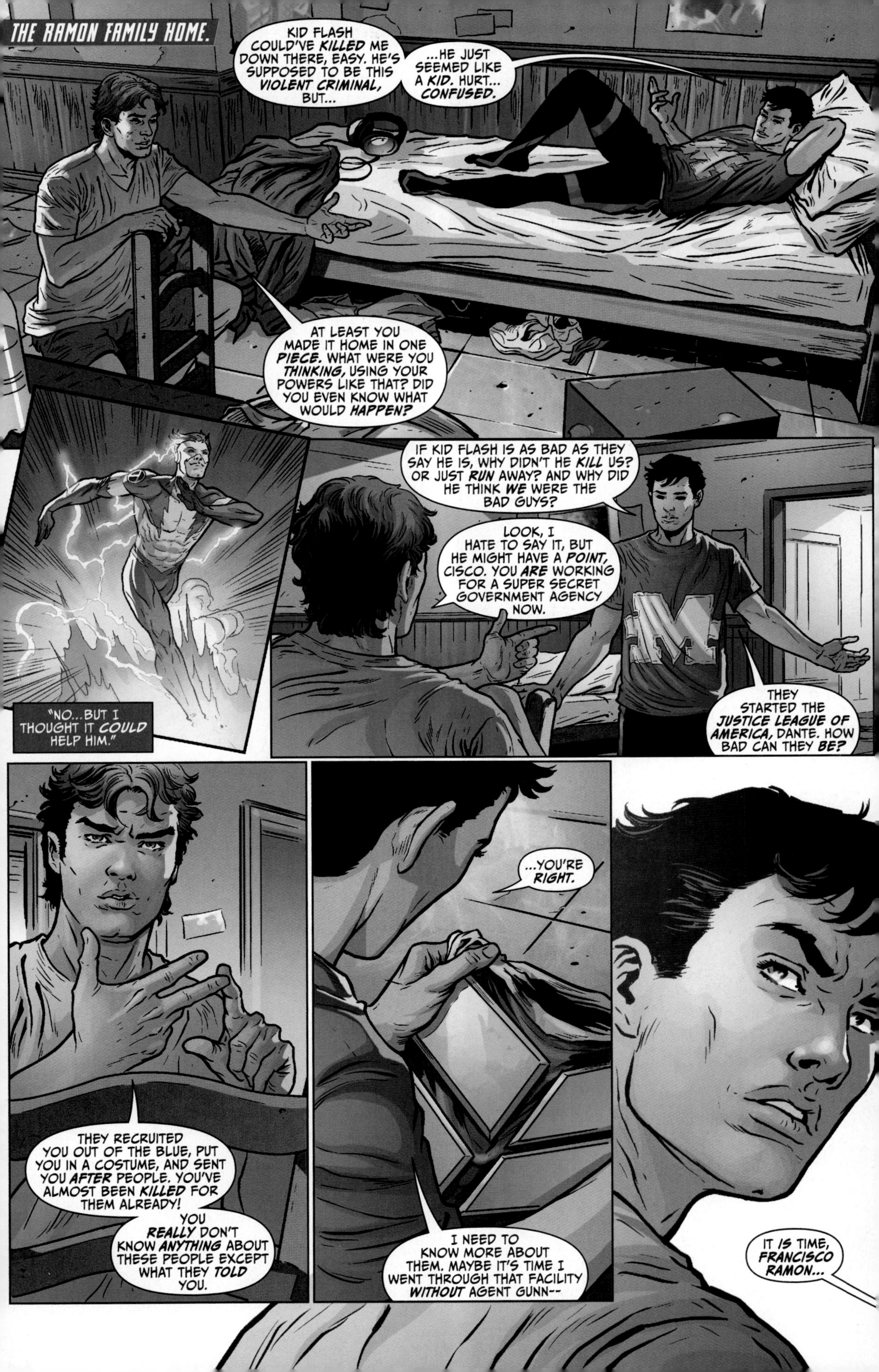
THE RAMON FAMILY HOME.
KID FLASH COULD'VE KILLED ME DOWN THERE, EASY. HE'S SUPPOSED TO BE THIS VIOLENT CRIMINAL, BUT...
...HE JUST SEEMED LIKE A KID. HURT... CONFUSED.
AT LEAST YOU MADE IT HOME IN ONE PIECE. WHAT WERE YOU THINKING, USING YOUR POWERS LIKE THAT? DID YOU EVEN KNOW WHAT WOULD HAPPEN?
"NO...BUT I THOUGHT IT COULD HELP HIM."
IF KID FLASH IS AS BAD AS THEY SAY HE IS, WHY DIDN'T HE KILL US? OR JUST RUN AWAY? AND WHY DID HE THINK WE WERE THE BAD GUYS?
LOOK, I HATE TO SAY IT, BUT HE MIGHT HAVE A POINT, CISCO. YOU ARE WORKING FOR A SUPER SECRET GOVERNMENT AGENCY NOW.
THEY STARTED THE JUSTICE LEAGUE OF AMERICA, DANTE. HOW BAD CAN THEY BE?
THEY RECRUITED YOU OUT OF THE BLUE, PUT YOU IN A COSTUME, AND SENT YOU AFTER PEOPLE. YOU'VE ALMOST BEEN KILLED FOR THEM ALREADY!
YOU REALLY DON'T KNOW ANYTHING ABOUT THESE PEOPLE EXCEPT WHAT THEY TOLD YOU.
...YOU'RE RIGHT.
I NEED TO KNOW MORE ABOUT THEM. MAYBE IT'S TIME I WENT THROUGH THAT FACILITY WITHOUT AGENT GUNN--
IT IS TIME, FRANCISCO RAMON...

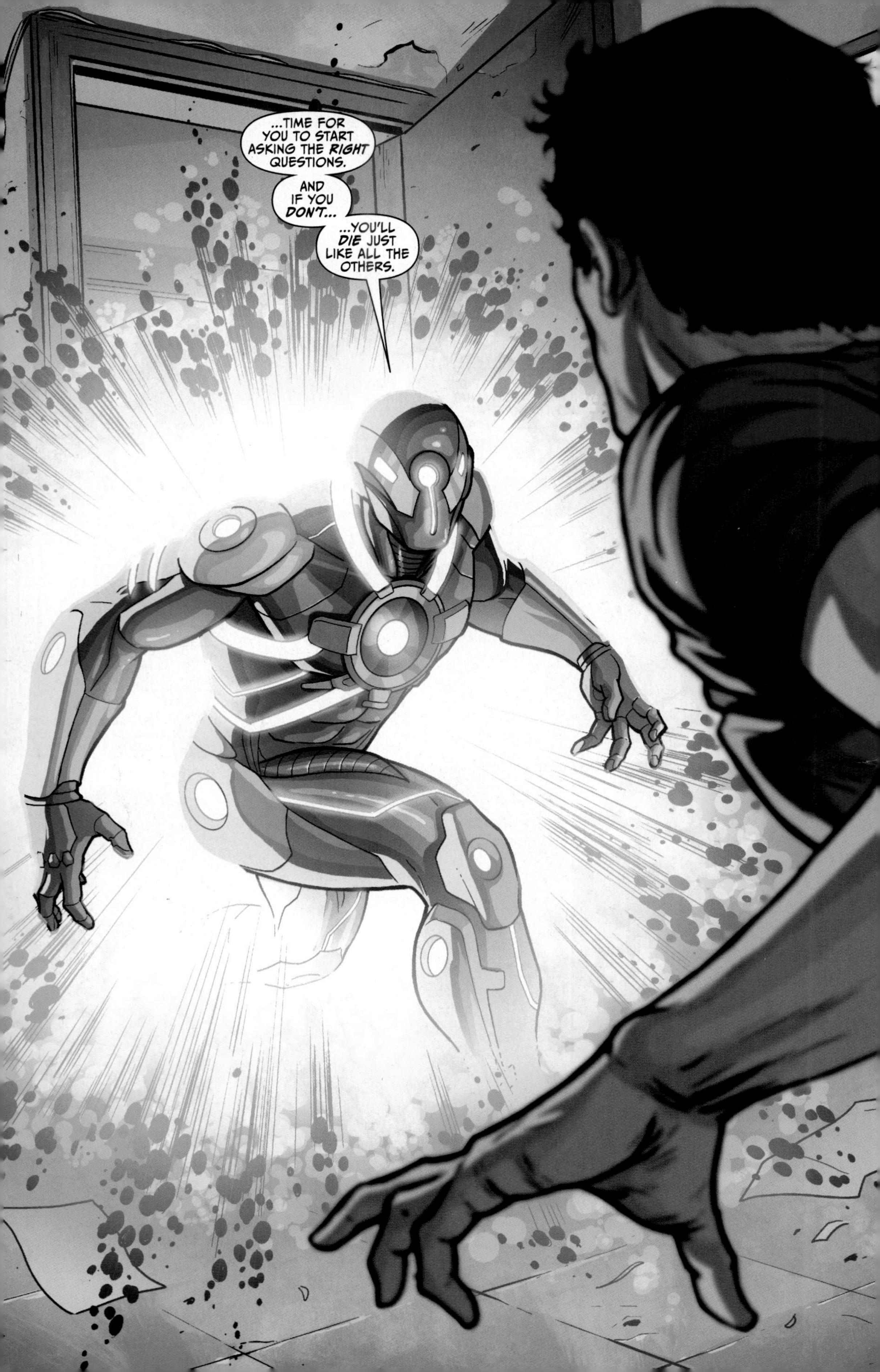
...TIME FOR YOU TO START ASKING THE RIGHT QUESTIONS.
AND IF YOU DON'T...
...YOU'LL DIE JUST LIKE ALL THE OTHERS.

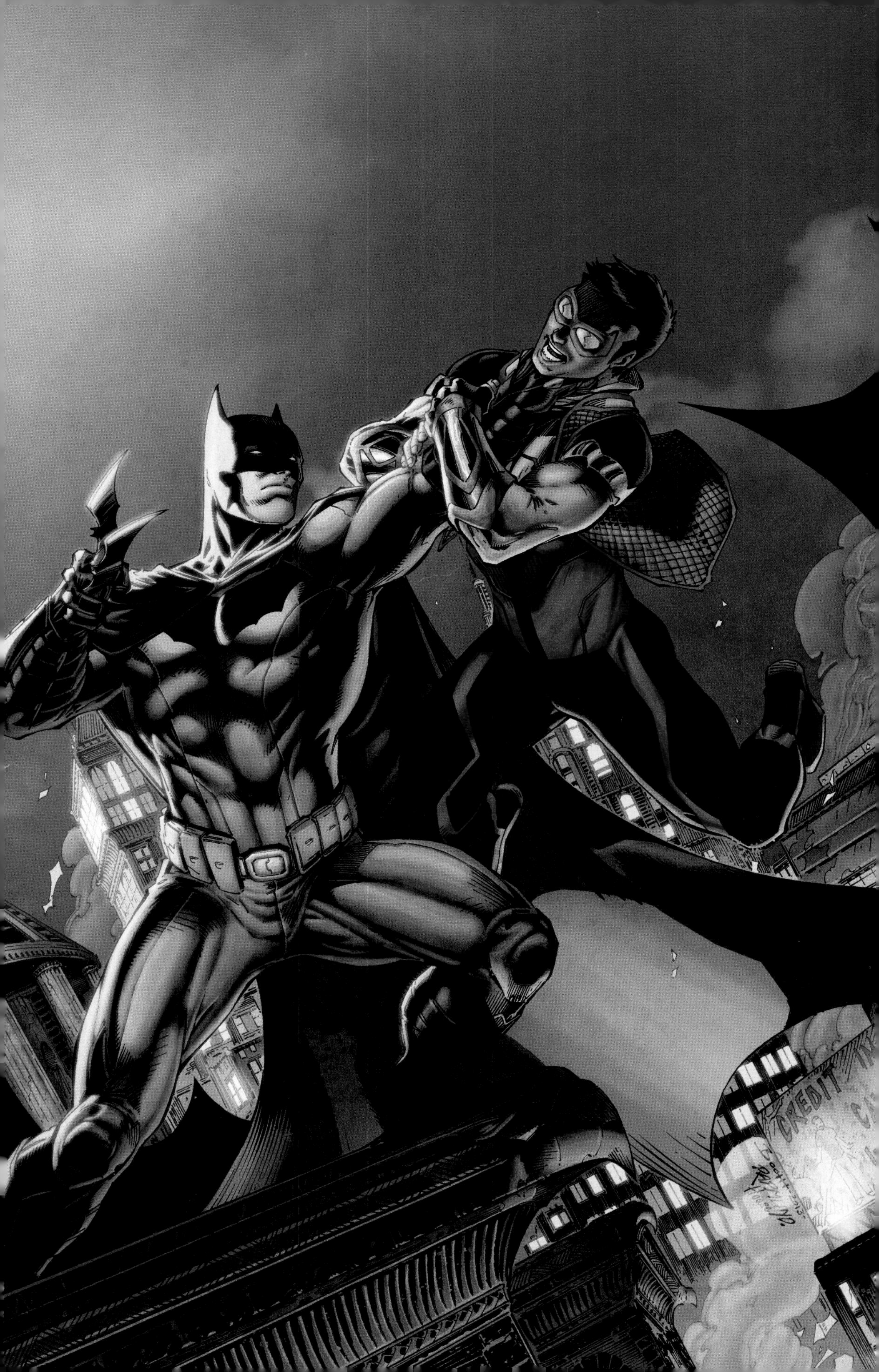
CREDIT

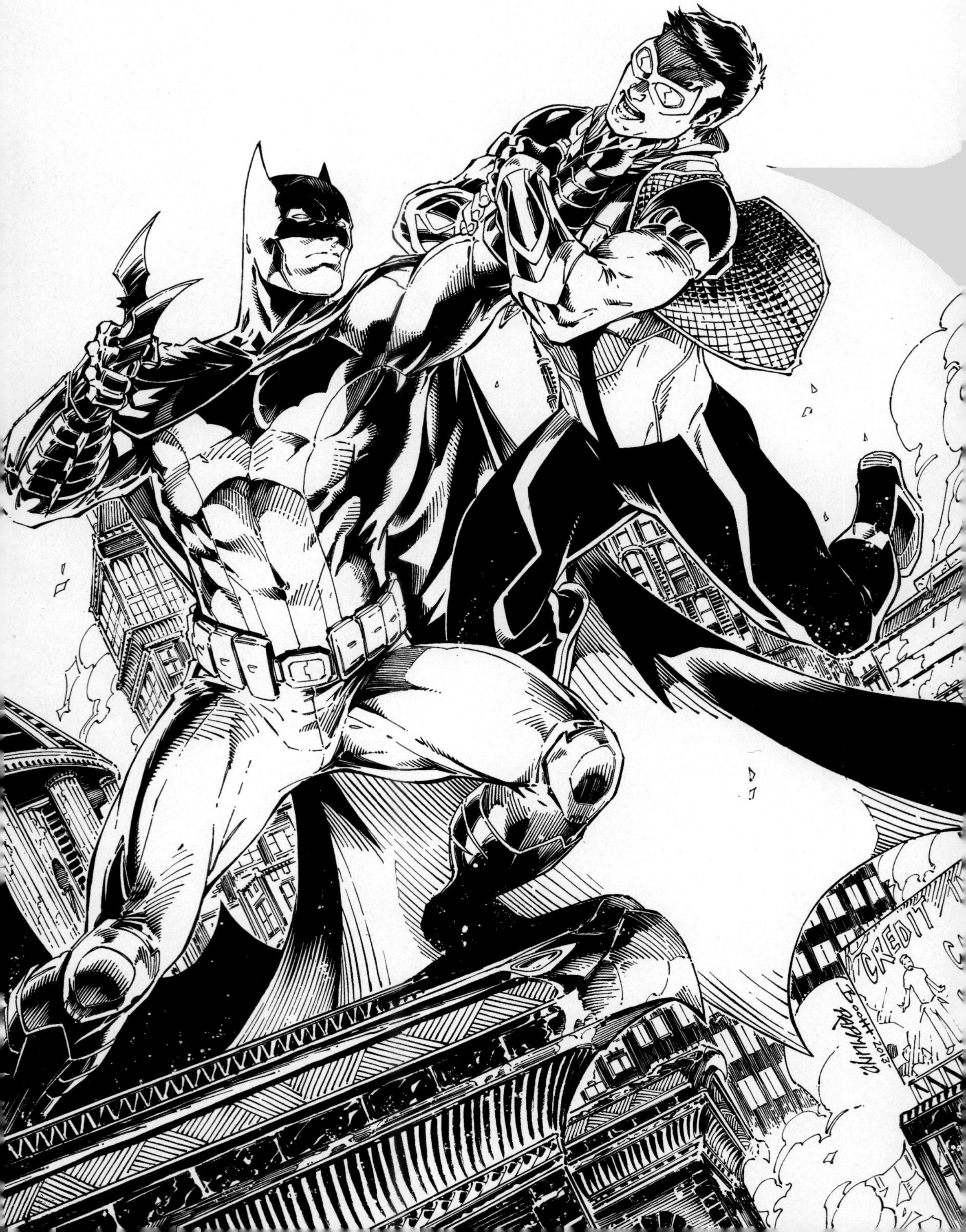
CREDIT

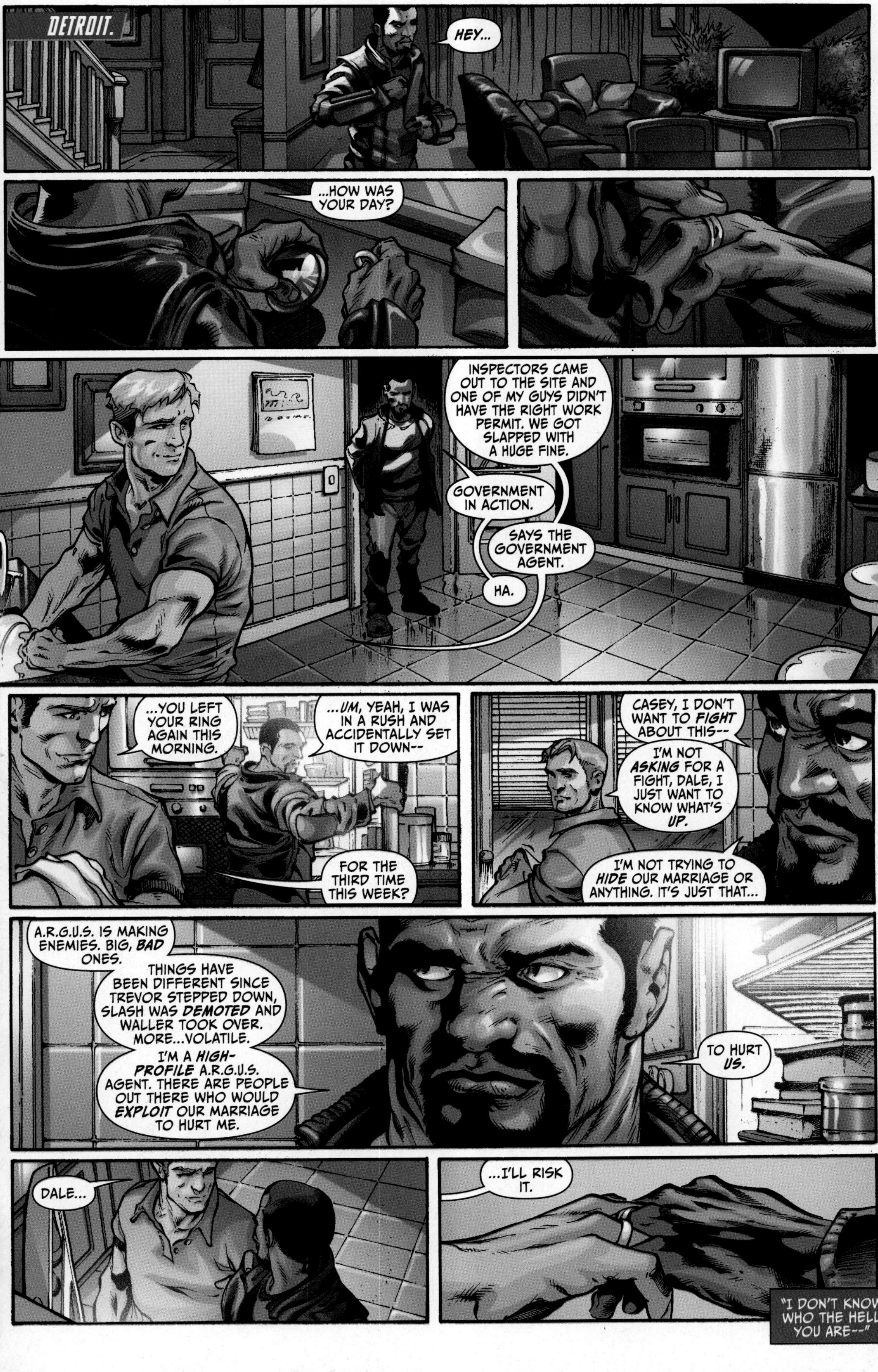
DETROIT.
HEY...
...HOW WAS YOUR DAY?
INSPECTORS CAME OUT TO THE SITE AND ONE OF MY GUYS DIDN'T HAVE THE RIGHT WORK PERMIT. WE GOT SLAPPED WITH A HUGE FINE.
GOVERNMENT IN ACTION.
SAYS THE GOVERNMENT AGENT.
HA.
...YOU LEFT YOUR RING AGAIN THIS MORNING.
...UM, YEAH, I WAS IN A RUSH AND ACCIDENTALLY SET IT DOWN--
FOR THE THIRD TIME THIS WEEK?
CASEY, I DON'T WANT TO FIGHT ABOUT THIS--
I'M NOT ASKING FOR A FIGHT, DALE, I JUST WANT TO KNOW WHAT'S UP.
I'M NOT TRYING TO HIDE OUR MARRIAGE OR ANYTHING. IT'S JUST THAT...
A.R.G.U.S. IS MAKING ENEMIES. BIG, BAD ONES.
THINGS HAVE BEEN DIFFERENT SINCE TREVOR STEPPED DOWN, SLASH WAS DEMOTED AND WALLER TOOK OVER. MORE...VOLATILE.
I'M A HIGH-PROFILE A.R.G.U.S. AGENT. THERE ARE PEOPLE OUT THERE WHO WOULD EXPLOIT OUR MARRIAGE TO HURT ME.
TO HURT US.
DALE...
...I'LL RISK IT.
"I DON'T KNOW WHO THE HELL YOU ARE--"

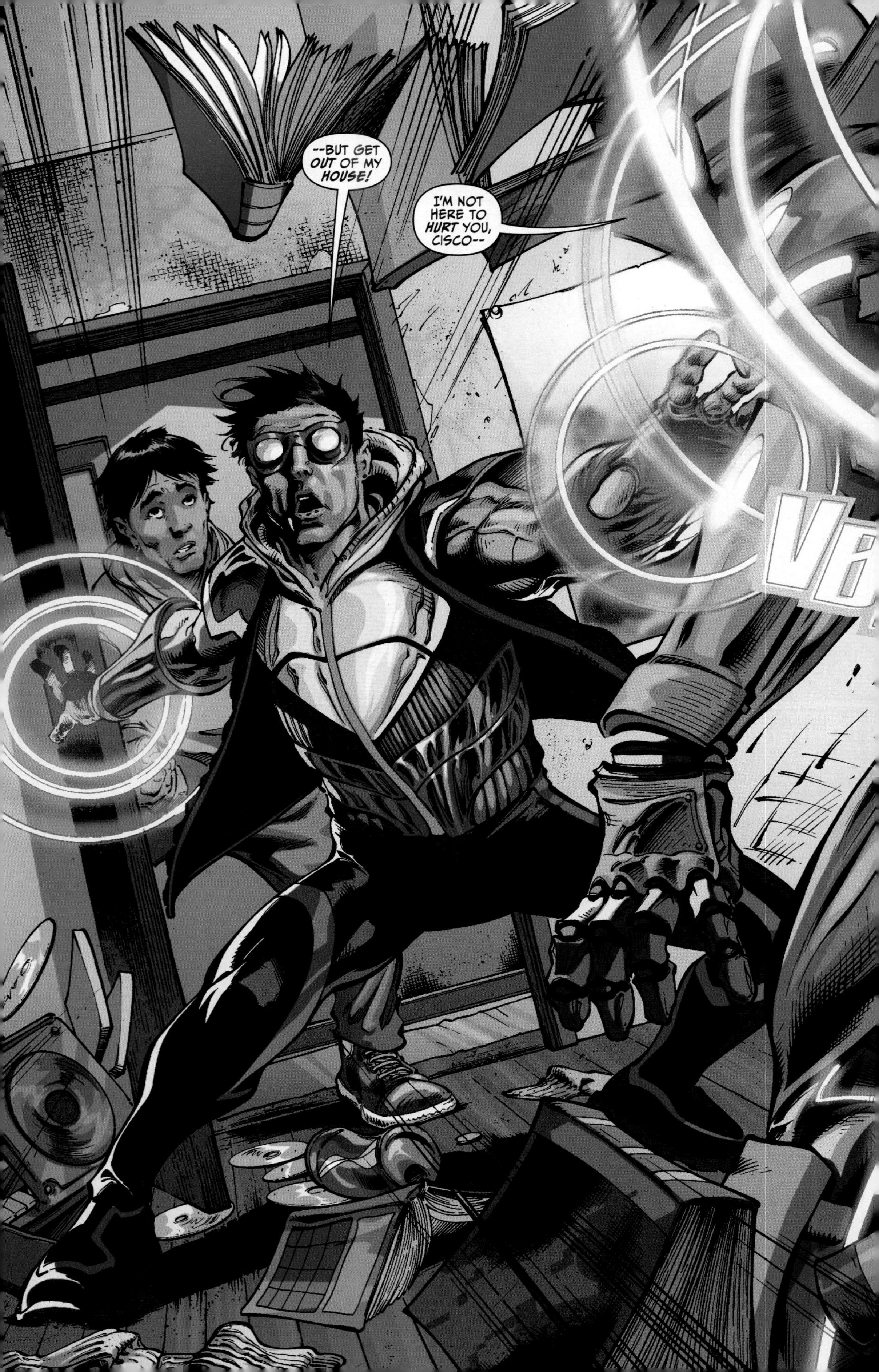
I'M NOT HERE TO HURT YOU, CISCO--
--BUT GET OUT OF MY HOUSE!

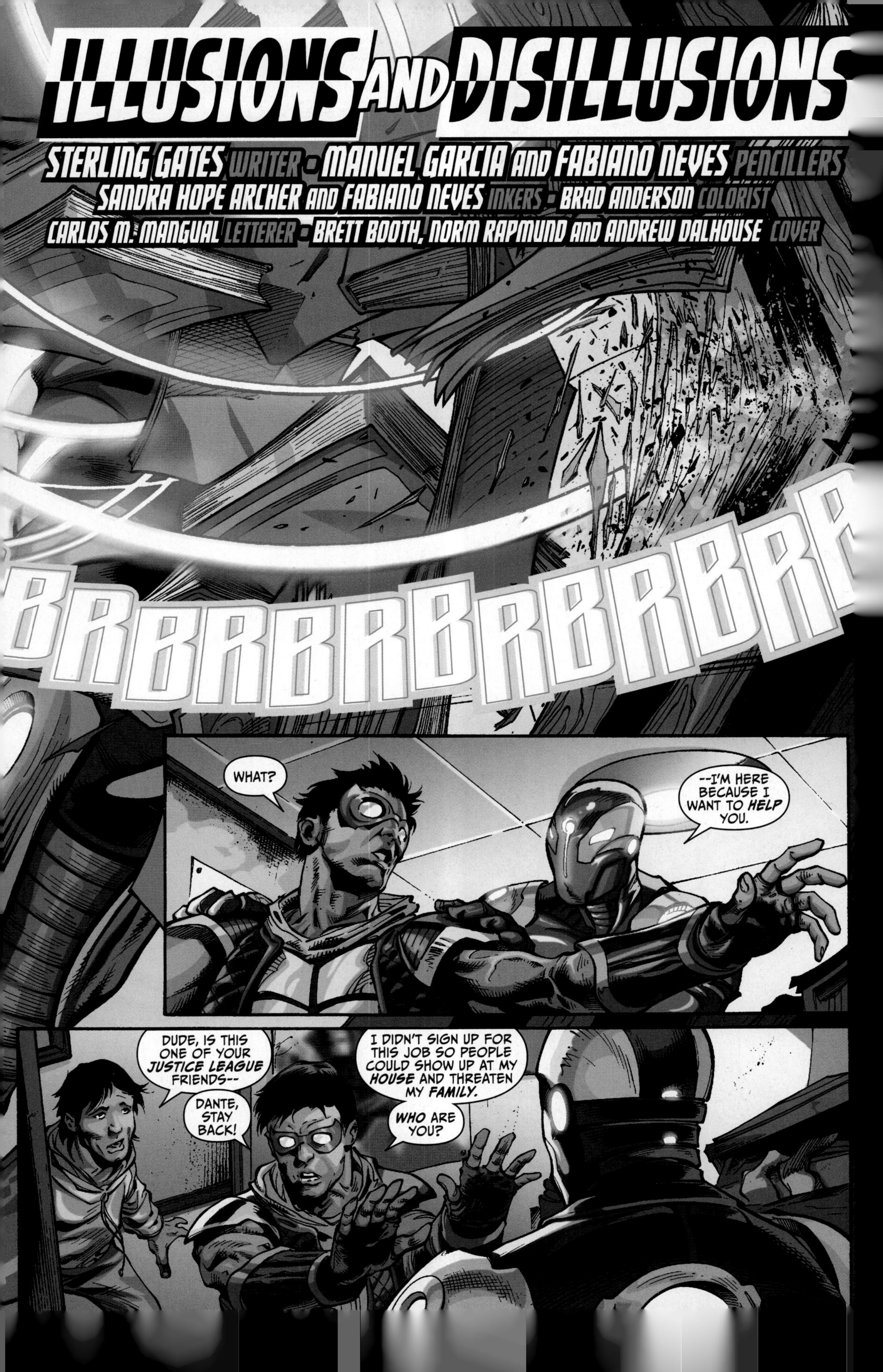
ILLUSIONS AND DISILLUSIONS
STERLING GATES WRITER • MANUEL GARCIA AND FABIANO NEVES PENCILLERS
SANDRA HOPE ARCHER AND FABIANO NEVES INKERS • BRAD ANDERSON COLORIST
CARLOS M. MANGUAL LETTERER • BRETT BOOTH, NORM RAPMUND AND ANDREW DALHOUSE COVER
BRBRBRBRBRBRBRA
WHAT?
--I'M HERE BECAUSE I WANT TO HELP YOU.
DUDE, IS THIS ONE OF YOUR JUSTICE LEAGUE FRIENDS--
DANTE, STAY BACK!
I DIDN'T SIGN UP FOR THIS JOB SO PEOPLE COULD SHOW UP AT MY HOUSE AND THREATEN MY FAMILY.
WHO ARE YOU?

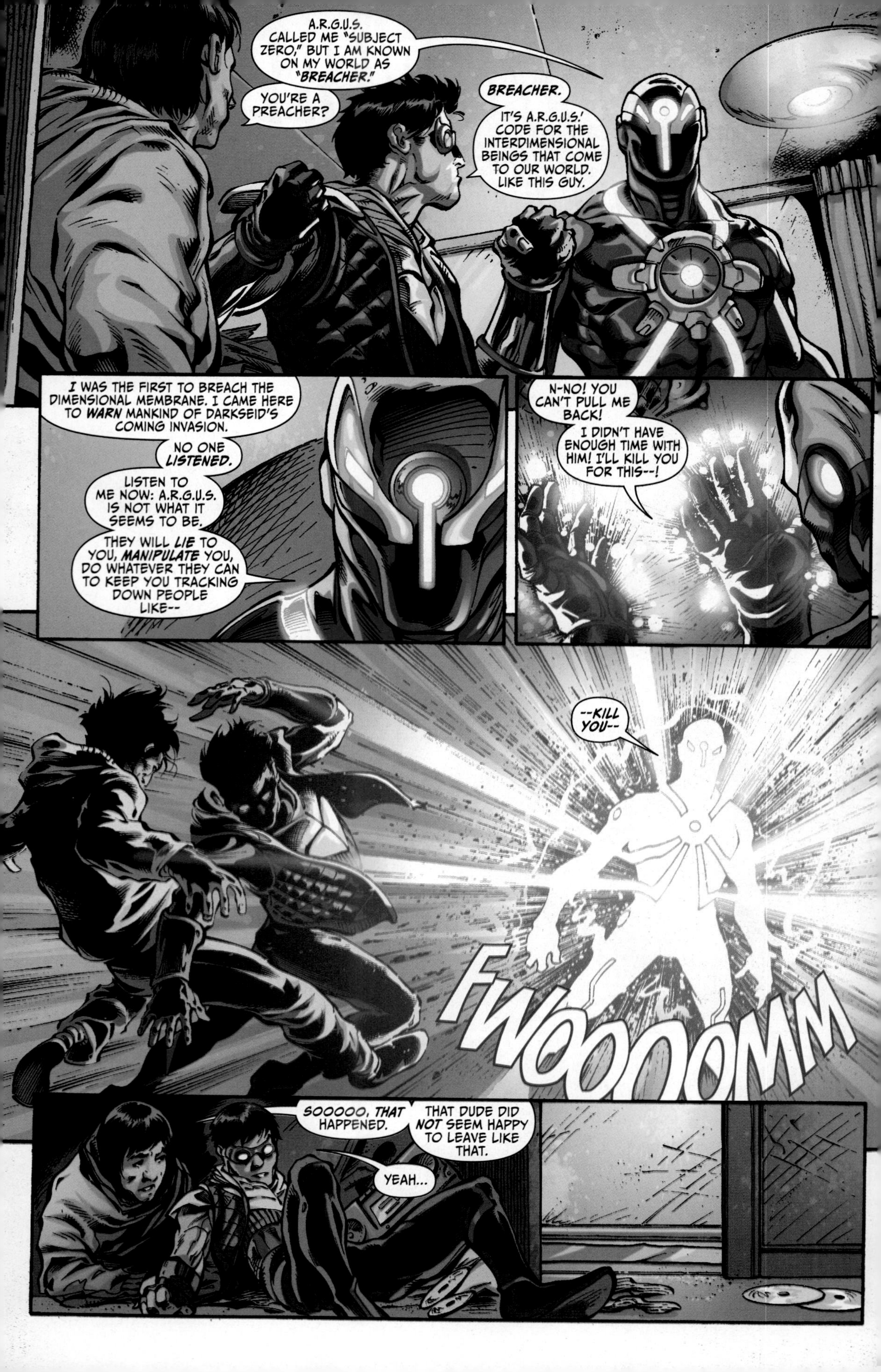
A.R.G.U.S. CALLED ME "SUBJECT ZERO," BUT I AM KNOWN ON MY WORLD AS "BREACHER."
YOU'RE A PREACHER?
BREACHER.
IT'S A.R.G.U.S.' CODE FOR THE INTERDIMENSIONAL BEINGS THAT COME TO OUR WORLD. LIKE THIS GUY.
I WAS THE FIRST TO BREACH THE DIMENSIONAL MEMBRANE. I CAME HERE TO WARN MANKIND OF DARKSEID'S COMING INVASION.
NO ONE LISTENED.
LISTEN TO ME NOW: A.R.G.U.S. IS NOT WHAT IT SEEMS TO BE.
THEY WILL LIE TO YOU, MANIPULATE YOU, DO WHATEVER THEY CAN TO KEEP YOU TRACKING DOWN PEOPLE LIKE--
N-NO! YOU CAN'T PULL ME BACK!
I DIDN'T HAVE ENOUGH TIME WITH HIM! I'LL KILL YOU FOR THIS--!
--KILL YOU--
FWOOOOMM
SOOOOO, THAT HAPPENED.
THAT DUDE DID NOT SEEM HAPPY TO LEAVE LIKE THAT.
YEAH...

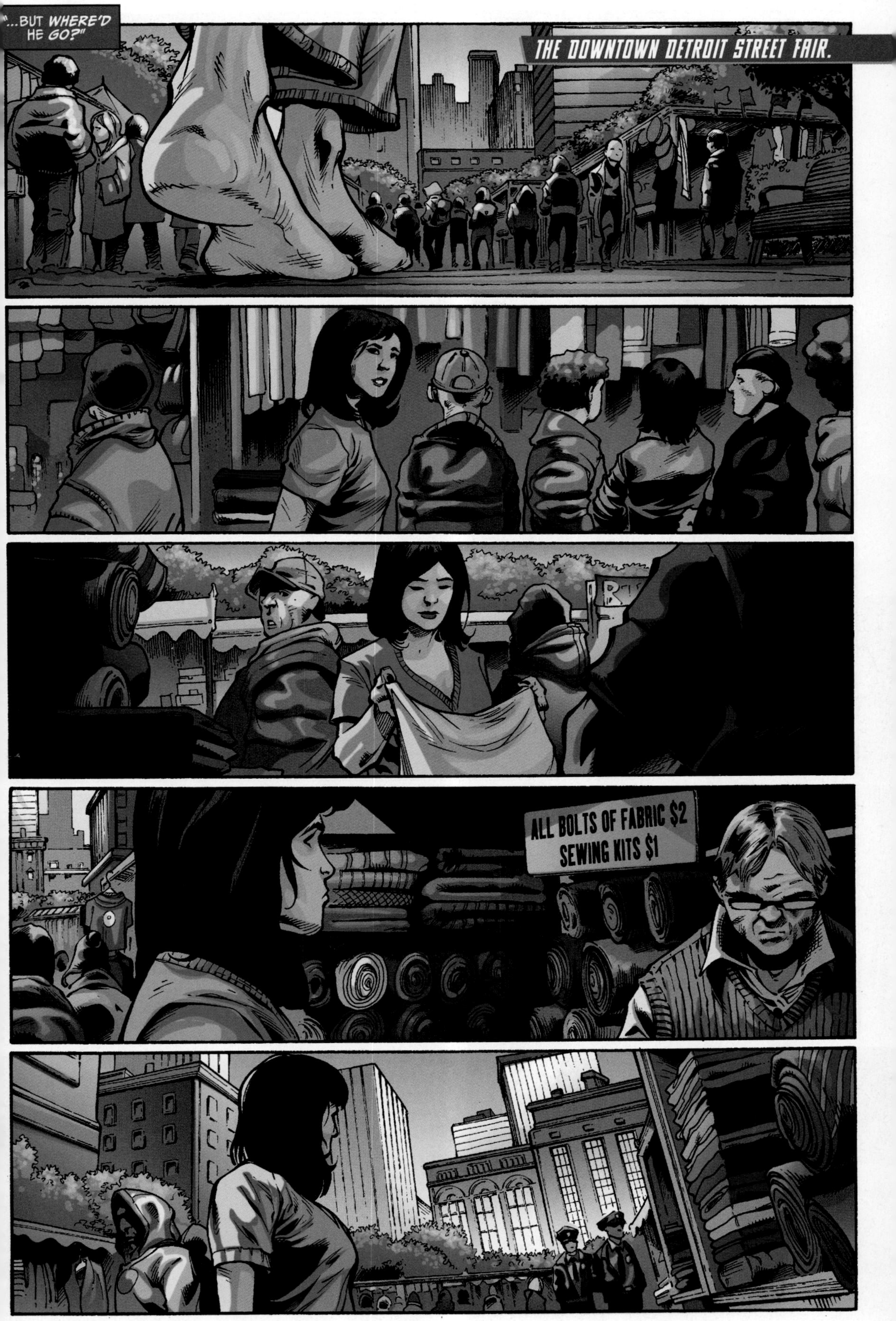
"...BUT WHERE'D HE GO?"
THE DOWNTOWN DETROIT STREET FAIR.
ALL BOLTS OF FABRIC $2
SEWING KITS $1

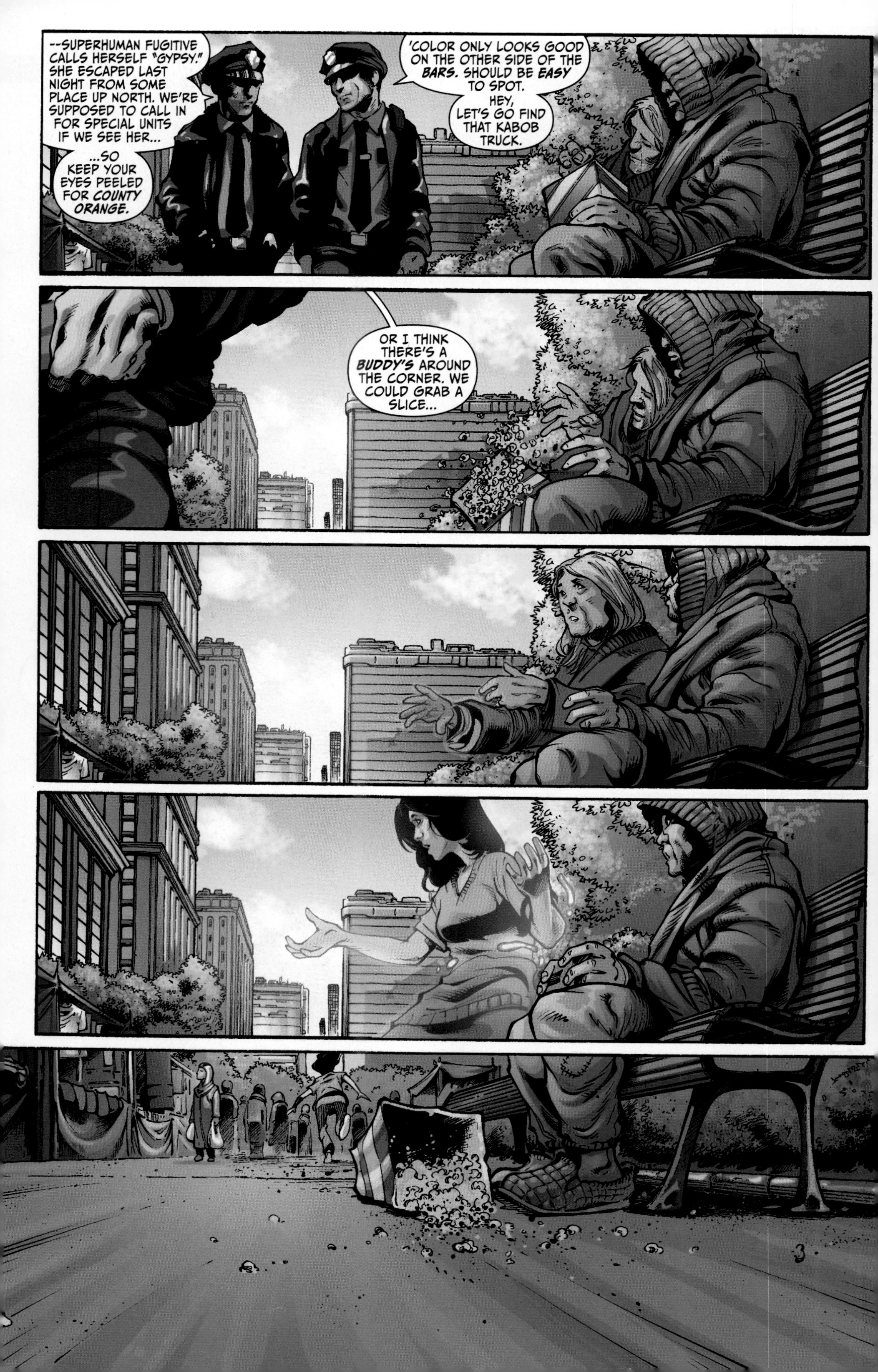
--SUPERHUMAN FUGITIVE CALLS HERSELF "GYPSY." SHE ESCAPED LAST NIGHT FROM SOME PLACE UP NORTH. WE'RE SUPPOSED TO CALL IN FOR SPECIAL UNITS IF WE SEE HER...
...SO KEEP YOUR EYES PEELED FOR COUNTY ORANGE.
'COLOR ONLY LOOKS GOOD ON THE OTHER SIDE OF THE BARS. SHOULD BE EASY TO SPOT.
HEY, LET'S GO FIND THAT KABOB TRUCK.
OR I THINK THERE'S A BUDDY'S AROUND THE CORNER. WE COULD GRAB A SLICE...

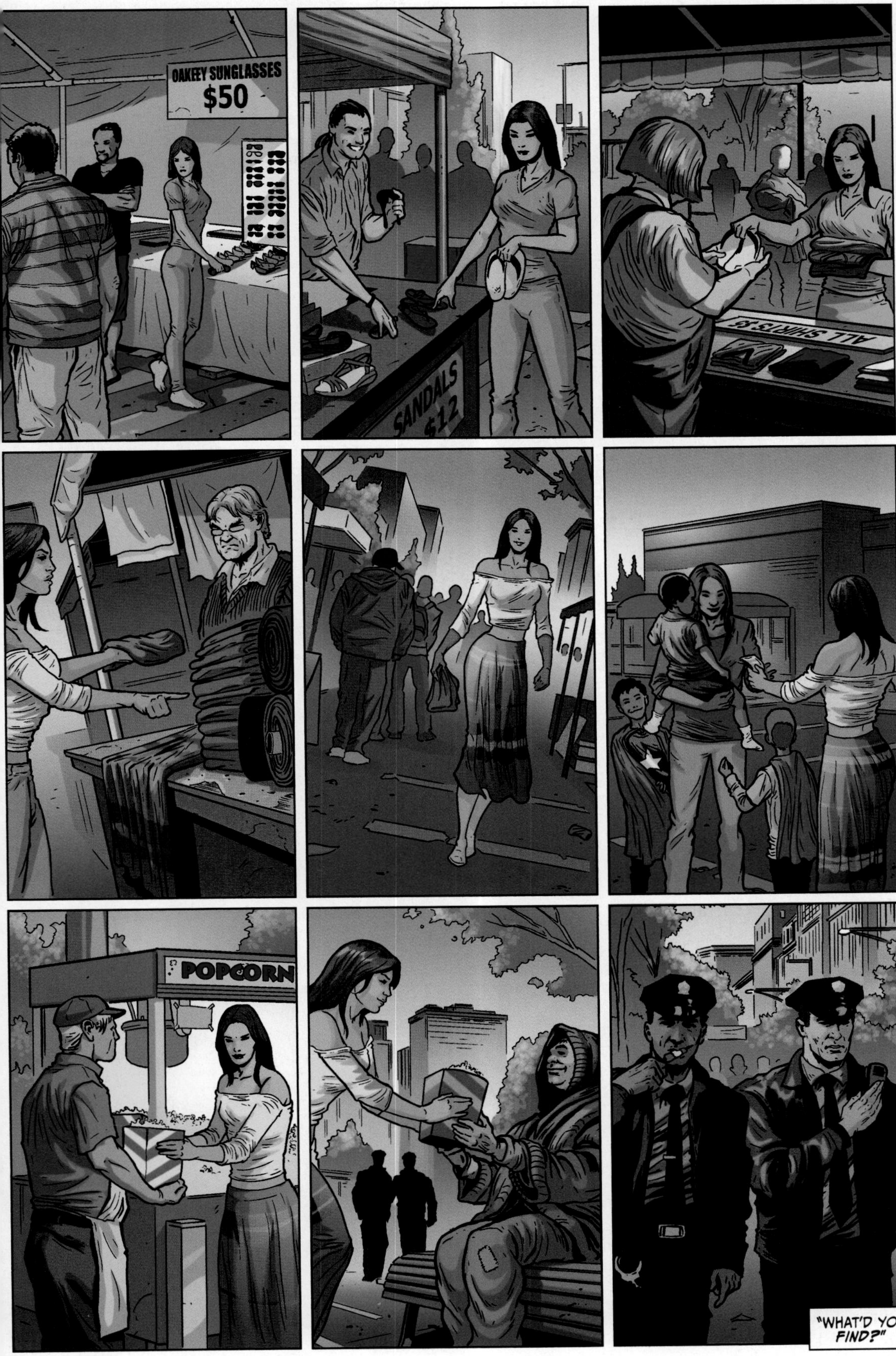
OAKEEY SUNGLASSES
$50
SANDALS
$12
ALL SHIRTS
POPCORN
"WHAT'D YOU FIND?"

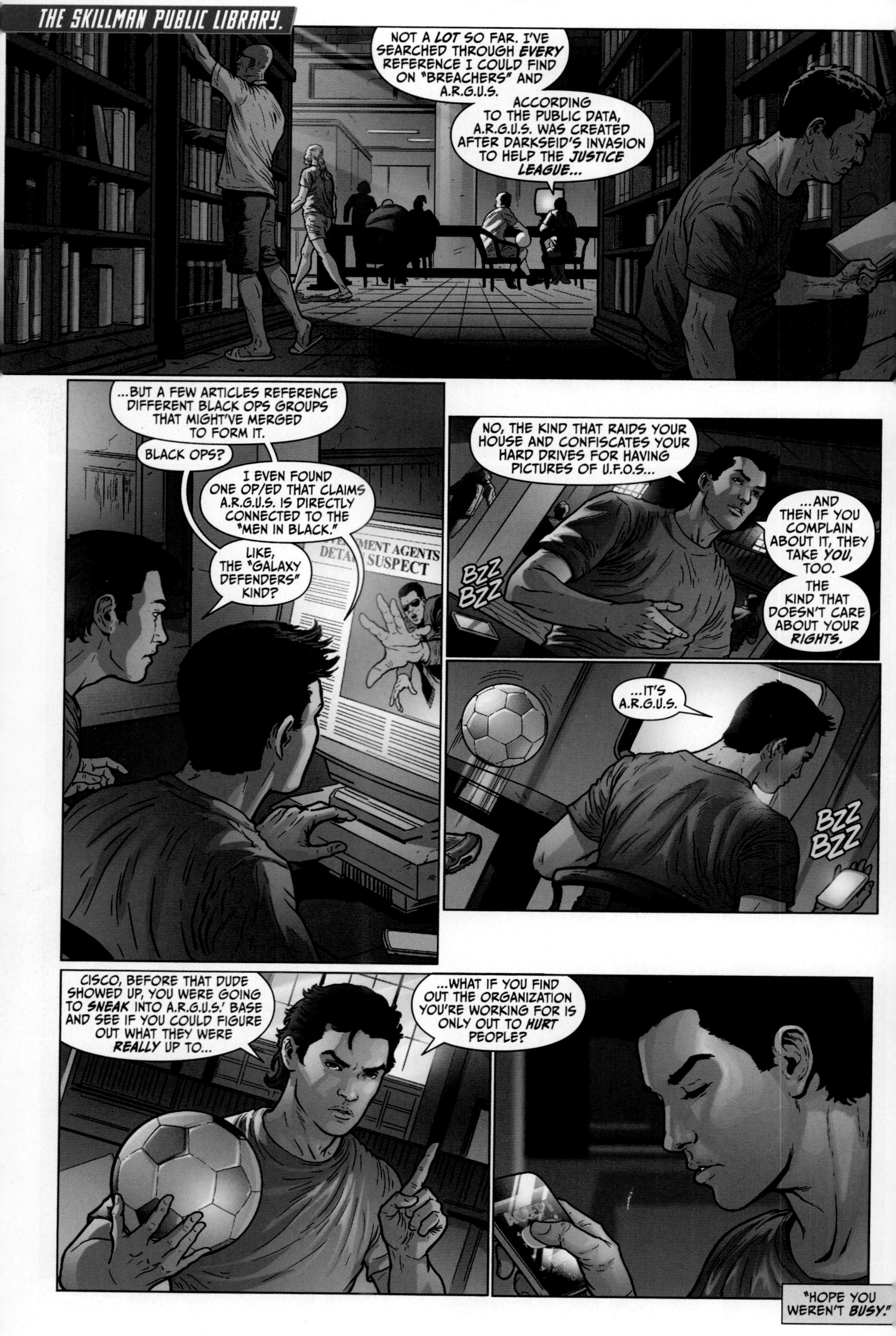
THE SKILLMAN PUBLIC LIBRARY.
NOT A LOT SO FAR. I'VE SEARCHED THROUGH EVERY REFERENCE I COULD FIND ON "BREACHERS" AND A.R.G.U.S.
ACCORDING TO THE PUBLIC DATA, A.R.G.U.S. WAS CREATED AFTER DARKSEID'S INVASION TO HELP THE JUSTICE LEAGUE...
...BUT A FEW ARTICLES REFERENCE DIFFERENT BLACK OPS GROUPS THAT MIGHT'VE MERGED TO FORM IT.
BLACK OPS?
I EVEN FOUND ONE OP/ED THAT CLAIMS A.R.G.U.S. IS DIRECTLY CONNECTED TO THE "MEN IN BLACK."
LIKE, THE "GALAXY DEFENDERS" KIND?
SUSPECT
NO, THE KIND THAT RAIDS YOUR HOUSE AND CONFISCATES YOUR HARD DRIVES FOR HAVING PICTURES OF U.F.O.S...
BZZ BZZ
...AND THEN IF YOU COMPLAIN ABOUT IT, THEY TAKE YOU, TOO.
THE KIND THAT DOESN'T CARE ABOUT YOUR RIGHTS.
...IT'S A.R.G.U.S.
BZZ BZZ
CISCO, BEFORE THAT DUDE SHOWED UP, YOU WERE GOING TO SNEAK INTO A.R.G.U.S.' BASE AND SEE IF YOU COULD FIGURE OUT WHAT THEY WERE REALLY UP TO...
...WHAT IF YOU FIND OUT THE ORGANIZATION YOU'RE WORKING FOR IS ONLY OUT TO HURT PEOPLE?
"HOPE YOU WEREN'T BUSY."

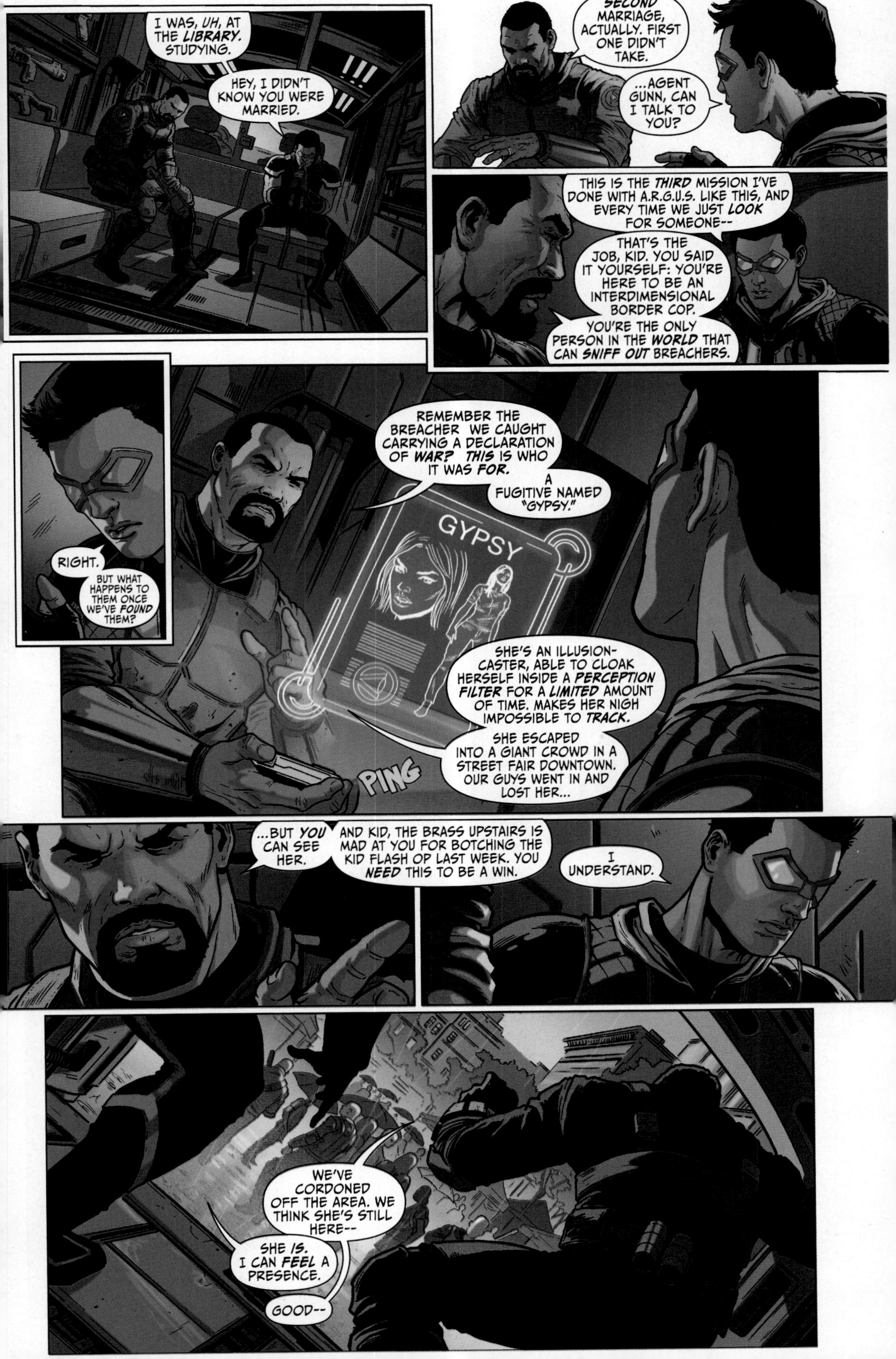
I WAS, *UH*, AT THE *LIBRARY.* STUDYING.
HEY, I DIDN'T KNOW YOU WERE MARRIED.
!!!
SECOND MARRIAGE, ACTUALLY. FIRST ONE DIDN'T TAKE.
...AGENT GUNN, CAN I TALK TO YOU?
THIS IS THE *THIRD* MISSION I'VE DONE WITH A.R.G.U.S. LIKE THIS, AND EVERY TIME WE JUST *LOOK* FOR SOMEONE--
THAT'S THE JOB, KID. YOU SAID IT YOURSELF: YOU'RE HERE TO BE AN INTERDIMENSIONAL BORDER COP.
YOU'RE THE ONLY PERSON IN THE *WORLD* THAT CAN *SNIFF OUT* BREACHERS.
RIGHT.
BUT WHAT HAPPENS TO THEM ONCE WE'VE *FOUND* THEM?
REMEMBER THE BREACHER WE CAUGHT CARRYING A DECLARATION OF *WAR? THIS* IS WHO IT WAS *FOR.*
A FUGITIVE NAMED "GYPSY."
GYPSY
SHE'S AN ILLUSION-CASTER, ABLE TO CLOAK HERSELF INSIDE A *PERCEPTION FILTER* FOR A *LIMITED* AMOUNT OF TIME. MAKES HER NIGH IMPOSSIBLE TO *TRACK.*
SHE ESCAPED INTO A GIANT CROWD IN A STREET FAIR DOWNTOWN. OUR GUYS WENT IN AND LOST HER...
PING
...BUT *YOU* CAN SEE HER.
AND KID, THE BRASS UPSTAIRS IS MAD AT YOU FOR BOTCHING THE KID FLASH OP LAST WEEK. YOU *NEED* THIS TO BE A WIN.
I UNDERSTAND.
WE'VE CORDONED OFF THE AREA. WE THINK SHE'S STILL HERE--
SHE *IS.* I CAN *FEEL* A PRESENCE.
GOOD--

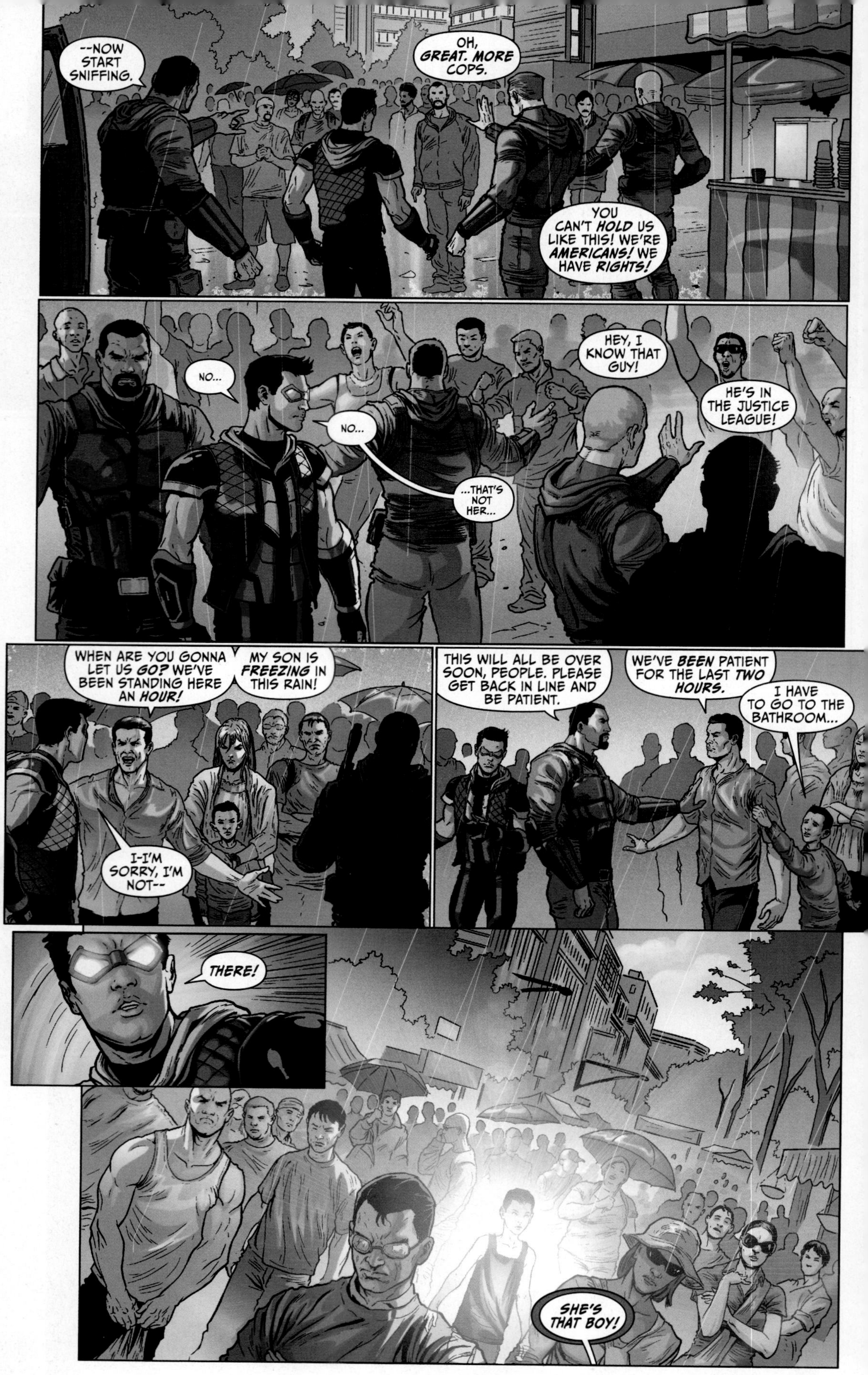
--NOW START SNIFFING.
OH, GREAT. MORE COPS.
YOU CAN'T HOLD US LIKE THIS! WE'RE AMERICANS! WE HAVE RIGHTS!
NO...
NO...
...THAT'S NOT HER...
HEY, I KNOW THAT GUY!
HE'S IN THE JUSTICE LEAGUE!
WHEN ARE YOU GONNA LET US GO? WE'VE BEEN STANDING HERE AN HOUR!
MY SON IS FREEZING IN THIS RAIN!
I-I'M SORRY, I'M NOT--
THIS WILL ALL BE OVER SOON, PEOPLE. PLEASE GET BACK IN LINE AND BE PATIENT.
WE'VE BEEN PATIENT FOR THE LAST TWO HOURS.
I HAVE TO GO TO THE BATHROOM...
THERE!
SHE'S THAT BOY!

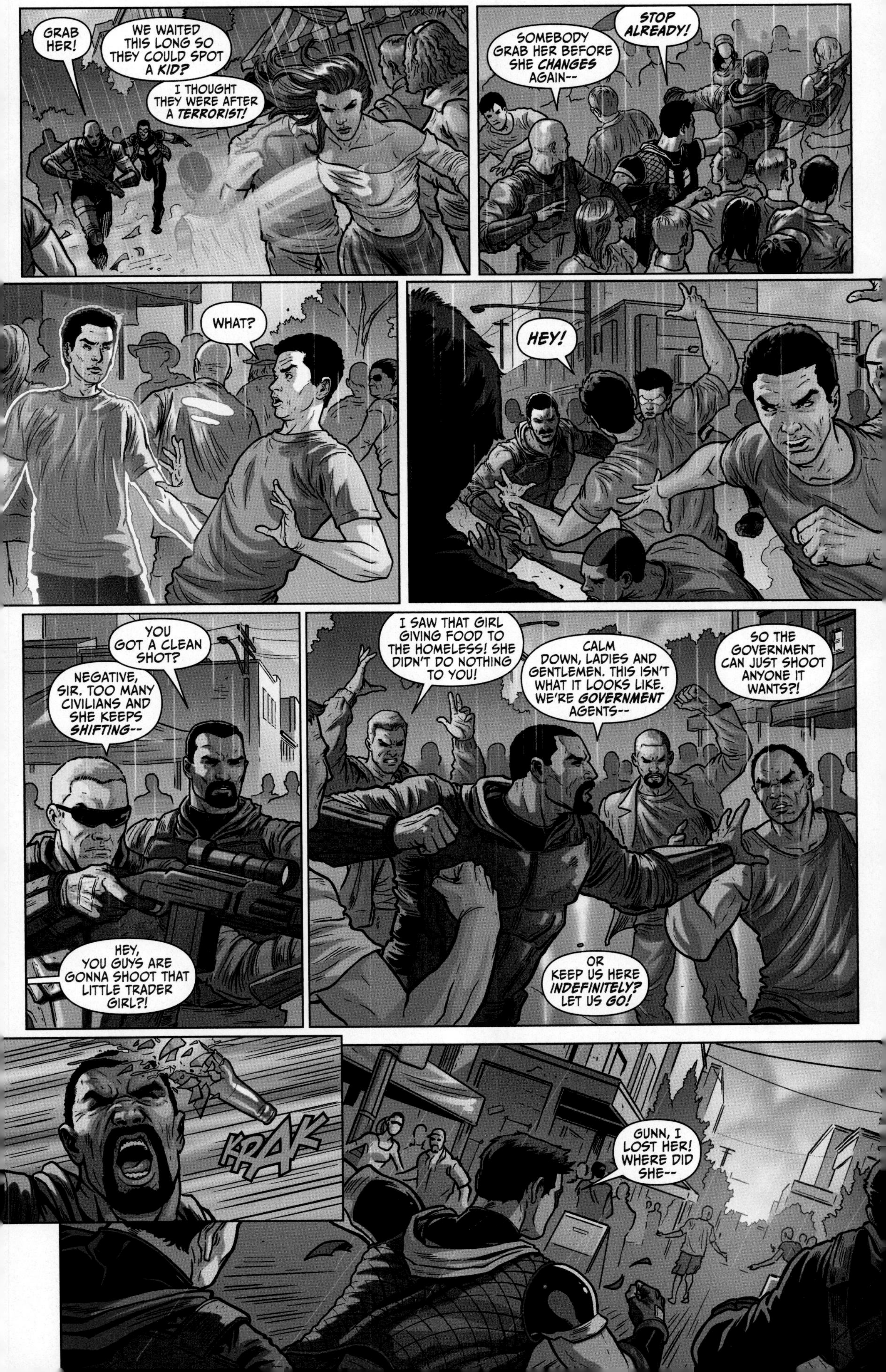
GRAB HER!
WE WAITED THIS LONG SO THEY COULD SPOT A KID?
I THOUGHT THEY WERE AFTER A TERRORIST!
SOMEBODY GRAB HER BEFORE SHE CHANGES AGAIN--
STOP ALREADY!
WHAT?
HEY!
YOU GOT A CLEAN SHOT?
NEGATIVE, SIR. TOO MANY CIVILIANS AND SHE KEEPS SHIFTING--
HEY, YOU GUYS ARE GONNA SHOOT THAT LITTLE TRADER GIRL?!
I SAW THAT GIRL GIVING FOOD TO THE HOMELESS! SHE DIDN'T DO NOTHING TO YOU!
CALM DOWN, LADIES AND GENTLEMEN. THIS ISN'T WHAT IT LOOKS LIKE. WE'RE GOVERNMENT AGENTS--
SO THE GOVERNMENT CAN JUST SHOOT ANYONE IT WANTS?!
OR KEEP US HERE INDEFINITELY? LET US GO!
KRAK
GUNN, I LOST HER! WHERE DID SHE--

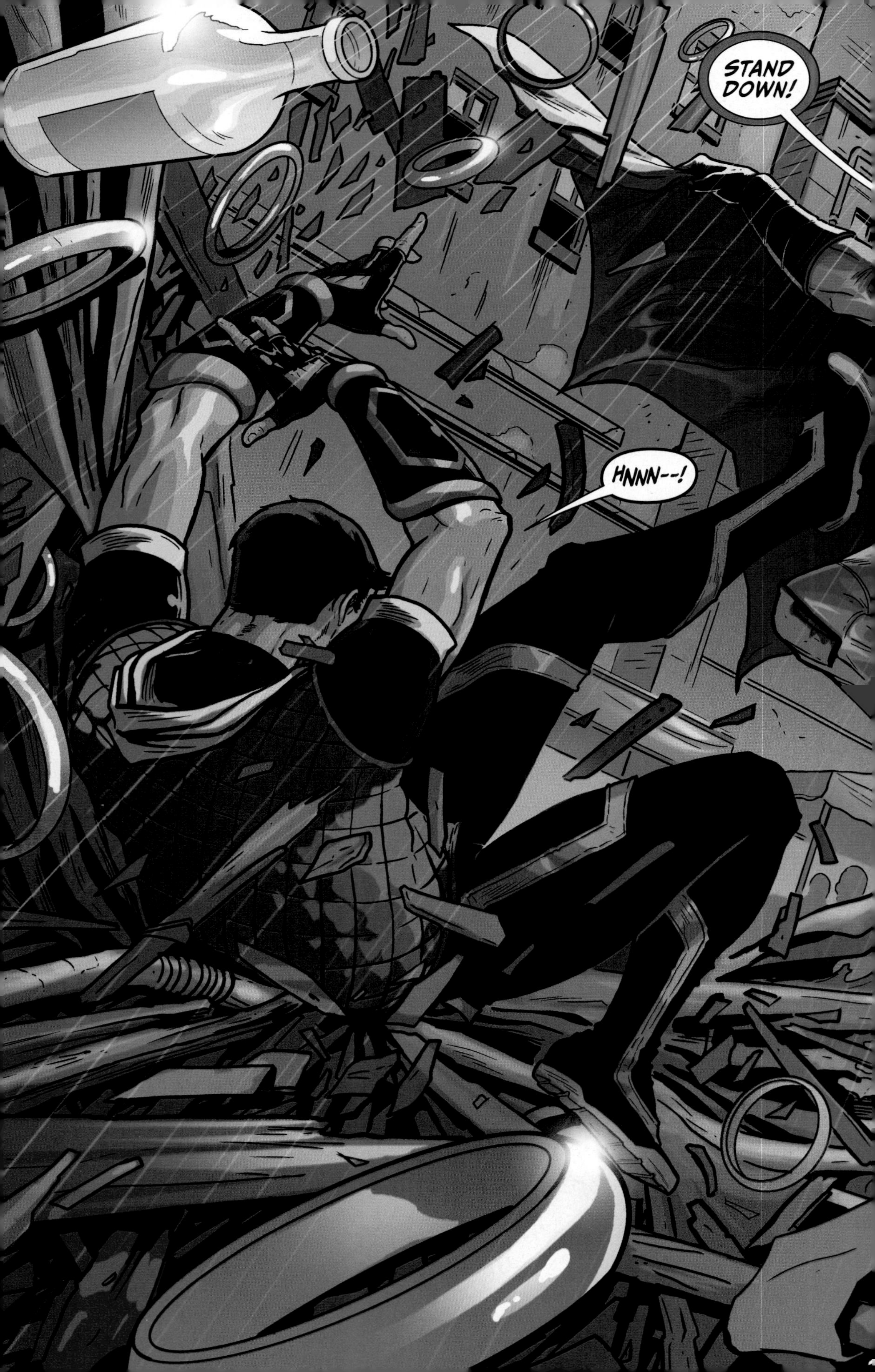
STAND DOWN!
HNNN--!

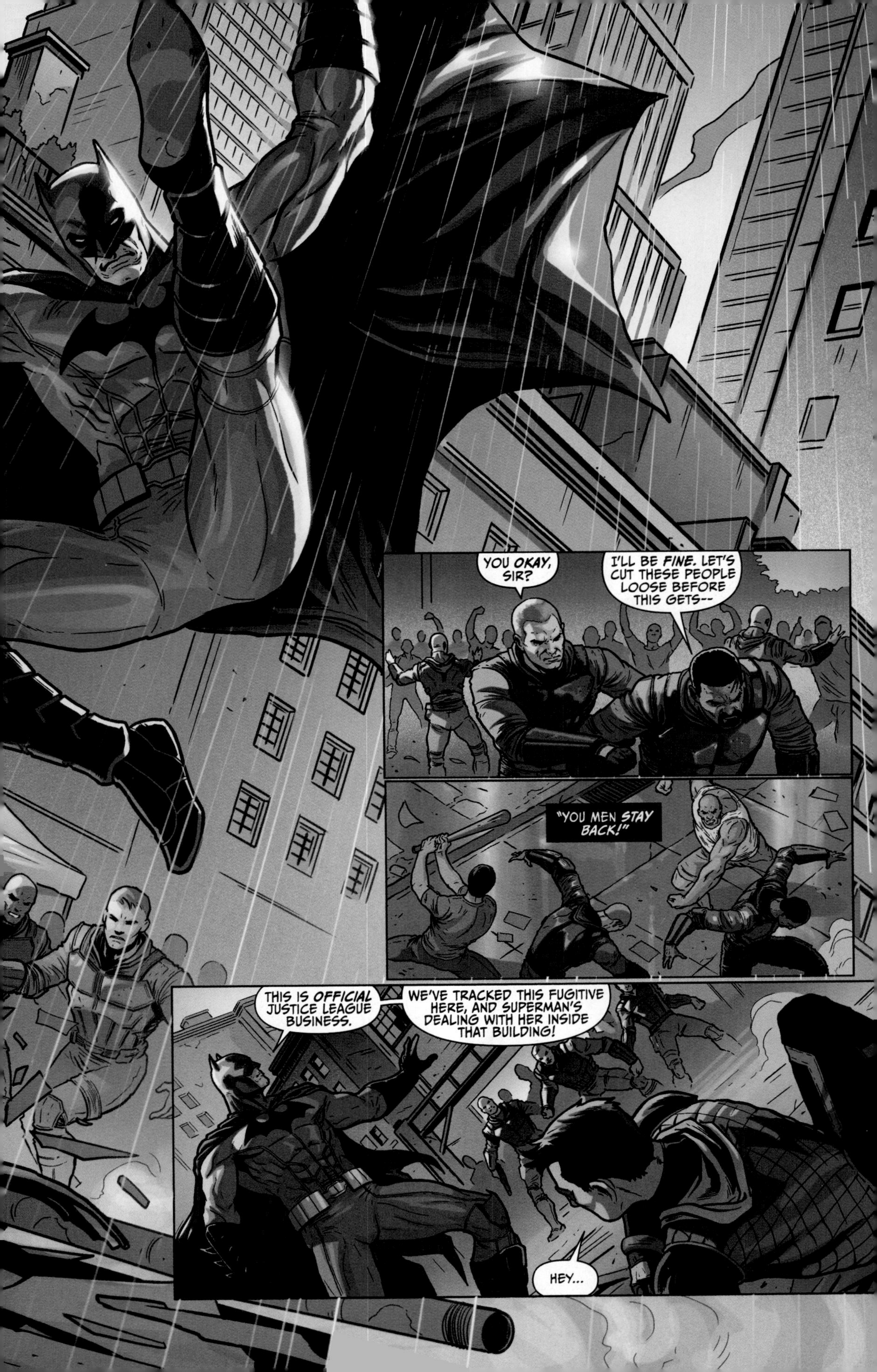
YOU OKAY, SIR?
I'LL BE FINE. LET'S CUT THESE PEOPLE LOOSE BEFORE THIS GETS--
"YOU MEN STAY BACK!"
THIS IS OFFICIAL JUSTICE LEAGUE BUSINESS.
WE'VE TRACKED THIS FUGITIVE HERE, AND SUPERMAN'S DEALING WITH HER INSIDE THAT BUILDING!
HEY...

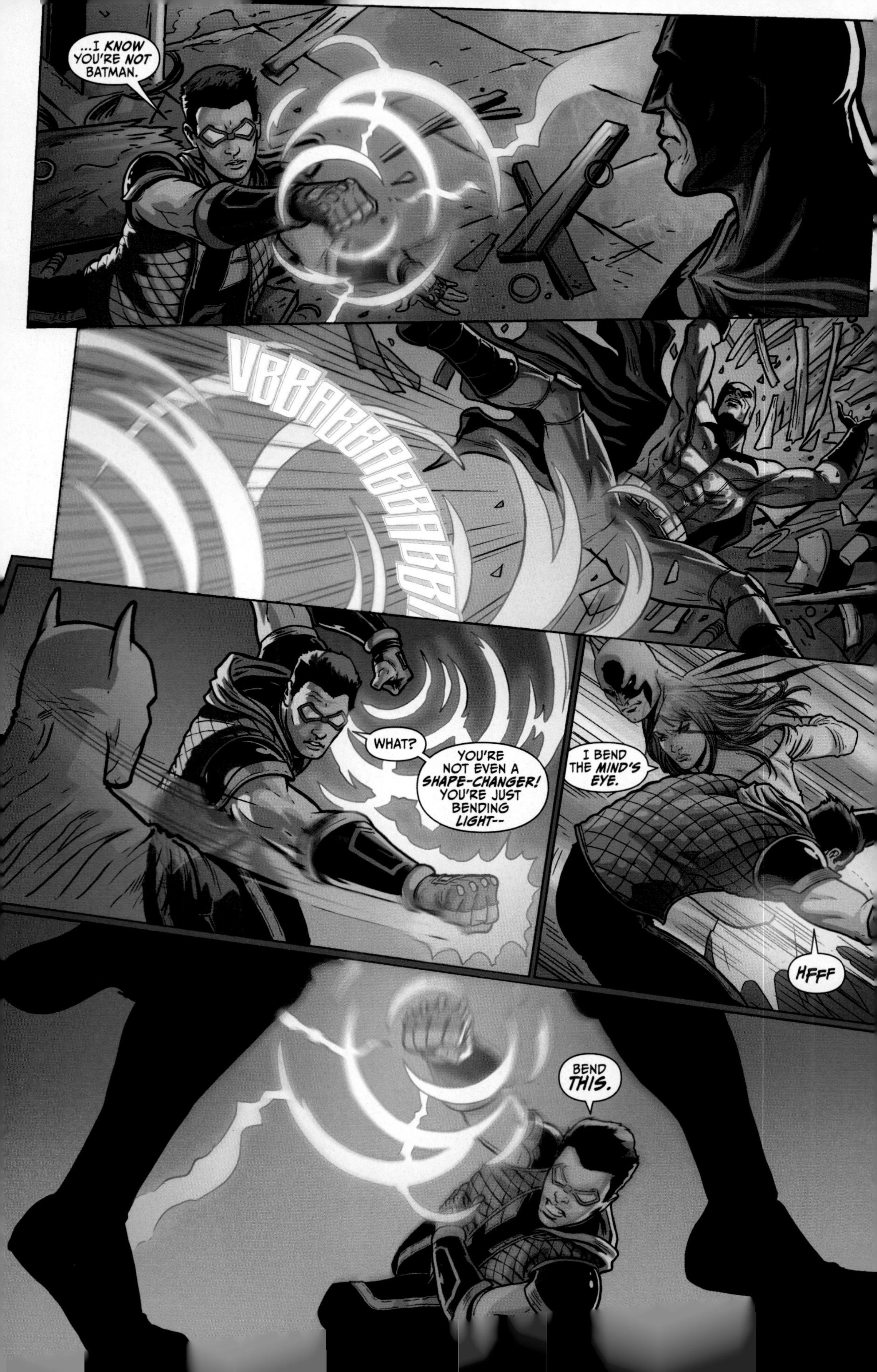
...I KNOW YOU'RE NOT BATMAN.
VBBRABBRABBRA
WHAT?
YOU'RE NOT EVEN A SHAPE-CHANGER! YOU'RE JUST BENDING LIGHT--
I BEND THE MIND'S EYE.
HFFF
BEND THIS.

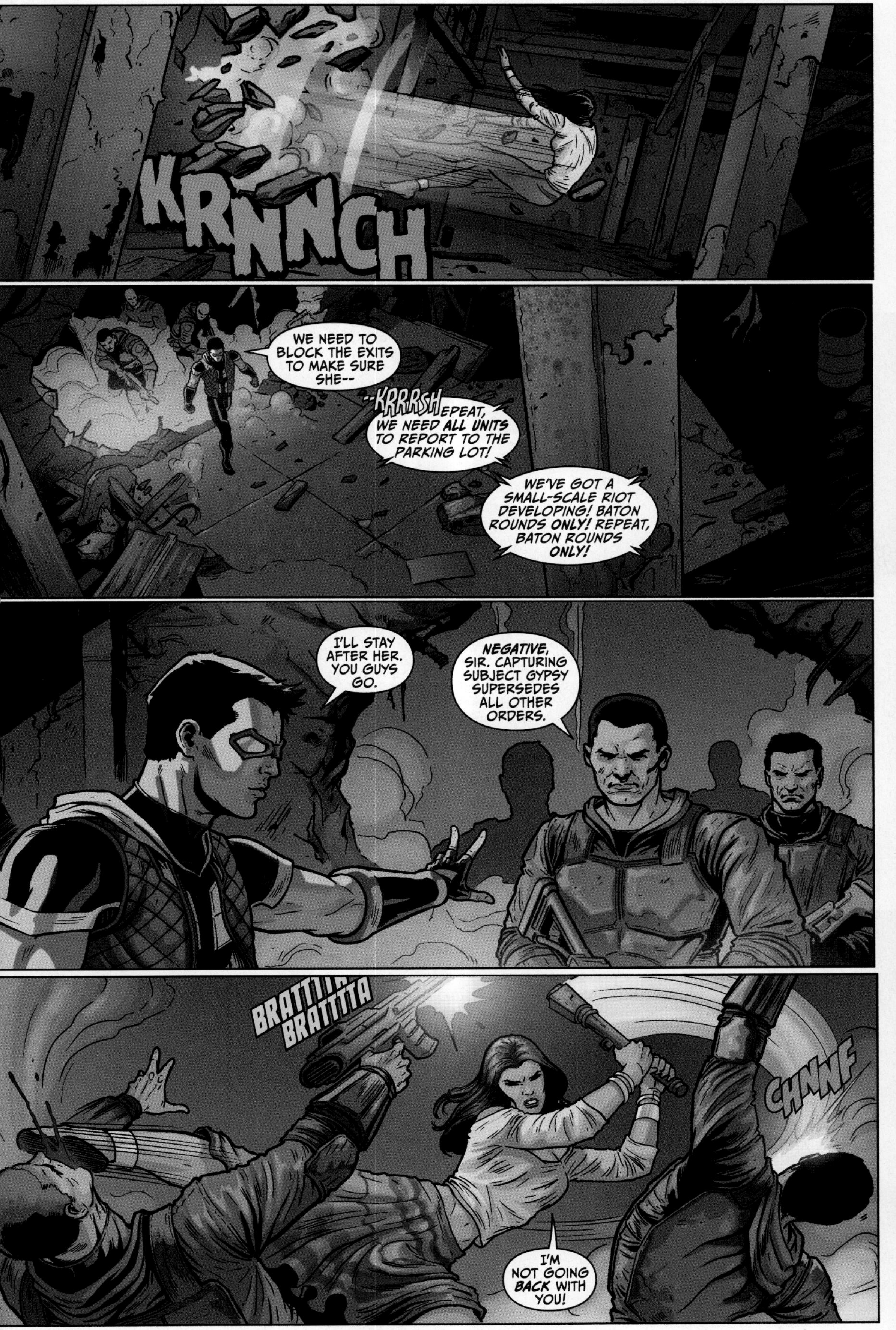
KRNNCH
WE NEED TO BLOCK THE EXITS TO MAKE SURE SHE--
--KRRRSH
EPEAT, WE NEED ALL UNITS TO REPORT TO THE PARKING LOT!
WE'VE GOT A SMALL-SCALE RIOT DEVELOPING! BATON ROUNDS ONLY! REPEAT, BATON ROUNDS ONLY!
I'LL STAY AFTER HER. YOU GUYS GO.
NEGATIVE, SIR. CAPTURING SUBJECT GYPSY SUPERSEDES ALL OTHER ORDERS.
BRATTTTA BRATTTTA
CHNNF
I'M NOT GOING BACK WITH YOU!

STOP!

VBBABBABBABBB

CHOOOM

--KAZZZT
CIVILIANS ARE DISPERSING!

LET'S GET MEDICAL IN HERE FOR CLEANUP!

I WON'T GO BACK TO THAT CAGE!

TAKE IT EASY. I'M NOT GONNA HURT YOU.

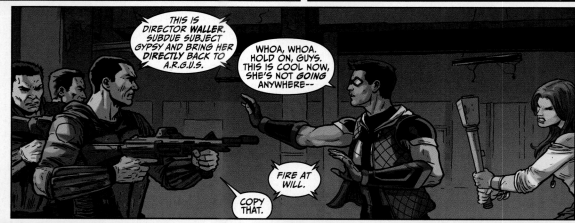

THIS IS DIRECTOR WALLER. SUBDUE SUBJECT GYPSY AND BRING HER DIRECTLY BACK TO A.R.G.U.S.

WHOA, WHOA. HOLD ON, GUYS. THIS IS COOL NOW, SHE'S NOT GOING ANYWHERE--

FIRE AT WILL.

COPY THAT.

VBRRAZT

THOOOM

NO!

AAAAH--!

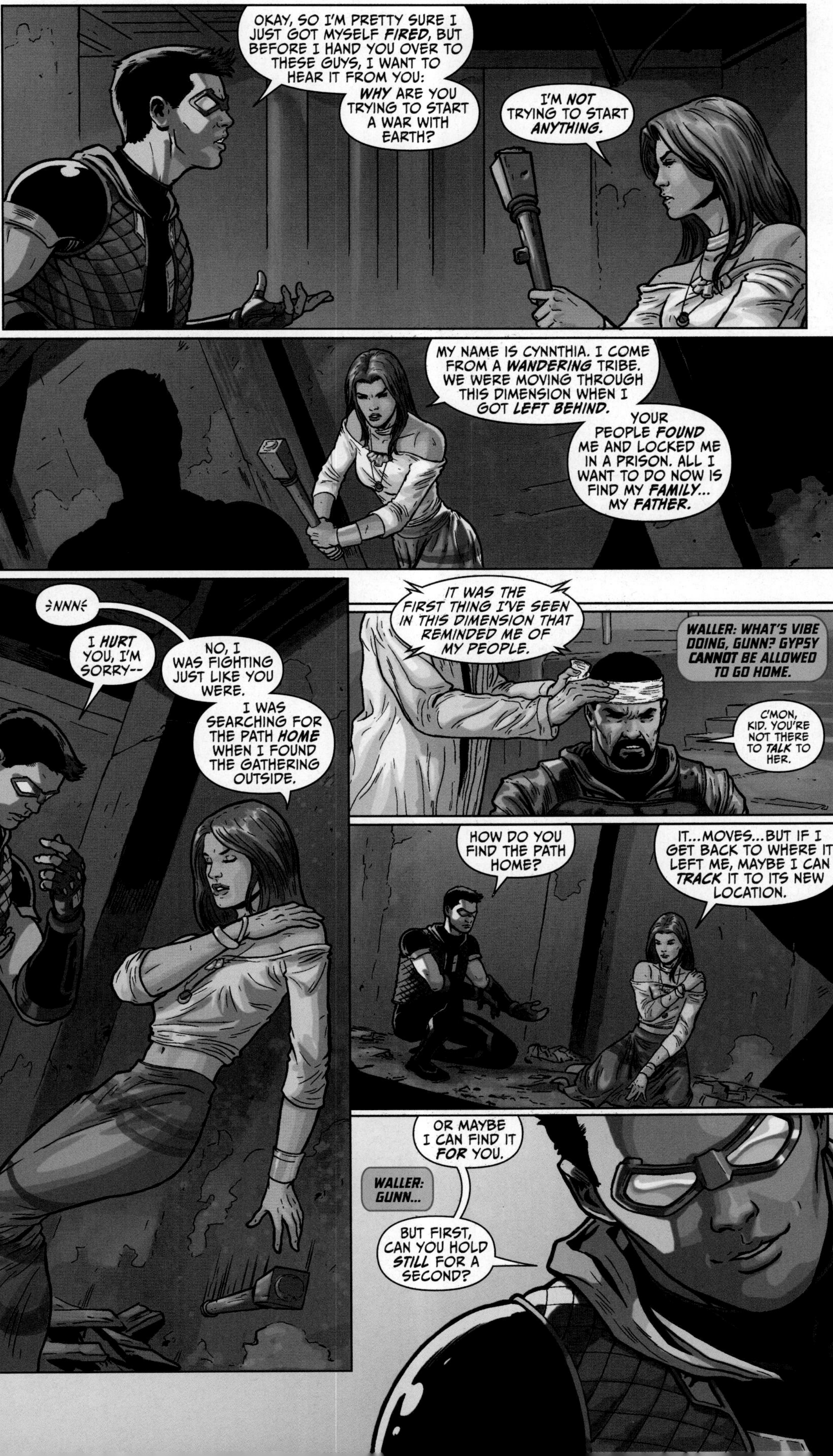
OKAY, SO I'M PRETTY SURE I JUST GOT MYSELF FIRED, BUT BEFORE I HAND YOU OVER TO THESE GUYS, I WANT TO HEAR IT FROM YOU: WHY ARE YOU TRYING TO START A WAR WITH EARTH?
I'M NOT TRYING TO START ANYTHING.
MY NAME IS CYNNTHIA. I COME FROM A WANDERING TRIBE. WE WERE MOVING THROUGH THIS DIMENSION WHEN I GOT LEFT BEHIND.
YOUR PEOPLE FOUND ME AND LOCKED ME IN A PRISON. ALL I WANT TO DO NOW IS FIND MY FAMILY... MY FATHER.
NNN
I HURT YOU, I'M SORRY--
NO, I WAS FIGHTING JUST LIKE YOU WERE.
I WAS SEARCHING FOR THE PATH HOME WHEN I FOUND THE GATHERING OUTSIDE.
IT WAS THE FIRST THING I'VE SEEN IN THIS DIMENSION THAT REMINDED ME OF MY PEOPLE.
WALLER: WHAT'S VIBE DOING, GUNN? GYPSY CANNOT BE ALLOWED TO GO HOME.
C'MON, KID. YOU'RE NOT THERE TO TALK TO HER.
HOW DO YOU FIND THE PATH HOME?
IT...MOVES...BUT IF I GET BACK TO WHERE IT LEFT ME, MAYBE I CAN TRACK IT TO ITS NEW LOCATION.
OR MAYBE I CAN FIND IT FOR YOU.
WALLER: GUNN...
BUT FIRST, CAN YOU HOLD STILL FOR A SECOND?

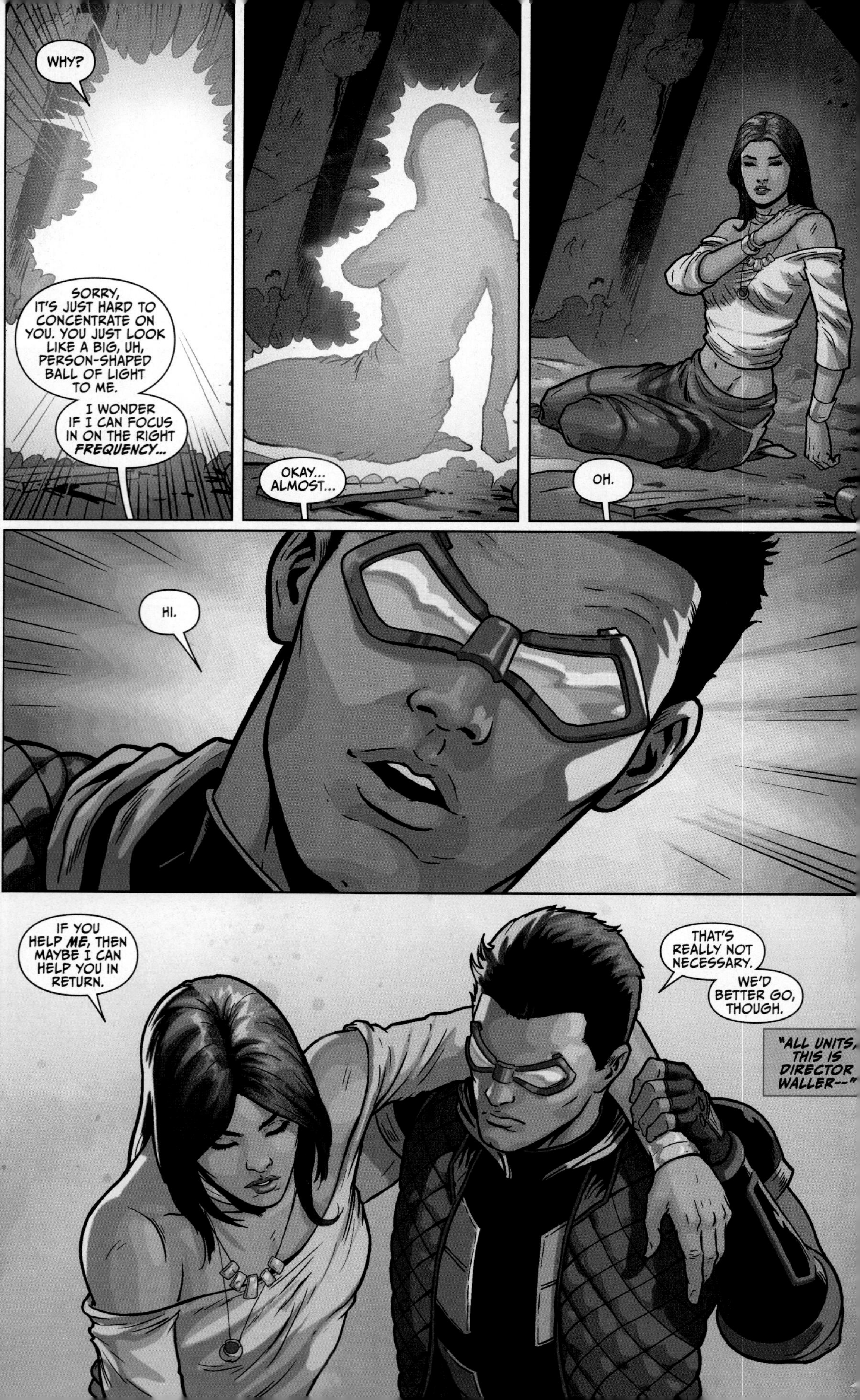
WHY?
SORRY, IT'S JUST HARD TO CONCENTRATE ON YOU. YOU JUST LOOK LIKE A BIG, UH, PERSON-SHAPED BALL OF LIGHT TO ME.
I WONDER IF I CAN FOCUS IN ON THE RIGHT FREQUENCY...
OKAY... ALMOST...
OH.
HI.
IF YOU HELP ME, THEN MAYBE I CAN HELP YOU IN RETURN.
THAT'S REALLY NOT NECESSARY.
WE'D BETTER GO, THOUGH.
"ALL UNITS, THIS IS DIRECTOR WALLER--"

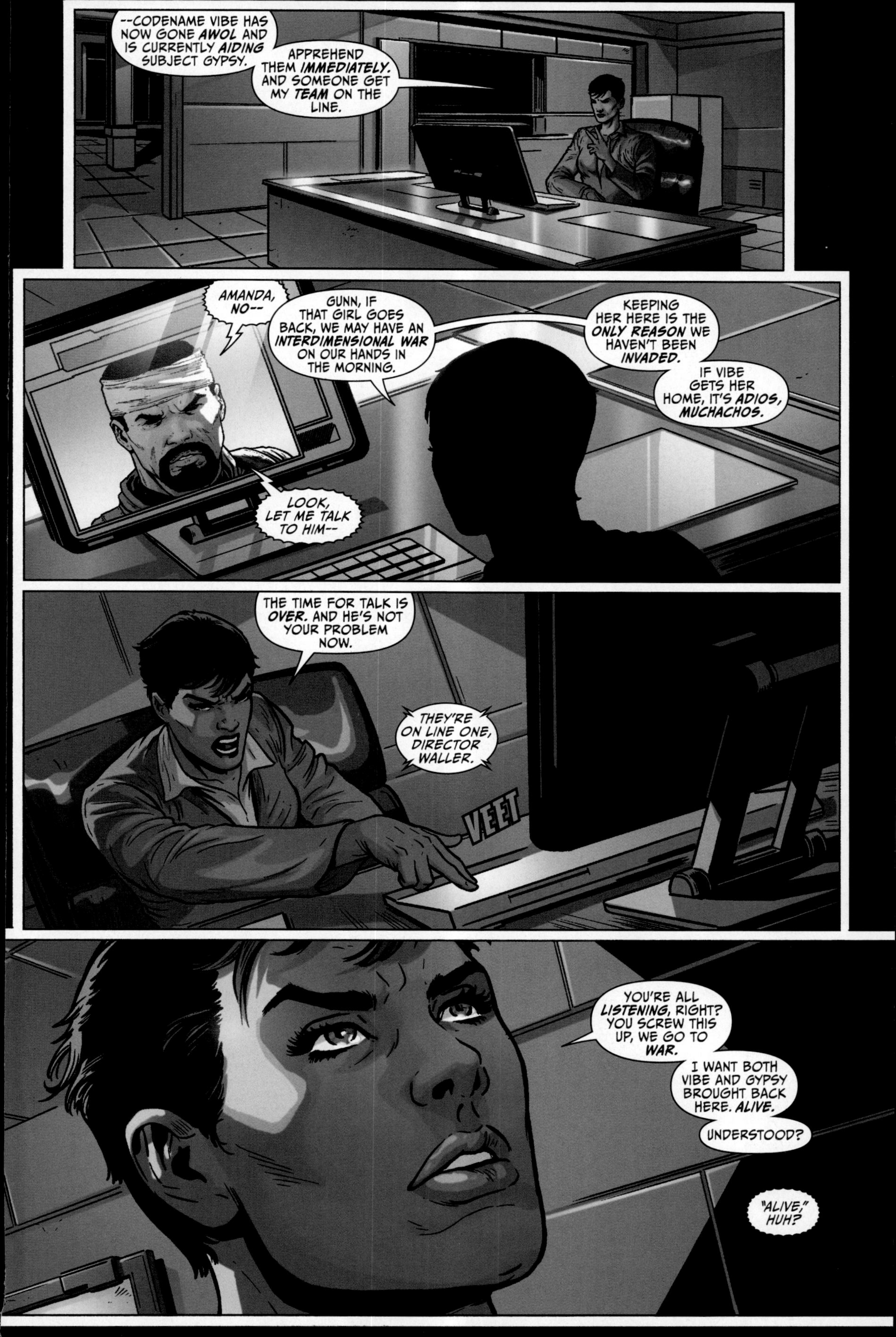
--CODENAME VIBE HAS NOW GONE AWOL AND IS CURRENTLY AIDING SUBJECT GYPSY.
APPREHEND THEM IMMEDIATELY. AND SOMEONE GET MY TEAM ON THE LINE.
AMANDA, NO--
GUNN, IF THAT GIRL GOES BACK, WE MAY HAVE AN INTERDIMENSIONAL WAR ON OUR HANDS IN THE MORNING.
KEEPING HER HERE IS THE ONLY REASON WE HAVEN'T BEEN INVADED.
IF VIBE GETS HER HOME, IT'S ADIOS, MUCHACHOS.
LOOK, LET ME TALK TO HIM--
THE TIME FOR TALK IS OVER. AND HE'S NOT YOUR PROBLEM NOW.
THEY'RE ON LINE ONE, DIRECTOR WALLER.
VEET
YOU'RE ALL LISTENING, RIGHT? YOU SCREW THIS UP, WE GO TO WAR.
I WANT BOTH VIBE AND GYPSY BROUGHT BACK HERE. ALIVE.
UNDERSTOOD?
"ALIVE," HUH?

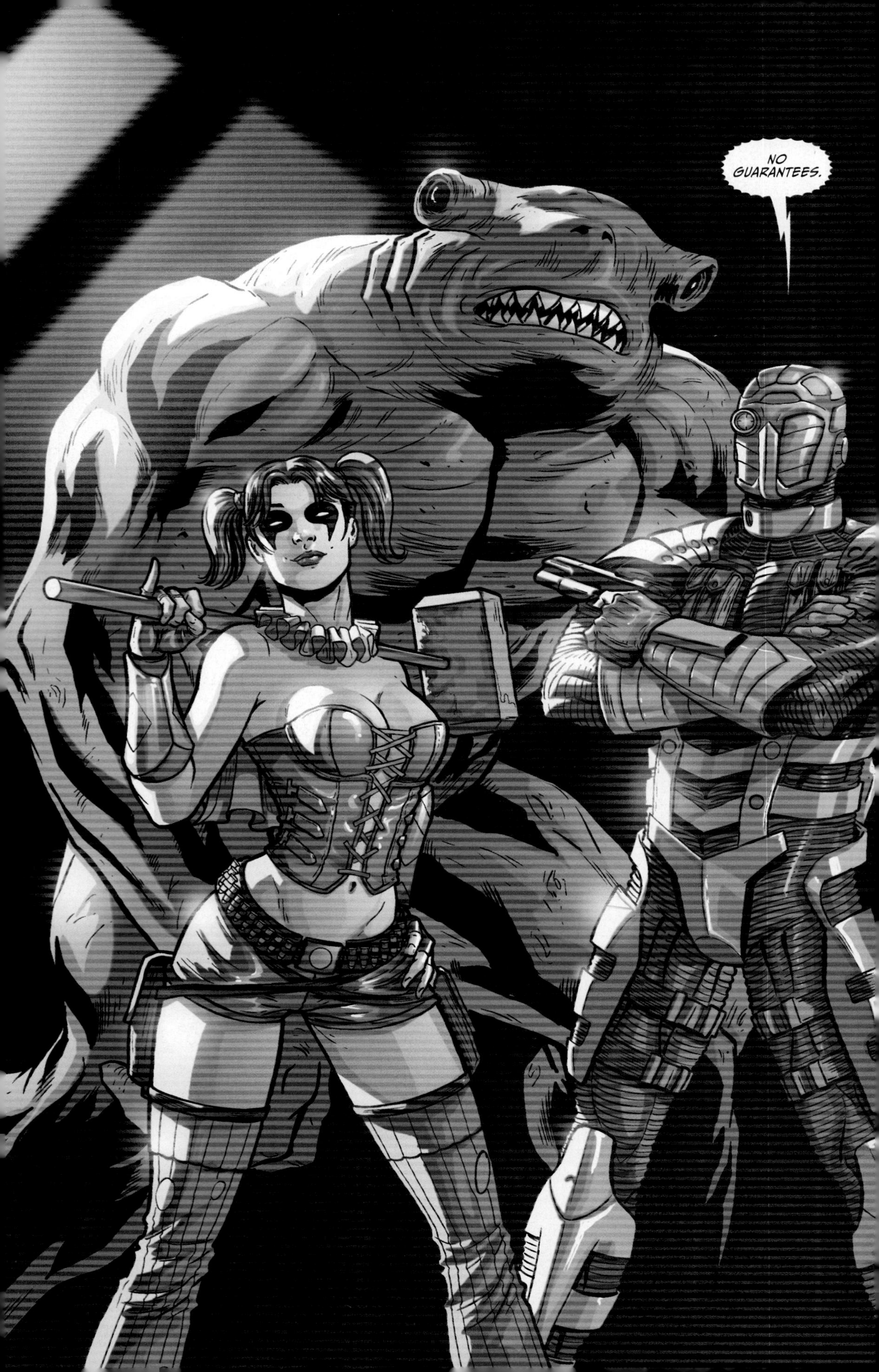
NO GUARANTEES.

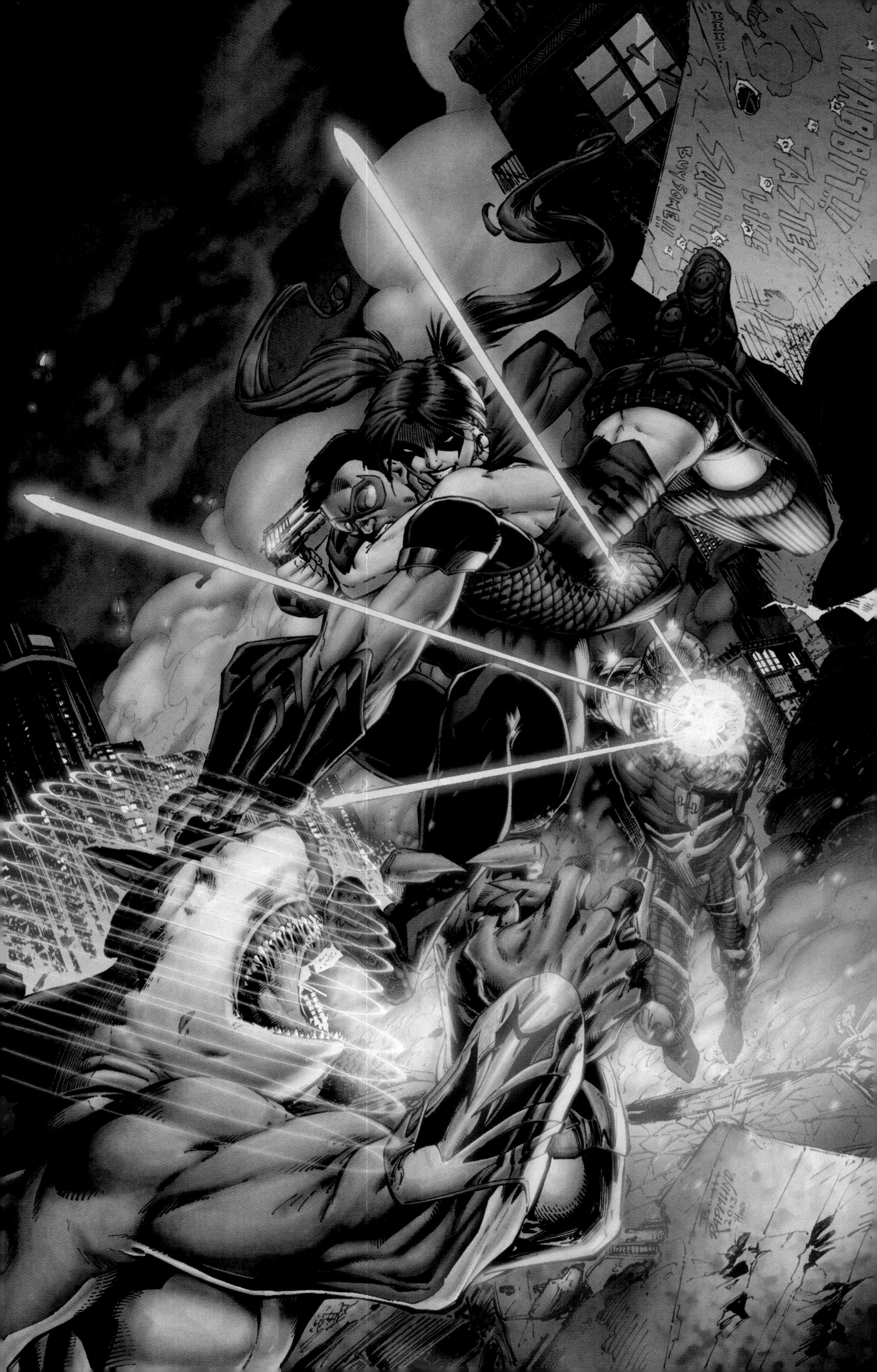
MMMM...
BUY SOME!!

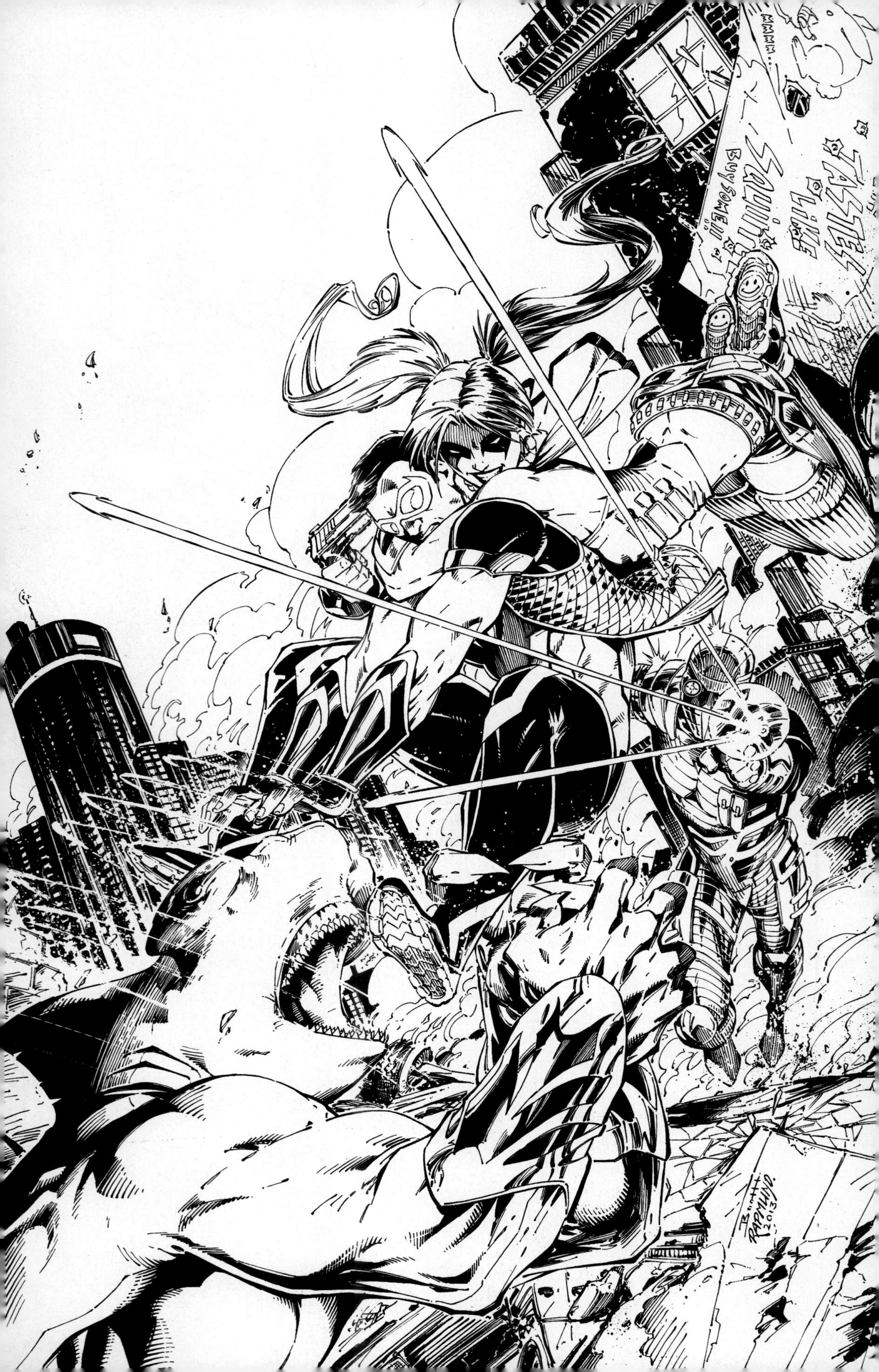
MMMM...
TASTES LIKE
BUY SOME!!

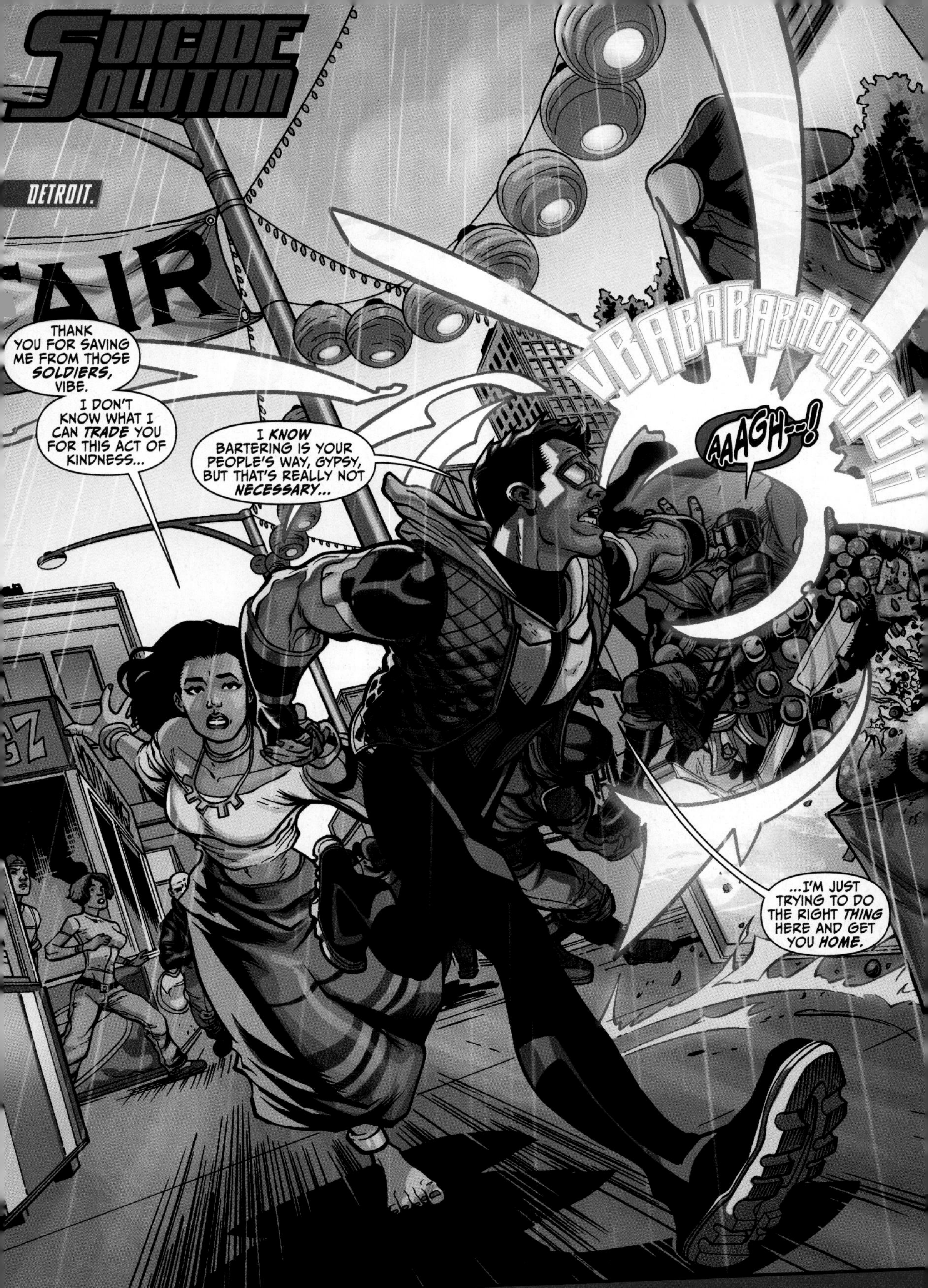
SUICIDE SOLUTION
DETROIT.
AIR
THANK YOU FOR SAVING ME FROM THOSE SOLDIERS, VIBE.
I DON'T KNOW WHAT I CAN TRADE YOU FOR THIS ACT OF KINDNESS...
I KNOW BARTERING IS YOUR PEOPLE'S WAY, GYPSY, BUT THAT'S REALLY NOT NECESSARY...
VBABABABABABABABH
AAAGH--!
...I'M JUST TRYING TO DO THE RIGHT THING HERE AND GET YOU HOME.

STERLING GATES writer PETE WOODS penciller SEAN PARSONS inker
BRAD ANDERSON colorist TAYLOR ESPOSITO letterer BRETT BOOTH, NORM RAPMUND AND ANDREW DALHOUSE cover

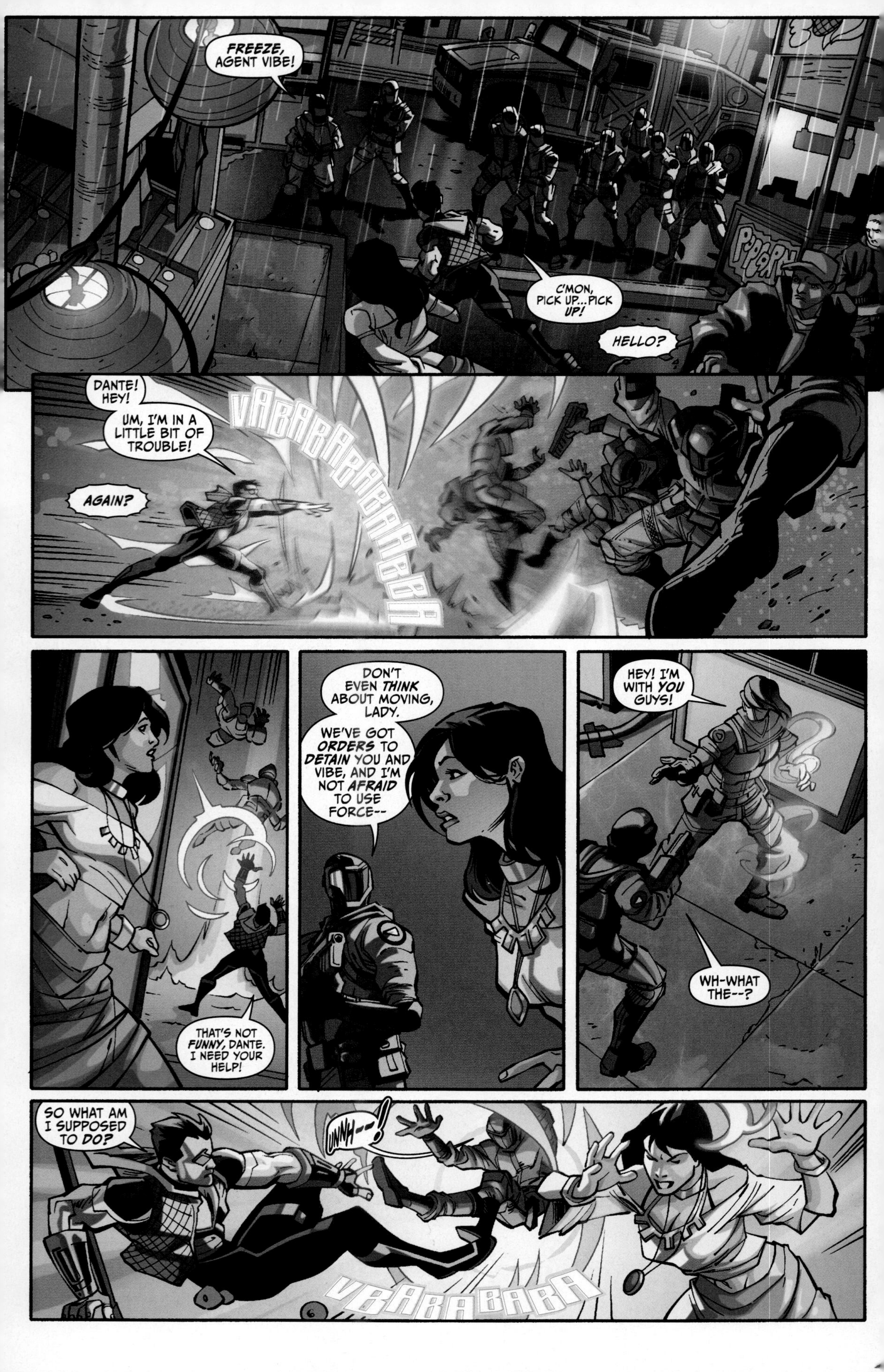
FREEZE, AGENT VIBE!
C'MON, PICK UP...PICK UP!
HELLO?
DANTE! HEY!
UM, I'M IN A LITTLE BIT OF TROUBLE!
VABABABABABABABA
AGAIN?
THAT'S NOT FUNNY, DANTE. I NEED YOUR HELP!
DON'T EVEN THINK ABOUT MOVING, LADY.
WE'VE GOT ORDERS TO DETAIN YOU AND VIBE, AND I'M NOT AFRAID TO USE FORCE--
HEY! I'M WITH YOU GUYS!
WH-WHAT THE--?
SO WHAT AM I SUPPOSED TO DO?
UNNH--!
VBABABABA

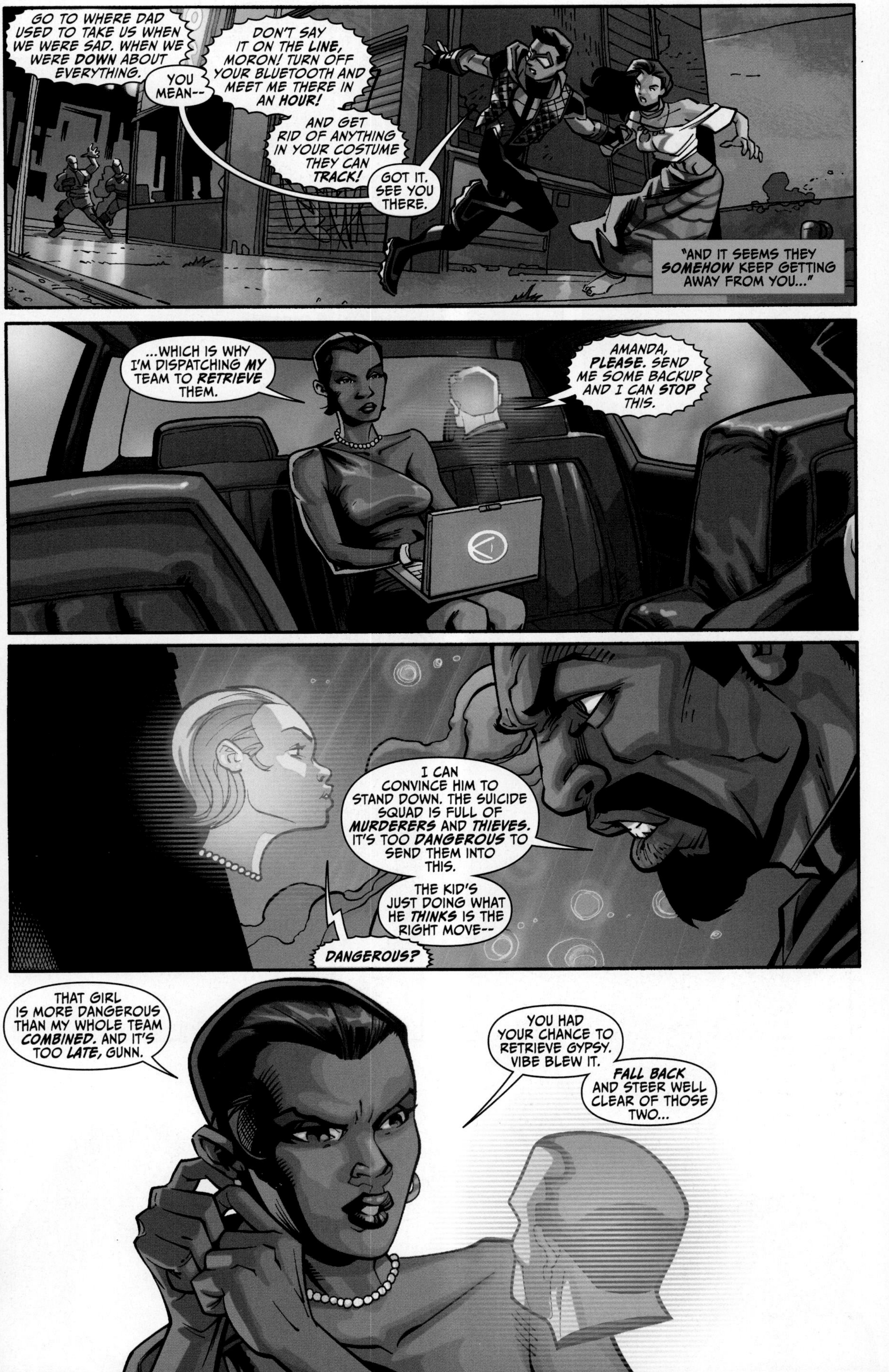
GO TO WHERE DAD USED TO TAKE US WHEN WE WERE SAD. WHEN WE WERE DOWN ABOUT EVERYTHING.
YOU MEAN--
DON'T SAY IT ON THE LINE, MORON! TURN OFF YOUR BLUETOOTH AND MEET ME THERE IN AN HOUR!
AND GET RID OF ANYTHING IN YOUR COSTUME THEY CAN TRACK!
GOT IT. SEE YOU THERE.
"AND IT SEEMS THEY SOMEHOW KEEP GETTING AWAY FROM YOU..."
...WHICH IS WHY I'M DISPATCHING MY TEAM TO RETRIEVE THEM.
AMANDA, PLEASE. SEND ME SOME BACKUP AND I CAN STOP THIS.
I CAN CONVINCE HIM TO STAND DOWN. THE SUICIDE SQUAD IS FULL OF MURDERERS AND THIEVES. IT'S TOO DANGEROUS TO SEND THEM INTO THIS.
THE KID'S JUST DOING WHAT HE THINKS IS THE RIGHT MOVE--
DANGEROUS?
THAT GIRL IS MORE DANGEROUS THAN MY WHOLE TEAM COMBINED. AND IT'S TOO LATE, GUNN.
YOU HAD YOUR CHANCE TO RETRIEVE GYPSY. VIBE BLEW IT.
FALL BACK AND STEER WELL CLEAR OF THOSE TWO...

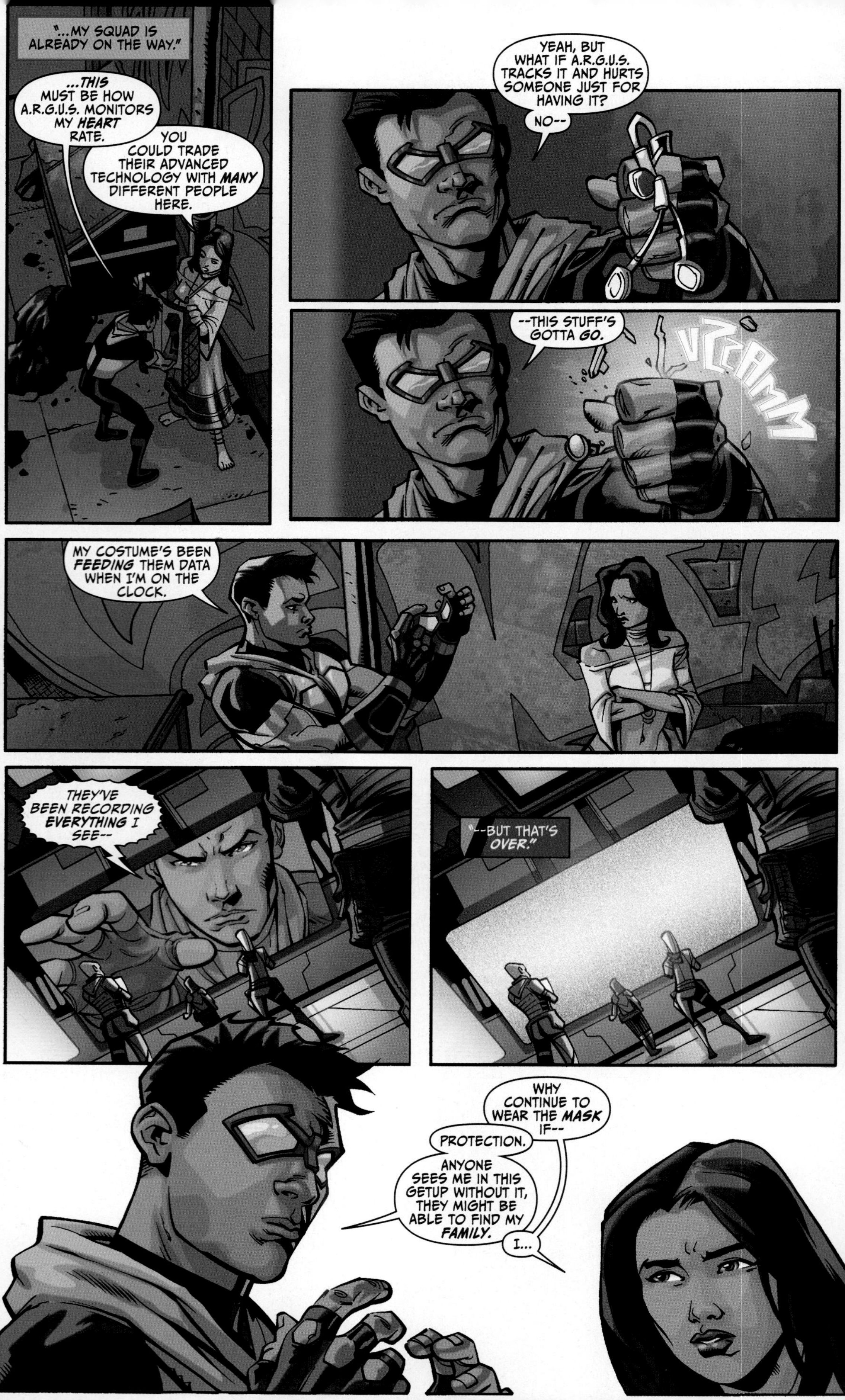
"...MY SQUAD IS ALREADY ON THE WAY."
...THIS MUST BE HOW A.R.G.U.S. MONITORS MY HEART RATE.
YOU COULD TRADE THEIR ADVANCED TECHNOLOGY WITH MANY DIFFERENT PEOPLE HERE.
YEAH, BUT WHAT IF A.R.G.U.S. TRACKS IT AND HURTS SOMEONE JUST FOR HAVING IT?
NO--
--THIS STUFF'S GOTTA GO.
VZZAMM
MY COSTUME'S BEEN FEEDING THEM DATA WHEN I'M ON THE CLOCK.
THEY'VE BEEN RECORDING EVERYTHING I SEE--
"--BUT THAT'S OVER."
WHY CONTINUE TO WEAR THE MASK IF--
PROTECTION.
ANYONE SEES ME IN THIS GETUP WITHOUT IT, THEY MIGHT BE ABLE TO FIND MY FAMILY.
I...

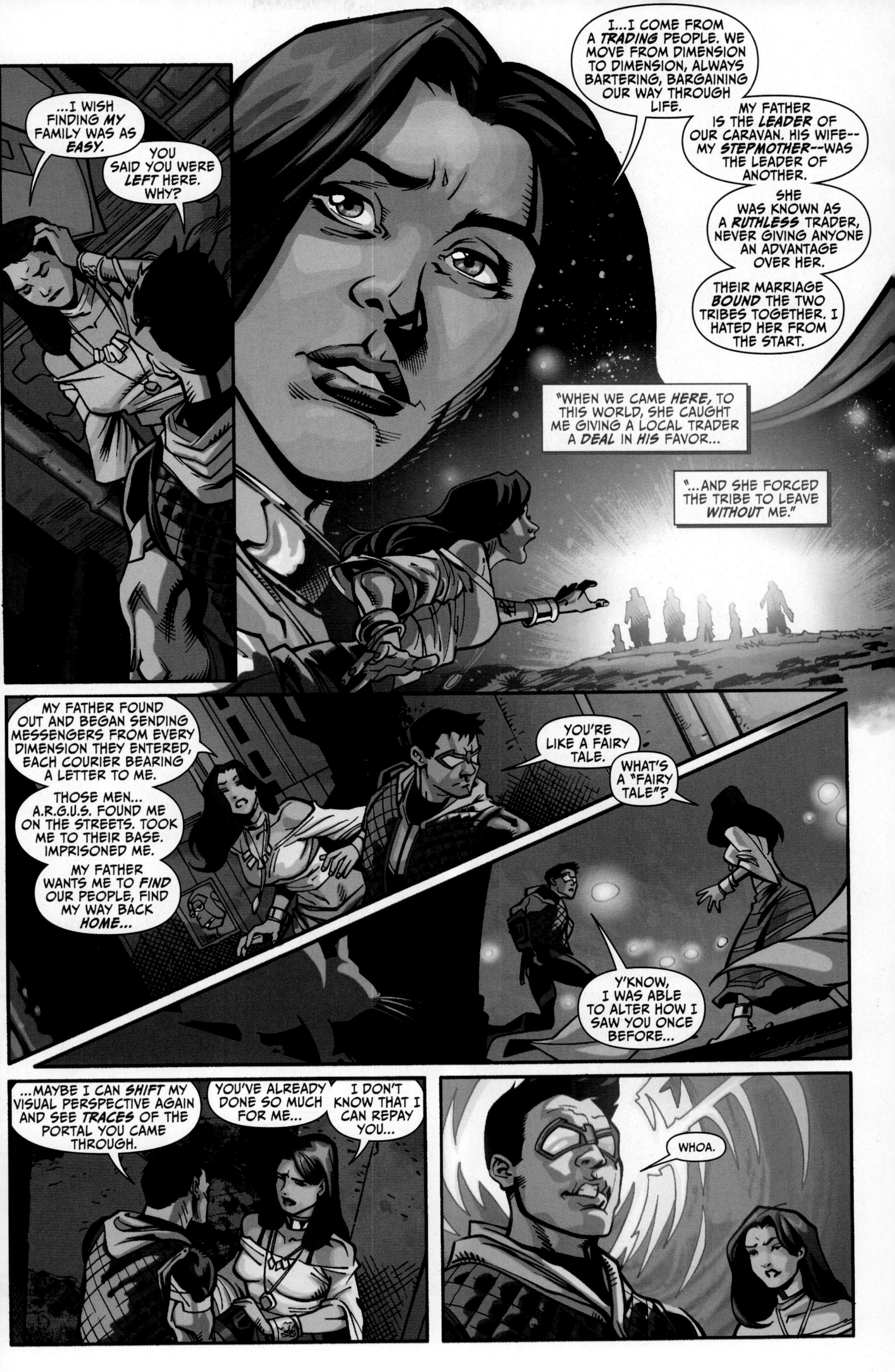
...I WISH FINDING MY FAMILY WAS AS EASY.
YOU SAID YOU WERE LEFT HERE. WHY?
I...I COME FROM A TRADING PEOPLE. WE MOVE FROM DIMENSION TO DIMENSION, ALWAYS BARTERING, BARGAINING OUR WAY THROUGH LIFE.
MY FATHER IS THE LEADER OF OUR CARAVAN. HIS WIFE-- MY STEPMOTHER--WAS THE LEADER OF ANOTHER.
SHE WAS KNOWN AS A RUTHLESS TRADER, NEVER GIVING ANYONE AN ADVANTAGE OVER HER.
THEIR MARRIAGE BOUND THE TWO TRIBES TOGETHER. I HATED HER FROM THE START.
"WHEN WE CAME HERE, TO THIS WORLD, SHE CAUGHT ME GIVING A LOCAL TRADER A DEAL IN HIS FAVOR...
"...AND SHE FORCED THE TRIBE TO LEAVE WITHOUT ME."
MY FATHER FOUND OUT AND BEGAN SENDING MESSENGERS FROM EVERY DIMENSION THEY ENTERED, EACH COURIER BEARING A LETTER TO ME.
THOSE MEN... A.R.G.U.S. FOUND ME ON THE STREETS. TOOK ME TO THEIR BASE. IMPRISONED ME.
MY FATHER WANTS ME TO FIND OUR PEOPLE, FIND MY WAY BACK HOME...
YOU'RE LIKE A FAIRY TALE.
WHAT'S A "FAIRY TALE"?
Y'KNOW, I WAS ABLE TO ALTER HOW I SAW YOU ONCE BEFORE...
...MAYBE I CAN SHIFT MY VISUAL PERSPECTIVE AGAIN AND SEE TRACES OF THE PORTAL YOU CAME THROUGH.
YOU'VE ALREADY DONE SO MUCH FOR ME...
I DON'T KNOW THAT I CAN REPAY YOU...
WHOA.

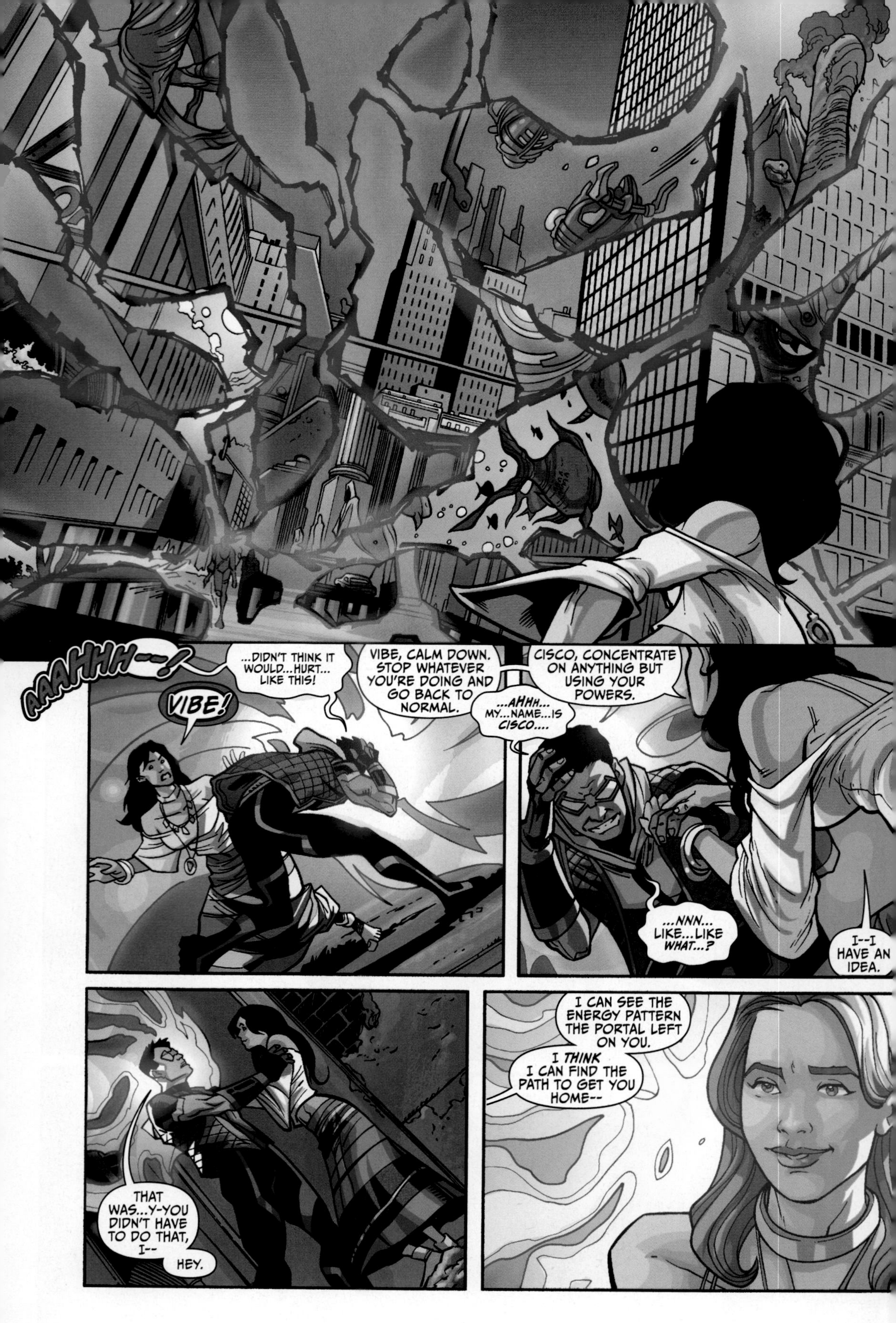
AAAHHH--!
...DIDN'T THINK IT WOULD...HURT... LIKE THIS!
VIBE!
VIBE, CALM DOWN. STOP WHATEVER YOU'RE DOING AND GO BACK TO NORMAL.
...AHHH... MY...NAME...IS CISCO....
CISCO, CONCENTRATE ON ANYTHING BUT USING YOUR POWERS.
...NNN... LIKE...LIKE WHAT...?
I--I HAVE AN IDEA.
THAT WAS...Y-YOU DIDN'T HAVE TO DO THAT, I--
HEY.
I CAN SEE THE ENERGY PATTERN THE PORTAL LEFT ON YOU.
I THINK I CAN FIND THE PATH TO GET YOU HOME--

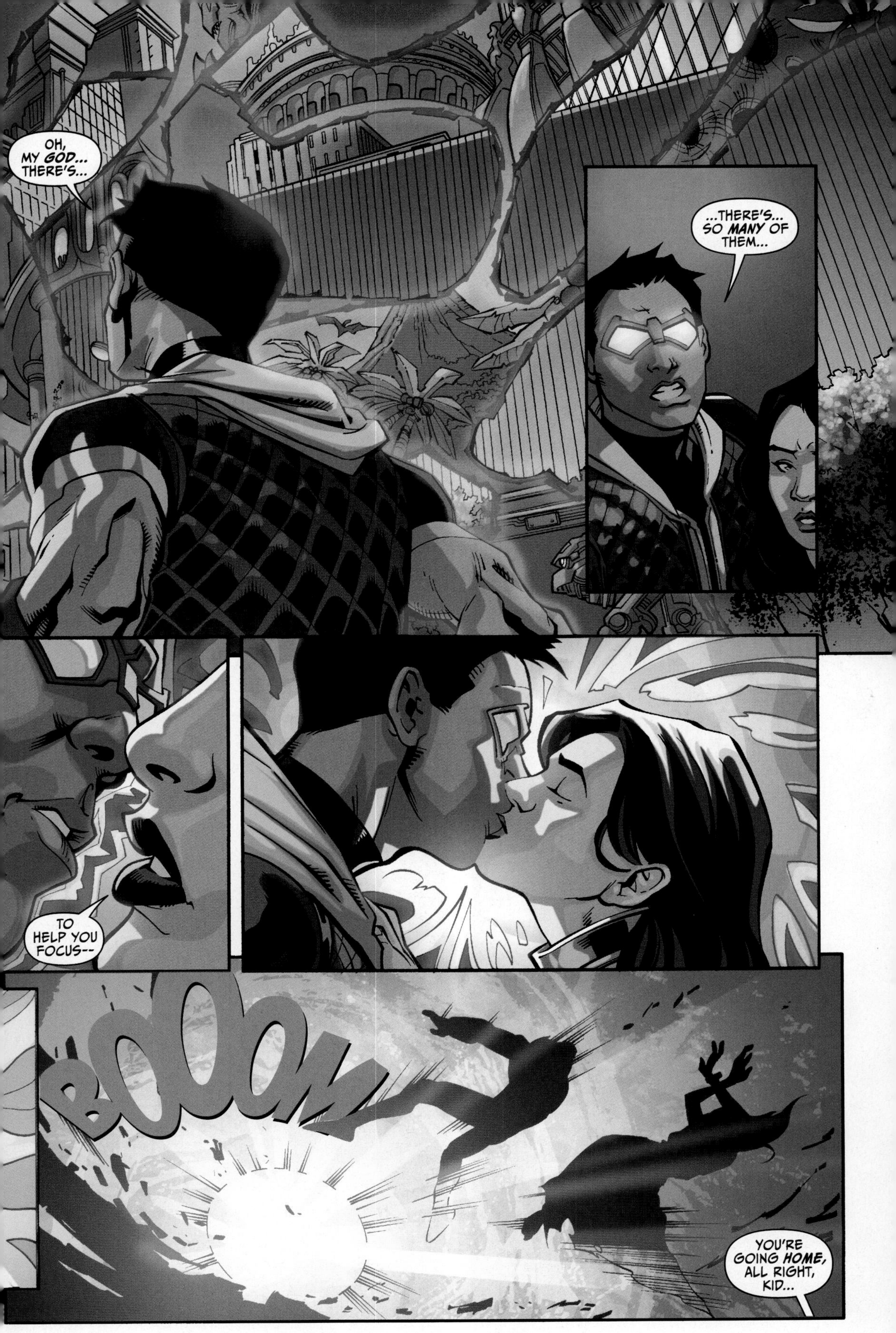
OH, MY GOD... THERE'S...
...THERE'S... SO MANY OF THEM...
TO HELP YOU FOCUS--
BOOOM
YOU'RE GOING HOME, ALL RIGHT, KID...

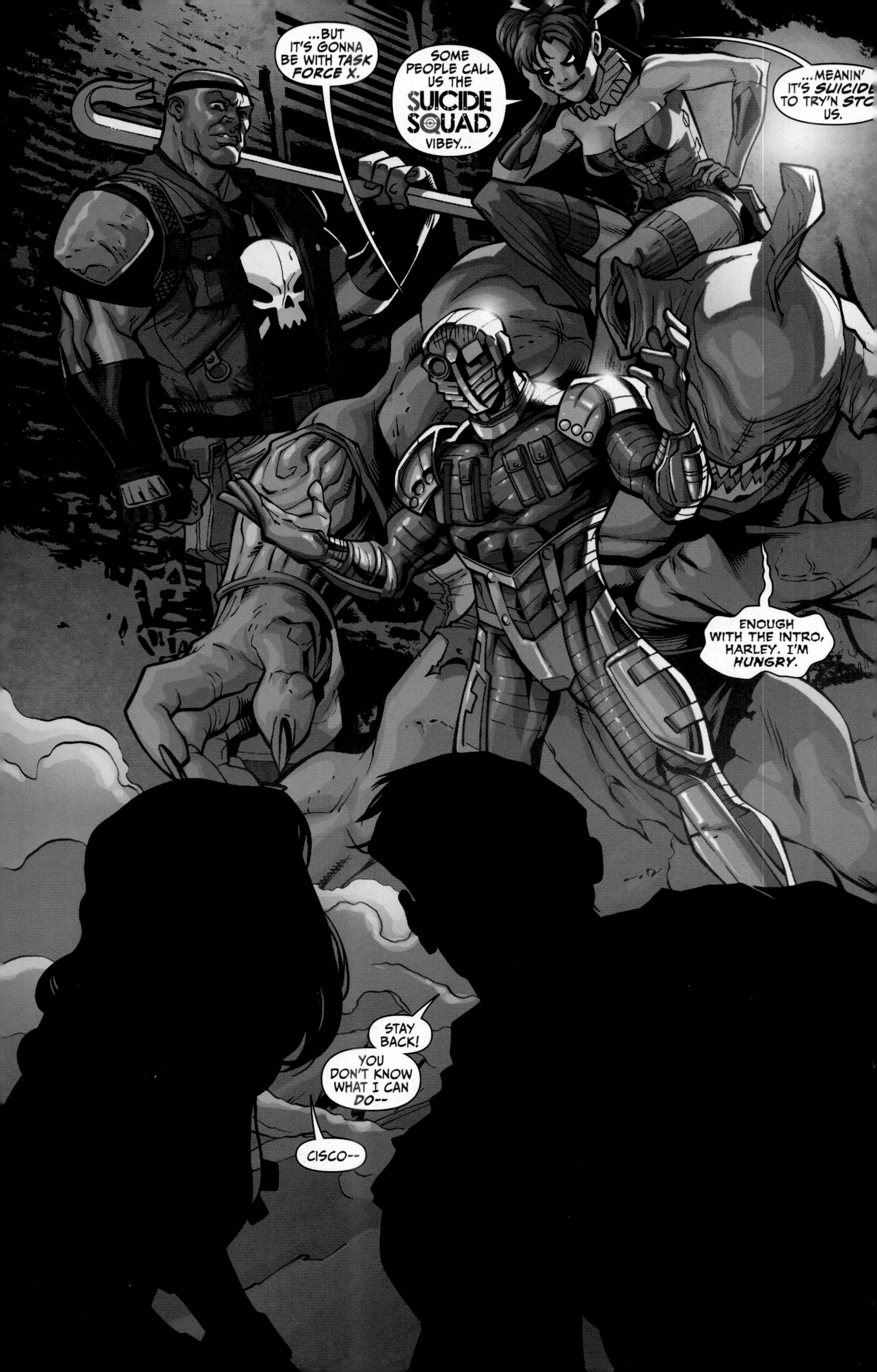
...BUT IT'S GONNA BE WITH TASK FORCE X.
SOME PEOPLE CALL US THE SUICIDE SQUAD, VIBEY...
...MEANIN' IT'S SUICIDE TO TRY'N STO
US.
ENOUGH WITH THE INTRO, HARLEY. I'M HUNGRY.
STAY BACK!
YOU DON'T KNOW WHAT I CAN DO--
CISCO--

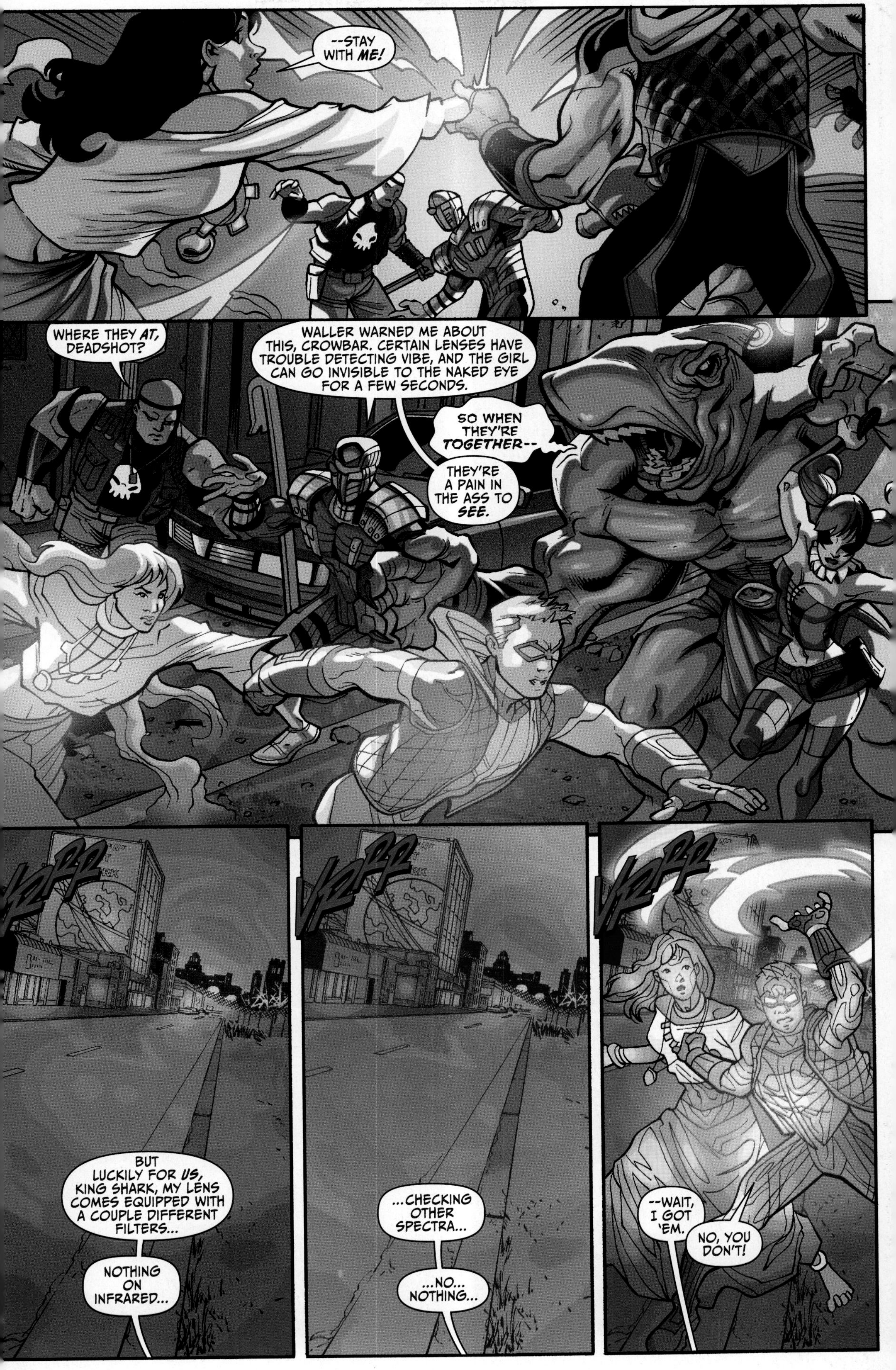
--STAY WITH ME!
WHERE THEY AT, DEADSHOT?
WALLER WARNED ME ABOUT THIS, CROWBAR. CERTAIN LENSES HAVE TROUBLE DETECTING VIBE, AND THE GIRL CAN GO INVISIBLE TO THE NAKED EYE FOR A FEW SECONDS.
SO WHEN THEY'RE TOGETHER--
THEY'RE A PAIN IN THE ASS TO SEE.
VRRR
BUT LUCKILY FOR US, KING SHARK, MY LENS COMES EQUIPPED WITH A COUPLE DIFFERENT FILTERS...
NOTHING ON INFRARED...
VRRR
...CHECKING OTHER SPECTRA...
...NO... NOTHING...
VRRR
--WAIT, I GOT 'EM.
NO, YOU DON'T!

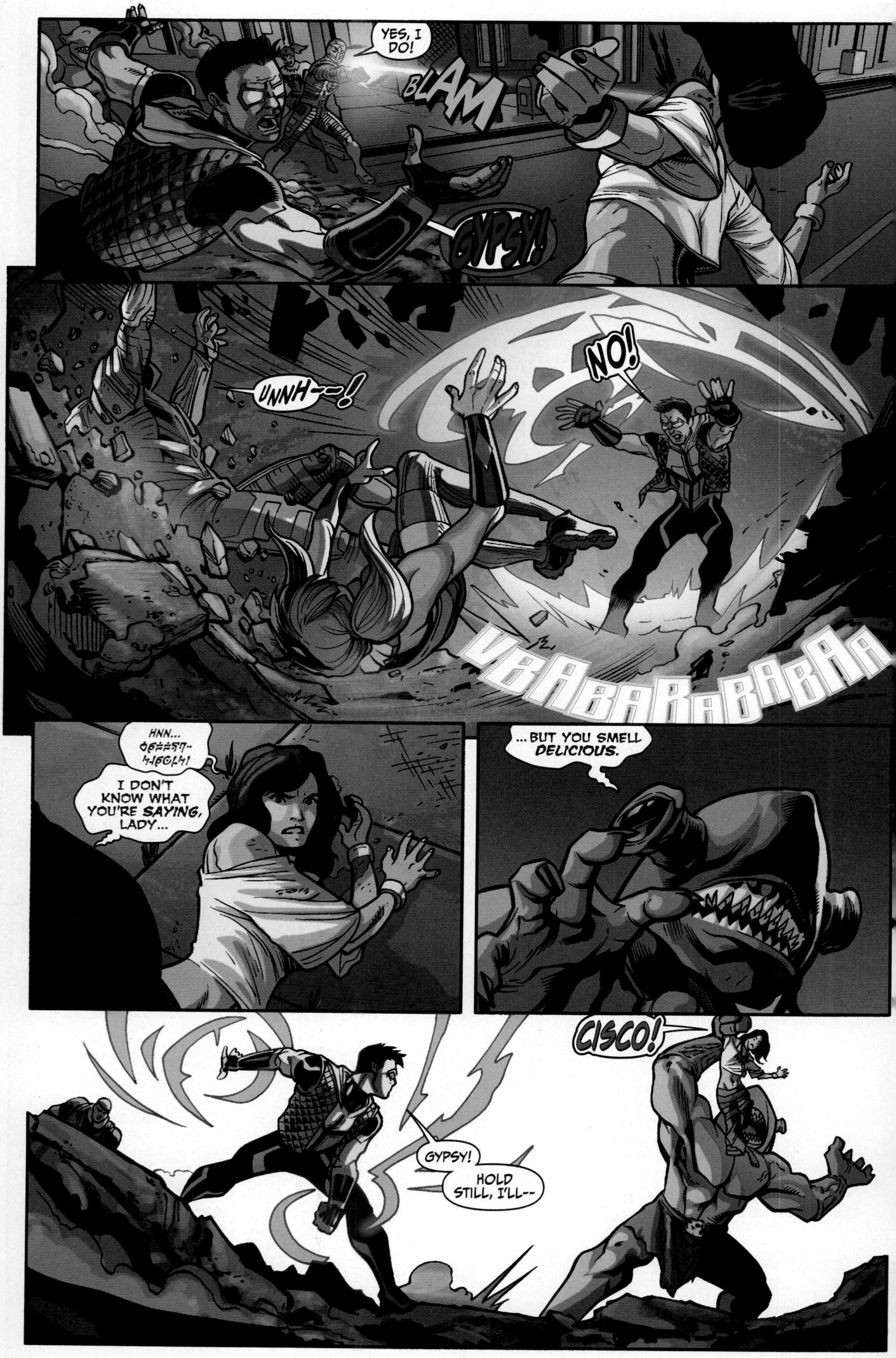
YES, I DO!
BLAM
GYPSY!
UNNH--!
NO!
VBABABABABAA
HNN...
I DON'T KNOW WHAT YOU'RE SAYING, LADY...
...BUT YOU SMELL DELICIOUS.
CISCO!
GYPSY!
HOLD STILL, I'LL--

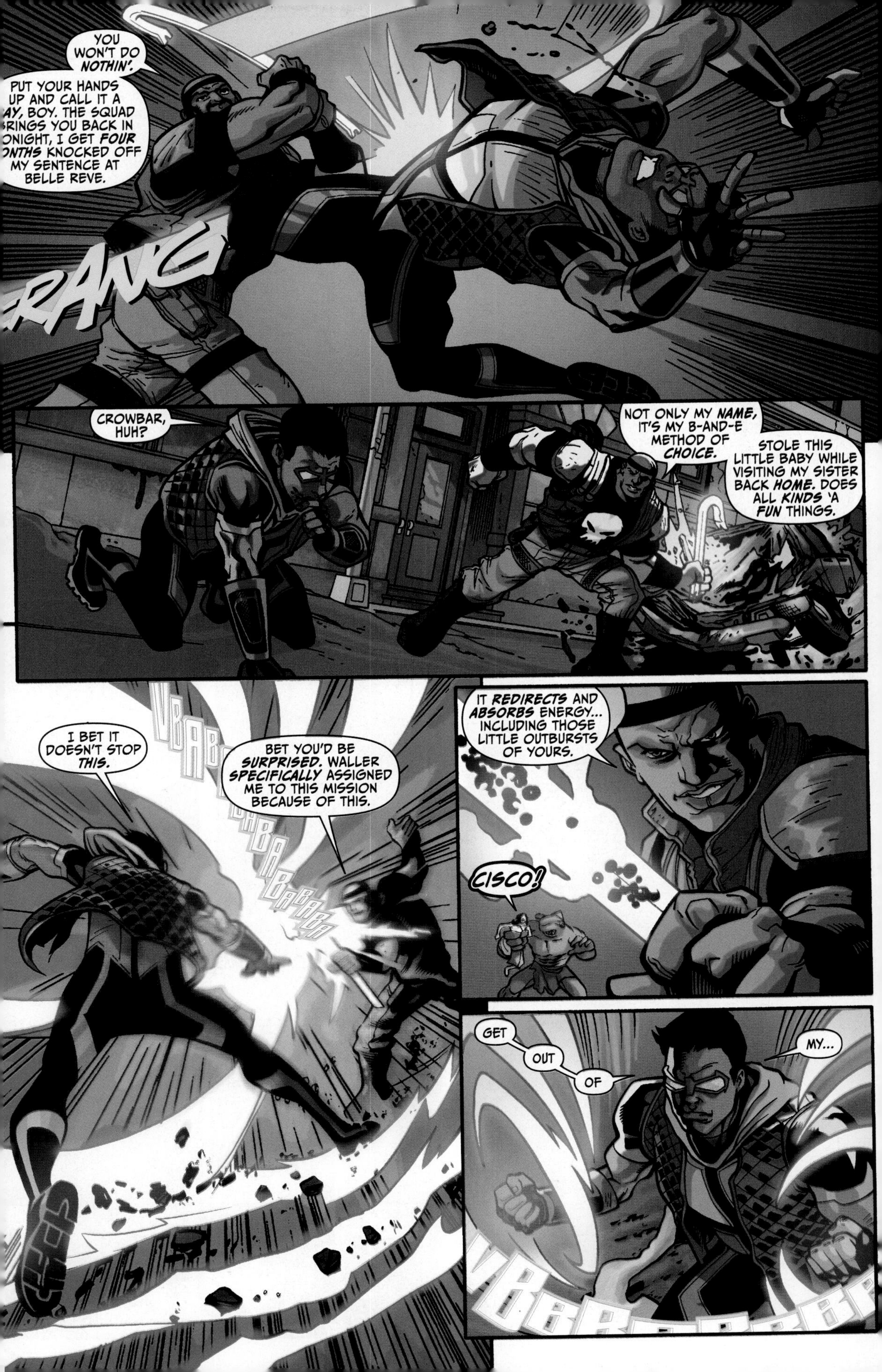
YOU WON'T DO NOTHIN'.
PUT YOUR HANDS UP AND CALL IT A DAY, BOY. THE SQUAD BRINGS YOU BACK IN TONIGHT, I GET FOUR MONTHS KNOCKED OFF MY SENTENCE AT BELLE REVE.
CRANG
CROWBAR, HUH?
NOT ONLY MY NAME, IT'S MY B-AND-E METHOD OF CHOICE.
STOLE THIS LITTLE BABY WHILE VISITING MY SISTER BACK HOME. DOES ALL KINDS 'A FUN THINGS.
I BET IT DOESN'T STOP THIS.
BET YOU'D BE SURPRISED. WALLER SPECIFICALLY ASSIGNED ME TO THIS MISSION BECAUSE OF THIS.
IT REDIRECTS AND ABSORBS ENERGY... INCLUDING THOSE LITTLE OUTBURSTS OF YOURS.
CISCO!
GET
OUT
OF
MY...

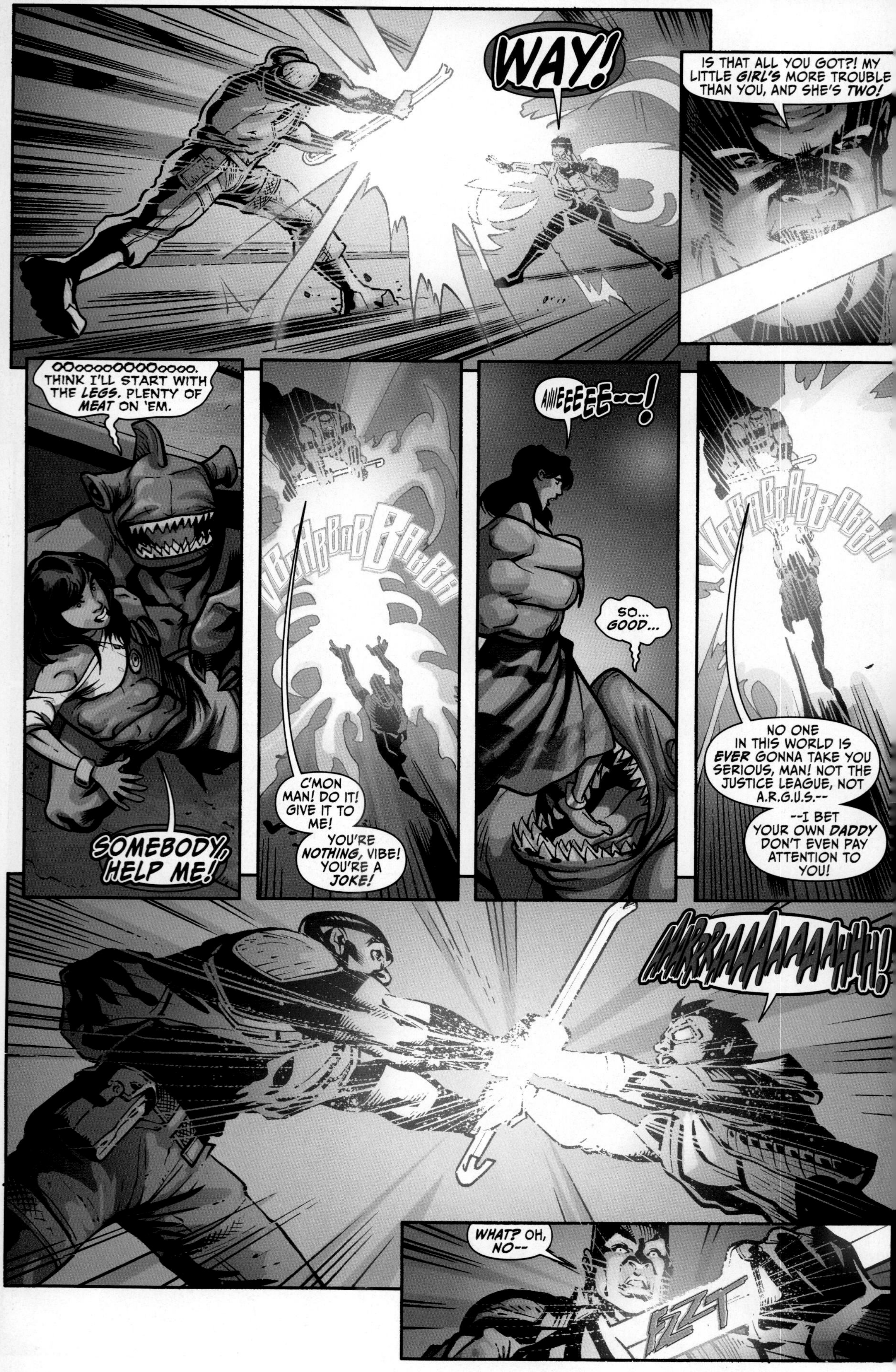
WAY!
IS THAT ALL YOU GOT?! MY LITTLE GIRL'S MORE TROUBLE THAN YOU, AND SHE'S TWO!
OOoooooOOOOoooo. THINK I'LL START WITH THE LEGS. PLENTY OF MEAT ON 'EM.
SOMEBODY, HELP ME!
VRBRRBRRBBRBBRR
C'MON MAN! DO IT! GIVE IT TO ME!
YOU'RE NOTHING, VIBE! YOU'RE A JOKE!
AIIIEEEEE--!
SO... GOOD...
VRBRBRRBBRBBRR
NO ONE IN THIS WORLD IS EVER GONNA TAKE YOU SERIOUS, MAN! NOT THE JUSTICE LEAGUE, NOT A.R.G.U.S.--
--I BET YOUR OWN DADDY DON'T EVEN PAY ATTENTION TO YOU!
AARRRAAAAAAAAHHH!
WHAT? OH, NO--
FZZT

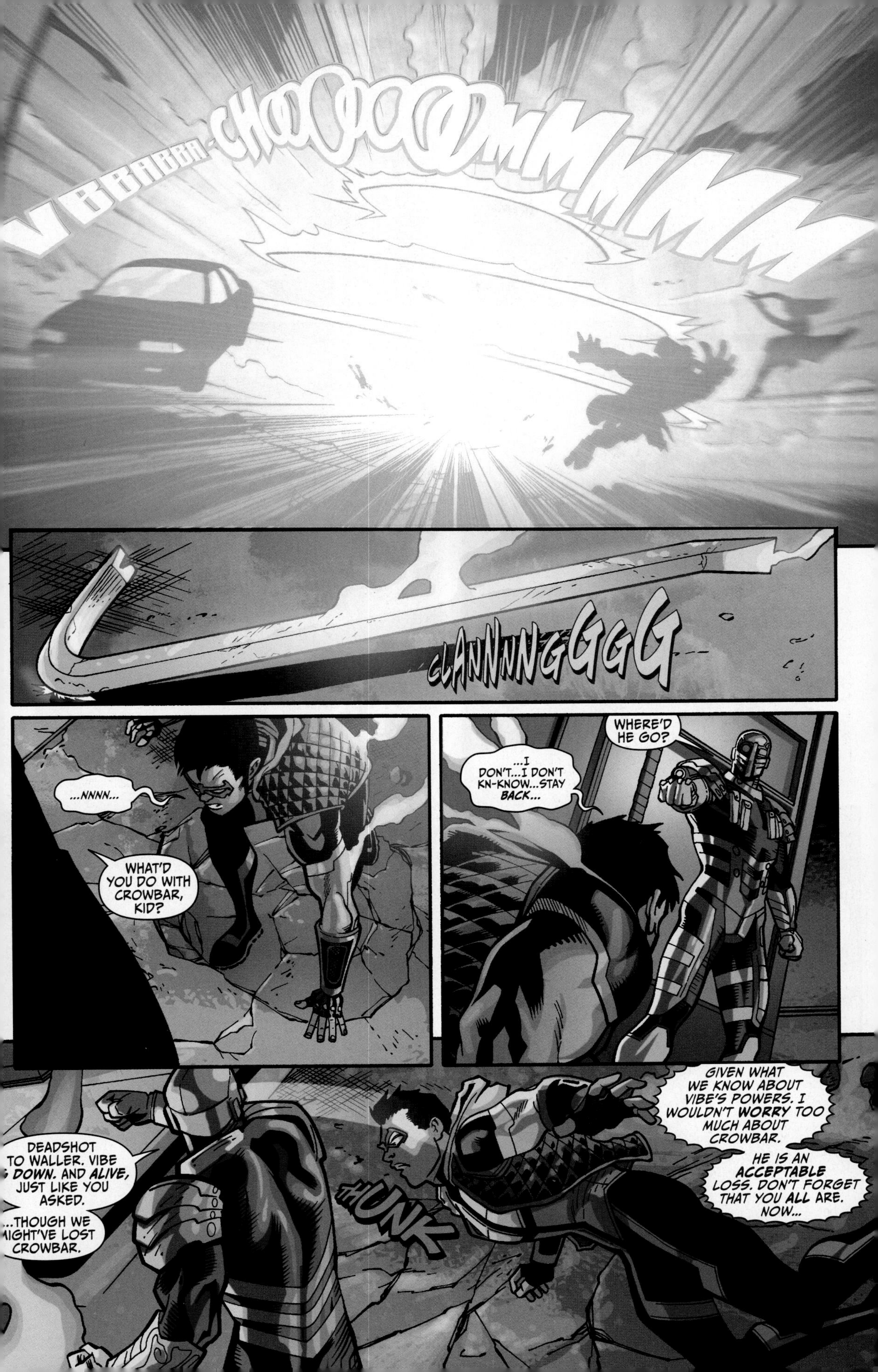
VBRABBA-CHOOOOOOMMMMMM
CLANNNNGGGG
...NNNN...
WHAT'D YOU DO WITH CROWBAR, KID?
WHERE'D HE GO?
...I DON'T...I DON'T KN-KNOW...STAY BACK...
DEADSHOT TO WALLER. VIBE IS DOWN. AND ALIVE, JUST LIKE YOU ASKED.
...THOUGH WE MIGHT'VE LOST CROWBAR.
THUNK
GIVEN WHAT WE KNOW ABOUT VIBE'S POWERS. I WOULDN'T WORRY TOO MUCH ABOUT CROWBAR.
HE IS AN ACCEPTABLE LOSS. DON'T FORGET THAT YOU ALL ARE. NOW...

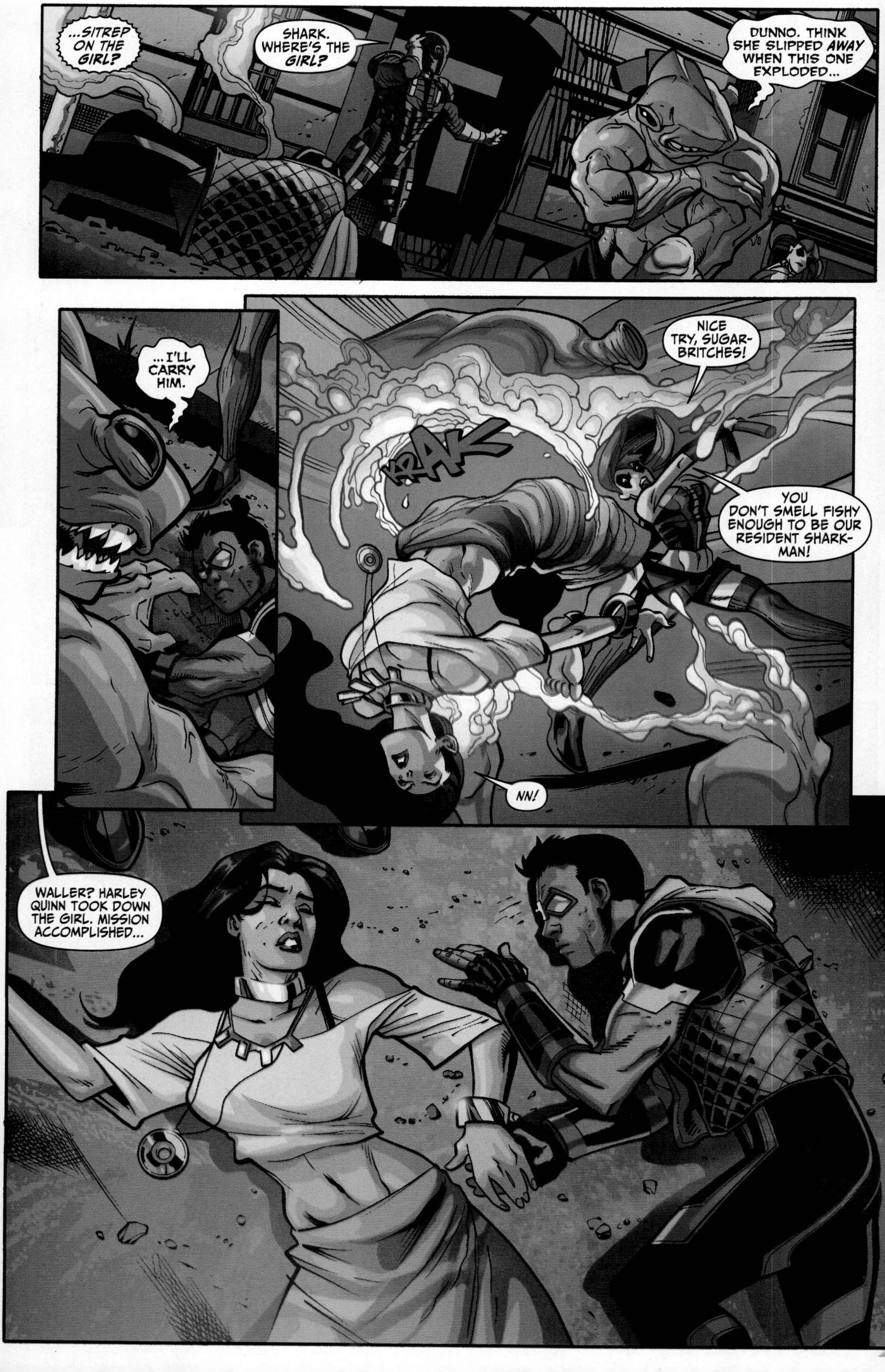

...SITREP ON THE GIRL?
SHARK. WHERE'S THE GIRL?
DUNNO. THINK SHE SLIPPED AWAY WHEN THIS ONE EXPLODED...
...I'LL CARRY HIM.
NICE TRY, SUGAR-BRITCHES!
KRAK
YOU DON'T SMELL FISHY ENOUGH TO BE OUR RESIDENT SHARK-MAN!
NN!
WALLER? HARLEY QUINN TOOK DOWN THE GIRL. MISSION ACCOMPLISHED...

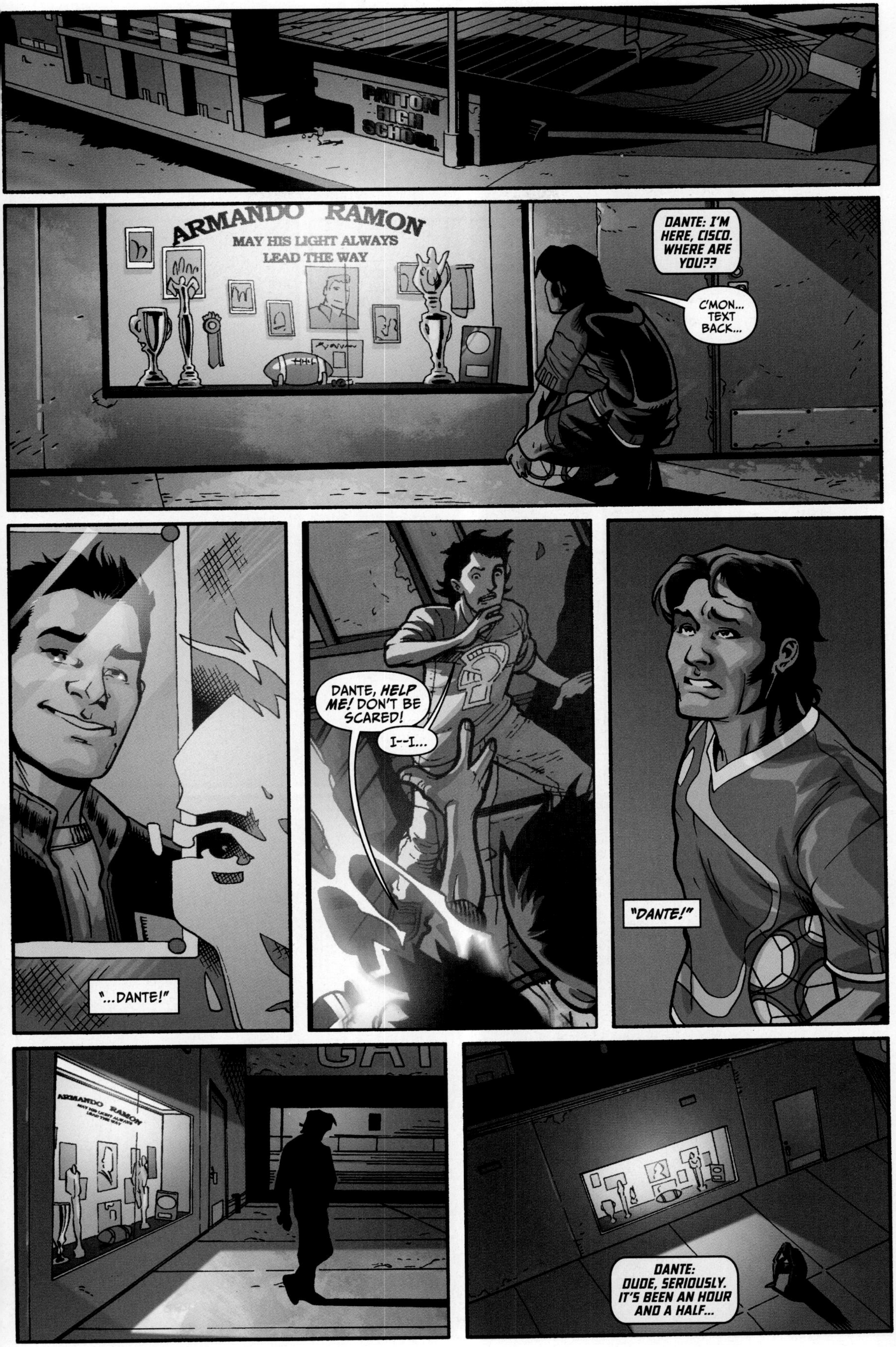
PATTON HIGH SCHOOL
ARMANDO RAMON
MAY HIS LIGHT ALWAYS LEAD THE WAY
DANTE: I'M HERE, CISCO. WHERE ARE YOU??
C'MON... TEXT BACK...
"...DANTE!"
DANTE, HELP ME! DON'T BE SCARED!
I--I...
"DANTE!"
ARMANDO RAMON
DANTE: DUDE, SERIOUSLY. IT'S BEEN AN HOUR AND A HALF...

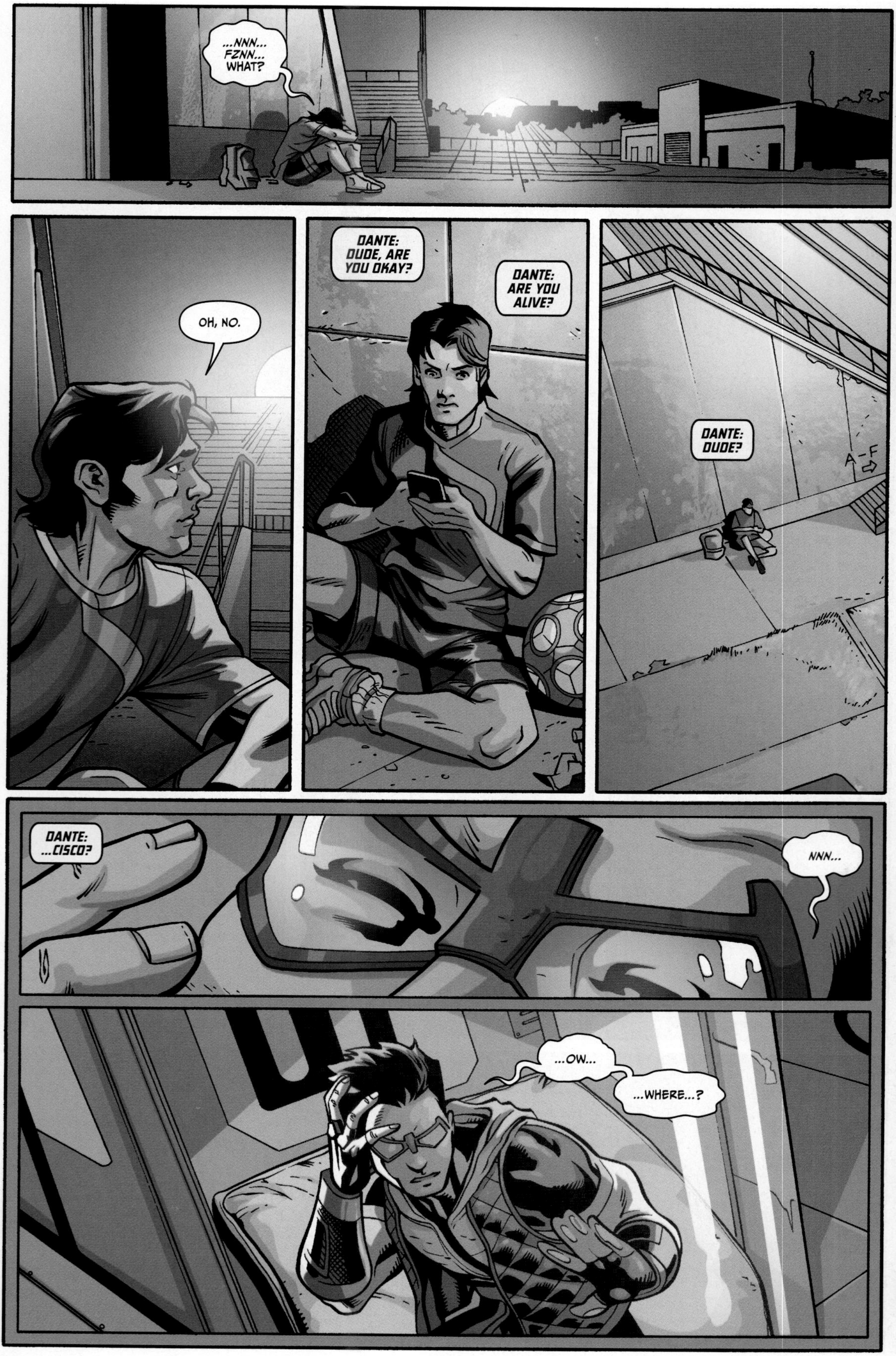
...NNN... FZNN... WHAT?
OH, NO.
DANTE: DUDE, ARE YOU OKAY?
DANTE: ARE YOU ALIVE?
DANTE: DUDE?
A – F
DANTE: ...CISCO?
NNN...
...OW...
...WHERE...?

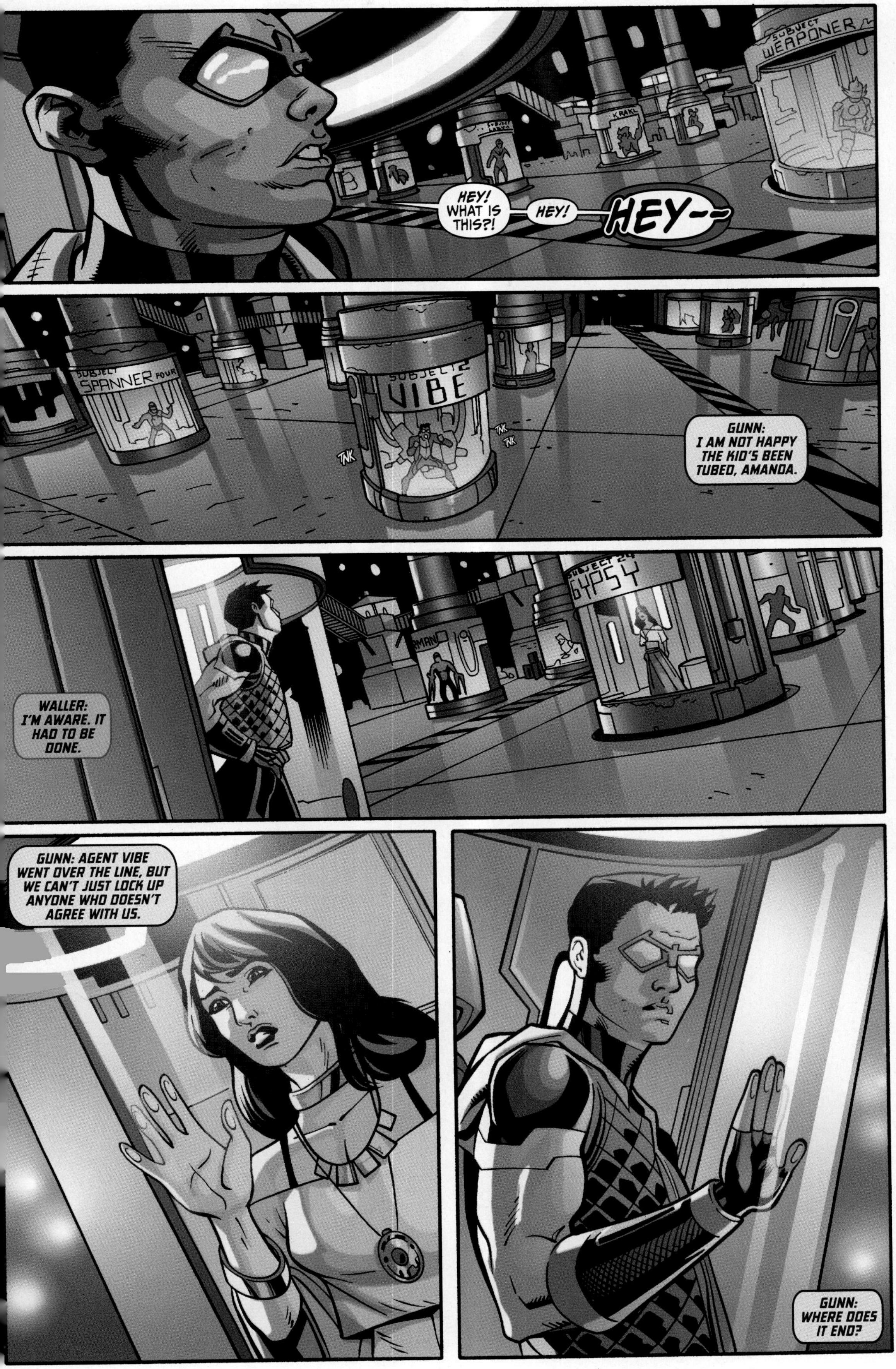
SUBJECT WEAPONER
KRAKL
HEY! WHAT IS THIS?!
HEY!
HEY--
SPANNER FOUR
VIBE
TNK
TNK
TNK
GUNN: I AM NOT HAPPY THE KID'S BEEN TUBED, AMANDA.
GYPSY
WALLER: I'M AWARE. IT HAD TO BE DONE.
GUNN: AGENT VIBE WENT OVER THE LINE, BUT WE CAN'T JUST LOCK UP ANYONE WHO DOESN'T AGREE WITH US.
GUNN: WHERE DOES IT END?

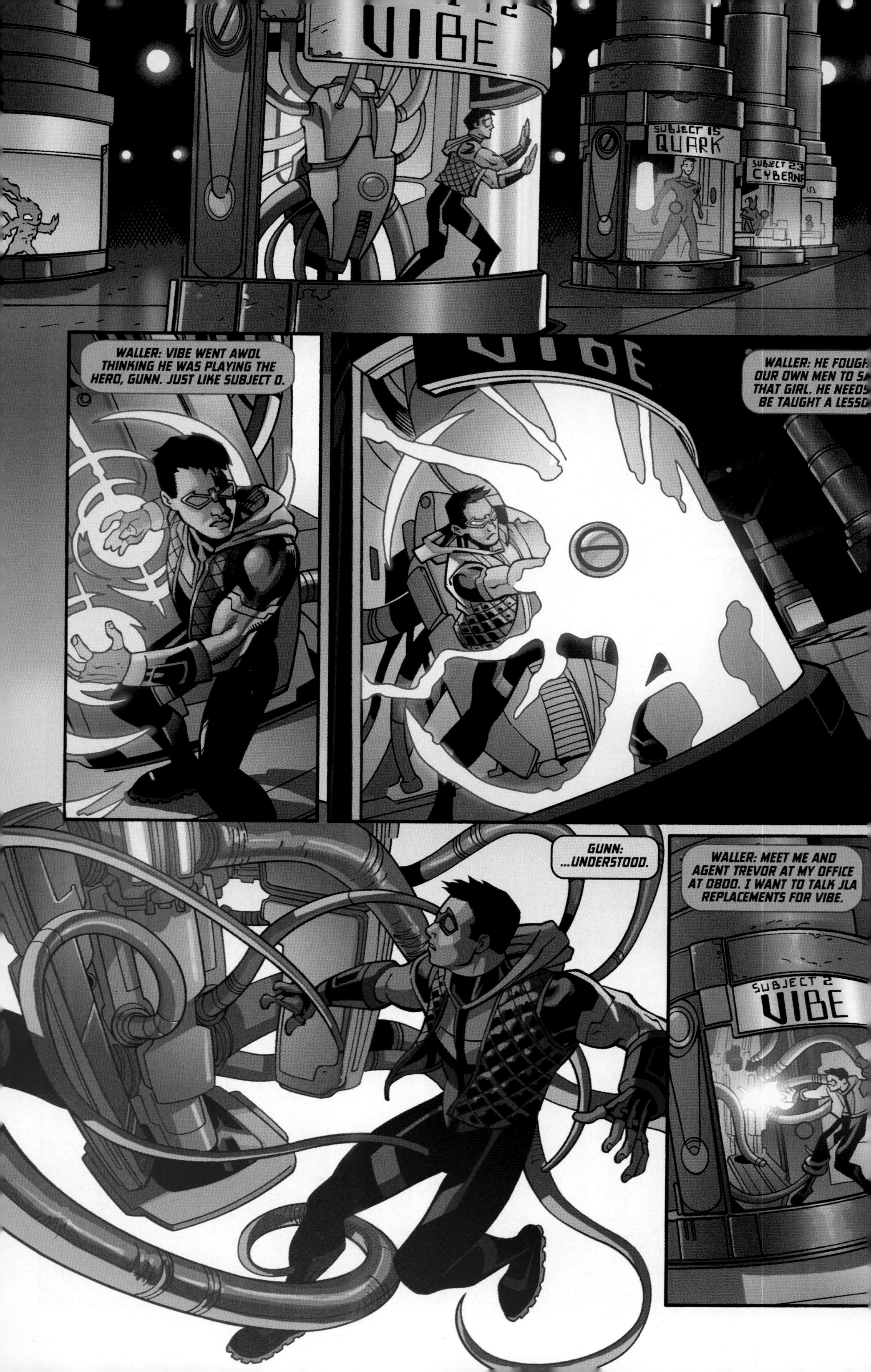
VIBE
SUBJECT 15
QUARK
SUBJECT 23
CYBERNA
WALLER: VIBE WENT AWOL THINKING HE WAS PLAYING THE HERO, GUNN. JUST LIKE SUBJECT 0.
WALLER: HE FOUGH OUR OWN MEN TO SA THAT GIRL. HE NEEDS BE TAUGHT A LESSO
GUNN: ...UNDERSTOOD.
WALLER: MEET ME AND AGENT TREVOR AT MY OFFICE AT 0800. I WANT TO TALK JLA REPLACEMENTS FOR VIBE.
SUBJECT 2
VIBE

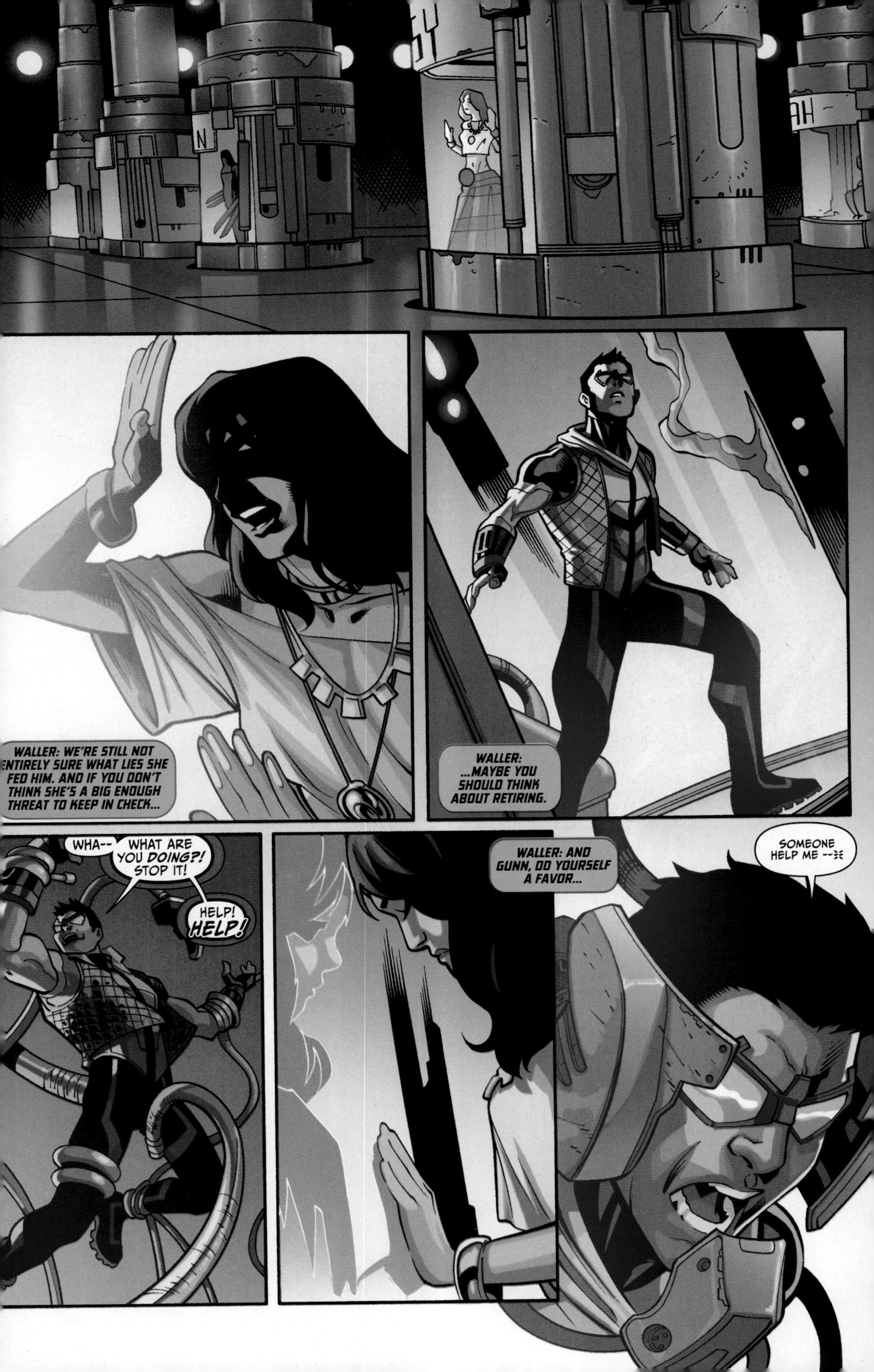
WALLER: WE'RE STILL NOT ENTIRELY SURE WHAT LIES SHE FED HIM. AND IF YOU DON'T THINK SHE'S A BIG ENOUGH THREAT TO KEEP IN CHECK...
WALLER: ...MAYBE YOU SHOULD THINK ABOUT RETIRING.
WHA--
WHAT ARE YOU DOING?! STOP IT!
HELP! HELP!
WALLER: AND GUNN, DO YOURSELF A FAVOR...
SOMEONE HELP ME --

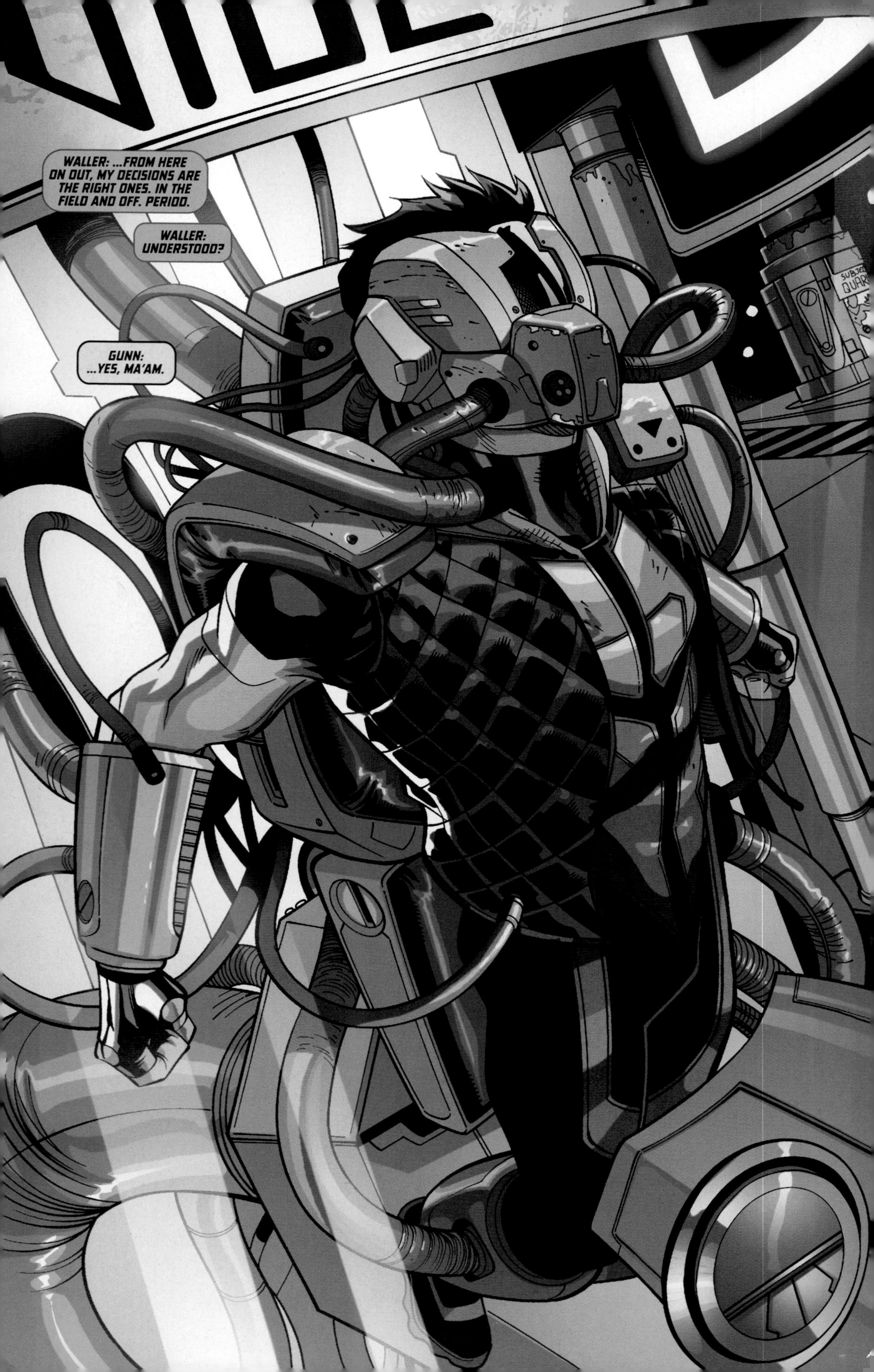
WALLER: ...FROM HERE ON OUT, MY DECISIONS ARE THE RIGHT ONES. IN THE FIELD AND OFF. PERIOD.
WALLER: UNDERSTOOD?
GUNN: ...YES, MA'AM.

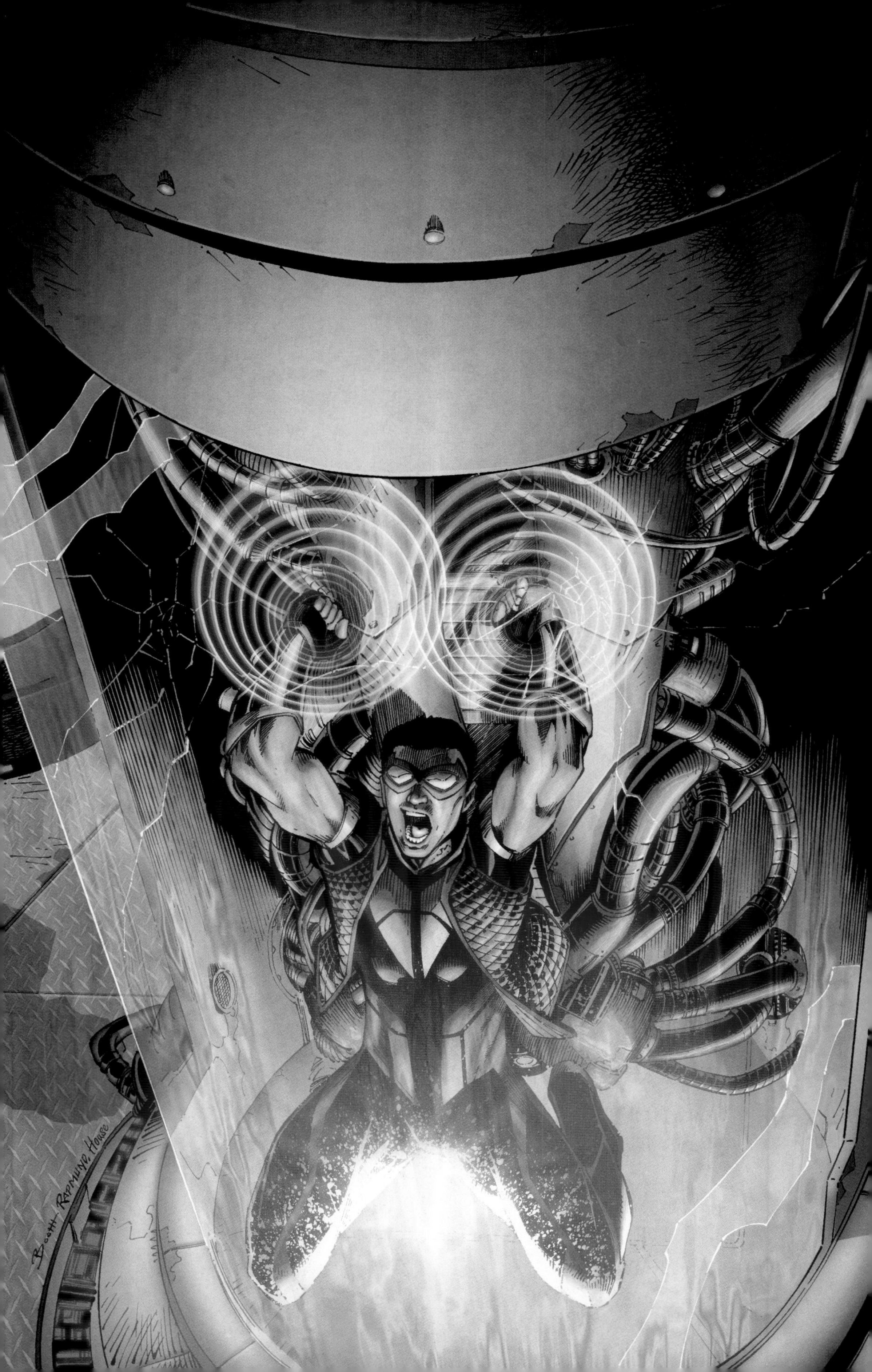
Booth Rapmund, House

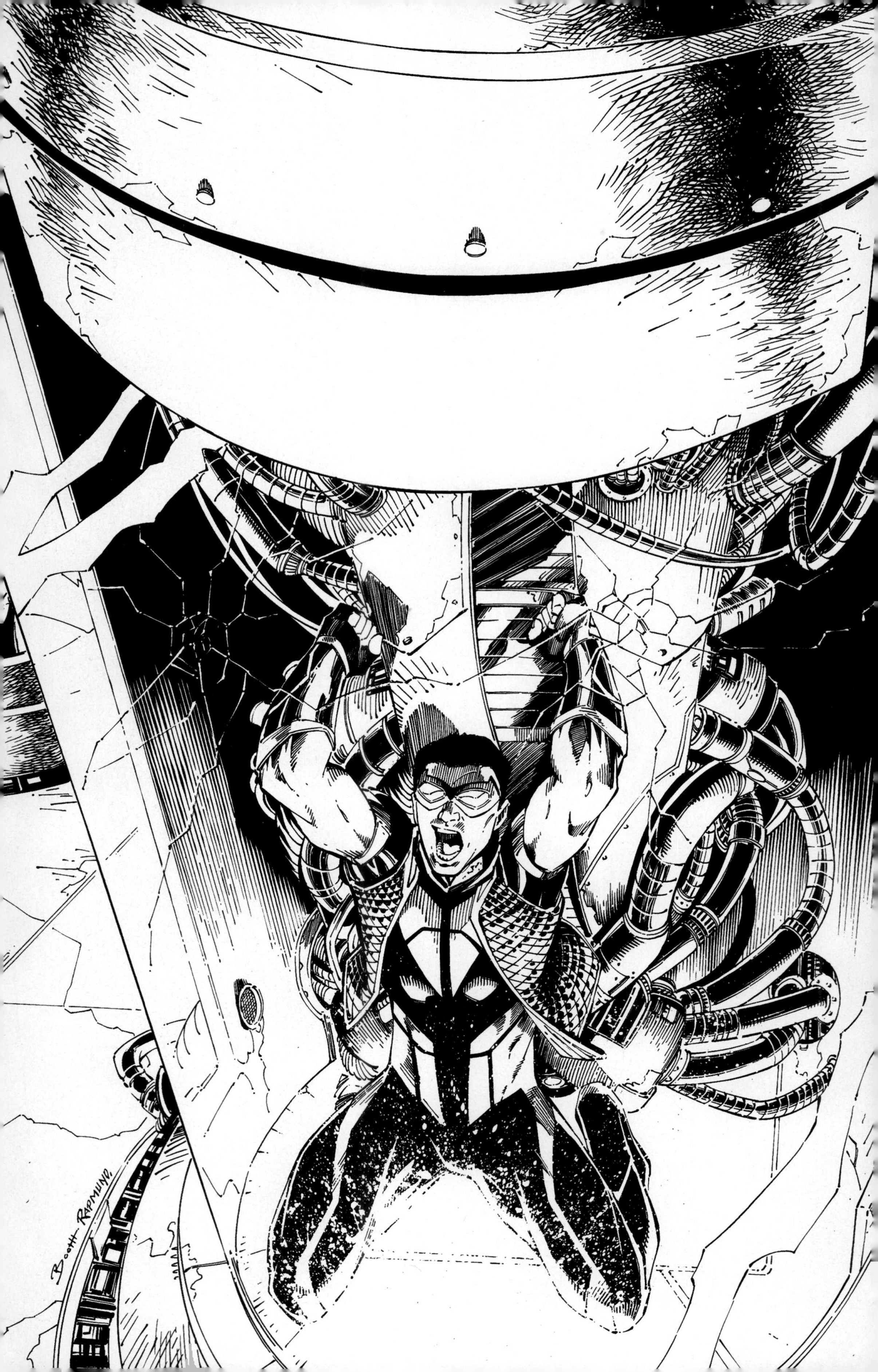
BOOTH RAPMUND

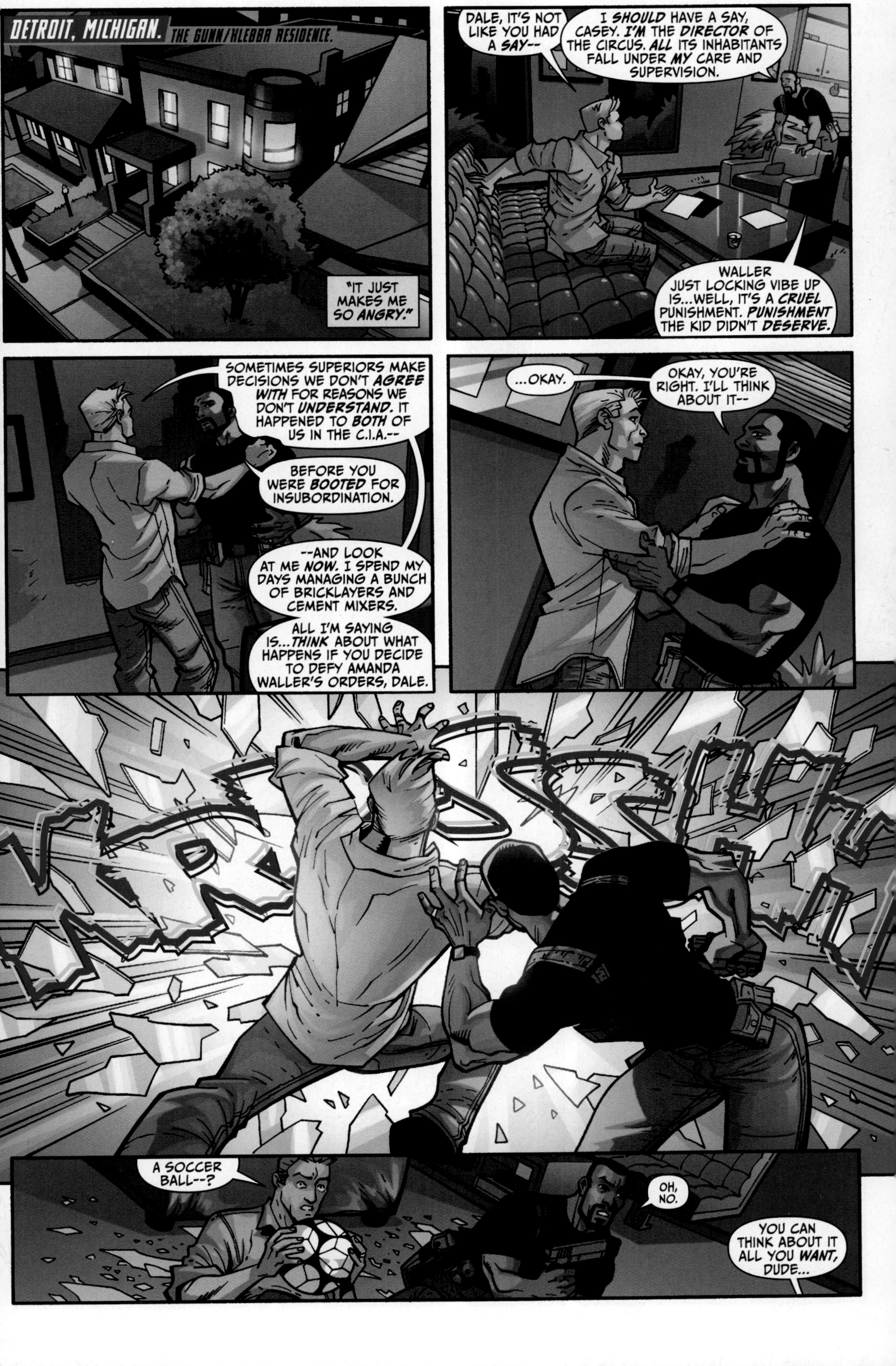

DETROIT, MICHIGAN.
THE GUNN/KLEBBA RESIDENCE.
"IT JUST MAKES ME SO ANGRY."
DALE, IT'S NOT LIKE YOU HAD A SAY--
I SHOULD HAVE A SAY, CASEY. I'M THE DIRECTOR OF THE CIRCUS. ALL ITS INHABITANTS FALL UNDER MY CARE AND SUPERVISION.
WALLER JUST LOCKING VIBE UP IS...WELL, IT'S A CRUEL PUNISHMENT. PUNISHMENT THE KID DIDN'T DESERVE.
SOMETIMES SUPERIORS MAKE DECISIONS WE DON'T AGREE WITH FOR REASONS WE DON'T UNDERSTAND. IT HAPPENED TO BOTH OF US IN THE C.I.A.--
BEFORE YOU WERE BOOTED FOR INSUBORDINATION.
--AND LOOK AT ME NOW. I SPEND MY DAYS MANAGING A BUNCH OF BRICKLAYERS AND CEMENT MIXERS.
ALL I'M SAYING IS...THINK ABOUT WHAT HAPPENS IF YOU DECIDE TO DEFY AMANDA WALLER'S ORDERS, DALE.
...OKAY.
OKAY, YOU'RE RIGHT. I'LL THINK ABOUT IT--
A SOCCER BALL--?
OH, NO.
YOU CAN THINK ABOUT IT ALL YOU WANT, DUDE...

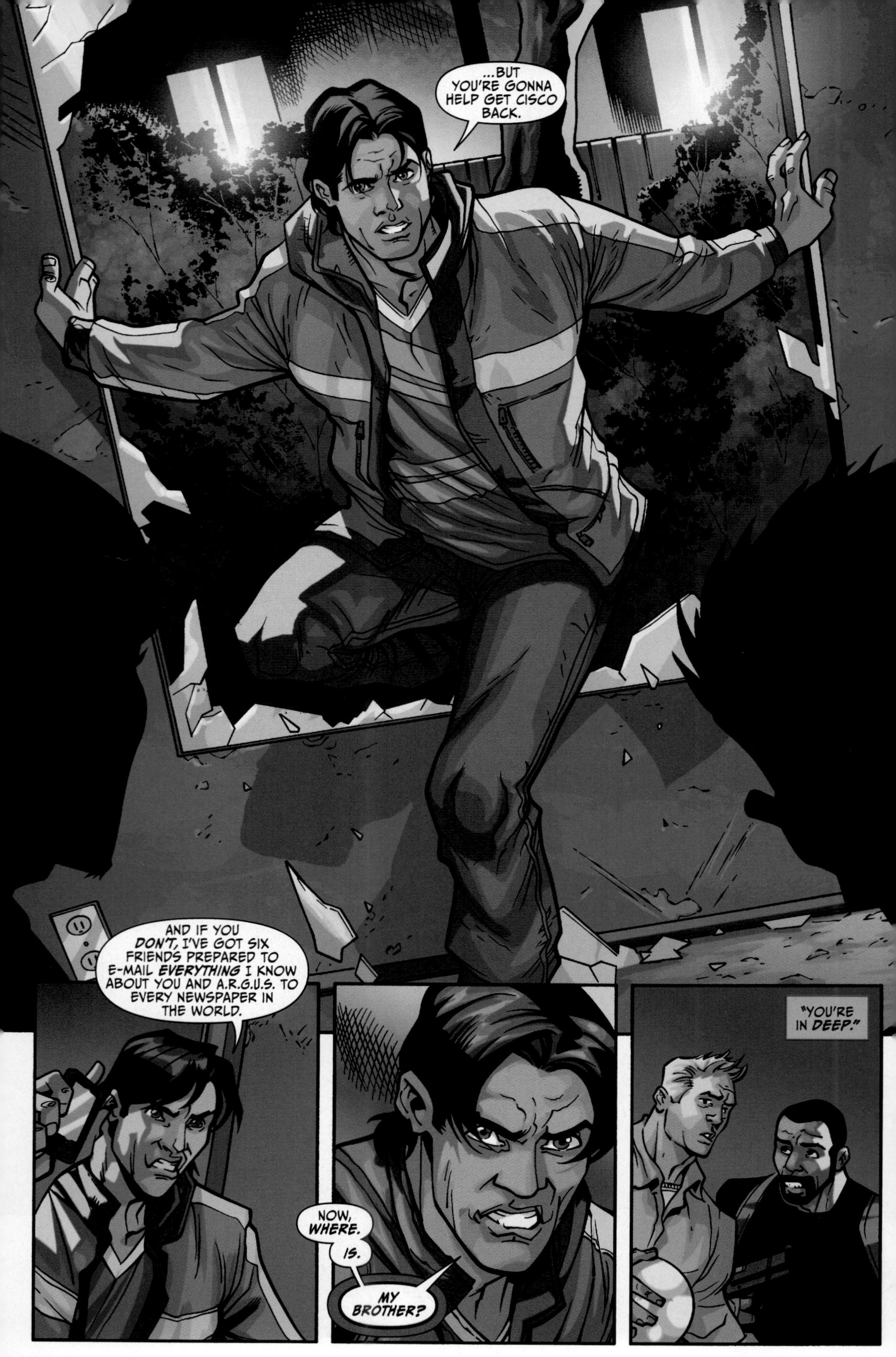
...BUT YOU'RE GONNA HELP GET CISCO BACK.
AND IF YOU DON'T, I'VE GOT SIX FRIENDS PREPARED TO E-MAIL EVERYTHING I KNOW ABOUT YOU AND A.R.G.U.S. TO EVERY NEWSPAPER IN THE WORLD.
NOW, WHERE.
IS.
MY BROTHER?
"YOU'RE IN DEEP."

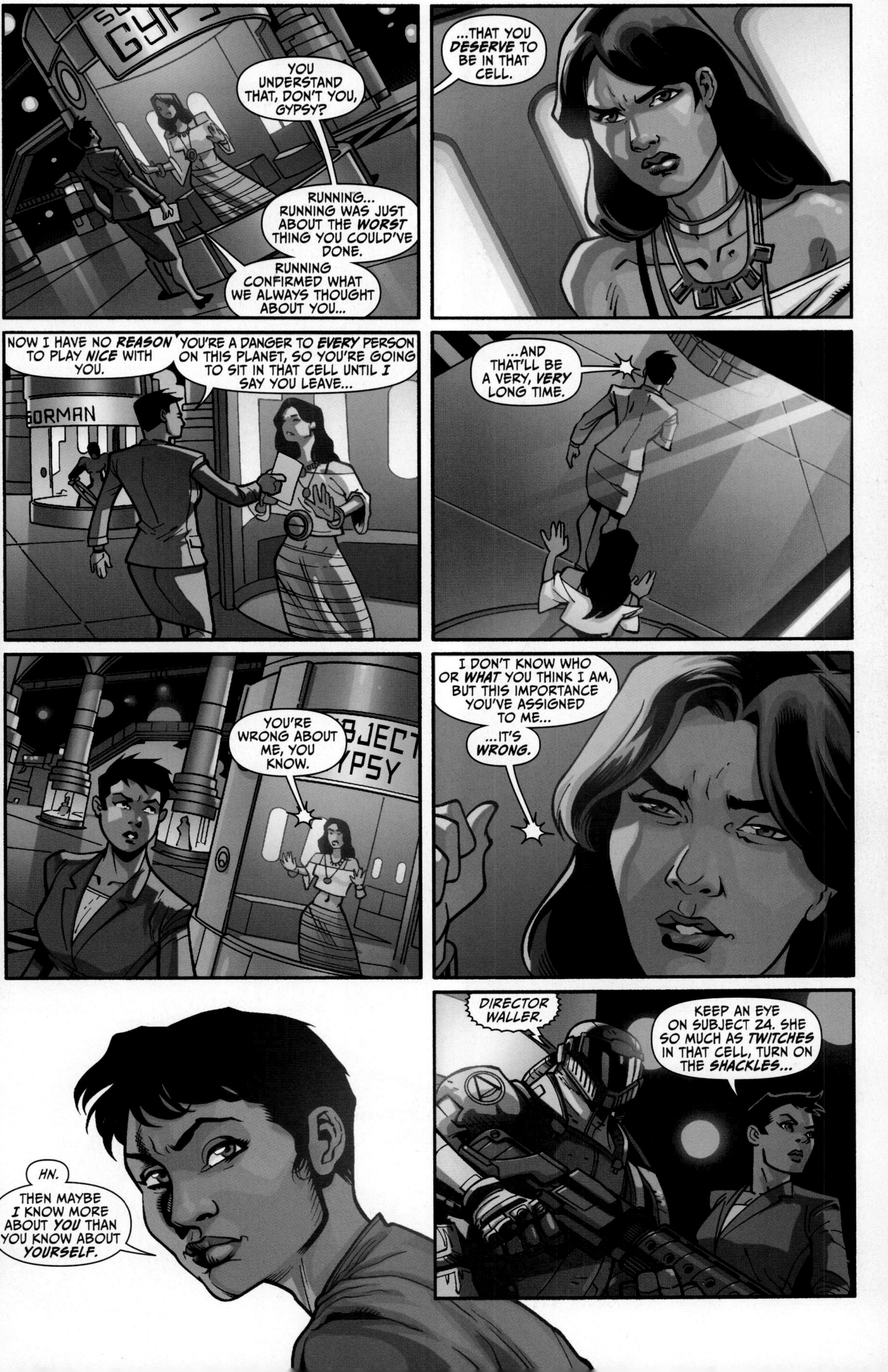
SUBJECT GYPSY
YOU UNDERSTAND THAT, DON'T YOU, GYPSY?
RUNNING... RUNNING WAS JUST ABOUT THE WORST THING YOU COULD'VE DONE.
RUNNING CONFIRMED WHAT WE ALWAYS THOUGHT ABOUT YOU...
...THAT YOU DESERVE TO BE IN THAT CELL.
NOW I HAVE NO REASON TO PLAY NICE WITH YOU.
YOU'RE A DANGER TO EVERY PERSON ON THIS PLANET, SO YOU'RE GOING TO SIT IN THAT CELL UNTIL I SAY YOU LEAVE...
GORMAN
...AND THAT'LL BE A VERY, VERY LONG TIME.
YOU'RE WRONG ABOUT ME, YOU KNOW.
SUBJECT GYPSY
I DON'T KNOW WHO OR WHAT YOU THINK I AM, BUT THIS IMPORTANCE YOU'VE ASSIGNED TO ME...
...IT'S WRONG.
HN.
THEN MAYBE I KNOW MORE ABOUT YOU THAN YOU KNOW ABOUT YOURSELF.
DIRECTOR WALLER.
KEEP AN EYE ON SUBJECT 24. SHE SO MUCH AS TWITCHES IN THAT CELL, TURN ON THE SHACKLES...

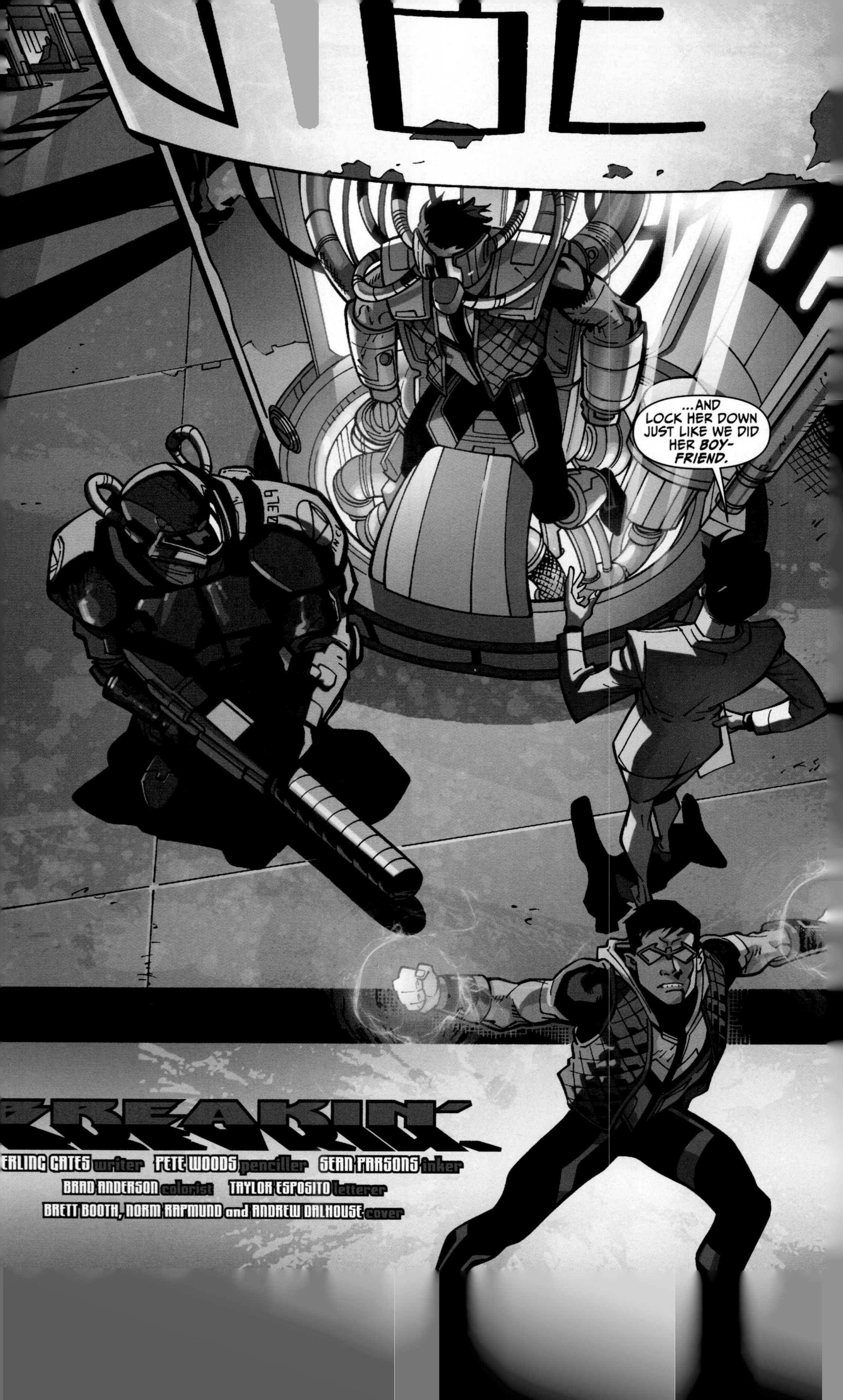
...AND LOCK HER DOWN JUST LIKE WE DID HER BOY-FRIEND.
BREAKIN'
ERLING GATES writer PETE WOODS penciller SEAN PARSONS inker
BRAD ANDERSON colorist TAYLOR ESPOSITO letterer
BRETT BOOTH, NORM RAPMUND and ANDREW DALHOUSE cover

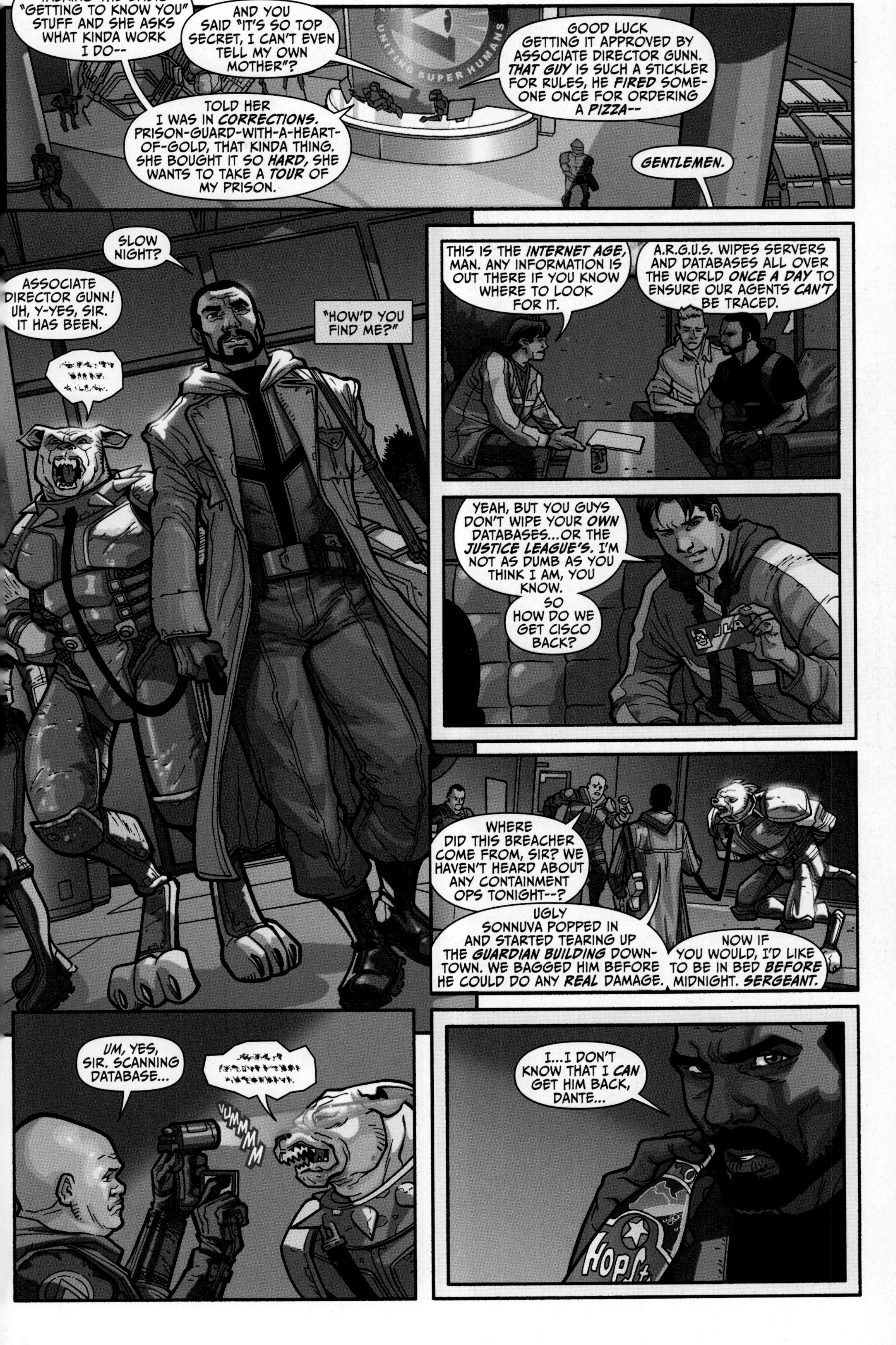
...SO WE'RE TALKING THE BASIC "GETTING TO KNOW YOU" STUFF AND SHE ASKS WHAT KINDA WORK I DO--
AND YOU SAID "IT'S SO TOP SECRET, I CAN'T EVEN TELL MY OWN MOTHER"?
TOLD HER I WAS IN CORRECTIONS. PRISON-GUARD-WITH-A-HEART-OF-GOLD, THAT KINDA THING. SHE BOUGHT IT SO HARD, SHE WANTS TO TAKE A TOUR OF MY PRISON.
GOOD LUCK GETTING IT APPROVED BY ASSOCIATE DIRECTOR GUNN. THAT GUY IS SUCH A STICKLER FOR RULES, HE FIRED SOME-ONE ONCE FOR ORDERING A PIZZA--
GENTLEMEN.
UNITING SUPER HUMANS
SLOW NIGHT?
ASSOCIATE DIRECTOR GUNN! UH, Y-YES, SIR. IT HAS BEEN.
"HOW'D YOU FIND ME?"
THIS IS THE INTERNET AGE, MAN. ANY INFORMATION IS OUT THERE IF YOU KNOW WHERE TO LOOK FOR IT.
A.R.G.U.S. WIPES SERVERS AND DATABASES ALL OVER THE WORLD ONCE A DAY TO ENSURE OUR AGENTS CAN'T BE TRACED.
YEAH, BUT YOU GUYS DON'T WIPE YOUR OWN DATABASES...OR THE JUSTICE LEAGUE'S. I'M NOT AS DUMB AS YOU THINK I AM, YOU KNOW.
SO HOW DO WE GET CISCO BACK?
JLA
WHERE DID THIS BREACHER COME FROM, SIR? WE HAVEN'T HEARD ABOUT ANY CONTAINMENT OPS TONIGHT--?
UGLY SONNUVA POPPED IN AND STARTED TEARING UP THE GUARDIAN BUILDING DOWN-TOWN. WE BAGGED HIM BEFORE HE COULD DO ANY REAL DAMAGE.
NOW IF YOU WOULD, I'D LIKE TO BE IN BED BEFORE MIDNIGHT. SERGEANT.
UM, YES, SIR. SCANNING DATABASE...
VUMMMM
I...I DON'T KNOW THAT I CAN GET HIM BACK, DANTE...

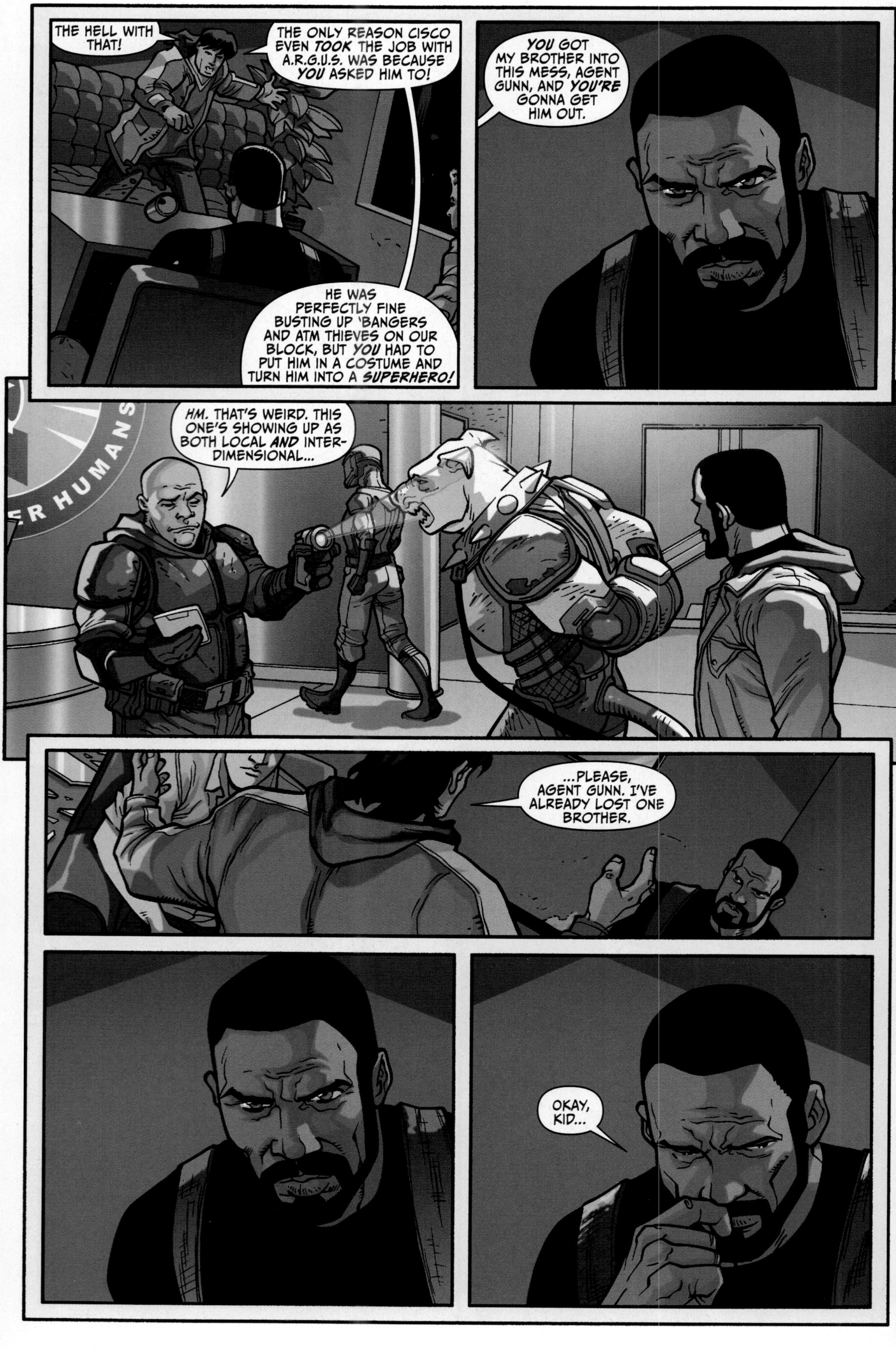
THE HELL WITH THAT!
THE ONLY REASON CISCO EVEN TOOK THE JOB WITH A.R.G.U.S. WAS BECAUSE YOU ASKED HIM TO!
HE WAS PERFECTLY FINE BUSTING UP 'BANGERS AND ATM THIEVES ON OUR BLOCK, BUT YOU HAD TO PUT HIM IN A COSTUME AND TURN HIM INTO A SUPERHERO!
YOU GOT MY BROTHER INTO THIS MESS, AGENT GUNN, AND YOU'RE GONNA GET HIM OUT.
HM. THAT'S WEIRD. THIS ONE'S SHOWING UP AS BOTH LOCAL AND INTER-DIMENSIONAL...
...PLEASE, AGENT GUNN. I'VE ALREADY LOST ONE BROTHER.
OKAY, KID...

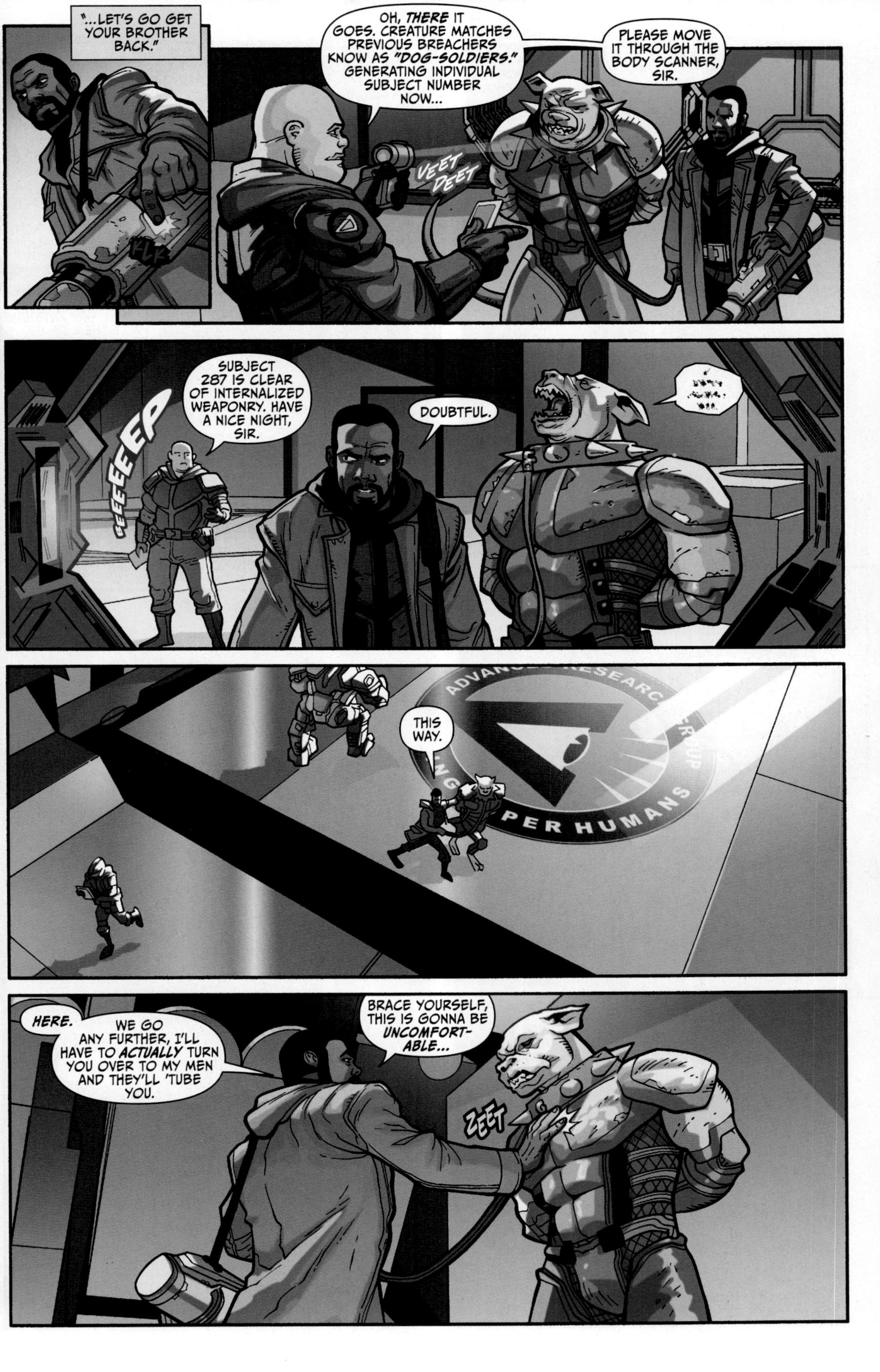
"...LET'S GO GET YOUR BROTHER BACK."
KLK
OH, THERE IT GOES. CREATURE MATCHES PREVIOUS BREACHERS KNOW AS "DOG-SOLDIERS." GENERATING INDIVIDUAL SUBJECT NUMBER NOW...
PLEASE MOVE IT THROUGH THE BODY SCANNER, SIR.
VEET DEET
SUBJECT 287 IS CLEAR OF INTERNALIZED WEAPONRY. HAVE A NICE NIGHT, SIR.
BEEEEEEP
DOUBTFUL.
ADVANCED RESEARCH GROUP
PER HUMANS
THIS WAY.
HERE.
WE GO ANY FURTHER, I'LL HAVE TO ACTUALLY TURN YOU OVER TO MY MEN AND THEY'LL 'TUBE YOU.
BRACE YOURSELF, THIS IS GONNA BE UNCOMFORT-ABLE...
ZEET

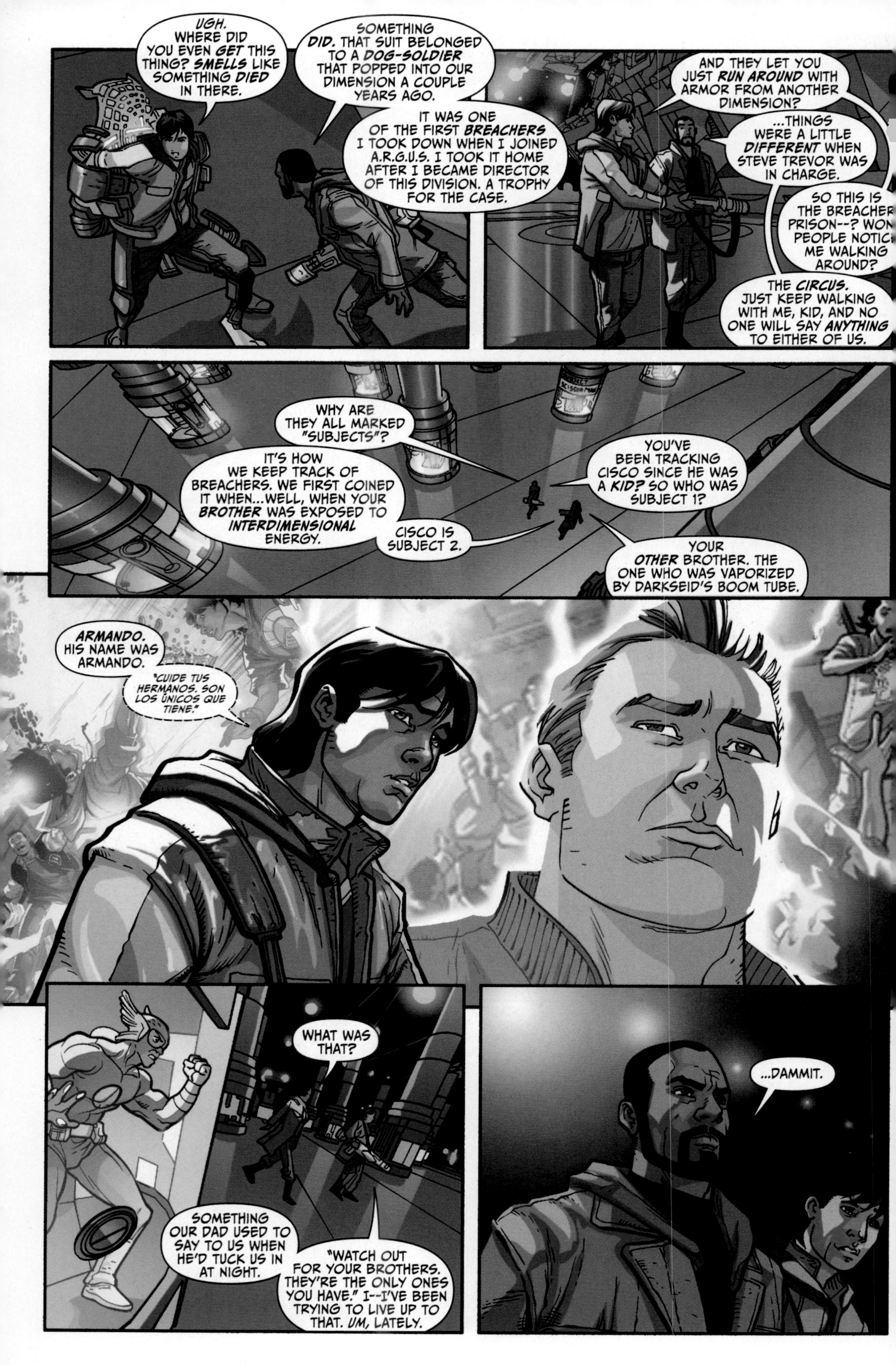

UGH. WHERE DID YOU EVEN GET THIS THING? SMELLS LIKE SOMETHING DIED IN THERE.
SOMETHING DID. THAT SUIT BELONGED TO A DOG-SOLDIER THAT POPPED INTO OUR DIMENSION A COUPLE YEARS AGO.
IT WAS ONE OF THE FIRST BREACHERS I TOOK DOWN WHEN I JOINED A.R.G.U.S. I TOOK IT HOME AFTER I BECAME DIRECTOR OF THIS DIVISION. A TROPHY FOR THE CASE.
AND THEY LET YOU JUST RUN AROUND WITH ARMOR FROM ANOTHER DIMENSION?
...THINGS WERE A LITTLE DIFFERENT WHEN STEVE TREVOR WAS IN CHARGE.
SO THIS IS THE BREACHER PRISON--? WON PEOPLE NOTIC ME WALKING AROUND?
THE CIRCUS. JUST KEEP WALKING WITH ME, KID, AND NO ONE WILL SAY ANYTHING TO EITHER OF US.
WHY ARE THEY ALL MARKED "SUBJECTS"?
IT'S HOW WE KEEP TRACK OF BREACHERS. WE FIRST COINED IT WHEN...WELL, WHEN YOUR BROTHER WAS EXPOSED TO INTERDIMENSIONAL ENERGY.
CISCO IS SUBJECT 2.
YOU'VE BEEN TRACKING CISCO SINCE HE WAS A KID? SO WHO WAS SUBJECT 1?
YOUR OTHER BROTHER. THE ONE WHO WAS VAPORIZED BY DARKSEID'S BOOM TUBE.
ARMANDO. HIS NAME WAS ARMANDO.
"CUIDE TUS HERMANOS. SON LOS ÚNICOS QUE TIENE."
WHAT WAS THAT?
SOMETHING OUR DAD USED TO SAY TO US WHEN HE'D TUCK US IN AT NIGHT.
"WATCH OUT FOR YOUR BROTHERS. THEY'RE THE ONLY ONES YOU HAVE." I--I'VE BEEN TRYING TO LIVE UP TO THAT. UM, LATELY.
...DAMMIT.

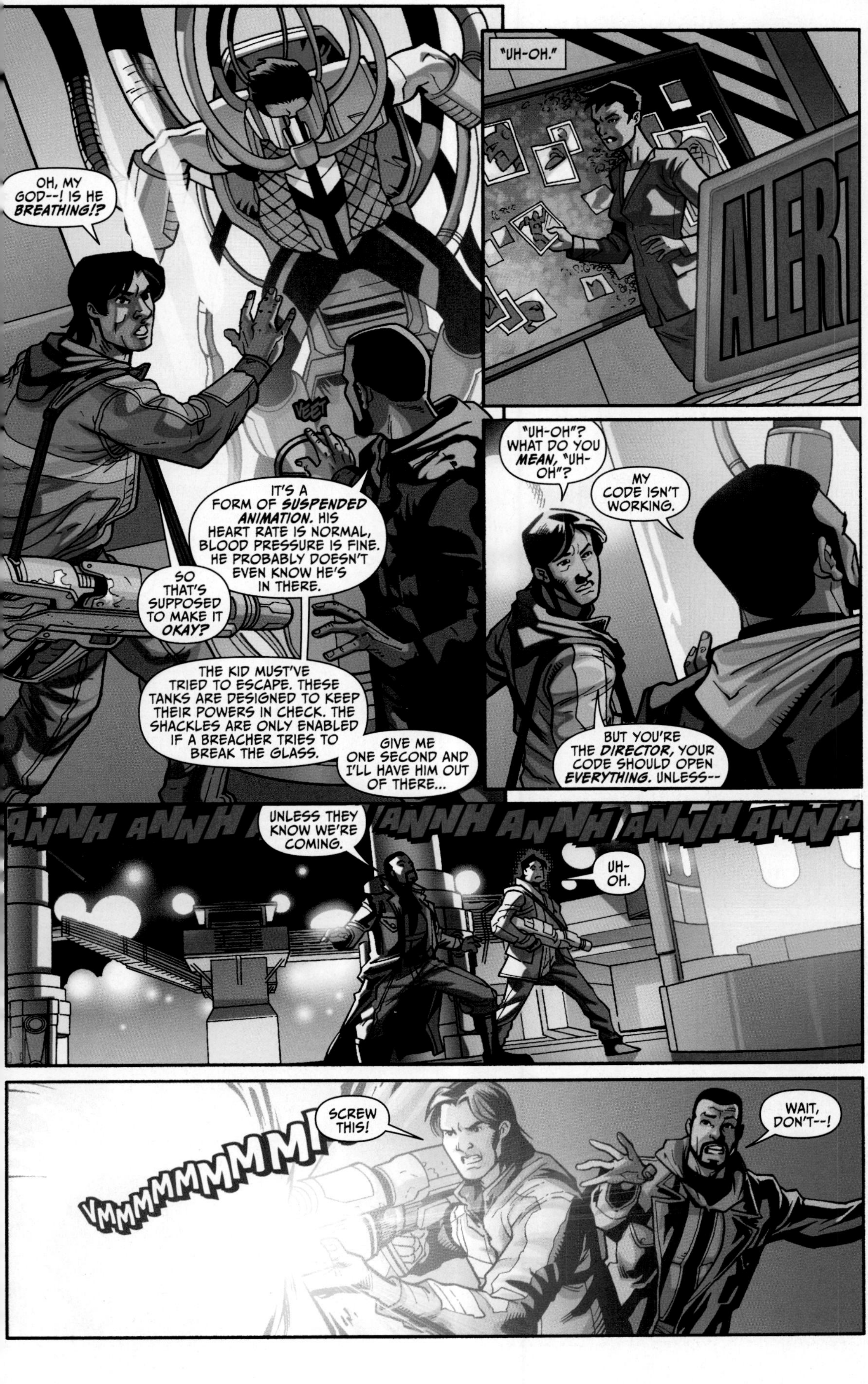

"UH-OH."
OH, MY GOD--! IS HE BREATHING!?
VEET
IT'S A FORM OF SUSPENDED ANIMATION. HIS HEART RATE IS NORMAL, BLOOD PRESSURE IS FINE. HE PROBABLY DOESN'T EVEN KNOW HE'S IN THERE.
SO THAT'S SUPPOSED TO MAKE IT OKAY?
THE KID MUST'VE TRIED TO ESCAPE. THESE TANKS ARE DESIGNED TO KEEP THEIR POWERS IN CHECK. THE SHACKLES ARE ONLY ENABLED IF A BREACHER TRIES TO BREAK THE GLASS.
GIVE ME ONE SECOND AND I'LL HAVE HIM OUT OF THERE...
"UH-OH"? WHAT DO YOU MEAN, "UH-OH"?
MY CODE ISN'T WORKING.
BUT YOU'RE THE DIRECTOR, YOUR CODE SHOULD OPEN EVERYTHING. UNLESS--
ANNH ANNH ANNH ANNH ANNH ANNH
UNLESS THEY KNOW WE'RE COMING.
UH-OH.
SCREW THIS!
VMMMMMMMMM!
WAIT, DON'T--!

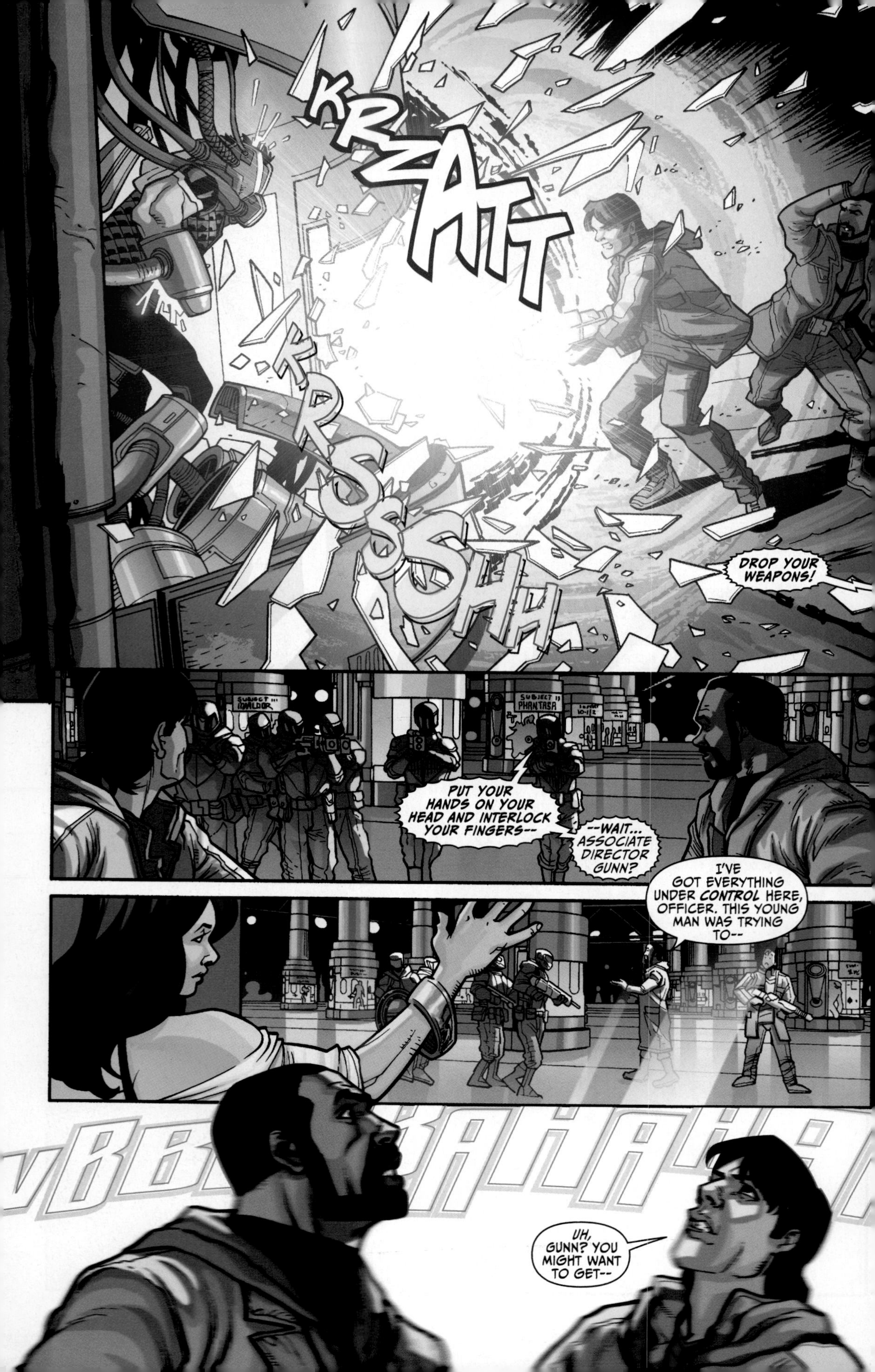
KRZATT
KRRSSSHH
DROP YOUR WEAPONS!
SUBJECT PHANTASA
PUT YOUR HANDS ON YOUR HEAD AND INTERLOCK YOUR FINGERS--
--WAIT... ASSOCIATE DIRECTOR GUNN?
I'VE GOT EVERYTHING UNDER CONTROL HERE, OFFICER. THIS YOUNG MAN WAS TRYING TO--
UH, GUNN? YOU MIGHT WANT TO GET--

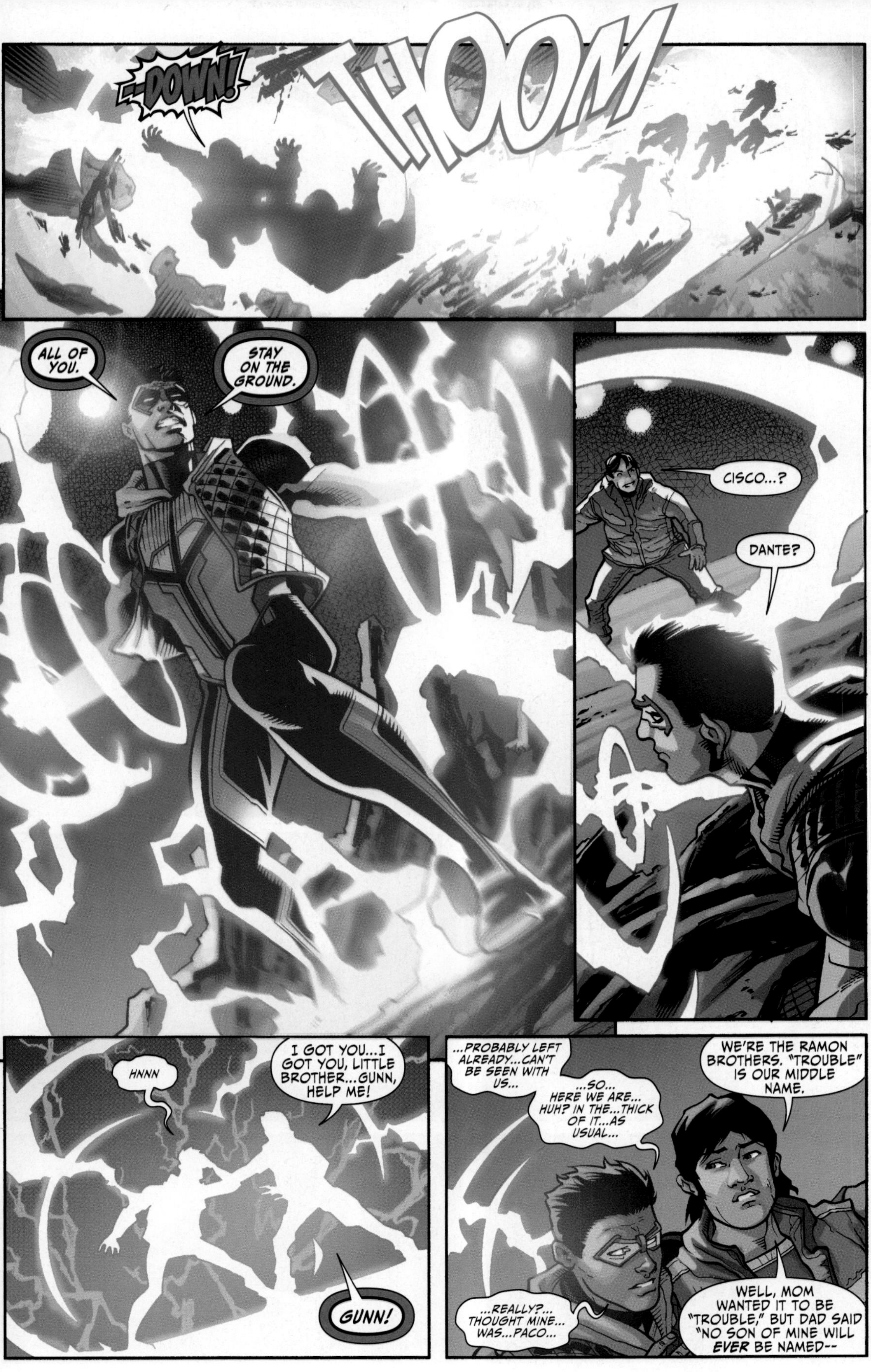
--DOWN!
THOOM
ALL OF YOU.
STAY ON THE GROUND.
CISCO...?
DANTE?
HNNN
I GOT YOU...I GOT YOU, LITTLE BROTHER...GUNN, HELP ME!
GUNN!
...PROBABLY LEFT ALREADY...CAN'T BE SEEN WITH US...
...SO... HERE WE ARE... HUH? IN THE...THICK OF IT...AS USUAL...
WE'RE THE RAMON BROTHERS. "TROUBLE" IS OUR MIDDLE NAME.
...REALLY?... THOUGHT MINE... WAS...PACO...
WELL, MOM WANTED IT TO BE "TROUBLE," BUT DAD SAID "NO SON OF MINE WILL EVER BE NAMED--

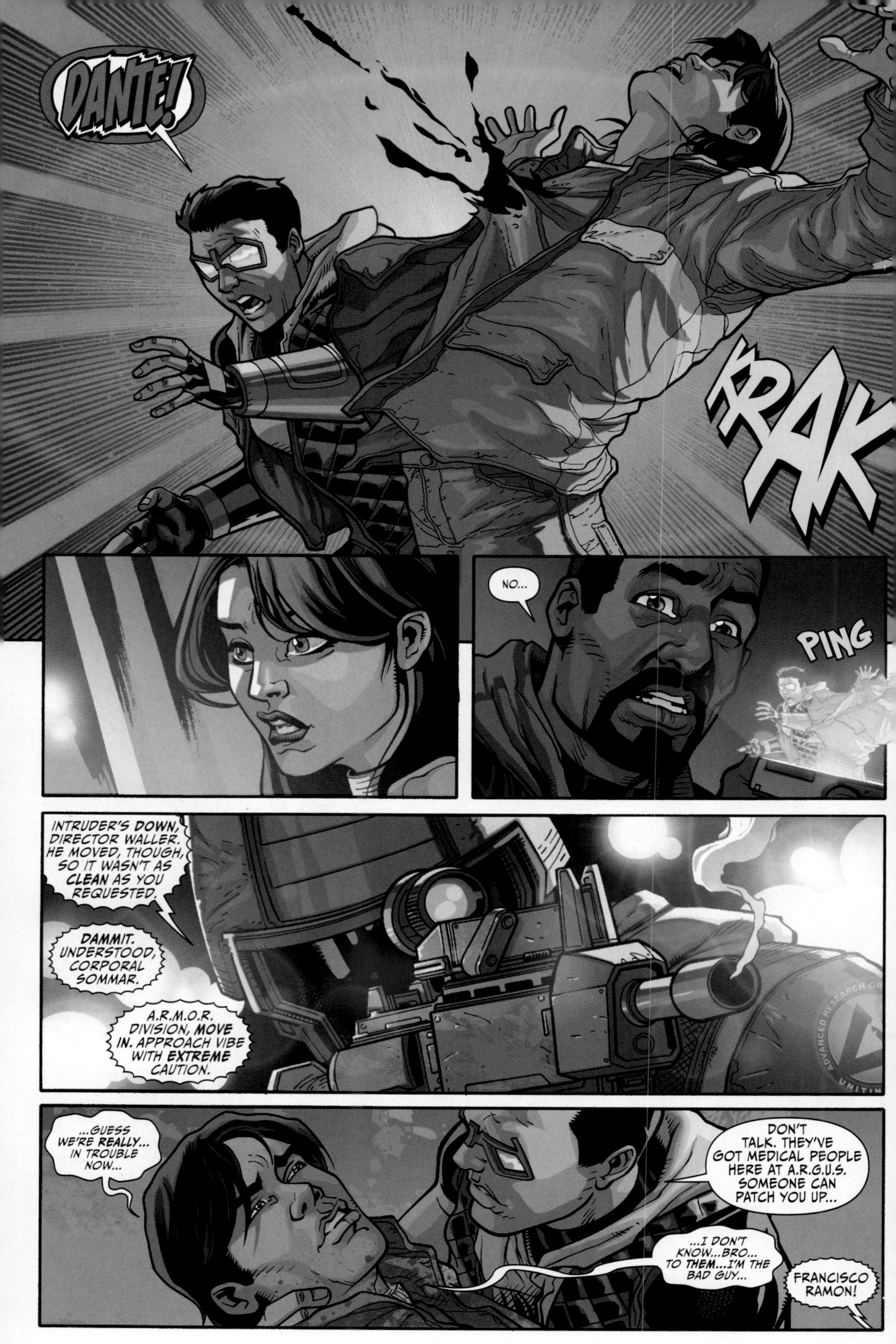
DANTE!
KRAK
NO...
PING
INTRUDER'S DOWN, DIRECTOR WALLER. HE MOVED, THOUGH, SO IT WASN'T AS CLEAN AS YOU REQUESTED.
DAMMIT. UNDERSTOOD, CORPORAL SOMMAR.
A.R.M.O.R. DIVISION, MOVE IN. APPROACH VIBE WITH EXTREME CAUTION.
...GUESS WE'RE REALLY... IN TROUBLE NOW...
DON'T TALK. THEY'VE GOT MEDICAL PEOPLE HERE AT A.R.G.U.S. SOMEONE CAN PATCH YOU UP...
...I DON'T KNOW...BRO... TO THEM...I'M THE BAD GUY...
FRANCISCO RAMON!

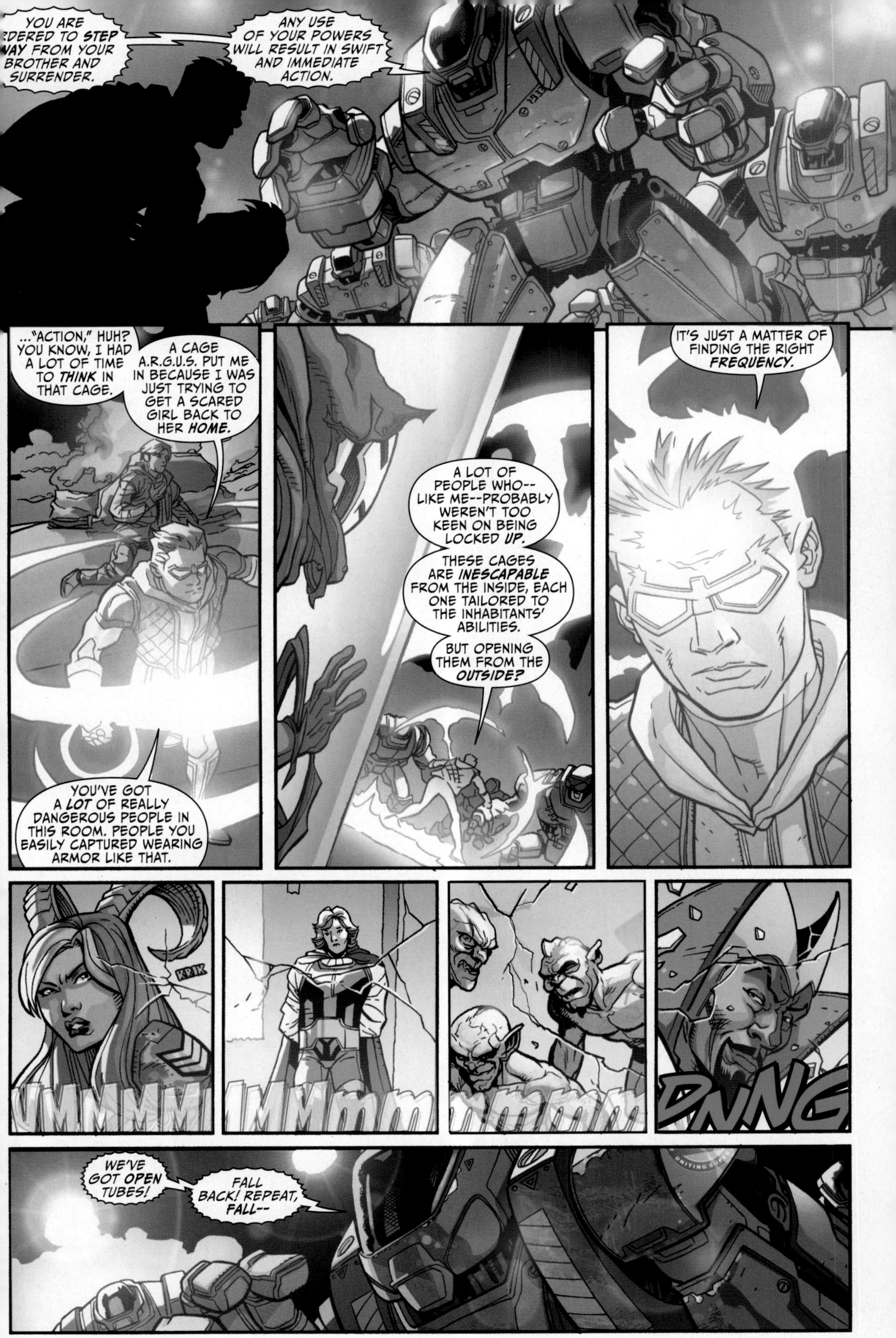

YOU ARE ...RDERED TO STEP ...WAY FROM YOUR BROTHER AND SURRENDER.
ANY USE OF YOUR POWERS WILL RESULT IN SWIFT AND IMMEDIATE ACTION.
..."ACTION," HUH? YOU KNOW, I HAD A LOT OF TIME TO THINK IN THAT CAGE.
A CAGE A.R.G.U.S. PUT ME IN BECAUSE I WAS JUST TRYING TO GET A SCARED GIRL BACK TO HER HOME.
YOU'VE GOT A LOT OF REALLY DANGEROUS PEOPLE IN THIS ROOM. PEOPLE YOU EASILY CAPTURED WEARING ARMOR LIKE THAT.
A LOT OF PEOPLE WHO-- LIKE ME--PROBABLY WEREN'T TOO KEEN ON BEING LOCKED UP.
THESE CAGES ARE INESCAPABLE FROM THE INSIDE, EACH ONE TAILORED TO THE INHABITANTS' ABILITIES.
BUT OPENING THEM FROM THE OUTSIDE?
IT'S JUST A MATTER OF FINDING THE RIGHT FREQUENCY.
KRIK
MMMMM
MMMMM
DNNG
WE'VE GOT OPEN TUBES!
FALL BACK! REPEAT, FALL--

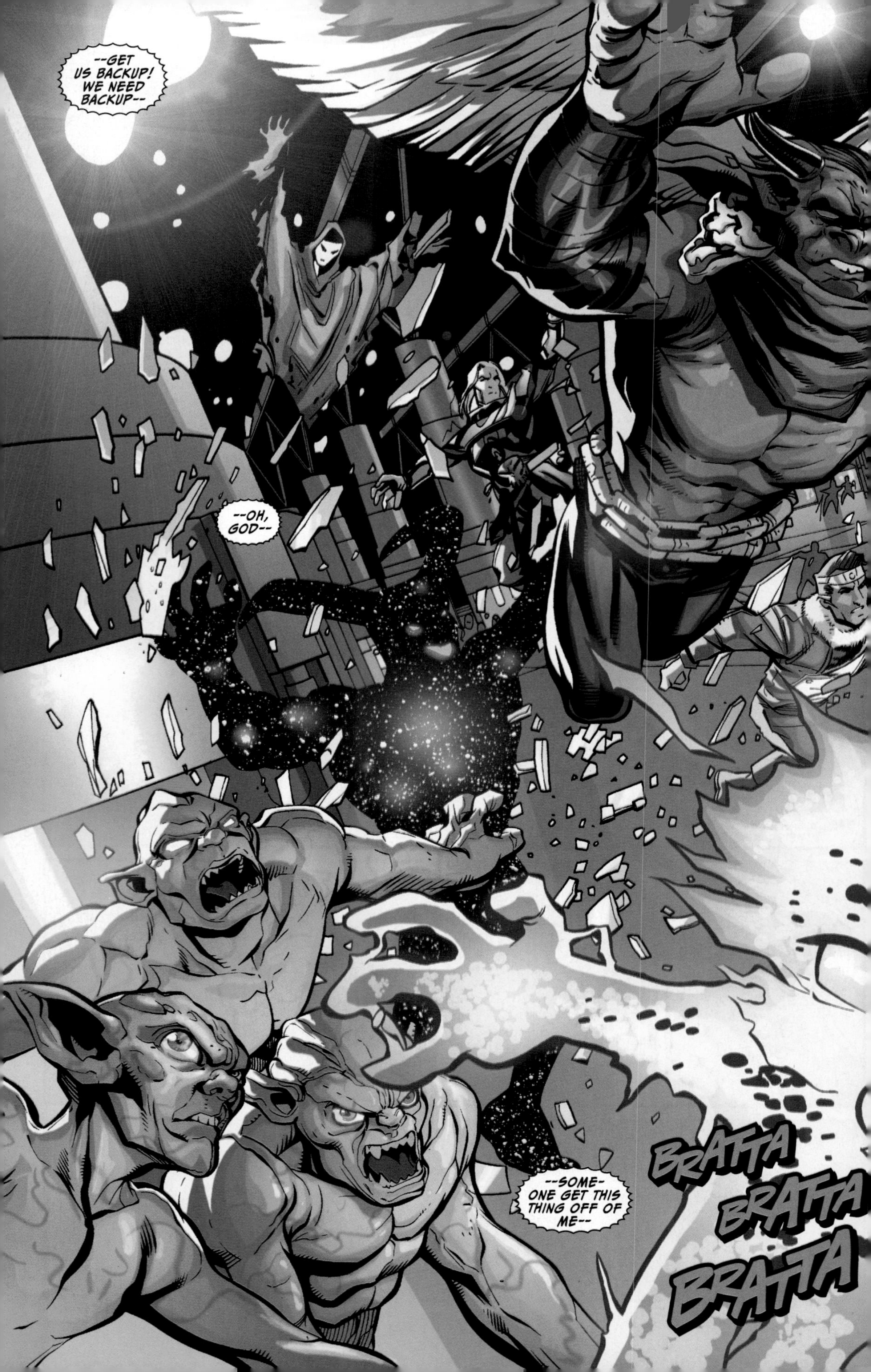
--GET US BACKUP! WE NEED BACKUP--
--OH, GOD--
--SOME-ONE GET THIS THING OFF OF ME--
BRATTA
BRATTA
BRATTA

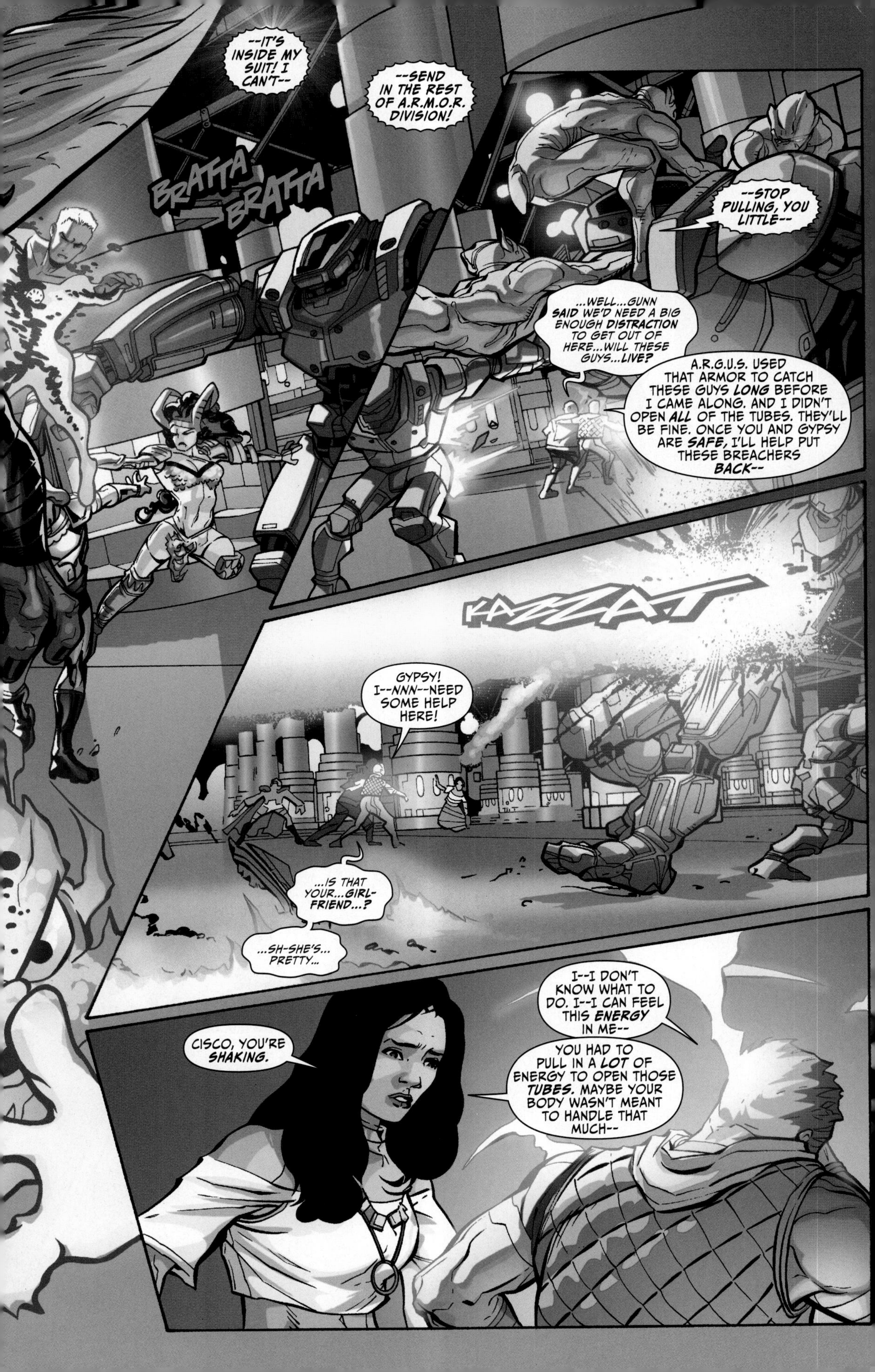
--IT'S INSIDE MY SUIT! I CAN'T--
--SEND IN THE REST OF A.R.M.O.R. DIVISION!
BRATTA BRATTA
--STOP PULLING, YOU LITTLE--
...WELL...GUNN SAID WE'D NEED A BIG ENOUGH DISTRACTION TO GET OUT OF HERE...WILL THESE GUYS...LIVE?
A.R.G.U.S. USED THAT ARMOR TO CATCH THESE GUYS LONG BEFORE I CAME ALONG. AND I DIDN'T OPEN ALL OF THE TUBES. THEY'LL BE FINE. ONCE YOU AND GYPSY ARE SAFE, I'LL HELP PUT THESE BREACHERS BACK--
KAZZAT
GYPSY! I--NNN--NEED SOME HELP HERE!
...IS THAT YOUR...GIRL-FRIEND...?
...SH-SHE'S... PRETTY...
CISCO, YOU'RE SHAKING.
I--I DON'T KNOW WHAT TO DO. I--I CAN FEEL THIS ENERGY IN ME--
YOU HAD TO PULL IN A LOT OF ENERGY TO OPEN THOSE TUBES. MAYBE YOUR BODY WASN'T MEANT TO HANDLE THAT MUCH--

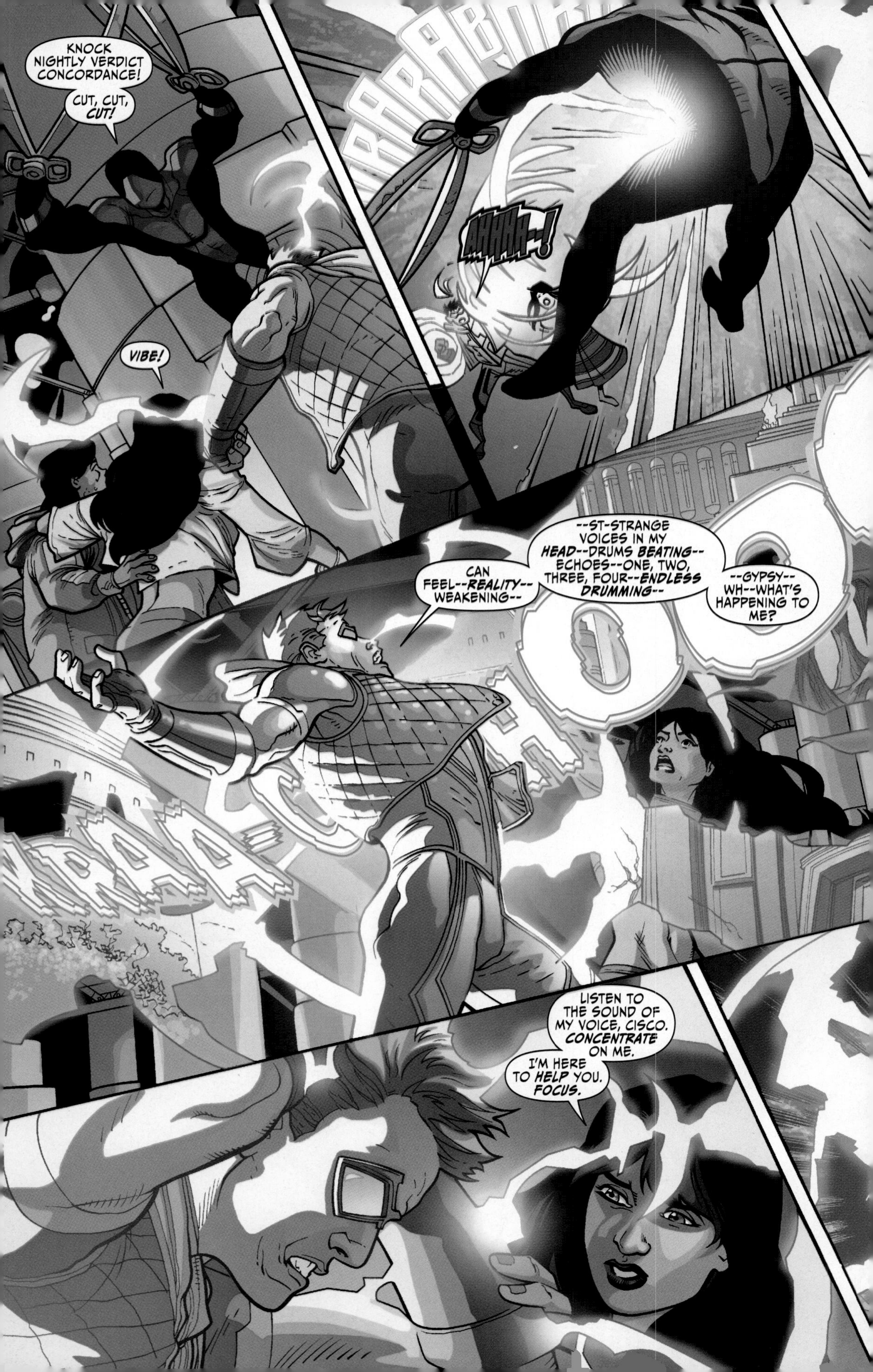

KNOCK NIGHTLY VERDICT CONCORDANCE!
CUT, CUT, CUT!
VIBE!
AHHHA--!
CAN FEEL--REALITY--WEAKENING--
--ST-STRANGE VOICES IN MY HEAD--DRUMS BEATING--ECHOES--ONE, TWO, THREE, FOUR--ENDLESS DRUMMING--
--GYPSY--WH--WHAT'S HAPPENING TO ME?
LISTEN TO THE SOUND OF MY VOICE, CISCO. CONCENTRATE ON ME.
I'M HERE TO HELP YOU. FOCUS.

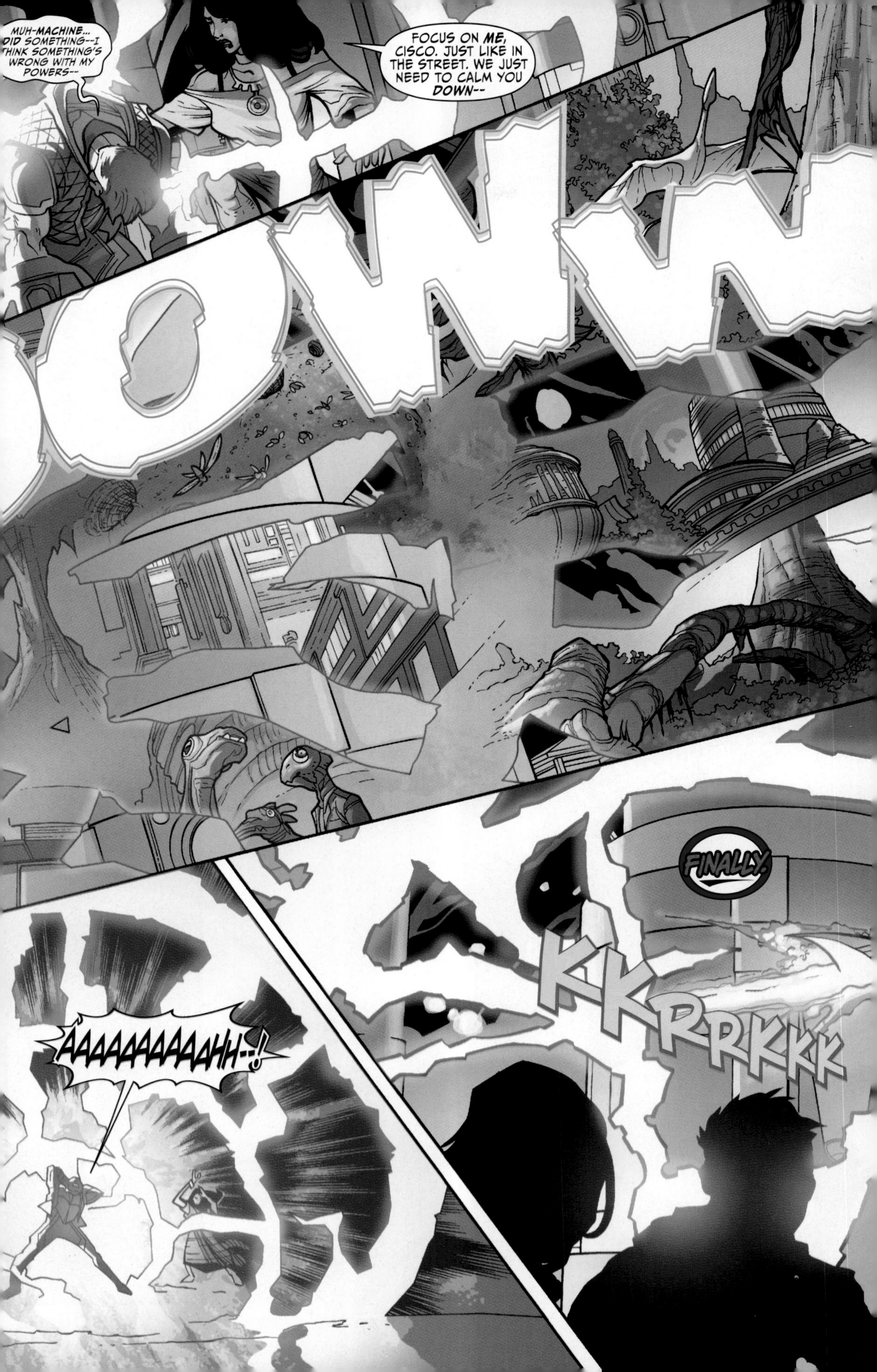
MUH-MACHINE... DID SOMETHING--I THINK SOMETHING'S WRONG WITH MY POWERS--
FOCUS ON ME, CISCO. JUST LIKE IN THE STREET. WE JUST NEED TO CALM YOU DOWN--
OWW
FINALLY.
AAAAAAAAAAHH--!
KKRRKKK

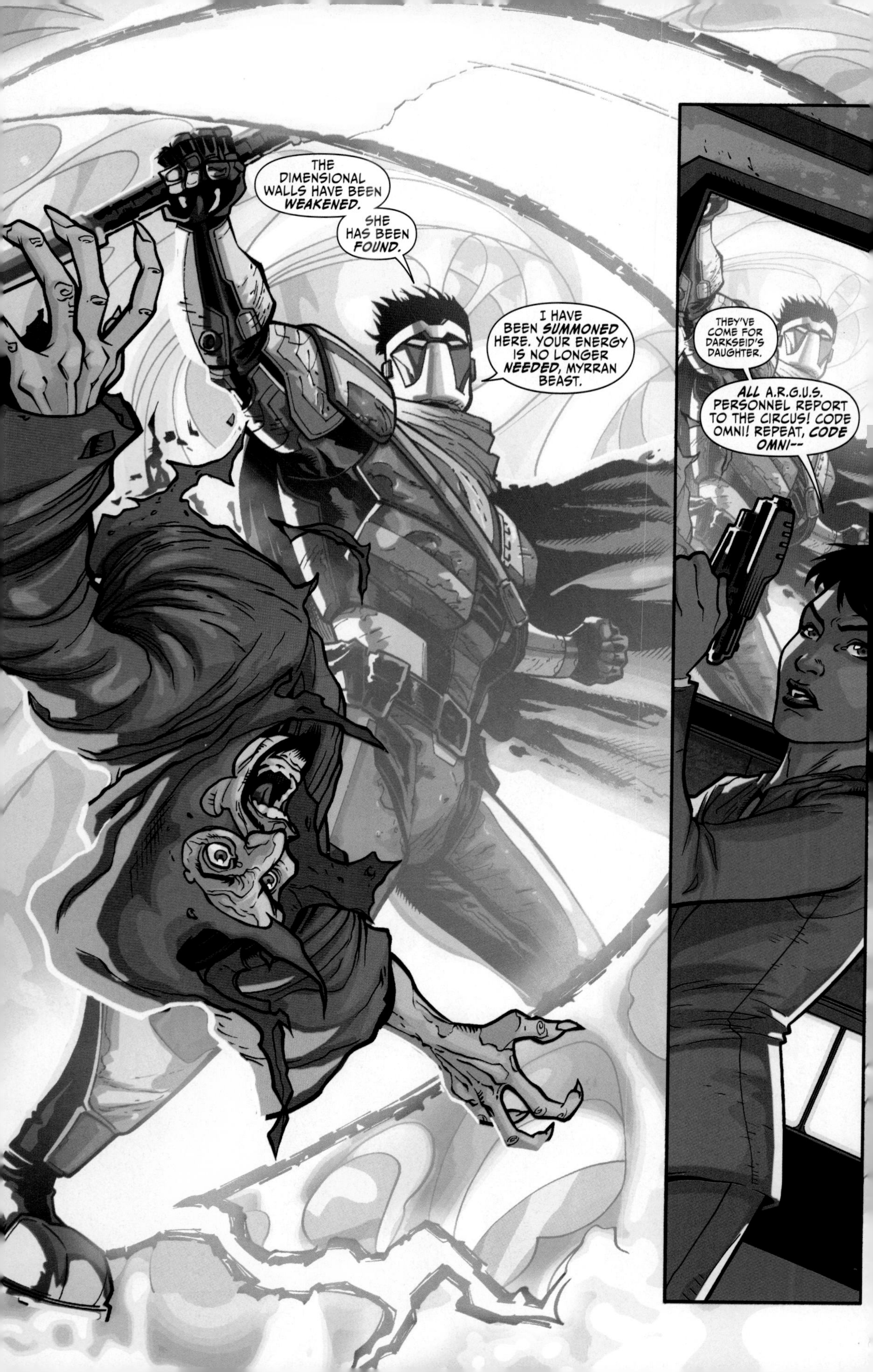
THE DIMENSIONAL WALLS HAVE BEEN WEAKENED.
SHE HAS BEEN FOUND.
I HAVE BEEN SUMMONED HERE. YOUR ENERGY IS NO LONGER NEEDED, MYRRAN BEAST.
THEY'VE COME FOR DARKSEID'S DAUGHTER.
ALL A.R.G.U.S. PERSONNEL REPORT TO THE CIRCUS! CODE OMNI! REPEAT, CODE OMNI--

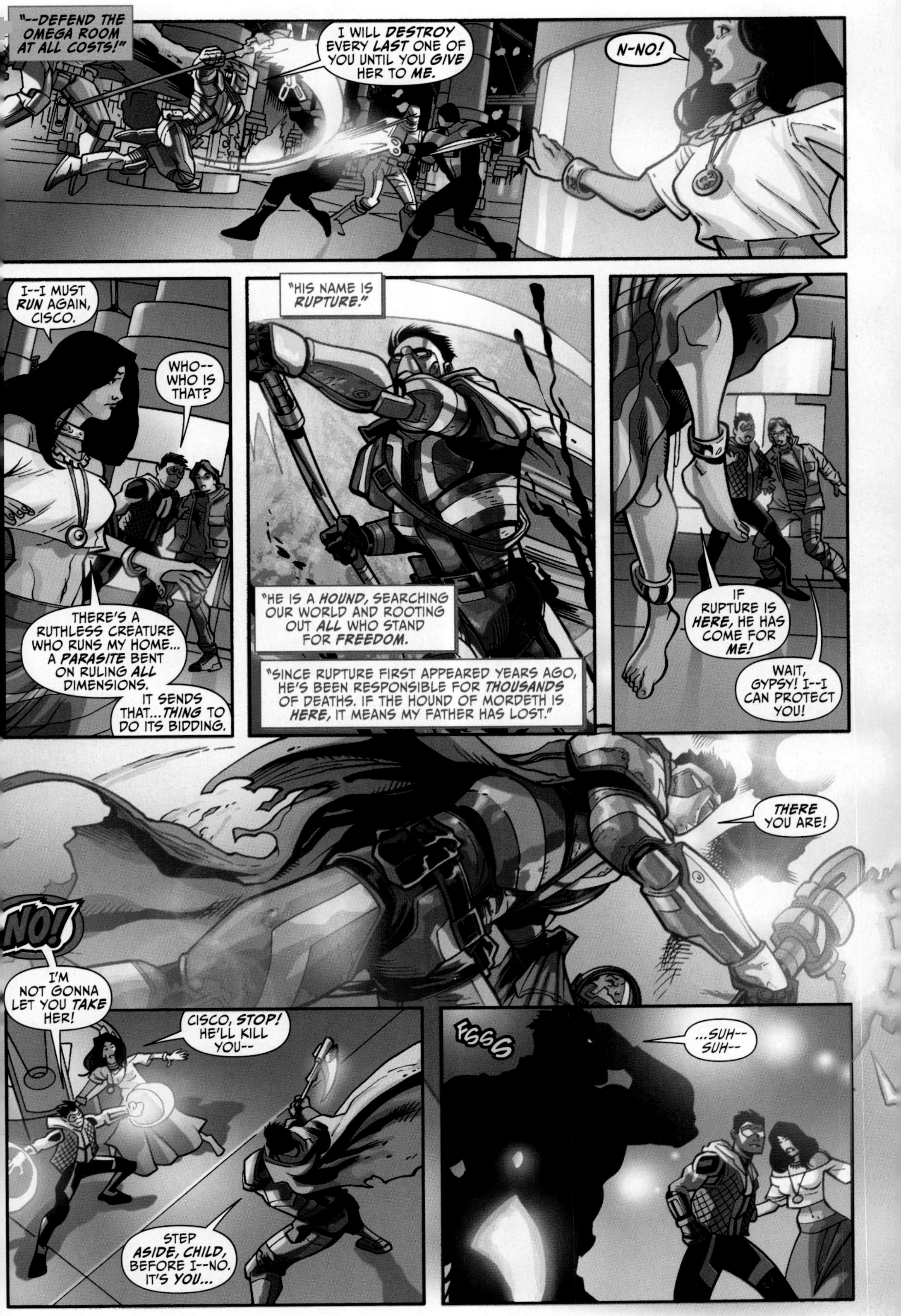
"--DEFEND THE OMEGA ROOM AT ALL COSTS!"
I WILL DESTROY EVERY LAST ONE OF YOU UNTIL YOU GIVE HER TO ME.
N-NO!
I--I MUST RUN AGAIN, CISCO.
WHO--WHO IS THAT?
THERE'S A RUTHLESS CREATURE WHO RUNS MY HOME... A PARASITE BENT ON RULING ALL DIMENSIONS.
IT SENDS THAT...THING TO DO ITS BIDDING.
"HIS NAME IS RUPTURE."
"HE IS A HOUND, SEARCHING OUR WORLD AND ROOTING OUT ALL WHO STAND FOR FREEDOM.
"SINCE RUPTURE FIRST APPEARED YEARS AGO, HE'S BEEN RESPONSIBLE FOR THOUSANDS OF DEATHS. IF THE HOUND OF MORDETH IS HERE, IT MEANS MY FATHER HAS LOST."
IF RUPTURE IS HERE, HE HAS COME FOR ME!
WAIT, GYPSY! I--I CAN PROTECT YOU!
THERE YOU ARE!
NO!
I'M NOT GONNA LET YOU TAKE HER!
CISCO, STOP! HE'LL KILL YOU--
STEP ASIDE, CHILD, BEFORE I--NO. IT'S YOU...
FSSS
...SUH--SUH--

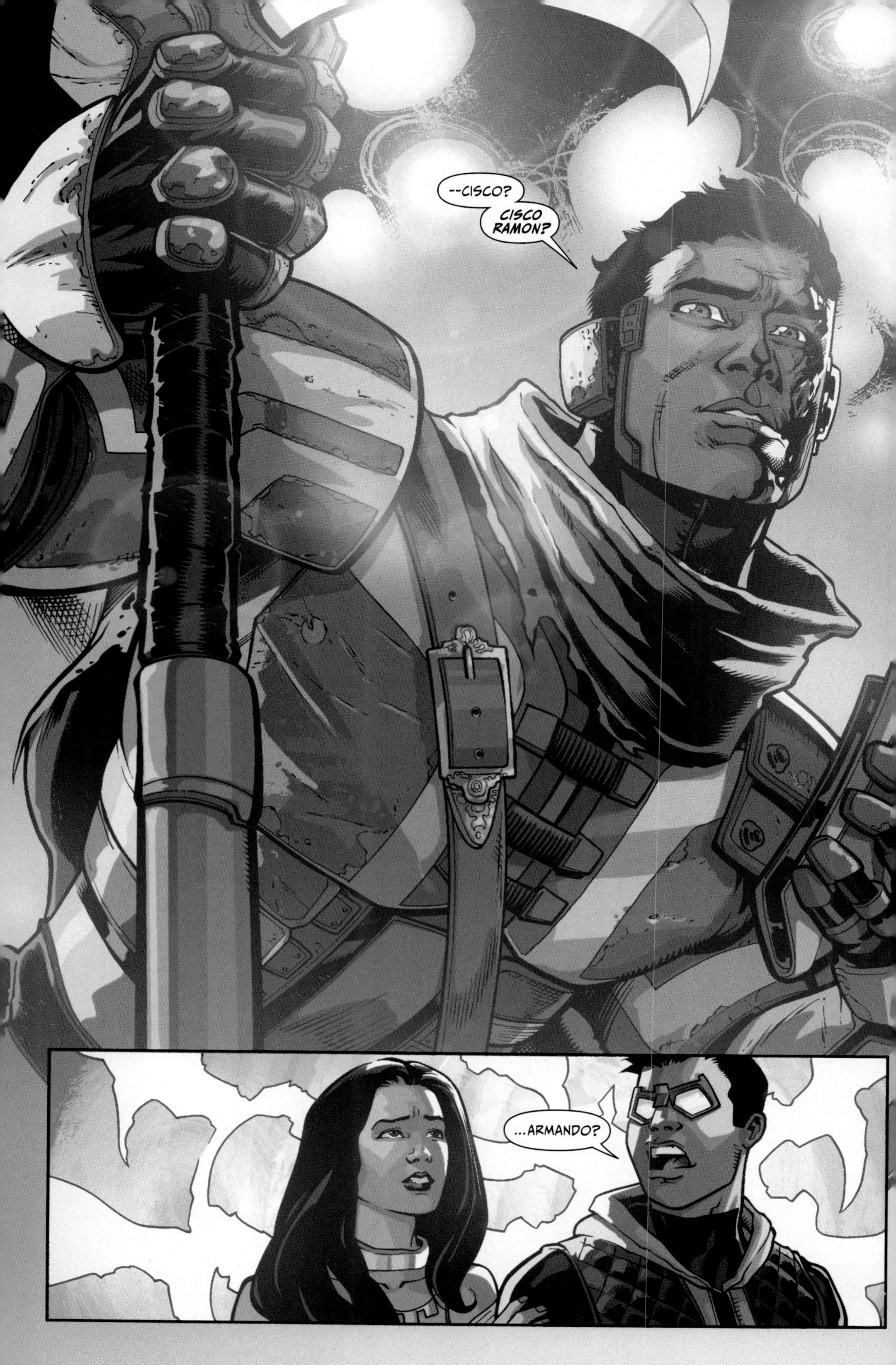
--CISCO?
CISCO RAMON?
...ARMANDO?

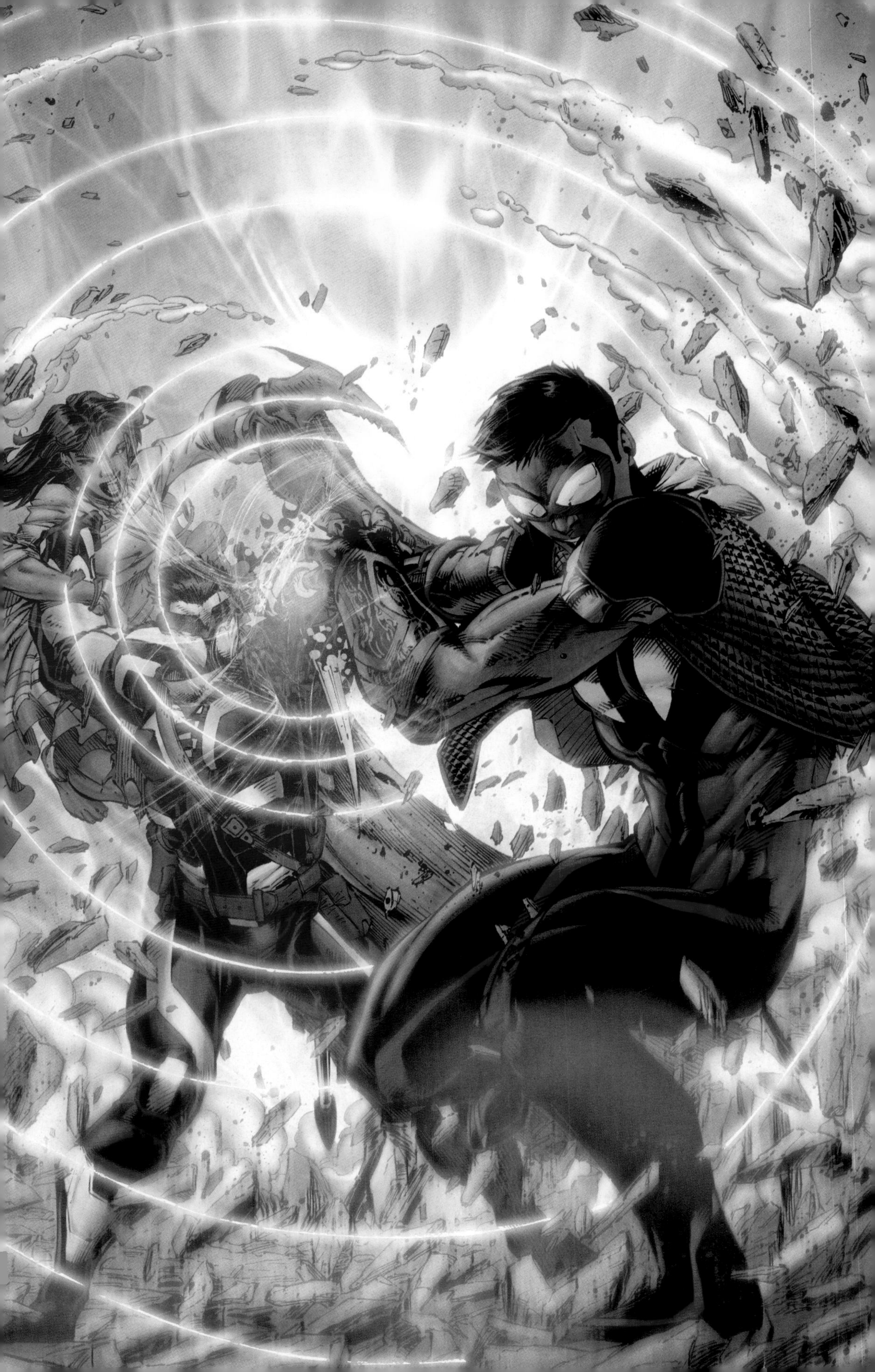

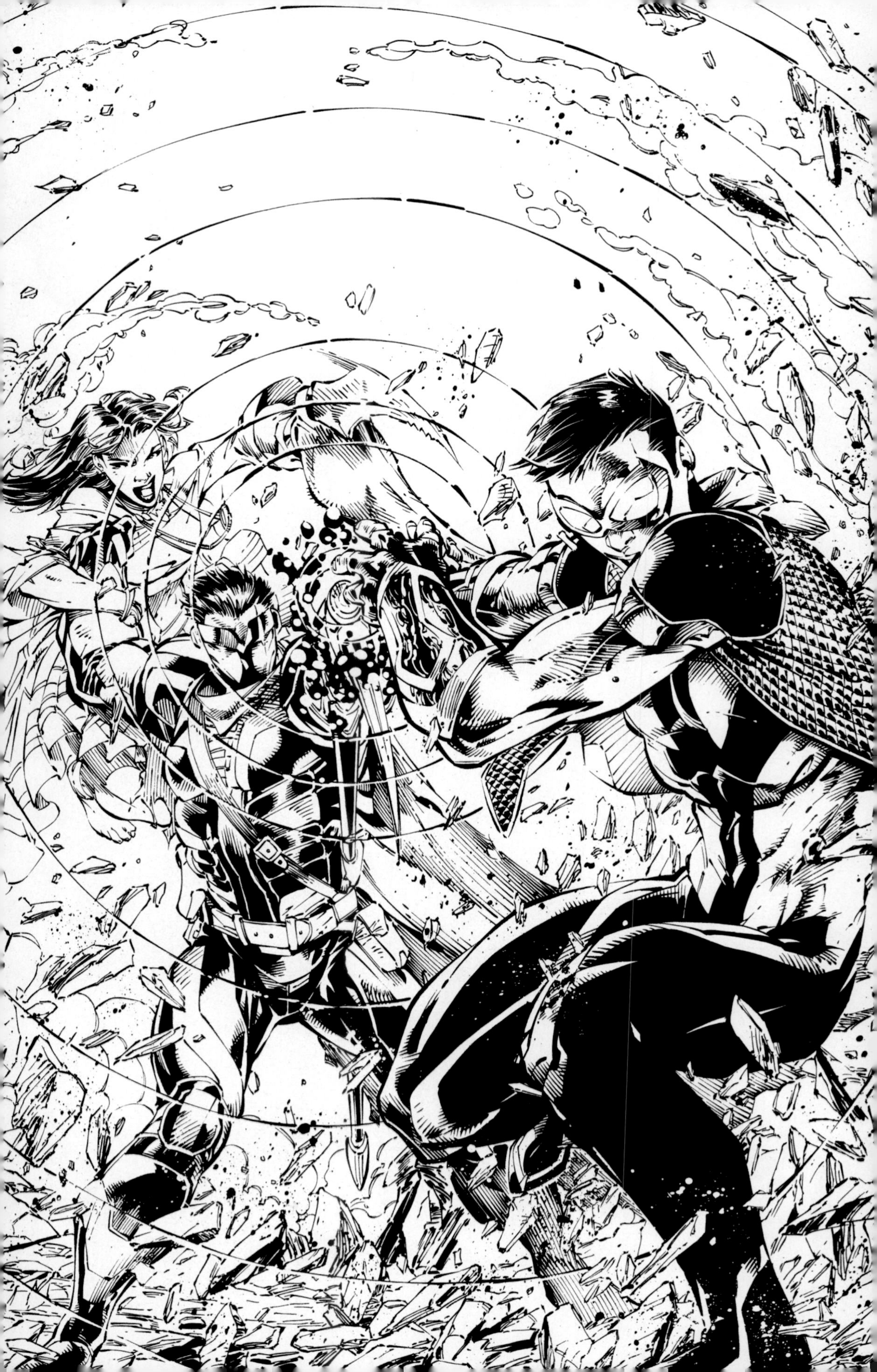

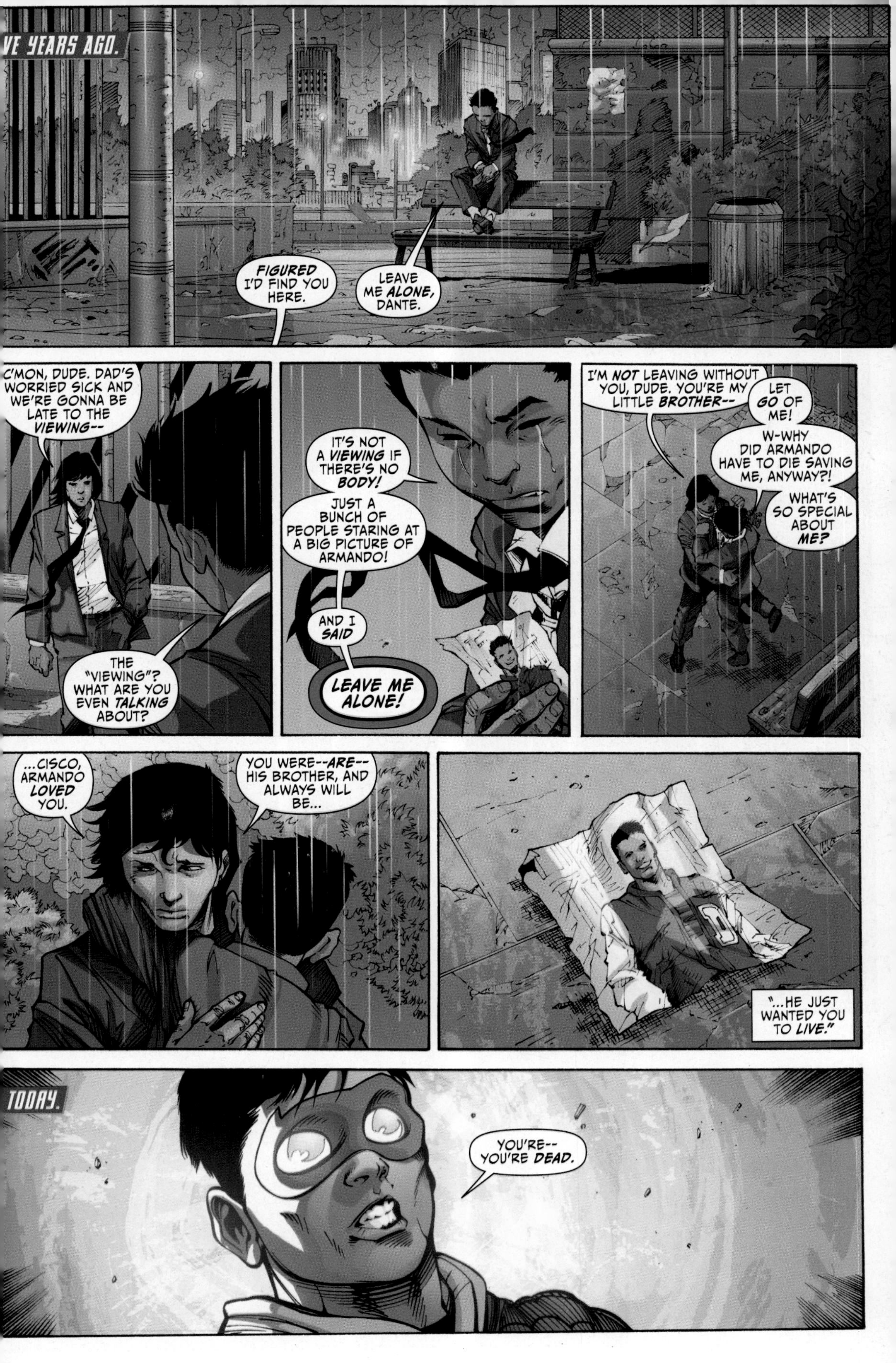
VE YEARS AGO.
FIGURED I'D FIND YOU HERE.
LEAVE ME ALONE, DANTE.
C'MON, DUDE. DAD'S WORRIED SICK AND WE'RE GONNA BE LATE TO THE VIEWING--
THE "VIEWING"? WHAT ARE YOU EVEN TALKING ABOUT?
IT'S NOT A VIEWING IF THERE'S NO BODY!
JUST A BUNCH OF PEOPLE STARING AT A BIG PICTURE OF ARMANDO!
AND I SAID
LEAVE ME ALONE!
I'M NOT LEAVING WITHOUT YOU, DUDE. YOU'RE MY LITTLE BROTHER--
LET GO OF ME!
W-WHY DID ARMANDO HAVE TO DIE SAVING ME, ANYWAY?!
WHAT'S SO SPECIAL ABOUT ME?
...CISCO, ARMANDO LOVED YOU.
YOU WERE--ARE--HIS BROTHER, AND ALWAYS WILL BE...
"...HE JUST WANTED YOU TO LIVE."
TODAY.
YOU'RE--YOU'RE DEAD.

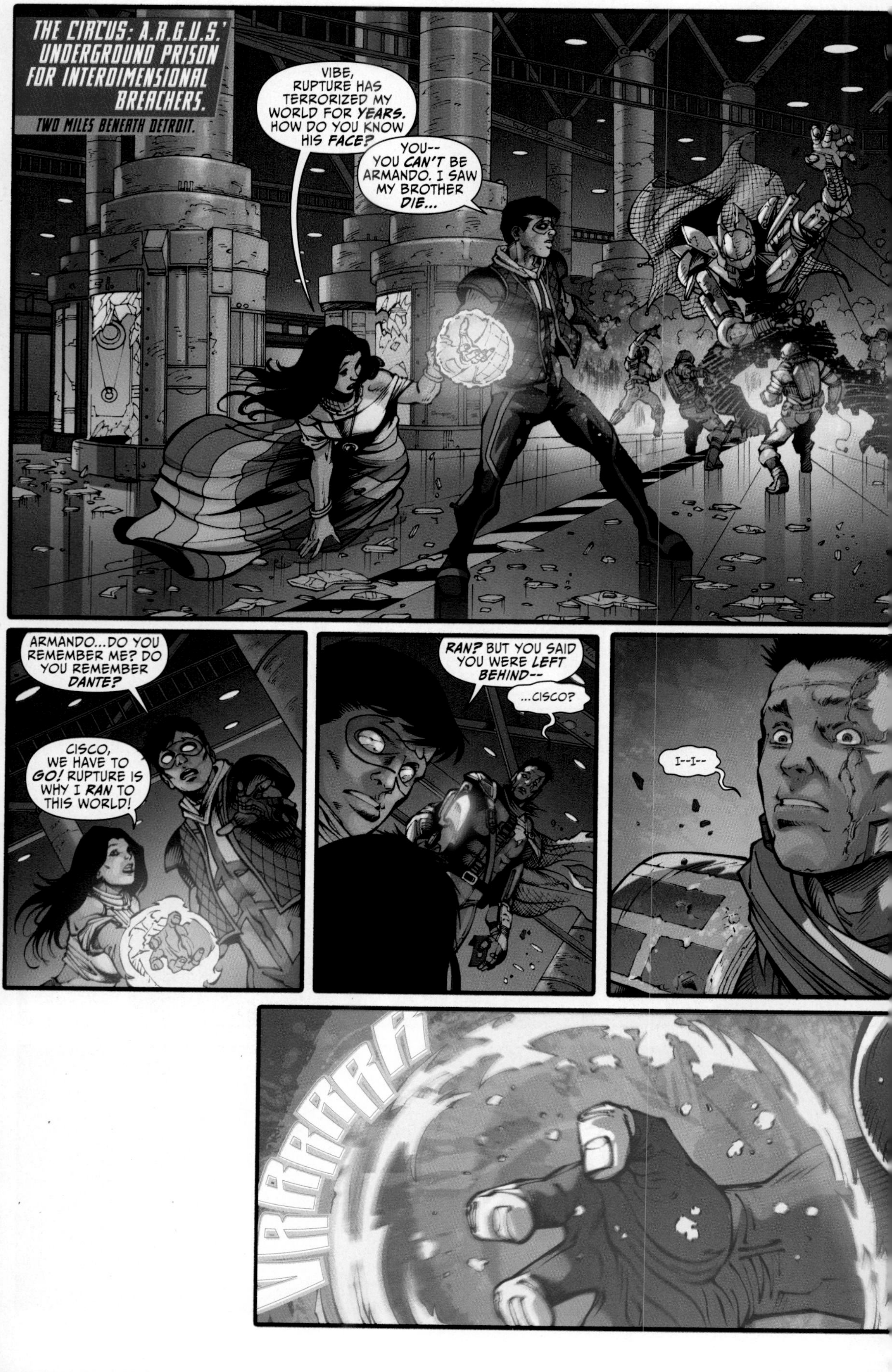
THE CIRCUS: A.R.G.U.S.' UNDERGROUND PRISON FOR INTERDIMENSIONAL BREACHERS.
TWO MILES BENEATH DETROIT.
VIBE, RUPTURE HAS TERRORIZED MY WORLD FOR YEARS. HOW DO YOU KNOW HIS FACE?
YOU-- YOU CAN'T BE ARMANDO. I SAW MY BROTHER DIE...
ARMANDO...DO YOU REMEMBER ME? DO YOU REMEMBER DANTE?
CISCO, WE HAVE TO GO! RUPTURE IS WHY I RAN TO THIS WORLD!
RAN? BUT YOU SAID YOU WERE LEFT BEHIND--
...CISCO?
I--I--
VRRRRRA

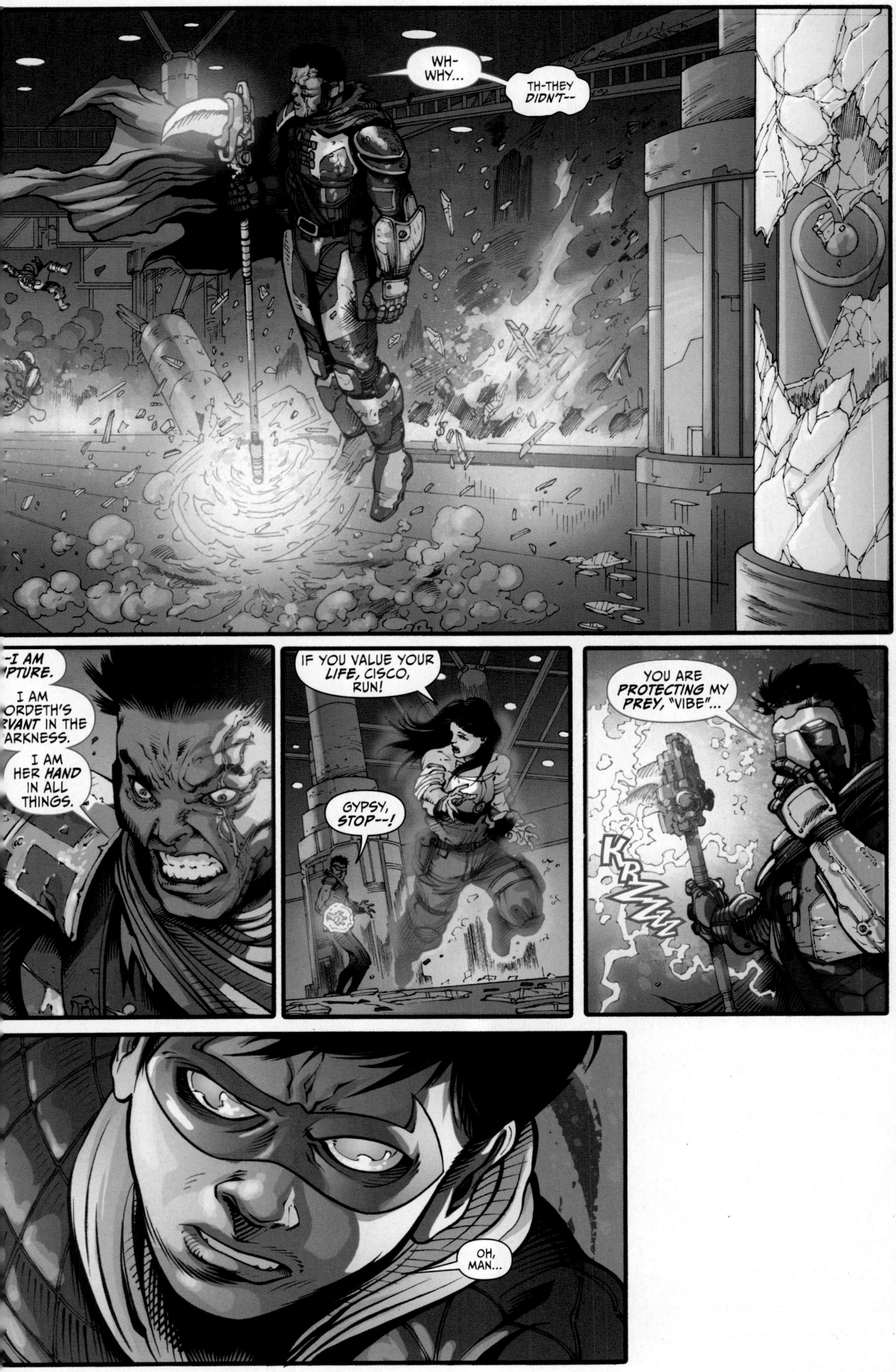

WH- WHY...
TH-THEY DIDN'T--
--I AM PTURE.
I AM ORDETH'S RVANT IN THE ARKNESS.
I AM HER HAND IN ALL THINGS.
IF YOU VALUE YOUR LIFE, CISCO, RUN!
GYPSY, STOP--!
YOU ARE PROTECTING MY PREY, "VIBE"...
KRZZZZ
OH, MAN...

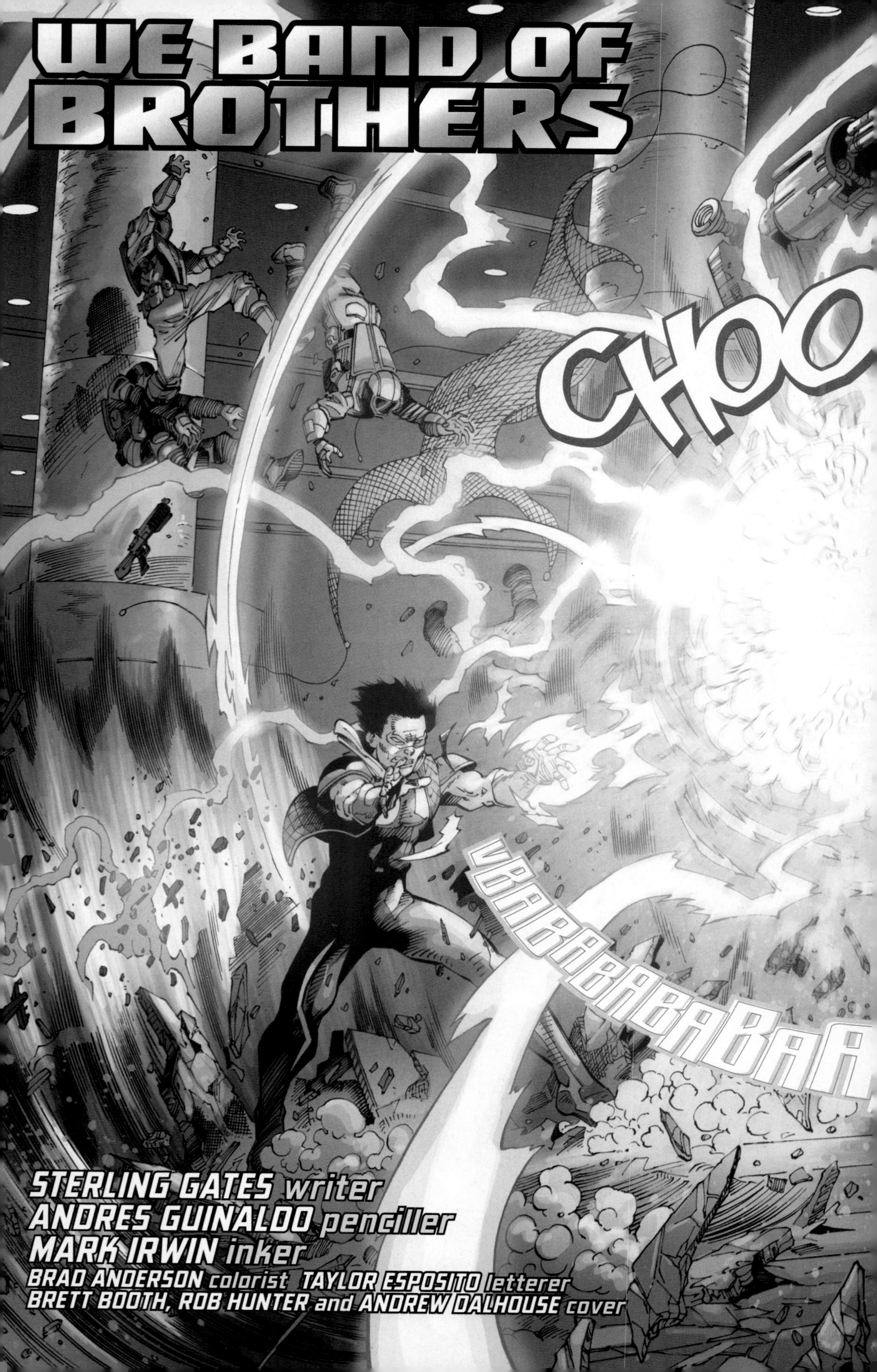
WE BAND OF BROTHERS
CHOOO
VBRRBBABABABAA
STERLING GATES writer
ANDRES GUINALDO penciller
MARK IRWIN inker
BRAD ANDERSON colorist TAYLOR ESPOSITO letterer
BRETT BOOTH, ROB HUNTER and ANDREW DALHOUSE cover

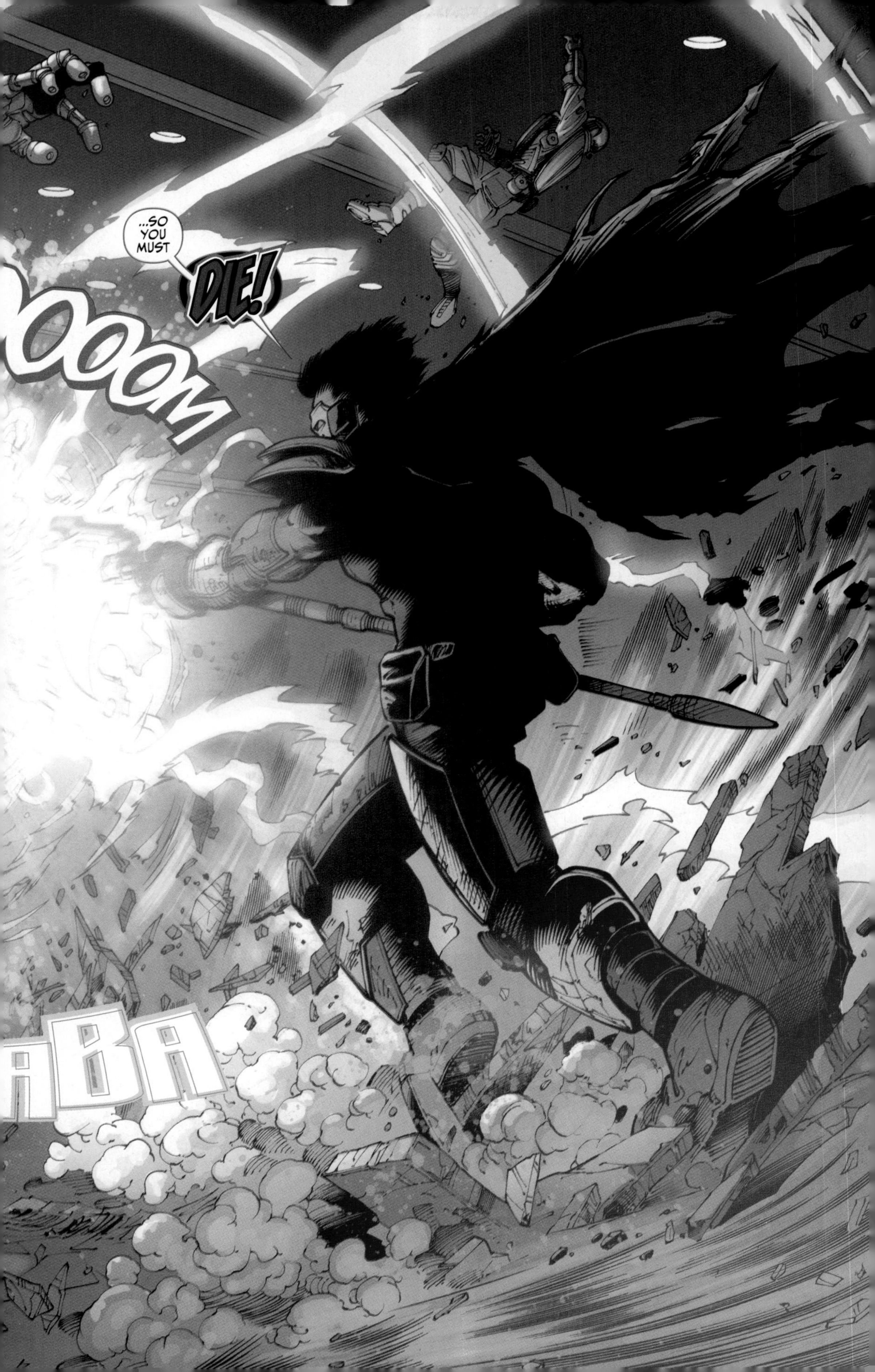

...SO YOU MUST
DIE!
OOOM
BA

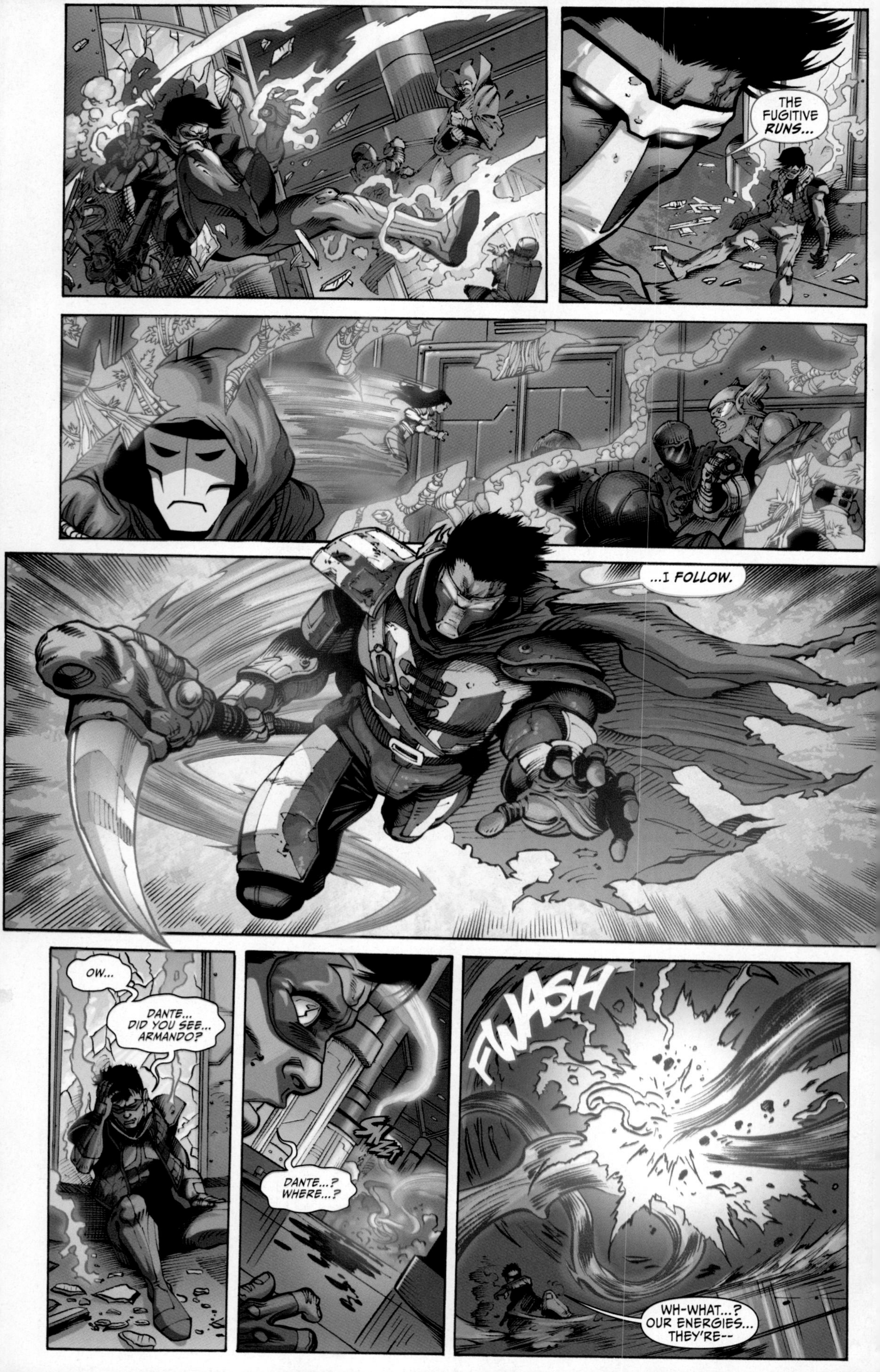

THE FUGITIVE RUNS...
...I FOLLOW.
OW...
DANTE... DID YOU SEE... ARMANDO?
DANTE...? WHERE...?
FWASH
WH-WHAT...? OUR ENERGIES... THEY'RE--

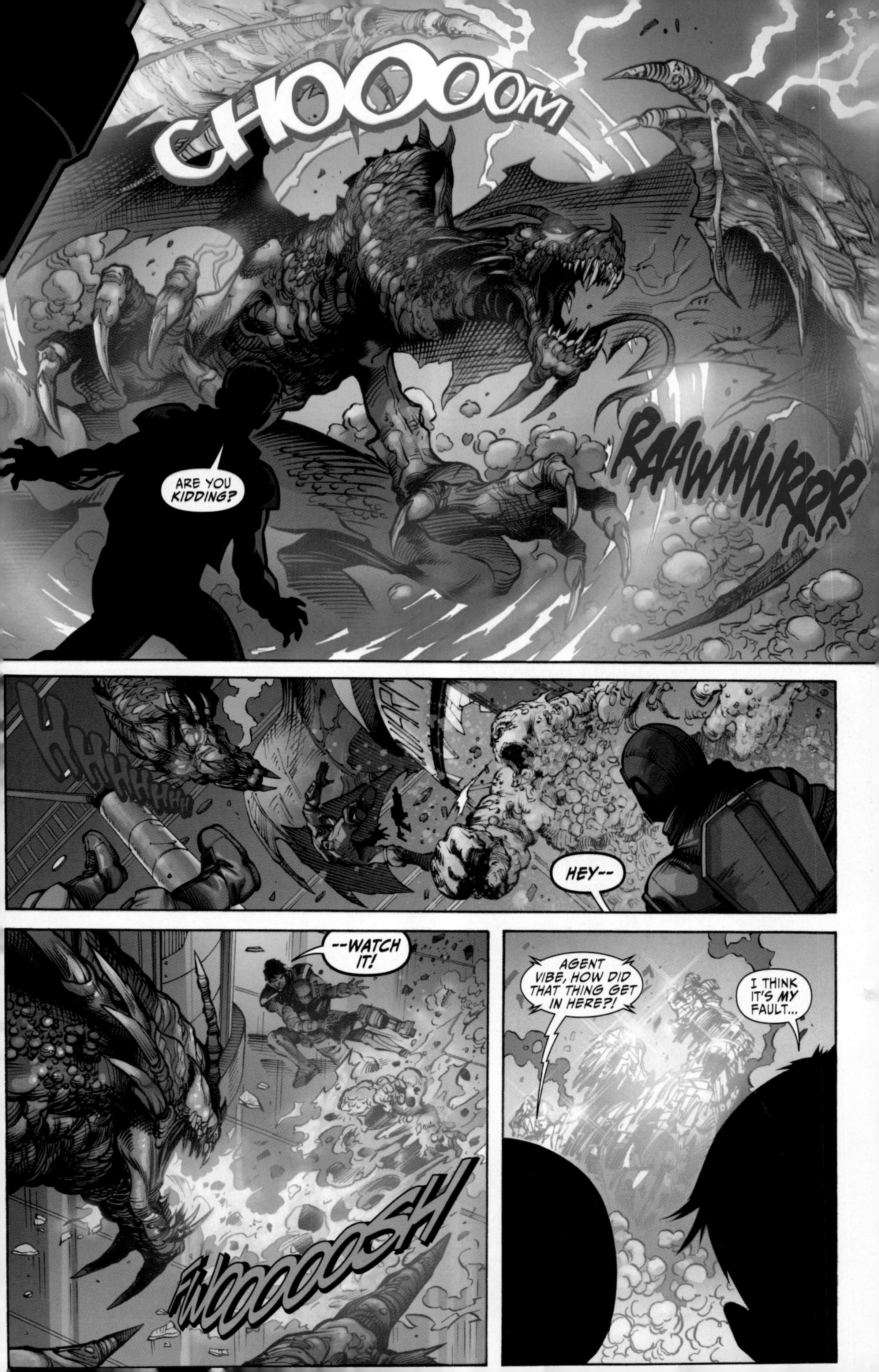
CHOOOOOM
ARE YOU KIDDING?
RAAWWWRRR
HEY--
--WATCH IT!
FWOOOOOSH
AGENT VIBE, HOW DID THAT THING GET IN HERE?!
I THINK IT'S MY FAULT...

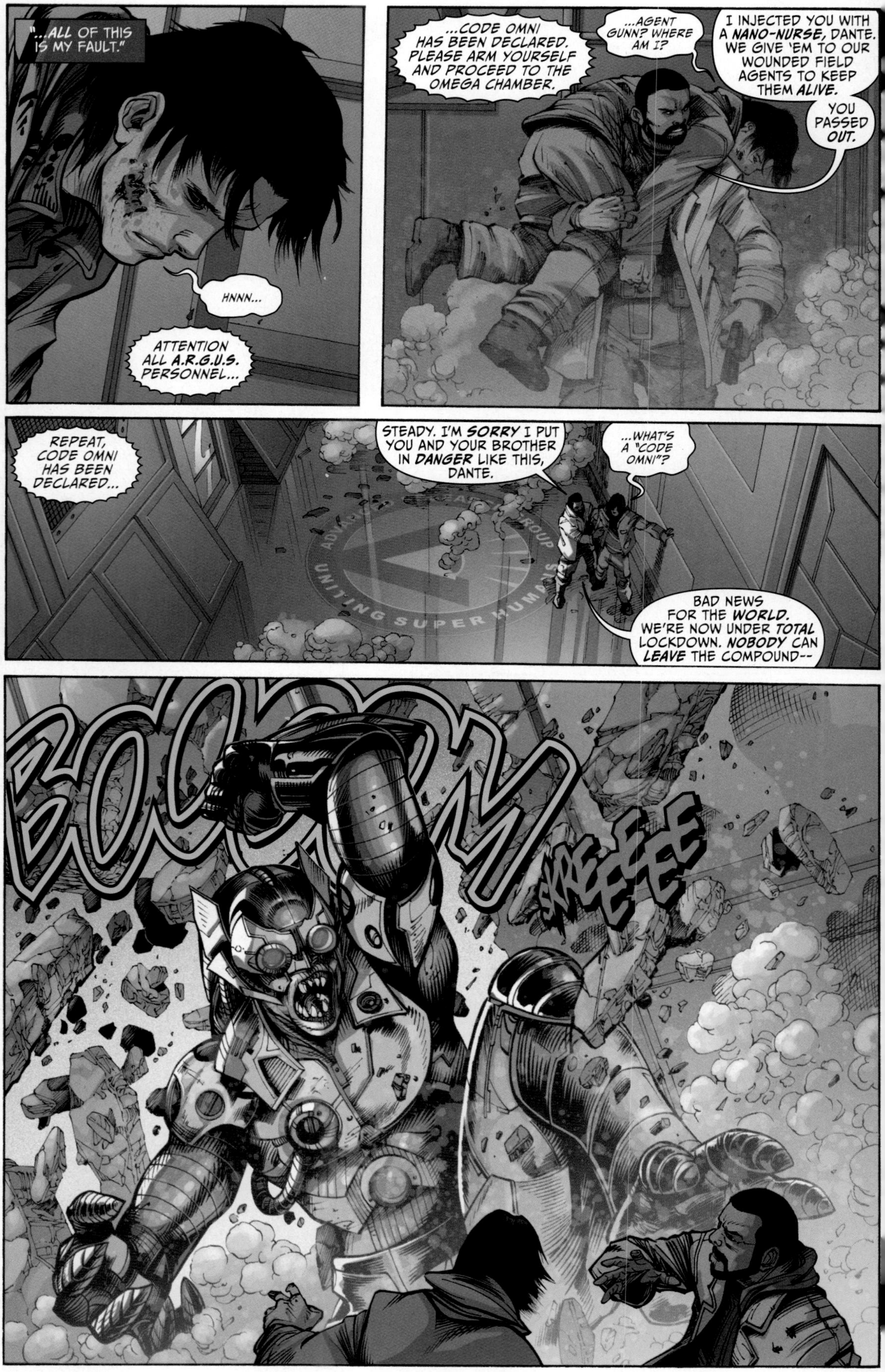
"...ALL OF THIS IS MY FAULT."
HNNN...
ATTENTION ALL A.R.G.U.S. PERSONNEL...
...CODE OMNI HAS BEEN DECLARED. PLEASE ARM YOURSELF AND PROCEED TO THE OMEGA CHAMBER.
...AGENT GUNN? WHERE AM I?
I INJECTED YOU WITH A NANO-NURSE, DANTE. WE GIVE 'EM TO OUR WOUNDED FIELD AGENTS TO KEEP THEM ALIVE.
YOU PASSED OUT.
REPEAT, CODE OMNI HAS BEEN DECLARED...
STEADY. I'M SORRY I PUT YOU AND YOUR BROTHER IN DANGER LIKE THIS, DANTE.
...WHAT'S A "CODE OMNI"?
UNITING SUPERHUMANS
BAD NEWS FOR THE WORLD. WE'RE NOW UNDER TOTAL LOCKDOWN. NOBODY CAN LEAVE THE COMPOUND--
BOOOOM
SKREEEEE

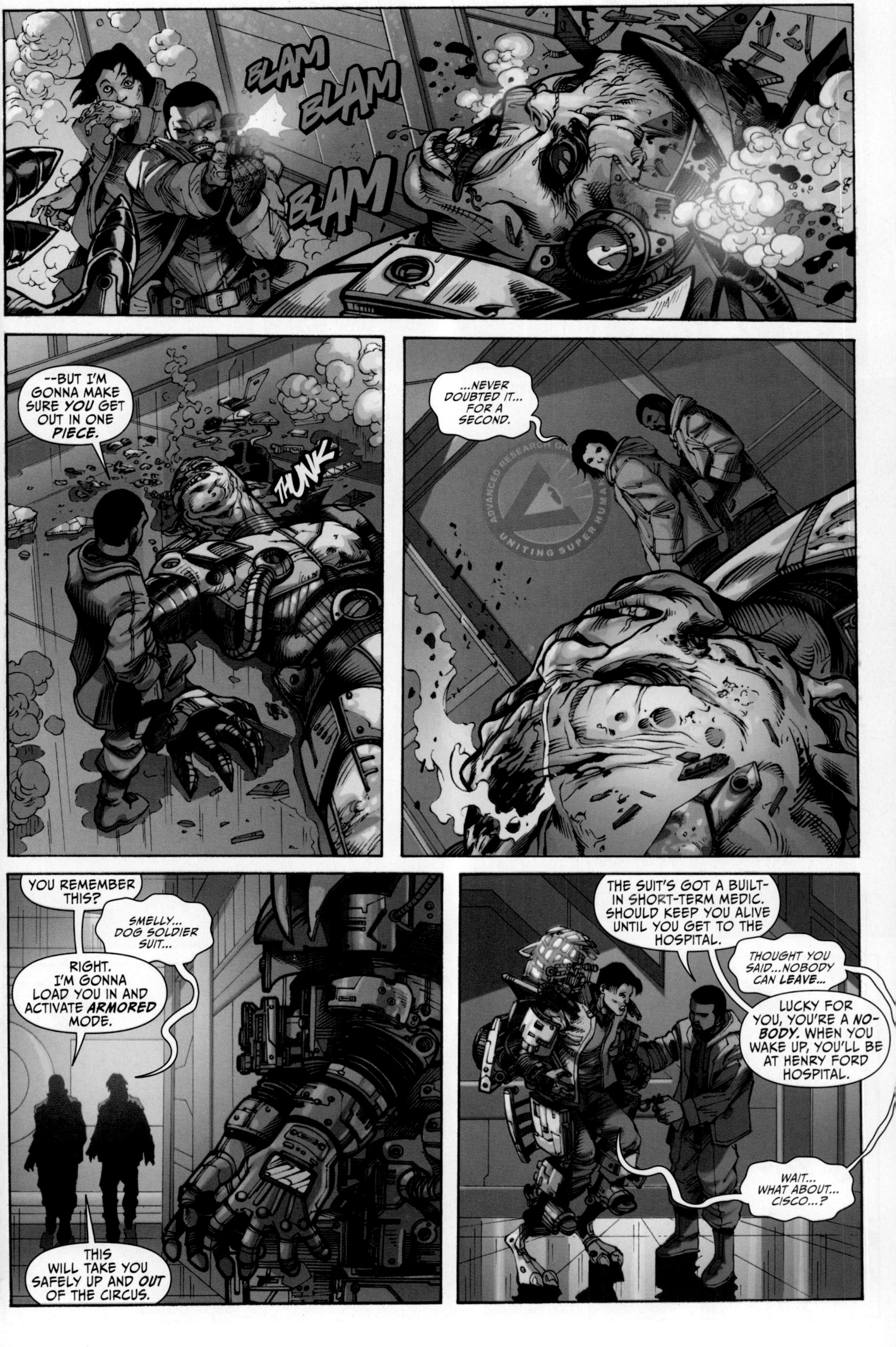
BLAM
BLAM
BLAM
--BUT I'M GONNA MAKE SURE YOU GET OUT IN ONE PIECE.
THUNK
...NEVER DOUBTED IT... FOR A SECOND.
ADVANCED RESEARCH GROUP
UNITING SUPER HUMANS
YOU REMEMBER THIS?
SMELLY... DOG SOLDIER SUIT...
RIGHT. I'M GONNA LOAD YOU IN AND ACTIVATE ARMORED MODE.
THIS WILL TAKE YOU SAFELY UP AND OUT OF THE CIRCUS.
THE SUIT'S GOT A BUILT-IN SHORT-TERM MEDIC. SHOULD KEEP YOU ALIVE UNTIL YOU GET TO THE HOSPITAL.
THOUGHT YOU SAID...NOBODY CAN LEAVE...
LUCKY FOR YOU, YOU'RE A NO-BODY. WHEN YOU WAKE UP, YOU'LL BE AT HENRY FORD HOSPITAL.
WAIT... WHAT ABOUT... CISCO...?

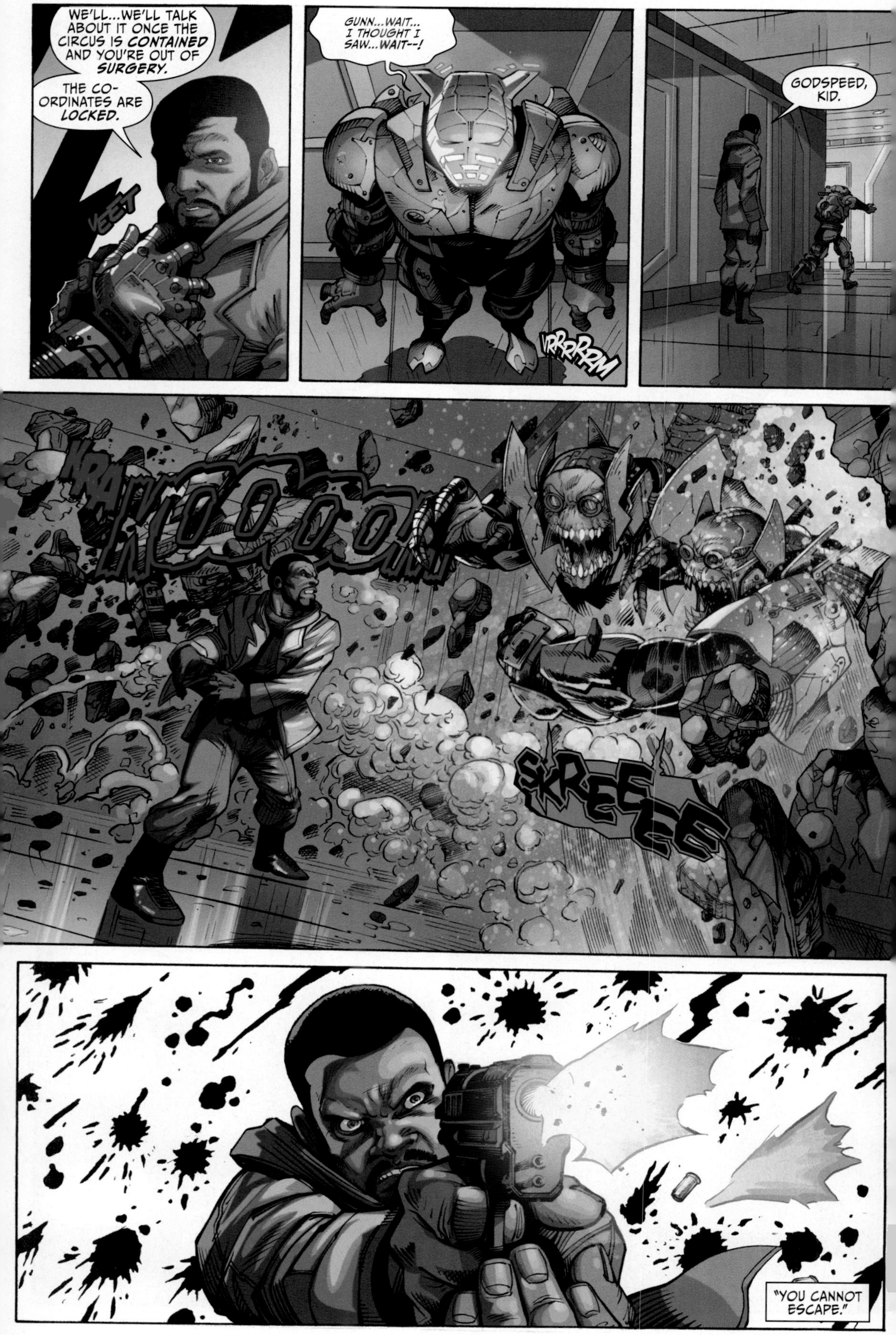
WE'LL...WE'LL TALK ABOUT IT ONCE THE CIRCUS IS CONTAINED AND YOU'RE OUT OF SURGERY.
THE CO-ORDINATES ARE LOCKED.
VEET
GUNN...WAIT... I THOUGHT I SAW...WAIT--!
VRRRRRM
GODSPEED, KID.
KRAKOOOOOM
SKREEEEE
"YOU CANNOT ESCAPE."

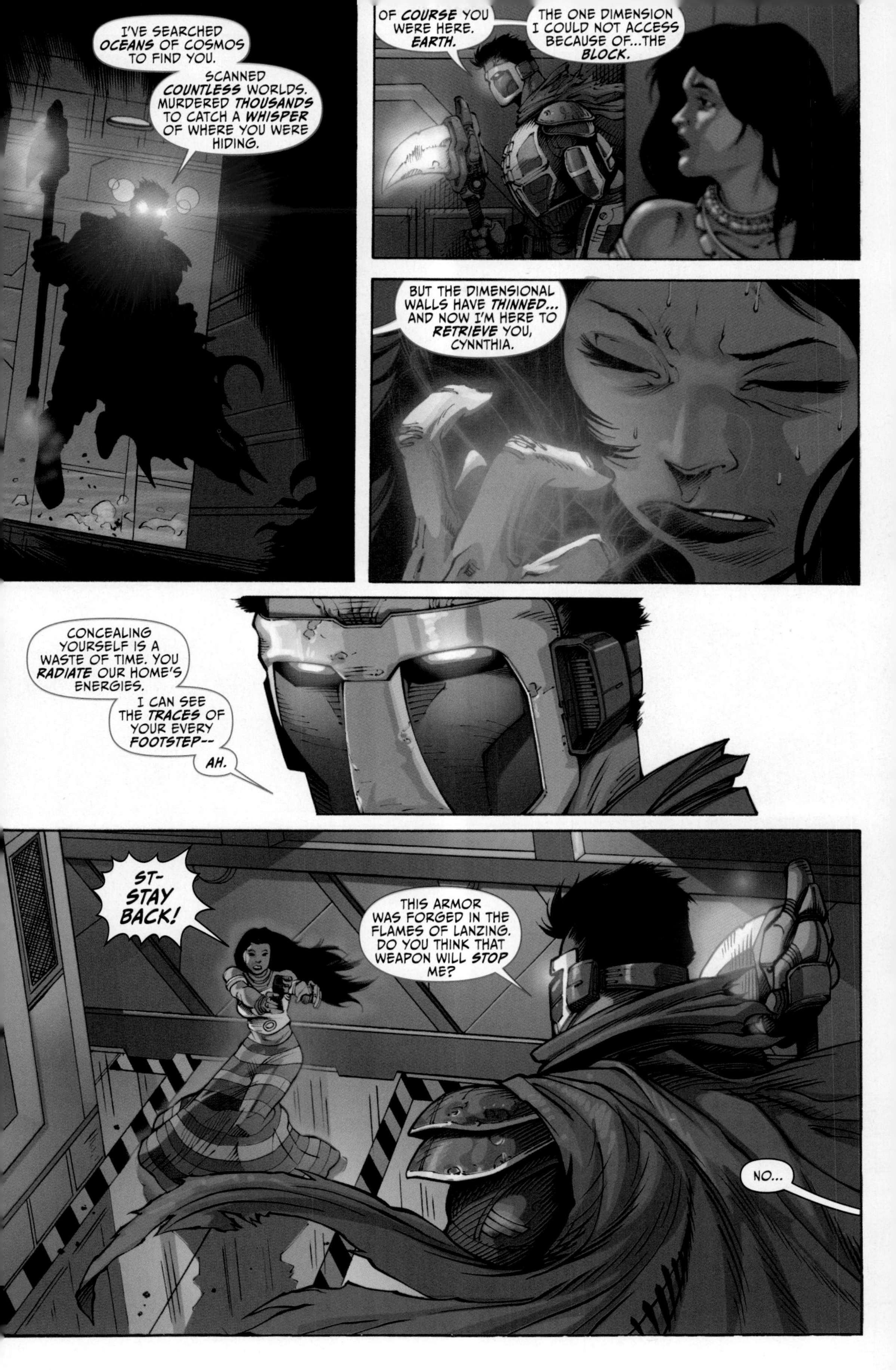

I'VE SEARCHED OCEANS OF COSMOS TO FIND YOU.
SCANNED COUNTLESS WORLDS. MURDERED THOUSANDS TO CATCH A WHISPER OF WHERE YOU WERE HIDING.
OF COURSE YOU WERE HERE. EARTH.
THE ONE DIMENSION I COULD NOT ACCESS BECAUSE OF...THE BLOCK.
BUT THE DIMENSIONAL WALLS HAVE THINNED... AND NOW I'M HERE TO RETRIEVE YOU, CYNNTHIA.
CONCEALING YOURSELF IS A WASTE OF TIME. YOU RADIATE OUR HOME'S ENERGIES.
I CAN SEE THE TRACES OF YOUR EVERY FOOTSTEP--
AH.
ST-STAY BACK!
THIS ARMOR WAS FORGED IN THE FLAMES OF LANZING. DO YOU THINK THAT WEAPON WILL STOP ME?
NO...

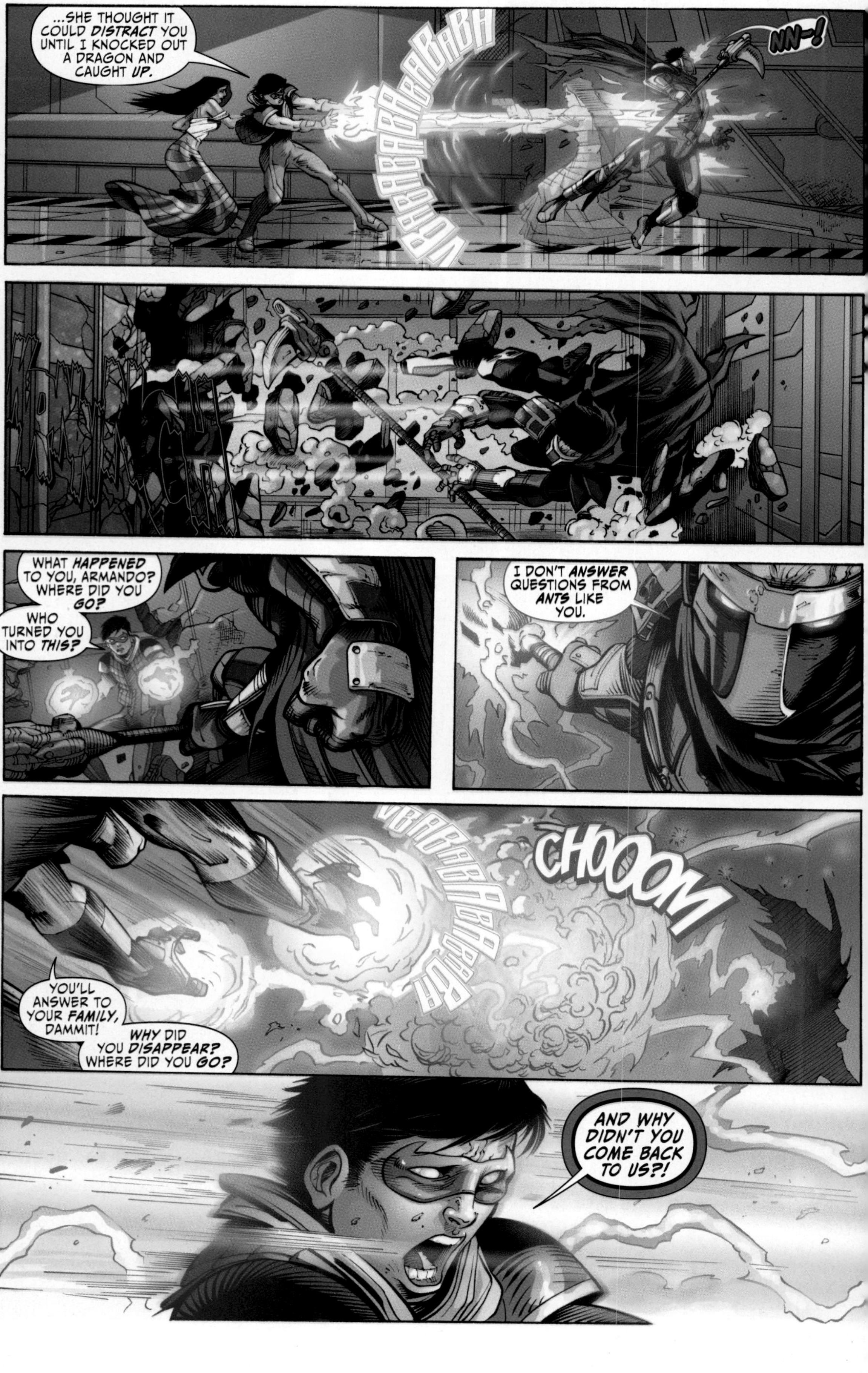
...SHE THOUGHT IT COULD DISTRACT YOU UNTIL I KNOCKED OUT A DRAGON AND CAUGHT UP.
VBRBBABABABABABA
NN-!
WHAT HAPPENED TO YOU, ARMANDO? WHERE DID YOU GO?
WHO TURNED YOU INTO THIS?
I DON'T ANSWER QUESTIONS FROM ANTS LIKE YOU.
VBRBBABABABABA
CHOOOM
YOU'LL ANSWER TO YOUR FAMILY, DAMMIT!
WHY DID YOU DISAPPEAR? WHERE DID YOU GO?
AND WHY DIDN'T YOU COME BACK TO US?!

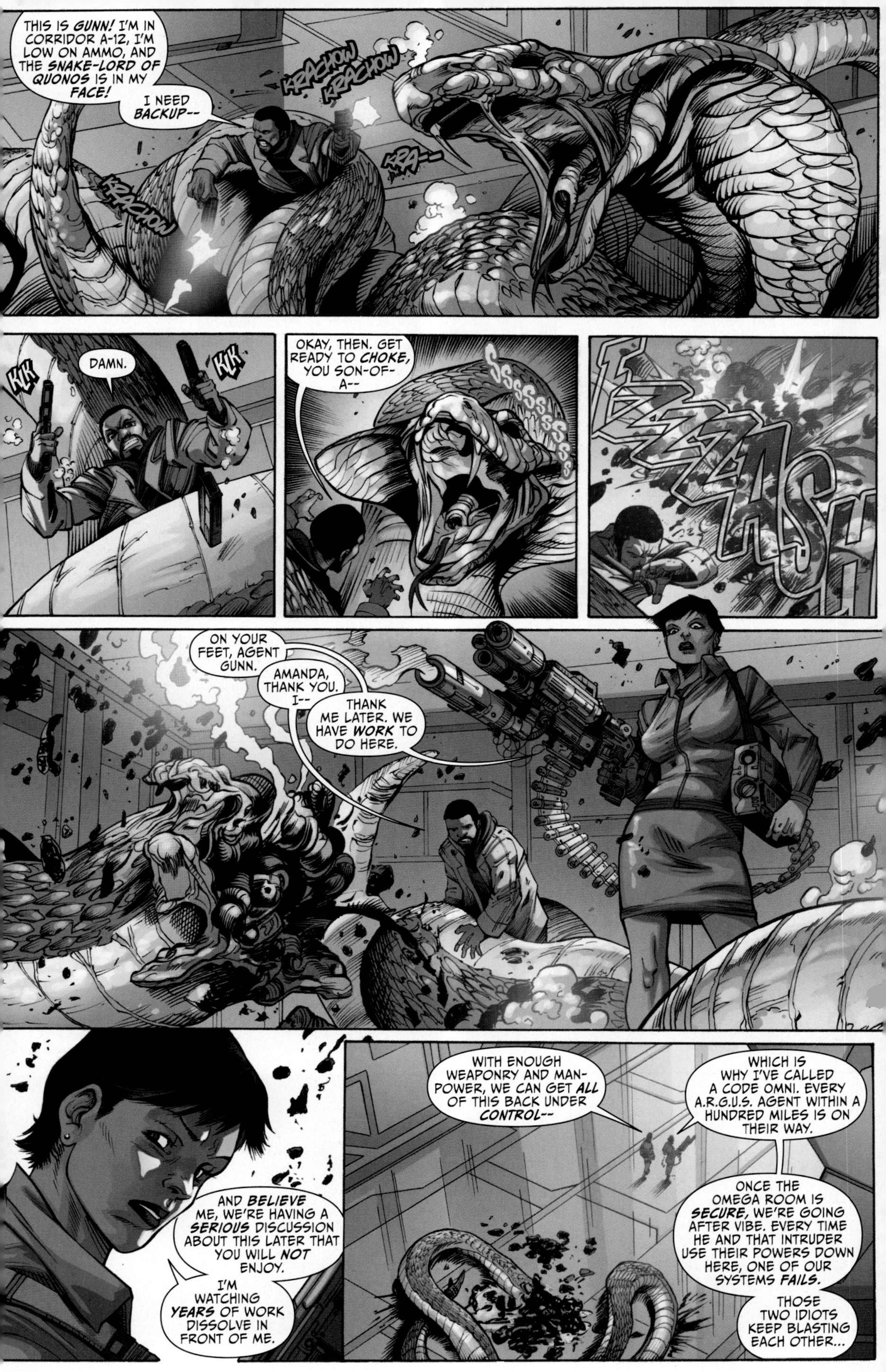

THIS IS GUNN! I'M IN CORRIDOR A-12, I'M LOW ON AMMO, AND THE SNAKE-LORD OF QUONOS IS IN MY FACE!
I NEED BACKUP--
KRACHOW
KRACHOW
KRA--
KRACHOW
KLIK
DAMN.
KLIK
OKAY, THEN. GET READY TO CHOKE, YOU SON-OF-A--
SSSSSSSSSSSS
ON YOUR FEET, AGENT GUNN.
AMANDA, THANK YOU. I--
THANK ME LATER. WE HAVE WORK TO DO HERE.
AND BELIEVE ME, WE'RE HAVING A SERIOUS DISCUSSION ABOUT THIS LATER THAT YOU WILL NOT ENJOY.
I'M WATCHING YEARS OF WORK DISSOLVE IN FRONT OF ME.
WITH ENOUGH WEAPONRY AND MAN-POWER, WE CAN GET ALL OF THIS BACK UNDER CONTROL--
WHICH IS WHY I'VE CALLED A CODE OMNI. EVERY A.R.G.U.S. AGENT WITHIN A HUNDRED MILES IS ON THEIR WAY.
ONCE THE OMEGA ROOM IS SECURE, WE'RE GOING AFTER VIBE. EVERY TIME HE AND THAT INTRUDER USE THEIR POWERS DOWN HERE, ONE OF OUR SYSTEMS FAILS.
THOSE TWO IDIOTS KEEP BLASTING EACH OTHER...

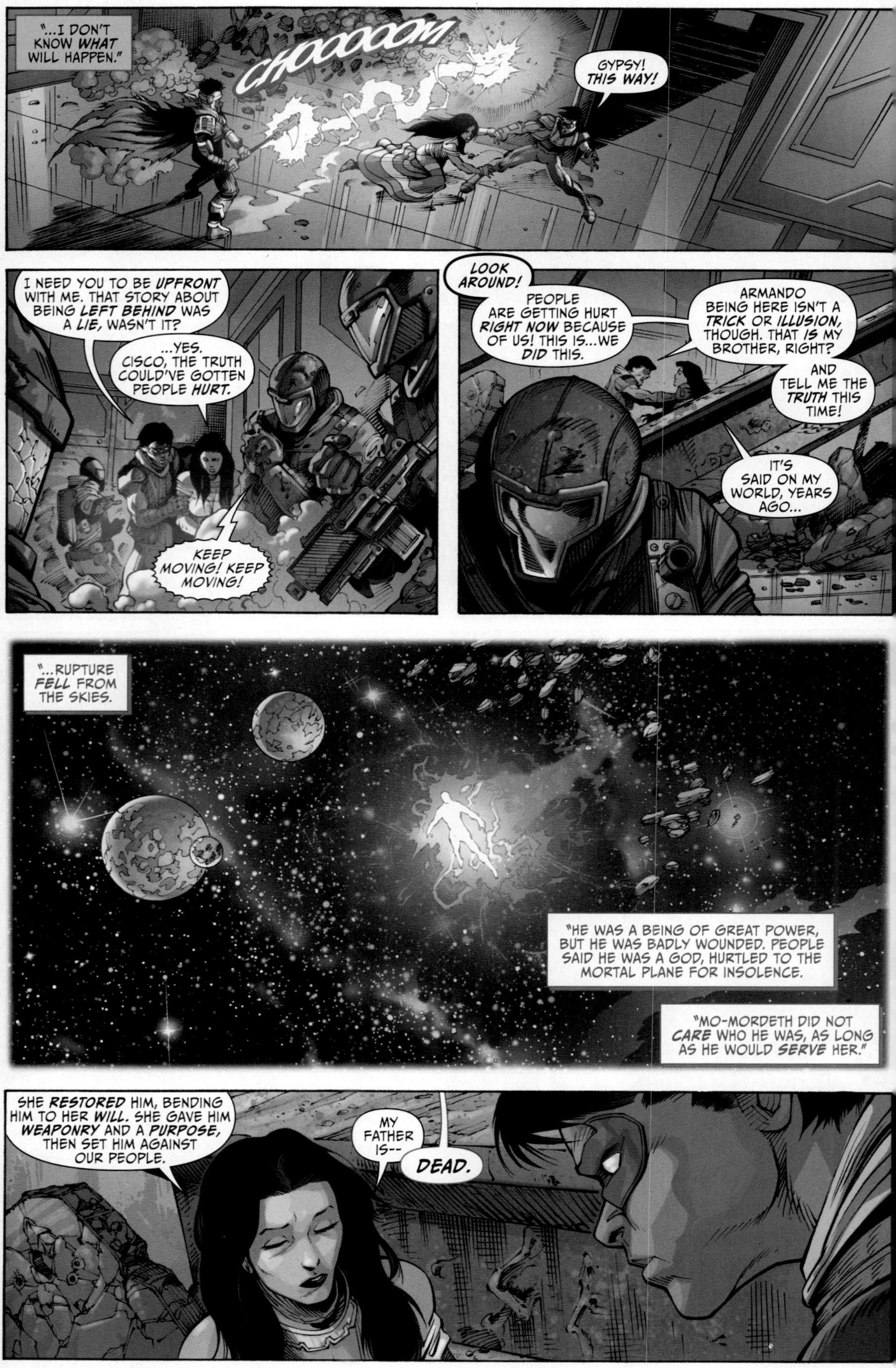

"...I DON'T KNOW WHAT WILL HAPPEN."
CHOOOOOM
GYPSY! THIS WAY!
I NEED YOU TO BE UPFRONT WITH ME. THAT STORY ABOUT BEING LEFT BEHIND WAS A LIE, WASN'T IT?
...YES. CISCO, THE TRUTH COULD'VE GOTTEN PEOPLE HURT.
KEEP MOVING! KEEP MOVING!
LOOK AROUND!
PEOPLE ARE GETTING HURT RIGHT NOW BECAUSE OF US! THIS IS...WE DID THIS.
ARMANDO BEING HERE ISN'T A TRICK OR ILLUSION, THOUGH. THAT IS MY BROTHER, RIGHT?
AND TELL ME THE TRUTH THIS TIME!
IT'S SAID ON MY WORLD, YEARS AGO...
"...RUPTURE FELL FROM THE SKIES.
"HE WAS A BEING OF GREAT POWER, BUT HE WAS BADLY WOUNDED. PEOPLE SAID HE WAS A GOD, HURTLED TO THE MORTAL PLANE FOR INSOLENCE.
"MO-MORDETH DID NOT CARE WHO HE WAS, AS LONG AS HE WOULD SERVE HER."
SHE RESTORED HIM, BENDING HIM TO HER WILL. SHE GAVE HIM WEAPONRY AND A PURPOSE, THEN SET HIM AGAINST OUR PEOPLE.
MY FATHER IS--
DEAD.

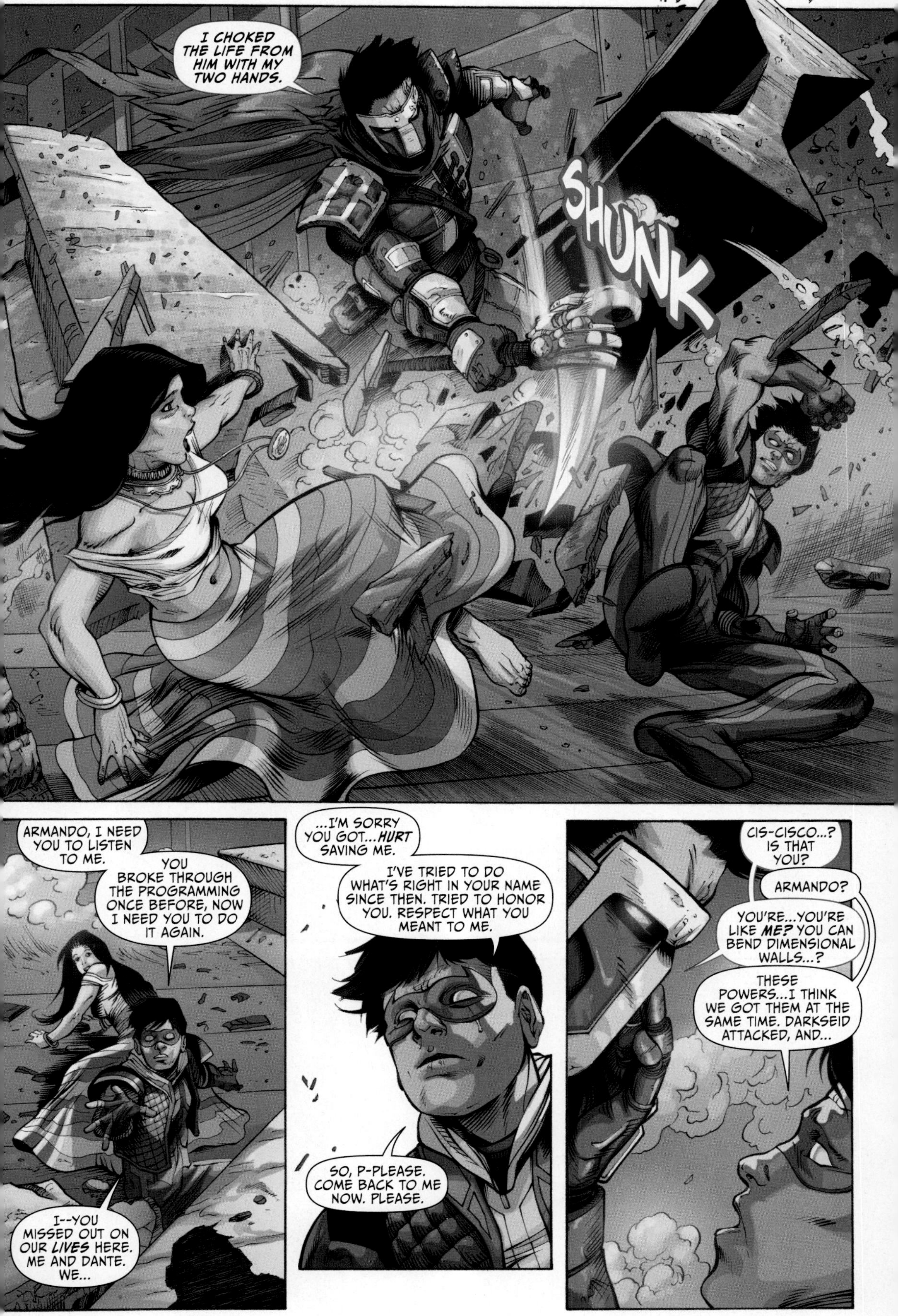

I CHOKED THE LIFE FROM HIM WITH MY TWO HANDS.
SHUNK
ARMANDO, I NEED YOU TO LISTEN TO ME.
YOU BROKE THROUGH THE PROGRAMMING ONCE BEFORE, NOW I NEED YOU TO DO IT AGAIN.
I--YOU MISSED OUT ON OUR *LIVES* HERE. ME AND DANTE. WE...
...I'M SORRY YOU GOT... *HURT* SAVING ME.
I'VE TRIED TO DO WHAT'S RIGHT IN YOUR NAME SINCE THEN. TRIED TO HONOR YOU. RESPECT WHAT YOU MEANT TO ME.
SO, P-PLEASE. COME BACK TO ME NOW. PLEASE.
CIS-CISCO...? IS THAT YOU?
ARMANDO?
YOU'RE... YOU'RE LIKE *ME?* YOU CAN BEND DIMENSIONAL WALLS...?
THESE POWERS... I THINK WE GOT THEM AT THE SAME TIME. DARKSEID ATTACKED, AND...

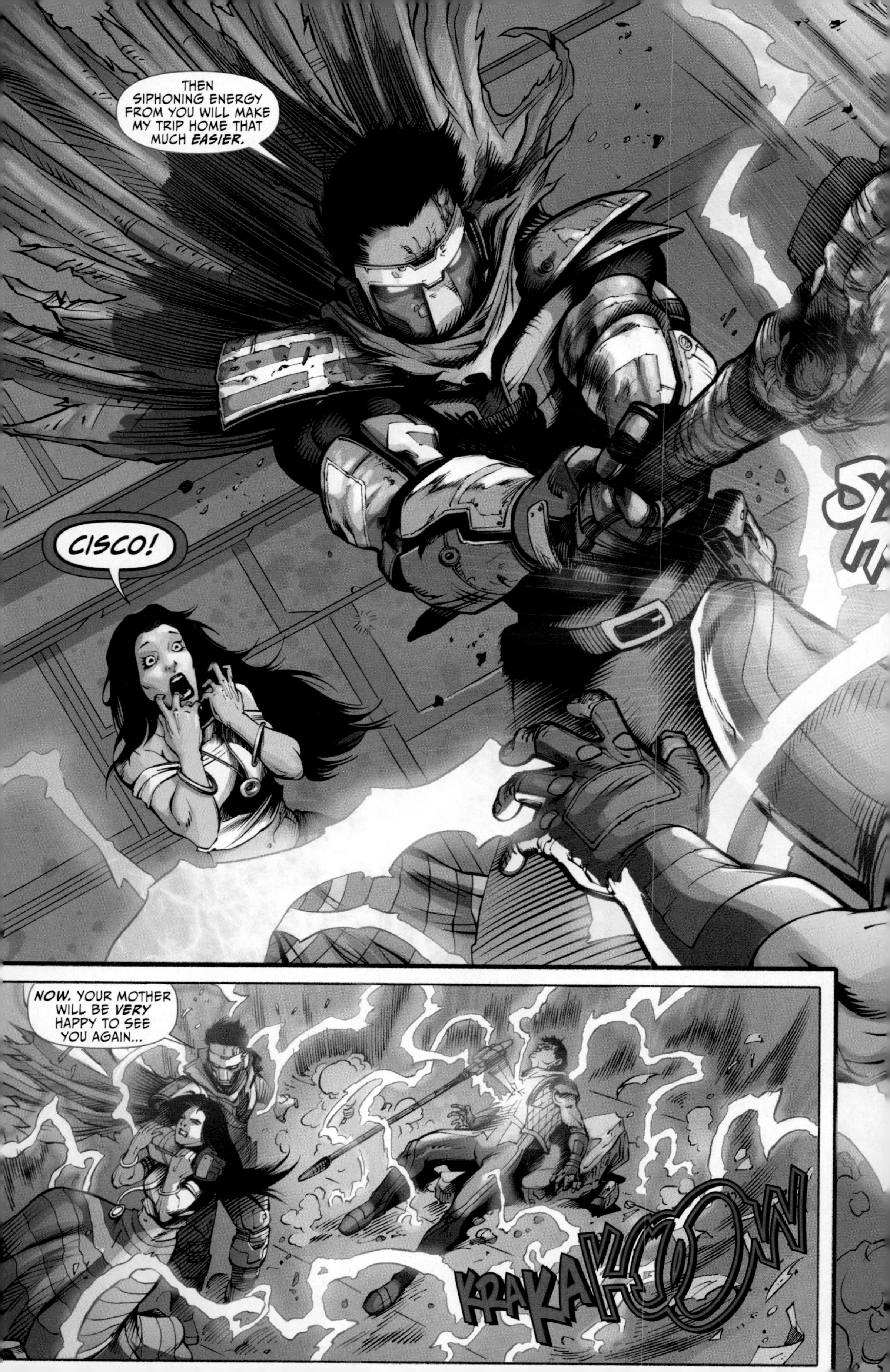
THEN SIPHONING ENERGY FROM YOU WILL MAKE MY TRIP HOME THAT MUCH *EASIER.*
CISCO!
NOW. YOUR MOTHER WILL BE *VERY* HAPPY TO SEE YOU AGAIN...
KRAKAKOOOW

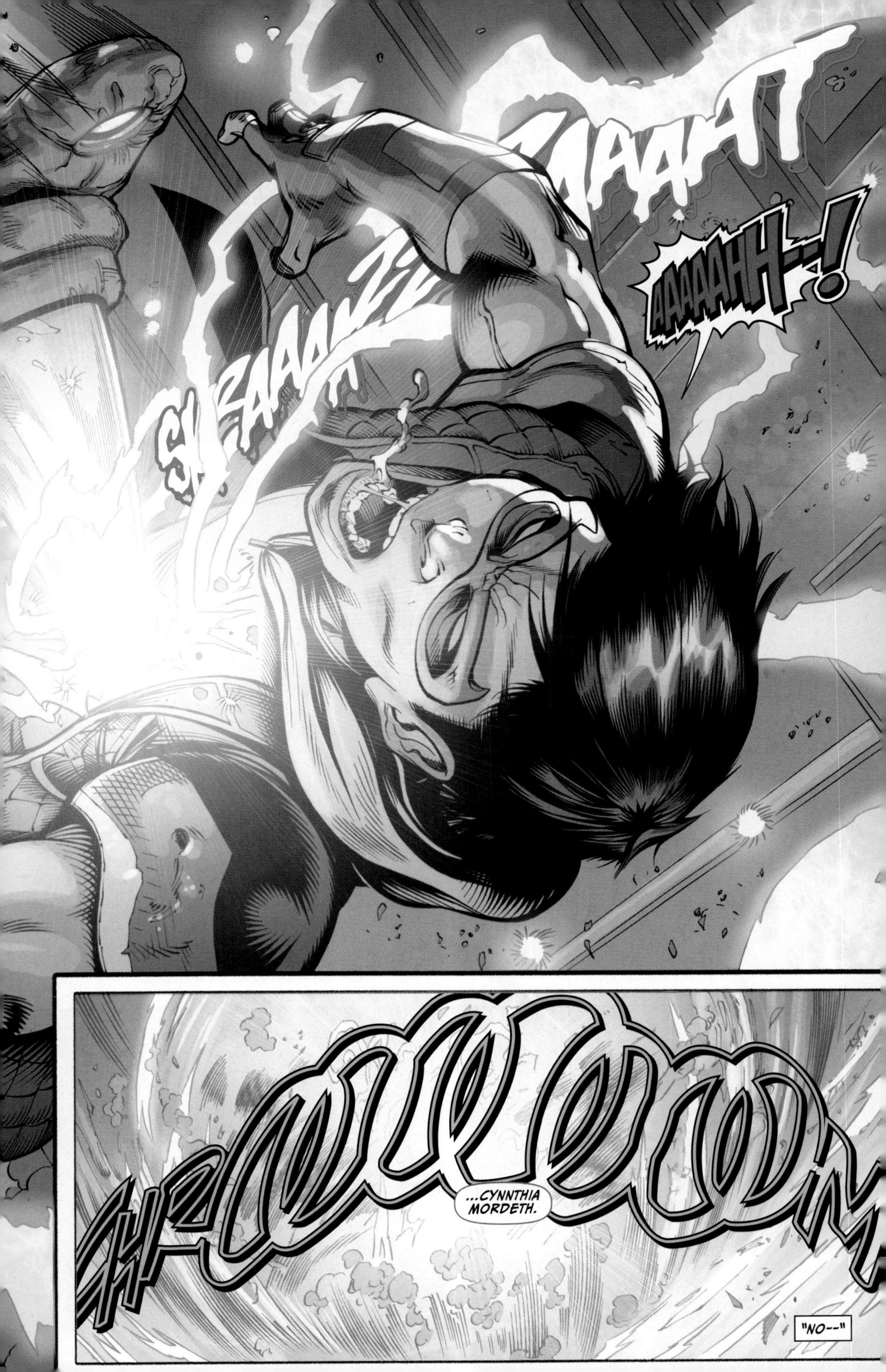
AAAAAHH--!
...CYNNTHIA MORDETH.
"NO--"

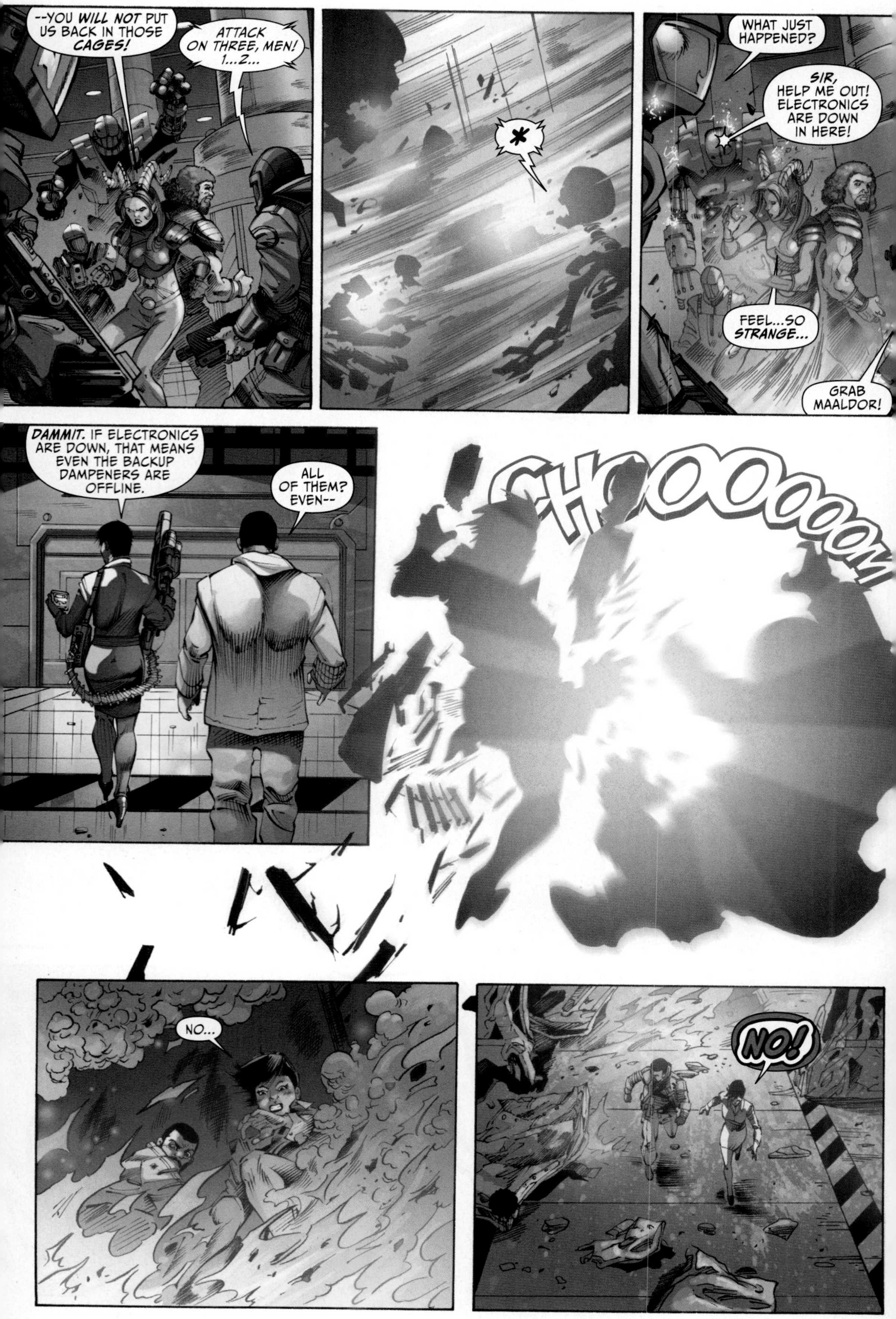
--YOU WILL NOT PUT US BACK IN THOSE CAGES!
ATTACK ON THREE, MEN! 1...2...
*
WHAT JUST HAPPENED?
SIR, HELP ME OUT! ELECTRONICS ARE DOWN IN HERE!
FEEL...SO STRANGE...
GRAB MAALDOR!
DAMMIT. IF ELECTRONICS ARE DOWN, THAT MEANS EVEN THE BACKUP DAMPENERS ARE OFFLINE.
ALL OF THEM? EVEN--
CHOOOOOOM
NO...
NO!

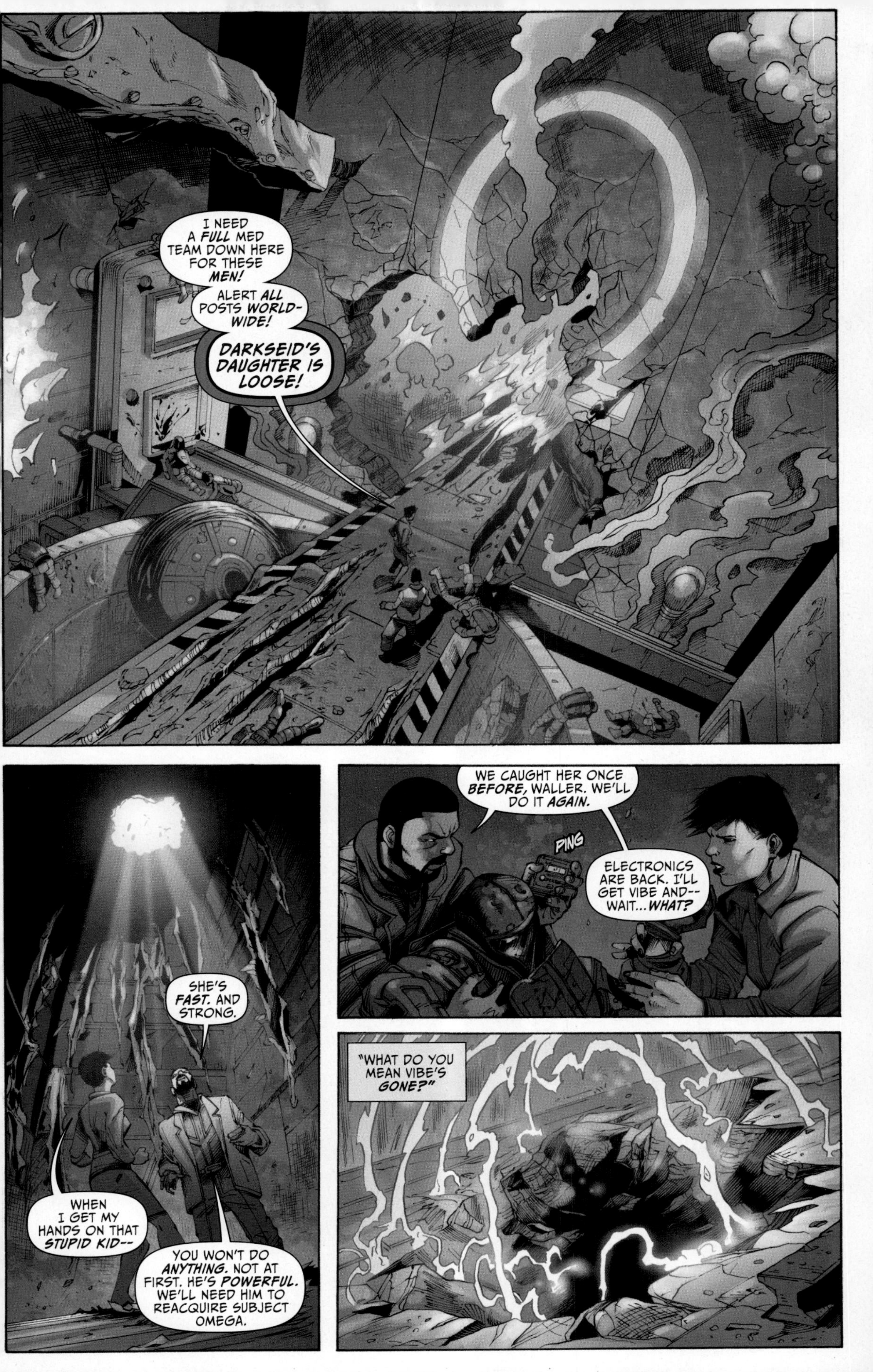
I NEED A *FULL* MED TEAM DOWN HERE FOR THESE *MEN!*
ALERT *ALL* POSTS *WORLD-WIDE!*
DARKSEID'S DAUGHTER IS LOOSE!
SHE'S *FAST.* AND STRONG.
WHEN I GET MY HANDS ON THAT *STUPID KID--*
YOU WON'T DO *ANYTHING.* NOT AT FIRST. HE'S *POWERFUL.* WE'LL NEED HIM TO REACQUIRE SUBJECT OMEGA.
WE CAUGHT HER ONCE *BEFORE,* WALLER. WE'LL DO IT *AGAIN.*
PING
ELECTRONICS ARE BACK. I'LL GET VIBE AND-- WAIT...*WHAT?*
"WHAT DO YOU MEAN VIBE'S *GONE?*"

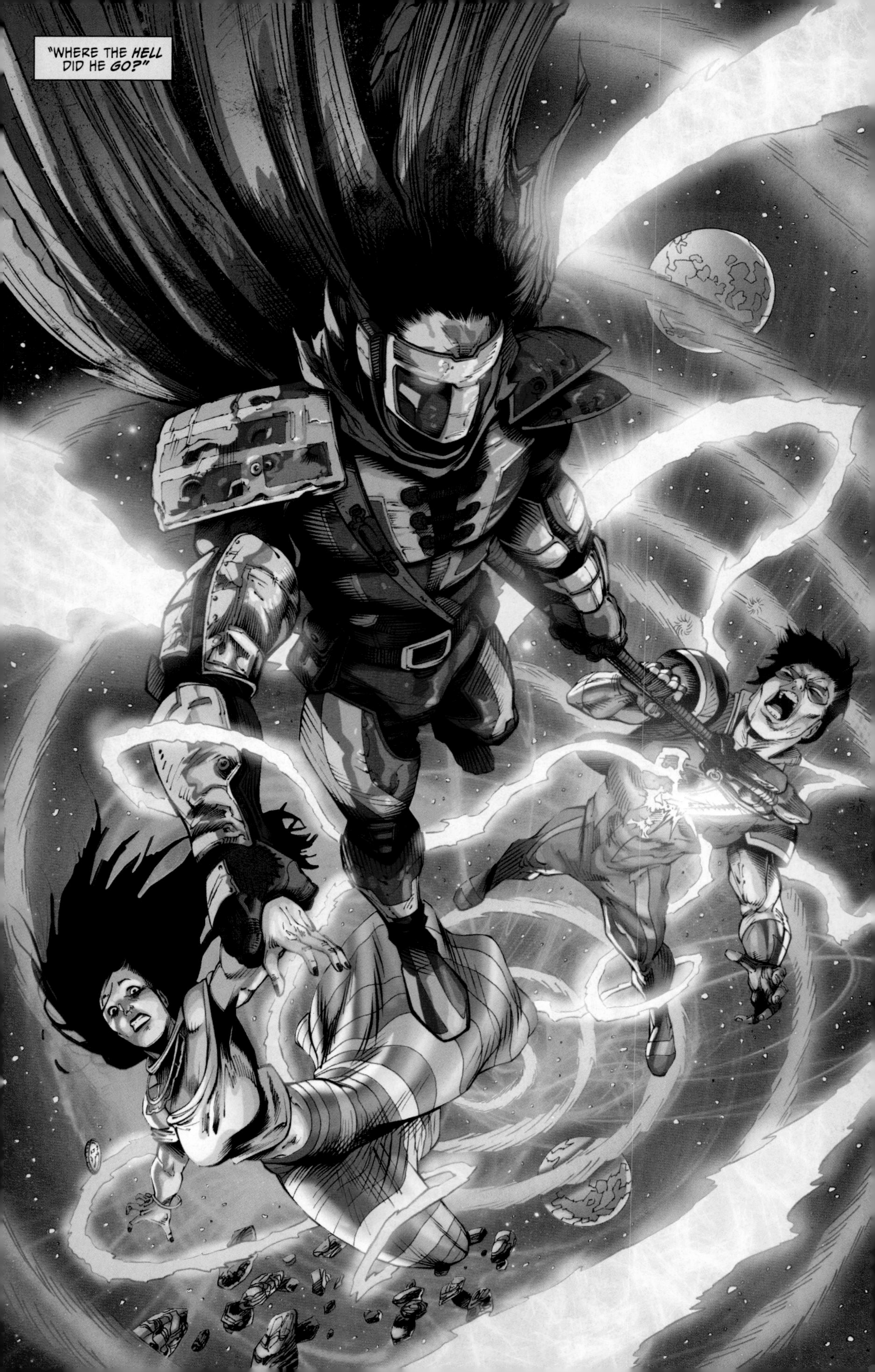
"WHERE THE HELL DID HE GO?"

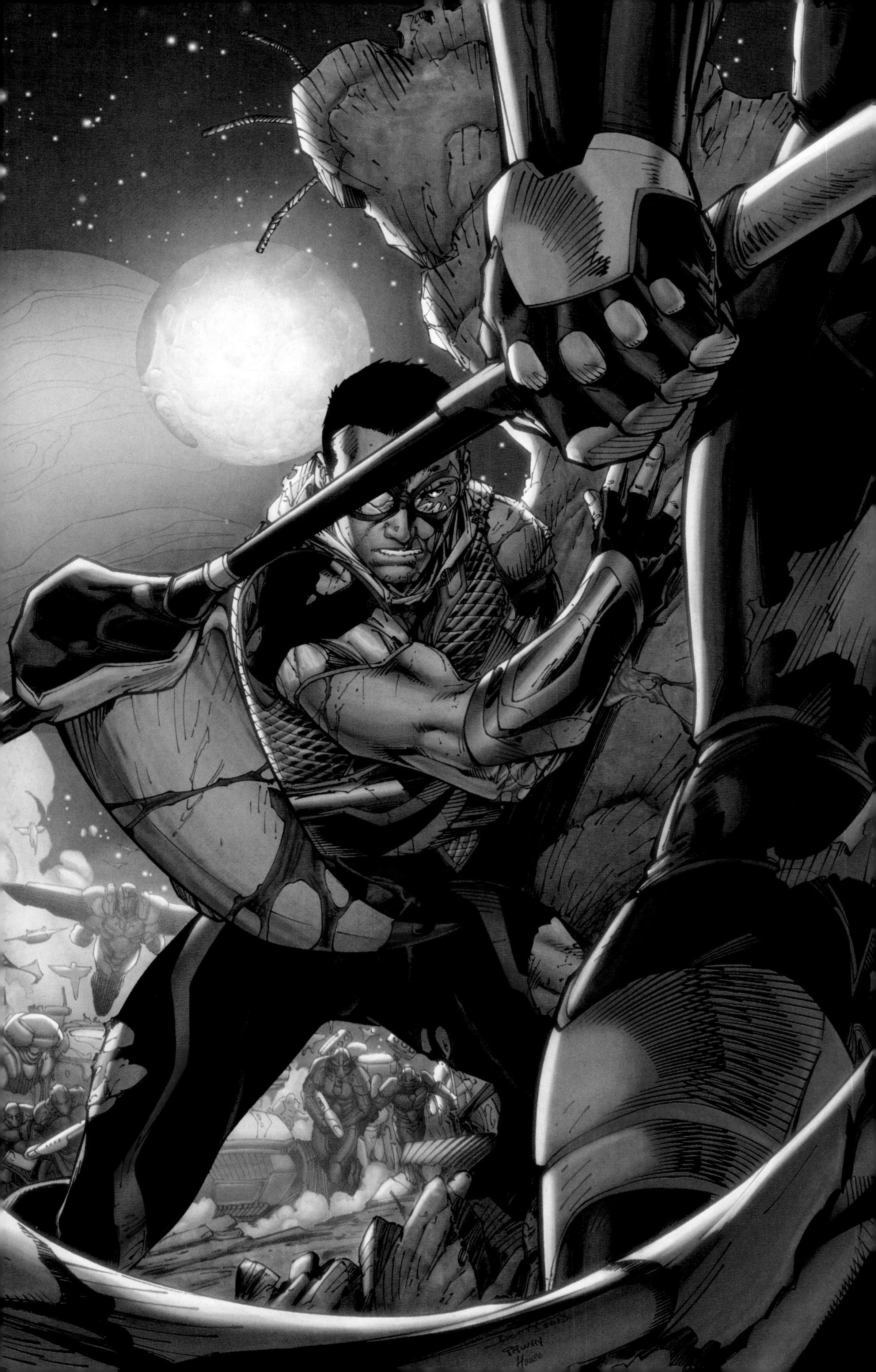

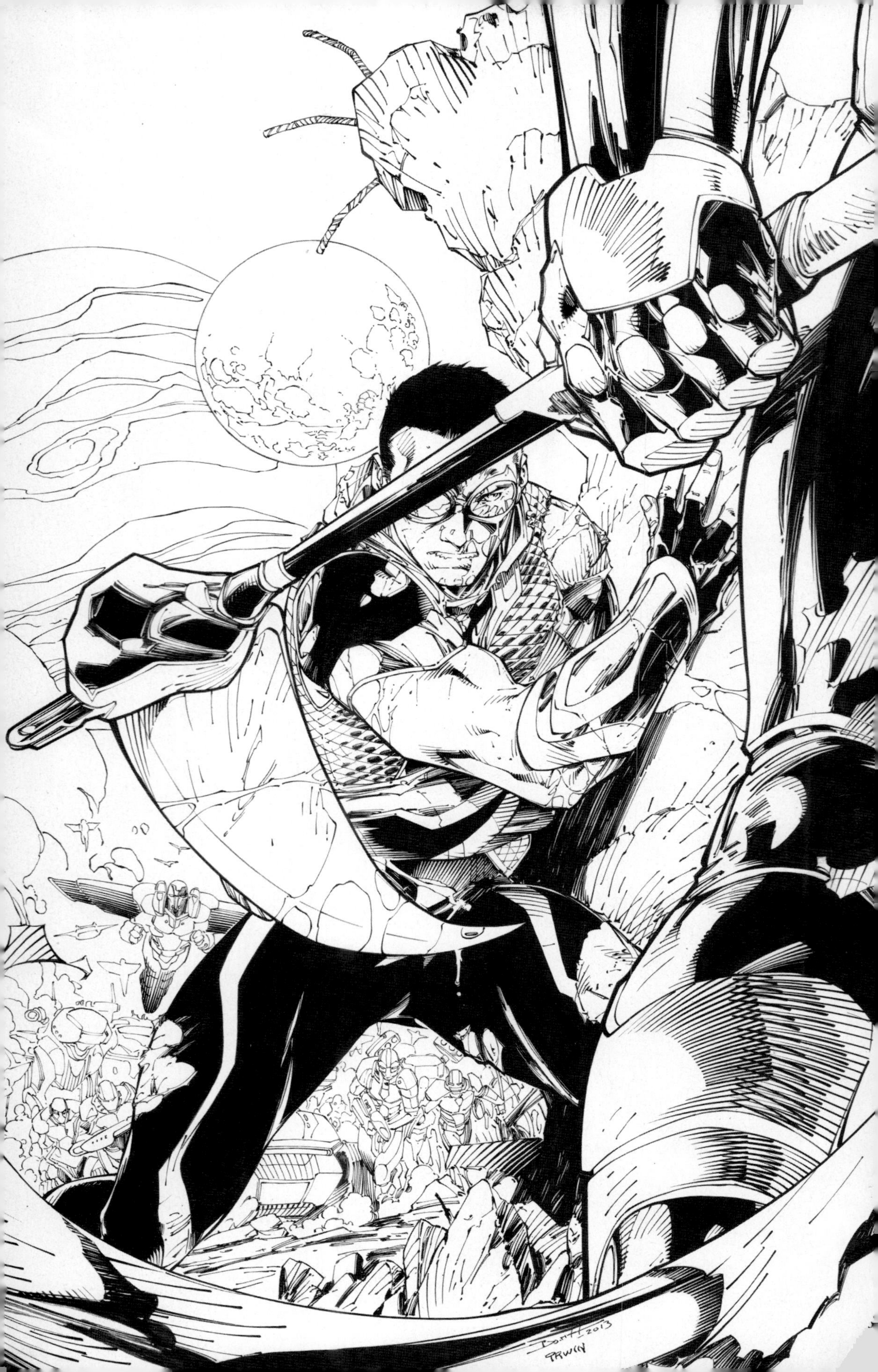

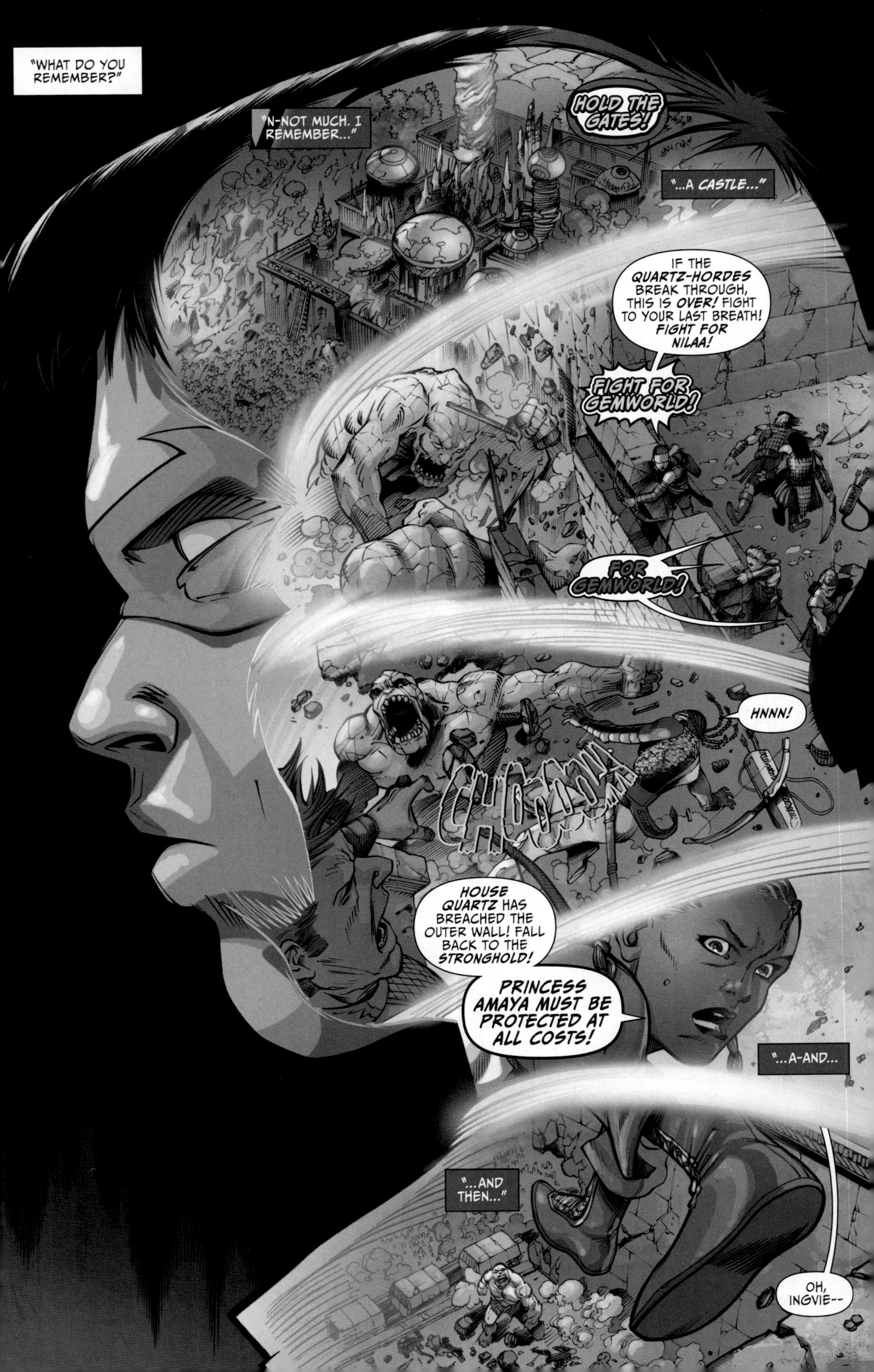
"WHAT DO YOU REMEMBER?"
"N-NOT MUCH. I REMEMBER..."
HOLD THE GATES!
"...A CASTLE..."
IF THE QUARTZ-HORDES BREAK THROUGH, THIS IS OVER! FIGHT TO YOUR LAST BREATH! FIGHT FOR NILAA!
FIGHT FOR GEMWORLD!
FOR GEMWORLD!
HNNN!
CHOOOM
HOUSE QUARTZ HAS BREACHED THE OUTER WALL! FALL BACK TO THE STRONGHOLD!
PRINCESS AMAYA MUST BE PROTECTED AT ALL COSTS!
"...A-AND...
"...AND THEN..."
OH, INGVIE--

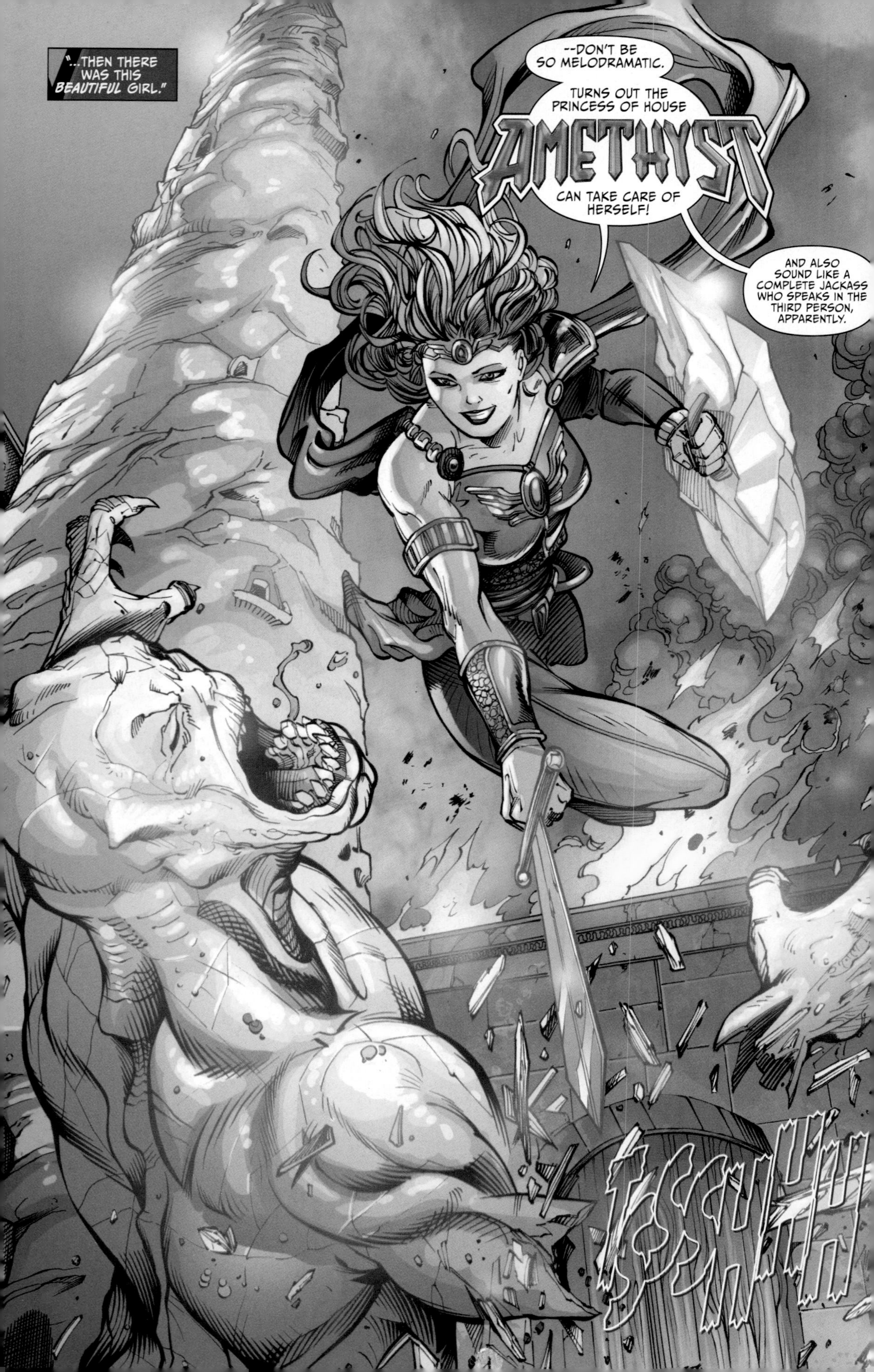
"...THEN THERE WAS THIS BEAUTIFUL GIRL."
--DON'T BE SO MELODRAMATIC.
TURNS OUT THE PRINCESS OF HOUSE AMETHYST CAN TAKE CARE OF HERSELF!
AND ALSO SOUND LIKE A COMPLETE JACKASS WHO SPEAKS IN THE THIRD PERSON, APPARENTLY.
TSSCHHHH

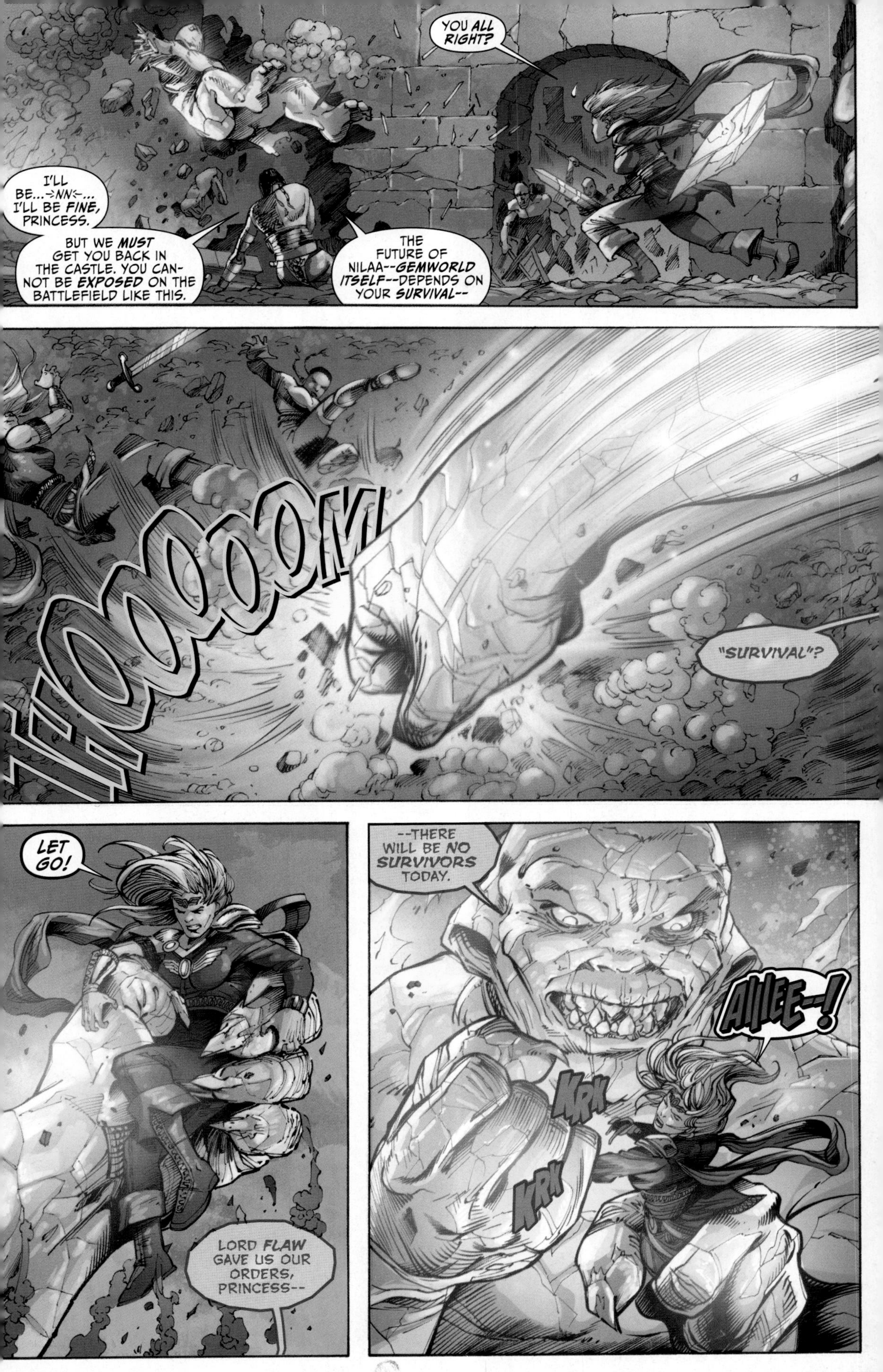
YOU ALL RIGHT?
I'LL BE...⊰NN⊱... I'LL BE FINE, PRINCESS.
BUT WE MUST GET YOU BACK IN THE CASTLE. YOU CAN-NOT BE EXPOSED ON THE BATTLEFIELD LIKE THIS.
THE FUTURE OF NILAA--GEMWORLD ITSELF--DEPENDS ON YOUR SURVIVAL--
WHOOOOOM
"SURVIVAL"?
LET GO!
LORD FLAW GAVE US OUR ORDERS, PRINCESS--
--THERE WILL BE NO SURVIVORS TODAY.
AIIEE--!
KRK
KRK

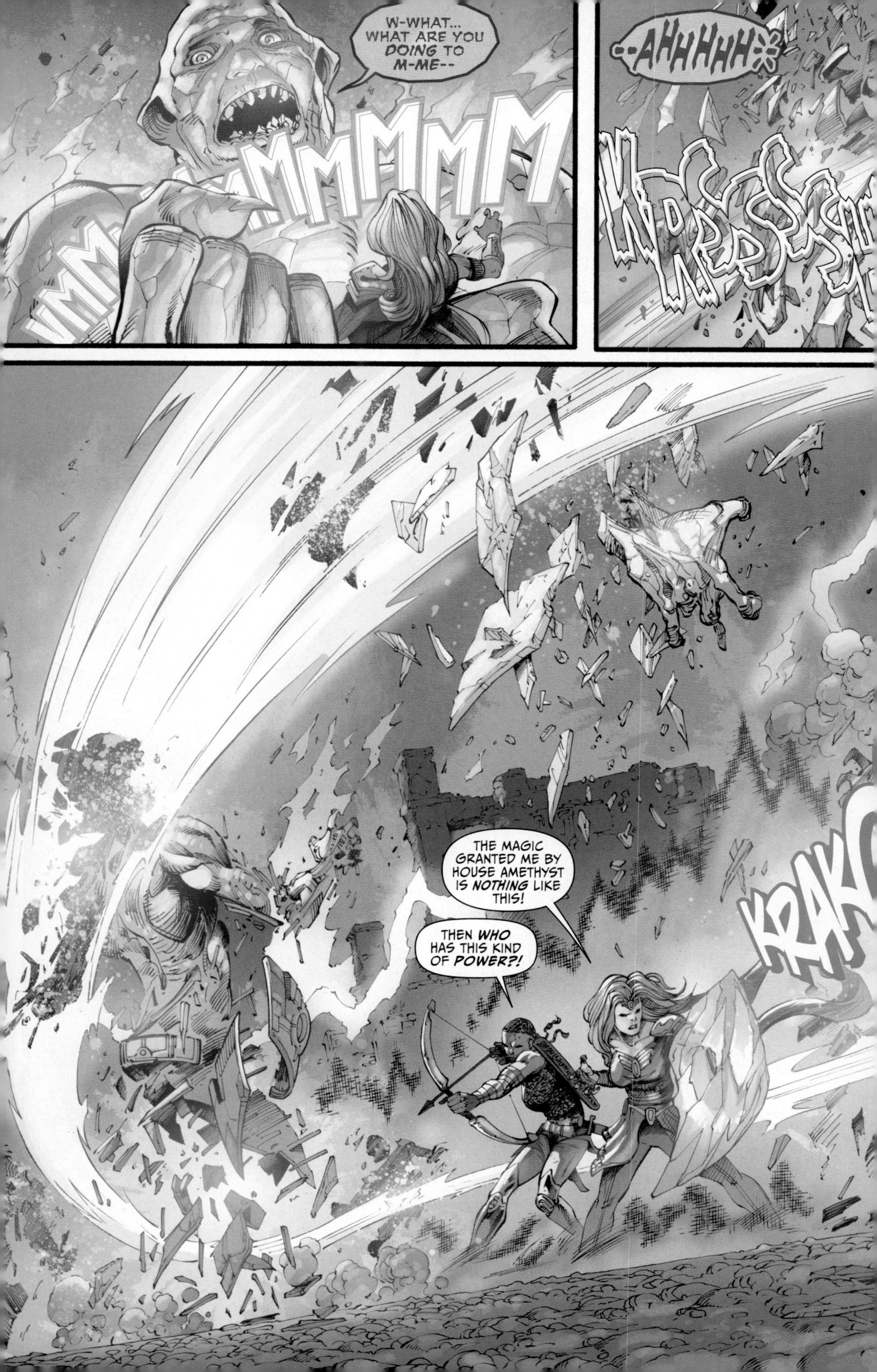
W-WHAT... WHAT ARE YOU DOING TO M-ME--
MMMMMMMM
--AHHHHH--
THE MAGIC GRANTED ME BY HOUSE AMETHYST IS NOTHING LIKE THIS!
THEN WHO HAS THIS KIND OF POWER?!

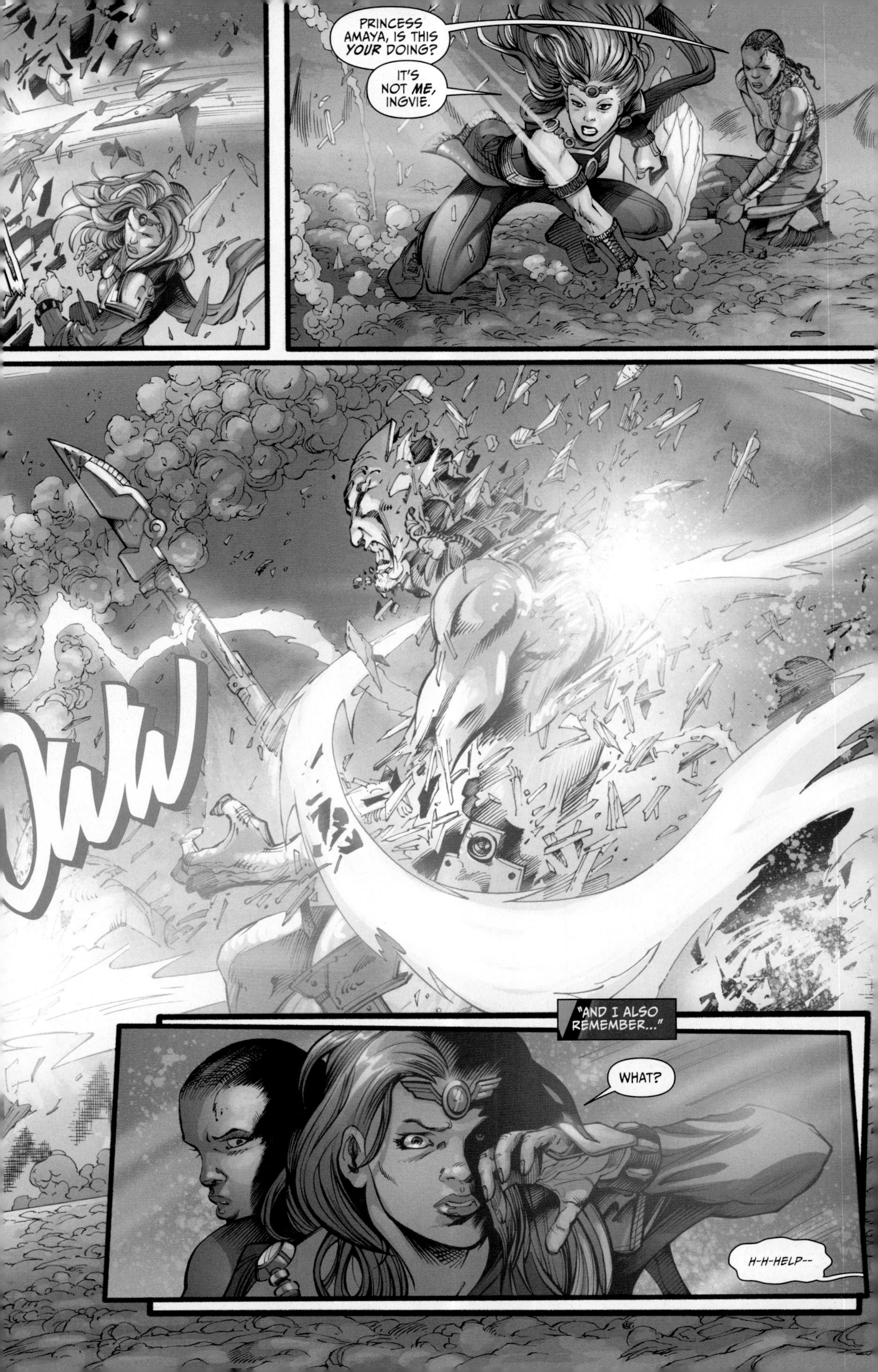
PRINCESS AMAYA, IS THIS YOUR DOING?
IT'S NOT ME, INGVIE.
"AND I ALSO REMEMBER..."
WHAT?
H-H-HELP--

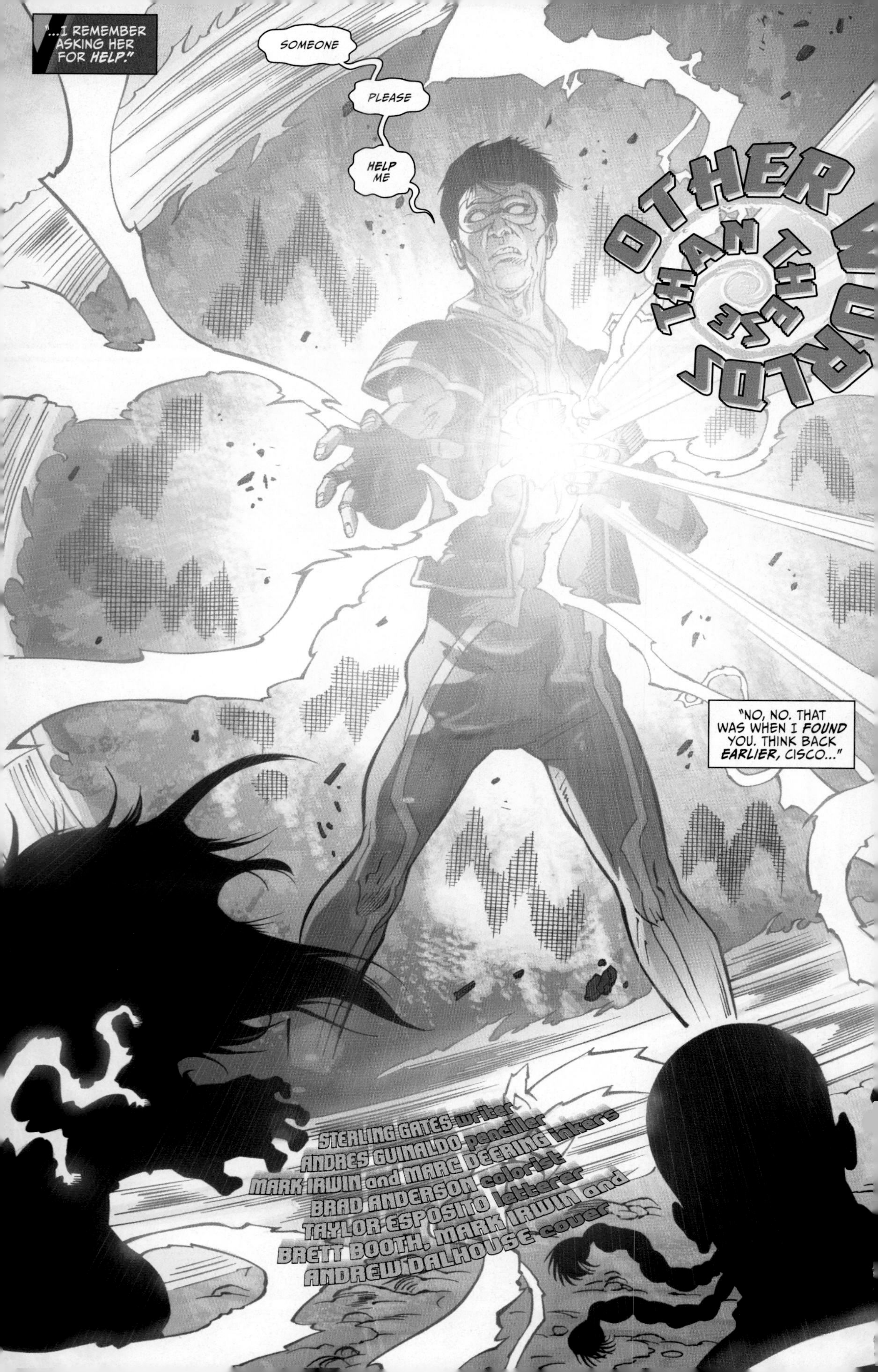
"...I REMEMBER ASKING HER FOR HELP."
SOMEONE
PLEASE
HELP ME
OTHER WORLDS THAN THESE
"NO, NO. THAT WAS WHEN I FOUND YOU. THINK BACK EARLIER, CISCO..."
STERLING GATES writer
ANDRES GUINALDO penciller
MARK IRWIN and MARC DEERING inkers
BRAD ANDERSON colorist
TAYLOR ESPOSITO letterer
BRETT BOOTH, MARK IRWIN and ANDREW DALHOUSE cover

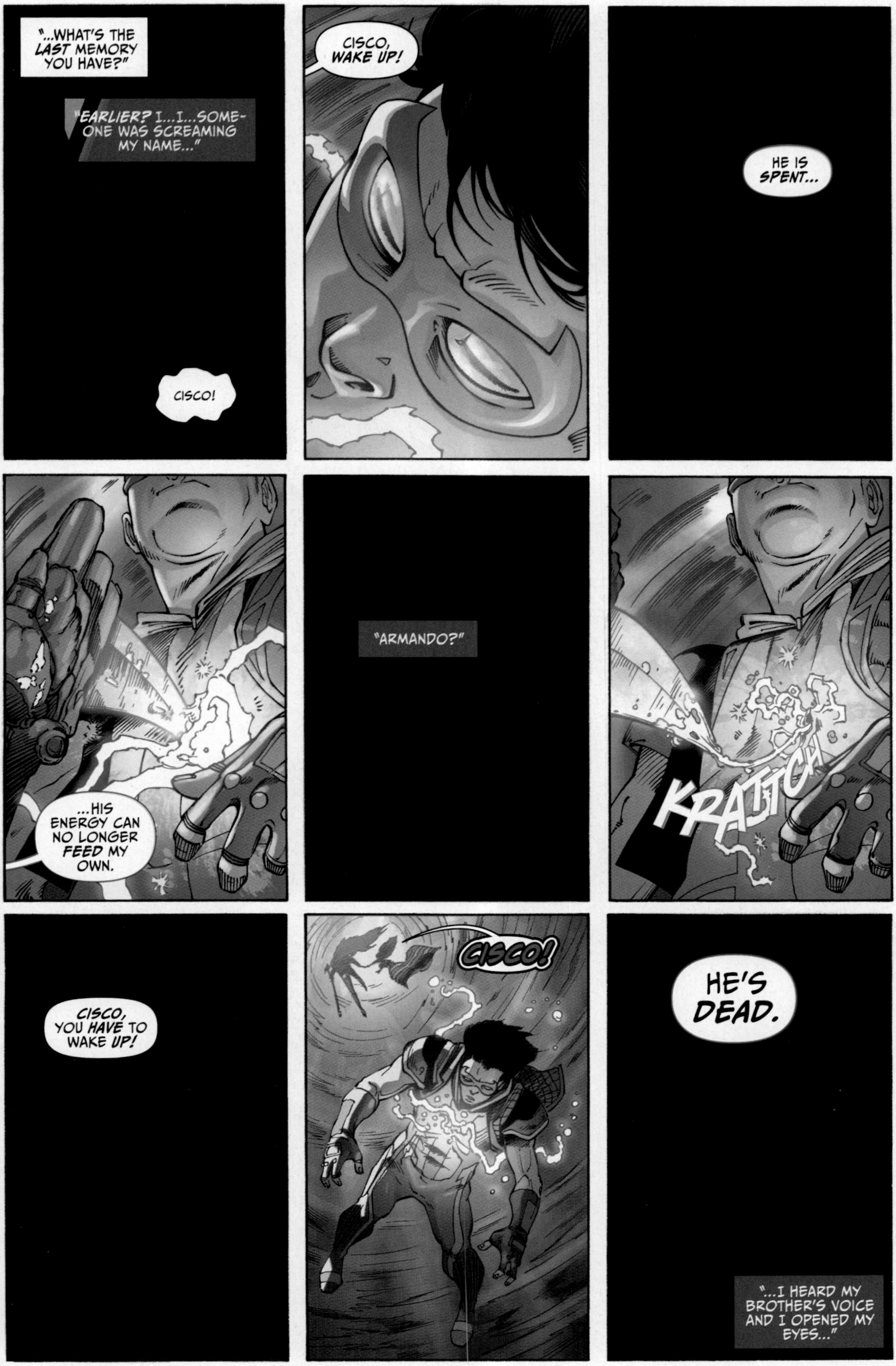
"...WHAT'S THE LAST MEMORY YOU HAVE?"
"EARLIER? I...I...SOME-ONE WAS SCREAMING MY NAME..."
CISCO!
CISCO, WAKE UP!
HE IS SPENT...
...HIS ENERGY CAN NO LONGER FEED MY OWN.
"ARMANDO?"
KRATTCH
CISCO, YOU HAVE TO WAKE UP!
CISCO!
HE'S DEAD.
"...I HEARD MY BROTHER'S VOICE AND I OPENED MY EYES..."

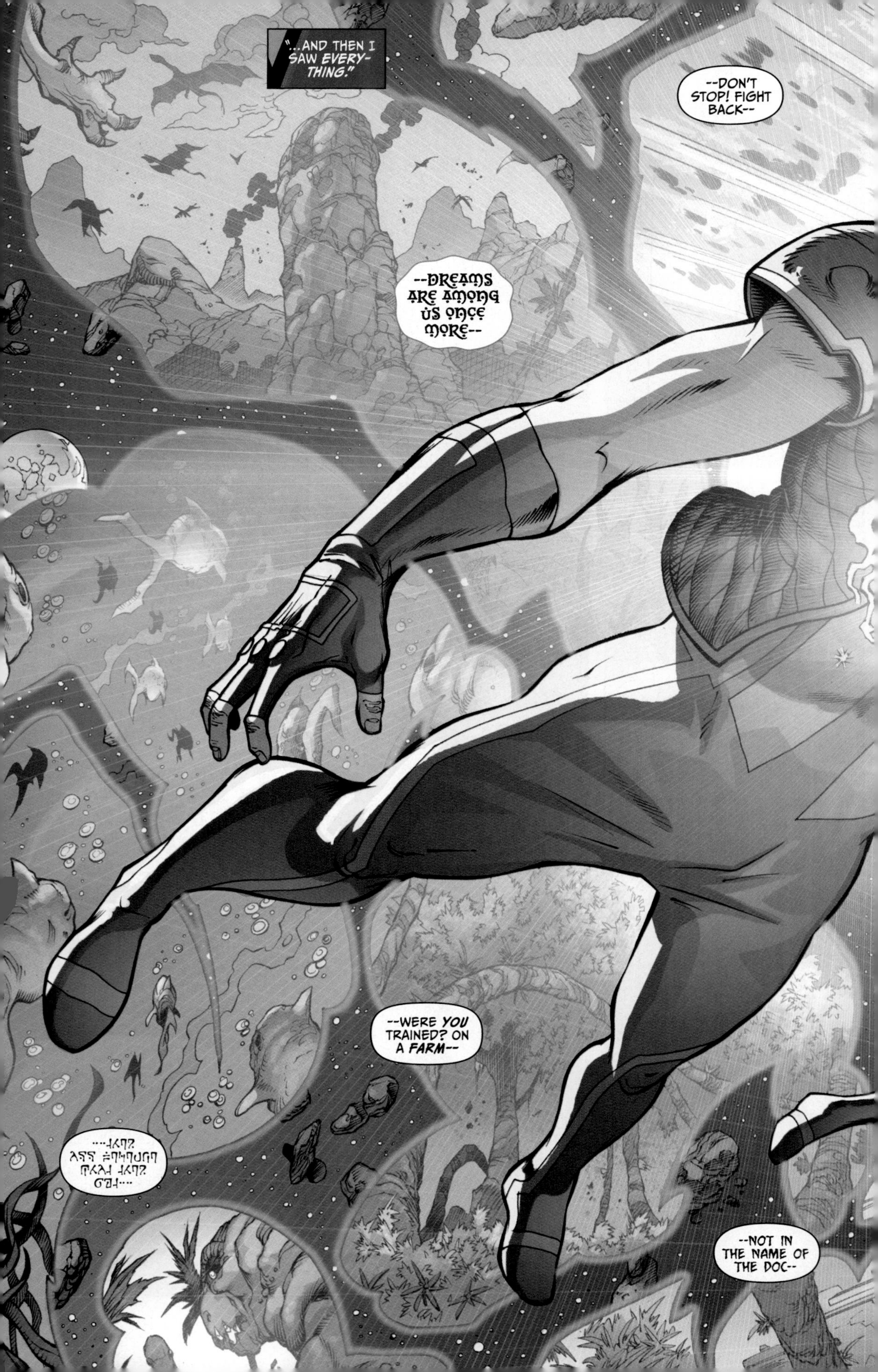
"...AND THEN I SAW EVERY-THING."
--DON'T STOP! FIGHT BACK--
--DREAMS ARE AMONG US ONCE MORE--
--WERE YOU TRAINED? ON A FARM--
--NOT IN THE NAME OF THE DOC--

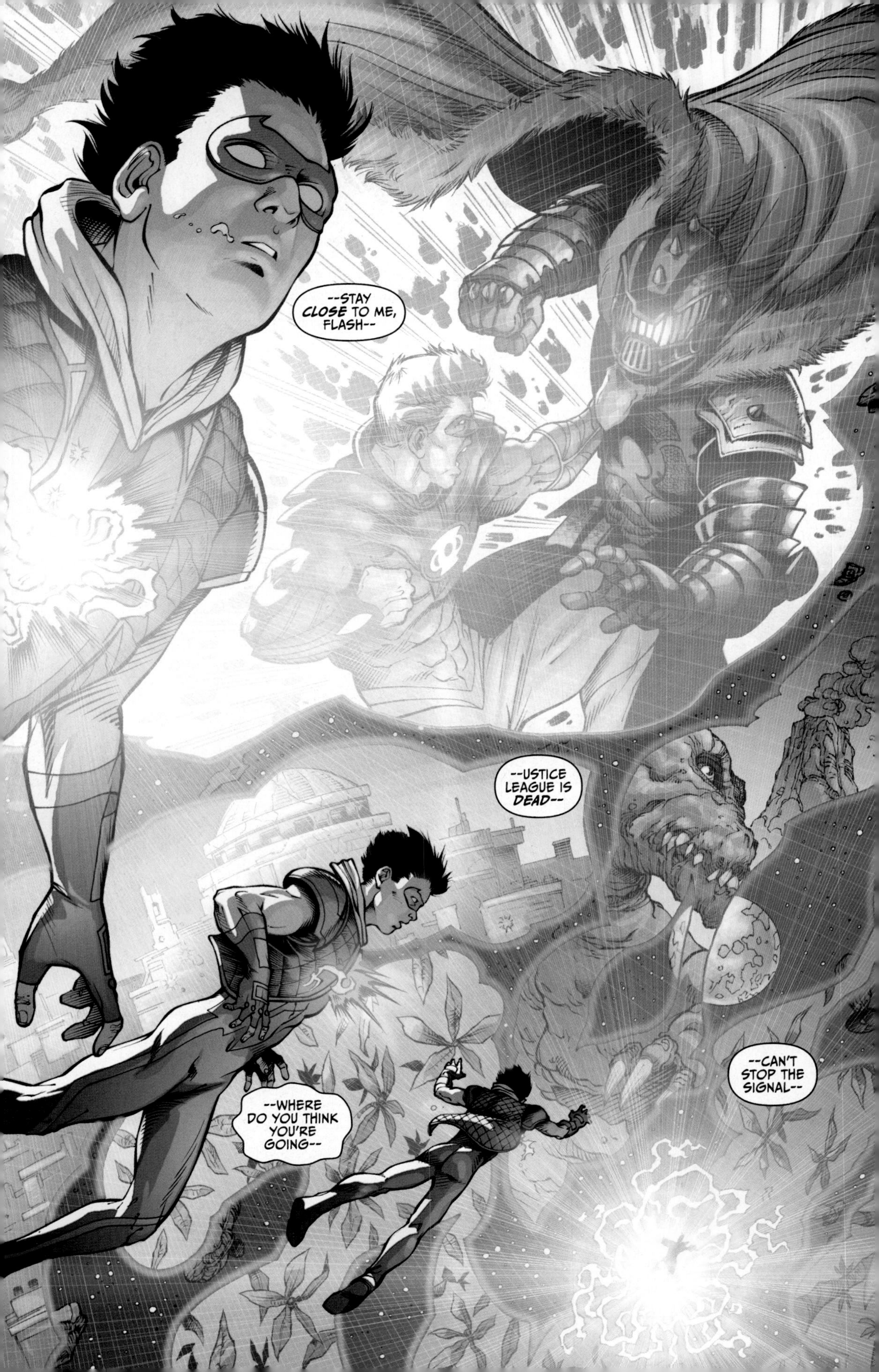
--STAY CLOSE TO ME, FLASH--
--USTICE LEAGUE IS DEAD--
--WHERE DO YOU THINK YOU'RE GOING--
--CAN'T STOP THE SIGNAL--

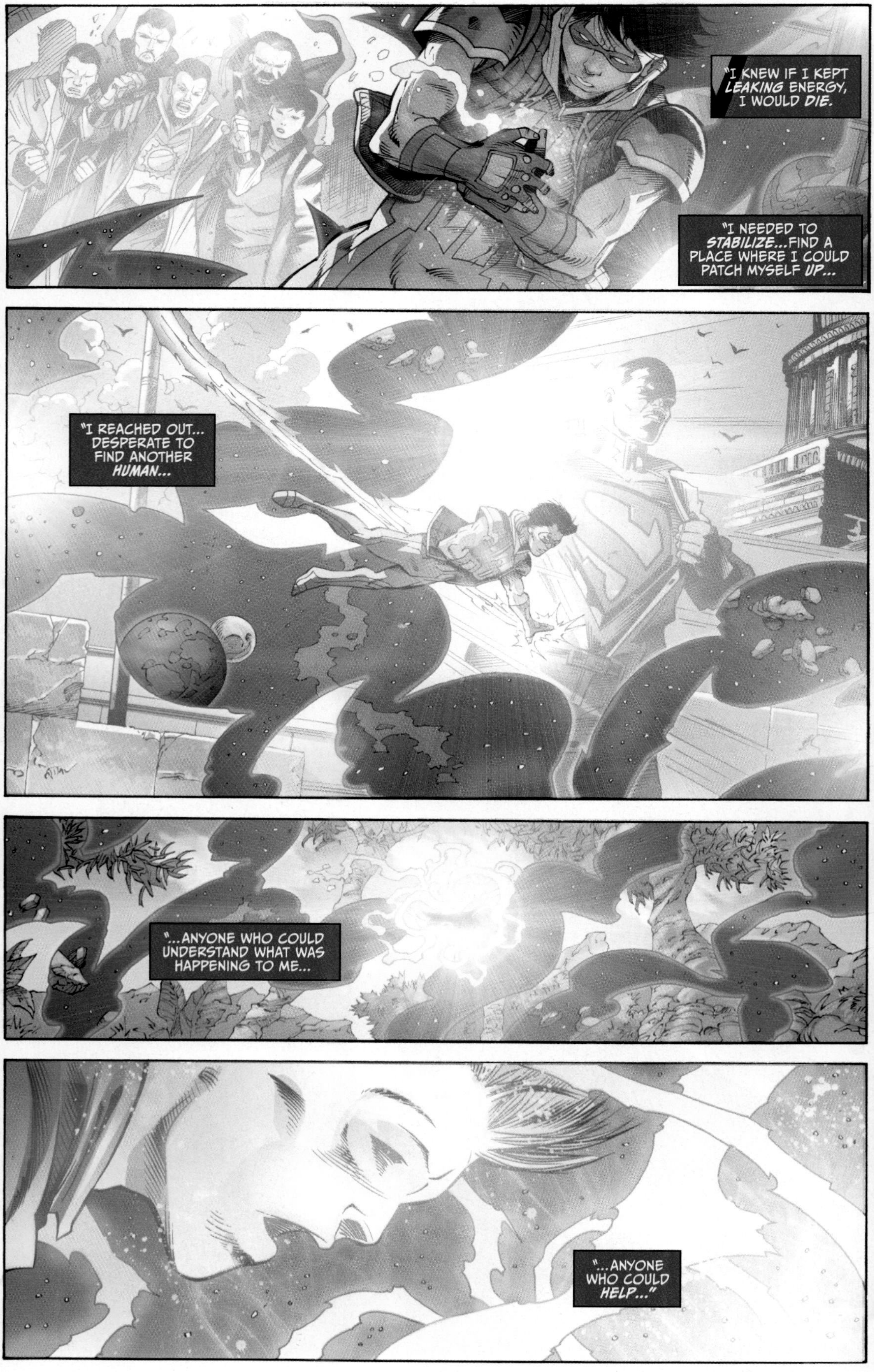
"I KNEW IF I KEPT LEAKING ENERGY, I WOULD DIE.
"I NEEDED TO STABILIZE...FIND A PLACE WHERE I COULD PATCH MYSELF UP...
"I REACHED OUT... DESPERATE TO FIND ANOTHER HUMAN...
"...ANYONE WHO COULD UNDERSTAND WHAT WAS HAPPENING TO ME...
"...ANYONE WHO COULD HELP..."

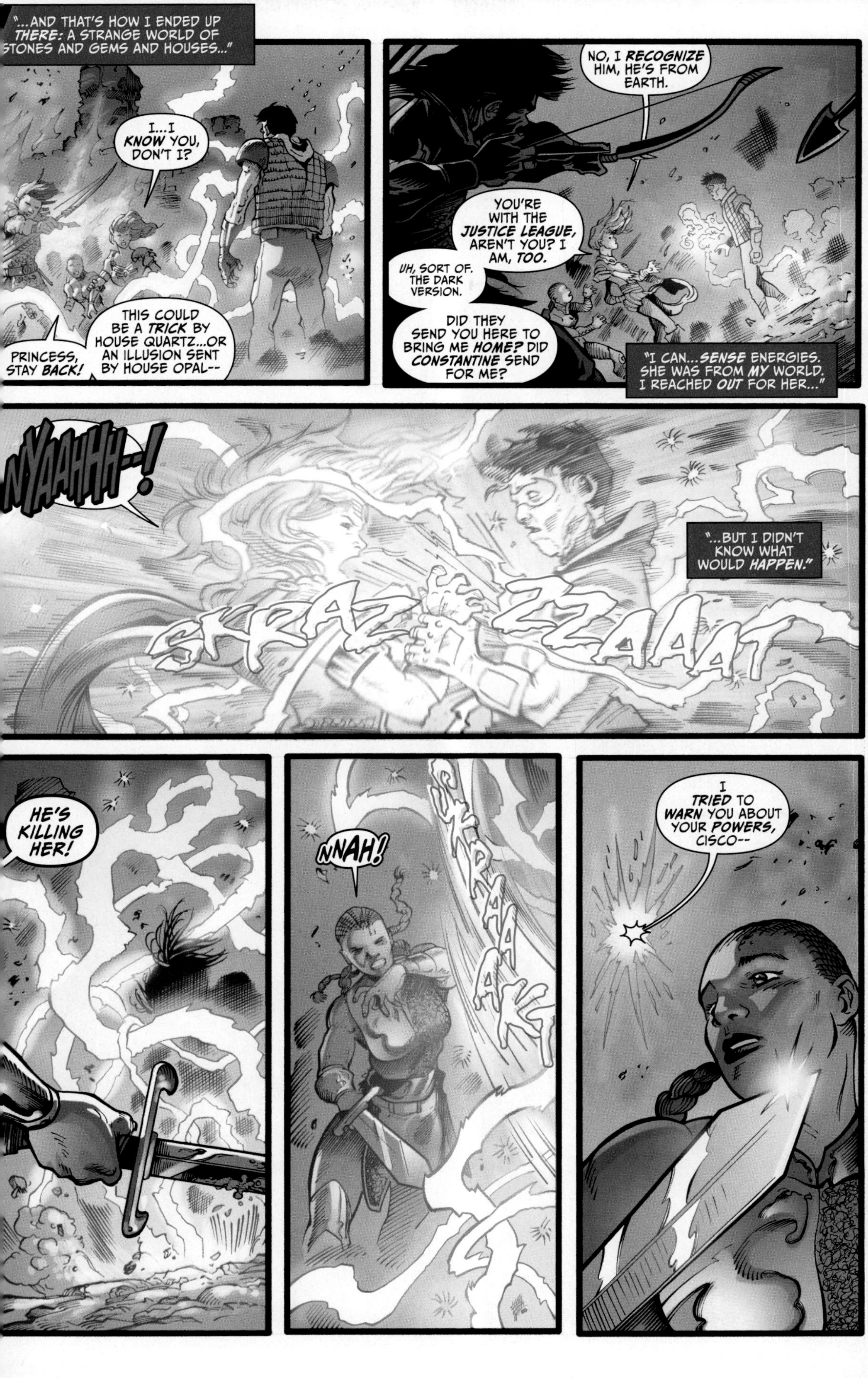
"...AND THAT'S HOW I ENDED UP THERE: A STRANGE WORLD OF STONES AND GEMS AND HOUSES..."
I...I KNOW YOU, DON'T I?
PRINCESS, STAY BACK!
THIS COULD BE A TRICK BY HOUSE QUARTZ...OR AN ILLUSION SENT BY HOUSE OPAL--
NO, I RECOGNIZE HIM, HE'S FROM EARTH.
YOU'RE WITH THE JUSTICE LEAGUE, AREN'T YOU? I AM, TOO.
UH, SORT OF. THE DARK VERSION.
DID THEY SEND YOU HERE TO BRING ME HOME? DID CONSTANTINE SEND FOR ME?
"I CAN...SENSE ENERGIES. SHE WAS FROM MY WORLD. I REACHED OUT FOR HER..."
NYAAHHH--!
"...BUT I DIDN'T KNOW WHAT WOULD HAPPEN."
SKRAZ ZZAAAAT
HE'S KILLING HER!
NNAH!
I TRIED TO WARN YOU ABOUT YOUR POWERS, CISCO--

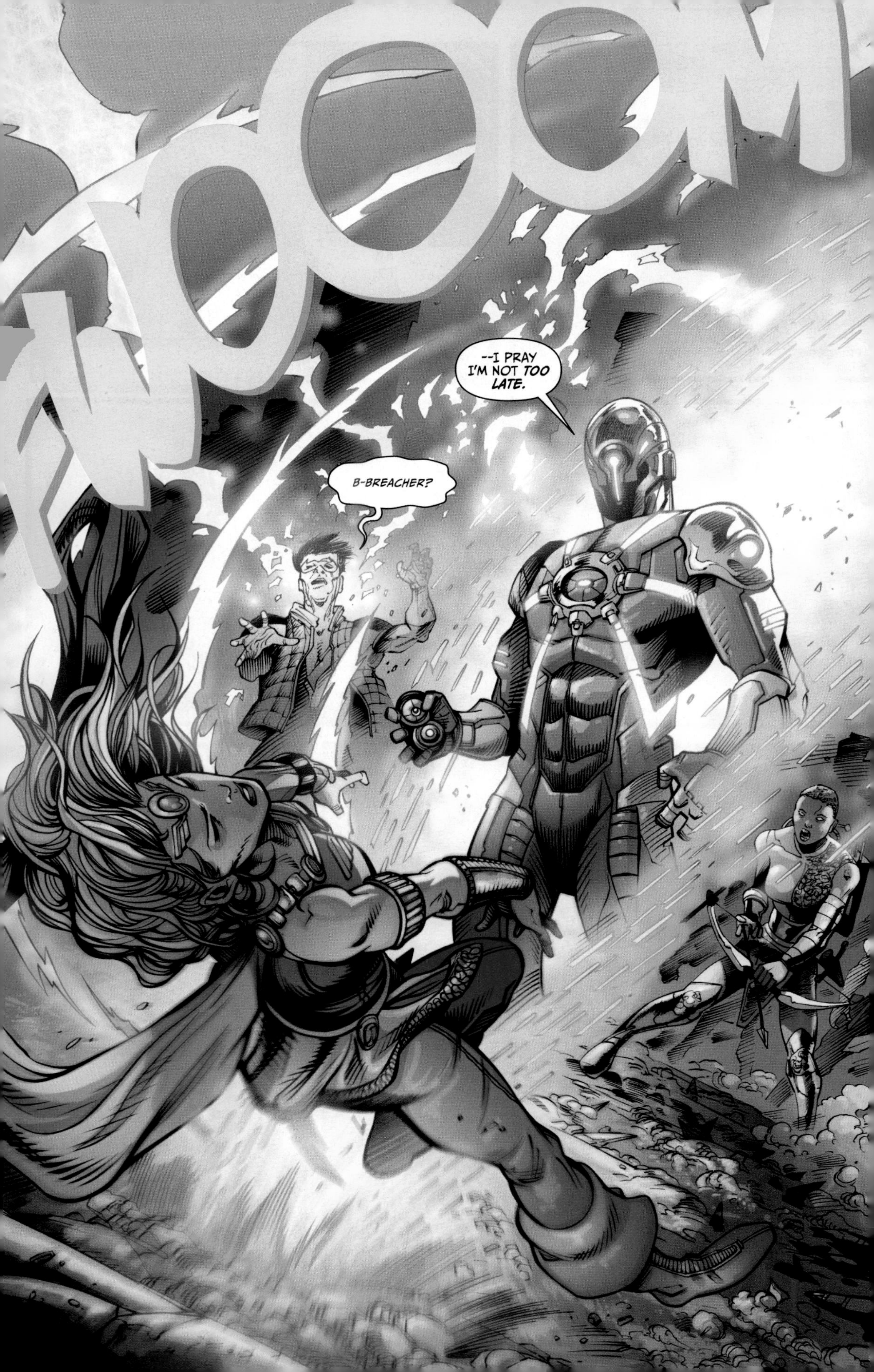
ZOOOM
--I PRAY I'M NOT TOO LATE.
B-BREACHER?

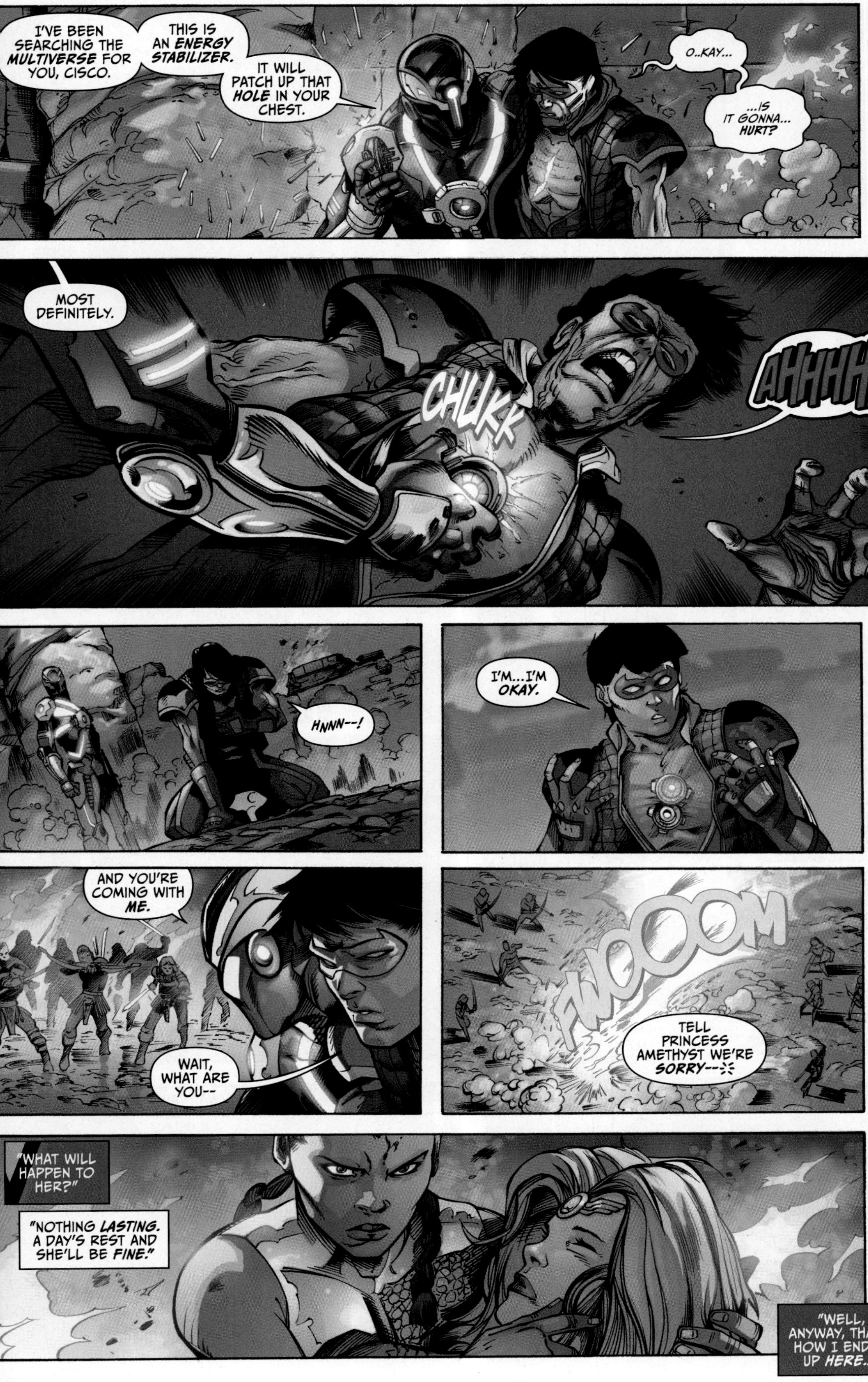
I'VE BEEN SEARCHING THE MULTIVERSE FOR YOU, CISCO.
THIS IS AN ENERGY STABILIZER.
IT WILL PATCH UP THAT HOLE IN YOUR CHEST.
O..KAY...
...IS IT GONNA... HURT?
MOST DEFINITELY.
CHUKK
AHHHH!
HNNN--!
I'M...I'M OKAY.
AND YOU'RE COMING WITH ME.
WAIT, WHAT ARE YOU--
FWOOOOM
TELL PRINCESS AMETHYST WE'RE SORRY--
"WHAT WILL HAPPEN TO HER?"
"NOTHING LASTING. A DAY'S REST AND SHE'LL BE FINE."
"WELL, ANYWAY, THAT'S HOW I ENDED UP HERE..."

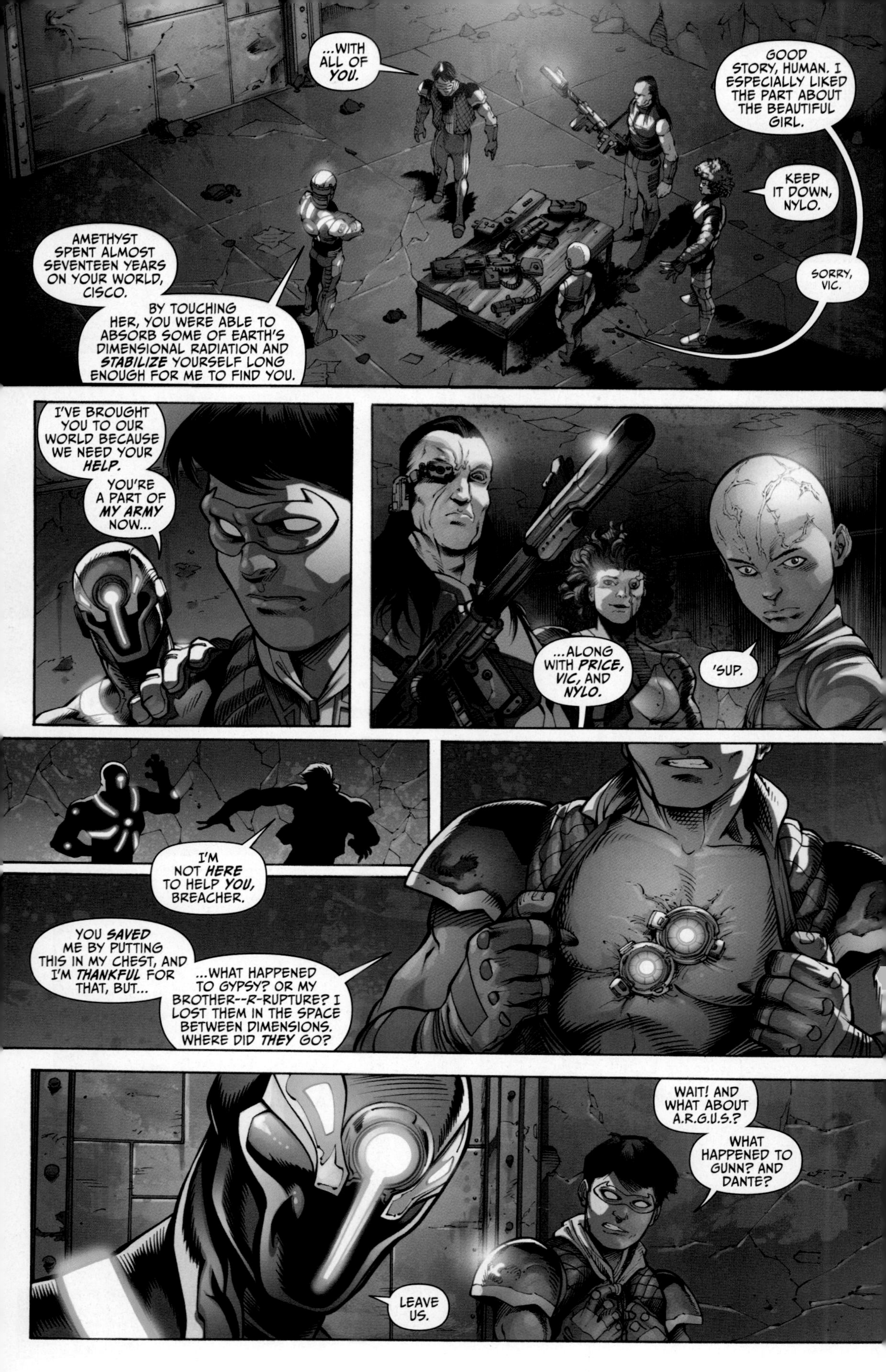
...WITH ALL OF YOU.
GOOD STORY, HUMAN. I ESPECIALLY LIKED THE PART ABOUT THE BEAUTIFUL GIRL.
KEEP IT DOWN, NYLO.
SORRY, VIC.
AMETHYST SPENT ALMOST SEVENTEEN YEARS ON YOUR WORLD, CISCO.
BY TOUCHING HER, YOU WERE ABLE TO ABSORB SOME OF EARTH'S DIMENSIONAL RADIATION AND STABILIZE YOURSELF LONG ENOUGH FOR ME TO FIND YOU.
I'VE BROUGHT YOU TO OUR WORLD BECAUSE WE NEED YOUR HELP.
YOU'RE A PART OF MY ARMY NOW...
...ALONG WITH PRICE, VIC, AND NYLO.
'SUP.
I'M NOT HERE TO HELP YOU, BREACHER.
YOU SAVED ME BY PUTTING THIS IN MY CHEST, AND I'M THANKFUL FOR THAT, BUT...
...WHAT HAPPENED TO GYPSY? OR MY BROTHER--R-RUPTURE? I LOST THEM IN THE SPACE BETWEEN DIMENSIONS. WHERE DID THEY GO?
WAIT! AND WHAT ABOUT A.R.G.U.S.?
WHAT HAPPENED TO GUNN? AND DANTE?
LEAVE US.

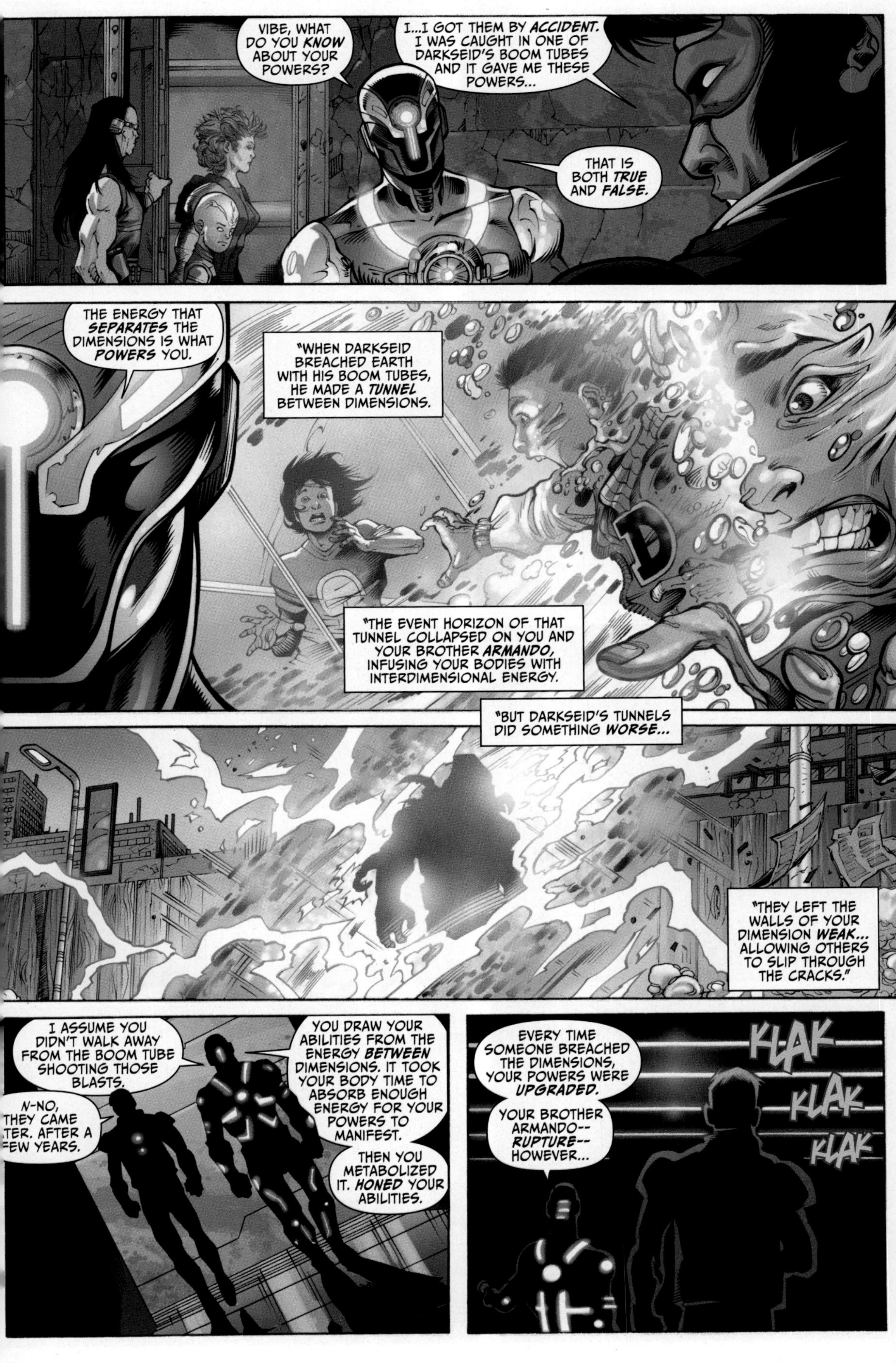

VIBE, WHAT DO YOU KNOW ABOUT YOUR POWERS?
I...I GOT THEM BY ACCIDENT. I WAS CAUGHT IN ONE OF DARKSEID'S BOOM TUBES AND IT GAVE ME THESE POWERS...
THAT IS BOTH TRUE AND FALSE.
THE ENERGY THAT SEPARATES THE DIMENSIONS IS WHAT POWERS YOU.
"WHEN DARKSEID BREACHED EARTH WITH HIS BOOM TUBES, HE MADE A TUNNEL BETWEEN DIMENSIONS.
"THE EVENT HORIZON OF THAT TUNNEL COLLAPSED ON YOU AND YOUR BROTHER ARMANDO, INFUSING YOUR BODIES WITH INTERDIMENSIONAL ENERGY.
"BUT DARKSEID'S TUNNELS DID SOMETHING WORSE...
"THEY LEFT THE WALLS OF YOUR DIMENSION WEAK... ALLOWING OTHERS TO SLIP THROUGH THE CRACKS."
I ASSUME YOU DIDN'T WALK AWAY FROM THE BOOM TUBE SHOOTING THOSE BLASTS.
N-NO, THEY CAME LATER. AFTER A FEW YEARS.
YOU DRAW YOUR ABILITIES FROM THE ENERGY BETWEEN DIMENSIONS. IT TOOK YOUR BODY TIME TO ABSORB ENOUGH ENERGY FOR YOUR POWERS TO MANIFEST.
THEN YOU METABOLIZED IT. HONED YOUR ABILITIES.
EVERY TIME SOMEONE BREACHED THE DIMENSIONS, YOUR POWERS WERE UPGRADED.
KLAK
KLAK
KLAK
YOUR BROTHER ARMANDO-- RUPTURE-- HOWEVER...

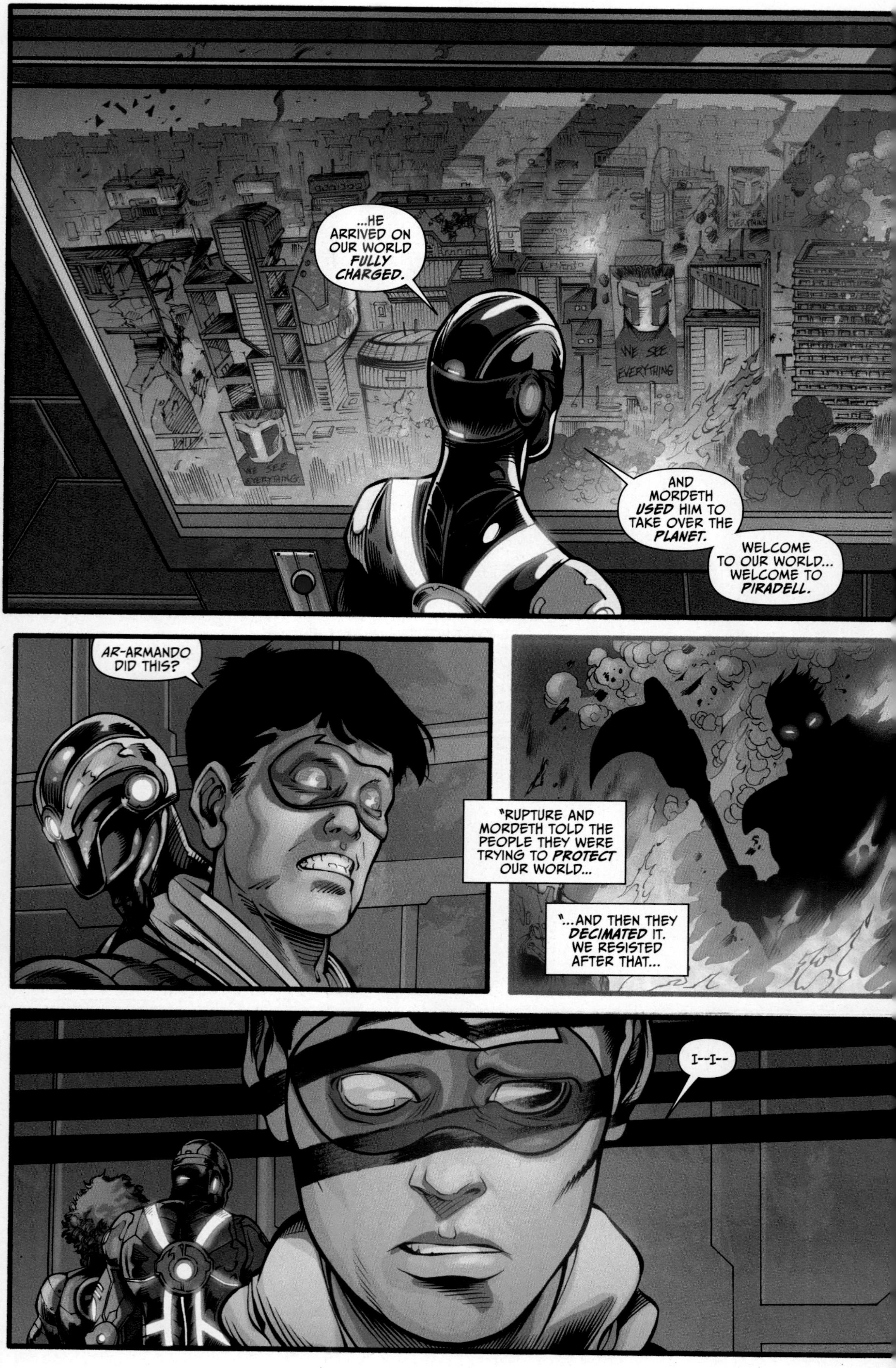
...HE ARRIVED ON OUR WORLD FULLY CHARGED.
WE SEE EVERYTHING
WE SEE EVERYTHING
WE SEE EVERYTHING
AND MORDETH USED HIM TO TAKE OVER THE PLANET.
WELCOME TO OUR WORLD... WELCOME TO PIRADELL.
AR-ARMANDO DID THIS?
"RUPTURE AND MORDETH TOLD THE PEOPLE THEY WERE TRYING TO PROTECT OUR WORLD...
"...AND THEN THEY DECIMATED IT. WE RESISTED AFTER THAT...
I--I--

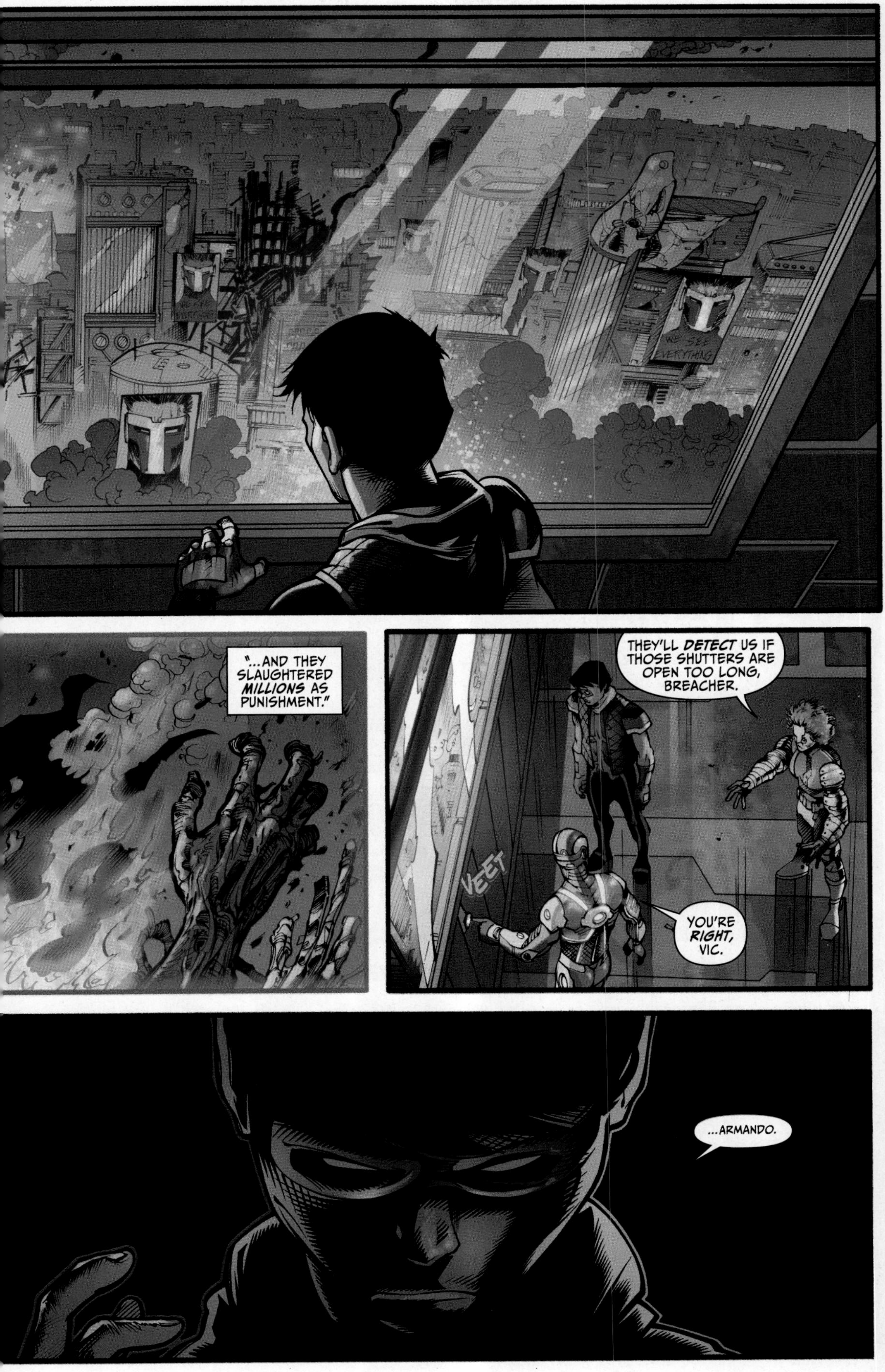
WE SEE EVERYTHING
"...AND THEY SLAUGHTERED MILLIONS AS PUNISHMENT."
THEY'LL DETECT US IF THOSE SHUTTERS ARE OPEN TOO LONG, BREACHER.
VEET
YOU'RE RIGHT, VIC.
...ARMANDO.

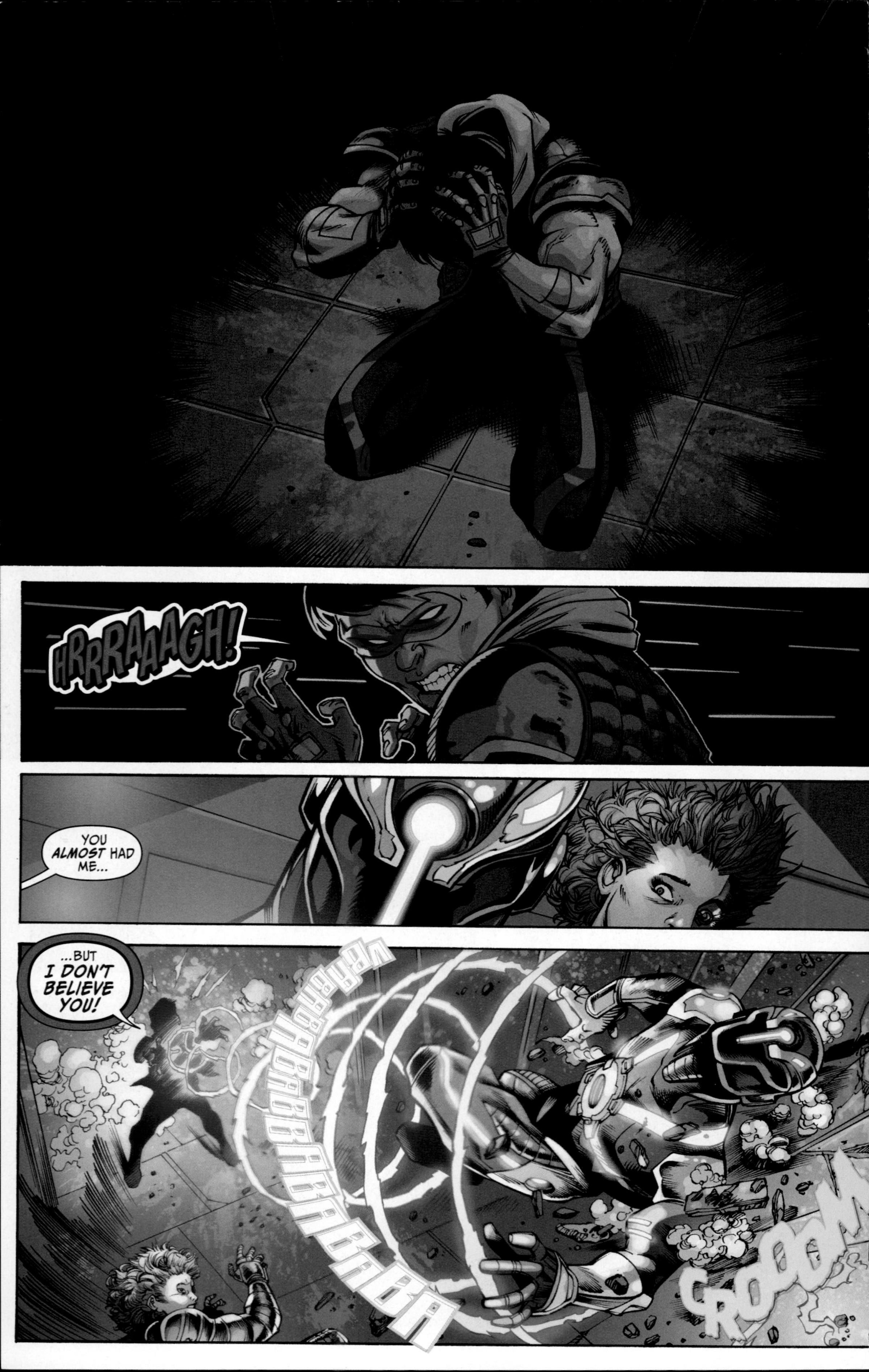
HRRRAAAGH!
YOU ALMOST HAD ME...
...BUT I DON'T BELIEVE YOU!

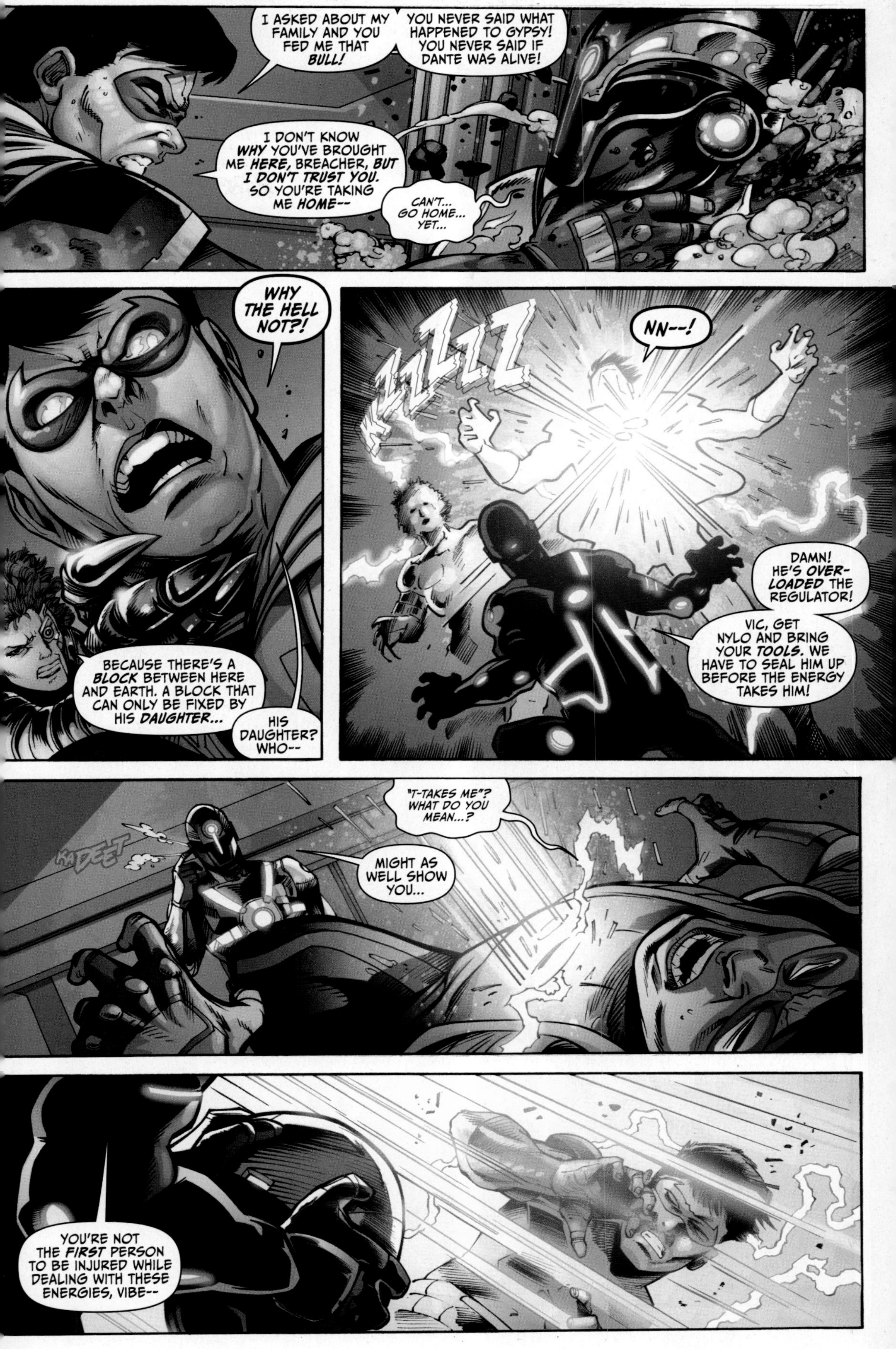

I ASKED ABOUT MY FAMILY AND YOU FED ME THAT BULL!
YOU NEVER SAID WHAT HAPPENED TO GYPSY! YOU NEVER SAID IF DANTE WAS ALIVE!
I DON'T KNOW WHY YOU'VE BROUGHT ME HERE, BREACHER, BUT I DON'T TRUST YOU. SO YOU'RE TAKING ME HOME--
CAN'T... GO HOME... YET...
WHY THE HELL NOT?!
BECAUSE THERE'S A BLOCK BETWEEN HERE AND EARTH. A BLOCK THAT CAN ONLY BE FIXED BY HIS DAUGHTER...
HIS DAUGHTER? WHO--
ZZZZZ
NN--!
DAMN! HE'S OVER-LOADED THE REGULATOR!
VIC, GET NYLO AND BRING YOUR TOOLS. WE HAVE TO SEAL HIM UP BEFORE THE ENERGY TAKES HIM!
KADEET
"T-TAKES ME"? WHAT DO YOU MEAN...?
MIGHT AS WELL SHOW YOU...
YOU'RE NOT THE FIRST PERSON TO BE INJURED WHILE DEALING WITH THESE ENERGIES, VIBE--

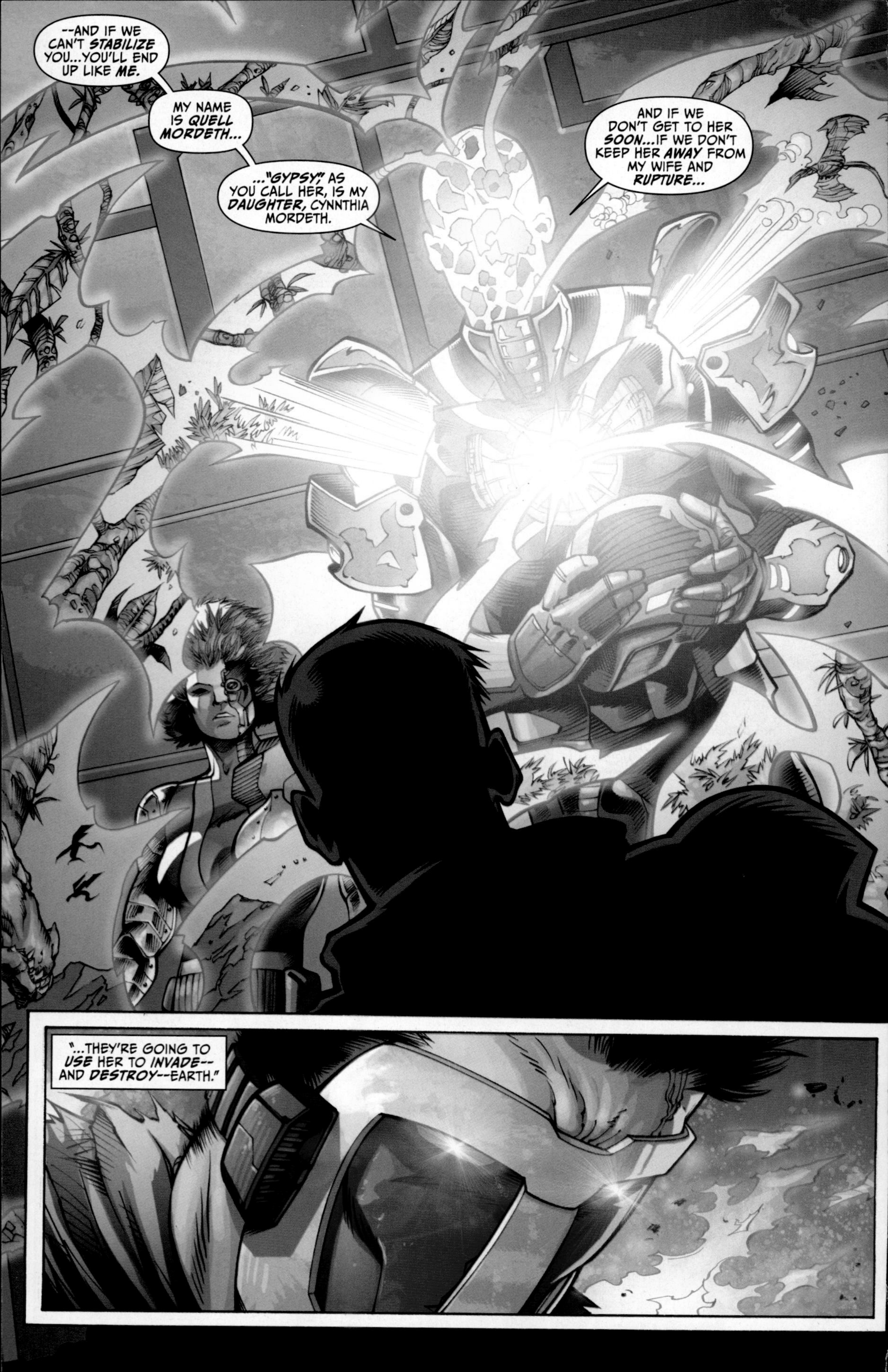
--AND IF WE CAN'T STABILIZE YOU...YOU'LL END UP LIKE ME.
MY NAME IS QUELL MORDETH...
..."GYPSY," AS YOU CALL HER, IS MY DAUGHTER, CYNNTHIA MORDETH.
AND IF WE DON'T GET TO HER SOON...IF WE DON'T KEEP HER AWAY FROM MY WIFE AND RUPTURE...
"...THEY'RE GOING TO USE HER TO INVADE--AND DESTROY--EARTH."

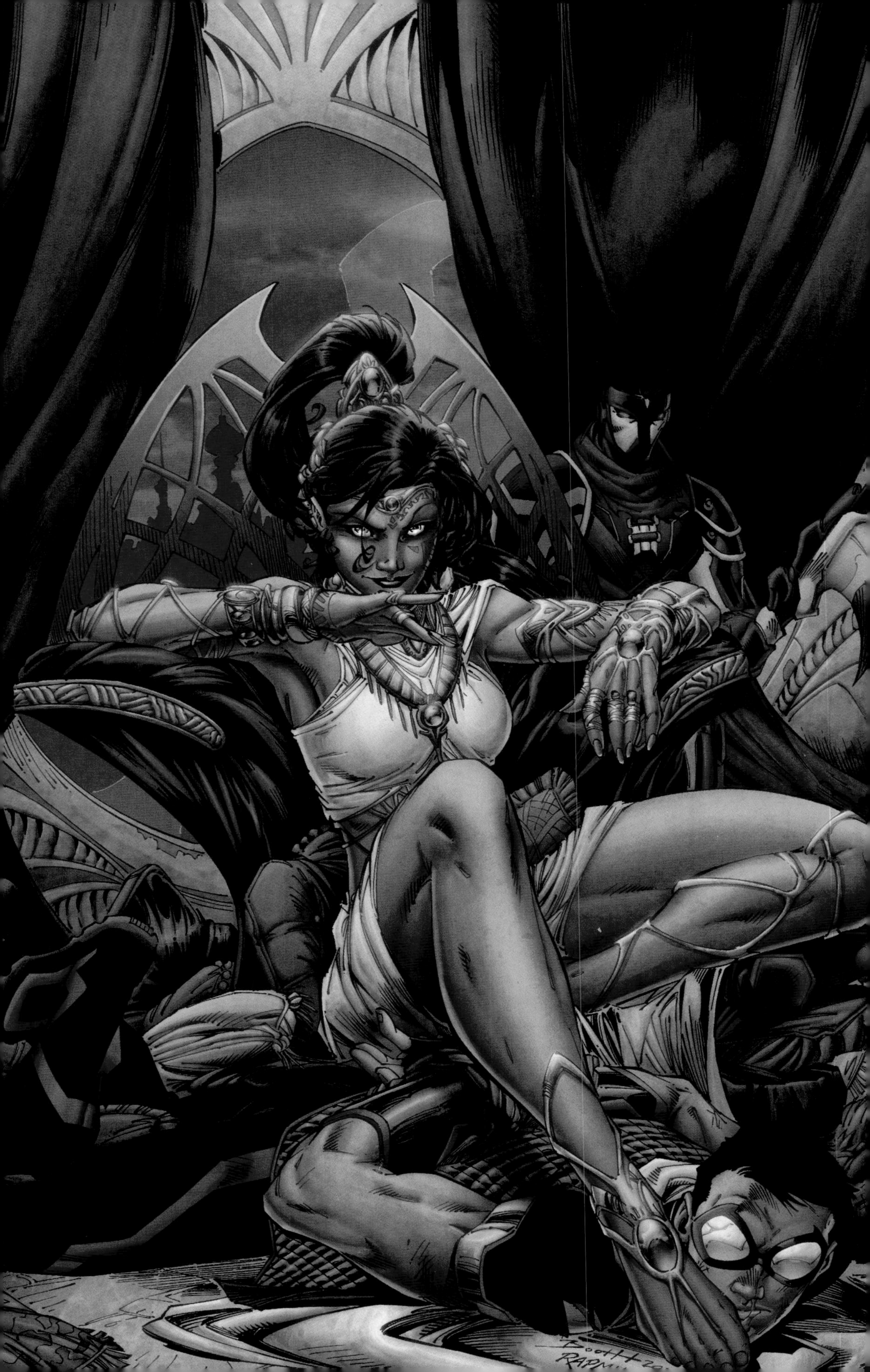

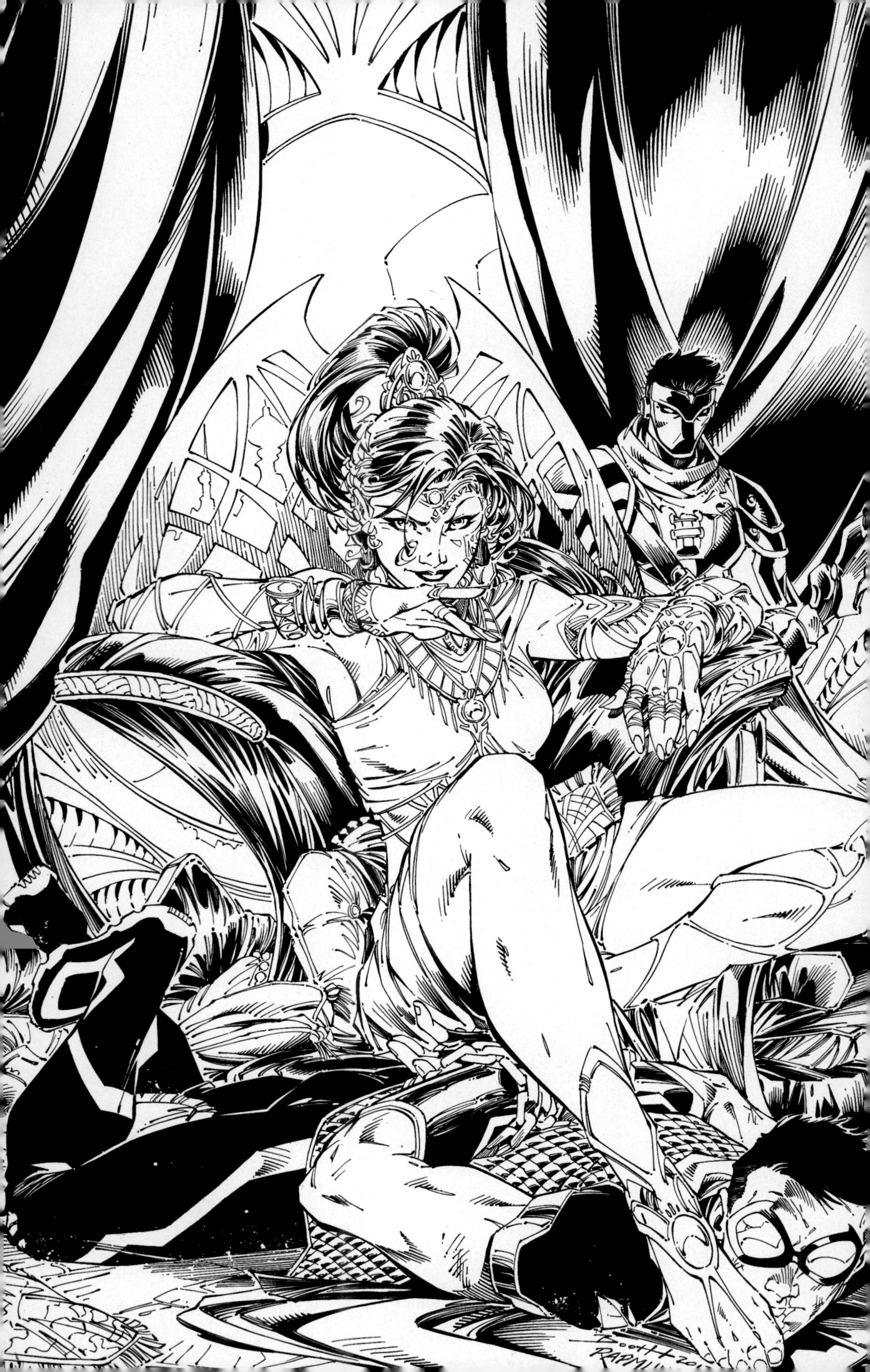

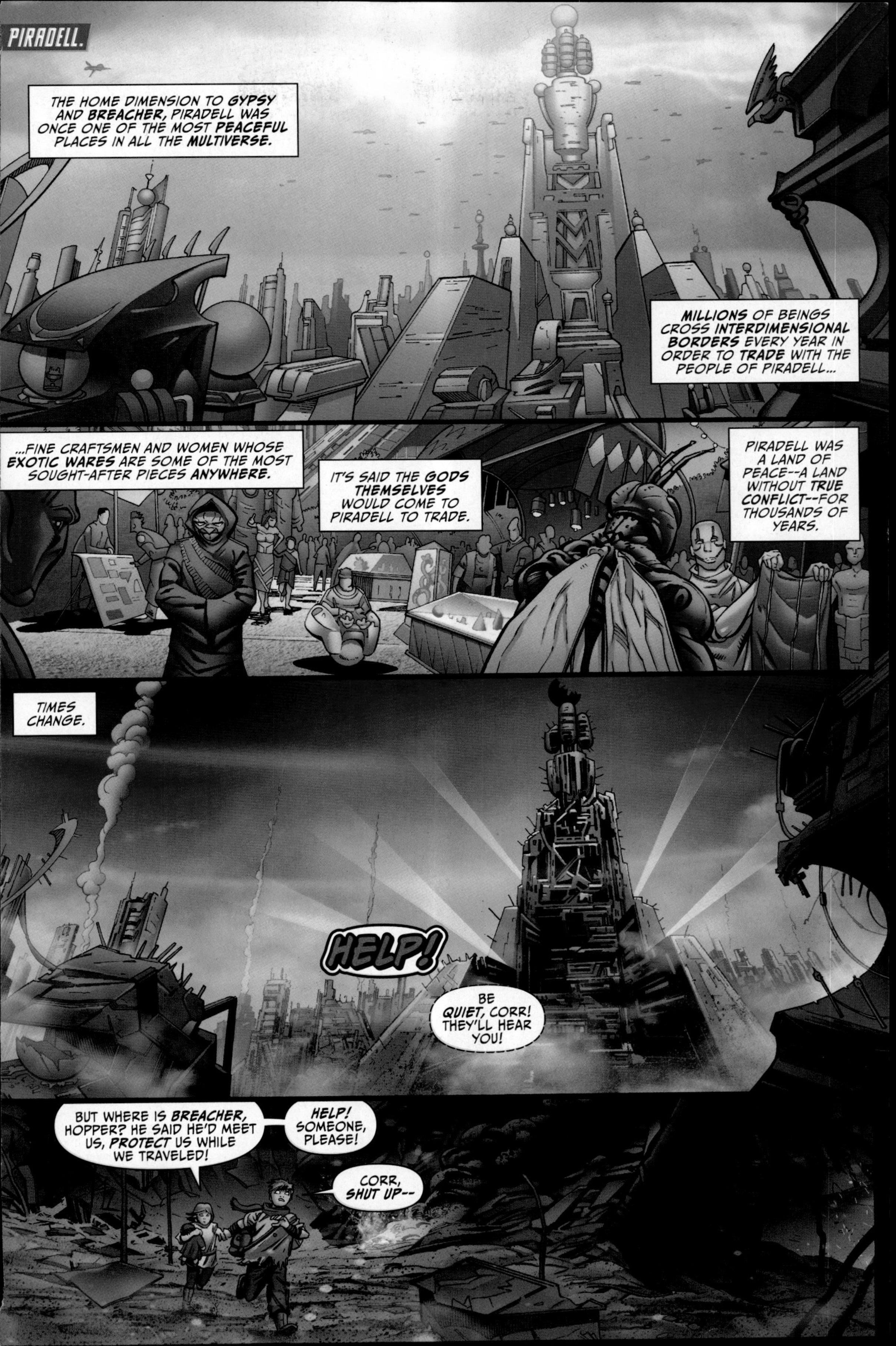
PIRADELL.
THE HOME DIMENSION TO GYPSY AND BREACHER, PIRADELL WAS ONCE ONE OF THE MOST PEACEFUL PLACES IN ALL THE MULTIVERSE.
MILLIONS OF BEINGS CROSS INTERDIMENSIONAL BORDERS EVERY YEAR IN ORDER TO TRADE WITH THE PEOPLE OF PIRADELL...
...FINE CRAFTSMEN AND WOMEN WHOSE EXOTIC WARES ARE SOME OF THE MOST SOUGHT-AFTER PIECES ANYWHERE.
IT'S SAID THE GODS THEMSELVES WOULD COME TO PIRADELL TO TRADE.
PIRADELL WAS A LAND OF PEACE--A LAND WITHOUT TRUE CONFLICT--FOR THOUSANDS OF YEARS.
TIMES CHANGE.
HELP!
BE QUIET, CORR! THEY'LL HEAR YOU!
BUT WHERE IS BREACHER, HOPPER? HE SAID HE'D MEET US, PROTECT US WHILE WE TRAVELED!
HELP! SOMEONE, PLEASE!
CORR, SHUT UP--

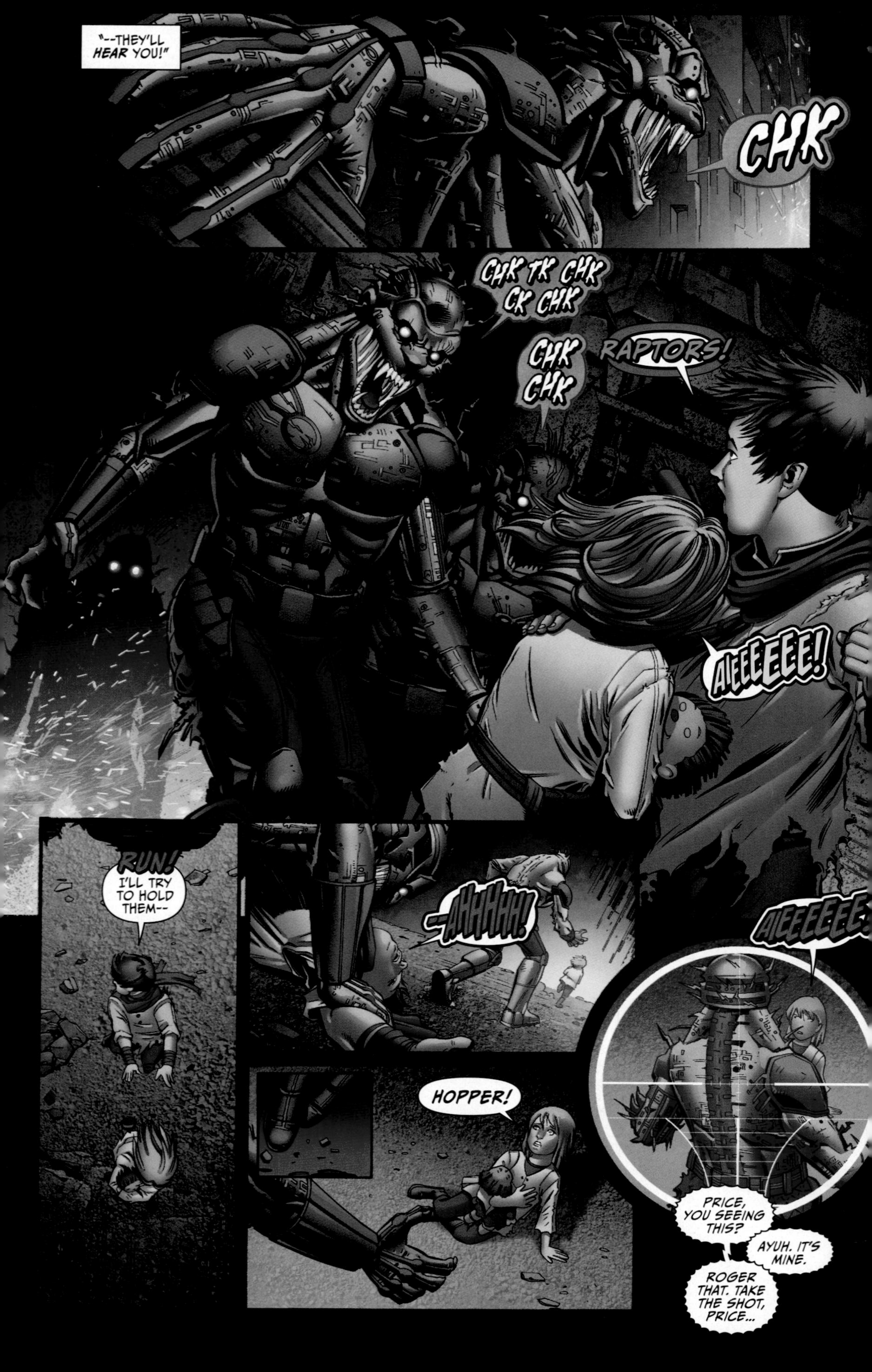
"--THEY'LL HEAR YOU!"
CHK
CHK TK CHK CK CHK
CHK CHK
RAPTORS!
AIEEEEEE!
RUN! I'LL TRY TO HOLD THEM--
--AHHHHH!
AIEEEEEE
HOPPER!
PRICE, YOU SEEING THIS?
AYUH. IT'S MINE.
ROGER THAT. TAKE THE SHOT, PRICE...

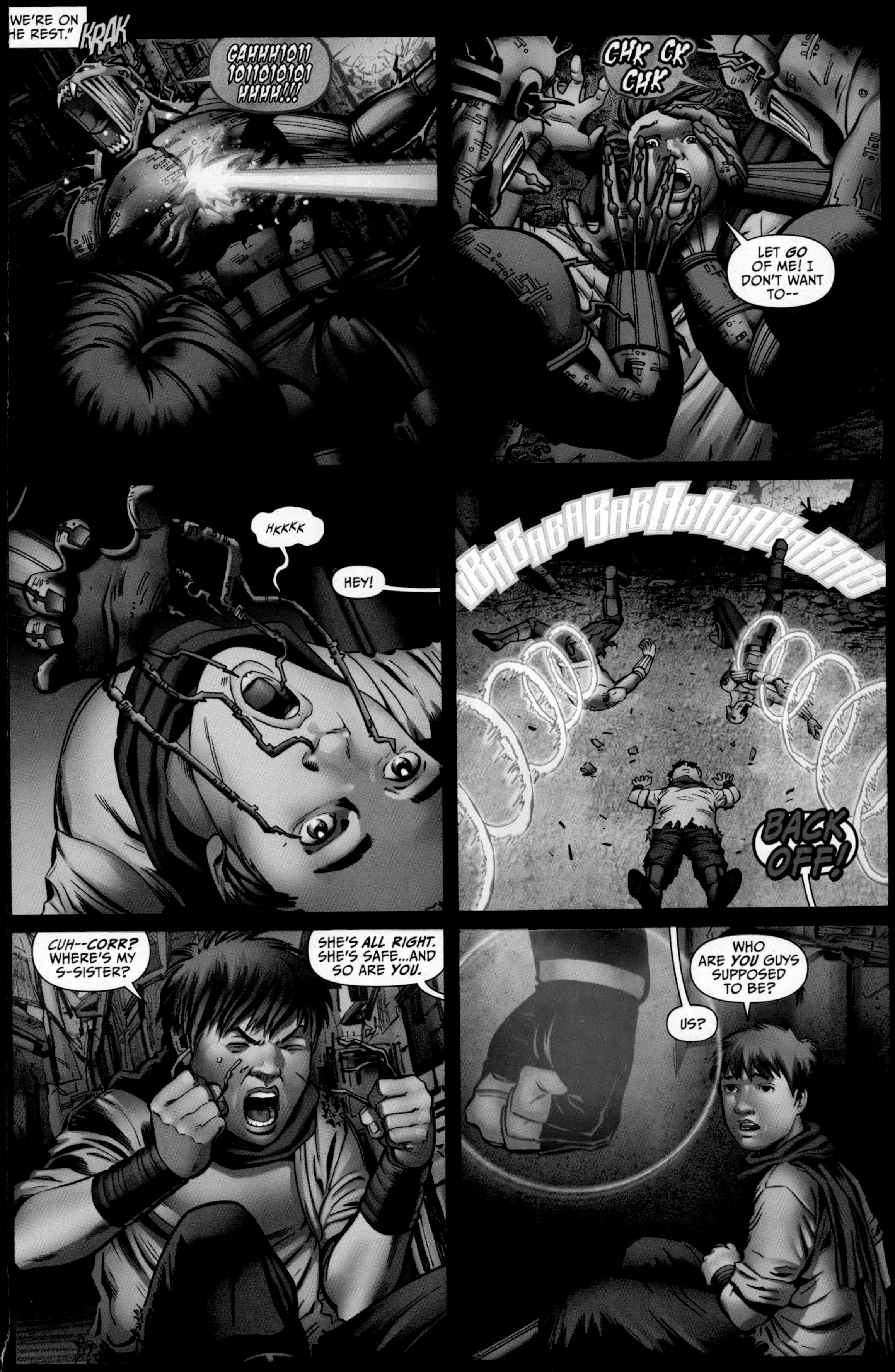
WE'RE ON
HE REST."
KRAK
GAHHH1011
1011010101
HHHH!!!
CHK CK
CHK
LET GO OF ME! I DON'T WANT TO--
HKKKK
HEY!
BABABABABABABABABAB
BACK OFF!
CUH--CORR? WHERE'S MY S-SISTER?
SHE'S ALL RIGHT. SHE'S SAFE...AND SO ARE YOU.
WHO ARE YOU GUYS SUPPOSED TO BE?
US?

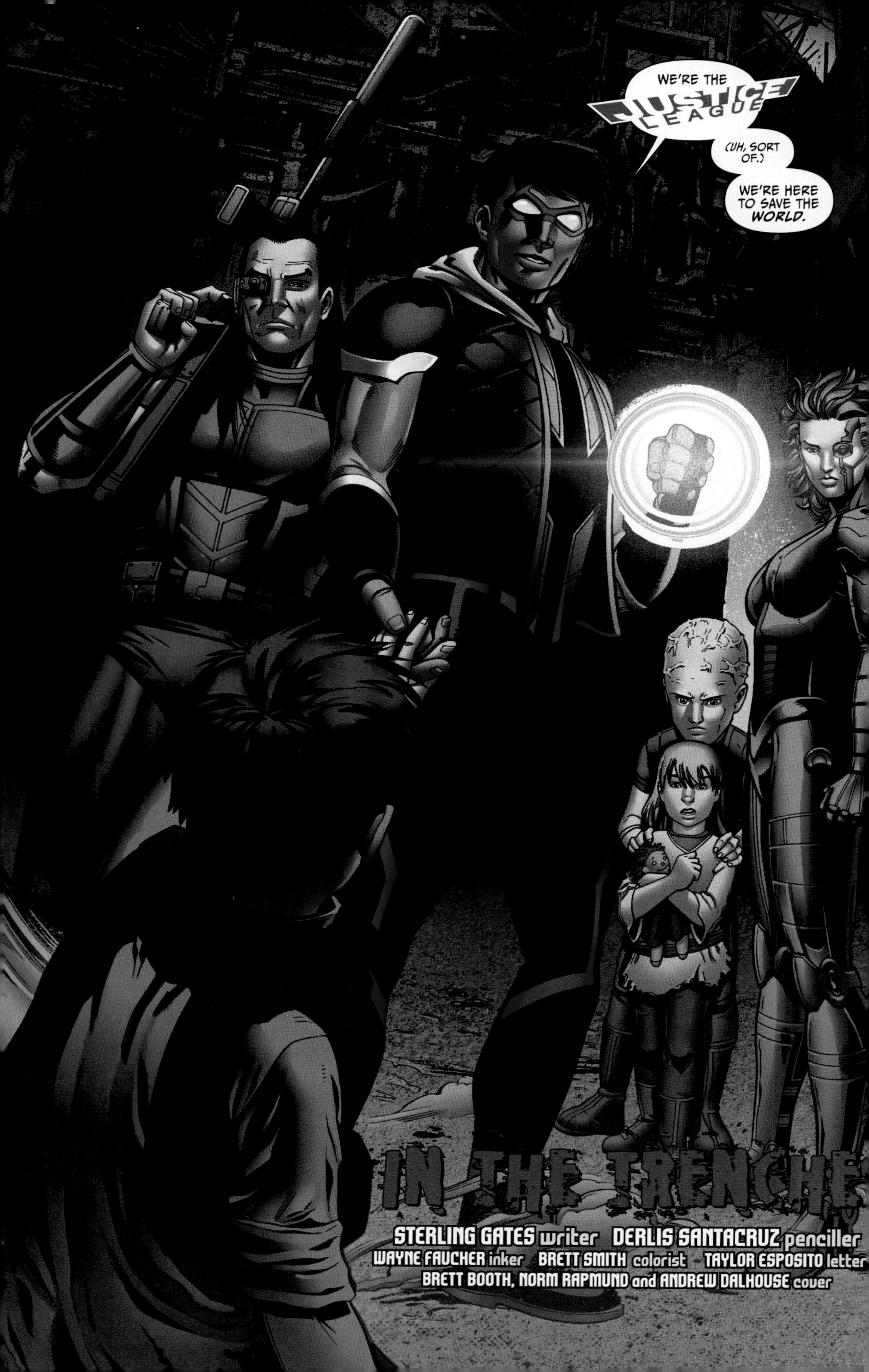
WE'RE THE JUSTICE LEAGUE
(UH, SORT OF.)
WE'RE HERE TO SAVE THE WORLD.
IN THE TRENCHE
STERLING GATES writer DERLIS SANTACRUZ penciller
WAYNE FAUCHER inker BRETT SMITH colorist TAYLOR ESPOSITO letter
BRETT BOOTH, NORM RAPMUND and ANDREW DALHOUSE cover

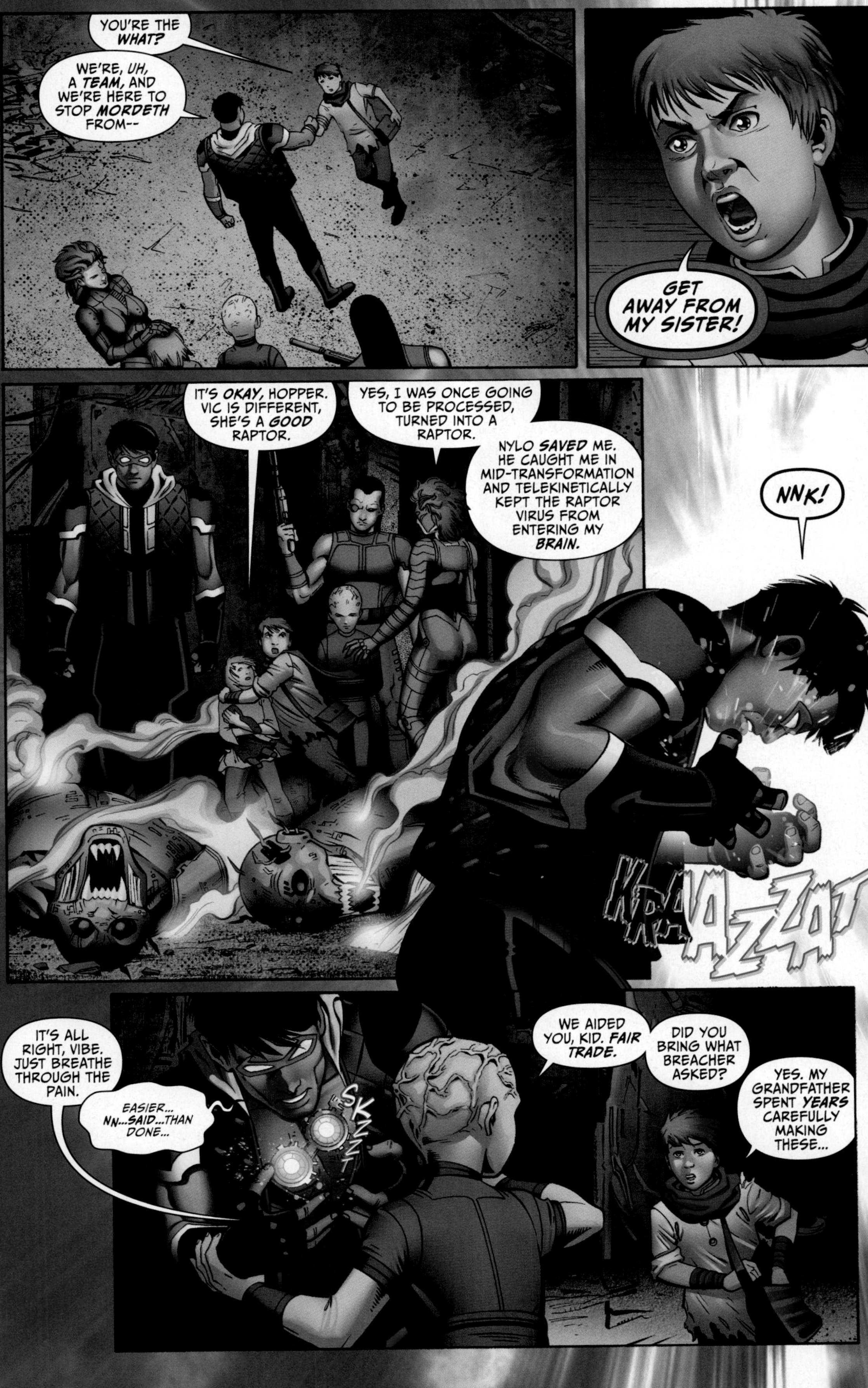

YOU'RE THE WHAT?
WE'RE, UH, A TEAM, AND WE'RE HERE TO STOP MORDETH FROM--
GET AWAY FROM MY SISTER!
IT'S OKAY, HOPPER. VIC IS DIFFERENT, SHE'S A GOOD RAPTOR.
YES, I WAS ONCE GOING TO BE PROCESSED, TURNED INTO A RAPTOR.
NYLO SAVED ME. HE CAUGHT ME IN MID-TRANSFORMATION AND TELEKINETICALLY KEPT THE RAPTOR VIRUS FROM ENTERING MY BRAIN.
NNK!
KRAAAZZAT
IT'S ALL RIGHT, VIBE. JUST BREATHE THROUGH THE PAIN.
EASIER... NN...SAID...THAN DONE...
SKZZZT
WE AIDED YOU, KID. FAIR TRADE.
DID YOU BRING WHAT BREACHER ASKED?
YES. MY GRANDFATHER SPENT YEARS CAREFULLY MAKING THESE...

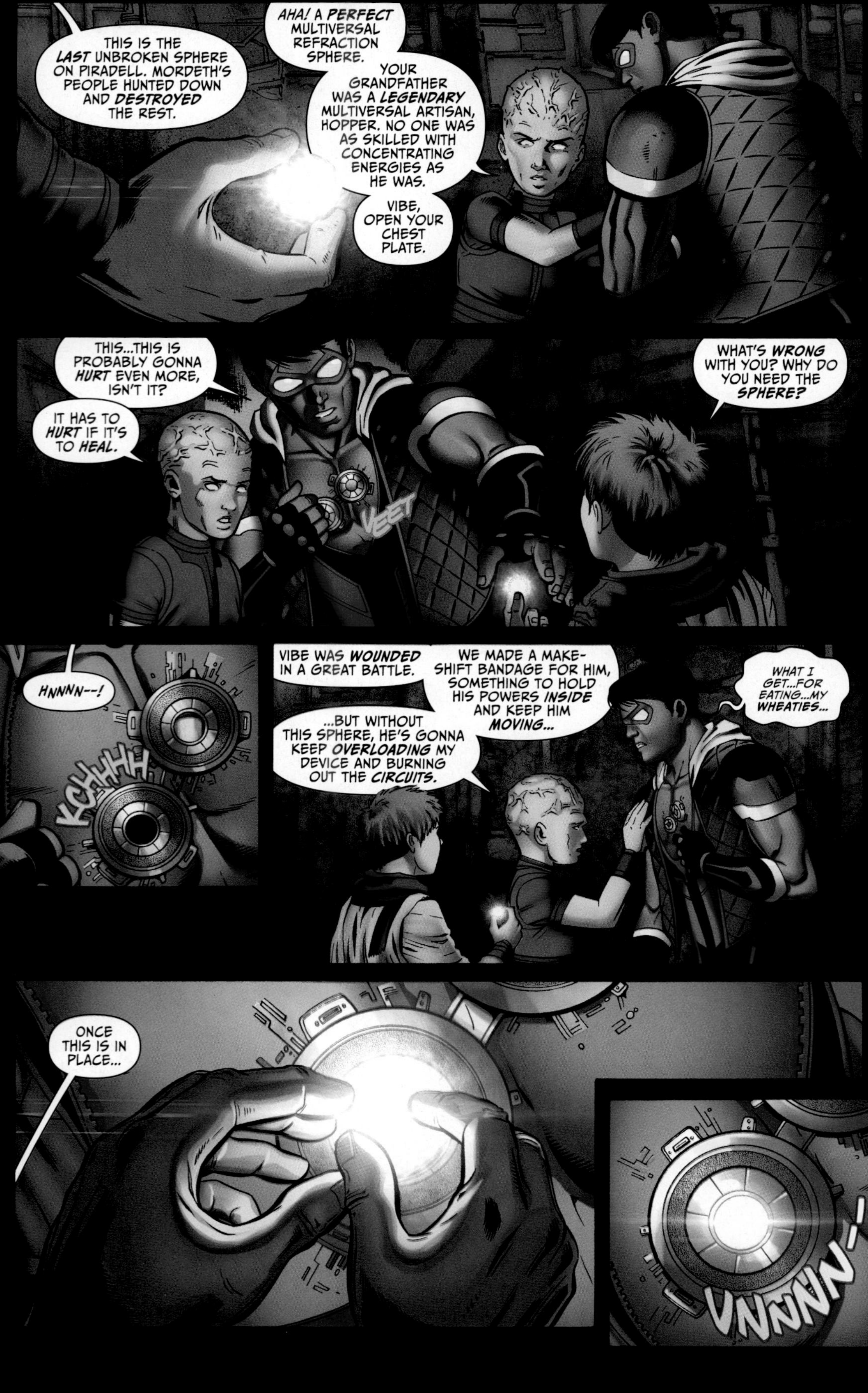
THIS IS THE LAST UNBROKEN SPHERE ON PIRADELL. MORDETH'S PEOPLE HUNTED DOWN AND DESTROYED THE REST.
AHA! A PERFECT MULTIVERSAL REFRACTION SPHERE.
YOUR GRANDFATHER WAS A LEGENDARY MULTIVERSAL ARTISAN, HOPPER. NO ONE WAS AS SKILLED WITH CONCENTRATING ENERGIES AS HE WAS.
VIBE, OPEN YOUR CHEST PLATE.
THIS...THIS IS PROBABLY GONNA HURT EVEN MORE, ISN'T IT?
IT HAS TO HURT IF IT'S TO HEAL.
VEET
WHAT'S WRONG WITH YOU? WHY DO YOU NEED THE SPHERE?
HNNNN--!
KCHHHH
VIBE WAS WOUNDED IN A GREAT BATTLE.
WE MADE A MAKE-SHIFT BANDAGE FOR HIM, SOMETHING TO HOLD HIS POWERS INSIDE AND KEEP HIM MOVING...
...BUT WITHOUT THIS SPHERE, HE'S GONNA KEEP OVERLOADING MY DEVICE AND BURNING OUT THE CIRCUITS.
WHAT I GET...FOR EATING...MY WHEATIES...
ONCE THIS IS IN PLACE...
VNNNN--

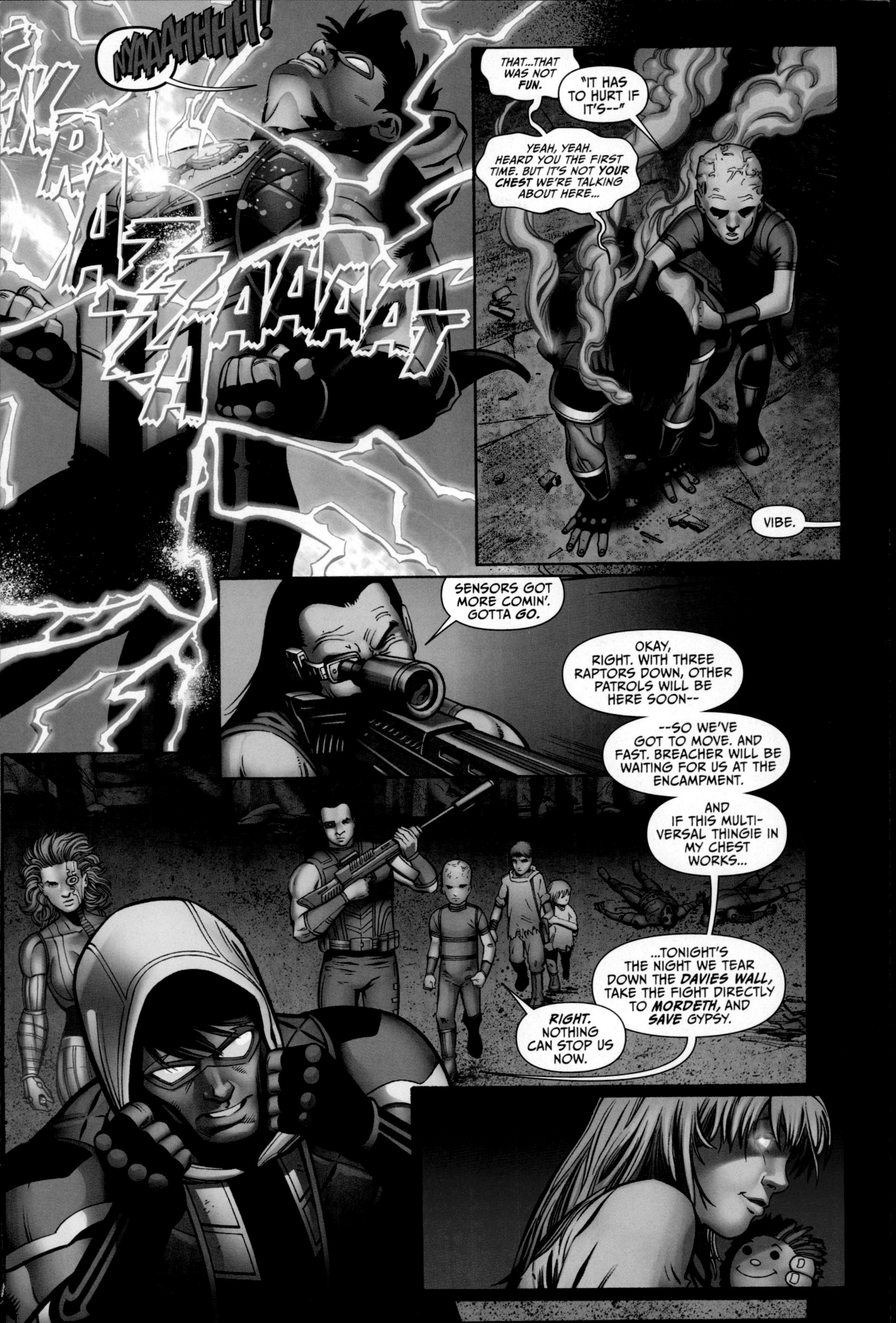
NYAAAHHHH!
KRAZZAAAAT
THAT...THAT WAS NOT FUN.
"IT HAS TO HURT IF IT'S--"
YEAH, YEAH. HEARD YOU THE FIRST TIME. BUT IT'S NOT YOUR CHEST WE'RE TALKING ABOUT HERE...
VIBE.
SENSORS GOT MORE COMIN'. GOTTA GO.
OKAY, RIGHT. WITH THREE RAPTORS DOWN, OTHER PATROLS WILL BE HERE SOON--
--SO WE'VE GOT TO MOVE. AND FAST. BREACHER WILL BE WAITING FOR US AT THE ENCAMPMENT.
AND IF THIS MULTI-VERSAL THINGIE IN MY CHEST WORKS...
...TONIGHT'S THE NIGHT WE TEAR DOWN THE DAVIES WALL, TAKE THE FIGHT DIRECTLY TO MORDETH, AND SAVE GYPSY.
RIGHT. NOTHING CAN STOP US NOW.

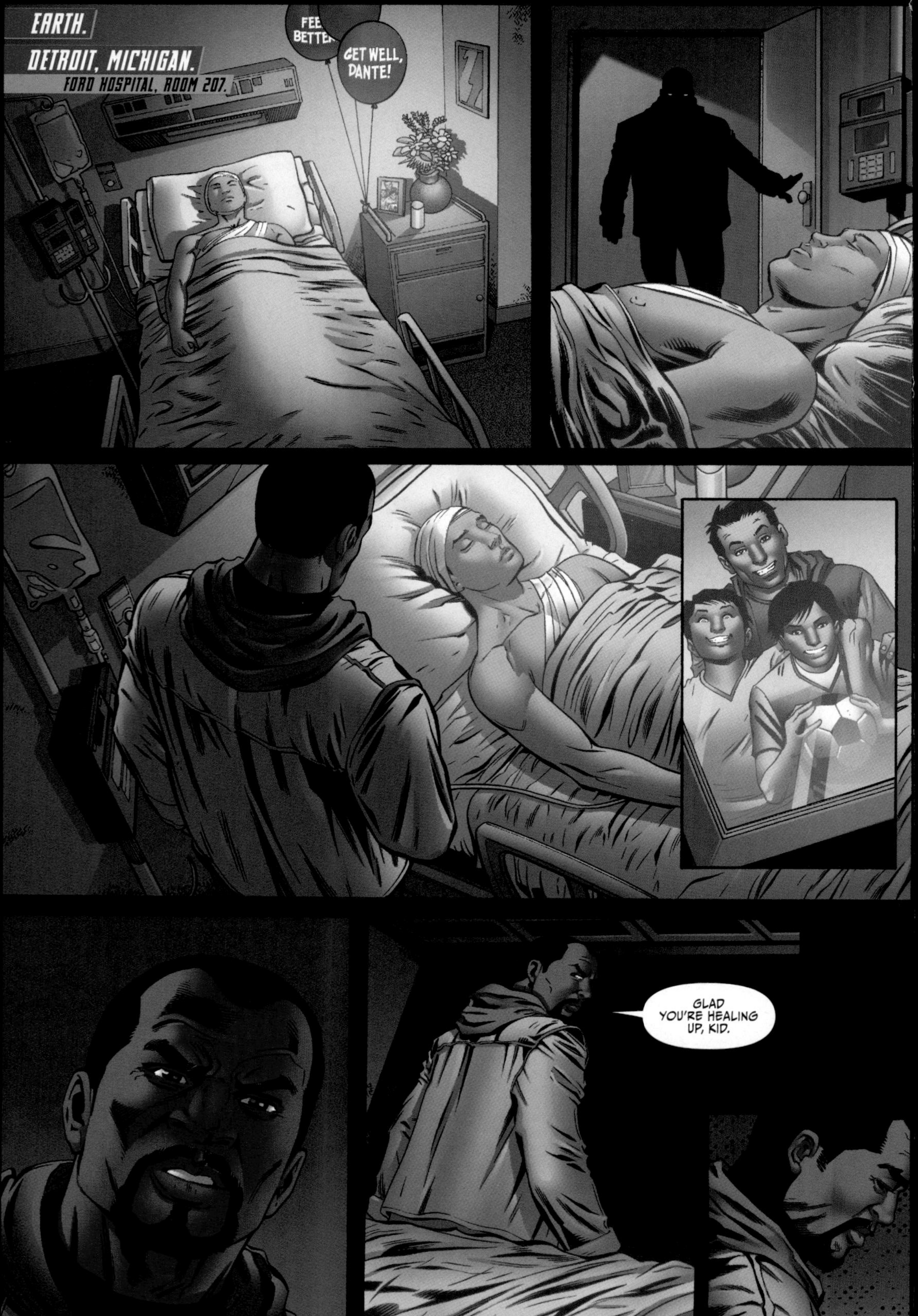
EARTH.
DETROIT, MICHIGAN.
FORD HOSPITAL, ROOM 207.
FEE BETTE
GET WELL, DANTE!
GLAD YOU'RE HEALING UP, KID.
DID YOU FIND HIM YET?

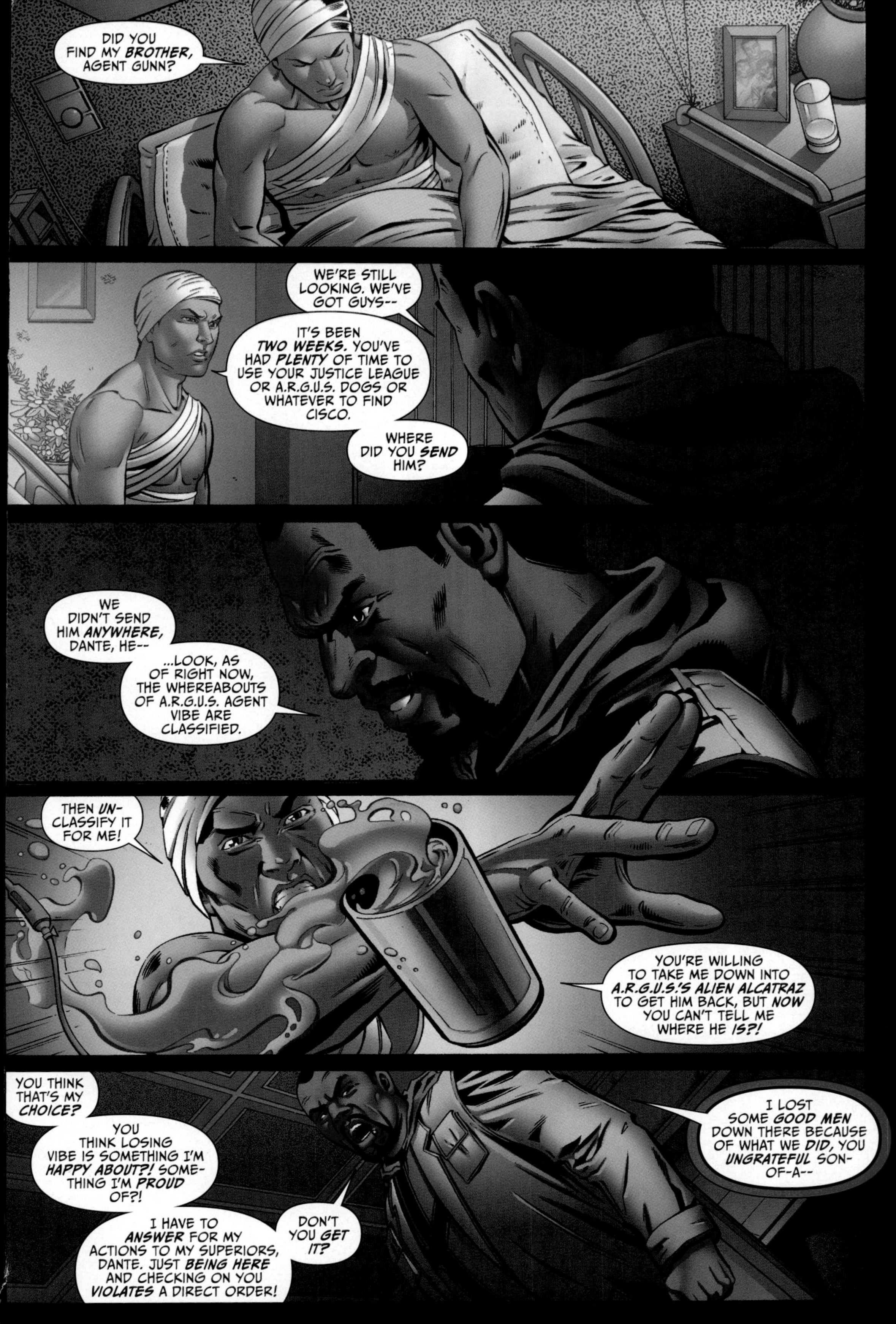
DID YOU FIND MY BROTHER, AGENT GUNN?
WE'RE STILL LOOKING. WE'VE GOT GUYS--
IT'S BEEN TWO WEEKS. YOU'VE HAD PLENTY OF TIME TO USE YOUR JUSTICE LEAGUE OR A.R.G.U.S. DOGS OR WHATEVER TO FIND CISCO.
WHERE DID YOU SEND HIM?
WE DIDN'T SEND HIM ANYWHERE, DANTE, HE--
...LOOK, AS OF RIGHT NOW, THE WHEREABOUTS OF A.R.G.U.S. AGENT VIBE ARE CLASSIFIED.
THEN UN-CLASSIFY IT FOR ME!
YOU'RE WILLING TO TAKE ME DOWN INTO A.R.G.U.S.'S ALIEN ALCATRAZ TO GET HIM BACK, BUT NOW YOU CAN'T TELL ME WHERE HE IS?!
YOU THINK THAT'S MY CHOICE?
YOU THINK LOSING VIBE IS SOMETHING I'M HAPPY ABOUT?! SOME-THING I'M PROUD OF?!
I HAVE TO ANSWER FOR MY ACTIONS TO MY SUPERIORS, DANTE. JUST BEING HERE AND CHECKING ON YOU VIOLATES A DIRECT ORDER!
DON'T YOU GET IT?
I LOST SOME GOOD MEN DOWN THERE BECAUSE OF WHAT WE DID, YOU UNGRATEFUL SON-OF-A--

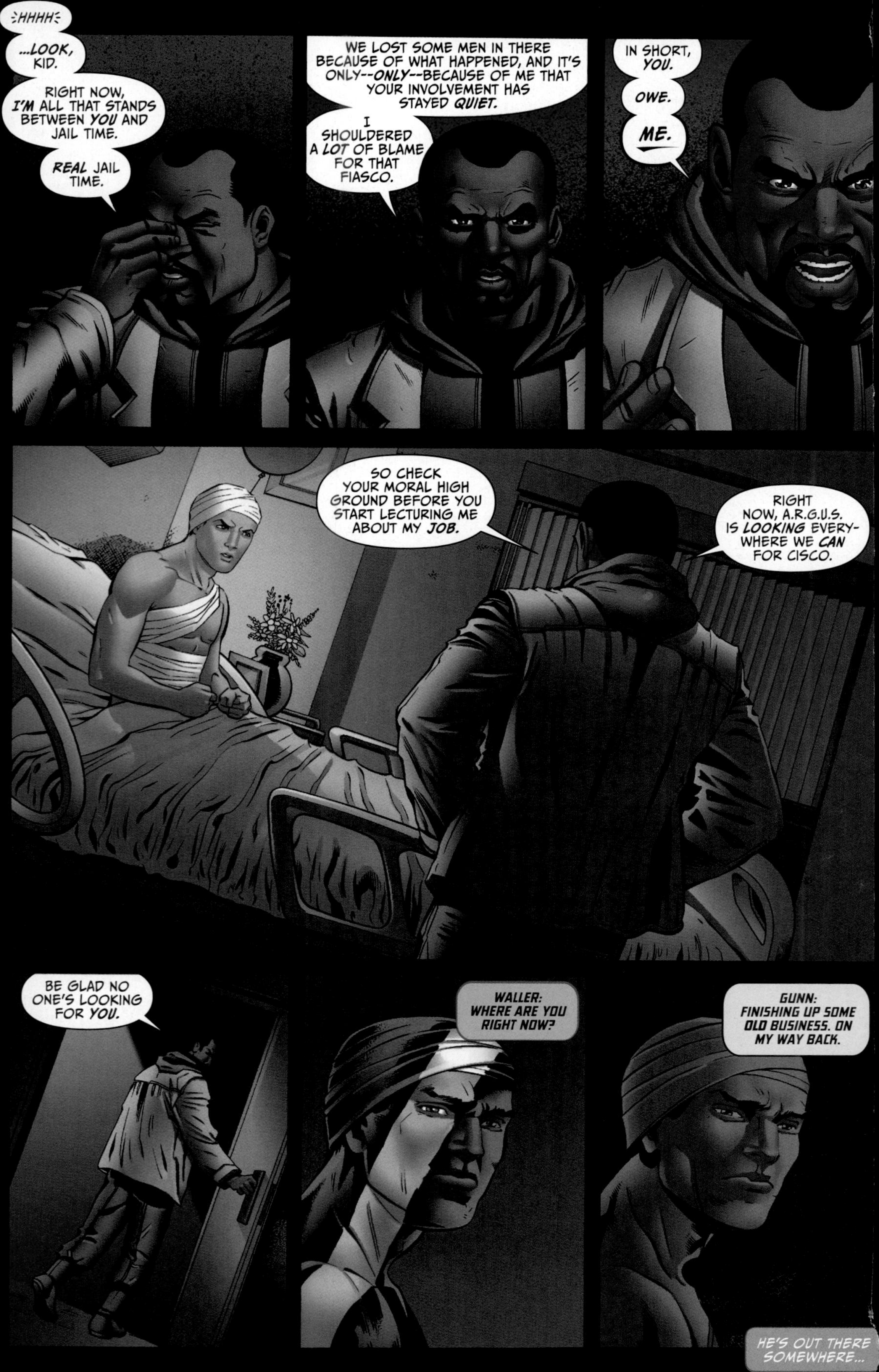
HHHH
...LOOK, KID.
RIGHT NOW, I'M ALL THAT STANDS BETWEEN YOU AND JAIL TIME.
REAL JAIL TIME.
WE LOST SOME MEN IN THERE BECAUSE OF WHAT HAPPENED, AND IT'S ONLY--ONLY--BECAUSE OF ME THAT YOUR INVOLVEMENT HAS STAYED QUIET.
I SHOULDERED A LOT OF BLAME FOR THAT FIASCO.
IN SHORT, YOU.
OWE.
ME.
SO CHECK YOUR MORAL HIGH GROUND BEFORE YOU START LECTURING ME ABOUT MY JOB.
RIGHT NOW, A.R.G.U.S. IS LOOKING EVERY-WHERE WE CAN FOR CISCO.
BE GLAD NO ONE'S LOOKING FOR YOU.
WALLER: WHERE ARE YOU RIGHT NOW?
GUNN: FINISHING UP SOME OLD BUSINESS. ON MY WAY BACK.
HE'S OUT THERE SOMEWHERE...

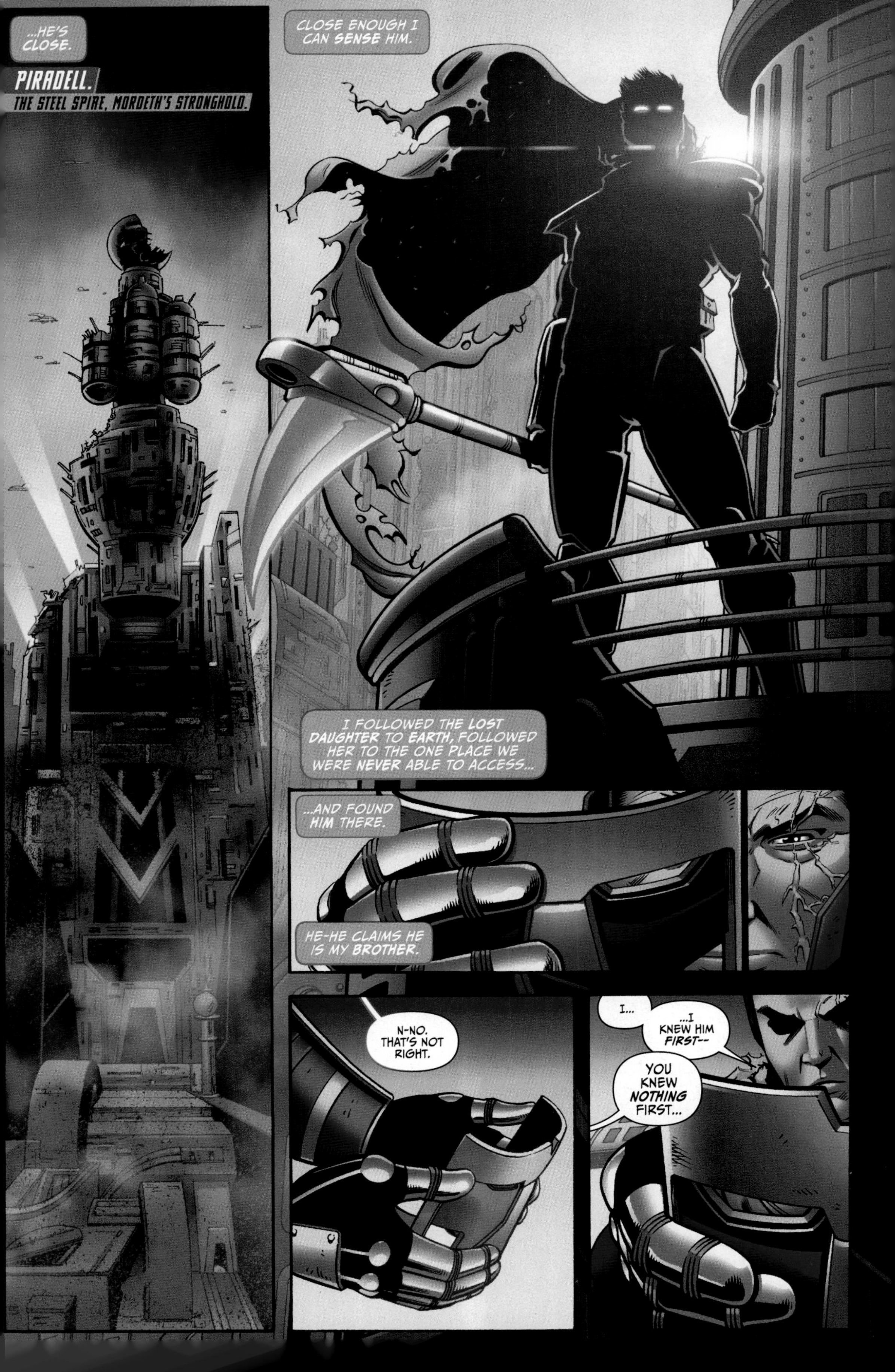
...HE'S CLOSE.
CLOSE ENOUGH I CAN SENSE HIM.
PIRADELL.
THE STEEL SPIRE, MORDETH'S STRONGHOLD.
I FOLLOWED THE LOST DAUGHTER TO EARTH, FOLLOWED HER TO THE ONE PLACE WE WERE NEVER ABLE TO ACCESS...
...AND FOUND HIM THERE.
HE-HE CLAIMS HE IS MY BROTHER.
N-NO. THAT'S NOT RIGHT.
I...
...I KNEW HIM FIRST--
YOU KNEW NOTHING FIRST...

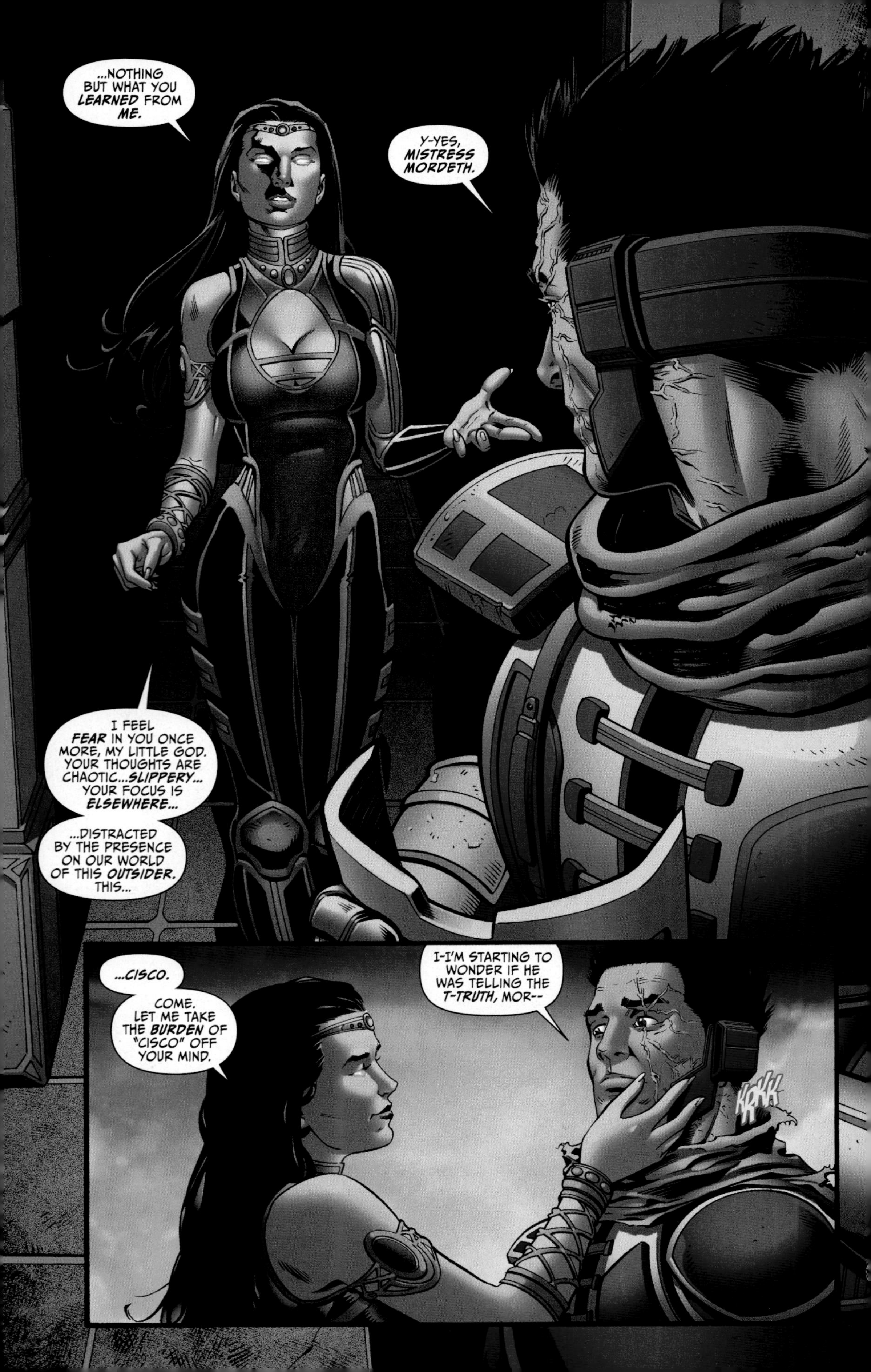
...NOTHING BUT WHAT YOU LEARNED FROM ME.
Y-YES, MISTRESS MORDETH.
I FEEL FEAR IN YOU ONCE MORE, MY LITTLE GOD. YOUR THOUGHTS ARE CHAOTIC...SLIPPERY... YOUR FOCUS IS ELSEWHERE...
...DISTRACTED BY THE PRESENCE ON OUR WORLD OF THIS OUTSIDER. THIS...
...CISCO.
I-I'M STARTING TO WONDER IF HE WAS TELLING THE T-TRUTH, MOR--
COME. LET ME TAKE THE BURDEN OF "CISCO" OFF YOUR MIND.
KRKK

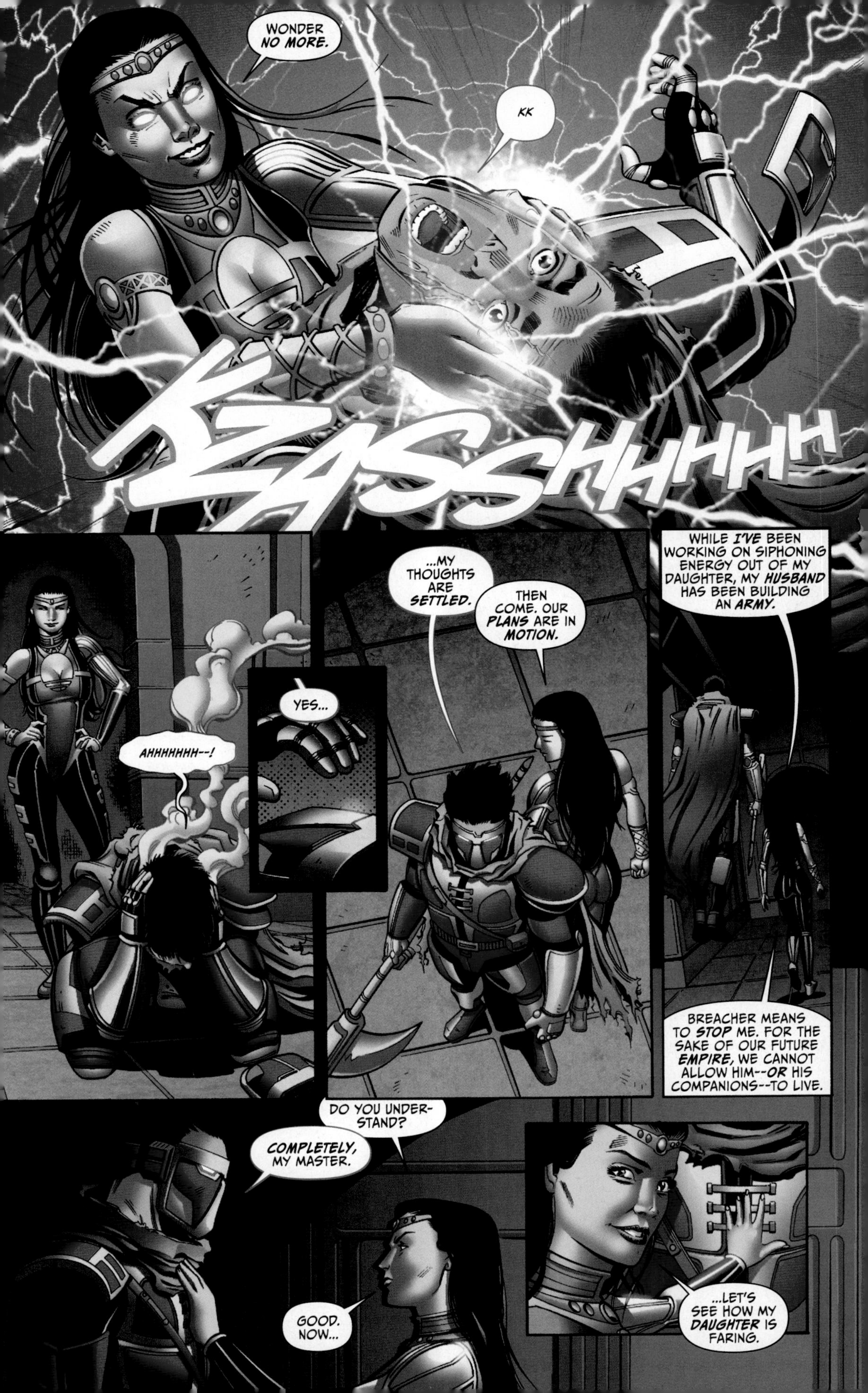
WONDER NO MORE.
KK
KZASSHHHHH
AHHHHHHH--!
YES...
...MY THOUGHTS ARE SETTLED.
THEN COME. OUR PLANS ARE IN MOTION.
WHILE I'VE BEEN WORKING ON SIPHONING ENERGY OUT OF MY DAUGHTER, MY HUSBAND HAS BEEN BUILDING AN ARMY.
BREACHER MEANS TO STOP ME. FOR THE SAKE OF OUR FUTURE EMPIRE, WE CANNOT ALLOW HIM--OR HIS COMPANIONS--TO LIVE.
DO YOU UNDER-STAND?
COMPLETELY, MY MASTER.
GOOD. NOW...
...LET'S SEE HOW MY DAUGHTER IS FARING.

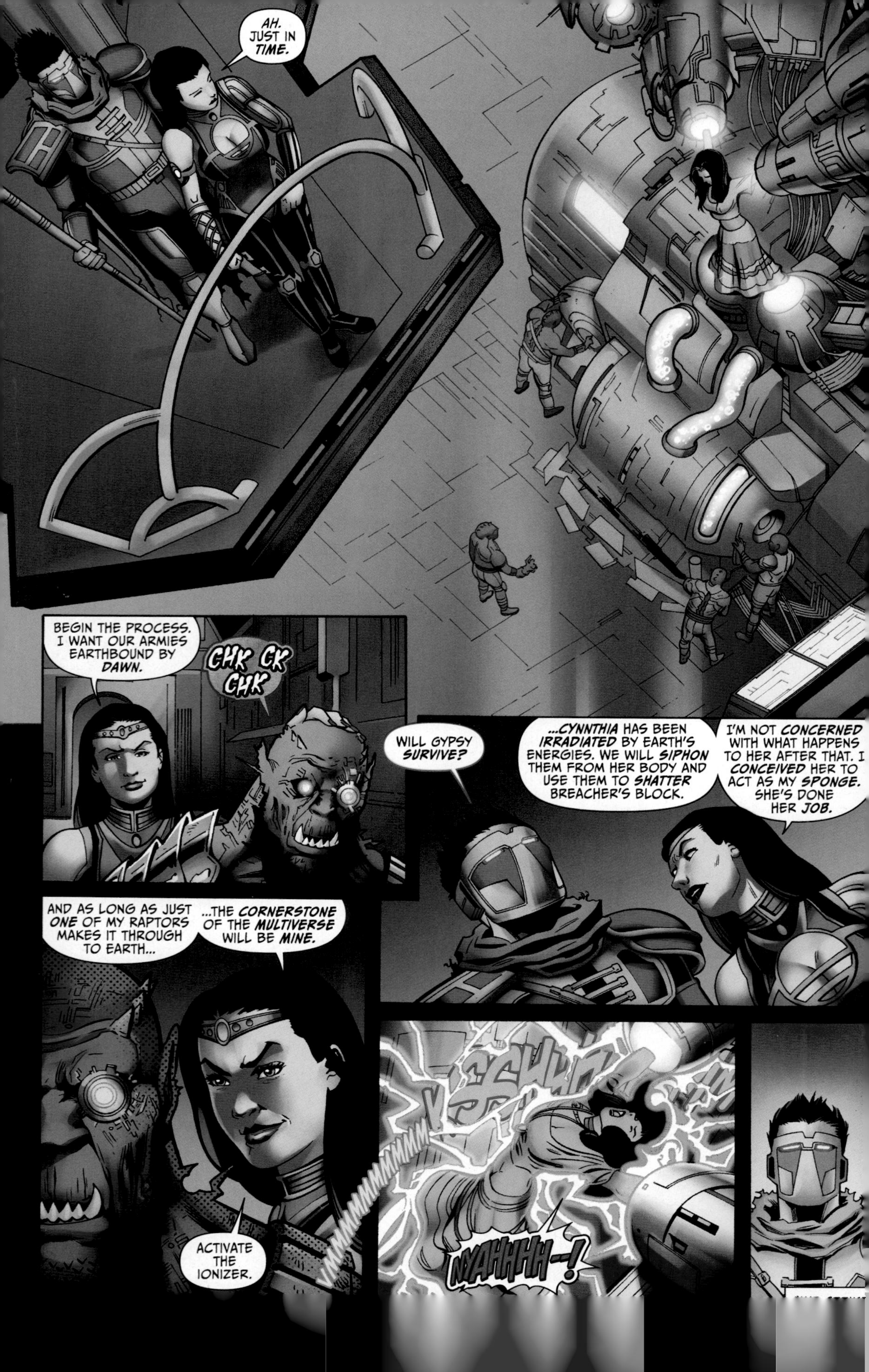

AH. JUST IN TIME.
BEGIN THE PROCESS. I WANT OUR ARMIES EARTHBOUND BY DAWN.
CHK CK CHK
WILL GYPSY SURVIVE?
...CYNNTHIA HAS BEEN IRRADIATED BY EARTH'S ENERGIES. WE WILL SIPHON THEM FROM HER BODY AND USE THEM TO SHATTER BREACHER'S BLOCK.
I'M NOT CONCERNED WITH WHAT HAPPENS TO HER AFTER THAT. I CONCEIVED HER TO ACT AS MY SPONGE. SHE'S DONE HER JOB.
AND AS LONG AS JUST ONE OF MY RAPTORS MAKES IT THROUGH TO EARTH...
...THE CORNERSTONE OF THE MULTIVERSE WILL BE MINE.
ACTIVATE THE IONIZER.
VMMMMMMMMMMMM!
NYAHHHH--!

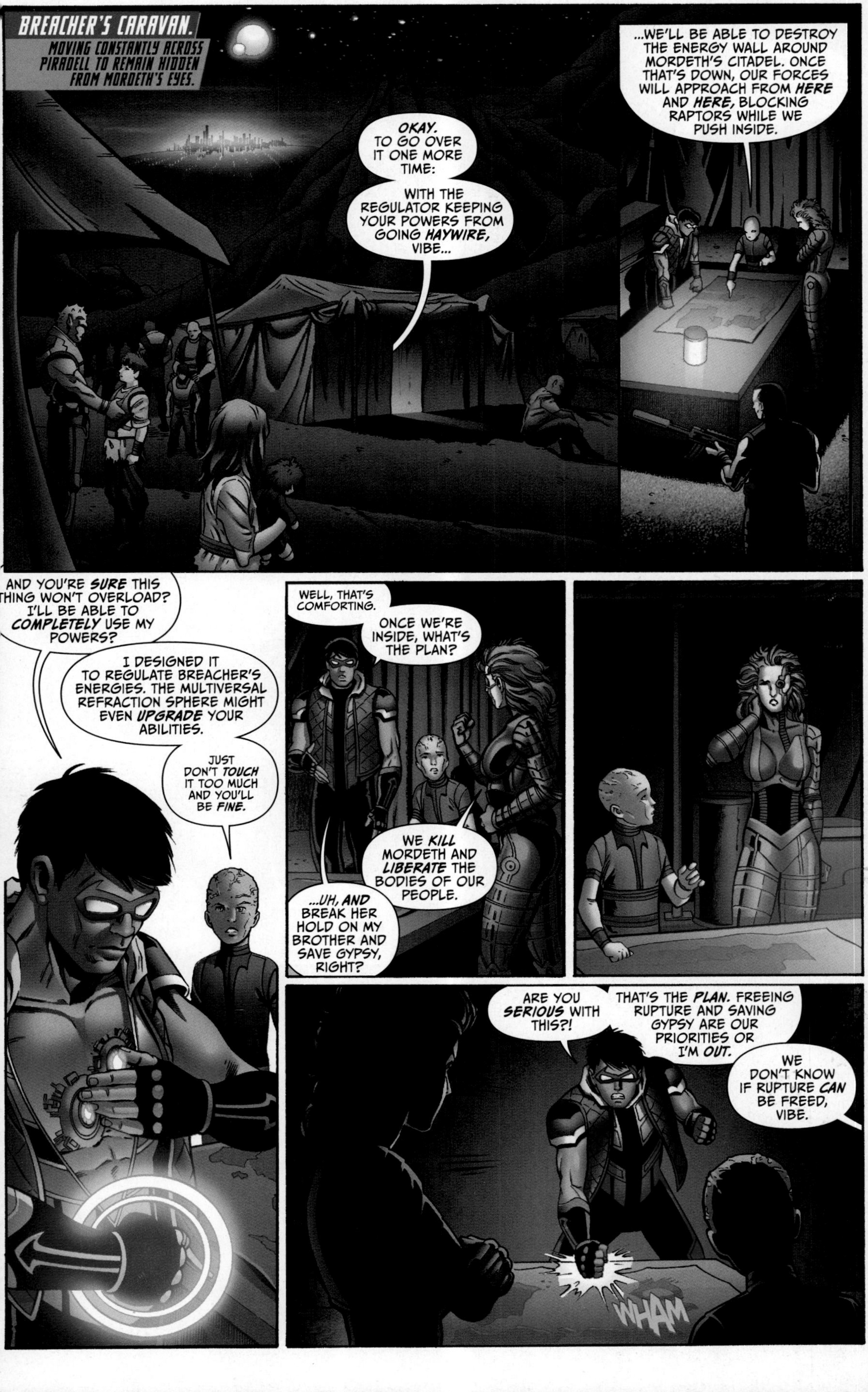
BREACHER'S CARAVAN.
MOVING CONSTANTLY ACROSS PIRADELL TO REMAIN HIDDEN FROM MORDETH'S EYES.
OKAY. TO GO OVER IT ONE MORE TIME:
WITH THE REGULATOR KEEPING YOUR POWERS FROM GOING HAYWIRE, VIBE...
...WE'LL BE ABLE TO DESTROY THE ENERGY WALL AROUND MORDETH'S CITADEL. ONCE THAT'S DOWN, OUR FORCES WILL APPROACH FROM HERE AND HERE, BLOCKING RAPTORS WHILE WE PUSH INSIDE.
AND YOU'RE SURE THIS THING WON'T OVERLOAD? I'LL BE ABLE TO COMPLETELY USE MY POWERS?
I DESIGNED IT TO REGULATE BREACHER'S ENERGIES. THE MULTIVERSAL REFRACTION SPHERE MIGHT EVEN UPGRADE YOUR ABILITIES.
JUST DON'T TOUCH IT TOO MUCH AND YOU'LL BE FINE.
WELL, THAT'S COMFORTING.
ONCE WE'RE INSIDE, WHAT'S THE PLAN?
WE KILL MORDETH AND LIBERATE THE BODIES OF OUR PEOPLE.
...UH, AND BREAK HER HOLD ON MY BROTHER AND SAVE GYPSY, RIGHT?
ARE YOU SERIOUS WITH THIS?!
THAT'S THE PLAN. FREEING RUPTURE AND SAVING GYPSY ARE OUR PRIORITIES OR I'M OUT.
WE DON'T KNOW IF RUPTURE CAN BE FREED, VIBE.
WHAM

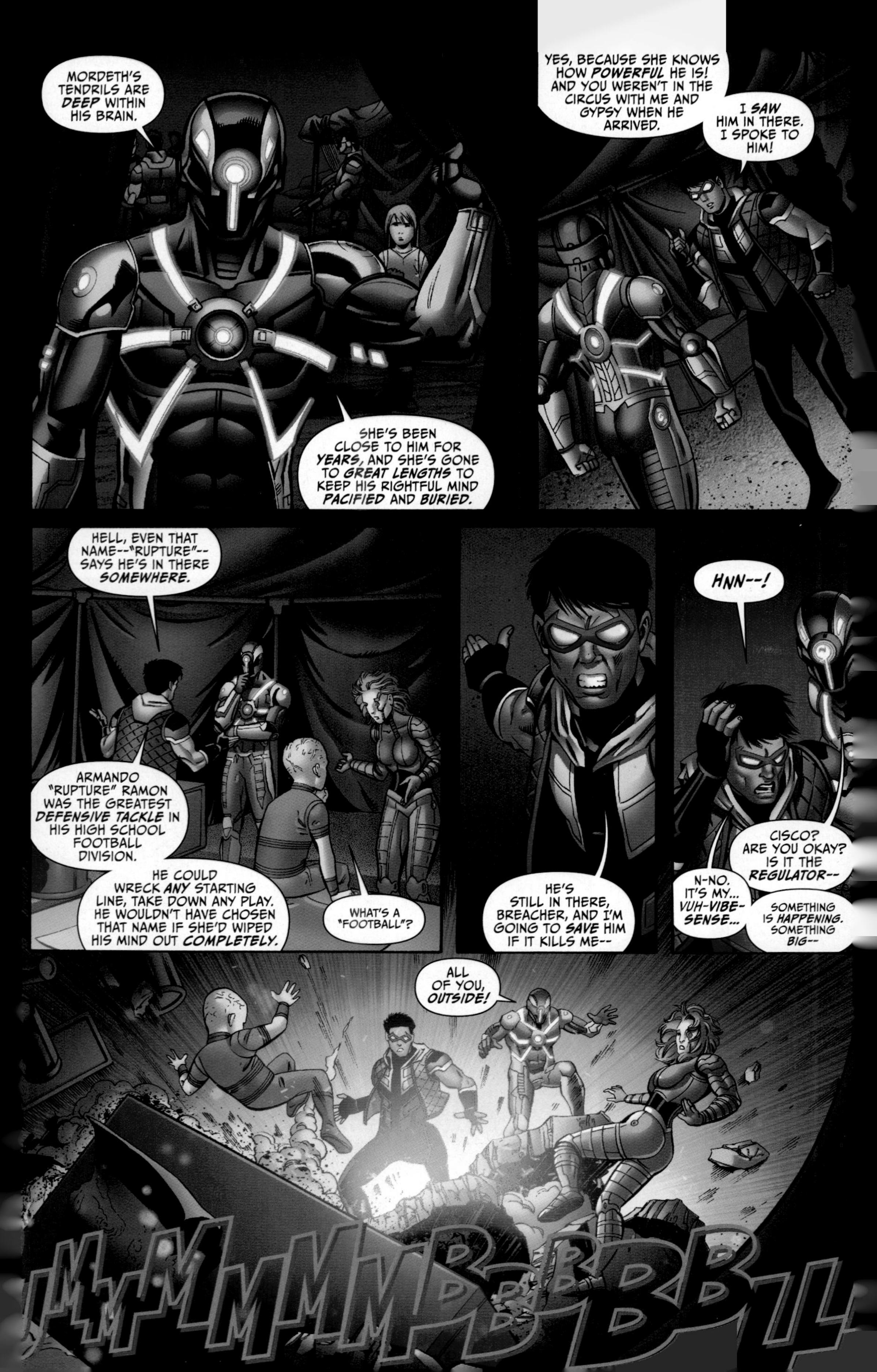
MORDETH'S TENDRILS ARE DEEP WITHIN HIS BRAIN.
SHE'S BEEN CLOSE TO HIM FOR YEARS, AND SHE'S GONE TO GREAT LENGTHS TO KEEP HIS RIGHTFUL MIND PACIFIED AND BURIED.
YES, BECAUSE SHE KNOWS HOW POWERFUL HE IS! AND YOU WEREN'T IN THE CIRCUS WITH ME AND GYPSY WHEN HE ARRIVED.
I SAW HIM IN THERE. I SPOKE TO HIM!
HELL, EVEN THAT NAME--"RUPTURE"--SAYS HE'S IN THERE SOMEWHERE.
ARMANDO "RUPTURE" RAMON WAS THE GREATEST DEFENSIVE TACKLE IN HIS HIGH SCHOOL FOOTBALL DIVISION.
HE COULD WRECK ANY STARTING LINE, TAKE DOWN ANY PLAY. HE WOULDN'T HAVE CHOSEN THAT NAME IF SHE'D WIPED HIS MIND OUT COMPLETELY.
WHAT'S A "FOOTBALL"?
HE'S STILL IN THERE, BREACHER, AND I'M GOING TO SAVE HIM IF IT KILLS ME--
HNN--!
CISCO? ARE YOU OKAY? IS IT THE REGULATOR--
N-NO. IT'S MY... VUH-VIBE-SENSE...
SOMETHING IS HAPPENING. SOMETHING BIG--
ALL OF YOU, OUTSIDE!
MMMMMBBBBB

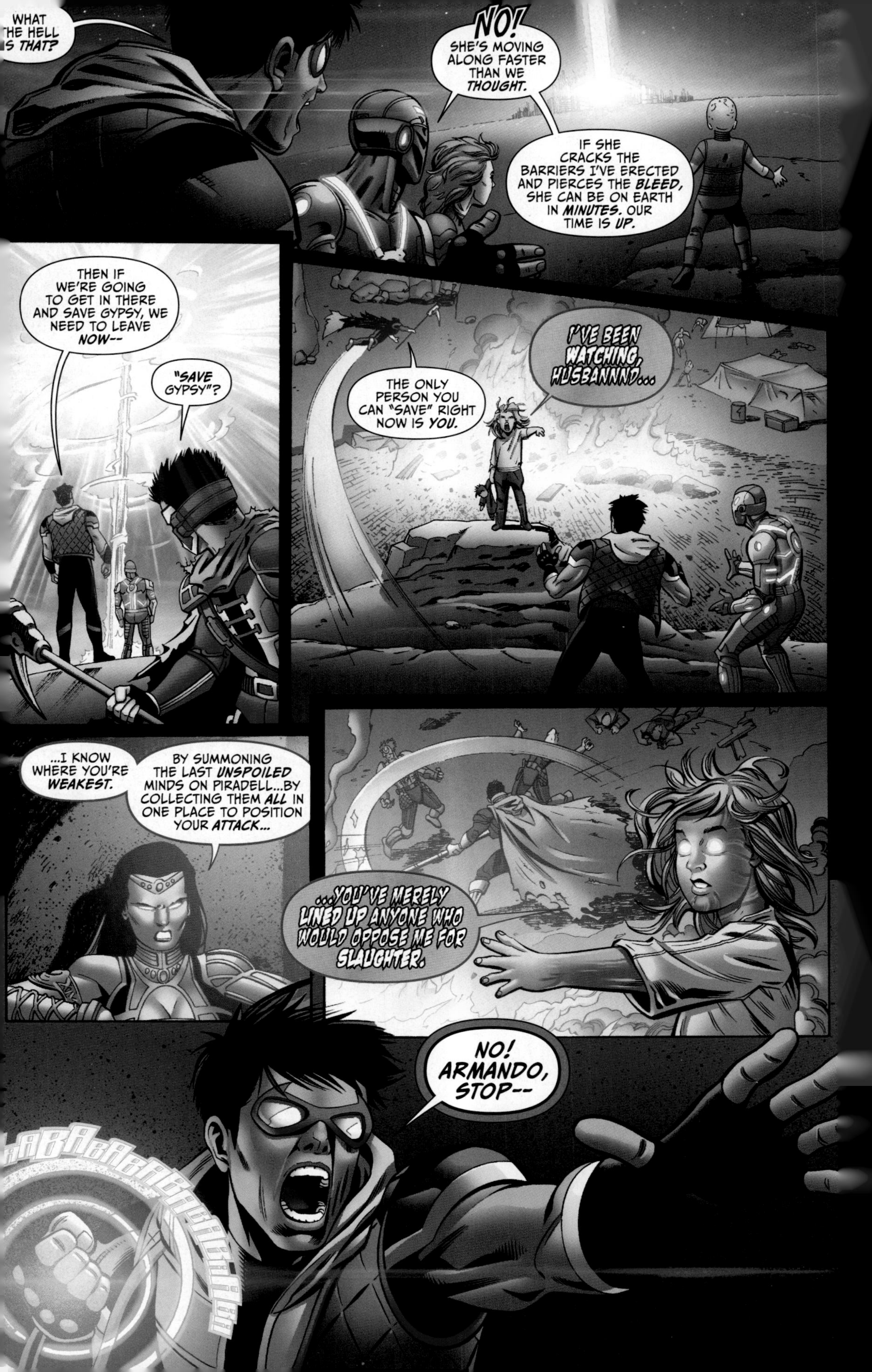

WHAT THE HELL IS THAT?
NO! SHE'S MOVING ALONG FASTER THAN WE THOUGHT.
IF SHE CRACKS THE BARRIERS I'VE ERECTED AND PIERCES THE BLEED, SHE CAN BE ON EARTH IN MINUTES. OUR TIME IS UP.
THEN IF WE'RE GOING TO GET IN THERE AND SAVE GYPSY, WE NEED TO LEAVE NOW--
"SAVE GYPSY"?
THE ONLY PERSON YOU CAN "SAVE" RIGHT NOW IS YOU.
I'VE BEEN WATCHING, HUSBANNND...
...I KNOW WHERE YOU'RE WEAKEST.
BY SUMMONING THE LAST UNSPOILED MINDS ON PIRADELL...BY COLLECTING THEM ALL IN ONE PLACE TO POSITION YOUR ATTACK...
...YOU'VE MERELY LINED UP ANYONE WHO WOULD OPPOSE ME FOR SLAUGHTER.
NO! ARMANDO, STOP--

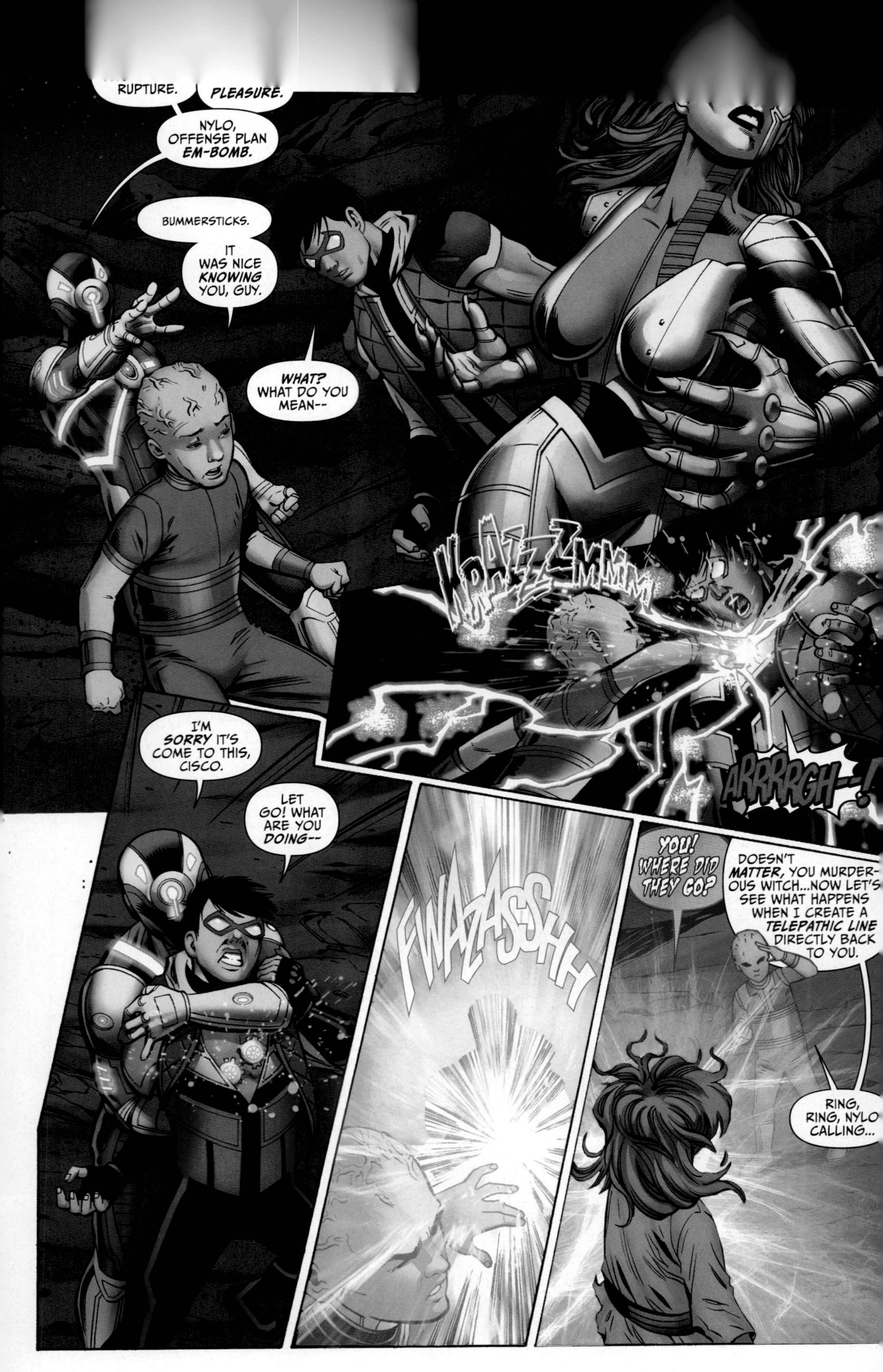
RUPTURE.
PLEASURE.
NYLO, OFFENSE PLAN EM-BOMB.
BUMMERSTICKS.
IT WAS NICE KNOWING YOU, GUY.
WHAT? WHAT DO YOU MEAN--
KRAZZZMMMM
ARRRRGH--!
I'M SORRY IT'S COME TO THIS, CISCO.
LET GO! WHAT ARE YOU DOING--
FWAZASSHH
YOU! WHERE DID THEY GO?
DOESN'T MATTER, YOU MURDEROUS WITCH...NOW LET'S SEE WHAT HAPPENS WHEN I CREATE A TELEPATHIC LINE DIRECTLY BACK TO YOU.
RING, RING, NYLO CALLING...

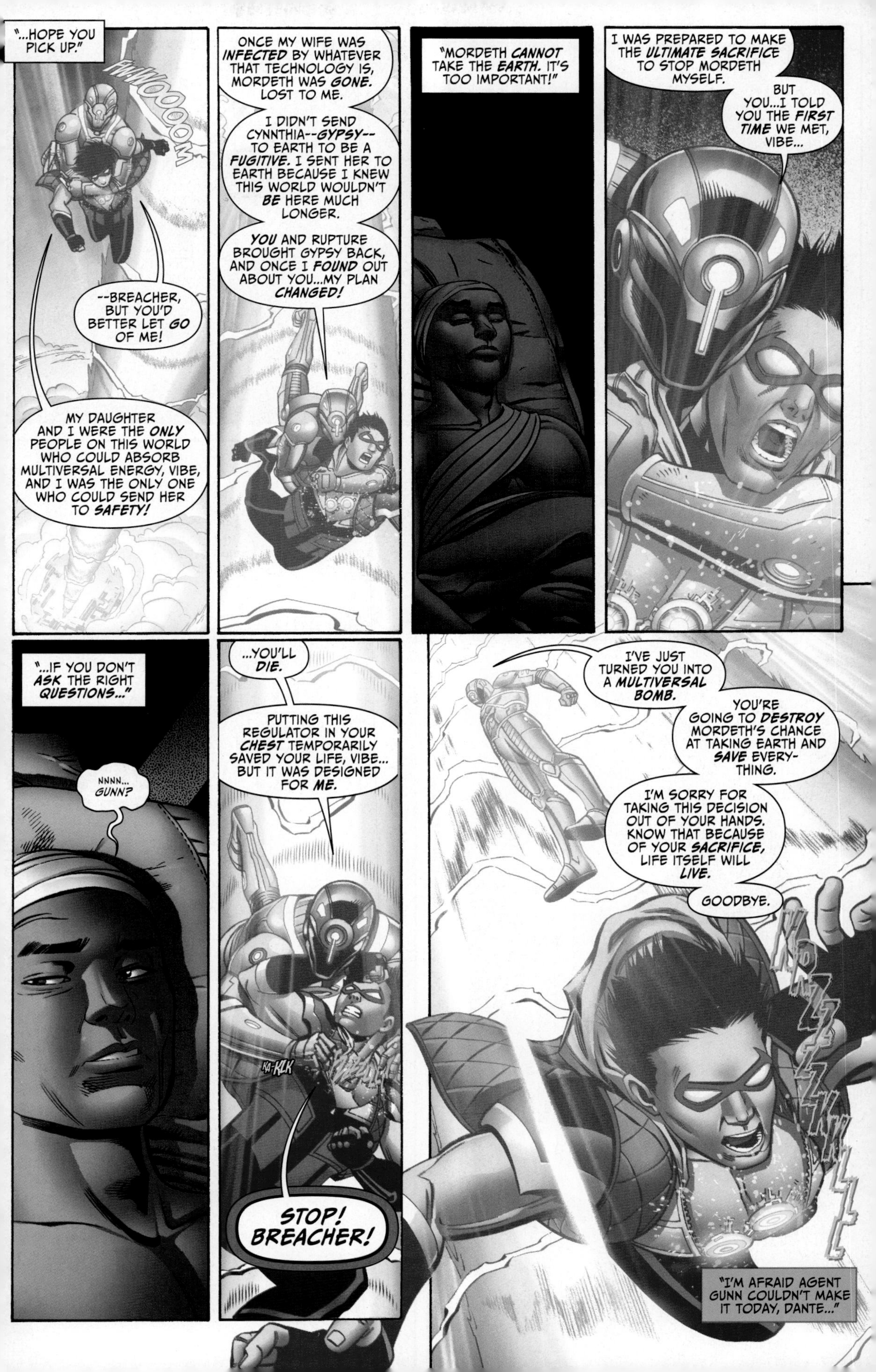
"...HOPE YOU PICK UP."
FWHOOOOOM
--BREACHER, BUT YOU'D BETTER LET GO OF ME!
MY DAUGHTER AND I WERE THE ONLY PEOPLE ON THIS WORLD WHO COULD ABSORB MULTIVERSAL ENERGY, VIBE, AND I WAS THE ONLY ONE WHO COULD SEND HER TO SAFETY!
ONCE MY WIFE WAS INFECTED BY WHATEVER THAT TECHNOLOGY IS, MORDETH WAS GONE. LOST TO ME.
I DIDN'T SEND CYNNTHIA--GYPSY--TO EARTH TO BE A FUGITIVE. I SENT HER TO EARTH BECAUSE I KNEW THIS WORLD WOULDN'T BE HERE MUCH LONGER.
YOU AND RUPTURE BROUGHT GYPSY BACK, AND ONCE I FOUND OUT ABOUT YOU...MY PLAN CHANGED!
"MORDETH CANNOT TAKE THE EARTH. IT'S TOO IMPORTANT!"
I WAS PREPARED TO MAKE THE ULTIMATE SACRIFICE TO STOP MORDETH MYSELF.
BUT YOU...I TOLD YOU THE FIRST TIME WE MET, VIBE...
"...IF YOU DON'T ASK THE RIGHT QUESTIONS..."
NNNN... GUNN?
...YOU'LL DIE.
PUTTING THIS REGULATOR IN YOUR CHEST TEMPORARILY SAVED YOUR LIFE, VIBE... BUT IT WAS DESIGNED FOR ME.
KA-KLK
STOP! BREACHER!
I'VE JUST TURNED YOU INTO A MULTIVERSAL BOMB.
YOU'RE GOING TO DESTROY MORDETH'S CHANCE AT TAKING EARTH AND SAVE EVERYTHING.
I'M SORRY FOR TAKING THIS DECISION OUT OF YOUR HANDS. KNOW THAT BECAUSE OF YOUR SACRIFICE, LIFE ITSELF WILL LIVE.
GOODBYE.
"I'M AFRAID AGENT GUNN COULDN'T MAKE IT TODAY, DANTE..."

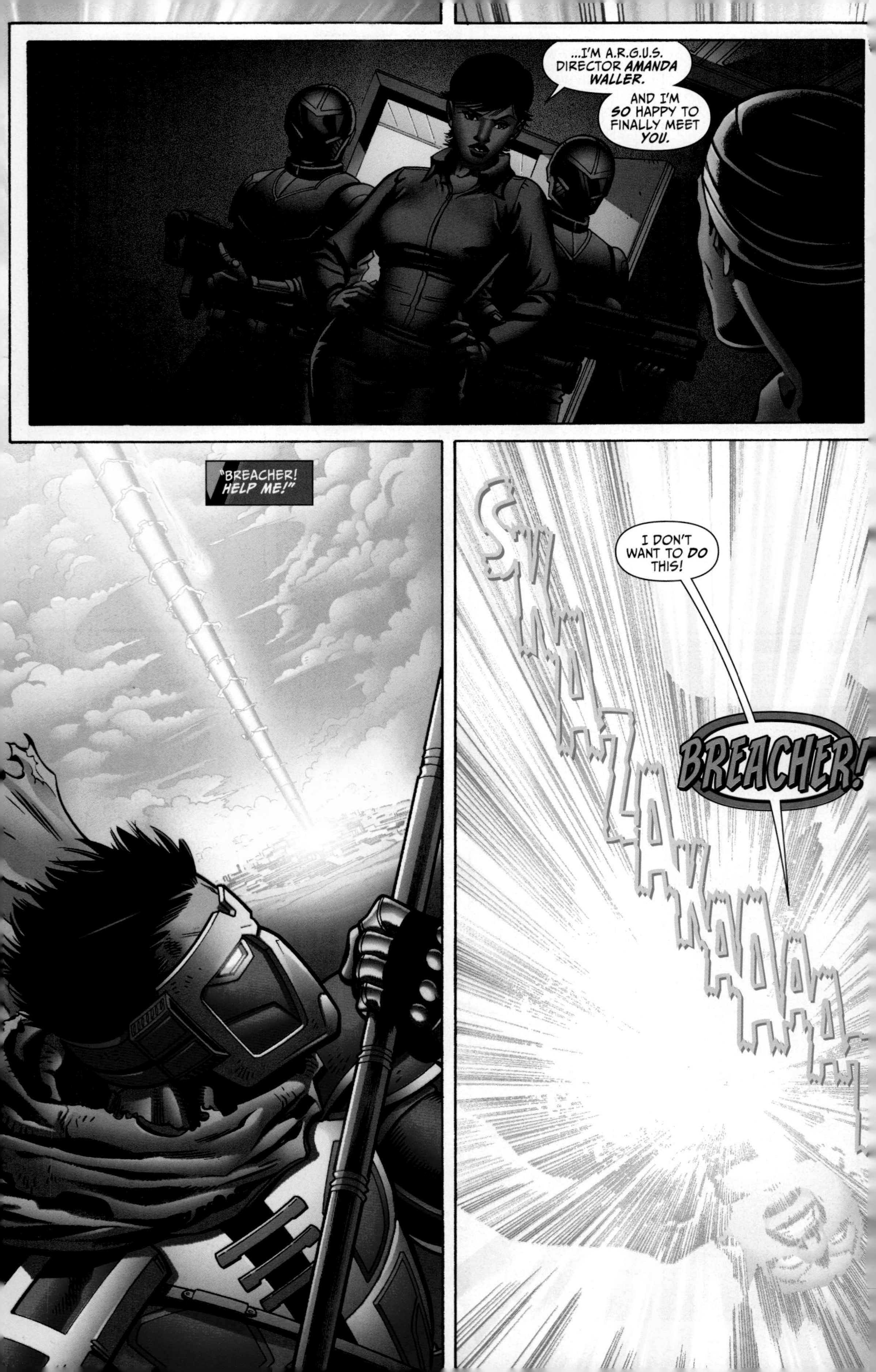
...I'M A.R.G.U.S. DIRECTOR AMANDA WALLER.
AND I'M SO HAPPY TO FINALLY MEET YOU.
"BREACHER! HELP ME!"
I DON'T WANT TO DO THIS!
BREACHER!

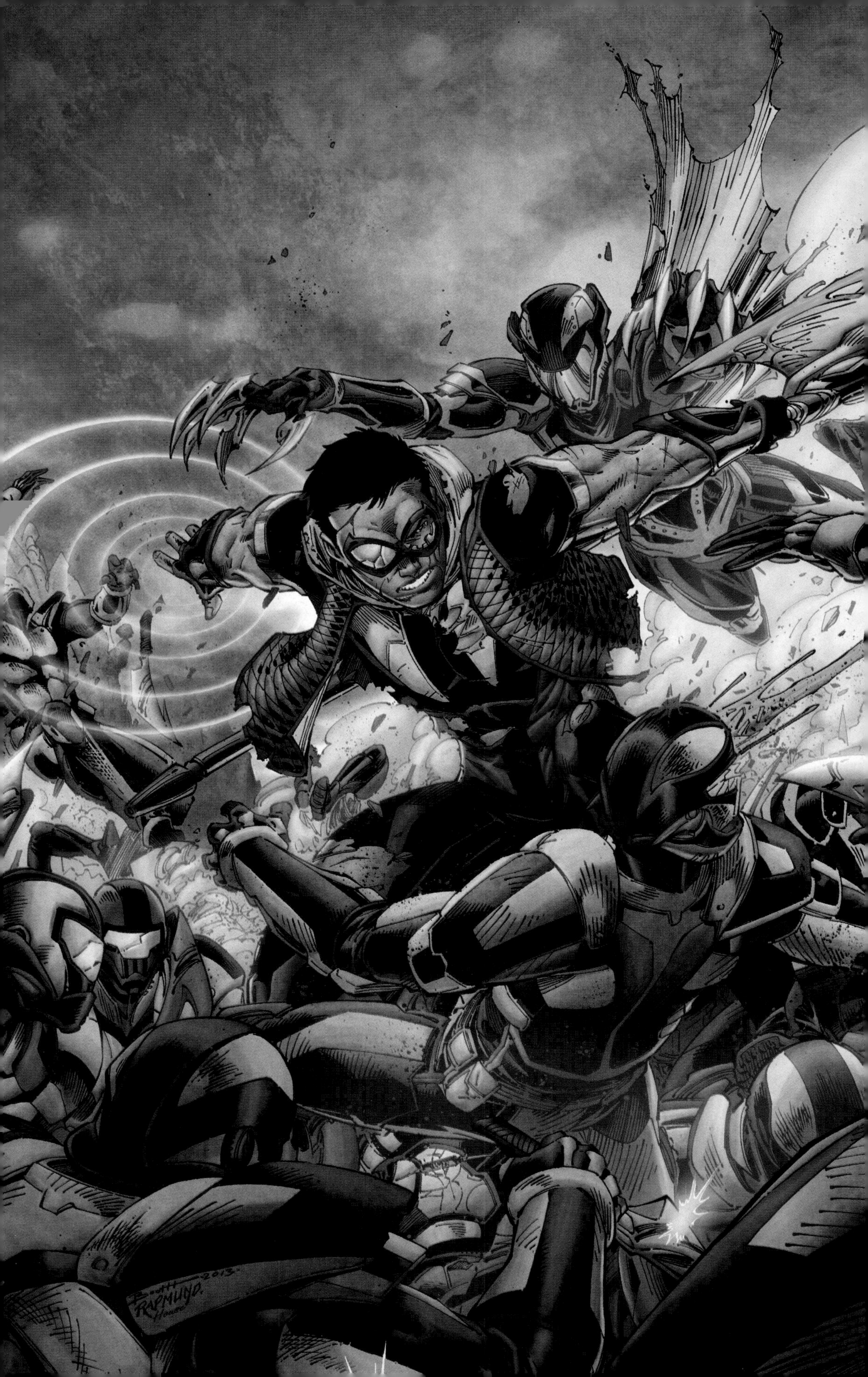
RAPMUND.
2013

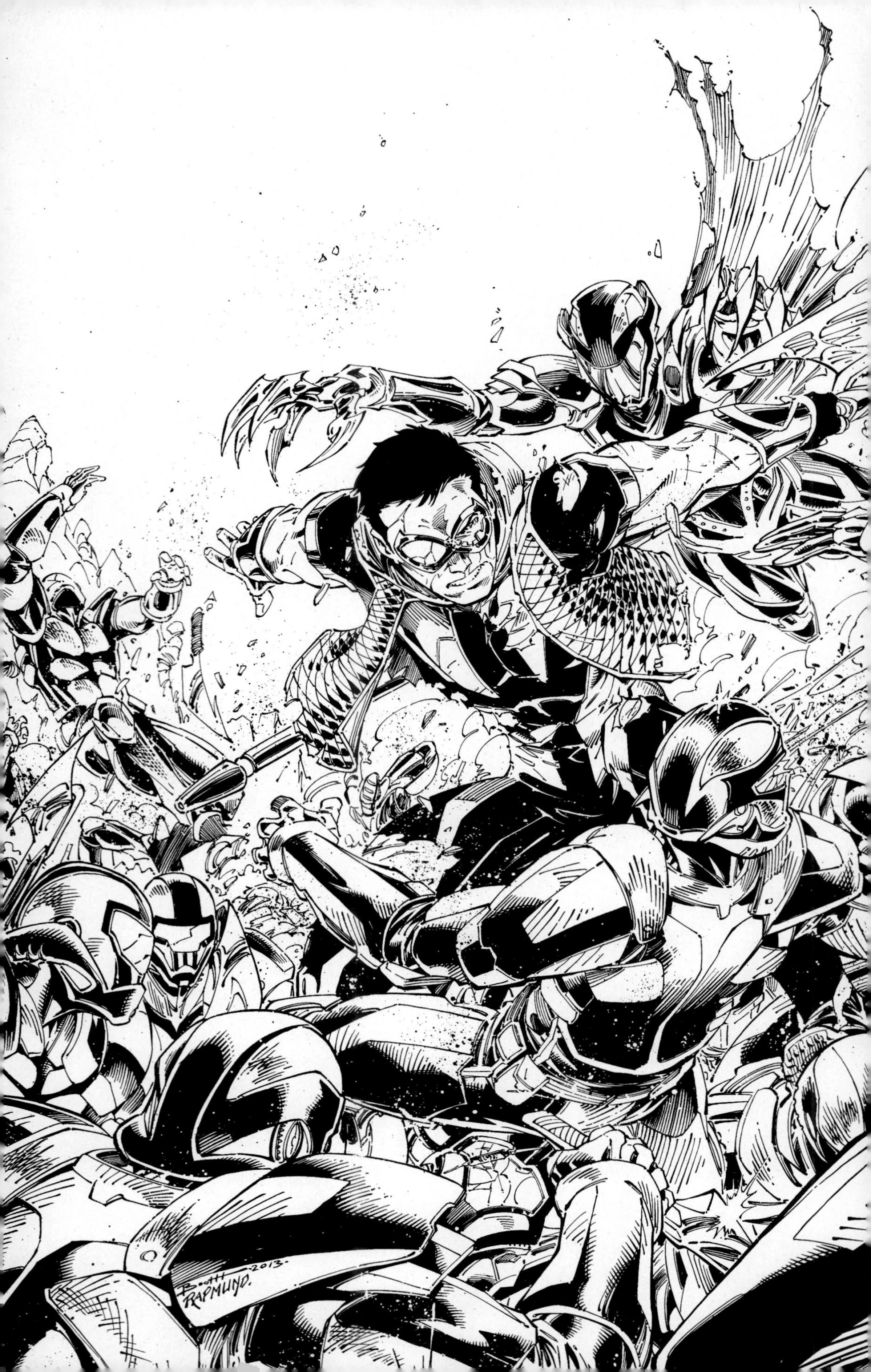
Booth
RAPMUND.
-2013-

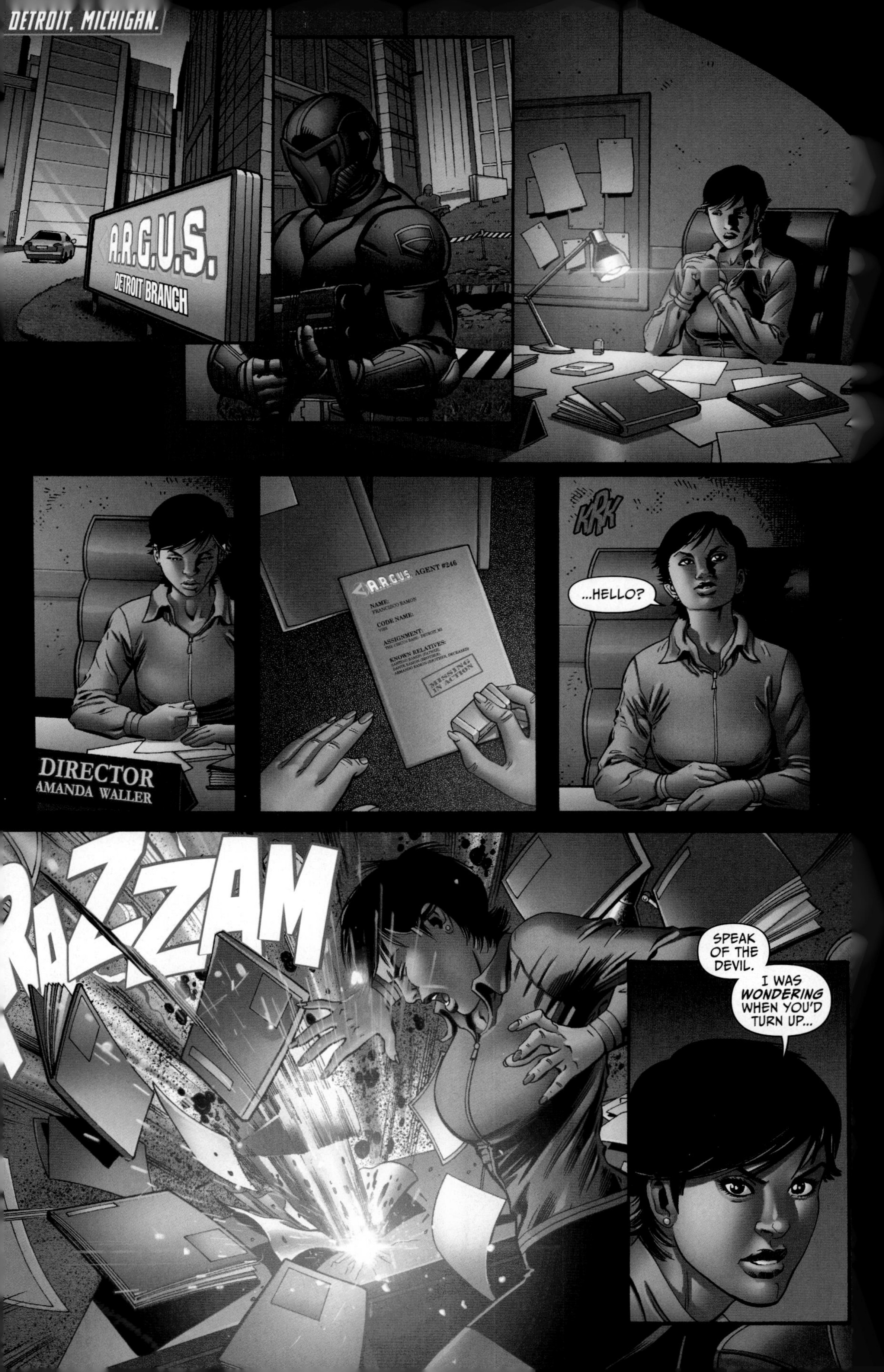
DETROIT, MICHIGAN.
A.R.G.U.S.
DETROIT BRANCH
DIRECTOR
AMANDA WALLER
A.R.G.U.S. AGENT #246
NAME:
FRANCISCO RAMON
CODE NAME:
VIBE
ASSIGNMENT:
THE CIRCUS BASE - DETROIT, MI
KNOWN RELATIVES:
SANTINO RAMON (FATHER),
DANTE RAMON (BROTHER),
ARMANDO RAMON (BROTHER, DECEASED)
MISSING IN ACTION
KRK
...HELLO?
RAZZAM
SPEAK OF THE DEVIL.
I WAS *WONDERING* WHEN YOU'D TURN UP...

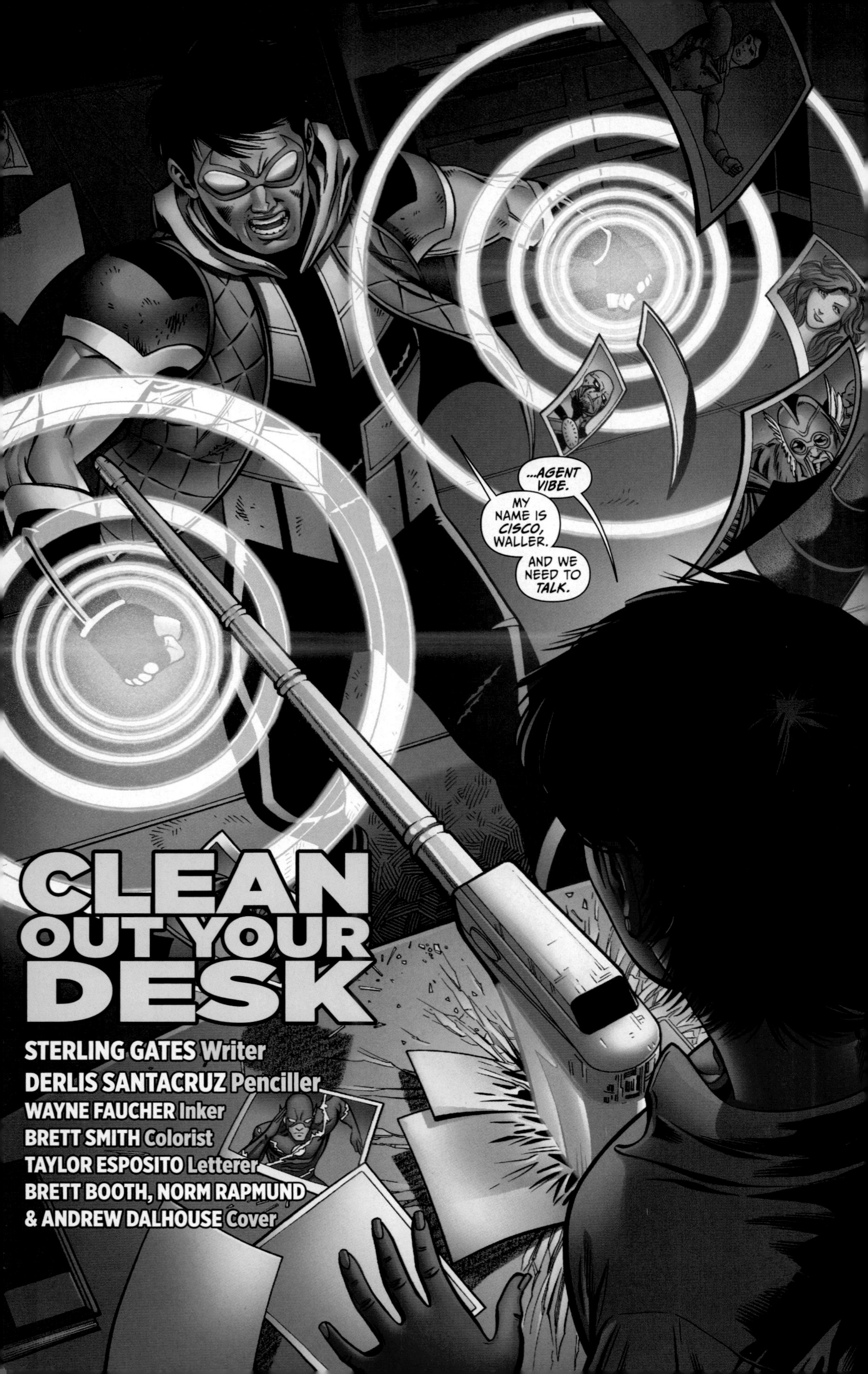
...AGENT VIBE.
MY NAME IS CISCO, WALLER.
AND WE NEED TO TALK.
CLEAN OUT YOUR DESK
STERLING GATES Writer
DERLIS SANTACRUZ Penciller
WAYNE FAUCHER Inker
BRETT SMITH Colorist
TAYLOR ESPOSITO Letterer
BRETT BOOTH, NORM RAPMUND & ANDREW DALHOUSE Cover

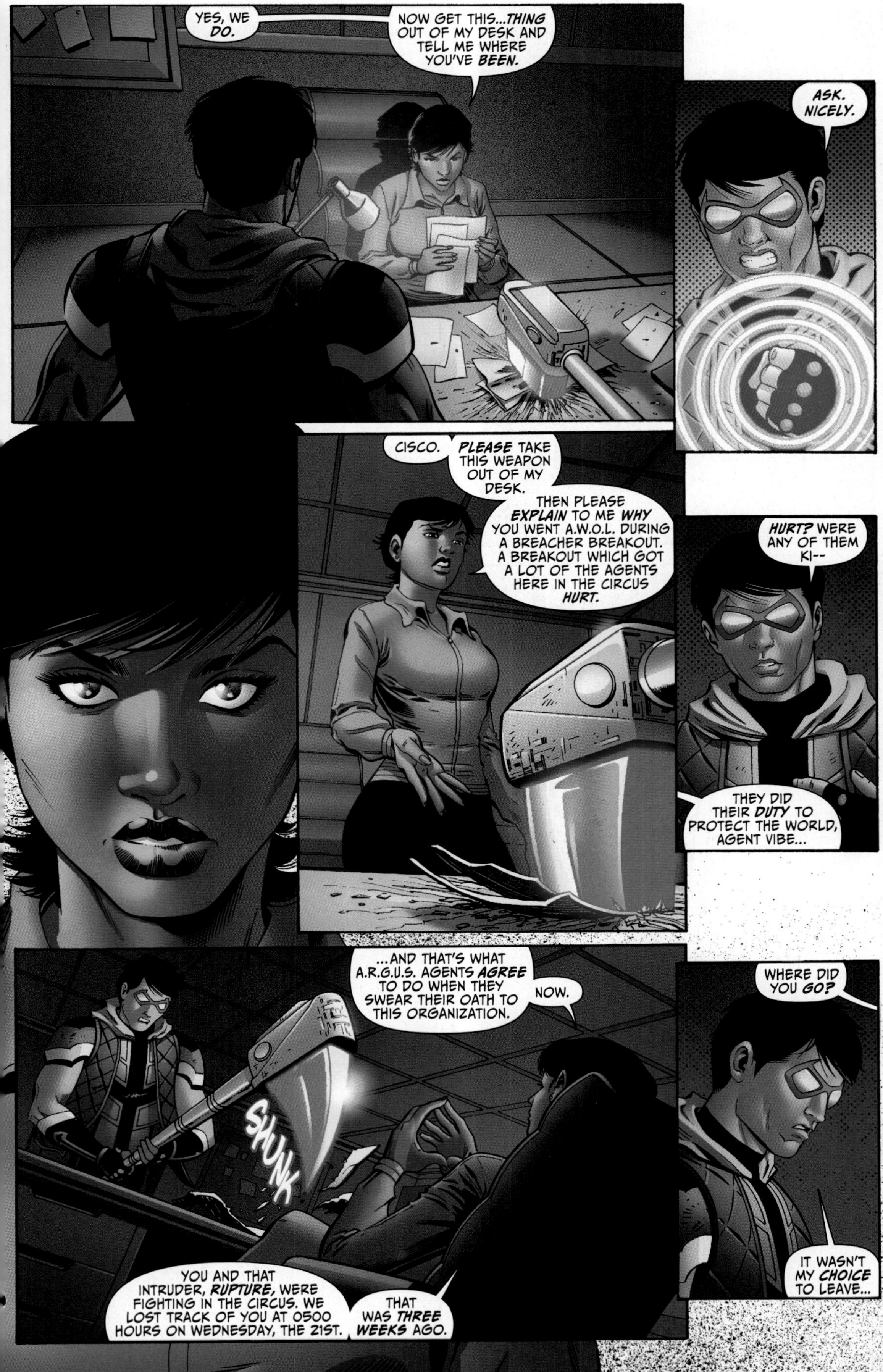
YES, WE DO.
NOW GET THIS...THING OUT OF MY DESK AND TELL ME WHERE YOU'VE BEEN.
ASK. NICELY.
CISCO. PLEASE TAKE THIS WEAPON OUT OF MY DESK.
THEN PLEASE EXPLAIN TO ME WHY YOU WENT A.W.O.L. DURING A BREACHER BREAKOUT. A BREAKOUT WHICH GOT A LOT OF THE AGENTS HERE IN THE CIRCUS HURT.
HURT? WERE ANY OF THEM KI--
THEY DID THEIR DUTY TO PROTECT THE WORLD, AGENT VIBE...
...AND THAT'S WHAT A.R.G.U.S. AGENTS AGREE TO DO WHEN THEY SWEAR THEIR OATH TO THIS ORGANIZATION.
NOW.
SHUNK
YOU AND THAT INTRUDER, RUPTURE, WERE FIGHTING IN THE CIRCUS. WE LOST TRACK OF YOU AT 0500 HOURS ON WEDNESDAY, THE 21ST.
THAT WAS THREE WEEKS AGO.
WHERE DID YOU GO?
IT WASN'T MY CHOICE TO LEAVE...

"...RUPTURE TOOK ME BACK TO GYPSY'S HOME DIMENSION.

"PIRADELL.

"I MET GYPSY'S *FATHER* THERE, A MAN CALLED *BREACHER*.

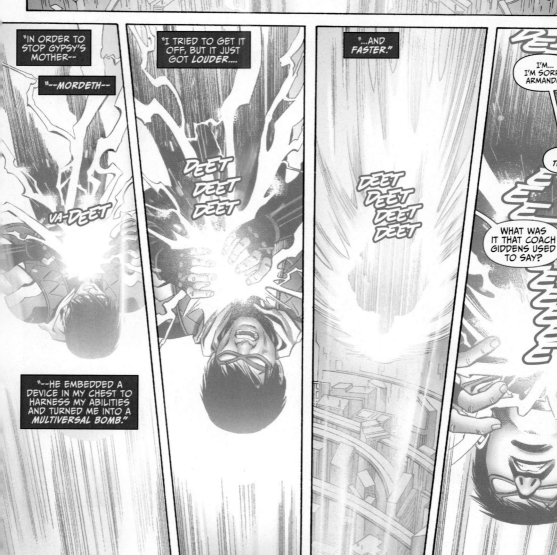

"IN ORDER TO STOP GYPSY'S MOTHER--

"--MORDETH--

VA-DEET

"--HE EMBEDDED A DEVICE IN MY CHEST TO HARNESS MY ABILITIES AND TURNED ME INTO A *MULTIVERSAL BOMB*."

"I TRIED TO GET IT OFF, BUT IT JUST GOT *LOUDER*....

DEET DEET DEET

"...AND *FASTER*."

DEET DEET DEET DEET

I'M... I'M SORRY, ARMANDO.

I TRIED.

WHAT WAS IT THAT COACH GIDDENS USED TO SAY?

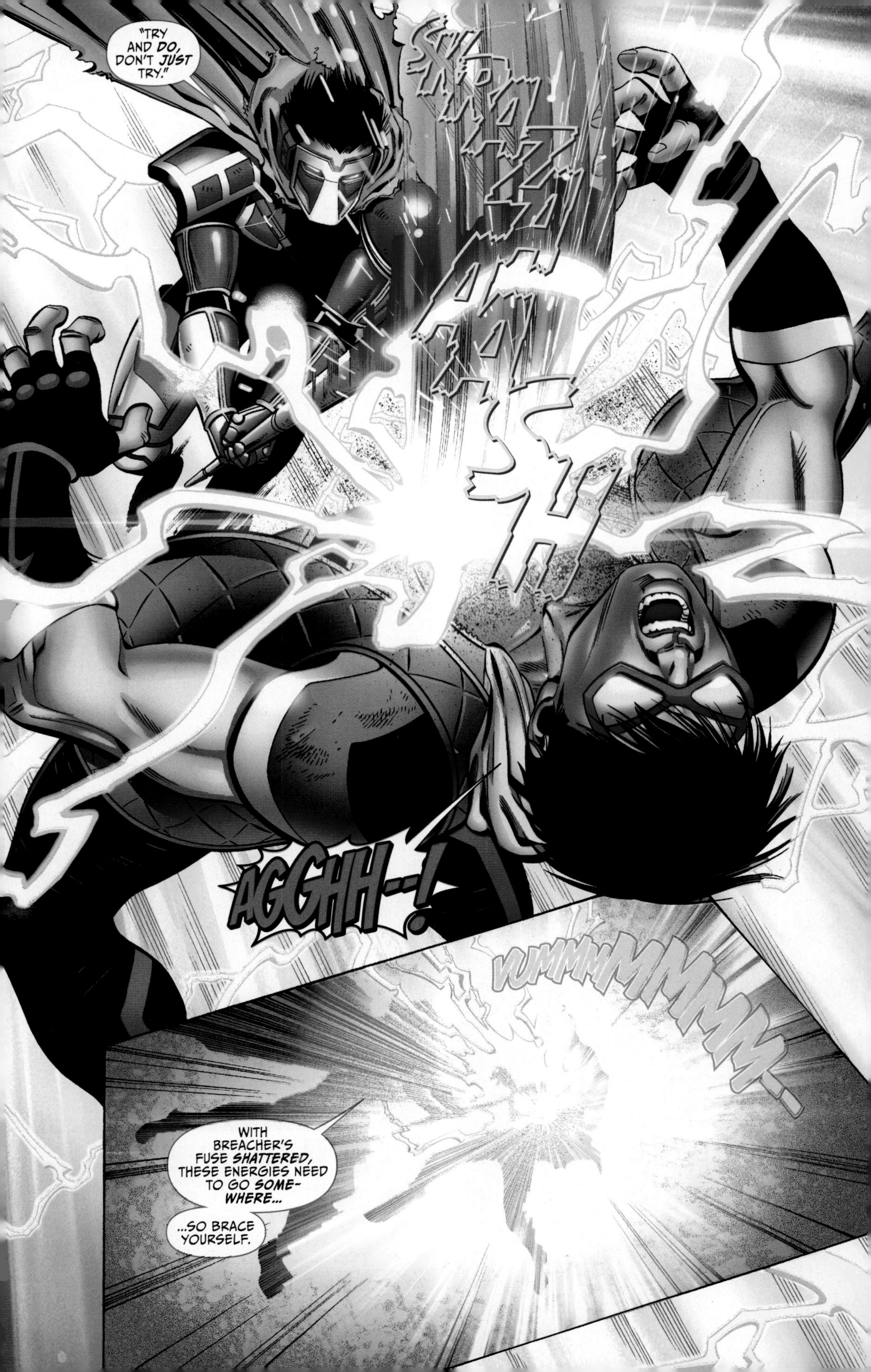
"TRY AND DO, DON'T JUST TRY."
AGGHH--!
VUMMMMMMMMM--
WITH BREACHER'S FUSE SHATTERED, THESE ENERGIES NEED TO GO SOME-WHERE...
...SO BRACE YOURSELF.

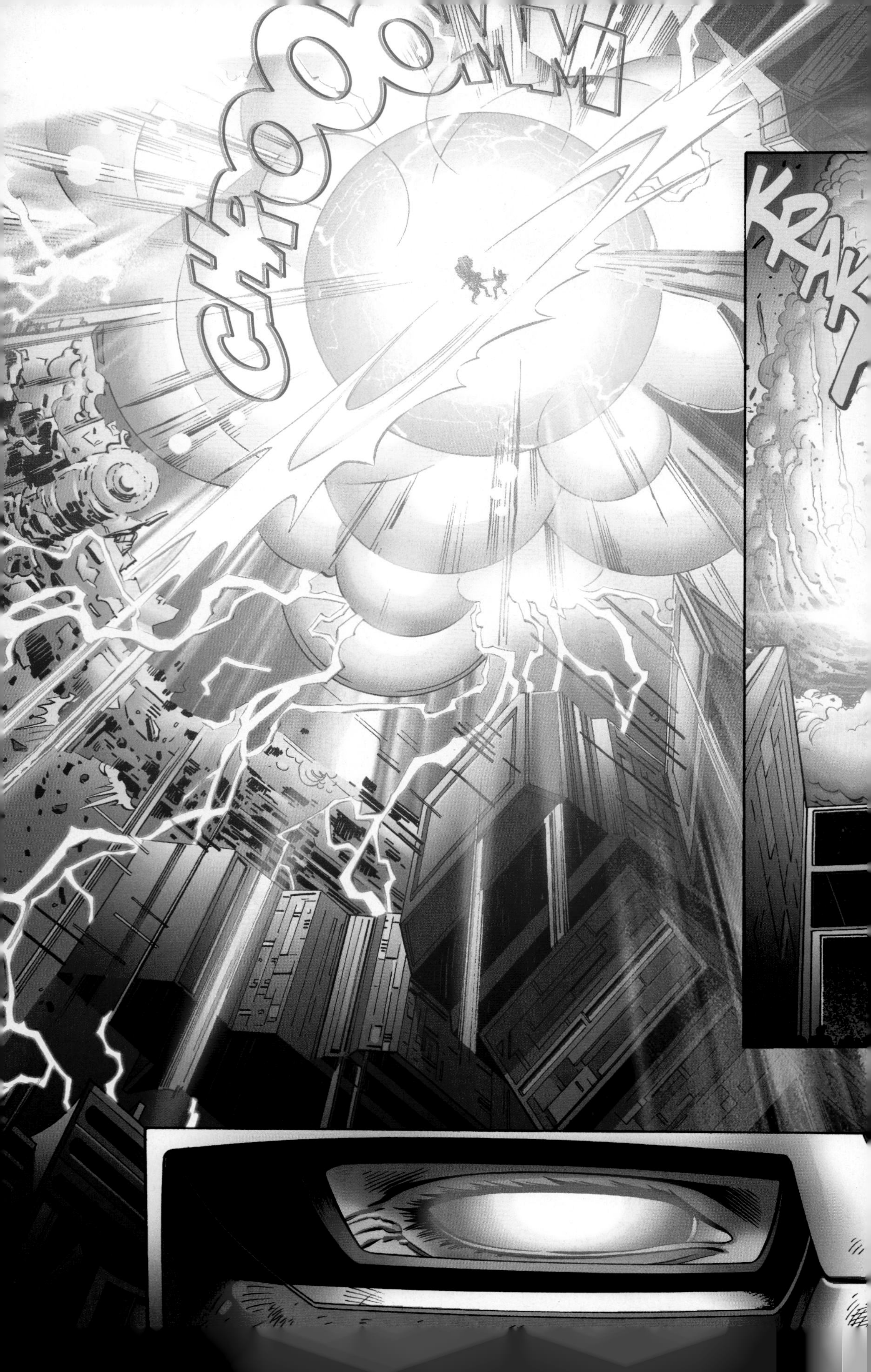
CHOOOMM!
KRAK

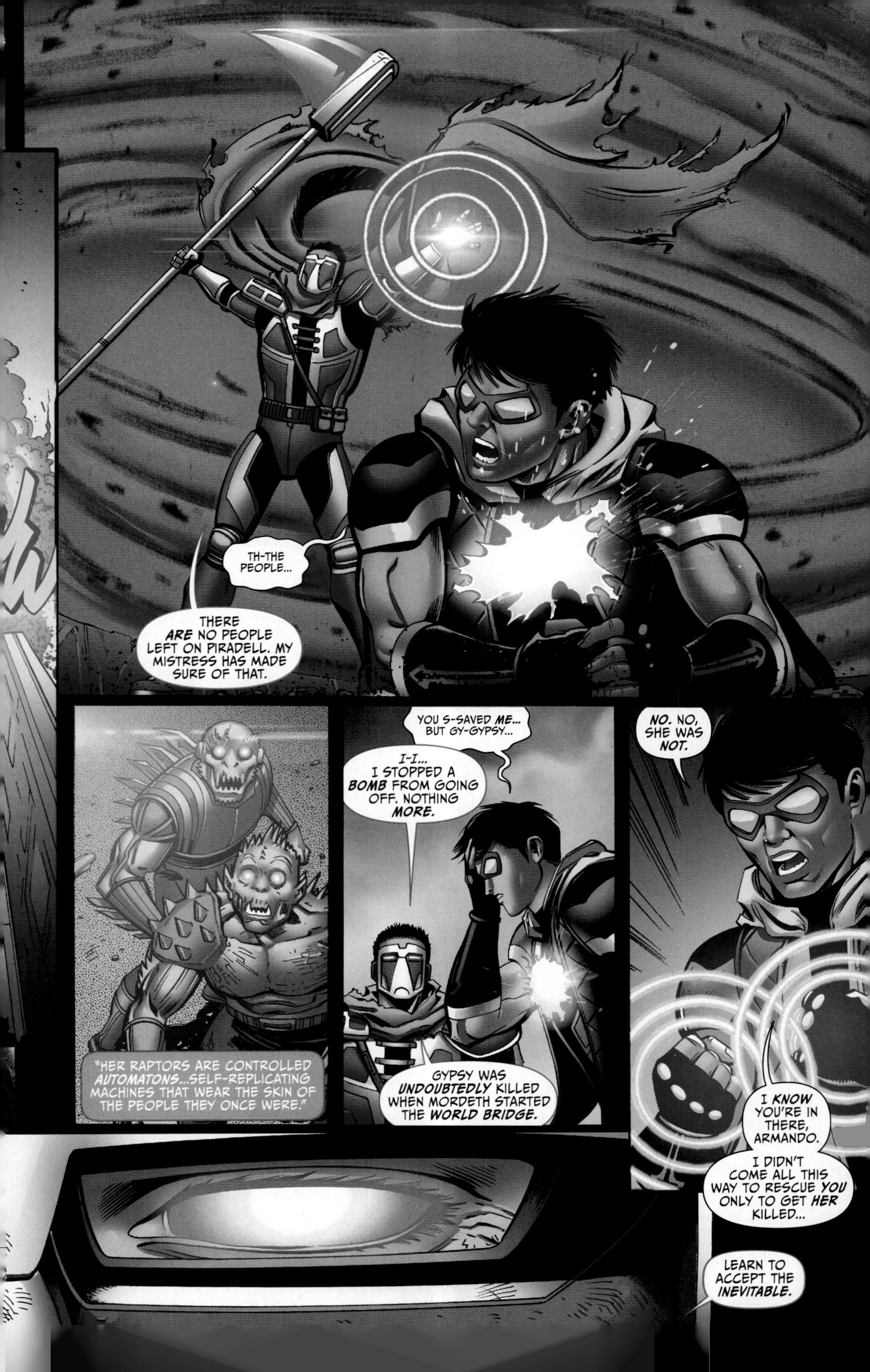
TH-THE PEOPLE...
THERE ARE NO PEOPLE LEFT ON PIRADELL. MY MISTRESS HAS MADE SURE OF THAT.
"HER RAPTORS ARE CONTROLLED AUTOMATONS...SELF-REPLICATING MACHINES THAT WEAR THE SKIN OF THE PEOPLE THEY ONCE WERE."
YOU S-SAVED ME... BUT GY-GYPSY...
I-I... I STOPPED A BOMB FROM GOING OFF. NOTHING MORE.
GYPSY WAS UNDOUBTEDLY KILLED WHEN MORDETH STARTED THE WORLD BRIDGE.
NO. NO, SHE WAS NOT.
I KNOW YOU'RE IN THERE, ARMANDO.
I DIDN'T COME ALL THIS WAY TO RESCUE YOU ONLY TO GET HER KILLED...
LEARN TO ACCEPT THE INEVITABLE.

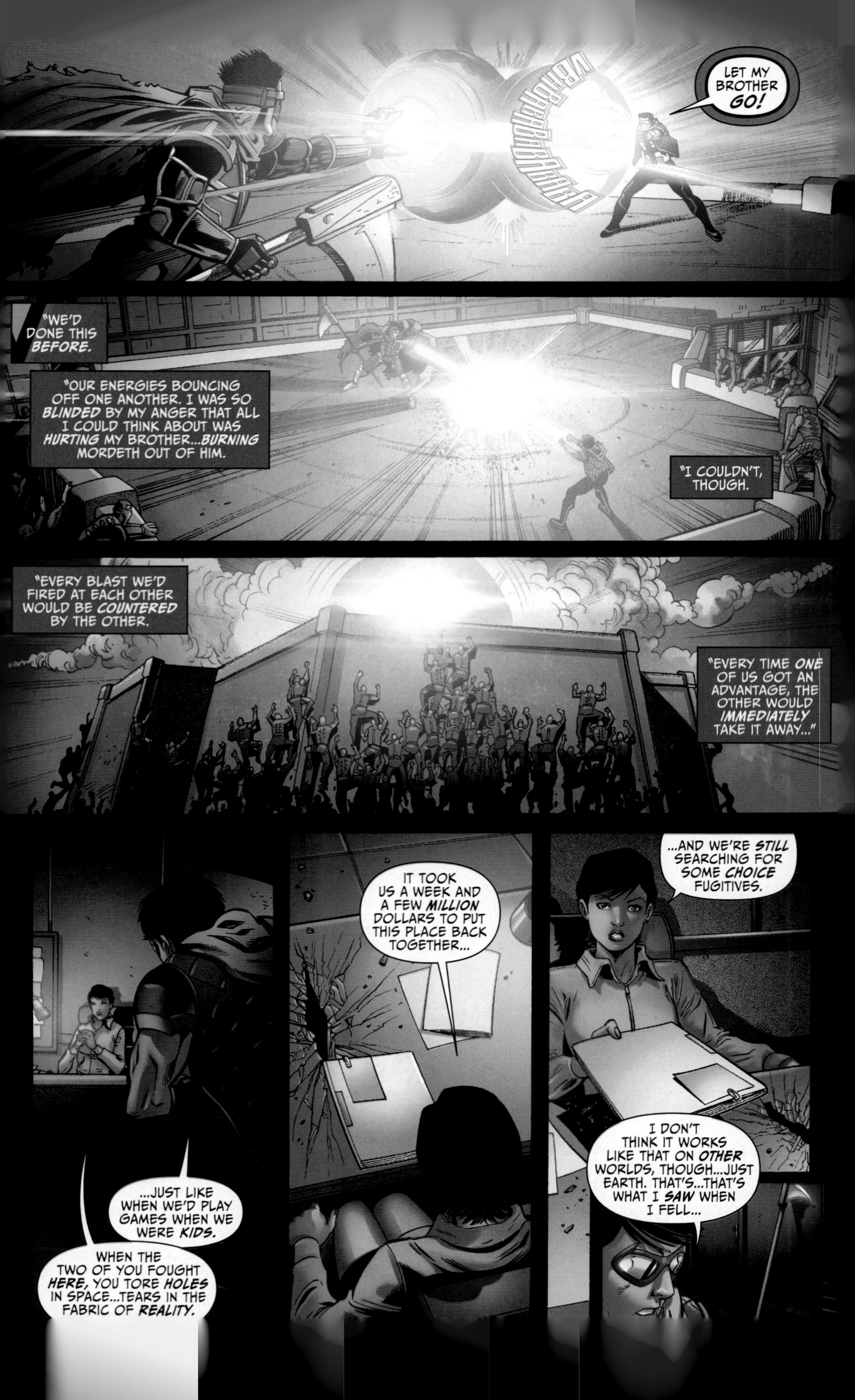
LET MY BROTHER GO!
"WE'D DONE THIS BEFORE.
"OUR ENERGIES BOUNCING OFF ONE ANOTHER. I WAS SO BLINDED BY MY ANGER THAT ALL I COULD THINK ABOUT WAS HURTING MY BROTHER...BURNING MORDETH OUT OF HIM.
"I COULDN'T, THOUGH.
"EVERY BLAST WE'D FIRED AT EACH OTHER WOULD BE COUNTERED BY THE OTHER.
"EVERY TIME ONE OF US GOT AN ADVANTAGE, THE OTHER WOULD IMMEDIATELY TAKE IT AWAY..."
...JUST LIKE WHEN WE'D PLAY GAMES WHEN WE WERE KIDS.
WHEN THE TWO OF YOU FOUGHT HERE, YOU TORE HOLES IN SPACE...TEARS IN THE FABRIC OF REALITY.
IT TOOK US A WEEK AND A FEW MILLION DOLLARS TO PUT THIS PLACE BACK TOGETHER...
...AND WE'RE STILL SEARCHING FOR SOME CHOICE FUGITIVES.
I DON'T THINK IT WORKS LIKE THAT ON OTHER WORLDS, THOUGH...JUST EARTH. THAT'S...THAT'S WHAT I SAW WHEN I FELL...

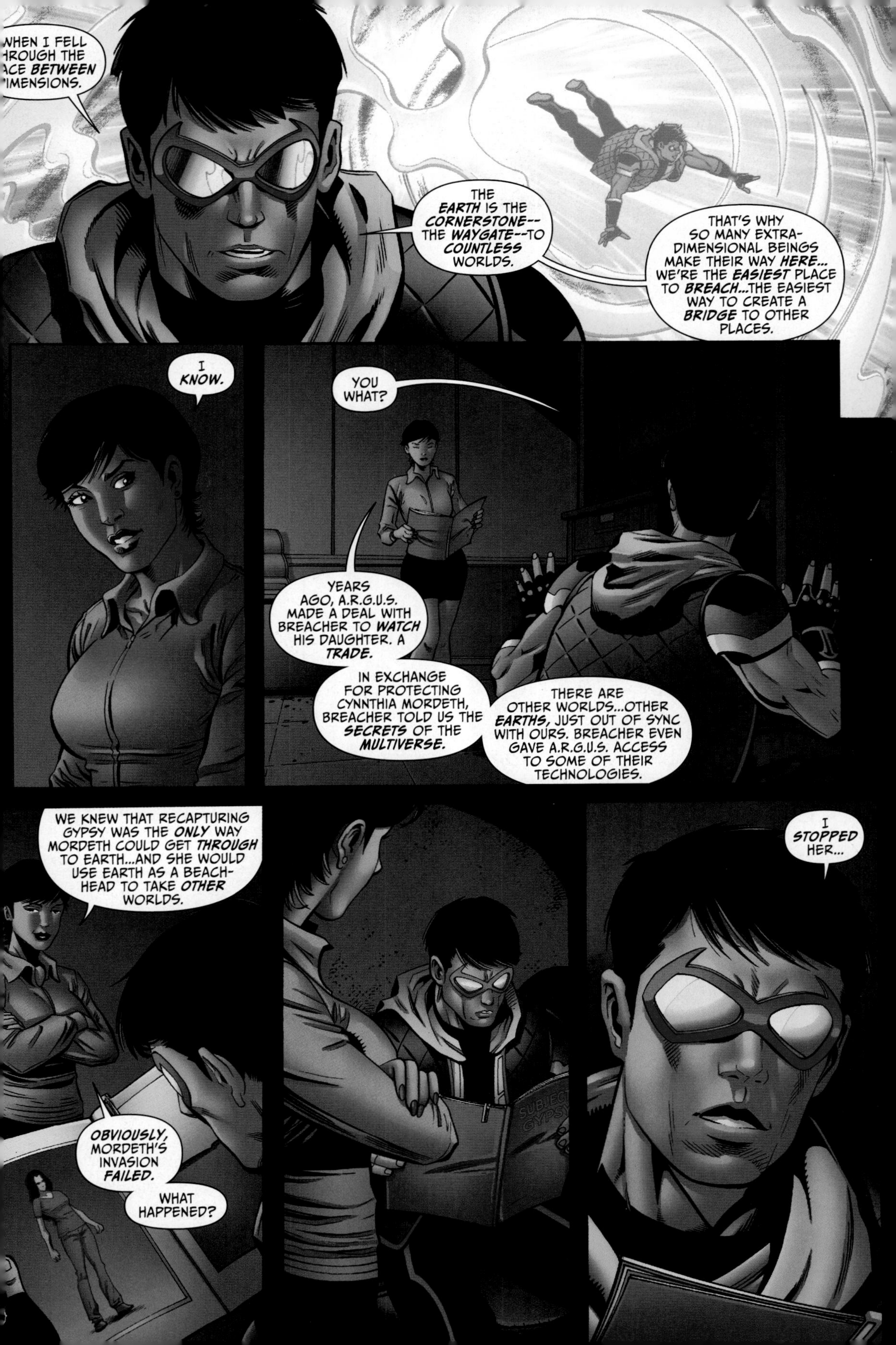
WHEN I FELL THROUGH THE ACE BETWEEN IMENSIONS.
THE EARTH IS THE CORNERSTONE-- THE WAYGATE--TO COUNTLESS WORLDS.
THAT'S WHY SO MANY EXTRA-DIMENSIONAL BEINGS MAKE THEIR WAY HERE... WE'RE THE EASIEST PLACE TO BREACH...THE EASIEST WAY TO CREATE A BRIDGE TO OTHER PLACES.
I KNOW.
YOU WHAT?
YEARS AGO, A.R.G.U.S. MADE A DEAL WITH BREACHER TO WATCH HIS DAUGHTER. A TRADE.
IN EXCHANGE FOR PROTECTING CYNNTHIA MORDETH, BREACHER TOLD US THE SECRETS OF THE MULTIVERSE.
THERE ARE OTHER WORLDS...OTHER EARTHS, JUST OUT OF SYNC WITH OURS. BREACHER EVEN GAVE A.R.G.U.S. ACCESS TO SOME OF THEIR TECHNOLOGIES.
WE KNEW THAT RECAPTURING GYPSY WAS THE ONLY WAY MORDETH COULD GET THROUGH TO EARTH...AND SHE WOULD USE EARTH AS A BEACH-HEAD TO TAKE OTHER WORLDS.
OBVIOUSLY, MORDETH'S INVASION FAILED.
WHAT HAPPENED?
SUBJECT GYPSY
I STOPPED HER...

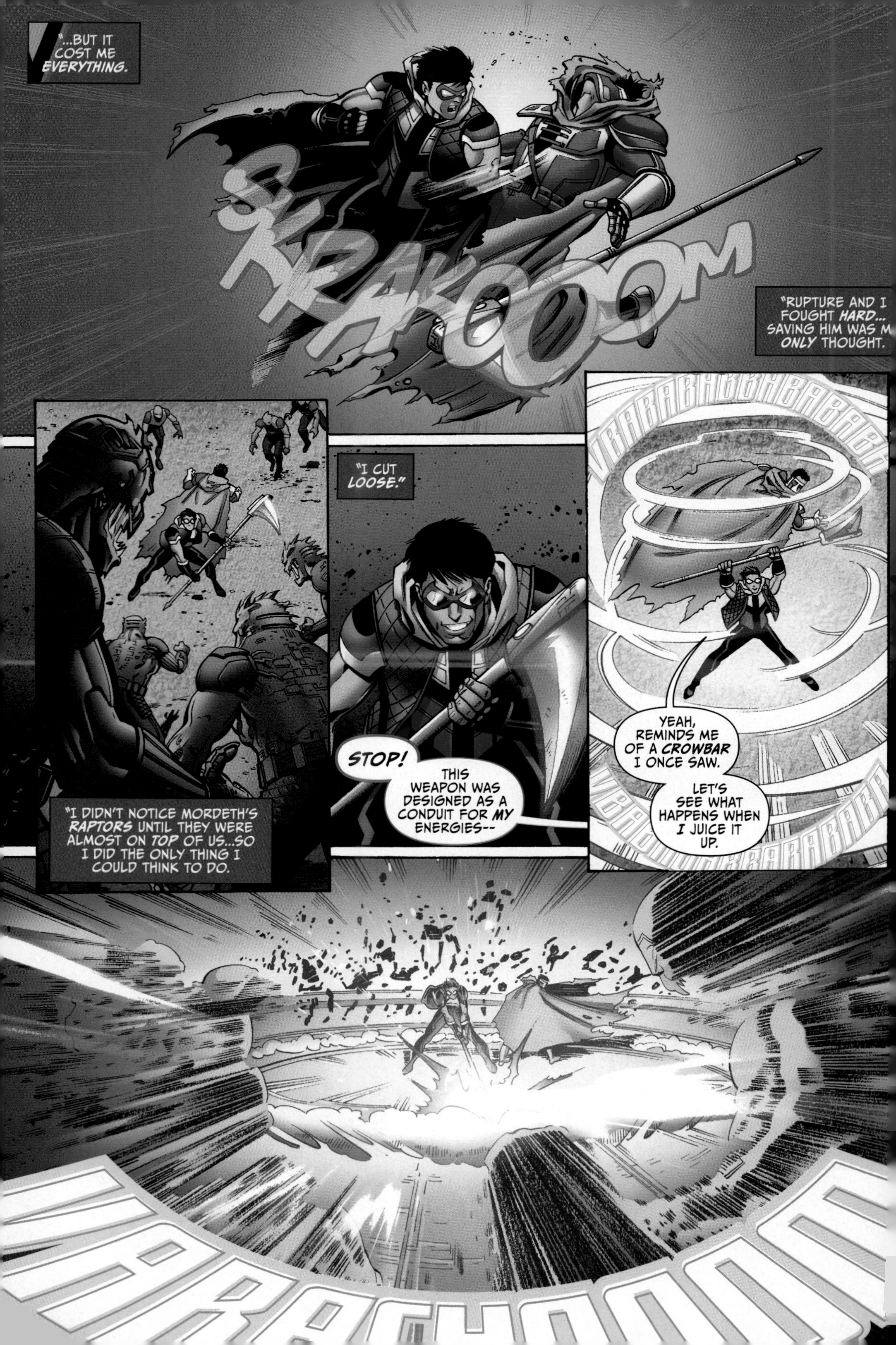
"...BUT IT COST ME *EVERYTHING*.
SKRAKOOOM
"RUPTURE AND I FOUGHT *HARD*... SAVING HIM WAS M *ONLY* THOUGHT.
"I DIDN'T NOTICE MORDETH'S *RAPTORS* UNTIL THEY WERE ALMOST ON *TOP* OF US...SO I DID THE ONLY THING I COULD THINK TO DO.
"I CUT *LOOSE*."
STOP!
THIS WEAPON WAS DESIGNED AS A CONDUIT FOR *MY* ENERGIES--
YEAH, REMINDS ME OF A *CROWBAR* I ONCE SAW.
LET'S SEE WHAT HAPPENS WHEN *I* JUICE IT UP.

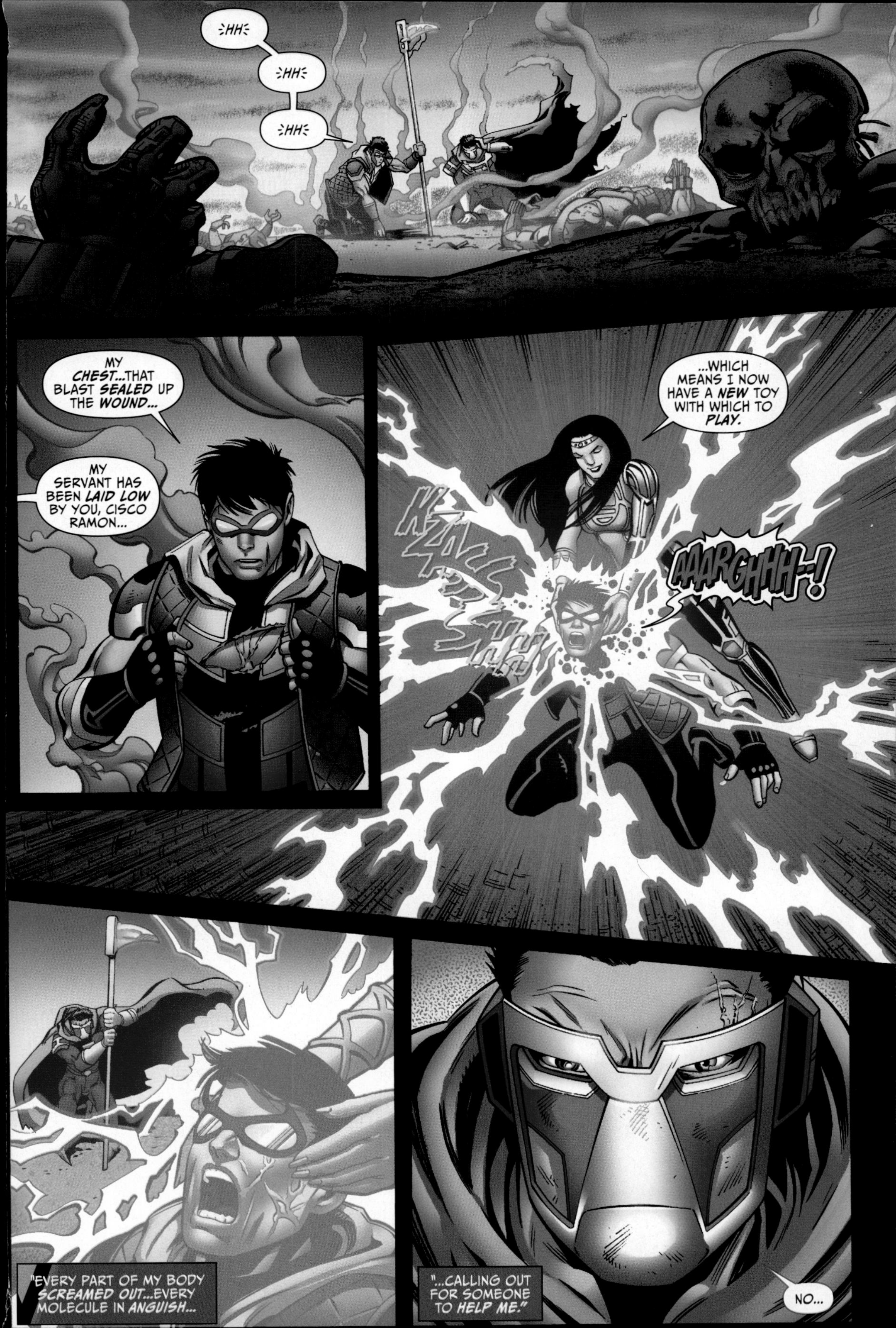
HH
HH
HH
MY CHEST...THAT BLAST SEALED UP THE WOUND...
MY SERVANT HAS BEEN LAID LOW BY YOU, CISCO RAMON...
...WHICH MEANS I NOW HAVE A NEW TOY WITH WHICH TO PLAY.
AAARGHHH--!
"EVERY PART OF MY BODY SCREAMED OUT...EVERY MOLECULE IN ANGUISH...
"...CALLING OUT FOR SOMEONE TO HELP ME."
NO...

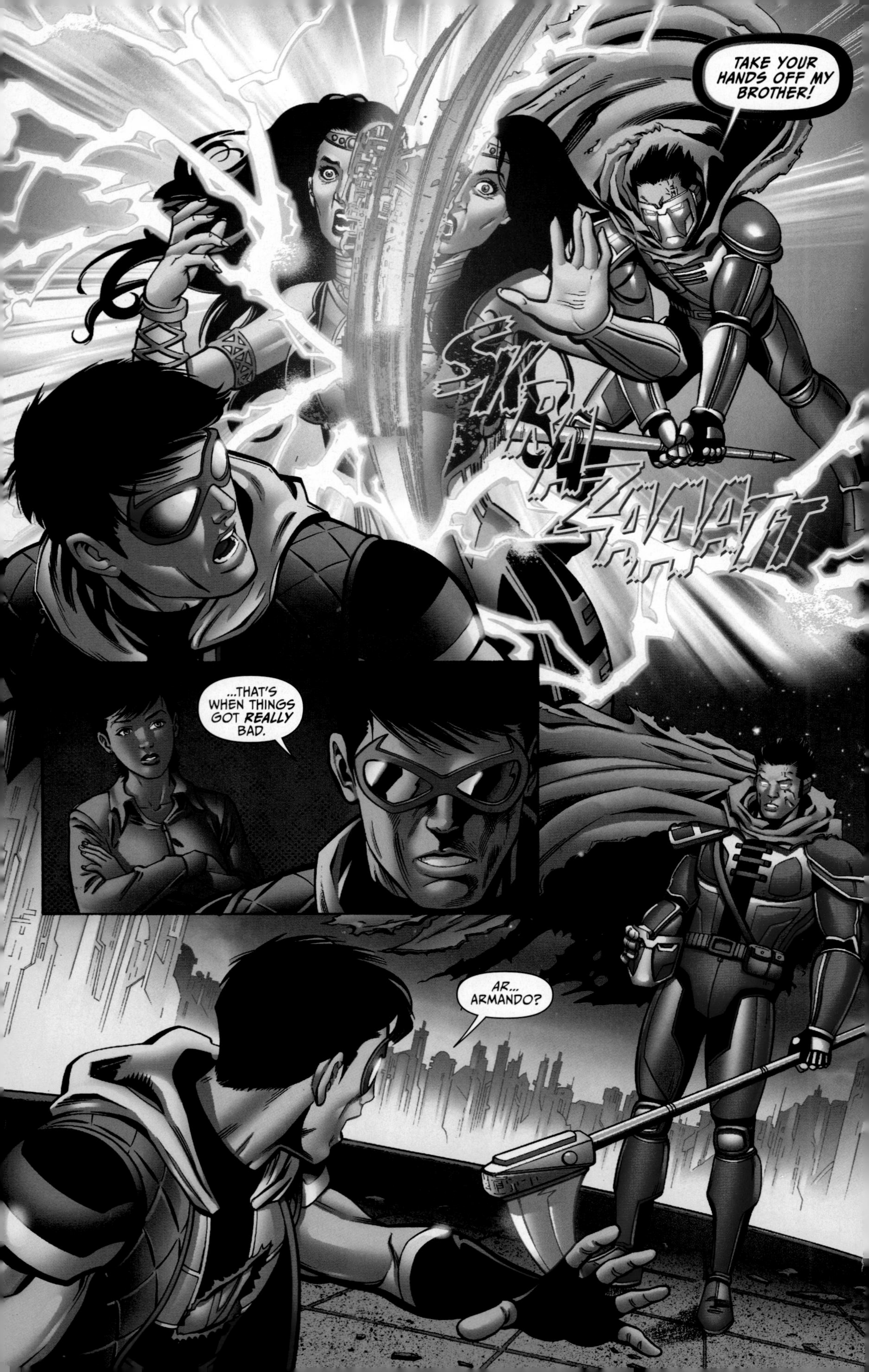
TAKE YOUR HANDS OFF MY BROTHER!
...THAT'S WHEN THINGS GOT *REALLY* BAD.
AR... ARMANDO?

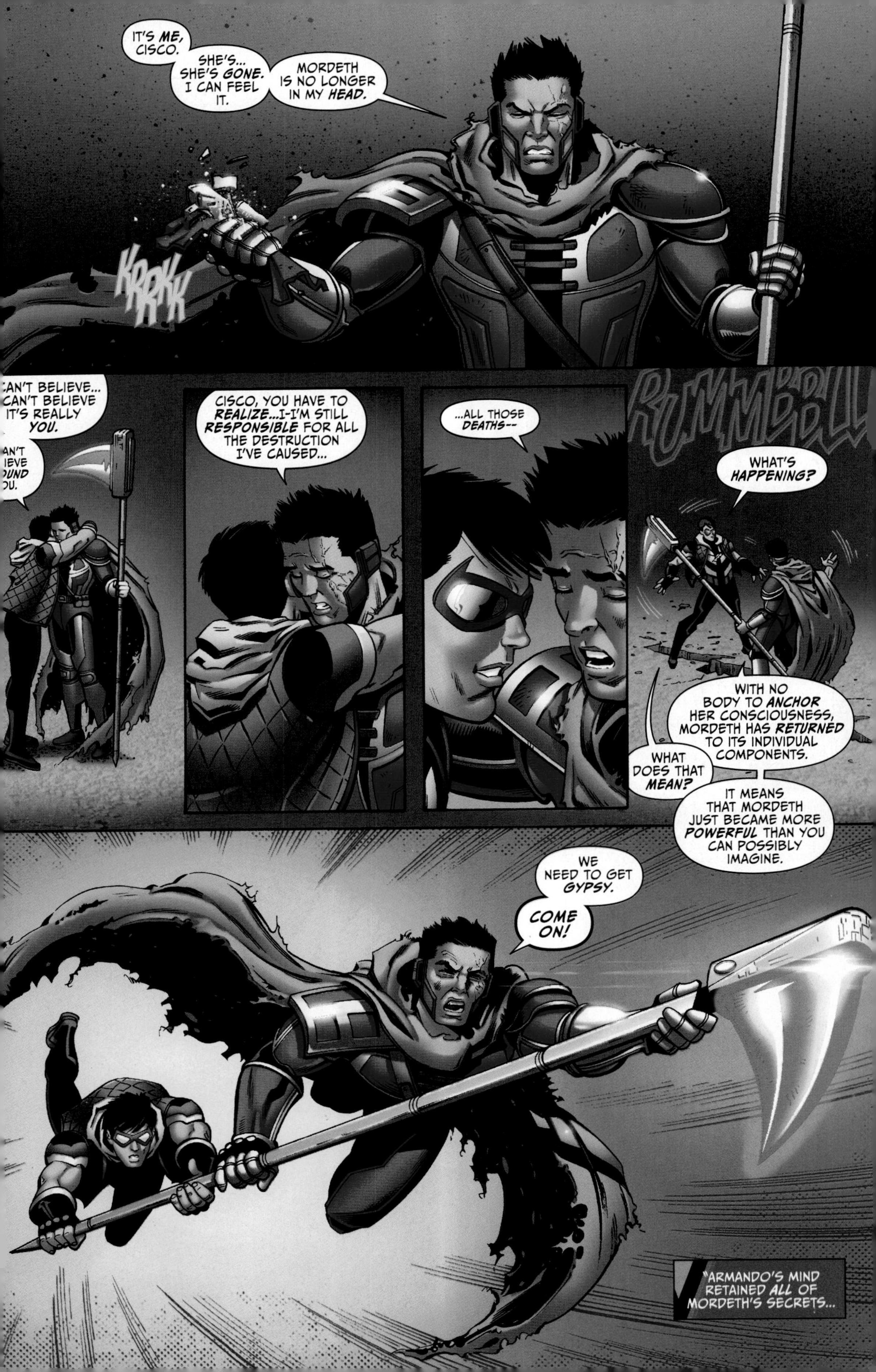
IT'S ME, CISCO.
SHE'S... SHE'S GONE. I CAN FEEL IT.
MORDETH IS NO LONGER IN MY HEAD.
KRKKK
CAN'T BELIEVE... CAN'T BELIEVE IT'S REALLY YOU.
CISCO, YOU HAVE TO REALIZE...I-I'M STILL RESPONSIBLE FOR ALL THE DESTRUCTION I'VE CAUSED...
...ALL THOSE DEATHS--
WHAT'S HAPPENING?
WITH NO BODY TO ANCHOR HER CONSCIOUSNESS, MORDETH HAS RETURNED TO ITS INDIVIDUAL COMPONENTS.
WHAT DOES THAT MEAN?
IT MEANS THAT MORDETH JUST BECAME MORE POWERFUL THAN YOU CAN POSSIBLY IMAGINE.
WE NEED TO GET GYPSY.
COME ON!
"ARMANDO'S MIND RETAINED ALL OF MORDETH'S SECRETS...

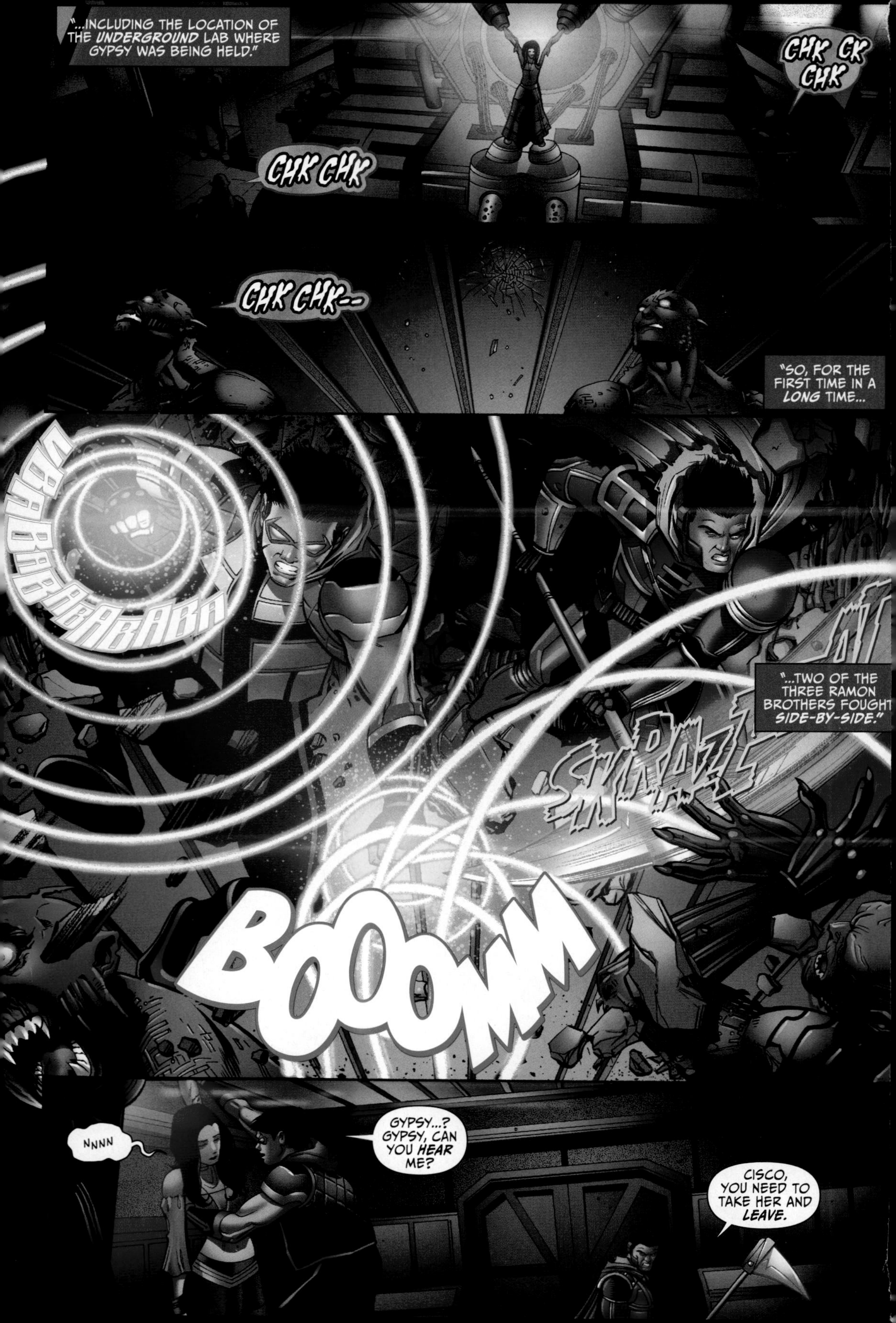
"...INCLUDING THE LOCATION OF THE UNDERGROUND LAB WHERE GYPSY WAS BEING HELD."
CHK CK CHK
CHK CHK
CHK CHK--
"SO, FOR THE FIRST TIME IN A LONG TIME...
"...TWO OF THE THREE RAMON BROTHERS FOUGHT SIDE-BY-SIDE."
SKRAZZ
BOOOMM
NNNN
GYPSY...? GYPSY, CAN YOU HEAR ME?
CISCO, YOU NEED TO TAKE HER AND LEAVE.

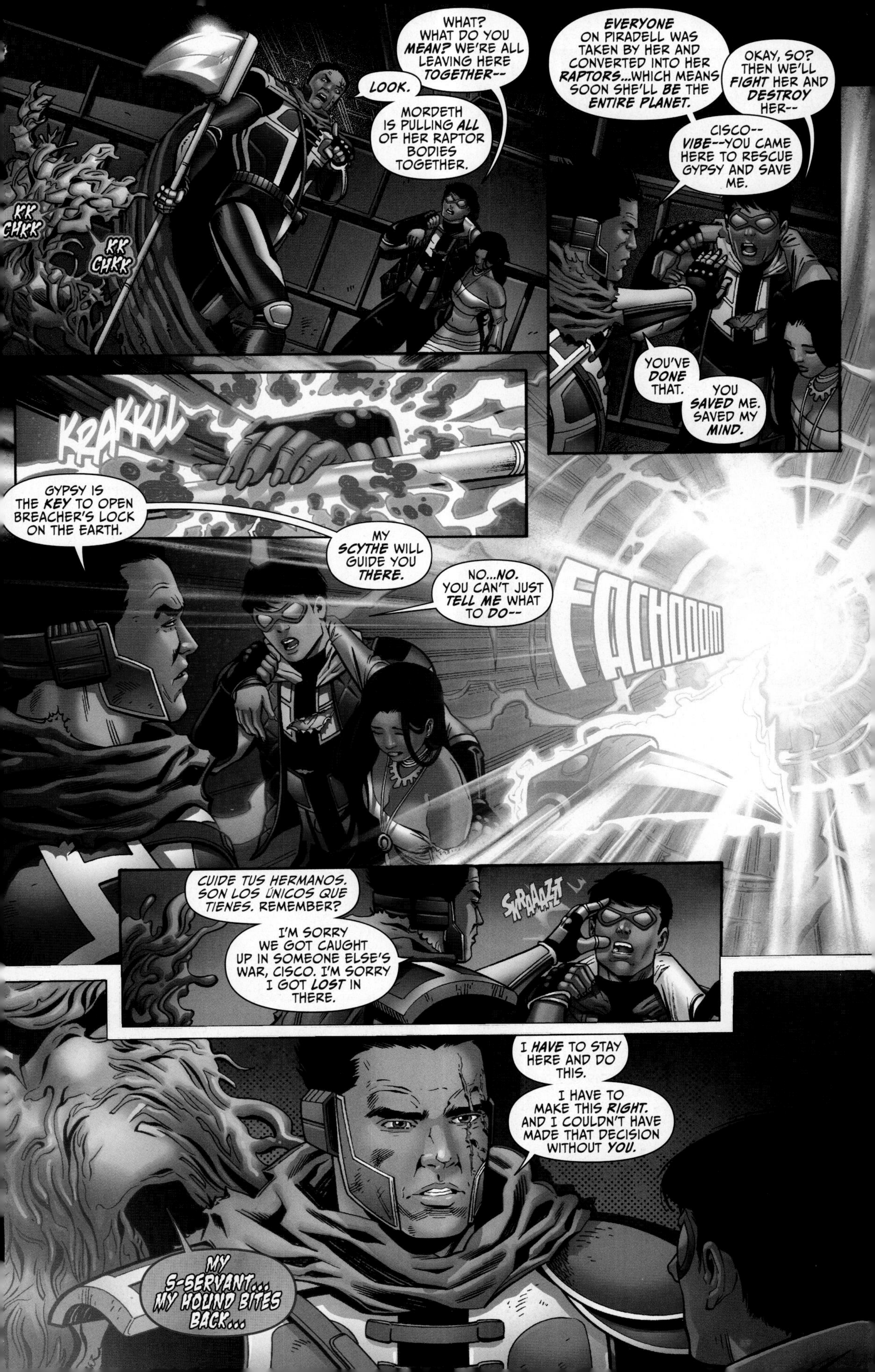

WHAT? WHAT DO YOU MEAN? WE'RE ALL LEAVING HERE TOGETHER--
LOOK.
MORDETH IS PULLING ALL OF HER RAPTOR BODIES TOGETHER.
KK CHKK
KK CHKK
EVERYONE ON PIRADELL WAS TAKEN BY HER AND CONVERTED INTO HER RAPTORS...WHICH MEANS SOON SHE'LL BE THE ENTIRE PLANET.
OKAY, SO? THEN WE'LL FIGHT HER AND DESTROY HER--
CISCO-- VIBE--YOU CAME HERE TO RESCUE GYPSY AND SAVE ME.
YOU'VE DONE THAT.
YOU SAVED ME. SAVED MY MIND.
KRAKKLL
GYPSY IS THE KEY TO OPEN BREACHER'S LOCK ON THE EARTH.
MY SCYTHE WILL GUIDE YOU THERE.
NO...NO. YOU CAN'T JUST TELL ME WHAT TO DO--
FACHOOOM
CUIDE TUS HERMANOS. SON LOS ÚNICOS QUE TIENES. REMEMBER?
I'M SORRY WE GOT CAUGHT UP IN SOMEONE ELSE'S WAR, CISCO. I'M SORRY I GOT LOST IN THERE.
SKRAAAZZT
I HAVE TO STAY HERE AND DO THIS.
I HAVE TO MAKE THIS RIGHT. AND I COULDN'T HAVE MADE THAT DECISION WITHOUT YOU.
MY S-SERVANT... MY HOUND BITES BACK...

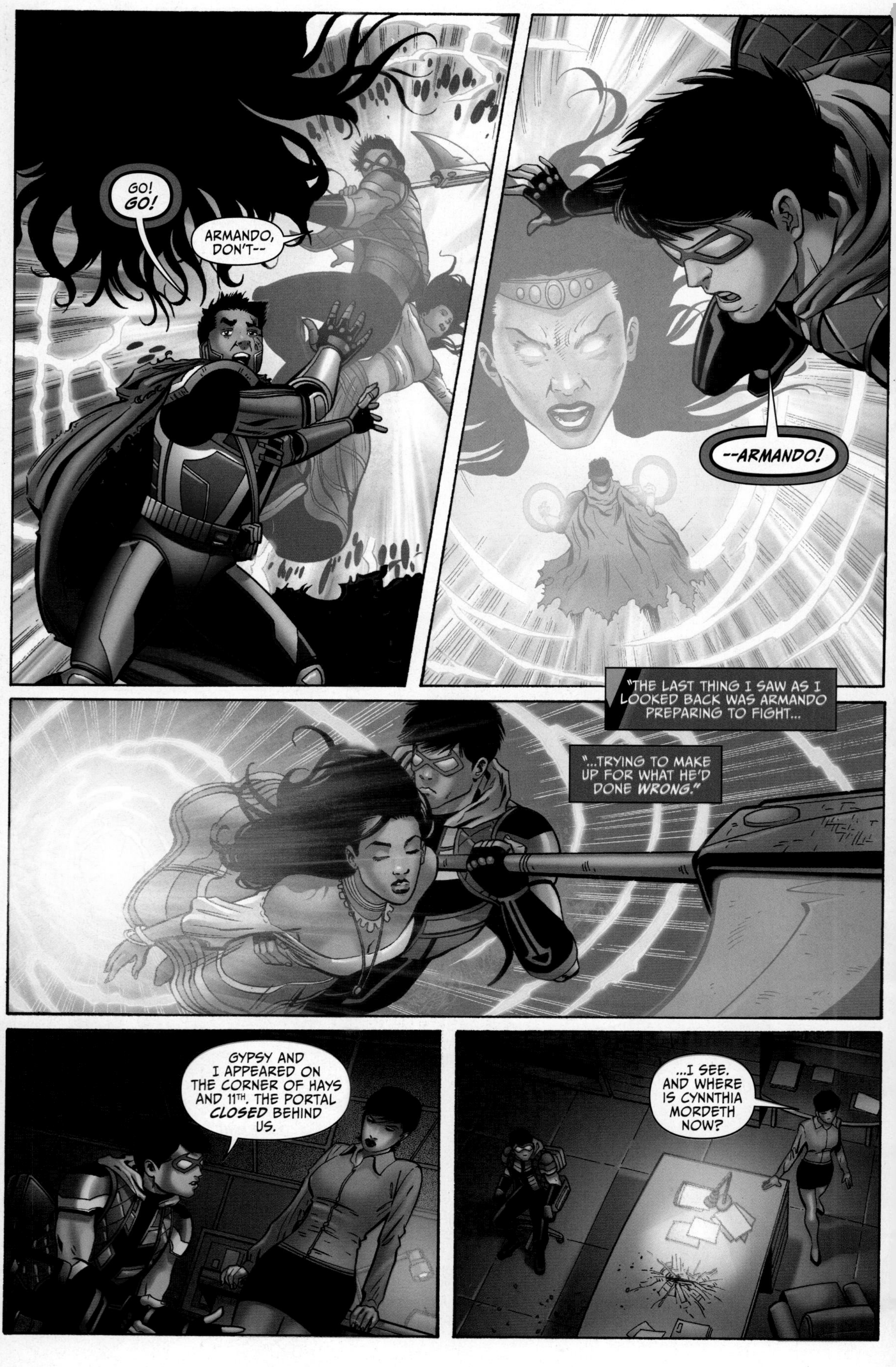
GO! GO!
ARMANDO, DON'T--
--ARMANDO!
"THE LAST THING I SAW AS I LOOKED BACK WAS ARMANDO PREPARING TO FIGHT...
"...TRYING TO MAKE UP FOR WHAT HE'D DONE WRONG."
GYPSY AND I APPEARED ON THE CORNER OF HAYS AND 11TH. THE PORTAL CLOSED BEHIND US.
...I SEE. AND WHERE IS CYNNTHIA MORDETH NOW?

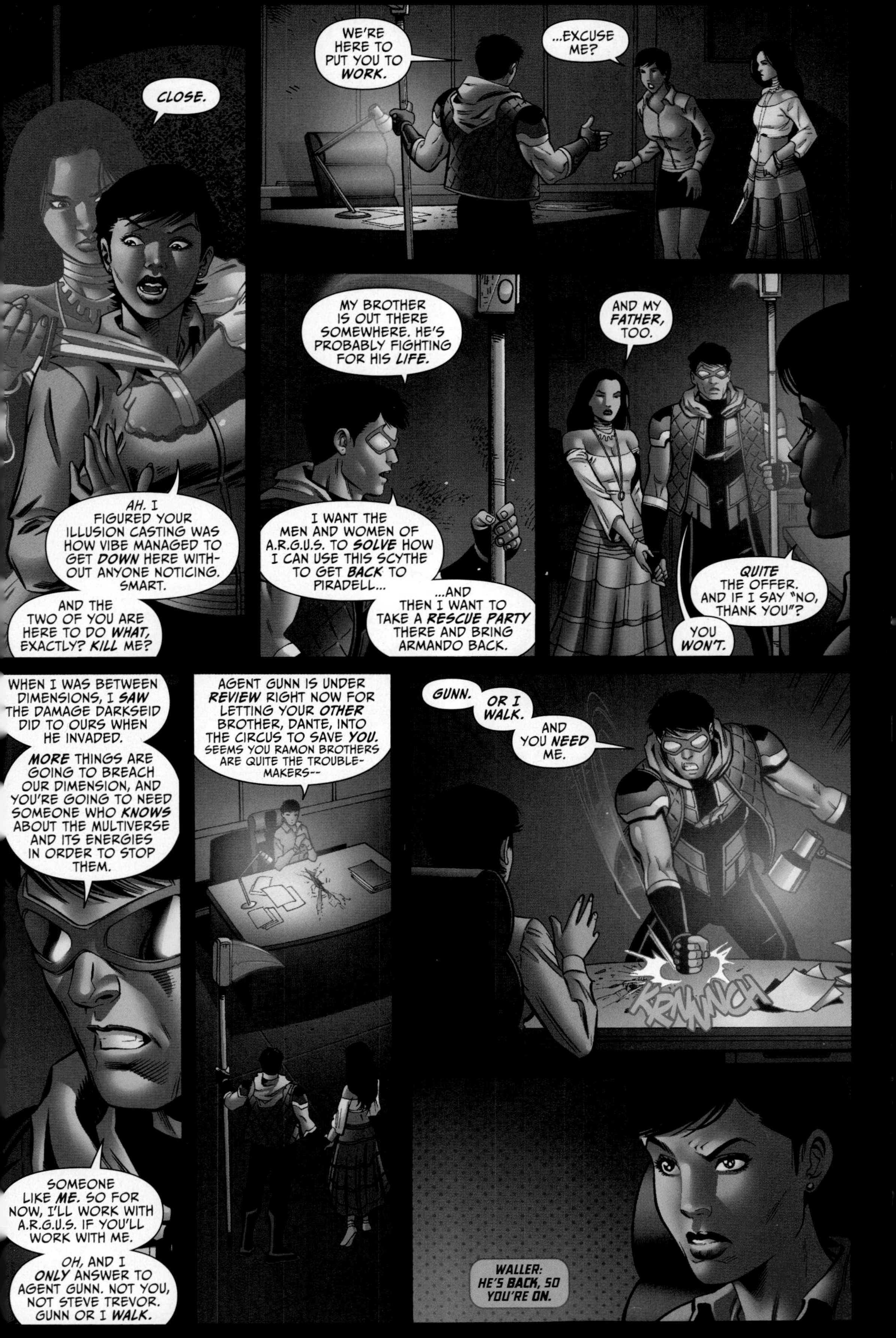
CLOSE.
WE'RE HERE TO PUT YOU TO WORK.
...EXCUSE ME?
AH. I FIGURED YOUR ILLUSION CASTING WAS HOW VIBE MANAGED TO GET DOWN HERE WITH-OUT ANYONE NOTICING. SMART.
AND THE TWO OF YOU ARE HERE TO DO WHAT, EXACTLY? KILL ME?
MY BROTHER IS OUT THERE SOMEWHERE. HE'S PROBABLY FIGHTING FOR HIS LIFE.
I WANT THE MEN AND WOMEN OF A.R.G.U.S. TO SOLVE HOW I CAN USE THIS SCYTHE TO GET BACK TO PIRADELL...
...AND THEN I WANT TO TAKE A RESCUE PARTY THERE AND BRING ARMANDO BACK.
AND MY FATHER, TOO.
QUITE THE OFFER. AND IF I SAY "NO, THANK YOU"?
YOU WON'T.
WHEN I WAS BETWEEN DIMENSIONS, I SAW THE DAMAGE DARKSEID DID TO OURS WHEN HE INVADED.
MORE THINGS ARE GOING TO BREACH OUR DIMENSION, AND YOU'RE GOING TO NEED SOMEONE WHO KNOWS ABOUT THE MULTIVERSE AND ITS ENERGIES IN ORDER TO STOP THEM.
SOMEONE LIKE ME. SO FOR NOW, I'LL WORK WITH A.R.G.U.S. IF YOU'LL WORK WITH ME.
OH, AND I ONLY ANSWER TO AGENT GUNN. NOT YOU, NOT STEVE TREVOR. GUNN OR I WALK.
AGENT GUNN IS UNDER REVIEW RIGHT NOW FOR LETTING YOUR OTHER BROTHER, DANTE, INTO THE CIRCUS TO SAVE YOU. SEEMS YOU RAMON BROTHERS ARE QUITE THE TROUBLE-MAKERS--
GUNN.
OR I WALK.
AND YOU NEED ME.
KRNNNCH
WALLER: HE'S BACK, SO YOU'RE ON.

WALLER: I'M RELYING ON YOU TO WATCH HIM.
KLEBBA TO GUNN. I DON'T SEE ANYTHING.
YOU SURE HE'S READING THIS RIGHT?
THE KID'S BEEN BATTING A THOUSAND LATELY. THAT ALARM IN HIS HEAD STARTS GOING OFF AND HE'S SPOT ON.
YOU WORK WITH HIM LONG ENOUGH, YOU SE HOW SERIOUS HE GOTTEN SINCE H STARTED.
WALLER: I'M TAKING A BIG RISK LETTING YOU ANYWHERE NEAR HIM.
YEAH, HE REMINDS ME OF A CERTAIN A.R.G.U.S. AGENT FROM BACK WHEN WE FIRST STARTED DATING.
YOU BARELY CRACKED A SMILE THE FIRST YEAR OF OUR RELATIONSHIP, DALE.
CUT THE CHATTER, AGENT KLEBBA.
I BROUGHT YOU ON THIS DETAIL TO SHOOT BREACHERS, NOT TO SHOOT OFF YOUR MOUTH. OVER.
HEH. WE'LL BE TALKING ABOUT THAT LATER...
KLEBBA TO ALL POINTS. I'VE GOT A BREACHER ENERGY SIGNATURE ENTERING OUR PLANE! OVER.
WALLER: WHO KNOWS HOW HE WOULD REACT IF HE KNEW THAT I WAS WORKING WITH YOU?
WALLER: YOU WOULD NEVER WANT TO BREAK THAT TRUST.
FZZZ ASH
WALLER: YOU'LL NEED HIS TRUST SO YOU CAN HAVE ACCESS TO HIM NIGHT AND DAY...
OKAY, FOLKS. HERE WE GO!
REMEMBER, AGENT VIBE IS LEAD, WE'RE JU THE BACKUP!

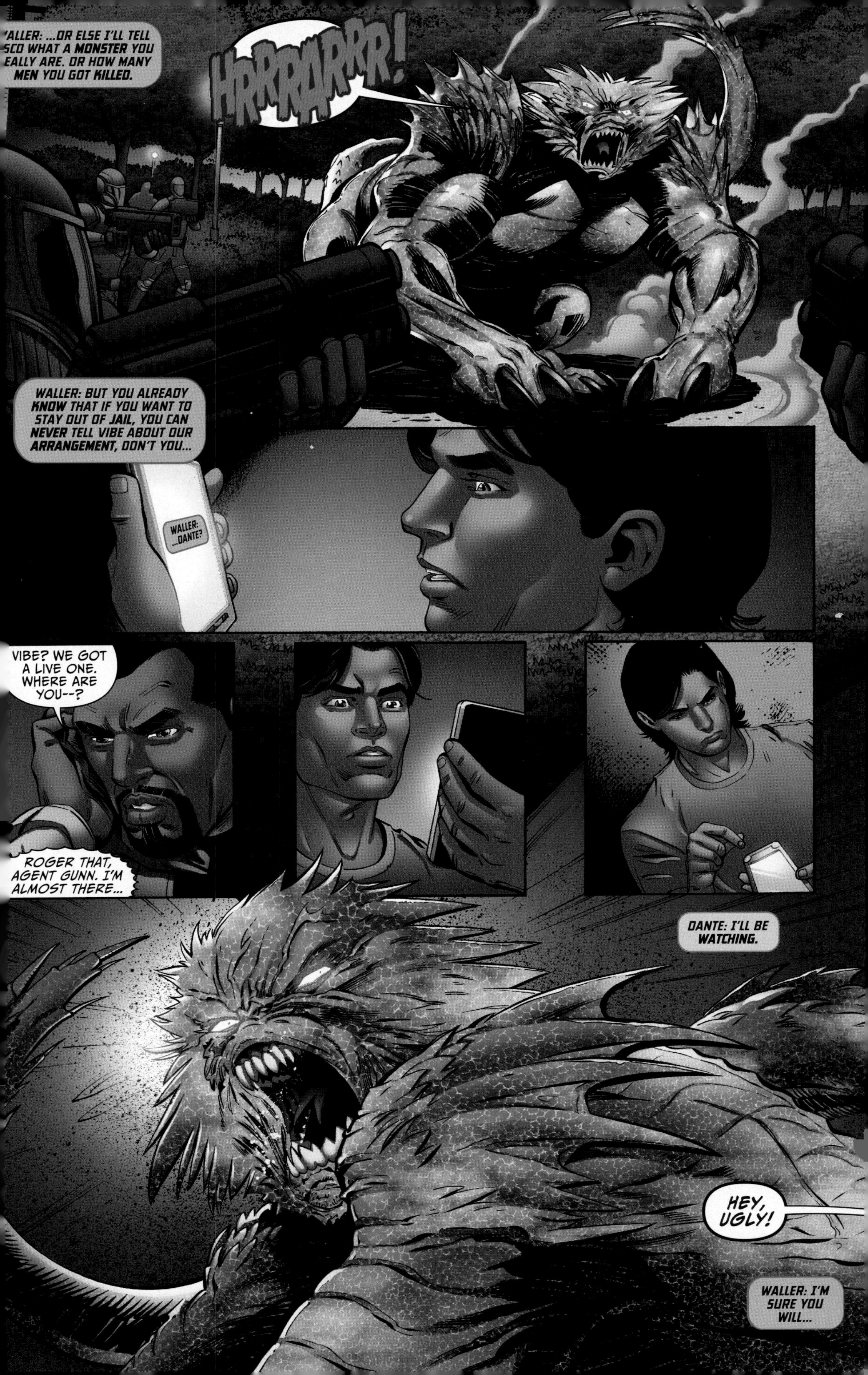

'ALLER: ...OR ELSE I'LL TELL
SCO WHAT A MONSTER YOU
EALLY ARE. OR HOW MANY
MEN YOU GOT KILLED.
HRRRARRR!
WALLER: BUT YOU ALREADY KNOW THAT IF YOU WANT TO STAY OUT OF JAIL, YOU CAN NEVER TELL VIBE ABOUT OUR ARRANGEMENT, DON'T YOU...
WALLER: ...DANTE?
VIBE? WE GOT A LIVE ONE. WHERE ARE YOU--?
ROGER THAT, AGENT GUNN. I'M ALMOST THERE...
DANTE: I'LL BE WATCHING.
HEY, UGLY!
WALLER: I'M SURE YOU WILL...

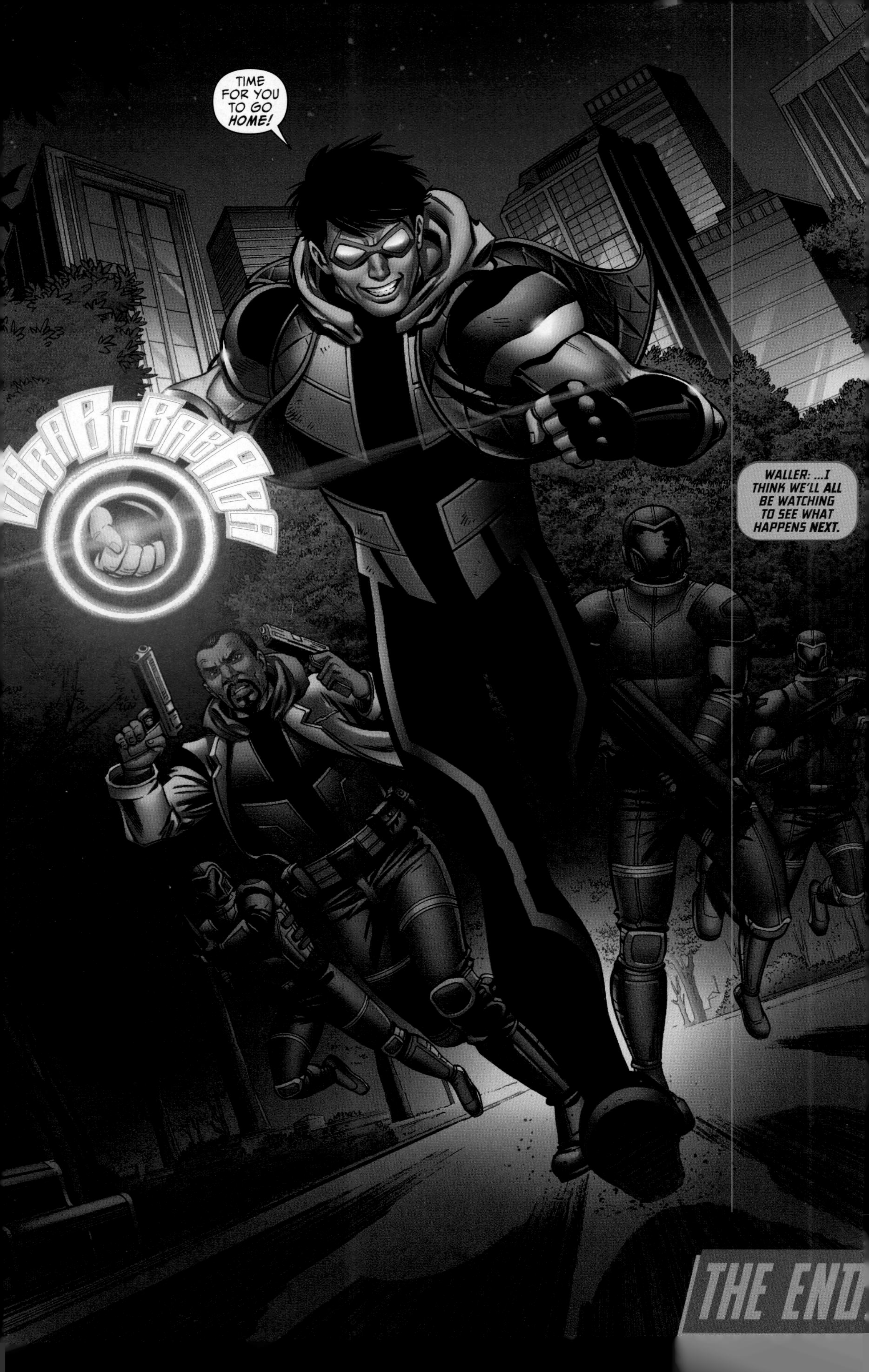
TIME FOR YOU TO GO HOME!
VABABABABABA!
WALLER: ...I THINK WE'LL ALL BE WATCHING TO SEE WHAT HAPPENS NEXT.
THE END

Design by Jim Lee

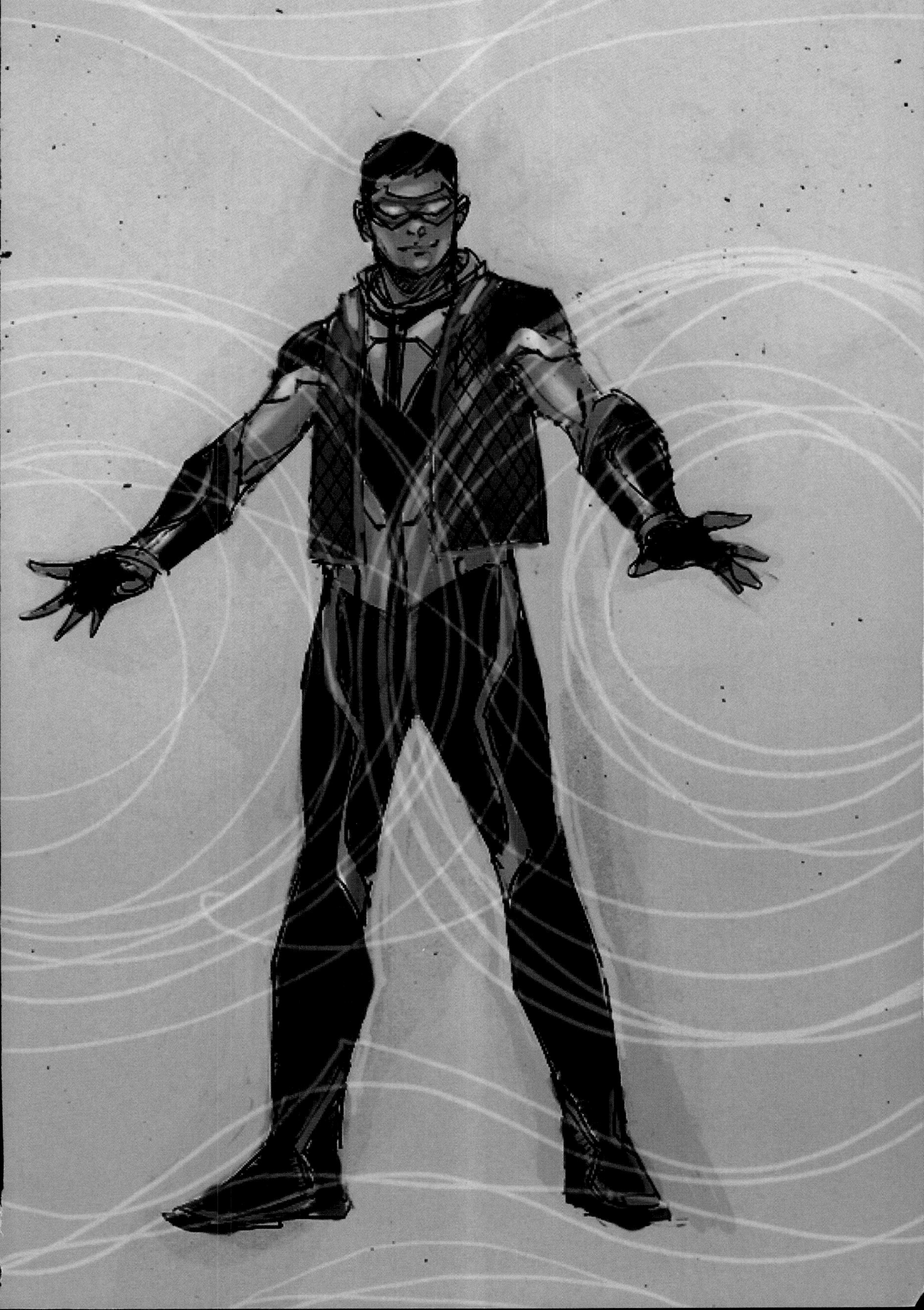

Sketches by Pete Woods

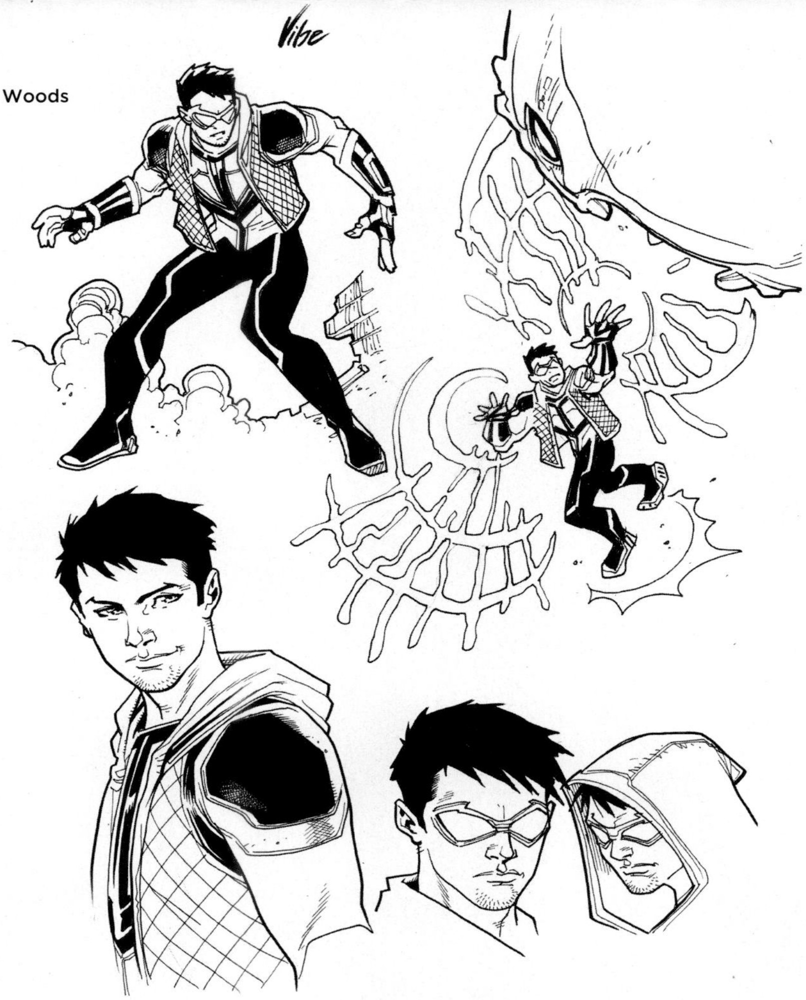
Vibe

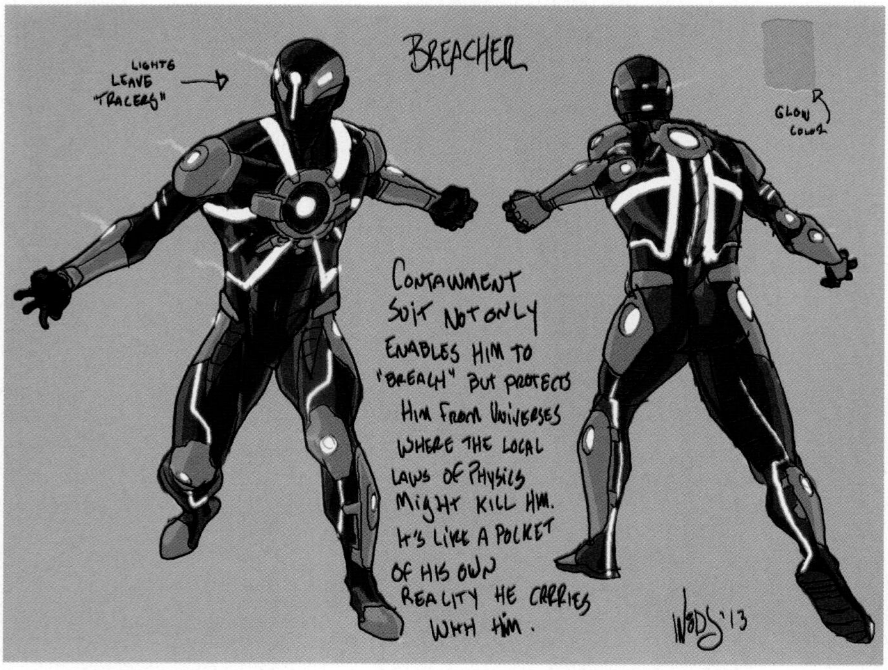
BREACHER
LIGHTS LEAVE "TRACERS"
GLOW COLOR
CONTAINMENT SUIT NOT ONLY ENABLES HIM TO "BREACH" BUT PROTECTS HIM FROM UNIVERSES WHERE THE LOCAL LAWS OF PHYSICS MIGHT KILL HIM. IT'S LIKE A POCKET OF HIS OWN REALITY HE CARRIES WITH HIM.
WOODS '13

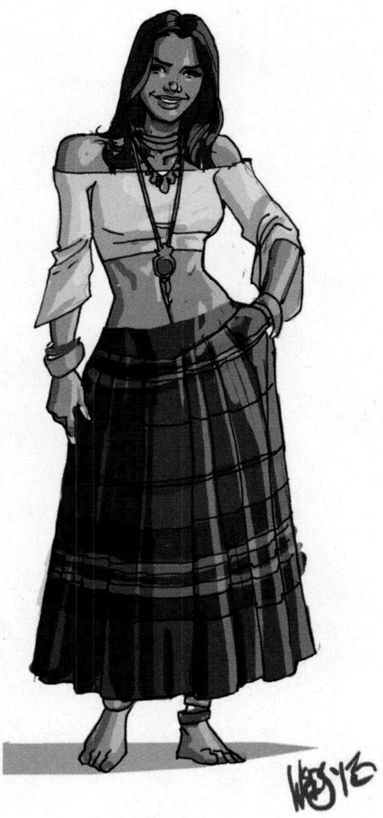

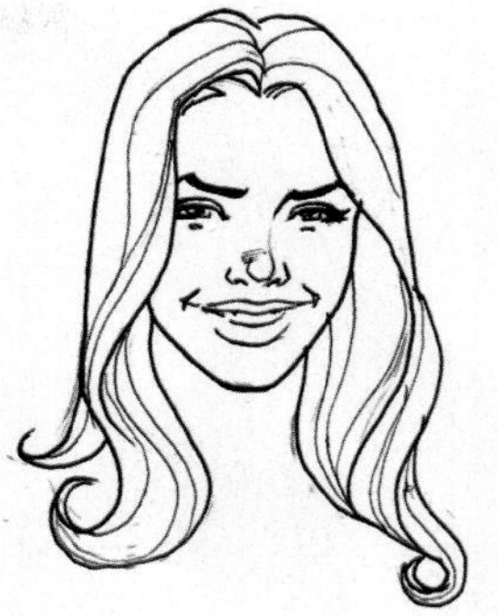

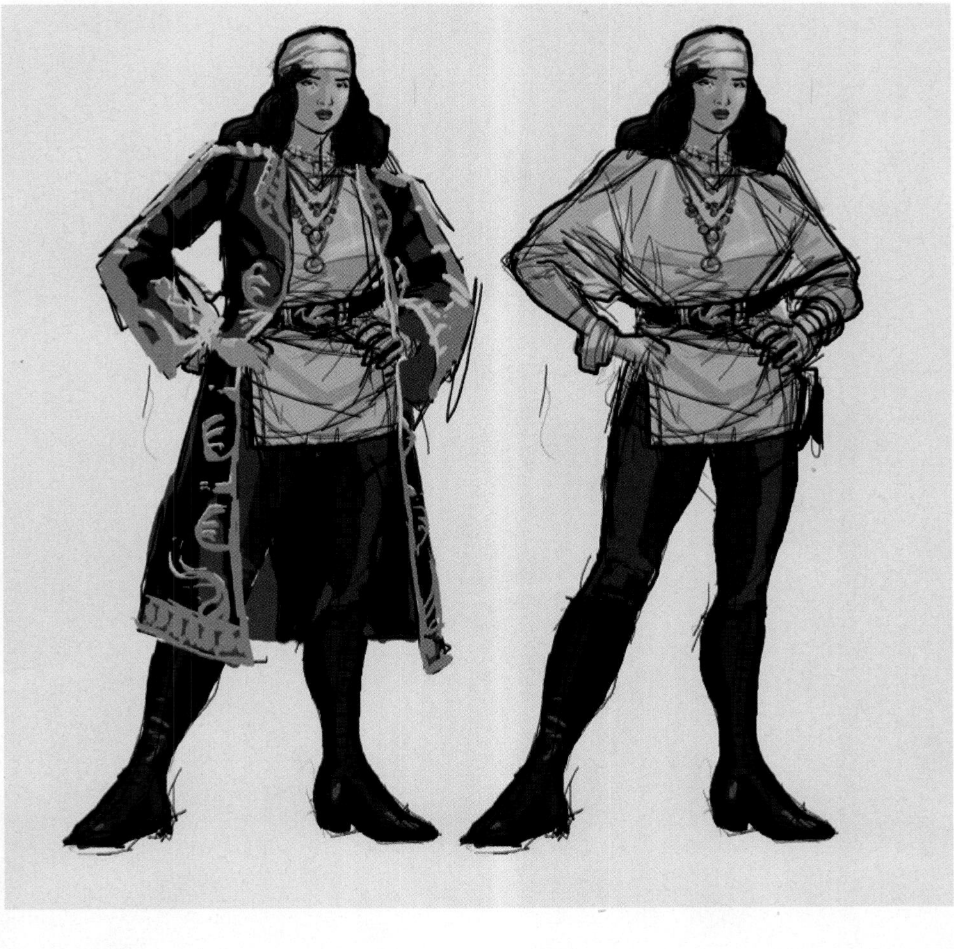

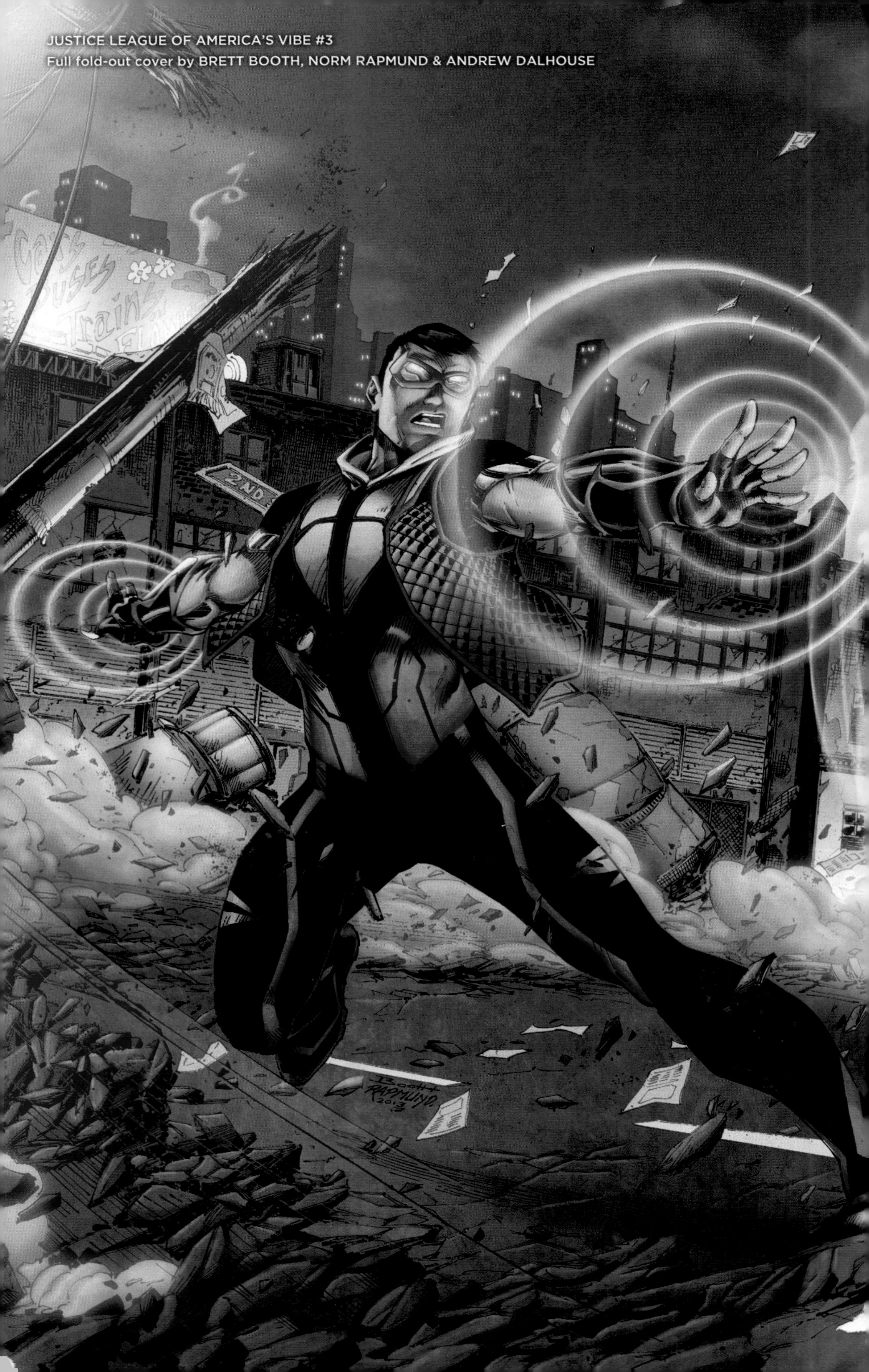
2ND
Trains

JUSTICE LEAGUE OF AMERICA'S VIBE #3
Full fold-out cover by BRETT BOOTH, NORM RAPMUND & ANDREW DALHOUSE

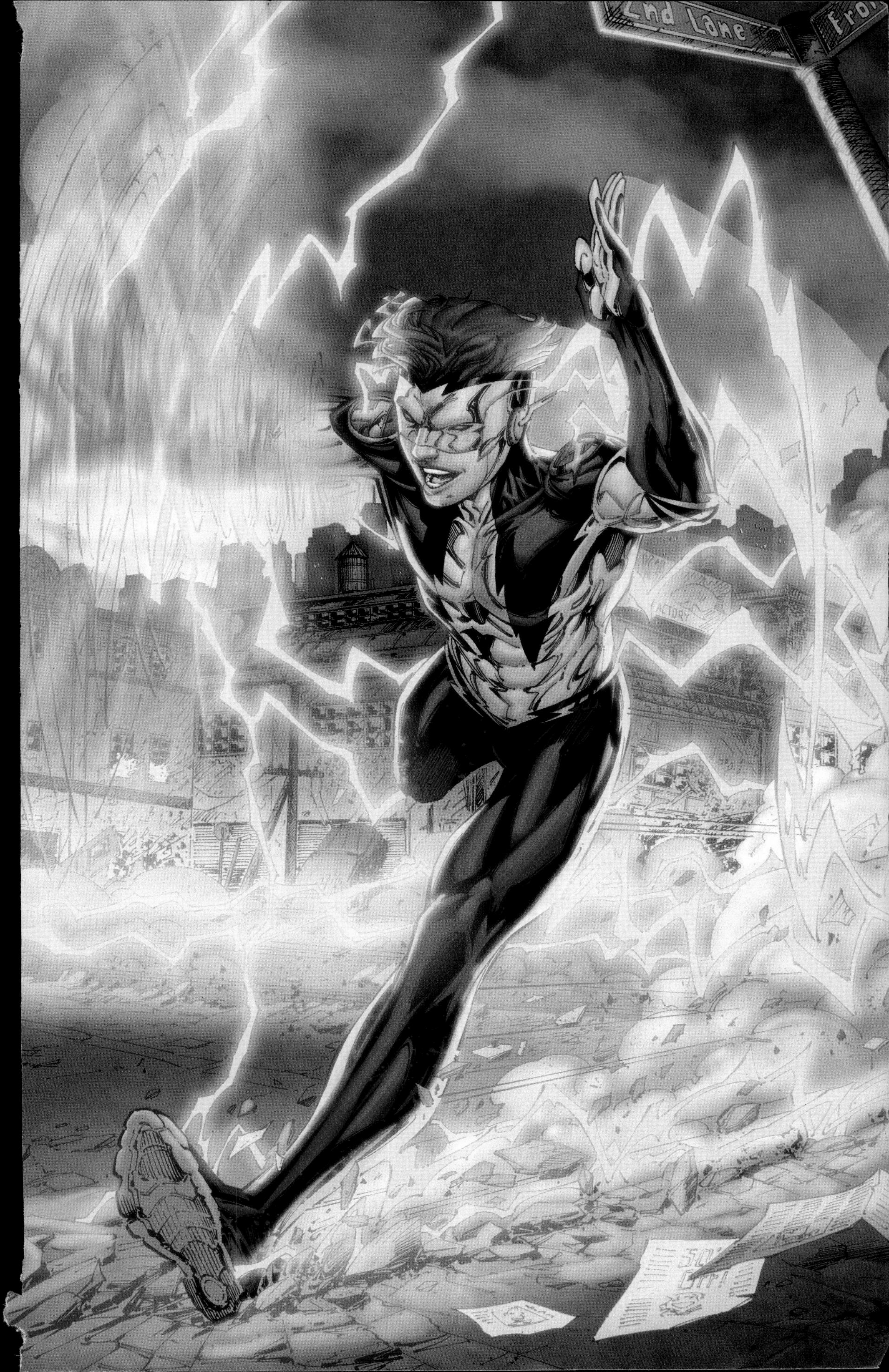
2nd Lane

Promo image by Pete Woods

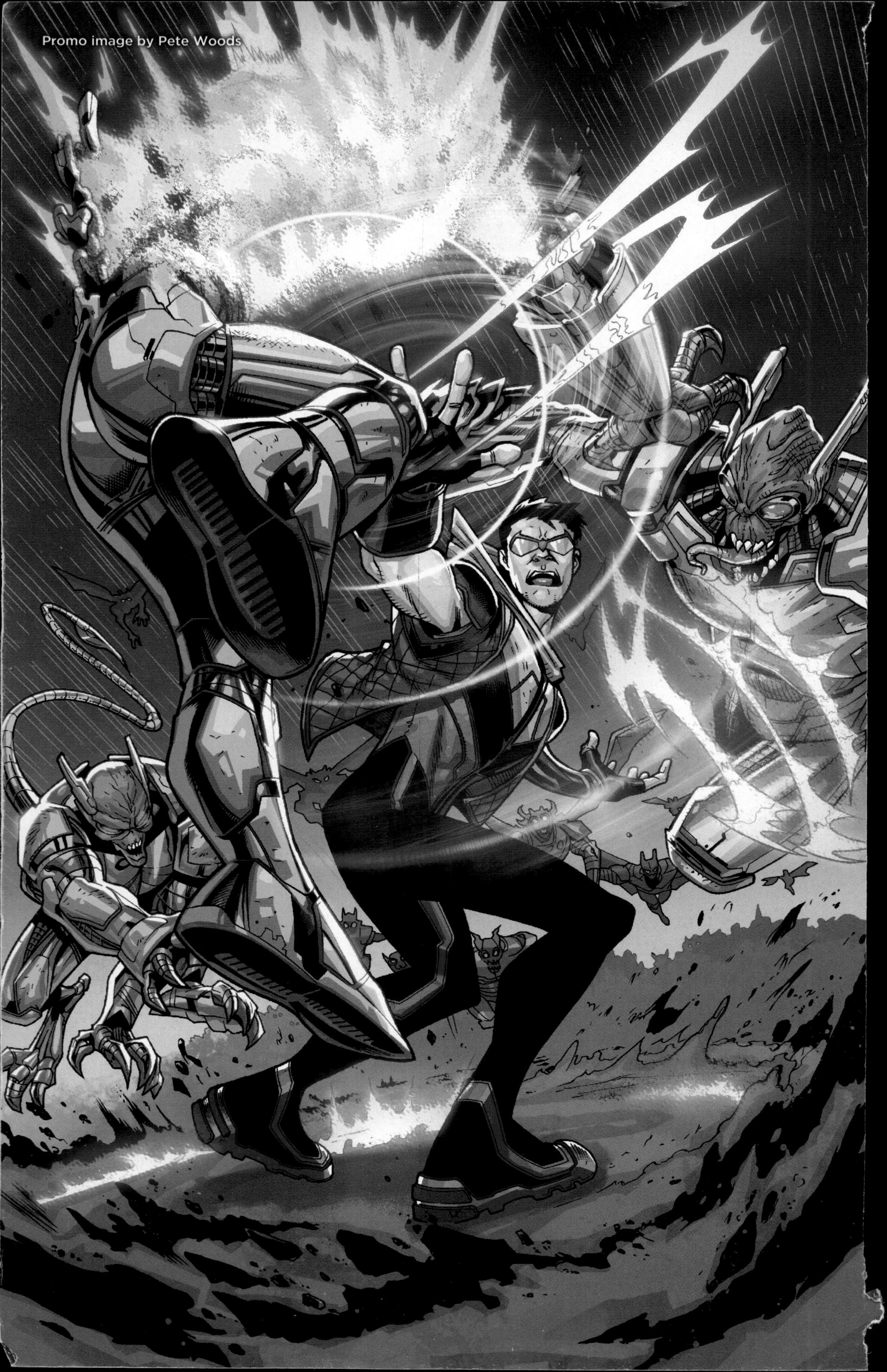